DIANA

The Life of a Troubled Princess

SALLY BEDELL SMITH is the author of the bestselling biography of William S. Paley, *In All His Glory, Reflected Glory: The Life of Pamela Churchill Harriman*, and the acclaimed history of the Kennedy White House, *Grace & Power*. She is currently working on a book about the Clinton White House. Ms. Smith began her career at *Time* magazine and has since worked at *TV Guide* and *The New York Times*. She joined *Vanity Fair* as a contributing editor in 1996. She lives in Washington, D.C., with her husband, Stephen G. Smith, editor of *U.S. News & World Report*, and their three children. She can be contacted via the website www.sallybedellsmith.com.

D1341497

DIANA

The Life of a Troubled Princess

SALLY BEDELL SMITH

Aurum

First published in Great Britain
1999 by Aurum Press Ltd
7 Greenland Street, London NW1 0ND
www.aurumpress.co.uk

This paperback edition published 2007

This edition published by arrangement with Random House, Inc.

A catalogue record for this book is available from the British Library.

ISBN-10: 1 84513 252 1
ISBN-13: 978 1 84513 252 1

10 9 8 7 6 5 4 3

2011 2010 2009 2008 2007

Design by Michael Mendelsohn at MM Design 2000, Inc.
Printed in the UK by CPI Bookmarque, Croydon, CR0 4TD

FOR JOAN AND BERNIE

Acknowledgments

This book began with a phone call from Peter Bernstein, then the publisher of Times Books at Random House, two days after the death of Diana, Princess of Wales. His hope, he said, was that I could "pull it all together" and write a "dignified analysis" that would "put her life in perspective." We agreed that it was vital that I finish the book before the mythology of Diana became so deeply rooted that even her friends would have trouble recalling her with clarity and perspective.

Achieving this goal kept me on a grueling course of travel, research, and writing. I shuttled back and forth between Washington and London—all told, I logged some four months in England—and at home I spent so much time in my study that I might as well have been abroad. My schedule required the loving patience of my husband, Stephen, and my three children, Kirk, Lisa, and David. I am deeply grateful to Gladys Campbell for overseeing the household whenever I was away, and to Carmel Park for doing the same when I was sequestered in my office. I am also indebted to my thoughtful neighbors, John and Annie Carter, and Robert and Maralyn Marsteller, for a hundred favors, big and small.

I owe enormous thanks to my dear friends Joan and Bernie Carl, for their boundless hospitality during my trips to London. Along with their lovely children, Alex, Andrew, and Jennifer, they embraced me as if I were a member of their family. I was cared for—make that hopelessly spoiled—by the rest of "Team Carl": Barry Crick, Britta Fahnemann, Colin Shanley, Tony Stephens, and Dulia Vieira. For their generosity, their friendship, their thoughtfulness, their warmth, and their laughter, I have dedicated this book to Joan and Bernie, with deep affection and gratitude.

Other friends helped keep me afloat with their ideas and encouragement. Maureen Orth, Sally Quinn, Martha Sherrill, and Marjorie Williams were invaluable sounding boards, by phone, over lunch, during long walks, and by e-mail. I'm indebted as well to Jill Abramson, Elizabeth Becker, Amy Bernstein, Tom Brokaw, Gahl Burt, Bob Colacello, Stefania Conrad, Frank Digiacomo, Dominick Dunne, Desmond Gorges, Jean Graham, Gale Hayman, Reinaldo Herrera, Jane Hitchcock, George Hodgman, Cathy Horyn, Ellen James, Jon Katz, Kim Masters, Mike and Sandy Meehan, Alyne Massey, Virginia Merriman, Howard and Susie Morgan, Sylvia Morris, Jill Scharff, Marilyn Schwartz, Wendy Stark, Evan Thomas, and Susan Watters for their suggestions about sources and lines of inquiry. In England I was fortunate to have the guidance of numerous friends and colleagues, including Ivo and Rachel Dawnay, Jane Harari, Warren Hoge, Annie and Patrick Holcroft, David Hooper, Anthony Holden, Anthony Lejeune, Suzanne Lobel, Grant Manheim, Stryker McGuire, Peter McKay, Linda Mortimer, Henry Porter, Carla Powell, William Shawcross, and Sally Taylor. As he has been in the past, Hugo Vickers was generous with his encyclopedic knowledge of the English upper class and the royal family.

Nearly 150 people agreed to be interviewed, and to some seventy who asked not to be named, I give my thanks for their time as well as their indispensable contributions. Those who spoke for the record offered equally important insights and information, for which I am endlessly thankful:

Richard Addis, Dr. Michael Adler, Violet Allen, Bruce Anderson, Jane Atkinson, Laurie Barrington, Peter Bart, Ross Benson, Carl Blade, Nicky Blair, Elsa Bowker, Paul Burrell, Timothy Burrill, Mark Canton, Graydon Carter, Felicity Clark, Michael Colborne, Michael Cole, Major Tim Coles, Bill Condon, Bob Daley, Hugh Davies, William Deedes, Nigel Dempster, Roberto Devorik, Sue Douglas, Deidre Fernand, Fiona Fraser, Johnny Gold, Corinna Gordon, Larry Gordon, Antonia Grant, Suzanne Gregard, Philippe Gudin, Robert Hardman, Jim Hart, William Haseltine, Nicholas Haslam, Max Hastings, Marie Helvin, Stuart Higgins, Christopher Hitchens, Anthony Holden, Mark Hollingsworth, Richard Ingrams, Paul Johnson, Penny Junor, Richard Kay, Andrew Knight, Sandy Lieberson, Marguerite Littman, Mark Lloyd, Jack Martin, Charlie Matthau, Mike Medavoy, Peter McKay, Piers Morgan, Charles Moore, Andrew Morton, Andrew Neil, Bruce Nelson, Farhad Novian, Clive Parsons, Melissa Prophet, David Puttnam, Anna Quindlen, Gail Rebuck, William Reilly, Annie Renwick, John Richardson, Peter Riva, Andrew Roberts, Vivienne Schuster, Nelson Shanks, Tina Sinatra, Cosima Somerset, Robert Spencer, Jim Stevenson, Nona Summers, James Tenner, Taki Theodoracopulos, John Tigrett, Jerry Tokofsky, Barbara Walters, Jack Weiner, Jerry Weintraub, James Whitaker, Michael White, and Fred Zolo.

My research assistant in London, Lucy Nichols, was intrepid, resourceful, and ever cheerful; my friend Jacqueline Williams brought her research expertise to bear once again in unearthing obscure documents and plumbing ancient newspaper archives. I was also ably assisted by Phil Murray, who transformed two shopping bags filled with clippings into orderly files and lists, as well as Peter Griggs and Mark Harnet, who transcribed tapes. At the Investigative Group International in Los Angeles, Dee Picken, Henry Kupperman, and Nancy Swain produced a thick stack of documents from an array of lawsuits and judgments against Dodi Fayed.

Vanity Fair editor Graydon Carter helped to jump-start the book by assigning me an article about Dodi Fayed in September 1997. As I proceeded with my reporting, Graydon provided editorial guidance and encouragement, not to mention a great deal of useful information. He was also kind enough to give me an extended leave so I could focus exclusively on the book. The magazine's executive literary editor, Wayne Lawson, steered me to useful sources and was always ready with artful editorial suggestions, and his former assistant Craig Offmam helped with research. Thanks as well to Robert Walsh, Pat Singer, Anne Phalon, Kris McNeil, and Pete Hyman for their attention to detail and accuracy.

At Random House, former president and publisher Harold Evans offered early and enthusiastic support for my project, for which I am exceedingly grateful. I was also fortunate to have Jonathan Karp as my editor at Times Books. Mindful of the time pressure, he instinctively understood when to leave me alone; when he weighed in he was invariably astute in his comments. Peter Bernstein's successor as publisher, Carie Freimuth, grasped immediately what the book was about and became an enthusiastic advocate. Mary Beth Roche and her associate TJ Snyder were great champions as well, offering imaginative ways to present the book to the public. I'm grateful to Jon Karp's assistant, Monica Gomez, to Martha Schwartz and Janet Wygal for their meticulous copy editing, to Heidi North for her design, and to Anke Steinecke for her careful legal review. Once again, Natalie Goldstein managed to dig up numerous revealing photographs, this time under tough time constraints. I also want to thank Kathy Schneider and Chad Bunning for their marketing expertise. My agent and longtime friend Amanda Urban asked all the right questions and represented me with her usual combination of loyalty and vigor.

I end these acknowledgments, as I customarily do, with a tribute to my wise and wonderful husband, Stephen G. Smith. His devotion and understanding sustained me through stressful periods when I didn't think I could complete the book in the allotted time. His editorial instincts saved me from making some serious organizational mistakes. He inspired the book's title. And he pored over the manuscript not once, but twice—first chapter by chapter, and again when it was complete—even as he wrestled with the demands of his job as editor of *U.S. News & World Report.* For his sense of structure, his feel for style and pace, his vigilance against murkiness and cliches, I cannot thank him—nor love him—enough.

Sally Bedell Smith
Washington, D.C.
May 1999

DIANA

The Life of a Troubled Princess

Introduction

IN September 1997, when I began my research on Diana, Princess of Wales, I had few preconceived ideas. I felt no partiality toward either Diana or her former husband, Charles, the Prince of Wales, though I had encountered each of them briefly and came away with impressions that seemed at odds with what I had read in the popular press.

I met Charles in the summer of 1991, as the couple were nearing their tenth wedding anniversary, on July 29. The British newspapers were filled with speculation about the state of their marriage. *The Sun* created a sensation when it published two articles by Andrew Morton describing Charles's fondness for Camilla Parker Bowles, a married woman he had known since 1971.

None of the articles mentioned that Camilla had been his mistress for the previous five years—an open secret in the aristocracy but unknown to the public at large. The tabloids had been similarly circumspect four months earlier when they reported that Diana's riding instructor, Major James Hewitt, had become infatuated with her after having "misread her friendliness." At the time, only Hewitt's family and a few of Diana's closest friends knew the two had been having an affair since 1986.

The British press did draw attention to the obvious signs of tension between Charles and Diana. "Set on separate ways in their private lives," *The Sunday Times* declared that May, "the Prince and Princess of Wales seem increasingly to be bringing their competition and conflict on to the public stage. It is an insidious process that could spell disaster for the monarchy."

On the afternoon of June 15 that year, my husband and I were taken by some English friends to the Guard's Polo Club in Windsor Park to watch a Pimms Cup match between a team sponsored by Perrier and a Canadian team called the Maple Leafs. Charles was there without Diana, who couldn't bear watching polo. He wasn't playing because his back was giving him problems; still, he appeared to be in good spirits, and he looked almost American in a blue blazer and sharply creased tan trousers with his slip-on shoes polished to a glistening mahogany.

After the match, we took refuge from the rain in a large tent. One member of our party, a woman in her late seventies, was a close friend of the Queen Mother's. When Charles saw his grandmother's friend, he kissed her on the cheek and called her by her first name. She made introductions all around, and we engaged in small talk. I noticed immediately how comfortable Charles seemed with older women. He was attentive and sweet to his grandmother's friend, solicitous of her health problems, inquiring about mutual friends.

Knowing his interest in holistic medicine, she told him of a practitioner who worked wonders on aching backs, but it turned out the man was a faith healer (much more the province of Diana than Charles), and Charles seemed to lose interest. When my husband made some observations about Charles's brother Prince Edward, with whom he had played court tennis—a forerunner of lawn tennis—at a club in New York several months earlier, Charles said something charming in response. In this familiar setting, chatting with people he knew and away from the prying eyes of the press, Charles was far more natural than the man shown on television performing his royal duties.

My only encounter with Diana was equally informal. In the summer of 1994, Diana and Charles had been legally separated for eighteen months, and their relationship had been further strained by his admission in a television documentary, broadcast in June, that he and Camilla Parker Bowles were lovers. That August, Diana was on vacation in Martha's Vineyard, the guest of the Brazilian ambassador Paolo Tarso Flecha de Lima, and his wife, Lucia, one of Diana's closest friends. A friend had invited me to the Vineyard for a visit with her family, and on August 16, I arrived with my children. An hour later, we were on a private beach for a small buffet lunch with Diana and the Flecha de Limas. Diana was mesmerizingly beautiful in a flowered bikini, her skin perfectly bronzed, her long-limbed figure exquisitely proportioned. My two younger children greeted her properly, but I had no time to brief my nineteen-year-old, who arrived late and breathless after sprinting down the hill. When I quickly whispered to him that the Princess of Wales was there, he exclaimed, "No way!" then whirled around to be introduced. He pumped her hand vigorously and said, "Hey, how are you doing?" She seemed genuinely tickled by his Yankee familiarity.

Otherwise, though, she was strikingly subdued. After a few feints at conversation around the buffet, I gave up. She seemed preoccupied, and she soon moved into a chair apart from the group to talk intently to our luncheon hostess, with whom she later took a long walk down the beach. I've pondered Diana's demeanor that day many times since. Here was one of the most charismatic women on the planet, yet she seemed almost without affect. I couldn't figure out whether she was dim and incurious, or troubled and sad. She had not been with her two sons in weeks, and she was surrounded by families with children about the same age as hers. I also knew she had spent the morning with Elizabeth Glaser, a prominent fundraiser for pediatric AIDS who was dying of the disease, which perhaps explained her subdued manner.

Only years later, when I was interviewing one of Diana's friends, did I hear the words that correctly summed up her manner that day: "At times," he said, "Diana could be fantastically vacant. She would just switch off. She was unhappy and would let herself give in. Sometimes she would not try a yard." Yet I also learned that she was often more alert than she seemed. In social settings, according to another of her close friends, "she would perceive small things. She could pick out all the details about a person, both physical and . . . personality [attributes]." After I met Diana on the Vineyard, she confided to a friend that she felt I was "closely observing" her— which I had been trying to do unobtrusively. Her behavior on the beach offered other glimpses of character traits: her intensity in pursuing a new friendship—in this case with our luncheon hostess—and her preference for taking the initiative in social situations in order to maintain control.

As I suspected, she had been deeply moved by her visit with Elizabeth Glaser, but I discovered that Diana was suffering for other reasons. The previous day, she had learned that a book about her affair with Hewitt (which had ended in 1991) would be published in the fall—based on their correspondence as well as interviews with him by author Anna Pasternak. Diana had wept inconsolably and had hardly eaten. She was obviously still preoccupied the following afternoon.

When Times Books asked me to consider writing a book about Diana shortly after her death in 1997 at thirty-six, I hesitated. Scores of books had already been written, most of them sensational or superficial or both, by turns condescending, prurient, and fawning. Many were simply newspaper accounts strung together by British tabloid reporters whose tone ranged from hagiography to character assassination, sometimes in the same volume: Diana would appear at one point as a self-possessed superwoman, only to be portrayed pages later as a self-loathing, weepy hysteric, with no explanation for such contradictory behavior.

As I did my own preliminary research, I found myself drawn to her emotional complexity, and I felt frustrated that no one had done enough reporting to make sense of her. The challenge was to separate her essential traits from the mythic personality that had been assigned to her, and then to show how these traits guided her behavior and her relationships. It was the prospect of finding the woman behind the public mask that drew me to the assignment.

Diana was a celebrity of almost unprecedented magnitude. As if royalty and photogenic beauty were not enough, she sent off wisps of desperate vulnerability—which were then confirmed by her wrenching personal confessions in the controversial 1992 book *Diana: Her True Story,* by Andrew Morton, and an equally controversial television interview with Martin Bashir on the BBC's *Panorama* program in 1995. When "ordinary" people met Diana, or even when they read about her or saw her on television, they often felt that her highs and lows reflected their own. It was this bond that brought out huge crowds of weeping mourners in the days after her death.

Among those who did know her, whether for years or months, Diana inspired proprietary feelings that grew stronger after her death. Perhaps because Diana had the ability to establish instant intimacy, or perhaps because she could be so intense, she inspired comparable feelings in others. After she died, various friends spoke of her with such assurance that it seemed as if she had confided in them all the secrets of her capacious personality. In fact, her friends supplied only partial and often contradictory views, because she was incapable of fully revealing herself to anyone. "She would tailor the truth about this aspect and that aspect of her life according to whom she was speaking to and what she thought they wanted to hear," wrote Simone Simmons, an "energy healer" who befriended Diana during the last four years of her life. "You have to fit the pieces of the puzzle together," one of her close friends told me. "Annabel Goldsmith [a friend in Diana's latter years] would see her in one light, I would see her in another."

Some who knew her had long declined to speak publicly about her, and others have spoken to me with extreme reluctance: Diana's hold over people—the fear of incurring her displeasure, of losing her friendship—remains even after her death. Another complicating factor is the Prince of Wales and his two sons. Few who knew Diana, even those who vehemently took her side in the marital wars with her husband, dare risk the wrath of the man who will someday be King. Some are genuinely fond of Princes William and Harry, and don't want to incur their disapproval, either. For these reasons, many of the people who spoke with me demanded strict pledges of confidentiality.

In addition to interviewing people who knew Diana, I have read thousands of newspaper articles and several dozen books about her. Many of these accounts are filled with conflicting assertions unsupported by evidence, with numerous anonymous quotes. Because I have no knowledge of the sources behind these statements, I decided against using anonymous quotes from secondary sources, unless I cite them for a specific purpose and identify their origin. Any unattributed quotations in this book are from my own interviews with sources I have judged knowledgeable and trustworthy. I have also included a detailed notes section to help guide the reader.

The British press will doubtless take a dim view of this book—in part because it presents an unflattering view of the role of the tabloid reporters, but also because they feel they "own" Diana. The British tabloids were as much players as observers in Diana's life; analyzing their impact on her is as important as understanding her relationship with her family, her husband, her lovers, and her friends.

While others have purported to tell Diana's "true story," "secret life," "real story," or "untold story," this book explores the interplay of Diana's character and temperament. It doesn't deal with quotidian details of Diana's life and her surroundings; nor does it attempt to be the final word, which would only be possible if everyone who knew her well agreed to speak unguardedly, on the record. The opening of Diana's archives would shed further light, although she shredded many sensitive documents, and after her death, friends and relatives destroyed medical records and what one friend called "incriminating" love letters.

It may ultimately be impossible to fully explain Diana because she was so mercurial. Even those close to her had trouble grasping what was going on in her mind. Her moods were volatile, causing her friends and relatives to walk on eggshells to avoid provoking her. "Sometimes she appeared to change from one moment to the next," her second cousin Robert Spencer told me. "One time she would be sweet and glad to see you, the next she would be distant." These frequent shifts in her personality reflected her fragile sense of herself and the turbulence of her emotions.

Richard Kay, a *Daily Mail* reporter who became one of Diana's confidants during the last five years of her life, often wrote about her with great certitude, but admitted to me that he wasn't sure how much he really knew about her. Only hours before she died on August 31, 1997, Diana called to tell him that "she had decided to radically change her life. She was going to complete her obligations . . . and then, around November, would completely withdraw from her formal public life. . . . It was a dream sequence I'd heard from her before, but this time I knew she meant it." Kay wrote those words the day after Diana's death, but eight months later, he said, "My feeling was at that time she meant it, but she could have changed the next week." It may be that recognizing such unpredictability is the beginning of wisdom about Diana, Princess of Wales.

Chapter 1

DIANA was driving through the English countryside one day in 1984 with Michael Shea, press secretary to the Queen, when they noticed a huge billboard ahead with an enormous photograph of Diana's face. "Oh no!" Diana exclaimed. "What's that?" As they came closer, they could see that the billboard was an advertisement for a book that had been written about her. Diana buried her face in her hands, exclaiming that she could no longer tell where her public image stopped and her private self began.

She spoke those words three years into her marriage to Prince Charles, but her anguished confusion stayed with her to the end. From the moment she stepped into the limelight in September 1980 to her violent death seventeen years later, Diana was swept along in an ever-expanding persona, even as she searched frantically for her own identity. When she first appeared on the world stage, Lady Diana Spencer was a nineteen-year-old who had been raised with limited expectations: that she marry a fellow aristocrat and fulfill her duty as a wife and mother. Her marriage to the future King of England thrust on her a public identity that she could never square with her muddled sense of self.

The world probably would have heard little of Diana Spencer had she not married the Prince of Wales. "She would either have been a country-woman, just like her sisters, and dissolved into the atmosphere," said a male friend who knew her from her teenage years, "or she would have married an achiever who offered more of a challenge but would have gone off and had an affair, and she would have divorced the husband in short order."

Diana lived only thirty-six years, all of them amid privilege and wealth: the first half in the rarefied cocoon of the British upper class, the second in the highly visible bubble of royal protocol and pageantry. Her married life was unnatural by any measure—"bizarre," her brother Charles, Earl

Spencer, called it in his eulogy of Diana. Much of her royal existence was lonely and regimented, but tabloid headlines invested its large and small events with high drama.

Simply assuming the title of princess transformed Diana. As Douglas Hurd, the former foreign secretary, put it, "She needed to be royal to succeed." But others have joined the royal family without becoming larger-than-life celebrities. Diana's extraordinary impact resulted to a great degree from her physical presence.

She was endowed with undeniable attributes. Her beauty was singular, especially her big blue eyes, the most expressive of all facial features. "They look so wondering and modest," a Norwegian photographer once remarked. Her height (five foot ten) and lithe figure allowed her to carry clothing exquisitely. If she had been a haughty ice queen, or even strikingly confident, her appeal would have been limited. What made her so charismatic was the combination of her looks and her air of accessibility. "She has a sympathetic face," her father once said, "the sort that you can't help but trust."

Diana had a knack for seeming to be open with people—offering the same small glimpses to everyone, while effectively masking what was really going on. "People adore her because whenever she speaks to them she reveals some small nugget of information about herself or her family," observed Catherine Stott in *The Sunday Telegraph* in 1984. "Nothing she says is ever embarrassing or indiscreet. People feel that they are getting more than they actually are from her." As one of Diana's former aides explained it, Diana knew just how far to go: "People would ask her the most intimate questions, and she knew how to answer them sweetly while actually blowing them off. But because all those intimate details were out there, people felt they knew her."

She lacked arrogance, and she connected effortlessly with her social inferiors. "She had the gift of making other people feel very good," said one of her friends. "She was a princess, but she could step down and make you feel special." With her informality and easy small talk, she seemed an outsider in her own class. Before marrying Charles she even worked as a housecleaner. "I am much closer to people at the bottom than to people at the top," she told *Le Monde* in the last interview before her death. Yet unlike her sister-in-law Sarah Ferguson, the Duchess of York, Diana maintained a regal dignity.

"I don't go by a rule book, I lead from the heart, not the head," Diana said. Her meager formal education enhanced her appeal as well. She frequently belittled her intelligence, saying she was "thick as a plank" or had a "brain the size of a pea." While she lacked intellectual curiosity and discipline, she had a practical, canny mind. "She was an entirely intuitive person," said journalist and historian Paul Johnson. "She was not particularly good at rational processes, but she could get on well with people because she could grasp ideas if they had emotional importance to her. She was very quick, and quick to sense what people wanted." One secret of her charm, according to interior designer Nicky Haslam, a friend for several years, was "she could appear to be talking about something to anyone. She was a conversational chameleon."

She had an agile, teasing sense of humor that included a sure grasp of the absurd and an instinct for punchy ripostes. During a party at Christie's auction house in London, "My friend Paolo said to Diana, 'Gosh, you're brown,'" recalled Haslam. "'W-8!' Diana said. I thought a minute and realized she meant she had been sitting in the sun outside Kensington Palace," her home in the London postal code W-8. "She was sharp as a sharp pencil," said a woman who knew her well, "fast with repartee. She got the point of stories. She got the point of all the people in the room."

But in the solitude of her apartment at Kensington Palace, the engaging public Diana often descended into a lonely, adolescent solipsism. "The time spent alone reviewing every situation and having no friends was for planning and plotting," said Haslam. Diana would dwell on her perceived inadequacies, ponder the betrayals of her past and present, and think obsessively about her enemies, both real and imagined. Her thoughts would plunge her into tears and sometimes vengeful schemes. At such moments, she made her worst decisions. "If you have a mind that doesn't connect together in a coherent way, and great instincts on the other hand, it is an interesting but odd mind," said film producer David Puttnam, a friend for more than a decade who adored her. "I don't like it that she sat around alone. When people like Diana put together bits of intuition and they don't have the ability to really analyze, they start spinning in space."

In public, Diana betrayed little evidence of her emotional storms—a testament to her stiff upper lip, her talent for disguise, and her determination to keep the lid on. "I always used to think Diana would make a very good actress because she would play out any role she chose," wrote her former nanny Mary Clarke.

Because of her quicksilver temperament, Diana could slip easily from one mood to another, confounding those around her. "If she would say we will do this or go here, she was totally reliable," said fashion entrepreneur Roberto Devorik, a longtime friend. "But in her actions, she was like a roller coaster." In his eulogy, her brother Charles lauded Diana's "level-headedness and strength." In some circumstances—giving advice or supporting friends in distress—she admirably displayed these traits. In many other situations, usually those in which she was emotionally involved, she could as easily be irrational and weak. "She was a curious mixture of incredible maturity and immaturity, like a split personality," said one of her friends. "It was so extraordinary how she handled ordinary people, but at the same time she did silly and childlike things. She was very impulsive."

Charles Spencer also praised her "honesty," but as he once admitted, "She had real difficulty telling the truth purely because she liked to embellish things." It was hard to take Diana's words at face value, since she so often said things to make a point, whether or not she contradicted a previous account. She had other motivations for dissembling as well—protecting herself or attracting attention—and throughout her adult life, her tendency to take liberties with the truth often caused problems.

Many of the people around Diana tolerated her dishonesty. "At least once . . . she lied to me outright," wrote her friend Clive James. "She looked me straight in the eye when she said this so I could see how plausible she could be when she was telling a whopper." Her friend Peter Palumbo believed that Diana's special circumstances excused her. "I would ask her whether this had happened or that had happened, and she would tell me a complete lie, which I believed," said Palumbo. "But I never held it against her because that was her way, and that was her character, and she was under a lot of pressure." Such "enabling" by her friends emboldened her to lie even more.

Diana had many fine traits that were evident both in public and in private: warmth, sweetness, affection, femininity, naturalness, grace, sensitivity, reserve, humility, wit, instinctive sympathy, thoughtfulness, generosity, kindness, courtesy, resilience, exuberance, energy, self-discipline, courage. "The nice side of her was fresh and unspoiled and almost childlike," said Nicholas Haslam. "Her nature was spontaneous."

But Diana also had darker traits that were largely hidden from the world. "Her dark side was that of a wounded trapped animal," noted her friend Rosa Monckton, "and her bright side was that of a luminous being." Diana's inability to see past her intense emotions and her failure to understand consequences often overwhelmed the better part of her nature, harming family and friends and creating misery for herself. As one of her relatives said, "She had a perfectly good character, but her temperament overtook her."

Indeed, Diana's unstable temperament bore all the markings of one of the most elusive psychological disorders: the borderline personality. This condition is characterized by an unstable self-image; sharp mood swings; fear of rejection and abandonment; an inability to sustain relationships; persistent feelings of loneliness, boredom, and emptiness; depression; and impulsive behavior such as binge eating and self-mutilation. Taken together, these characteristics explain otherwise inexplicable behavior. Throughout her adult life, Diana experienced these symptoms severely and chronically. While she received periodic treatment for some of her problems—her eating disorder and her depression—neither Diana nor anyone close to her came to grips with the full extent of her illness.

There were numerous reasons for this failure, among them Diana's own ambivalence toward treatment, an ingrained mistrust of psychiatry in the British upper class, and hostility in the press toward mental illness. But mostly it was Diana's dazzling public persona that lulled even her friends and family into disbelieving that anything could be seriously wrong with her—a common fate of the borderline. In the months before her death, Diana's erratic behavior and anguished outbursts showed that she needed help more than ever, but she was too isolated and tormented to find it.

For more than a decade, it fell to Britain's tabloid hacks (as the reporters cheerfully call themselves) to shape Diana's image. The British tabloids cater mainly to blue-collar readers, and circulation rather than advertising provides the bulk of their revenues. Consequently, they clamor for attention with sensationalism and titillation. These newspapers include the gaudy "red tops" (*The Sun, Mirror, Daily Star, News of the World, Sunday Mirror, Sunday People*) as well as the bourgeois midmarket *Mail* (daily and Sunday), *Express* (daily and Sunday), *Evening Standard,* and from 1984 until it closed in 1995, *Today,* a color tabloid modeled on *USA Today.*

The tabloids felt favorably disposed toward Diana most of the time: Promoting her was good for business. But if Diana crossed them, or misbehaved in their eyes, the hacks would scold and attack her, then patronizingly praise her when she came to heel. "Slowly she is adjusting," wrote tabloid veteran James Whitaker in a typical column at the end of 1983, when she seemed "no longer quite so obsessive in her determination . . . to keep her private life totally private."

Tabloid coverage of Diana was marked by some facts, but more often by guesswork, exaggeration, and outright fiction. Reporters wrote thousands of words on her setbacks, yet somehow managed to turn her life into a triumphant progression. Every six months or so, the press would offer a string of articles commenting on Diana's new "maturity," "confidence," and "strength."

"New confidence" was an especially popular theme, and the hacks invoked it on the slightest evidence: a different hairstyle, an adjustment in her wardrobe, a more poised demeanor. The real ingredients of confidence—stability, commitment, clarity, maturity—were sadly absent in her private life. Even in her last year, Diana was so terrified of silence and solitude that she called friends numerous times each day. According to Diana's energy healer Simone Simmons, "We would speak for hours a day—eight hours was not unusual, although the record was fourteen. She spent nearly every free minute of the day on the telephone." Diana relied heavily on alternative therapists such as Simmons (who, among other tasks, "ghost-hopped" Diana's house by standing in doorways and "willing" away "hostile spirits") and unconventional treatments such as colonic irrigation, in which the bowel is flushed with purified water through a plastic tube inserted in the rectum.

Rather than traveling a steady upward path, Diana actually staggered between advances and retreats. In her public role, Diana methodically became more skilled and assured, while privately her turbulence persisted. "You could see how she was evolving in the sense that she was . . . very, very professional," said Dr. Michael Adler, Chairman of the National AIDS Trust, who helped guide Diana in her work with AIDS patients. But in fundamental ways, Diana moved very little. She began her adult life looking for a man to take care of her, which is where she ended her life, with Egyptian playboy Dodi Fayed.

"There was a tremendous fight all the time to believe in herself," said her friend Elsa Bowker. "She wasn't steady because she didn't believe in herself." Another longtime friend observed: "She had so many compartments, so many periods and changes. It is difficult to knit into a coherent picture. What was applicable for her in 1989 was not so in 1994."

In the early years of the Waleses' marriage, the tabloids periodically hinted at deeper problems. These accounts were gleaned from dinner-party gossip and tidbits supplied, often for a fee, by disaffected staff from the royal household. Like social anthropologists, the reporters also relied on visual cues, divining meaning from the scantiest evidence, such as body language and facial expressions. Having introduced various alarming assertions about Diana—using such inflammatory terms as "fiend" and "monster"—the tabloids would then capriciously reverse course and resume their gushing coverage as if the troubles didn't exist.

These twists and turns were part of the game; the tabloids were simply keeping a great story at a constant boil. Coverage of Diana often had as much to do with complicated turf wars among journalists as with the subject at hand. "If you look through the record of the eighties, you find totally contradictory stories week after week," said Richard Ingrams, longtime editor of *Private Eye,* which kept close tabs on the coverage. "I can't think of anyone who was consistently well informed about the royal family."

At the same time, the British "broadsheets"—the respectable upmarket British papers such as *The Times* and *The Daily Telegraph*—largely ignored the saga of Diana and Charles, considering it inappropriate and frivolous to follow the personal lives of the royal family. "We felt we had a responsibility to give the royal family the benefit of any doubt," said Max Hastings, editor of *The Telegraph* from 1986 to 1995. "I didn't think our audience would thank us for emblazoning our front pages with the rumor and gossip that had been in the tabloids." Whenever the broadsheets did cover Charles and Diana's relationship, they offered the official version, endorsed by the public relations spokesmen for the royal family: a marriage that endured some small bumps but benefited from a solid foundation of mutual affection and duty to the monarchy.

In 1992, the Diana saga took a perilous turn with the publication of *Diana: Her True Story,* by Andrew Morton, a former tabloid reporter. The fairy tale, it was clear, had gone horribly wrong. The royal love match turned out to be a sad tale of adultery, mental illness, betrayal, mistrust, and revenge. Diana's secret tape-recorded interviews with an intermediary supplied the basic message of the book. Presented as the "true story," the book was actually her highly emotional perception of events, shaped by psychotherapy as well as astrological readings and alternative therapists who reinforced her efforts to assign blame. The account was one-sided and filled with inconsistencies that mirrored Diana's own tendency to embellish and contradict herself. It was Diana's view of the world, but the public came to accept the book as reality.

The Wales marriage ruptured following the Morton book, polarizing opinion among friends and the public. Most writers found it easier, and more appealing to their readers, to sympathize with Diana and demonize Charles. To an astonishing degree, they took the book's word at face value. In the last five years of her life, Diana actively encouraged their efforts by courting an array of British journalists. "It is an undisputed fact that the Princess connived with the media and exploited it for her own interests," wrote Sir David English, the late chairman of Associated Newspapers and one of her most ardent advocates, "just as much as we exploited her for ours."

As a result, Diana's version was reinforced by sympathetic chroniclers, especially tabloid reporters James Whitaker and Richard Kay, as well as various friends, therapists, and astrologers such as Penny Thornton. Even James Hewitt's bodice-ripping tale published in 1994 reinforced Diana's spin, with his own self-aggrandizing role woven through. Diana's televised interview the following year with Martin Bashir essentially cemented the Diana viewpoint.

Allies of the Prince of Wales tried to even the score, circulating a pro-Charles version of events that portrayed Diana as unstable and manipulative. But journalists took a jaundiced view of Charles's aristocratic friends, and despite the Prince's earnestness and a basic sincerity, he simply couldn't compete with Diana's more endearing qualities of warmth and empathy. He was further defeated by his own awkwardness and his reluctance to hobnob with the press. Diana's champions also tapped into a natural sympathy for her grievances against a royal family known to be aloof, chilly, and preoccupied by duty. A sober authorized biography of the Prince by Jonathan Dimbleby did little to undercut the prejudices against Charles.

After Diana's death, Simon Jenkins of *The Times* called her "the paradigm unhappy woman of today. She was a spokeswoman for those with impossible husbands, worried about their appearance, wrestling with divorce, careers, children, trying to match impossible expectations." In a sense, Diana had ceased to be a person and had become a symbol—of victimhood, rebellion, and emotional authenticity.

Because of its constant repetition as well as its compelling dramatic elements, Diana's life story often strayed from the facts. The lore regarding the divorce of Diana's parents is especially revealing. According to a 1992 account in the *Evening Standard*, the case was "publicly and bloodily fought out in the courts." That same year, the *Daily Mail* recounted that during her childhood Diana had "watched her parents publicly tear their marriage apart." On the first anniversary of Diana's death, MTV ran a biography set to music that even included a fake newspaper with the oversized headline THEIR DIVORCE WAS A TERRIFIC SCANDAL; EVERYONE TOOK SIDES to illustrate the film's assertion that when Diana's parents divorced, "a fierce custody battle" was "played out in the press."

In fact, nothing of the sort happened. A family member familiar with the Spencer archives recalled, "I have never seen a single clipping. I can't see any reason why it would have been in the papers. They weren't high-profile people." Indeed, while the Spencers' divorce and custody disputes were known to a small circle of aristocrats, the proceedings were conducted in private and only attracted discreet notices in the *Daily Telegraph* and the *Evening Standard*.

The reporters who covered Diana thought nothing of changing the story to suit the needs of the moment. Writing about Diana's problems at the end of 1982, royal reporter James Whitaker had noted Charles's solicitude, but reprising the episode for his book on the troubled Wales marriage eleven years later, he said he had actually concluded early on, "It was clear to me he did not love her at all." This assertion was even more puzzling in light of Whitaker's January 1982 report in the *Daily Star* that declared, "Prince Charles has finally fallen hopelessly in love with his wife—more deeply than even he believed he could."

A more egregious example is the way Diana's chroniclers appropriated the phrase "three of us in this marriage," which Diana introduced in her 1995 *Panorama* interview. Martin Bashir began a line of inquiry with

"Around 1986 . . . according to the biography written by Jonathan Dimbleby . . . he says that your husband renewed his relationship with Mrs. Camilla Parker Bowles. Were you aware of that?" Diana replied: "Yes, I was, but I wasn't in a position to do anything about it." She further observed that she knew Charles had gone back to Camilla "by the change of behavioral pattern in my husband." In that context—from 1986 onward—Diana noted, "there were three of us in this marriage, so it was a bit crowded."

Not only did many journalists ignore the fact that, including James Hewitt, there were actually four in the marriage at that point, they consistently used Diana's remark to demonstrate that Charles continued his physical relationship with Camilla throughout his marriage. Thus, in the book *The Day Diana Died,* the author Christopher Andersen stated flatly, "From the beginning, Diana said, 'there were three of us in this marriage.' "

Because of Diana's worldwide celebrity, every character trait, gesture, action, and utterance was amplified. "She lived in an extreme state," said her friend Cosima Somerset. "There was no normal middle ground." Diana's potent public image drove expectations for her behavior impossibly high. Diana was clearly delighted when flattering articles bolstered her fragile sense of herself, yet the incessant scrutiny and bursts of invective drove her to despair. As early as 1983, she took to calling tabloid reporters the "wolf pack," and in the last few years of her life, according to a man close to her, when she felt despondent over her press coverage she would drive to Beachy Head on the south coast and contemplate suicide, only to be drawn back by thoughts of her two sons.

Instead of building a shield, as Charles did by declining to read what was said and written about him, Diana got pulled into a process she found fascinating and terrifying. As perception and reality became more confused, Diana's insecurities grew. From the beginning, Diana devoured everything written about her, and she viewed herself through the prism of the press. The Heisenberg uncertainty principle took over: The act of being watched warped her self-image and behavior. She herself once said, "I didn't like myself. I was ashamed because I couldn't cope with the pressures . . . I felt compelled to perform."

In his eulogy, her brother Charles offered one perplexing observation against considerable evidence to the contrary. "She remained intact, true to herself," he said. In some respects—certain signature traits such as her mischievous wit and her easy rapport—this was accurate. Habits drummed into her by an upper-class background persisted throughout her life: fulfilling her public engagements, for example, or writing instantaneous thank-you notes. As her friend Rosa Monckton observed, "Whenever things got too much for her she would say to herself, 'Diana, remember you're a Spencer' . . . and she would then get on with whatever she had to do."

Yet she tended to define herself in terms of the approval of others. "I think essentially that she was an ill person," said Dr. Michael Adler of the National AIDS Trust. "She was very, very insecure. She didn't believe in herself. There was not a sort of real center to her personality. Her identity was created for her, and she increasingly got herself into personal problems, which highlighted her inadequacies."

When she started out, she appeared to be a typical Sloane Ranger—an ill-educated girl with a perfect pedigree and good manners, but little else to prepare her for the rough-and-tumble ahead. Her identity was incomplete and unsatisfactory, her self-esteem shaky, especially regarding her intellectual ability. What's more, she had certain juvenile preconceptions of her future, an idealized version of marriage that was fed by the fairy-tale romances written by her stepgrandmother, Barbara Cartland.

The royal family imposed a new identity on her, which was glamorized by the press and the demands of her international celebrity. She was expected to be a wife and mother as well as a royal spokesperson and stylish symbol. As she tried to fulfill her duties, she felt that neither the royal family nor the press adequately praised her. The tabloids would create one image of her, and she would react, at times unwittingly, to a view of herself that the public had accepted but that often had little basis in fact. "As she expressed it to friends," wrote Charles's biographer Jonathan Dimbleby, ". . . she did not know who she really was."

Seeing herself over and over in photographs and on television only deepened her insecurities. "She scoured the newspapers for photographs of herself with an eagerness unalloyed by familiarity," wrote Dimbleby. "Not for the first time, it seemed to [Charles and Diana's] friends that she was searching for her own identity in the image of a princess that smiled back at her from every front page."

Diana felt inadequate to the burgeoning expectations, so she continually sought a new persona that would please everyone, mutating to fit the predominant impression and placate criticism. As Sam McKnight, one of her many hairstylists, observed, "Her whole life appears to have been a series of transformations, and I guess it was, but I think she made it like that because she had to transform and transform until she found her true self." Diana's constantly changing hairstyles were only the most visible evidence of her shifting identities. "The haircut was a way to have a strong image," said her friend Roberto Devorik. "She changed it according to her moods. When she went to the excess of cutting it too short or making it too wet, she wanted to make a statement or fight a moment of her life. When it was looser and softer, I think she was feeling better about herself."

When Diana began actively spinning her own story in 1991 by collaborating with journalists, she declared, "From now on, I am going to own myself and be true to myself. I no longer want to live someone else's idea of what and who I should be. I am going to be me." But she was still obsessed by the expectations of others. "Whatever I do," she said toward the end of her life, "it's never good enough for some people."

Living as a celebrity did incalculable damage to Diana, whose emotional underpinnings were tenuous to begin with. "It is the inability to see oneself from the inside," said a friend who was privy to Diana's psychological torment. "There is always a reflection, a distortion. Who one is and what one's contributions are may be perfectly ordinary and valuable, but they are skewed by the distortion of fame. It is difficult to see oneself in that circumstance."

Chapter 2

Diana's childhood was shattered in late 1967 "when Mummy decided to leg it." Diana was only six. Andrew Morton wrote that she "sat quietly at the bottom of the cold stone stairs at her Norfolk home, clutching the wrought-iron banisters while all around her there was a determined bustle. She could hear her father loading suitcases into the boot of a car, then Frances, her mother, crunching across the gravel forecourt, the clunk of the car door being shut and the sound of a car engine revving and then slowly fading as her mother drove through the gates of Park House and out of her life."

As was so often the case, Diana's memory shifted with various re-tellings. Debbie Frank, one of Diana's astrologers, recalled that Diana told her with similar clarity, "I will always remember [my mother] packing her evening dresses into the car and saying, 'Darling, I'll come back.' I sat on the steps waiting for her to return but she never did." Frank wrote, "She could recall it as if it happened yesterday. In fact she told me the story again over our final lunch." According to Ross Benson of the *Sunday Express,* Diana also remembered "cowering behind a curtain, listening to her parents berating each other in the most dreadful terms" and then "her mother's footsteps walking away down the hallway for the last time."

Diana described the episode to many of her friends. "I remember her telling me about her mother leaving," Cosima Somerset said, "that it was the most painful thing in her life, that the children weren't told why she was leaving, and that she was leaving permanently." Diana's abandonment became a central feature of her psychology. "Her mother left at the moment Diana adored her," said Diana's friend Elsa Bowker. "Diana told me she loved her father, but he couldn't replace [her] mother. She said to me, 'I have been unhappy all my life.'"

The marriage of Diana's parents had started out as a whirlwind love match. Johnnie, then known as Viscount Althorp, was the son of the 7th Earl Spencer and Lady Cynthia Hamilton, a daughter of the Duke of Abercorn. Born in 1924, Johnnie was tall and handsome, wealthy and socially prominent—a "catch" for the women of his generation. He was educated at Eton, then went on to Sandhurst, and served in the Royal Scots Greys during World War II, seeing action in France, Belgium, and Holland.

The Spencers were one of England's grand families. Originally sheep farmers, they made a fortune in wool trading from medieval times onward, and acquired vast tracts of land in Warwickshire, Northamptonshire, Buckinghamshire, and Hertfordshire. In 1508, John Spencer built the family seat at Althorp, a 121-room house on 13,000 acres. The Spencer earldom originated in 1765, and in the following years the family bought more land in what is now Greater London's Clapham, Wandsworth, and Wimbledon.

The Spencers were related to royalty (Charles II and James II) as well as other noble families. Along with the Bedfords, Devonshires, Sutherlands, Westminsters, Norfolks, Carlisles, and Egertons, the Spencers led the Whig aristocracy that governed Britain in the eighteenth and nineteenth centuries. The Whigs were the "most serious, exclusive and illustrious cousinhood, held together by birth, blood and breeding," wrote historian David Cannadine. "They were the very embodiment of glamour and grandeur, high rank and high living."

When Diana said to herself "Remember you're a Spencer," it was no idle reminder. Being a Spencer was a vital element of her character. Along with the other Whigs, the Spencers derived their power from the Revolution of 1688, when they helped topple the pro-Catholic James II, limited the power of the monarchy, and guaranteed that the throne would eventually pass to George of Hanover in Germany, whose mother, Sophia, was the granddaughter of James I. When he took the English throne as George I, the Whigs ascended to the dominance that would continue through the early nineteenth century. "Diana was brought up to believe her family was much grander than the royal family," said historian Paul Johnson. "The Whigs are the most arrogant families in the world."

At the same time, the Whigs "tended to be populist and anti-monarch[ist], or at least for a feeble monarchy, not a strong monarchy," said Johnson. "Despite their calm assumption of effortless superiority," wrote David Cannadine, the Whigs "claimed a rapport with the people denied to most patricians." This combination of Whig grandeur and populism passed down through the generations to Diana's father, and to Diana herself. "It was instinctive for her," Paul Johnson said. "She didn't know Whigs."

The Spencers used their riches to amass an extraordinary collection of paintings, porcelain, and rare books, much of which filled the vast rooms of Althorp House. Diana's grandfather Jack, the 7th Earl Spencer, was known as the "curator earl" for his intensely serious stewardship of Althorp and its collections. Jack Spencer was "intolerant of differences and he was a perfectionist," said Fiona Fraser, his niece. Behind his back, he was called, ironically, "Jolly Jack." "He was very frightening when we were small," said a Spencer cousin. "I think that made Johnnie slightly reticent."

The relationship between Jack Spencer and his son Johnnie was "uneasy," according to Charles Spencer. "Grandfather found it hard to accept that his custodianship of Althorp was to be limited by his own mortality. . . . For his part, my father was wary of Grandfather's temper." Father and son were also fundamentally incompatible. Johnnie's interests ran to outdoor activities such as farming and shooting. He had neither his father's intellect nor his passion for Althorp's treasures.

The enduring image of Johnnie Spencer dates to Diana's engagement and wedding. Although he was only fifty-seven, he had suffered a severe stroke three years earlier, and his unsteady gait and slightly slurred speech made him seem a dim and doddering Colonel Blimp. Yet as a young man, he had great charm, a formidable memory, and surprising shrewdness. Whenever he gave a speech, he spoke fluently, amusingly, and without notes.

"He was a good steady Englishman who wouldn't have set the Thames on fire, but he was great fun," said one of his relatives. Shy as a young boy, Johnnie grew confident after his service in the military but retained his gentle manner and sweet thoughtfulness. Johnnie was endearingly down-to-earth, with a warm geniality that extended to people of all classes. "I found him to be adorable," his cousin Fiona Fraser said. "He was not buttoned-up, like a lot of patrician men. If he felt joy, he would show it." Perhaps his most memorable "unstuffy" moment was snapping pictures with the tourists outside Buckingham Palace on the day Diana's engagement was announced.

"He was in many ways not a twentieth-century figure, nor even a nineteenth-century one," said his friend Lord St. John of Fawsley, "but an illegal immigrant from the eighteenth century, when the aristocracy lived fully and at ease with their neighbors. He was the perfect gentleman, but one never afraid to speak openly about his emotions. The words of love were on his lips."

Yet to some who knew him, Johnnie seemed contradictory. One woman who knew Johnnie during her debutante season considered him "amazingly good-looking, but . . . odd and unpredictable and moody." In his softness, Johnnie seemed disconcertingly weak—all the more so because he was drawn to women who were tougher than he was. "Johnnie Spencer liked strong women," said one of his cousins. "He was motivated by them." Frances Roche had many appealing qualities, but above all, Robert Spencer recalled, "Frances was dominant."

Johnnie and Frances Burke Roche had met briefly during his visits to the royal residence at Sandringham in his role as equerry to King George VI, who died in February 1952. Frances was a daughter of the 4th Baron Fermoy and his wife, Ruth, who had been such close friends of George VI that they leased one of his homes, Park House, on the Sandringham Estate in Norfolk.

Johnnie and Frances began what she described as a "rather fast romantic courtship" after her London coming-out ball in April 1953, when he was twenty-nine and she was seventeen. Johnnie had been unofficially engaged for some months to seventeen-year-old Lady Anne Coke, the eldest daughter of the Earl and Countess of Leicester, who found him "sweet, amusing, charming . . . and a very good dancer." But he was dazzled by Frances, one of the prettiest and most popular of the Season's debutantes. That summer he broke his engagement to Lady Anne and proposed marriage to Frances during a tennis game at Park House.

"It was a real love match from his standpoint," Robert Spencer said. "He wrote me a letter after they were engaged, and it was very passionate about her." The age gap was never an issue, as Frances later explained, because "for four generations we've married men much older than ourselves. My grandmother's husband was fifteen years older than [she], and my parents had twenty-three years between them—he was double her age when they married."

While the Spencers were pure English stock, Frances considered herself a "mongrel." "It really upsets me when the papers say I'm English," she once said. "There's not a drop of English blood in my body. I'm half Scots, a quarter Irish and a quarter American." The Fermoys came from Ireland, where Diana's great-great-grandfather Edmund Burke Roche was elected to Parliament and became a baron in the mid–nineteenth century. His son James Roche, who would succeed as the 3rd Baron Fermoy late in life, married an American named Frances (Fanny) Work, whose father was a prosperous stockbroker descended from one of the bricklayers who helped build Independence Hall in Philadelphia. As with many such alliances in the late nineteenth century, James Roche conferred a title on an eager American woman, and Fanny Work supplied a financial infusion to a cash-strapped aristocratic family.

But the marriage foundered, and Fanny took her three children, including twin sons Maurice and Francis, to New York. Having little use for

Europeans, Frank Work told his daughter that her children would inherit his fortune only if they became American citizens and never returned to England. Fanny educated Maurice and Francis at St. Paul's School, in New Hampshire, and at Harvard.

In 1911, Frank Work died and left each of the twins $2.9 million (roughly £28 million apiece today). Neither son wished to become an American citizen, so they successfully challenged the conditions imposed by Frank Work's will, collected most of their inheritance, and went to England in 1921. Their father, the 3rd Baron Fermoy, had died the previous year, which allowed Maurice to claim the title of 4th Baron. Instead of returning to Ireland, where civil unrest had made life inhospitable for the Anglo-Irish, Maurice settled in England at Norfolk and was elected to Parliament.

On a trip to Paris a decade later, Maurice met a Scottish woman named Ruth Gill, who was studying piano at the Paris Conservatoire of Music. The daughter of a colonel from Aberdeen, Ruth was "a very ambitious woman," said a childhood friend of the Spencers. "Her roots were quite humble, and she had achieved everything herself. She had been a concert pianist, and she was very beautiful." Maurice and Ruth fell in love and married in 1931, when she was twenty-three and he was forty-six.

By then Maurice was part of the inner circle of the Duke of York and his wife, the former Lady Elizabeth Bowes-Lyon, the youngest daughter of the 14th Earl of Strathmore. When the Duke of York became King George VI, the Fermoys ascended the social ladder even further. Ruth and Queen Elizabeth, the Queen Mother, were inseparable friends, in part because of their shared love of music. Ruth would eventually become the Queen Mother's Woman of the Bedchamber, a position she would hold until her death.

The Fermoys had three children: Mary in 1934, Frances in 1936, and Edmund in 1939. Like most aristocratic children, they were raised largely by nannies and governesses. Frances considered her father "the most compassionate, sensitive, and glorious man I have ever met." Charming and intelligent, but also austere and enigmatic, Ruth was a courtier to the core, well versed in protocol and intensely loyal to the monarch and his family. "I don't think I've ever known anyone with as much confidence," Frances recalled. "She made up her mind and went for it. She didn't waver over anything." Both Frances and her sister fulfilled Ruth's social aspirations by finding suitable upper-class husbands: Mary married Anthony Berry, the son of Viscount Kemsley, but the alliance of Frances with the more prestigious Spencer family was even more satisfying.

A streak of instability ran through the Roche family. Frances's sister Mary struggled through three failed marriages and lived reclusively in London after her mother's death. Edmund Roche, who became the 5th Baron Fermoy in 1955, had a history of depression for which he sought treatment in 1969, but continued to suffer from black moods. In 1984, at age forty-five, he died after shooting himself in the chest.

Although Frances grew eccentric as she aged, she was always tough and determined. Educated at Downham, a second-tier boarding school for girls in Hertfordshire, she displayed a keen intelligence, a strong interest in art history and music, and a natural athleticism. "She has a very quick mind," said Johnnie's first cousin Fiona Fraser, "stronger on the cerebral side rather than the imaginative, intuitive side." According to a friend of the Spencers, Frances was clever: "She could do the *Times* crossword puzzle in six minutes, things like that." To some, she seemed brittle and coolly matter-of-fact. Yet according to Fraser, she was "good with people, and she could bring out the best in them." Much like Johnnie, Frances was known to be democratic rather than snobbish, with a rollicking sense of humor. Above all, she seemed sure of herself at an early age. "Frances has an inner strength," continued Fraser. "She is the most confident woman I have ever spent time with."

Shortly after Frances and Johnnie's engagement, Johnnie left for a six-month royal tour. He had previously served as an aide to the governor of South Australia after World War II, and while an equerry to King George VI, Johnnie Spencer had pledged to help him when he visited Australia. After the King's death, Johnnie kept his commitment to the new Queen, Elizabeth II. Decades later, Diana confronted a similar situation when Charles spent five weeks in Australia soon after their engagement. While Diana was traumatized by the departure of her fiancé for even a short trip, her mother took Johnnie's commitment to his duty in stride, occupying herself by traveling to Florence and Paris with Johnnie's cousin Fiona to study art history and languages.

Frances and Johnnie were married in June 1954 in Westminster Abbey, with more than 1,000 guests, including Queen Elizabeth, Prince Philip, and numerous members of the royal family. Decades later, Frances would describe her wedding—and Diana's as well—as "mirages of happiness." Yet she would also say, paradoxically, that she had been "immensely happy for a long time" with Johnnie. For their honeymoon, Frances and Johnnie toured Europe, then spent their first year together in a house on the grounds of Althorp. Nine months after their wedding, their first daughter, Sarah, was born—a "honeymoon baby," as Frances liked to call her.

Frances didn't care for Althorp, which she considered a place of "enormous sadness" that was "strange . . . like you're . . . locked in [a museum] after it's shut." The gloomy atmosphere was aggravated by the tension between Johnnie and his father. In the beginning, Jack Spencer got along reasonably well with Frances. "She was very attractive and intelligent and forthright and a strong woman," Fiona Fraser said. "And he respected all that," but Frances had an independent streak that didn't sit well with the Spencers. "They were a very, very conservative family," recalled another cousin. "Frances could have stepped out of line and they could have been sharp with her. Frances didn't fit in. They always expected her to do the right thing and open the right show, but . . . Frances had quite a bit of character."

After the death of Frances's father in 1955, she and Johnnie moved away from Althorp and into Park House at Sandringham, where she had grown up, and Johnnie became a gentleman farmer. Frances's substantial inheritance from her American forebears enabled her to spend £20,000 (£200,000 at today's values) on 236 acres of land to double her husband's holding.

At the beginning, Frances and Johnnie seemed the ideal couple, with her forthrightness balancing his diffidence. They lived the country life, traveled abroad, and socialized with their aristocratic friends. "I was blissfully happy and immensely busy having children," Frances recalled.

It was in building their family that Frances and Johnnie encountered their first heartache. As in any aristocratic dynasty, they felt considerable pressure to produce a boy who would inherit the Spencer title and estate. Two years after Sarah's birth, they had a second daughter, Jane, who was born six weeks prematurely. Then on January 12, 1960, Frances gave birth at Park House to a boy. "I never saw him, never held him," she said years later. "I was told he needed help and I could see him later on. He never came back. . . . He was an eight-pound baby who had a lung malfunction, which meant he couldn't survive." The boy, named John Spencer, died when he was eleven hours old.

The death of their son shattered Frances and Johnnie and had a profound impact on their marriage. A number of accounts have alleged that Johnnie responded cruelly to Frances afterward. "Thwarted in his wish for a son, he lashed out," wrote Johnnie's biographer Angela Levin. According to Diana's biographer Andrew Morton, Johnnie forced Frances to visit doctors in London "for intimate tests" to determine if she had a problem— an ordeal Morton described as a "humiliating and unjust experience."

"It was a dreadful time for my parents," Charles Spencer said years later, "and probably the root of their divorce, because I don't think they ever got over it." Like most men of his upbringing and class, Johnnie Spencer probably lacked what Angela Levin described as an "instinctive understanding of how to help his young wife recover from a severe emotional and physical trauma." Frances did say years later, with a trace of bitterness, "One had to keep a stiff upper lip and get on with it. I was crying about what had happened, and I was told, 'You'll have another child.'"

"The death of John was a deep tragedy in their lives," Fiona Fraser said. "Afterwards, there was a sadness in both of them that had not been there."

The death hit Frances especially hard. "She had been married six years, and the marriage went wrong," said Robert Spencer. "Frances was depressed, and, not surprisingly, she became pregnant again as soon as possible."

The result of that pregnancy was Diana, born on July 1, 1961, eighteen months after the birth and death of John. Diana's father was thirty-seven at the time, and her mother twenty-five. Johnnie declared Diana "a perfect physical specimen," but he still needed an heir. In Diana's adult life, the circumstances of her birth—"the girl who was supposed to be a boy"—assumed enormous significance in her mind as the first of a series of rejections that would splinter her self-esteem. Diana recalled wondering during her childhood if she was a "nuisance to have around." As she analyzed those feelings later, she came to believe that she had been a disappointment because she followed the son who died, that her parents had still longed for a son and had considered it a "bore" to have to "try again." Frances and Johnnie did try again, and on May 20, 1964, when Diana was nearly three, her mother gave birth to Charles Edward Maurice Spencer.

By all accounts, Frances and Johnnie treated Diana as they had their two other girls—and didn't consider her an inferior substitute for their dead son. "Diana was a different soul [from John]," Frances said later, "so it is wrong that a child should ever be considered a replacement." Friends and family didn't recall Diana's talking about feelings of rejection or unworthiness during her childhood. "I don't know what to say about Diana['s] saying she was unwanted because she was born a girl," said Robert Spencer. "I never saw any of that, but I don't know what was going on inside her head."

Nor is it possible to know what signals Diana may have picked up from her parents in her first few years, when maternal attachment is considered so vital to forming a secure sense of self. It was a time, as Robert Spencer observed, when Frances "was feeling pressure to have another boy, and the marriage seemed to be under stress." The nub of Diana's insecurity was her nagging belief that had John survived, she would not have been born. "She said she felt rejected because the whole family was under the shock of John's birth and death," said one of her close friends. "They didn't treat her differently, but she always felt this way. Her father liked her very much, but maybe at the first moment he didn't. Or maybe it was her own imagination. Her mother had five children, and Diana felt rejected. Her self-esteem was very low."

In the years following her brother's birth—when Diana was aged three to six—her parents' marriage unraveled. Various tabloid writers have alleged that the marriage was "violent and unhappy," as Penny Junor wrote in

Charles: Victim or Villain?, her 1998 book on Prince Charles. Longtime tabloid reporter James Whitaker even claimed that Diana's psychological problems were not at all due to her "motherless years," but rather the "violent scenes which went on before Frances . . . finally quit [her marriage]."

After Johnnie Spencer's death in 1992, tabloid reporters toughened these accusations about his behavior. In *Diana vs. Charles: Royal Blood Feud*, his 1993 book on Diana and Charles, James Whitaker said flatly that Johnnie was "a wife beater. There was little doubt in the minds of Norfolk society—and in the wider world—that it was so." Others joined the chorus, including Angela Levin, who wrote that his bullying was "believed to have extended to physical violence."

Members of the Spencer family have said such charges are false, and Johnnie and Frances themselves described the disintegration of their relationship in sad but undramatic terms. "Over the last three years we spent together we just drifted apart, and there was nothing either of us could do about it," said Frances in 1997. Johnnie acknowledged as much in a 1981 interview: "We hadn't fallen apart. We'd drifted apart."

Johnnie and Frances's friends in Norfolk found it hard to believe that there could have been violence in their marriage. "It was never discussed at the time," said Fiona Fraser. "My mother lived in Norfolk and she knew nothing of it." Nor did others close to Johnnie believe he was prone to physical abuse. One Spencer relative said emphatically that Johnnie was "the least violent man I ever met." A friend similarly described Johnnie as "odd, gentle, and weak, not capable of cruelty." Robert Spencer said that his cousin Johnnie "showed no evidence of brutal behavior. Johnnie could be insensitive and unimaginative and dominated by his wife." A woman who had known Johnnie since 1971 said, "He was more a pacifist gentleman than an aggro [aggressive] one."

If anything, the Spencer family appeared to be a rather prosaic English aristocratic household. Johnnie came and went on the periphery, leaving the nurturing to the women, especially the nannies and governesses; yet neither parent appeared disengaged from the children. "She was a wonderful mother and spent a lot of time with her children," said Fiona Fraser, "and he was a wonderful father." Janet Thompson, the nanny who arrived when Diana was three, recalled that on return from her days off, she would find that Frances had slept in the nanny's nursery bed to be with the children.

Frances had always been "very stay-at-home," said one Spencer relative, while Johnnie had wanted to go abroad and travel. But in these years a shift took place, and Frances became restless, while Johnnie seemed more settled and dull. As one of his friends explained to Angela Levin, "He was a reasonably intelligent man who never had his brain taken out of its box. . . . It was never used or stretched." While Johnnie stayed behind in Norfolk, Frances began traveling more frequently to London, where she joined the dinner party circuit. "Frances had lots of 'go,' " a Spencer cousin explained. "Living in Norfolk, she was a bit bored."

It was not so much that Frances yearned for a sparkling city life; although she would keep an apartment in London for years, she would never give up the country ways she loved. But after more than ten years of marriage, she was nearing her thirtieth birthday, and she seemed to feel she was missing something. With the exception of boarding school and little more than a year at Althorp, Frances had essentially never left home. "She went off for her own reasons," said a man who was close to her for several decades. "She was definitely looking. John's death had a major impact. She got engaged at seventeen, married at eighteen, Johnnie was twelve years older, and she wanted something else." She also had the means to find it. "She was financially independent, an almost totally rare thing in an Englishwoman," said one of her Norfolk neighbors. "That gave her latitude."

If Johnnie did have a dark side, it likely was manifested in words, not actions. As his son Charles acknowledged, "There is a thing called the Spencer temper. We are renowned for having a very bad temper." Johnnie's temper was more an expression of exasperation than abuse. On those infrequent occasions when he showed his anger, it was without "the remotest threat of violence," a Spencer relative said. "I remember at a dinner party, Raine [Johnnie's second wife] had been talking and talking, and he wanted to get a word in," said one of Johnnie's neighbors. "He shouted, 'Will you shut up!' "

Johnnie himself confirmed such behavior in several interviews that offered naively revealing glimpses of his contradictory attitudes as a husband dealing with a forceful woman: equal measures of traditional chauvinism, admiration, and compensatory bravado for his own self-effacing manner. "I don't touch [Raine] physically or even shake her, but don't worry about suggesting it. Maybe I should," he said with a smile to Jean Rook of the *Daily Express* in 1981. "She's an amazing person, but you've got to control her. When I'm cross, I'm very direct with her. I shout, 'Now bloody well listen to me for a minute,' and she does." On the other hand, he said, "She grumbles that I'm too soft and kind and nice with people, and that I'm too idle. I don't work hard enough . . . but I'm very strong, strong steel underneath, so we do have our very occasional rows. When I jump on her, she jumps back at me, but it doesn't worry me. She always comes round to my decision in the end."

Diana was notably restrained when talking with friends about her parents' relationship. "She once told me that her father was not a good husband to her mother, but she went no further," said a close friend of Diana's.

After the accusations of wife-beating came out, a member of the Spencer family asked Frances directly about it. "She said it was not true, that he was the most gentle and mild-mannered man," said the family member, who added, "It's too ludicrous. It wasn't in his makeup; and secondly, both Frances and Raine were married to him, and they both say it didn't happen."

Frances did, however, give Johnnie reason to be angry with her. In the summer of 1966, she found what she was seeking when she met Peter Shand Kydd at a London dinner party. "It wasn't love at first sight," she later said, "but I do remember we made each other laugh." Shand Kydd's family had made its money in the wallpaper trade, but Peter had little appetite for business. He had run a sheep station, or ranch, in Australia, and when he ran into financial problems, he had returned to London. He was handsome and full of charm, but he was also the married father of three children. Peter Shand Kydd has been described as a "bohemian" and a "*bon viveur*," which would seem to imply that he offered Frances something more urbane than she had with Johnnie, but Shand Kydd was an equally dedicated countryman, although decidedly livelier.

At the end of 1966, the Spencers and the Shand Kydds went skiing together in Courchevel, France. Recalled Frances, "That's when we realized there was a strong attraction." Frances and Shand Kydd began having an affair, and early in 1967, he left his wife of sixteen years. During Frances's visits to London the following spring and summer, she met Shand Kydd secretly at an apartment in South Kensington. "Peter wasn't responsible for our separation," Frances later insisted. "If Johnnie and I had had a strong marriage, it wouldn't have happened." Others weren't so sure. "She fell in love with Peter Shand Kydd," Robert Spencer said. "I don't think she would have left Johnnie to be on her own."

When Frances told Johnnie in the late summer of 1967 that she wanted a separation, he was thunderstruck. "It was a terrible shock," he said in 1981. "We had fourteen years together, and I was very upset—distraught." Asked how many of those fourteen years had been happy, he said, "I had thought all of them, until the moment we parted." Friends and relatives were equally astonished, because the marriage was considered a great success. One cousin entertained Johnnie and Frances shortly before Frances left. "I thought they seemed perfectly happy," recalled the cousin.

Frances walked out in September 1967, but not as a "bolter," as she has often been described in the tabloid press. The day after her departure, with Johnnie's blessing, Diana and her younger brother Charles, aged three, along with their nanny, joined Frances at her apartment in London. She had enrolled Diana in the Frances Holland School and Charles in a nearby kindergarten. The two older daughters, Sarah and Jane, were already away at boarding school. Before Frances left, she explained to her four children that she and their father would have a "trial separation." "It was something I put a lot of thought into," Frances recalled.

Throughout the autumn of 1967, Diana and Charles shuttled to Norfolk on weekends, or their father came to London for visits. Andrew Morton later described Charles's memory of "playing quietly on the floor with a train set while his mother sat sobbing on the edge of the bed, his father smiling weakly at him in a forlorn attempt to reassure his son that everything was all right." Frances acknowledged the pain of these meetings, saying, "Of course there were tears . . . from all my children. It would be ridiculous to suggest that it [was] anything other than traumatic." Yet she hastened to add, "It was better for them that we separated, as there was such an air of tension in the house."

When the family reunited in Norfolk for the Christmas holidays, Diana's father played his trump card. Without telling Frances, he had registered Diana and Charles at new schools near his home, after calling in his lawyers. According to Frances, "He refused to let [Diana and Charles] return to me and applied to the court for their permanent return to Norfolk, and this was granted. The courts were closed for Christmas, and I could do nothing."

"I was devastated," recalled Frances, who had no choice but to return to London once again—this time on her own. It was probably this highly charged second departure that fueled Diana's memory of the footsteps crunching on gravel, the car door slamming, and the fading sound of the car's engine, filling her with sadness, confusion, anger, insecurity—and guilt. Indeed, according to Diana's friend and energy healer Simone Simmons, Diana "always felt especially bleak at Christmas. The season reminded her of her mother's departure."

Events moved swiftly after Frances left for good at the end of 1967. She and Johnnie spoke "only through lawyers," said Frances. "I desperately tried to make contact personally, but it wasn't fruitful." On April 10, 1968, Peter Shand Kydd's wife Janet was granted a divorce, with custody of their three children. The next day, just two newspapers, *The Times* and *The Daily Telegraph*, carried brief accounts of the decision. *The Telegraph* ran four sentences, noting the cause as "adultery by Mr. Peter Shand Kydd with Viscountess Althorp." The following June, Frances went to court with her own custody plea, which she lost.

That December, Frances filed for divorce on the grounds of her husband's cruelty, an action that prompted one sentence in *The Times*. Johnnie quickly responded with his own petition charging her with adultery. It was Frances's cruelty charge that led many journalists to conclude that Johnnie had physically abused her. According to James Whitaker, Johnnie made his own counterclaim because he was "fearful the details of cruelty to her would become public"—a puzzling notion, since the proceedings were closed, and there was no coverage of the case in the press. Whitaker further alleged that "Frances declined to give evidence of his cruelty because her lawyers advised her against doing so."

Those who knew the situation have said that Frances's charge was a standard legal device at the time. "In those days, [an accusation of] mental cruelty was one of the more discreet ways to get a divorce," said Fiona Fraser. More significantly, another member of the Spencer family said that Frances "only accused [Johnnie] of mental cruelty basically to blackmail him into a divorce that he didn't want to give."

Frances had no defense against the adultery charge; she had already been identified as an adulteress in the Shand Kydd divorce, which Peter had not contested. What she didn't anticipate was Johnnie's stubborn fight for custody of the children: he summoned a string of character witnesses, including Frances's mother, Lady Fermoy, in an extraordinary rejection of her own daughter. The more charitable view was that Ruth felt the children would be happier in the country than in London. Said one neighbor, "Ruth lived down the road, and she saw Johnnie a lot. I suppose she felt Frances had behaved badly." Others saw a more insidious reason: modestly born Ruth Gill couldn't bear to see her grandchildren leave the prestigious embrace of the Spencers.

Neither the Spencer children nor their friends and relatives knew the specifics of the courtroom testimony at the time. It was not until 1982, with the publication of more than a dozen biographies about Diana, that particulars of the Spencer divorce became widely known. The story of the bitterness between Diana's parents spilled into the tabloids after Frances issued a statement to biographer Gordon Honeycombe, who wrote *Year of the Princess,* explaining why she was not a "bolter." As the *Daily Mail* noted that August, "Only now is the full story emerging of a family split that has produced the effect of Earl Spencer remaining close to his mother-in-law Ruth, Lady Fermoy."

Diana and her siblings had learned in the mid-seventies what their grandmother had done. While Diana shared her mother's hurt and resentment, she didn't turn against her grandmother. One reason, according to a Spencer relative, was that the children "hardly knew [Lady Fermoy], anyway." It was only well into Diana's marriage, when Ruth Fermoy took Prince Charles's side as she had with Johnnie, that Diana grew to hate her grandmother. "A courtier to the end," explained the Spencer relative, Ruth Fermoy "wanted Diana to stay in the marriage, no matter how bad it was, in order to spare the royal family the embarrassment of a divorce."

Diana's unwavering antagonism was evident in her comments to Morton: "My grandmother tried to lacerate me in any way she could. She fed the royal family with hideous comments about my mother, so whenever I mention her name the royal family come down on me like a ton of bricks. Mummy came across very badly because grandmother did a real hatchet job."

On April 15, 1969, the court granted Johnnie his divorce. According to the *Evening Standard*, Johnnie was given his decree "on the ground of the adultery of thirty-two-year-old Viscountess Althorp with Mr. Peter Shand Kydd. Lady Althorp did not proceed with the petition which she had filed. Her husband denied her allegations of cruelty." The account continued, "Adultery was alleged at an address in Queens Gate, South Kensington, in April and May 1967. The judge ordered that the wife and Mr. Shand Kydd should pay jointly an agreed £3,000 [£19,000 at today's values] for the husband's costs." The two paragraphs in *The Telegraph* the following day contained the additional information that Johnnie "was granted custody of his four children."

As a leading divorce judge described the situation to Diana's biographer Gordon Honeycombe, "The fact that the father was staying in the family home and that he wanted the children to stay there with him would have been the most powerful factor in coming to the decision about custody." Explained Honeycombe, "Several factors worked against Lady Althorp. . . . The weight of aristocratic opinion was against her, as was her own mother. And Norfolk, where the children had spent nearly all their lives, was a better place to bring them up than London. The law itself favored the father, who happened to be the son of an earl. Custody of children involved in a divorce case is invariably given to the mother, unless she is mentally deranged, a drug addict—or married to a nobleman. His rank and title give him prior claims." In the divorce of Diana's parents, the final condition seemed to prevail. Said Honeycombe, "It reflects the aristocracy's view of women."

That May, Frances married Peter Shand Kydd. Two years later, in July 1971, she reopened the custody question, and after a five-day hearing behind closed doors was rejected again. Throughout these disputes, Johnnie freely permitted the children to visit Frances on weekends in London and on the West Sussex coast, where she and Peter bought a house shortly after their wedding.

For different reasons, each of Diana's parents was undone by the separation and divorce. Frances had lost her children, and her mother had repudiated her, which "unbalanced" Frances, said Robert Spencer. "It was a very emotional period for Diana," he added. Even more troubling was Johnnie's state of mind. "He was really miserable after the divorce, basically shell-shocked. He used to sit in his study the whole time," Charles Spencer recalled. Johnnie's "body language was appalling," said his friend Rupert Hambro. "He walked with a stoop and he wasn't concentrating on what was going on." Recalled another friend, "He used to come over and visit my sister and just talk to her and then thank her for listening to him."

But Johnnie couldn't bring himself to talk to his children about the divorce, which left Diana and Charles mystified and uneasy. Diana recalled that not only was her father silent about the divorce, neither she nor her brother asked about it. Charles remembered "asking where [my mother] was, and being told that she'd gone away on holiday, then asking every day and sensing that something was very wrong but not understanding at all, really. . . . I can remember that, as a child, you know if somebody's lying to you."

Johnnie clearly intended no harm by his silence, which seemed a predictable response for a nobleman of his generation, but it worsened the situation, especially for Diana. At age six, she had witnessed distressing tension and strong emotions in her parents: anxiety, anger, and grief. Naturally reticent, she was unable to speak about either their reaction or her own, and she kept her feelings inside. At a time when a healthy child should be building a strong bond with parents based on love and trust, Diana was emotionally adrift, her mother gone and her father sinking ever deeper into melancholy.

Chapter 3

> *The emotional drama we grow up in can be, even without our knowing it, an imprint for life. It stays with us and shapes who we are and our expectations. What we observe in our parents' relationship to each other and to ourselves provides emotional signposts for what each of us feels entitled to get out of life.*
>
> —SUSIE ORBACH (WITH LUISE EICHENBAUM),
> Diana's therapist from 1993 to 1997

WHEN Diana Spencer first hit the tabloid headlines in September 1980, the press and the public glossed over her parents' divorce, neglecting to consider the damage it might have caused her. The fairy tale couldn't have a dark side. Diana was portrayed as the perfect mate for Prince Charles: well-born, pretty, virginal, and charming. She was from a "broken home," but the tabloid reporters responsible for creating her image regarded the Spencer divorce as an unfortunate incident that Diana had simply brushed away. (Indeed, in their quest for scandal, they were far more focused on futile attempts to uncover a secret lover.)

Diana's chroniclers focused on her willfulness as evidence that she had come through the divorce unscathed. In his portrait of Diana's troubled childhood in the *Daily Star* on July 1, 1981, James Whitaker wrote, "It is hard to imagine it now but this sequence of events shattered Diana. It was worse for her because she loved her mother and father so much, and like anybody of that age couldn't really understand what was going on." Continued Whitaker, "Outwardly happy she may have appeared, but I am told she often suffered 'like mad.' " Nevertheless, Whitaker concluded on a typically upbeat note, "Diana's tremendous strength and depth of character brought her through it all."

Over and over, those who knew Diana in her childhood and adolescence insisted, "She was just an ordinary girl." As a child, especially when she was in supportive surroundings, she seemed even more adept at shielding herself from emotional turmoil than she was as an adult. To most of those around her, Diana's personality and demeanor seemed little changed after her mother left home. But if anyone had bothered to dig more deeply, some clues would doubtless have been apparent.

As difficult as it is to diagnose mental illness in adults, it is even harder with children because their personalities are still developing—yet warning signs are often evident. Virginia Woolf once wrote that from an early age she had "never been able to become part of life; as if the world was complete and I was outside of it, being blown forever outside the loop of time. Other people seemed to live in a real world but I often fell down into nothingness." According to psychiatrist E. James Anthony, Woolf's description suggested the early stages of serious psychological problems. Her words differ little from Diana's confession of childhood isolation to Andrew Morton: "I always felt very different from everyone else, very detached. . . . I always had this thing inside me that I was different. I didn't know why. I couldn't even talk about it but in my mind it was there. . . . I felt I was in the wrong shell."

By the time Diana began divulging intimate details of her life to Morton in 1991, she had been through a number of psychotherapists, as well as several less conventional spiritual advisers and astrologists. She had grown accustomed to reaching into her past for painful memories, many of them at odds with the Diana seen by others as she was growing up. "I don't know what she was talking about," said a Norfolk friend of the Spencer children. "They had dogs, rabbits, guinea pigs, swimming, and school parties, and she had a sunny disposition. I saw no storm clouds."

Diana's most astute friends and relatives did see signs of troubling behavior at various stages of her youth. These manifestations, which seem highly significant in retrospect, included moodiness, fearfulness (of the dark, of being alone), depression, obsessive behavior, food bingeing, academic difficulties, anxiety, distractibility, detachment, and insecurity—all of which occurred against the backdrop of prolonged separation from her mother.

The divorce severed virtually all contact between Frances and Johnnie. "Between their divorce . . . and my father's death [in 1992], they hardly spoke," said Charles Spencer, "so I've never really thought of them as a unit in any way." Diana and her brother had to deal with constant unpredictability. "It was a very unhappy childhood," Diana recalled. "Parents were busy sorting themselves out. . . . Too many changes over nannies, very unstable, the whole thing, generally unhappy and being detached from everybody else."

The children treated their nannies badly, especially after their mother left. Diana recalled that she and Charles dealt with nannies they disliked by sticking pins in their chairs and tossing their clothing out the window. The two children would view their nanny as a threat if she tried to usurp their mother's position. Not surprisingly, some nannies responded with cruelty. "Diana and I had a nanny who—when we did something wrong—would bang our heads together," said Charles. "Or if one of us did something wrong, would bang our head against the wall." Charles also recalled having "three or four nannies during those years who were exceptionally nice." Unfortunately, none stayed very long.

Even as a little girl, Diana could put up a brave front. In home movies filmed by her father, she comes across as an extroverted gamine, gaily striking poses for the camera and running around, as her brother Charles remarked in a television interview, "like a little bee. . . . She was very energetic, always on the move." Diana took pride in her self-control. "I've got what my mother's got," she said. "However bloody you're feeling you can put on the most amazing show of happiness." Given the extent of her distress, it was remarkable that she could maintain a pleasing exterior, especially at such an early age. Only those closest to her were aware of her insecurity below the surface. "As a child, she was deeply unhappy," her brother Charles privately admitted to a friend. "I don't remember her being a sunny child."

Not surprisingly, accounts of her demeanor before and after the divorce are contradictory. In some respects, she appeared to change very little. Janet Thompson, the nanny who came to Park House three years before the separation, recalled that at age three, Diana had been fearful of the dark and required frequent reassurance. Yet Diana was hardly meek and retiring. "Diana could not be called a difficult child, but she could be obstinate," Thompson said. "Even in those days she knew what she wanted and how she wanted things done. . . . She wasn't easy. Some children that young will do as they are told immediately, but Diana wouldn't—it was always a battle of wills. She was full of spirit. But she was a lovely child, and after she had been reasoned with she would usually cooperate . . . eventually."

Although willful, Diana had a finely tuned sensibility from the outset. "She was very modest," said her father's cousin Fiona Fraser, "and she was like that before Johnnie and Frances separated. She was deeply perceptive from an early age, observing everything."

In *Diana Princess of Wales,* her 1982 biography, Penny Junor described Diana's behavior in late 1967 and early 1968 as "on the go all day long and quite exhausting to be with. This seemed to be her method of dealing with her problems. She refused to allow herself to think or to notice that Mummy wasn't there." Junor also noted that Diana "began to talk far more than anyone ever remembers her talking either before or later in her life. She chattered constantly from the moment she got up in the morning to the time she went to bed."

Junor's book has some weight because it was partly sanctioned. Diana answered a "long list of questions" submitted by the author to the Queen's press secretary, Michael Shea, who also read the manuscript for accuracy. In addition, members of Diana's family checked material about her early years. Still, Junor's disquieting description of Diana's sudden volubility did not disturb the conventional wisdom, which said her withdrawal and reticence began when her mother left. In one typical account, British writer Ingrid Seward claimed that Diana "became introverted and nervous and acquired [a] lifetime's habit of always looking down." A more plausible reason for looking down came from her mother, who had the same habit as a child. "In school I was taught to keep my head up and smile," Frances said. "I was always dropping it to hide my height."

A reliable description of Diana's moods and behavior can be found in *Little Girl Lost: The Troubled Childhood of Princess Diana by the Woman Who Raised Her,* a 1986 book by Mary Clarke, who joined the Spencers as their nanny in 1971—four years after the separation—and worked for the family for two years. Within the family, Diana was anything but shy: "ever so talkative," recalled Clarke, "warm and friendly, genuinely interested in whatever was going on." Diana had a tendency to giggle, Clarke noted, "especially when she was nervous."

Clarke also discovered that Diana was "very sensitive." Of the four Spencer children, she had been "most affected" by her parents' divorce. Clarke's description hinted at some of Diana's more extreme traits as an adult: her tendency to want "everything very clear-cut," for example, which presaged the difficulty she had with ambiguities in personal relationships. Most telling was the report Clarke heard from other staff that Diana "fluctuated between being very bright and happy and quiet and moody. . . . She was confused."

An unnerving aspect of that confusion was her tendency to lie. When Charles Spencer described her "difficulty telling the truth," he wondered "whether a psychologist would say it was the trauma of the divorce." Spencer also told a friend he considered this dishonesty "a classic sign of attention-seeking, trying to get attention by being naughty."

She was so afraid of the dark that she described her feeling as an "obsession," and she recalled the night-time sound of her brother sobbing for their mother from his room on the other side of the house. (Her brother, who has said his childhood "wasn't particularly happy," admitted, "a lot of my childhood is a blank. I've been told that when my mother left, I used to cry the whole time, sob all night . . . but I have to say I can't remember it.")

According to astrologer Penny Thornton, Diana said "her early life had indeed been awful. She talked about the constant loneliness she felt, and the lack of attention; [she said] that no one took the time to 'really listen' and give her the deep affection she required."

Diana submerged her own needs by looking after her father. She may have yearned for someone to care for her, but seemed to find some solace in taking on this maternal role. By one newspaper account, Diana was often seen "trailing after her father, offering to make him cups of tea and cook him cake. Many's the time he begged her to 'run along with your sisters,' but Diana was obdurate. The thought had grown in her mind that her father needed protection, and she saw herself in this protector's role, adopting a gravitas beyond her years. . . . She made 'looking after daddy' her big childhood task."

Like many children, Diana took comfort in what psychiatrists call "transitional objects," which serve as maternal substitutes. She kept twenty stuffed animals—"my family," she called them—on her bed, with a "midget space" for herself. She was allowed to take only one of her animals to boarding school, so she chose a "green hippo" and painted its eyes fluorescent. When it was dark, she allayed her fears with the illusion that the hippo was looking at her.

Until the end of her life, Diana kept her menagerie on a sofa at the foot of her bed. As her lover James Hewitt observed, they "lay in a line, about thirty cuddly animals—animals that had been with her in her childhood, which she had tucked up in her bed at Park House and which had comforted her and represented a certain security." When she traveled in her adult years, Diana even took a favorite teddy bear with her; once, on a trip to New York City, she discovered that she had left her bear in Washington, D.C., which prompted a dash to the FAO Schwarz toy store for a replacement.

Charles Spencer once said that because they had divorced parents, the Spencer children became "a self-contained unit, in a way." They had in common a self-deprecating sense of humor, and an affinity for nicknames: Diana was "Duch," Charles was "The Admiral," Sarah was "Ginge." But by virtue of age and temperament, the siblings reacted differently to the divorce. Since Sarah and Jane were off at boarding school when Johnnie and Frances separated, the aftershocks fell hardest on Diana and Charles, who formed a close bond.

From the time he was a baby, Diana had nurtured Charles, who described himself as "an introspective and shy little boy." He was more intellectually gifted than Diana, which made her feel inferior. While Diana claimed not to be jealous of her brother's academic superiority, she yearned to do as well as he did.

Diana's relationship with her sisters was more distant. "Their growing up was done out of my sight," she said, since she saw them only during vacations and considered them "very independent." She felt a natural affinity with Charles because she saw him as more of a kindred spirit than Sarah or Jane. "Like me he will always suffer," she said. Diana felt that her two sisters were perfectly content "being detached" from the problems of their family.

Many of their friends thought Diana had traits in common with her eldest sister, Sarah, the most headstrong of the four siblings. "I didn't like being a girl with red hair," Sarah once told a reporter. "I'm a redhead with a terrible temper. When I was a child I tended to break the furniture." Diana also had a hot temper, which shocked members of the royal family when they saw it firsthand; in her youth, Diana usually managed to suppress her rage.

Whatever Sarah took on, she did well—learning languages, mastering the piano, playing games—all of which Diana struggled with. Because Sarah was so capable, outgoing, and confident, Diana idolized her. Whenever Sarah came home from school, Diana waited on her like a servant, washing her clothes, making her bed, running her bath, packing her suitcase. Diana prided herself on taking care of her sister, but there was also a competitive side to her relationship with Sarah that would come and go over the years.

Jane, the second sister, was highly intelligent, quiet, and thoughtful. She was the most levelheaded of the Spencer children, and Diana respected her without being dominated, as she was by Sarah. "Jane and Diana had this thing of holding their head down and looking up with the eyes," said Felicity Clark, a former *Vogue* editor who knew both sisters. "They had remarkably similar voices, but characterwise, they were fairly different."

Of the four siblings, Diana was the least self-assured. "She felt . . . her opinion didn't count," said a close friend of Diana. When Diana was feeling good about herself and her abilities—particularly in swimming and dancing—she was genuinely exuberant, "confident about her gracefulness," said Charles Spencer. "She loved to show off what an excellent swimmer she was," recalled nanny Mary Clarke. "She would shout, 'Look at me! Look at me!' "

The years after the divorce were difficult for Diana's father. One of Johnnie's childhood friends visited him in Norfolk in the early seventies and found him "rather sad. His clothes looked as if he needed a wife." It was obvious that he still loved Frances. "For five or six years, he was very crestfallen," said Fiona Fraser. "He gradually got his confidence back."

In accounts of Diana's life, it has often been said that Ruth Fermoy stepped into the maternal breach, visiting Park House frequently. But Ruth's manner was aloof, not nurturing, and she had little tolerance for brooding. Her advice to Diana's elder sisters on handling the family crisis was "Cheer up and grin and bear, because worse things happen at sea, my little sailors." Ruth also had a life of her own, and her all-important royal connections. According to a Spencer relative, the Spencer children saw Ruth Fermoy as "a background figure"; she visited only four or five times a year, although she lived nearby in Norfolk. She spent much of her time in an apartment in Eaton Square.

Johnnie was a conscientious parent who treated his children with kindness. Jean Lowe, headmistress of the nearby Silfield School that Diana and Charles attended, said that Johnnie "was a wonderful father. He used to see that they'd got their wellies and they'd got their homework. He used to do the school run when he was able to." When Diana turned seven, Johnnie hired a camel for a surprise birthday party, a treat intended to reward her for working hard at school. Johnnie was a stickler for manners, so much so that Diana later said she would go into a "panic" if she hadn't written a thank-you note within twenty-four hours. Each day, Johnnie made an effort to have tea with his two younger children, a ritual he savored. "He was never happier than when he was eating Marmite sandwiches and drinking glasses of milk in the nursery," said a neighbor. Whenever there was an important event in Diana's life—"every step she took," he once said—Johnnie recorded it with his camera.

Diana and her brother appreciated the example Johnnie set and the values he taught. "My father always said, 'Treat everybody as an individual and never throw your weight around,'" Diana said. Somewhat more poignantly, Charles considered "one of [Johnnie's] greatest achievements as a father . . . [was] that never, ever did he say anything against my mother in front of his children." Johnnie also made an effort to know his children's friends, and he could recall, with surprising clarity, details of the friends' school courses and sports, as well as particulars about their families.

But as a reserved English gentleman, Johnnie's inbred formality and diffident temperament limited his effectiveness as a parent. "He was of a generation that didn't kiss and cuddle the children," explained Jean Lowe of Silfield School. "Diana wanted . . . physical touch. When she used to come up and read to me, she would lean on me, and she obviously wanted that, and that, I suppose, was what was missing." Mary Clarke, who observed Johnnie daily during the two years she worked at Park House, considered him a "very kind, understanding man who was very anxious to do his best for the children, even though he was not quite sure of himself with them." Clarke could see that Johnnie "tried so hard. He would ask them about their games and their pets, but they only answered his questions; they never started a conversation." In time, though, as Johnnie became more comfortable, Diana and Charles "became more relaxed with their father."

In his traditional role before the divorce, Johnnie had been free to come and go in the household as he pleased, attending to his duties (farming, local government, army reserves, charitable activities) and his sporting pursuits. Once he was in charge, the inconsistency of his presence became more troubling to Diana. "There were long periods in the evenings and at weekends when Diana was unoccupied and when Johnnie couldn't always guarantee to be there," wrote Penny Junor. Diana became noticeably worried whenever her father went away—much as she would when Prince Charles and others she loved had to leave her. "She did fret about Johnnie if he was gone for long," wrote Junor. "She would always ask, 'When's Daddy coming home?' " These memories doubtless prompted Diana's comment to her astrologer Penny Thornton about "constant loneliness," and Diana's anxiety about abandonment during her father's absences may well have led to her hatred of solitude as an adult. From her school days onward, Diana thrived when she was surrounded by other people, which brought her relief from the emptiness she said she felt on her own.

In later years, both Diana and her brother spoke openly of their love for their father. In the view of their cousin Robert Spencer, Diana was "particularly fond of her father, especially since he was the parent left behind." Indeed, one of the more unjust calumnies made in the tabloid press was James Whitaker's assertion that "to be left in the custody of a man they knew had been unkind to their mother was a burden [the Spencer children] had to endure." When Diana was in the throes of her own difficult marriage, however, she did express resentment of her father, complaining to Penny Thornton—unfairly, it seems—that he had been "distant and remote, and if he wasn't being unreachable, he was being angry and intolerant." According to Thornton, Diana felt that her father "had driven her mother away, yet at the same time she felt utterly abandoned by Frances."

Diana's contradictory feelings were aggravated by the tensions surrounding weekend visits to her mother. Mary Clarke, who accompanied Diana on these unsettling journeys, recalled that she invariably said on her departure, "Poor Daddy, I feel so sad leaving him on his own"; after parting from her mother, as well: "Poor Mummy, I feel so sad leaving her on her own." Until the Morton revelations, little else was said about these visits. In her 1982 biography of Diana, Penny Junor had emphasized the stoicism shown by both parents and children. Before and after the weekend visits, "there were no tears," wrote Junor, "and Frances didn't allow herself to show any emotion either. . . . Both parents did their utmost to make their separation as easy and painless as possible for the children."

Diana's own recollections were considerably more raw: "I can remember Mummy crying an awful lot," Diana recalled. The moment Diana and her brother arrived for the weekend, Frances began to weep. When the children asked why she was crying, she told them that she couldn't bear to have them leave after only a day—a reply that was "devastating" to nine-year-old Diana. According to one of Diana's close friends, Diana said that in addition to weeping, Frances denigrated Johnnie during their visits. Not only did Diana have to deal with knowing her mother had been so dissatisfied that she had left home, she also had to console Frances while feeling conflicted about her father—a heavy load for a young girl.

The immediate consequences of these traumatic weekend trips, according to Mary Clarke, were Diana's increased willfulness and a tendency to "make unfavorable remarks about her father." Johnnie didn't help matters with his inability to cope with Diana and Charles on their return. "After he made them welcome, he would normally retire to his study and leave me to return equilibrium to the house," said Mary Clarke. While at Park House, Diana didn't say a word about her mother.

The scars on her children, especially Diana and Charles, caused Frances profound sadness. "It was agonizing for her," said cousin Fiona Fraser. Nevertheless, in 1972, Frances and Peter Shand Kydd made a radical move by relocating to a hill farm on the remote Isle of Seil off the west coast of Scotland. Somewhat defensively, Frances later explained, "Peter and I had no wish to distance ourselves from anyone. We just wanted to live in Scotland." Yet the move made routine weekend visits impossible and effectively cut off regular maternal contact when Diana was only eleven.

Children normally worship their parents without recognition of their quirks and flaws until adolescence or adulthood. A natural reaction for a girl in Diana's situation would be to fault her own inadequacies for her mother's departure. "She never felt good enough as a child, blaming herself for her mother's leaving and subsequently living with a stark sense that those she loved would abandon her," wrote Diana's astrologer Debbie Frank. Only later, when she was in her twenties and thirties, did Diana shift the blame for her misfortunes. "Diana said her mother was not there when she needed her," said her friend Roberto Devorik, echoing other friends to whom Diana had made the same complaint.

As a child, Diana didn't talk about her guilt, but an incident she recounted to Andrew Morton showed how burdened she had been. At age nine, she was asked to be a bridesmaid in a cousin's wedding, and she had to choose between dresses given to her by her father and mother. Although she couldn't recall which dress she wore, she did remember feeling "totally traumatized" that her choice might signal that she favored one parent over the other. The impulse to inflate such small dilemmas into full-blown crises became more powerful as Diana grew older.

The push and pull between Johnnie and Frances meant that they often placated Diana when they should have set limits. "She learned how to manipulate her parents by playing one off against the other," explained one of her close friends. "They both wanted her attention, so they indulged her." Diana boasted that she was her "father's favorite" and freely admitted she could "get away with murder." Combined with her numerous insecurities, this kind of power allowed Diana to expect people to accept her terms, establishing behavior patterns that would lead to trouble later in life. "The problem was," said her cousin Robert Spencer, "few people had said no to her."

The ultimate effect of Diana's turbulent childhood was her sense that she could not depend on either of her parents. A feeling of healthy dependence—the certainty that parents are "there" for a child—is the usual path to security and confidence in later life. In her insecurity, Diana eventually became obsessively dependent in her search for a provider of the continuous love and understanding she needed.

Chapter 4

A FEW years after the divorce, Diana's father decided to send her to boarding school, which, under ordinary circumstances, probably would have caused scarcely a ripple. In the English upper class, boarding school was a time-honored ritual: boys tended to go off at age eight; most girls left several years later. For boys, boarding school marked the start of a rigorous education. For girls, with the exception of a handful of demanding public schools such as Cheltenham and Roedean, the aim was more social than academic. Girls learned the basics of English, maths, language, history, and science, but boarding schools primarily taught them how to live together and develop habits of responsibility, good manners, neatness, discipline, and tolerance. Johnnie and Frances had both gone away to school, so it was natural that their children should do the same.

Diana was only nine when her father decided to send her to Riddlesworth Hall, two hours' drive from Park House. She had done reasonably well at the local day school, Silfield, where she had been enrolled since January 1968, following the chaotic autumn of separations and quarrels. On Diana's arrival at Silfield, a teacher had noted she was "beginning to gain confidence in her work." Two years later, she was "very good but she must be careful where she puts capital letters!" Shortly afterward, the assessment caught some emerging problems: "Unfortunately, Diana has a defeatist attitude where her weaknesses are concerned which must change if she is to achieve an overall improvement."

By one journalist's description, Diana's classroom demeanor was "bright and chatty," while another called her "quiet and shy." In all likelihood, she showed both sides of her personality. Diana recalled feeling uncomfortable at Silfield because she was the only student with divorced parents, which made her believe that she was "horribly different." The school staff waited for Diana's cheerful demeanor to crack, and when it didn't, they concluded that she had a strong core of resilience.

With 120 students between the ages of seven and thirteen, Riddlesworth offered a nurturing environment and a student body that included other girls from divorced families. One cousin and several friends were already there, so Diana would be in familiar company from the beginning. The headmistress was Elizabeth Ridsdale, a warm and wise woman the girls called "Riddy." The philosophy of the school seemed ideal for Diana's emotional and academic needs: "a stable family atmosphere in which a child can develop naturally and happily, where individual freedom and the discipline of a community are in easy balance, a sense of security can be achieved, and every child will have the opportunity to be good at something."

But when Johnnie described his Riddlesworth plan to Diana, she recalled feeling rejected. Having become accustomed to looking after her father, she tried to dissuade him from sending her off. "I used to make threats," she said, "like, 'If you love me, you won't leave me' "—the same sort of entreaty she used with Prince Charles when she didn't want him to go away.

She enrolled in Riddlesworth, nevertheless, in the fall of 1970. After some initial homesickness, she adjusted well in the school's friendly atmosphere. When Mary Clarke first arrived at Park House several months later, she was sent to retrieve Diana for a visit home. Diana greeted her with "those downcast eyes" that she had "whenever she met anybody new," recalled Clarke; but "the longer Diana spent at Riddlesworth, the more settled and happy she became. She made lots of friends, I think because she posed no threat to anyone. She was generous-natured, openhearted, imaginative."

Diana later said she "adored" Riddlesworth, where her talents and attributes were reinforced. She won a trophy for swimming, took extra dancing lessons, received an award for the best guinea pig, and earned the Legatt Cup, the school's prize for "helpfulness." "She was overtaken by the busyness of the place," wrote Penny Junor, ". . . alive and full of go, always wanting to dash on to the next thing. . . . She was happy to fit in. . . . Not the sort of girl the others looked up to, but the sort they liked to have around. She was a girl who wanted to be liked."

Junor also reported that Diana was "a teacher's dream: well-mannered, eager to please, friendly, pleasant, even-tempered and always cooperative." That assessment doesn't quite square with Diana's own recollection: "I was very naughty in the sense of always wanting to laugh and muck about rather than sit tight looking at the four walls of the schoolroom." At least in part because of her inattention, Diana was only an average student. Riddy's evaluation at the end of Diana's third year was typically mixed: "Diana has been outstandingly helpful this term. She has proved herself efficient and a good organizer. If only she would put the same enthusiasm into her work, she could move mountains. There are occasional lapses when she becomes rather quarrelsome, but these are much fewer than in the past."

After three years at Riddlesworth, Diana was accepted at West Heath, the boarding school for older girls that Sarah and Jane had attended. The only requirement for admission was neat handwriting. Located an hour outside London in Kent, West Heath was an ideal safe harbor for a girl trying to navigate adolescence under difficult circumstances. In some ways, the school was so comforting that it mitigated the mood shifts, turbulent relationships, identity crises, and challenges to authority that make up the normal developmental challenges faced by a teenager.

"It was a very unsophisticated place, and we weren't encouraged to be sophisticated," said a woman who went to West Heath with Diana. "We used to get cross about it, and complain that we were cocooned. London schools were allowed to do things we weren't allowed to do. We never met boys at the end of the drive. Several schools allowed girls to smoke and drink in the sixth form. But West Heath was old-fashioned. We didn't grow up very quickly. It was very small, a hundred and twenty [students] in all. There were very small classes. Everyone came out confident and happy, and there was very little angst. Maybe Diana was miserable, but I wasn't aware. It was a relaxed place."

Diana was twelve when she entered West Heath in the fall of 1973. Her sixteen-year-old sister Jane was a school leader and stellar student, having passed eleven O-level exams (the tests sat at fifteen or sixteen and now called GCSEs, the results of which determine the choice of A-level subjects for the two sixth-form years at secondary school).

Sarah fared less well. She had been successful at West Heath, playing lacrosse, netball, tennis, and cricket, appearing in school plays, winning prizes in diving, and passing six O-level exams. But despite her obvious aptitude, Sarah decided "I wasn't university material" and opted for rebellion instead. "I used to drink because I was bored," she recalled. "I would drink anything: whiskey, Cointreau, gin, sherry or, most often, vodka, because the staff couldn't smell that." One day in 1971 when she was drunk, she got caught, and was expelled from school.

The following year, Sarah rebounded at finishing school in Switzerland, where she became fluent in French; she then moved on to Vienna to study piano at a music conservatory and earn a diploma for German proficiency. On Sarah's return to England in the spring of 1973, Johnnie gave her a grand debutante party in Norfolk, and she came out during the

London "Season." By the time Diana settled in at West Heath, Sarah was eighteen and working in London at *Vogue* as an editorial assistant.

Presiding over West Heath was Ruth Rudge, a longtime Latin teacher turned principal. Flinty, astute, and sensible, Rudge, like Elizabeth Ridsdale, played to the strengths of her students. "The school gave a certain security to girls when they needed it," said the mother of one of Diana's schoolmates. "If they wanted to dance, they did. If they wanted to play music, they did." Ruth Rudge's initial assessment of Diana showed an awareness of her personality's undercurrents, as well as the means to soothe them. When Diana came to West Heath, she was "wary of adults, often prickly with her peers," Rudge later observed. "She was lucky enough to find herself in a group of lively, talented, caring individuals, some of whom she already knew, and soon gained confidence in her new surroundings and found her niche socially."

Rudge had spotted Diana's streak of suspicion. "She was wary of people until she trusted them," Rudge said. "She had a number of knocks, particularly from adults. . . . Once she trusted you, it was fine." Diana was tougher on herself in her Morton interviews: Her conduct at first was "ghastly," she said. She became a "bully" because her sister Jane held a position of power as a prefect. But after some of the girls retaliated against Diana for her bossy behavior, she became "completely calm and sorted out."

Neither Rudge nor Violet Allen, the matron who supervised dormitory life and ran the infirmary, actually witnessed Diana's bullying, although one school report admonished that "she must try to be less emotional in her dealings with others." Rudge was well aware of Diana's feistiness: "She was a very strong character. She went about getting what she wanted. She could verbally defend herself quite well."

Diana also bragged to Morton about nearly being expelled from West Heath after sneaking out one night on a dare. She described the episode vividly, complete with police cars, the arrival of both her parents, and her mother's tart expression of pride—"I didn't think you had it in you"—instead of a rebuke. Yet Ruth Rudge had no recollection of any such incident: "I would have been involved," said Rudge. "It doesn't ring any bell at all."

Diana's schoolmate Carolyn Bartholomew recalled her friend as "buoyant and noisy . . . full of life, a bubbly character," while other students remembered her as more private and controlled, with her emotions well-hidden. In fact, depending on circumstances and her own level of confidence, Diana could be either. When Diana assessed her schoolgirl behavior for Andrew Morton, she was so contradictory that she seemed to be speaking in riddles. "I was always looking for trouble," she said, and in the next breath, "I always knew how to behave. There was a time to be quiet and a time to be noisy. I could always tune in to which it should be." Ruth Rudge understood these complexities, as she noted in a tribute written after Diana's death: "The compassion and caring, the stresses and harassments, her ease and friendliness as well as the swift retaliation for wrongs she felt done to her, all marked and recorded in her later life, were evident in her school days."

Diana's temper may have flared when schoolmates crossed her, but for the most part she maintained her agreeable facade and aimed to please. The school encouraged her to focus on what she did well, and rewarded her achievements. She found fulfillment in helping younger students as well as needy people in the community: the mentally handicapped at a local asylum, and an elderly woman she visited each week. Diana enjoyed learning to play the piano—her favorite piece was Dvořák's *Slavonic Dance in G Minor*—but her technique, though energetic, didn't match that of Jane or Sarah, much less her grandmother Ruth Fermoy, who had played professionally. Diana's forte was dance, and she took lessons in ballet, tap, and ballroom. She practiced diligently, and in 1976, she won the school dance competition. She was equally proficient in swimming and diving, winning awards in each sport four years straight.

In her last year, Diana was named a prefect, as her sister Jane had been, and she carried out her leadership role so responsibly that she was awarded a special prize for service—an award "for anyone who has done things that otherwise might have gone unsung," said Ruth Rudge. "She was dependable in her own doings, reliable, and went out of her way to help people. She was generous with her time." Once after Diana had been discharged from the infirmary during an epidemic, she came back to help Violet Allen serve meals to the other ailing girls. "She had a very caring heart," said Allen.

More than five years had passed since her parents' split, but Diana was still troubled by it. "Mostly it was a traumatic time for her," said Allen. "We had quite a few girls from divorced families, and she came and talked to me quite a lot. Of course she missed her mother and father. The others who had divorces felt the same way. Some accepted it, and some had more difficulty with it. No doubt about it, Diana found it difficult to accept. She was vulnerable in some things. I can't put a finger on it, but it probably all had to do with the insecurity and breakup of [her parents'] marriage."

Yet Diana held her sadness in check, as she had at Silfield and Riddlesworth. "Most of the girls from a divorced family would come in and have a little weep," said Allen. "I never saw her cry. She probably kept a lot to herself." Allen's observation was strikingly similar to the Riddlesworth staff's, who noticed that Diana "was always very controlled, never likely, as they put it, to have 'boo-hooed' under any circumstances."

No school could protect Diana from further dislocations in the family, however. She was hit hard by the death of her favorite grandmother, Lady Cynthia Spencer, in 1972. A bigger blow came when her grandfather Jack, the 7th Earl Spencer, died on June 9, 1975, causing the family to leave Norfolk and move to Althorp, where Johnnie would take over as the 8th Earl Spencer. "A terrible, terrible wrench," Diana called her departure from Park House at fourteen. Her brother Charles considered it "a difficult phase in all our lives: uprooted from our childhood haunts and friends, and marooned in the middle of a park the size of Monaco." The 121-room house reminded Charles of "a chilling time warp, complete with the permeating smell of Trumper's hair oil and the ubiquitous tocking of Grandfather's clocks." According to Junor, Diana "never grew to be fond" of Althorp.

Shortly after the move, the Spencer children were shocked to learn that Johnnie, then fifty-two, had married Raine, the forty-six-year-old Countess of Dartmouth, in a quiet ceremony on July 14, 1976—without notifying any of them in advance. Raine was a handsome woman with a meticulous bouffant hairstyle and a controversial image. Her family, the McCorquodales, had been minor gentry who made money in the printing business. Her mother was the flamboyant romance novelist Barbara Cartland, and one of her cousins, Neil McCorquodale, would later marry Diana's sister Sarah. Raine was known for her involvement in London government, where she earned a reputation for outspokenness. She had a keen intelligence, enormous energy, and big ambitions.

Johnnie and Raine fell in love in the early seventies when they worked together on a book about historic buildings for the Greater London Council. Raine had been married for twenty-eight years to the Earl of Dartmouth and had four children. "When I met Johnnie he was a very lonely and unhappy man who'd been divorced for years," Raine once said. By the time Johnnie brought Raine to his daughter Sarah's debutante party in 1973, the affair was already the stuff of gossip; Raine left her husband in 1974. Like Johnnie, Gerald Dartmouth won custody of the children when he divorced Raine in 1976 after naming Johnnie—his former friend from Eton days—as the corespondent.

Johnnie was besotted with Raine, and friends and relatives could see that he was in high spirits once again. "When Raine came into his life, he was vulnerable to her gushing flattery and settled for her," said a Spencer relative. She even charmed Johnnie's famously grumpy father, and other relatives as well. "In the beginning I was very much for Raine," said Robert Spencer. "I thought she would be good for Johnnie, and that she would be a good chatelaine for Althorp. Everyone was for her, really. Everyone except the children."

Diana and her siblings took an instant dislike to Raine, primarily because they didn't want to share their father with someone they barely knew. Diana recalled that Raine "used to . . . pour us with presents, and we all hated her so much because we thought she was going to take Daddy away from us." Raine's overbearing and tactless manner made matters worse, prompting the Spencer children to call her "Acid Raine." "She dominated him and wouldn't let them get close to him," said a friend of the Spencer sisters. "They were hurt that their father would drop everything and rush to this woman who had him under wraps. She wouldn't let them come home without giving her a date three months before. She ruled his life and spent his money."

In one revealing episode, Diana enlisted a friend to write a nasty anonymous note to Raine after coming across a letter her future stepmother had sent to Johnnie about plans for redoing the decor at Althorp. (Diana's habits of reading other people's mail and eavesdropping were aspects of her suspicious nature that would cause problems in her marriage.) Diana's mistrust of Raine hardened as the new Countess Spencer orchestrated the sale of Althorp treasures to pay inheritance taxes and finance elaborate renovations. "They minded terribly what she did to Althorp," said another Spencer cousin. "It was so overpolished and overgilded and overshiny. There was a gap with the children. If they could make it awkward for her, they did it. She was tough enough to take it, but they kept their distance."

Although Diana spoke bitterly in later years about her hatred of her stepmother, Raine clung to a more benign view of her youngest stepdaughter. In a 1981 interview, Raine recalled that Sarah "resented" her and Jane ignored her for two years, but Diana "was sweet, always did her own thing."

Raine joined the Spencer family at an especially difficult time for Sarah. After securing the job at *Vogue,* Sarah began what she described as an "intense love affair" with Gerald Grosvenor, the Duke of Westminster, who had been one of the escorts at her debutante party. Early in 1975, Sarah went to Australia, where her mother and stepfather owned a farm in New South Wales. On her return to London three months later, her relationship with Gerald Grosvenor ended, setting off Sarah's two-year ordeal with eating disorders.

"Sarah was very attractive and there were always little dramas in her love life," said a friend. "Her eating disorder had more to do with being rejected by a man than anything else." Sarah herself attributed her condition to the ruptured love affair, plus what she described as "domestic upheavals concerning my family," which created a situation she considered "catastrophic." Within a month of her return from Australia, recalled Sarah, "I just stopped eating. I would toy with a couple of pieces of lettuce, and if I forced a meal down I would just bring it up again."

Sarah's diminished appetite and weight loss were so alarming that her mother arranged for her to be admitted to hospital in May 1975. "I sought a lot of medical help," Frances said. Instead of improving, Sarah dropped seven pounds in two weeks. On leaving the hospital, she was no better, and she continued to struggle for the next year. Sarah's weight plummeted from 8 stone to 5½ stone, which on her five-foot-seven frame made her look "like something out of a concentration camp," said Sarah. "I couldn't find any normal clothes to fit me and did my shopping in the children's department." She didn't seek treatment because, as she said, "one behaves like an alcoholic. You will just not admit there is a problem. You end up believing you are beautiful, looking so thin."

Around the time of Johnnie's wedding to Raine in July 1976, Sarah escaped to Africa, where she spent several months traveling through Kenya, Rhodesia, and South Africa with two friends. On returning to England at the end of the year, she got a job working for a London real estate company, but, she said, "I was really in a physical mess, although of course I wouldn't admit it."

Sarah later acknowledged that she suffered from anorexia nervosa, the eating disorder dating from the mid–nineteenth century that is characterized by self-imposed starvation diets, but she also engaged in the binge eating and self-induced vomiting that define bulimia nervosa. ("Bulimia" comes from the Greek word *limos,* meaning "hunger," coupled with *bous,* meaning "bull" or "ox"; the term can mean either "hunger as great as that of an ox," or "hungry enough to consume an entire ox.") Although bulimia nervosa was not identified as a specific disorder until 1979, its symptoms had been seen in cases of anorexia such as Sarah's. "Sarah was sick after meals," recalled a friend from those years. "She was tiny. The only thing that kept her alive was Coca-Cola."

During this tense period, Diana visited Sarah at her apartment in Eaton Mews South on weekends away from West Heath. While bulimics and anorexics typically try to disguise the patterns of their fasting, overeating, and "inappropriate compensatory behaviors" such as vomiting, Sarah's friends and family saw through her subterfuges. Diana worried about her sister along with everyone else, but "she didn't try to play a role" in helping Sarah, said one of Sarah's friends.

It wasn't until several months before her death that Diana revealed how much she had been affected by watching Sarah's illness. Previously, Diana had always said her own eating disorder had been provoked by Charles's unfeeling treatment of her during her engagement. To psychiatrists and other mental health professionals, such a sudden emergence at that age seemed implausible without some history of eating problems. Finally, in May 1997, Diana told patients at Roehampton Priory, a private clinic outside London, that she first had symptoms of bulimia nervosa in the mid-seventies. "It started because Sarah was anorexic and I idolized her so much that I wanted to be like her," Diana said. "I never really understood why two sisters would develop such similar diseases, but we did, and I can only put it down to me wanting to emulate everything she did."

Diana's analysis made sense up to a point, as she did worship Sarah and was impressionable, but she failed to take into account other factors that seemed to govern her personality and behavior. One element might have been the influence of her mother, who admitted to her own difficulties with eating. Shortly after Diana's visit to Roehampton Priory, an interviewer asked Frances about stories that she had problems with alcohol. "I don't think I have," replied Frances, but added, somewhat elliptically, "I have a problem with eating, when I get fussed. . . . I don't think there is anything wrong with my eating. . . . It's only when I'm under pressure. . . . My problem has simply been not noticing if I haven't eaten."

There are strong indications that Diana began bingeing as a teenager in response to stressful situations. Diana may have been able to effectively cover up her bouts of purging, but the evidence of overeating was obvious. Both Ruth Rudge and Violet Allen at West Heath observed that Diana ate with gusto. "She was often seen lurking near the pantry, whether for leftovers to bolster her healthy appetite, as I suspected, or because she actually enjoyed domesticity, as she assured me," noted Ruth Rudge. Rudge also remembered Diana's "midnight feasts, bringing food back illegally into the school." Diana "loved food," wrote Penny Junor in her 1982 biography, "particularly baked beans, and she'd help herself to anything up to four bowls of All-Bran every morning." Diana herself recalled, "I ate and ate and ate. It was always a great joke—let's get Diana to have three kippers at breakfast and six pieces of bread, and I did all that."

The administrators at West Heath were attuned to anorexia, but not bulimia, which had yet to be identified by the psychiatric community. Although Diana had a tendency to put on weight quickly, she didn't balloon in a way that conformed to her eating habits. As one of Diana's relatives observed, "She used to eat a lot. She probably had to get rid of it somehow." The need to purge requires elaborate secrecy. "It is so easy to hide," said a woman close to the royal family who suffered from bulimia. "You get clever about running taps, putting on the radio. The deception with bulimia is huge." Diana had the capacity for secret behavior, as was evident in one of her descriptions of West Heath days: She recalled sneaking downstairs after lights-out, turning on her music, and dancing ballet routines for "hours on end" without being discovered.

Bulimic symptoms can be motivated by any number of impulses, but one is the need to impose some control—over the body as well as the mind—in uneasy circumstances. Such a situation occurred when Diana had to leave her childhood home in 1976. As the movers were packing up the family's belongings, Diana found the scene unbearable. She called Alex Loyd, one of her neighbors, and together the two girls gathered all the peaches in the Park House larder. They then went to the beach and devoured the entire cache. But no one took much notice of Diana's overeating in those days, and her symptoms seemed to be intermittent as well, limited by the protective environment of West Heath.

In addition to bingeing and purging, Diana kept things together in other ways that verged on obsessive behavior. From a very early age, she had been unusually neat. Even as a six-year-old, she had kept an immaculate bedroom, with her clothing and her toys perfectly arranged. Diana's cousin Robert Spencer noticed that she "was always washing or tidying or ironing. That was a nervous streak in her."

Diana's preoccupation carried over to school, where she seemed to find relief in cleaning up after the other girls. "I would go in sometimes and she would be there with a dustpan and brush," said matron Violet Allen. "I think perhaps some of the other girls thought she was excessively tidy. It could be, I suppose, her wanting to control her situation." In light of Diana's later loss of control in her private life, her behavior seems significant. "Diana had strong character traits that held her glued together," said Dr. Kent Ravenscroft, a child and adolescent psychiatrist and psychoanalyst. "She was a good girl cleaning up her bad feelings when she cleaned up around her. She had the urge to do untidy things, to be messy, but she used her character and upbringing and strength to hold on. Her tidiness was a way of managing."

In class, she wrote copious essays, recalling that the words "just came out of the pen, on and on and on"—not unlike her burst of compulsive chattering following her parents' breakup. Diana's late-night dancing for hours on end, she said, "always released tremendous tension in my head." She used exercise throughout her life as a way of dealing with stress or depression.

Diana's friendships at school weren't nearly as intense as they would be in adulthood, largely due to Ruth Rudge's West Heath policy that forbade "best friends," which helped avoid some of the tensions of teen friendship. Explained Rudge, "I didn't allow best friends because they break up and cause terrible traumas. Diana had no trouble making friends. There were about twenty-five of them in that particular group." Diana found safety in the group activities encouraged by Rudge, so the West Heath policy suited her emotional needs and prevented her relationships from getting out of hand.

The biggest source of anxiety for Diana, even at low-key West Heath, was the classroom. On one hand, she recalled liking all her courses, but she was easily distracted and rarely spoke in class. She failed to develop either intellectual rigor or curiosity; her sole passion was escaping into the romantic fiction of her stepgrandmother Barbara Cartland. Diana "wrote a lot," said Ruth Rudge. "But if you are writing for exams, you have to be concise and shape things up. She had suffered a lot. Her mind wasn't on her lessons, and the groundwork wasn't there. It was 'bitty and piecey.' She had a lot of catching up to do. As with anyone with other things on her mind, she would go off in daydreams."

Rudge attributed Diana's middling academic performance directly to the divorce. "Any child from a broken home is under more pressure than not," said Rudge. "Children cope with death better than with a broken home. Death is absolutely traumatic, but one copes. The other, a broken home, one doesn't really cope with at all."

Diana suffered no stigma at West Heath for her academic record. Indeed, even in the late seventies, many upper-class girls were not expected to pursue a university degree, and none of Diana's friends did. "She wouldn't have been made to feel inferior by the girls at school," said the mother of one of Diana's classmates. "The emphasis there was on sport and music and giggling. They learned what was necessary."

Despite the school's positive reinforcement of her talents, Diana's academic difficulties bothered her. "At the age of fourteen, I just remember thinking that I wasn't very good at anything, that I was hopeless," Diana recalled. At the time, Diana gave no indication of such feelings, according to Ruth Rudge and Violet Allen. But Diana's difficulties in the classroom foreshadowed some of the problems she would have in adulthood: poor concentration, lack of intellectual discipline, and inability to focus on anything for long.

At fifteen, Diana faced her O-level exams. Even for students with no plans for college, "If you wanted to get a job you had to get the O levels," said a woman who attended West Heath with Diana. "They were important. It was the first hurdle." When Diana took her O levels in June 1977 she failed them all: English literature, English language, history, art, and geography. The following autumn she took them again, and failed each one yet again. The explanation, according to Andrew Morton, was that she "froze." Penny Junor offered a similar reason, that "exams made her panic. . . . She forgot everything she ever knew," but added that Diana's friends also blamed her "sheer laziness and the fact that she was never pushed."

Still, it was highly unusual to fail every O level. After all, Diana's sister Sarah had passed six, and Jane eleven. Principal Ruth Rudge said she did not detect exam apprehension in Diana. "I never remember walking around with her and feeding her aspirins the night before, which I have done a number of times with other girls," said Rudge. "I didn't see any signs of panic when she took exams."

In hindsight, the magnitude of Diana's failure looks like a warning signal. Her intelligence was perfectly adequate, so there was no logical reason for her to perform so badly. It could have been a willful act, a sign of acute but hidden anxiety, or distraction due to trouble at home. Whatever the reason, it was the one moment in her youth when she was subjected to the kind of stressful demands she would encounter as Princess of Wales.

In later years, Diana openly bemoaned her early lack of self-esteem, and complained that no one took the time to listen to her. Paradoxically, she also talked about her dream as a young girl of doing "something special" and following a "winding road . . . going somewhere different, but I had no idea where." Diana expressed no urge to achieve on her own; rather, she spoke of wanting to marry a prominent man, which was a touchingly limited yearning to advance slightly beyond marriage to a garden-variety aristocrat. Nevertheless, Diana's tabloid chroniclers inflated this claim into a noteworthy aspiration. Richard Kay of the *Daily Mail* wrote that "it was well known in the family that Diana believed, even when she was very little, that she would grow up to marry someone important." Her astrologer Penny Thornton wrote that "according to Diana, her father would also tell her when she was little that he knew she was destined for great things."

But as so often happened, Diana's recollections differed markedly from the way others saw her. "She didn't talk that way as a child," said one of her relatives. "None of us had any great hopes for Diana. She was just another child." A *Woman's Own* interview with Johnnie Spencer seven years after Diana's marriage seconded that judgment, noting that he "never had her marked down to be a princess. . . . He hadn't really addressed himself to her future." Said Johnnie, "I always thought she'd do something involved with children, like child care." Once again, Diana's interpretation of her childhood showed a disparity between her "ordinary girl" exterior and the thoughts she said were churning in her mind.

Having twice failed her O levels, Diana had to leave West Heath at sixteen. Early in 1978, she enrolled in the Institute Alpin Videmanette near Gstaad in Switzerland, only the second time she had traveled outside England. The institute was a classic "finishing school," offering classes in shorthand and typing as well as "domestic science" courses in cooking and dressmaking that were designed to prepare girls for marriage. All classes were in French, and Diana was expected to learn the language, as Sarah had done.

Diana later said she felt completely unnerved by the school. She was one of only nine English-speaking girls out of sixty, she arrived five months after the school year had begun, and her French was so inferior that she would speak only English. "Diana felt totally left out," said the mother of one of her West Heath friends. "She was at a boarding school where, if you were English, it was not easy. Most of the girls were Spanish or Italian. It was too clannish."

Diana did make friends with the English girls, and joined them for skiing lessons, but she was deeply homesick. In her frantic effort to escape, she behaved in an obsessive fashion. She recalled writing "something like one hundred twenty letters" to her parents during the first month—roughly four a day. "I just wrote and wrote," Diana said. "I felt out of place there. . . . It was just too claustrophobic for me." After six weeks, her parents relented, and she was back in England by March. Rather poignantly, she made frequent visits to West Heath to see her old friends, and Violet Allen couldn't help observing that during her short time abroad, Diana had lost a noticeable amount of weight.

In retrospect, Diana's failure at finishing school showed how she could react when she felt exposed and insecure. After a chaotic early home life, she had spent seven years in boarding school's institutional setting. In many respects, Riddlesworth and West Heath had benefited Diana. Surrounded by jolly girls from similar backgrounds, her days were so packed with activities that she had little opportunity for loneliness. She had to live within the rules, which imposed a useful structure on a girl accustomed to having her own way. She found mother substitutes in the matrons who oversaw dormitory life. Above all, Riddlesworth and West Heath had given Diana an atmosphere of stability and reassurance that reined in her anxieties. As Ruth Rudge observed, "If Diana was in a safe and secure environment, she was fine."

Chapter 5

BECAUSE of her incomplete education and her age—still four months shy of her seventeenth birthday—Diana presented a dilemma for her mother and father when she returned to England in March 1978. Both her sisters had landed in London at eighteen with sufficient credentials to secure respectable jobs at *Vogue* magazine. Sarah had certificates from schools in Switzerland and Austria, topped off by a course in speedwriting. After graduating with distinction from West Heath, Jane had studied art for six months in Italy, and completed a secretarial course before joining *Vogue*. Sarah and Jane had each been launched into "society," although Jane's debut was less elaborate than Sarah's, but Diana had no debutante party, and she didn't navigate the social hurdles of the London Season. The reason, according to her friends and relatives, was that "coming out" had grown unfashionable, and Diana had no interest in any party presided over by her stepmother.

At first, Diana occupied herself helping Jane prepare for her marriage in April 1978 to Robert Fellowes, a former neighbor from Norfolk who worked as the Queen's assistant private secretary. Following the wedding, Diana's parents got her a job in the country as a nanny for some family friends. Diana said she couldn't wait to go to London, although her parents had told her she couldn't settle there until she was eighteen. Three months later, Diana managed to get her way and moved into her mother's house, at 69 Cadogan Place in Chelsea. "By the late seventies, Diana was definitely on good terms with her mother," Robert Spencer said. "It happened after Raine came on the scene."

Although Frances was living in Scotland, Diana wasn't left entirely on her own. She had two roommates—Laura Grieg, a friend from West Heath, and Sophie Kimball, whom Diana knew from her Swiss finishing school. Diana enjoyed her family's financial support, and two years later, at eighteen, she would come into an inheritance from her American great-grandmother Fanny Work that would allow her to buy her own London apartment, but Diana lacked the training to find a promising job. Prodded by her parents, she tried her hand at a three-month cooking course, which led to only a few jobs providing canapés for cocktail parties. She then signed on for a three-year training course to teach ballet, again at her mother's suggestion.

As an apprentice teacher at the ballet studio run by Betty Vacani in Kensington, Diana was responsible for working with more than a dozen two-year-olds. In theory, this seemed an ideal situation, combining her love of dance with her enjoyment of small children. But Diana felt over-whelmed, not only by the number of pupils but by the pressure of provid-ing instruction while gimlet-eyed mothers and nannies observed the classes. Much as she had at finishing school, Diana felt unsettled when she was away from her comfortable group of friends. After three months, Diana quit without explanation. By Morton's account, Diana couldn't con-tinue because she had torn "all the tendons in her left ankle" in a skiing ac-cident. Another version had her injuring her leg "slightly." When someone from the Vacani studio finally called to inquire about her absence, Diana said that she had hurt her foot and could no longer continue.

By this time, Diana's difficulty with making long-term commitments was more apparent than ever, although she was not the sort to lead an in-dolent life. "She did not hang about," said Robert Spencer. "Doing some-thing useful was always in her character." Diana needed to keep herself occupied, but she drifted through temporary work—low-stress, unde-manding jobs such as housecleaning and child care that drew on her agree-able demeanor. Describing her experience later, she derided her employers as "velvet hairbands" and expressed resentment that "nobody thanked me" for the work she did as a cleaner.

In the fall of 1979, Diana secured her first permanent employment as a part-time assistant at the Young England Kindergarten, which was run by Kay King, an older graduate of West Heath. "When it came to children, [Diana] had this incredible ability to get down to their level," said King. "They responded so well to her, she was completely at ease with them. They weren't a threat in any way." Six months later, Diana found a second job as a baby-sitter for an American family living in elegant Belgrave Square. These positions offered Diana reassuring routines that bolstered her confidence and made her feel needed: playing for hours on the floor with her American charge and taking him for long walks in his stroller, or-ganizing artwork for the kindergarten pupils, and tidying up at the end of the day.

Diana may have been surrounded by the bustle and temptations of a big city, but her life was a remarkably cloistered extension of her West Heath days. Her roommates and other friends were from boarding school or her childhood in Norfolk. They ran together as a group and shared the same taste in books, movies, and clothing—tweed skirts and cardigans, Laura Ashley shirts set off by pearls, sturdy shoes. Diana and her friends fit the definition of Sloane Rangers, young women (their male counterparts were known as "Hooray Henrys") whose lives revolved around the shops and restaurants of Sloane Square. "Diana was pure state-of-the-art Sloane," said Peter York, the style critic who originated the term in the seventies.

Diana's crowd led an utterly "square" existence, lacking even the social pressures of drinking, smoking, and drugs, all of which they avoided: "There were still pockets of innocence then," explained a man who befriended Diana in 1980. Their socializing consisted of small dinner parties, evenings at the movies or a favorite restaurant, excursions to the ballet, and house parties in the country. This was "the new school of born-again old-fashioned girls who play it safe and breed early," wrote Tina Brown in *Vanity Fair*, "postfeminist, postverbal," with a "femininity . . . modeled on a fifties concept of passive power" and "total absence of intellectual curiosity."

Although Andrew Morton characterized Diana as a "loner by inclination and habit" during these years, she actually seemed to shrink from seclusion. As at West Heath, Diana found security in the swarm of her friends, where she functioned largely on the surface and found fun in giggles and practical jokes. "I kept myself to myself," she recalled. Observed Rory Scott, an admirer who was a lieutenant in the Royal Scots Guards, "You always felt that there was a lot you would never know about her." Anything outside Diana's element threatened her equilibrium, however. "Diana didn't enjoy parties much," wrote Penny Junor. "She went if she knew she was going to meet friends there . . . but she didn't go just for the sake of a party, and she had no interest in meeting new people. She hated nightclubs too . . . possibly because they were full of the sort of flamboyant, sophisticated people with whom she felt at her most insecure."

Diana also conspicuously avoided intimate relationships with the young men in her group. "She just wasn't that involved with boys," said the mother of one of her friends. "She often said, 'Let's go out with the girls.' She preferred that." Diana had reached her full five foot ten height, and she certainly was pretty, but her mousey-brown hair was styled boyishly, she was slightly plump, and she wore juvenile clothing. Diana held her head down primarily to disguise her height, and she blushed easily. Yet Diana was good company, and men were drawn to her, though she kept her distance. Rory Scott found her "sexually attractive," he recalled, "and the relationship was not a platonic one as far as I was concerned, but it remained that way."

Another admirer, George Plumptre, wrote decades later in Diana's obituary for *The Daily Telegraph* that "Lady Diana's life in London lacked one element for which the press were to search ceaselessly and in vain—boyfriends. It seemed that she was happy to enjoy the company of a close and fairly small circle, and that she had no desire to form any serious attachment."

Characteristically, Diana offered differing explanations for her early relationships with men. The most dramatic, as revealed in her interviews with Morton, reflected her then-secret belief that she was destined to marry someone important. Diana explained that she was the only girl among her contemporaries who didn't have a boyfriend "because I knew somehow that I had to keep myself very tidy for whatever was coming my way." Diana did indeed project a quaintly virginal image for the swinging seventies. "She was an unusual thing, a good girl, fantastically innocent," said a longtime male friend. "I never heard any evidence Diana had sex before marriage, which was as rare as rocking-horse shit." Perhaps because of the trauma of her parents' divorce, Diana suffered from anxiety when it came to the opposite sex. "I had never had a boyfriend," Diana also said. "I'd always kept them away, thought they were all trouble—and I couldn't handle it emotionally. I was very screwed up, I thought."

By shutting the door on meaningful relationships with young men, Diana created an emotional vacuum in her life. She didn't learn the responsibilities that come with commitment—the sort of "practice" relationships that can provide valuable experience prior to marriage—nor was she exposed to the give and take of healthy interdependence with a man.

Diana also continued to have a low opinion of herself despite her devil-may-care facade. She was self-conscious about being plump, although if she was bingeing and purging she kept it well disguised. When Diana was feeling tense during her days at the Vacani ballet studio, she was known to dash across the street to "tuck into a good-sized chicken portion." During her cooking course in the fall of 1978, Diana "got terribly fat," she recalled. "My fingers were always in the saucepans." Her friend Rory Scott vividly remembered the time when Diana gobbled a one-pound bag of sweets while playing bridge.

Diana's refuge in compulsive neatness—another way she imposed control when feeling overwhelmed—was more obvious. At the apartment she bought at eighteen in Colherne Court, she took charge of the cleaning. During dinner parties she was known to rise even before the meal was finished so she could start washing up, because she couldn't bear the sight of dirty dishes.

Diana's arrival in London coincided with a significant turning point for her sister Sarah. Back in June 1977, Sarah—still so thin her bones nearly poked through her skin—had been working for a London real estate company. In spite of her illness, at twenty-two she was an eligible young woman, and she had been invited by the Queen to join her house party at Windsor Castle during the races at Ascot. That weekend, Prince Andrew introduced Sarah to Prince Charles, then twenty-eight, whom she had known from afar as a child at Sandringham.

According to Sarah, Charles greeted her by tactlessly asking, "Do you have anorexia?" "I, of course, like an alcoholic, said that I hadn't," she recalled. "But although I knew I hadn't fooled him, he did not persist." They enjoyed each other's company nevertheless, and six weeks later she checked herself into the Regent's Park Nursing Home to treat her eating disorder. "It is mind over matter and I had finally sorted myself out," Sarah said later. Although numerous accounts said that Charles had helped her toward recovery, Sarah credited "my mother and just common sense." "Within a week she had put on a stone [14 pounds]," recalled one of Sarah's friends. "She would eat and a nurse would prevent her from going to the loo."

It is difficult to account for the relative ease with which Sarah threw off her eating disorder once she committed herself to effective treatment, compared with Diana's inability to conquer her symptoms throughout two decades of affliction. "Bulimia ranges from fad bulimic people to people with serious personality disorders," explained child and adolescent psychiatrist Dr. Kent Ravenscroft, who has a special expertise in eating disorders. "If your bulimia is a passing skirmish, or a passing neurotic period of young to middle adolescence, it can be brief. . . . If it is embedded in a larger disorder, it can be difficult to treat."

By mid-July 1977, Sarah and the Prince of Wales were an item. One reporter even noted in the *Daily Express,* the "touching side to this friendship": "Lady Sarah . . . has been suffering from anorexia nervosa [and] . . . a member of her family tells me, 'Sarah has been in and out of hospital in recent months, and she has been seeing Prince Charles in between times.' " Sarah became a regular at Charles's polo games, and she joined him during the royal family's holiday at Balmoral, in Scotland, at the end of the summer. "He makes me laugh and I enjoy being with him," she told *The Sun* in November, adding rather boldly, "I have two or three other boyfriends, and I go out with them just as much." However, one of the tabloid reporters who tracked her at the time, *The Sun*'s James Whitaker, undercut Sarah's apparent nonchalance by reporting that a "friend" of Sarah's told him, "She is crazy about the Prince. You should see her bedroom. The whole wall is covered in photographs of him."

So which was it: smitten or indifferent? According to a friend since childhood, while Sarah was flattered that the Prince of Wales was paying attention to her, "She realized quite early he was not for her. She didn't fancy him." Charles's longtime valet Stephen Barry later wrote, "I never thought there was anything in it" with Sarah. To Barry, she was little more than "the girl next door" from Norfolk days. This was also a time when the late twenty-something heir to the throne seemed especially fickle in his romances. "His closest friends began to worry about the rate with which young women came in and out of his life, too often—it seemed to them—picked up and discarded on a whim," wrote his authorized biographer Jonathan Dimbleby, "but he seemed to derive precious little joy from these encounters."

Nevertheless, Sarah Spencer invited Prince Charles to Althorp for a pheasant shoot in November 1977. Diana was about to take her O-level exams for the second time, and she came home for the weekend from West Heath. Diana had supposedly been mooning over Prince Charles from afar for years. "When she was twelve, Diana attended the exclusive West Heath School in Kent," wrote *Time* magazine in a typical account, "where she hung a picture of Charles above her bed." The story of the picture was untrue, and its origins reveal something of how the tabloid press concocted vital parts of the Diana saga: "After the investiture of the Prince of Wales in 1969," said West Heath headmistress Ruth Rudge, "Cecil King, then at the *News of the World,* sent his granddaughter Lorna, who was at West Heath, a large picture of the investiture. We put it on the wall in a bedroom. Later, when the press decided to descend on the school, we happened to be by this particular bedroom. I pulled open the door and said, 'I expect Diana slept in here sometime,' because in the course of their school life, the girls changed rooms and roommates at the end of each term. The reporters rushed up to this picture under which Diana might have slept and gazed, and made it a big deal."

With thirteen years between them, Diana and Charles had scarcely crossed paths during her childhood at Sandringham, so the weekend at Althorp was the first time they had been properly introduced. The circumstance of their meeting, in a plowed field at Nobottle Wood on the estate, has taken on totemic significance. In their own recollections, however, neither professed to be overwhelmed by the other. "His first impression," wrote Dimblebly, "was that she was, as his friends put it, 'jolly' and 'bouncy,' an unaffected teenager who was relaxed, irreverent and friendly."

Diana's account was more uneasy, complicated by her self-doubts as well as a surge of competition with her older sister. "The first impact was 'God, what a sad man,' " Diana recalled. "My sister was all over him like a bad rash, and I thought, 'God, he must really hate that' "—an astute observation for a sixteen-year-old, although it's more likely that Diana was applying her retrospective knowledge of Charles's aversion to public displays of affection. Diana described herself as a "fat, podgy, no-makeup, unsmart lady," but admitted that she tried to attract Charles's attention by being noisy, which he seemed to enjoy. At a dance given by the Spencers that evening, Charles asked her to show him Althorp's picture gallery. She was about to comply when Sarah intervened and told Diana to "push off."

The next day at the shoot, Diana ignored her sister's admonition and took up position next to Charles. Diana was "sort of amazed" that he paid attention to her. "Why would anyone like him be interested in me?" she wondered, "and it WAS interest." Diana's explanation: "He was charm itself." Diana may well have developed a full-blown crush that weekend, yet no evident spark was struck between them. One of the tabloids subsequently reported that Sarah and Charles "were seen walking around the corridors hand in hand," and several weekends later Sarah was a guest of the royal family at Sandringham.

However Sarah might have felt about the Prince of Wales, her head seemed to be turned by the publicity. According to *The Sun*'s James Whitaker, Sarah kept a scrapbook filled with clippings about her relationship with Charles that she intended to "show [her] grandchildren one day."

The following February, Charles invited Sarah to join a group of friends for a ten-day skiing holiday in Klosters, Switzerland. Tabloid reporters trailed her around the slopes, and photographers took her picture. Back in London, she made a crucial mistake by meeting two of her new tabloid friends—James Whitaker and the *Daily Mail*'s Nigel Nelson—at a Mayfair restaurant. She showed up in a long blue skirt and a green vinyl parka, and over a meal of smoked salmon and fish pie, Sarah revealed how she felt about the Prince of Wales.

After characterizing him as "a romantic who falls in love easily," she said, "I'm not in love with Prince Charles. I'm a whirlwind sort of lady, as opposed to a person who goes in for slow-developing courtships. I can assure you that if there was to be any engagement between Prince Charles and myself, then it would have happened by now. I wouldn't marry anyone I didn't love—whether it was the dustman or the King of England. If he asked me I would turn him down. . . . He doesn't want to marry anyway. He's not ready for marriage yet. . . . Our whole approach has always been a brotherly-sisterly one, never anything else. . . . There's no question of me being the future Queen of England. I don't think he's met her yet."

On February 18, 1978, the *Daily Mail* and *The Sun* published Sarah's comments about her relationship with Charles, along with a brief reference to her history of anorexia. "This is the first time one of Charles's girlfriends has talked publicly and frankly about her relationship with the Prince," Nelson wrote in the *Mail*. The *News of the World* was positively gleeful the next day, proclaiming, "What a girl! Prince Charles will be lucky indeed if he finds one to match her for candor, charm and common sense."

Yet it wasn't until more than a month later that Sarah got into serious trouble for her indiscretion. Whitaker wrote a longer article based on the interview for the widely read *Woman's Own* magazine, under the byline Jeremy Slazenger, one of his six pseudonyms. (A gossip columnist in the *Daily Express* later described Whitaker as a "panicky perspiring figure who begs me not to reveal his true identity.") Whitaker, as Slazenger, recycled Sarah's comments about Prince Charles, along with her descriptions of her drinking and expulsion from boarding school, a detailed account of her battle with anorexia, and her claim to have had "thousands of boyfriends." According to Whitaker, Sarah told him that when she called Charles to alert him to the article, he remarked, "You've just done something extremely stupid." Sarah frantically tried to backpedal, telling the *Daily Mail* that her comments were obtained "by foul means," perhaps forgetting that a shortened version had already appeared in two tabloids, including the *Mail*. "My sister Sarah spoke to the press," Diana later told Mary Robertson, her employer in London, "and frankly . . . that was the end of her."

Nevertheless, Diana seemed intrigued by Sarah's brush with fame. When James Whitaker showed up to cover her sister Jane's wedding in April 1978 at the Guard's Chapel in London, Diana recognized the tabloid reporter and approached him. "I know who you are, you're the wicked Mr. Whitaker," she said. "Who are you?" Whitaker asked. "I'm Sarah's baby sister," Diana replied. "I know all about you."

Chapter 6

SARAH Spencer was correct when she said Prince Charles was "not ready for marriage yet." "He was a complete bachelor," said Michael Colborne, who worked as an aide to Charles from 1975 to 1985. "I think if he hadn't had the pressure to produce an heir to the throne, he might not have married."

Nevertheless, Charles's romantic entanglements had become a tabloid press preoccupation as the young prince approached his thirtieth birthday in November 1978—a benchmark he had rashly set for himself during an interview with *Woman's Own* magazine in February 1975. "I've fallen in love with all sorts of girls," Charles had said, "but I've made sure I haven't married the first person I've fallen in love with. . . . I personally feel that a good age for a man to get married is around 30."

With those jaunty words, Charles inadvertently issued a challenge to the tabloid hacks, who had already been amusing themselves with reports on the dashing young naval officer—an "action man" who parachuted out of airplanes, flew jets, skied, surfed, and played polo. By pushing himself to the limit physically, Charles was showing the world that he was a made of stronger stuff than anyone might have anticipated a decade earlier.

As a young boy born in the first years of the postwar baby boom, Charles had been strikingly timid, with a sensitive, easily wounded nature. Like most of his aristocratic contemporaries, he had been cared for largely by servants, and his relationship with his parents had been highly ritualized: half-hour sessions with his mother in the mornings, ninety-minute intervals in the evenings. Even in her days as Princess Elizabeth, his mother had been diverted by the burden of her public duties, and when she became Queen at twenty-five, she grew even more distant.

Neither parent was emotionally demonstrative, and both were often away on official tours during Charles's birthdays and holidays. According to his official biographer Jonathan Dimbleby, they both had a "deep if inarticulate love for their son," yet their way of life prevented them from sharing much of it with Charles. His father was an intelligent, robust character who utterly lacked the sensitivity required to motivate a diffident boy. Philip viewed Charles's manner as weak, and in his irritation mocked and criticized the boy, often unfairly. Charles reacted by withdrawing further into his shell, while his mother declined to intervene. Explained Dimbleby, "she was not indifferent so much as detached, deciding that in domestic matters she would submit entirely to the father's will."

Charles found emotional solace from two women: his nanny, Mabel Anderson, and his grandmother Queen Elizabeth, the Queen Mother. Anderson was a constant presence from Charles's infancy, providing physical affection and moral support—the very sort of "surrogate mother" Diana Spencer could have used. During his parents' prolonged absences, Charles also spent a great deal of time with his grandmother, who cuddled him, regaled him with stories, and nurtured his interest in art and music. His connection with the Queen Mother was "the most intimate of the Prince's relationships within the family . . . for him a vital source of praise and encouragement," wrote Dimbleby.

From his earliest years, Charles's education groomed him to inherit the throne from his mother. He had a governess until age five, when he was sent to Hill House, the London preparatory school, in an effort to expose him to everyday life outside the royal cloister. Like Diana, he was an indifferent student. At age nine, he went to Cheam, a boarding school in Berkshire, where his father had done well. Charles felt lost, but managed to hide his unhappiness. Although he emerged as a school leader by the end of his five years at Cheam, he had little enthusiasm for the place.

When Charles turned thirteen, his father marched him into another alma mater, Gordonstoun in Scotland, which prided itself on instilling physical and mental toughness—just the thing to bring out a reticent boy, in Prince Philip's view. The Queen Mother had wanted her grandson to attend Eton instead. Located in the shadow of Windsor Castle, Eton would have offered Charles the camaraderie of boys more like himself, but Philip's preference prevailed.

The rigors of Gordonstoun's infamous cold showers, early morning runs, and mandatory dress code of shorts year-round seemed of dubious value. Yet in theory, the school's egalitarian ethos and the diversity of its student body offered a sensible way to broaden the horizons of a privileged royal prince. In practice, the culture of humiliation among the boys—cruel taunts and gratuitous punches, organized gangs of older bullies who preyed on younger students—proved harrowing for Charles. Because of his position, Charles felt the brunt of this malicious treatment. "I simply dread going to bed as I get hit all night long," he wrote in one letter.

A loner by nature, Charles became even more so at Gordonstoun. "I'm not a gregarious person," Charles later said. "I have always preferred my own company or just a one-to-one." Yet Charles did well academically, passing five O levels. Thanks to several gifted teachers, he gained confidence as an artist by learning pottery, and as an actor by playing the lead in *Macbeth*. He also learned the cello, prompting his grandmother's best friend Ruth Fermoy to pronounce him a "sensitive musician"—a judgment she declined to bestow on her granddaughter Diana's piano-playing. Nevertheless, Charles remained afflicted by low self-esteem, which was only intensified by being bullied at Gordonstoun and his parents' inability to applaud his achievements.

Prince Philip posed one more character-building challenge after Charles turned seventeen: a sabbatical in the Australian outback at a school called Timbertop. Charles was reluctant at first. When he left, he told his grandmother that he would wear two watches. "I have one set to Australian time and the other to English time," he said, "so I can think about what you are doing at all times." As at Gordonstoun, the emphasis at Timbertop was on fostering initiative and self-reliance, and this time the lessons stuck. Charles thrived on learning to prepare meals, cutting down trees for fuel, and hiking in the wilderness.

He also made some friends and found what Dimbleby called a "surrogate elder brother" in his father's equerry, David Checketts, who served as an aide to the young prince. Charles spent weekends with Checketts, his wife, and three children. It was the Prince's first exposure to real family life, and he could relax in the informality of the Checketts household. In Australia, Charles was able "to find himself—free of Gordonstoun, away from his parents, away from the British press, away from the suffocating certainties of royal life," wrote Dimbleby.

The experience made Charles's last year at Gordonstoun more bearable. He was also appointed head boy, which offered new responsibilities such as serving as the intermediary between students and staff, as well as privileges. Rather than living in a communal dormitory, Charles had his own bedroom, which adjoined the apartment of his art teacher, Robert Waddell, who stimulated his intellectual curiosity during long conversations about music, art, history, and archaeology. In such encounters, Charles's boarding school years differed significantly from Diana's. He may have endured his classmates' tyrannies, but because he was male, and the heir to the throne at that, teachers took a keen interest in making the most of him intellectually. At eighteen, Charles passed his A levels and secured admission to Trinity College, Cambridge.

At Cambridge, Charles fell in with the sort of young men he would have known at Eton: aristocrats who spent their free time hunting, shooting, fishing, and playing polo. He joined the drama group, in which he appeared in a revue, spent a term at University College of Wales to learn Welsh, and submitted to his first radio and television interviews as part of his investiture as Prince of Wales in 1969. Charles was a diligent but less than dazzling student; however, when he earned a "lower second-class degree" in history in 1970, he became the first future king to graduate from college. At the suggestion of his father and his great-uncle Lord Mountbatten, Charles entered the Royal Naval College at Dartmouth in the autumn of 1971 for a career in the service—once again following his father's path.

Unable to talk to his parents about intimate subjects, Charles turned to Mountbatten for advice on his late-blooming interest in romance. Mountbatten encouraged him to "sow his wild oats," and offered the use of his home, Broadlands, as a safe haven for trysts, away from the nosy press.

Shortly after Charles turned twenty-three in November 1971, a friend from Cambridge named Lucia Santa Cruz, the daughter of the Chilean ambassador, introduced him to someone she considered "just the girl" for him. Her name was Camilla Shand, and she was a year older than Charles. The daughter of Major Bruce Shand, a wine merchant and avid huntsman, Camilla was related to Lord Ashcombe of the Cubitt family that built much of fashionable Belgravia in London. She was also the great-granddaughter of Alice Keppel, the longtime lover of King Edward VII. Gossip columnist Nigel Dempster wrote that the connection prompted Camilla to greet Charles on their first meeting "with a searching look," and say, "My great-grandmother was the mistress of your great-grandfather." (According to Dempster, when he printed this anecdote in July 1981, Camilla's husband, Andrew Parker Bowles, told him it was "dashed accurate.")

Camilla was known to be quick-witted, and she was full of the confidence that Diana lacked. She had been through a similarly unchallenging education, topped off by school in Switzerland and a turn as a popular London debutante. She was also attractive to men: "She has laughing eyes," said a friend of the Shands. "She is an intensely warm, maternal, laughing creature, with enormous sex appeal." For a young girl, Camilla had an engaging directness, and an earthy streak that came through in what another friend described as a "slightly sexy, ginny voice" deepened by cigarette smoking. "She is about dogs and gumboots, and a cozy life," continued the friend. She shared Charles's self-deprecatory humor and fondness for the absurd, as well as his love of the country and its range of sporting pursuits. Most of all, Camilla made him feel secure, not least because she was so comfortable in her own skin. "He always liked older women," said a friend of the Queen's who knew Charles from childhood. "He is able to relax with them." "With all the intensity of first love," wrote Dimbleby, Charles "lost his heart to [Camilla] almost at once."

Years later, with the release of the infamous "Camillagate" tape in 1992—a telephone conversation between Charles and Camilla, surreptitiously recorded in 1989—it would become clear that Camilla knew how to please the Prince, and perhaps to manipulate him as well. Although much attention would focus on the silly sexual banter (especially Charles's desire to be reincarnated as Camilla's Tampax to "live inside [her] trousers"), the more revealing aspect of the tape was Camilla's solicitude toward him: her eagerness to read one of his speeches, to mop his brow, soothe his doubting ego, and encourage him at every turn ("I think, as usual, you're underestimating yourself. . . . You're a clever old thing, an awfully good brain lurking there, isn't there?").

At the time of her first encounter with Charles, Camilla had been dating Andrew Parker Bowles, a handsome officer in the Household Cavalry whose father, Derek, was a close friend and distant relative of the Queen Mother's. Nearly a decade older than Charles, Parker Bowles had become friendly with the Prince through polo and hunting. Parker Bowles was a ladies' man, and his relationship with Camilla had been through its ups and downs.

By mid-1972 Charles and Camilla had struck up a relationship, and began spending time together in London and at the Mountbatten estate. In Camilla's company, Charles became "more confident," according to Dimbleby; nevertheless, he had no intention of marrying for a while, and he faced a long tour at sea starting the following January. Charles and Camilla spent their last weekend together that December at Broadlands, but he didn't ask her to wait for him. Writing to his great-uncle, Charles noted that it was "the last time I shall see her for eight months."

When Charles was at sea, he wrote about Camilla in his journal from time to time, but the couple didn't correspond. She took up again with Andrew Parker Bowles, and in April 1973, Charles learned that Camilla would marry the cavalry officer that July. Charles wrote to a friend that it seemed unfair, after "such a blissful, peaceful and mutually happy relationship," that he and Camilla had been able to enjoy only six months together. He lamented that he had "no one" to return to in England, adding, "I suppose the feeling of emptiness will pass eventually."

Charles heard the news about Camilla while he was on vacation at the home of Mountbatten's daughter Patricia Brabourne on Eleuthera in the

Caribbean, yet by then he had already found a diversion in the Brabournes' daughter Amanda Knatchbull. "I must say, Amanda really has grown into a very good-looking girl—most disturbing," Charles wrote to Mountbatten two days before he confided his gloomy thoughts about losing Camilla.

Prodded by his great-uncle, Charles started to correspond with Amanda, and Mountbatten began to steer the couple toward the possibility of marrying. "Perhaps being away and being able to think about life and about the future (and her) has brought ideas of marriage into a more serious aspect," Charles wrote to Mountbatten in 1974. He noted that Amanda was "incredibly affectionate and loyal, with a glorious sense of fun and humor—and she's a country girl as well, which is even more important."

Other women shuttled in and out of Charles's life during these years, usually unknown to the press. But when he left the Royal Navy in December 1976, he moved into the tabloid sights. Except for King Edward VIII's abdication to marry Wallis Simpson in 1936, reporters had taken only a superficial interest in the royals; but the Prince of Wales had caught their attention, and once he passed his thirtieth birthday, the tabloid hacks became obsessed with the ultimate scoop. As Harry Arnold, the veteran tabloid reporter, described it, "Our editor said . . . 'We want to be the first to tell the British public who Prince Charles is going to marry.' "

By 1978, Charles had given no indication who that might be. But behind his mercurial approach to romance, he had been establishing a set of guiding principles for his ideal bride, which he had set out in a series of informal manifestos that went all the way back to 1969, when he granted a TV interview for his investiture. Part romance, part pragmatism, his statements revealed an earnest yearning for a soulmate who would share his interests and his devotion to duty, and who would show him the deference he had come to expect from everyone around him. His words also revealed a sense of foreboding about the responsibilities that his wife would inevitably assume.

Looking distinctly nervous as he broached such private thoughts, Charles told the TV interviewer in 1969, "You've got to remember . . . in my position you're going to marry somebody who perhaps one day is going to become Queen, and you've got to choose somebody very carefully, I think, who can fulfill this particular role because people like you [the interviewer], perhaps, would expect quite a lot from somebody like that, and it's got to be somebody pretty special." Although much would later be made of the need for Charles to marry a virgin, that was not a specific requirement per se. Rather, as royal historian Hugo Vickers wrote, "His bride needed to have a character of such irrefutable dignity that such questions were irrelevant."

Mountbatten subsequently urged Charles (with his own granddaughter in mind, no doubt) to "choose a suitable and sweet-charactered girl before she meets anyone else she might fall for." In 1974, the same year as Mountbatten's exhortation, Charles emphasized the need for a wife to adapt to her husband's world: "A woman not only marries a man; she marries into a way of life into which she's got a contribution to make," he told Kenneth Harris of *The Observer*. "She's got to have some knowledge of it, some sense of it, or she wouldn't have a clue about whether she's going to like it. And if she didn't have a clue, it would be risky for her, wouldn't it?" Marriage, he said, was "the last decision on which I want my head to be ruled by my heart."

The following year, Charles discussed the premium he also placed on compatibility and shared interests. "My marriage has to be forever," he said, adding, "A lot of people get the wrong idea of what love is all about. It is rather more than just falling madly in love with somebody and having a love affair for the rest of your married life. . . . It's basically a very strong friendship. As often as not you have shared interests and ideas in common and also have a great deal of affection. And I think where you are very lucky is when you find the person attractive in the physical and the mental sense. To me marriage . . . seems to be one of the biggest and most responsible steps to be taken in one's life. . . . Marriage is something you ought to work at. I may easily be proved wrong but I intend to work at it when I get married."

In his *Woman's Own* interview with Douglas Keay in February 1975, Charles pursued yet another crucial theme: He wanted "a secure family unit in which to bring up children, to give them a happy, secure upbringing—that is what marriage is all about. Essentially one must be good friends, and love I'm sure will grow out of friendship and become deeper and deeper." Yet Charles was beginning to doubt the intentions of various women he had met. "You must get married at once," TV broadcaster Alistair Cooke told Charles over lunch in 1976. "Yes, well, it's not that easy," Charles replied. "You see, every time a girl tells me that she loves me, I have to ask myself whether she really loves me or just wants to be Queen. And whoever I choose is going to have a jolly hard job, always in my shadow, having to walk a few steps behind me, all that sort of thing."

The year Charles turned thirty, an increasingly impatient Mountbatten gave him a jolt by warning that he was "beginning on the downward slope which wrecked your uncle David's [Edward VIII] life and led to his disgraceful abdication and his futile life ever after." Charles was starting to feel the pressure, telling a friend in April 1979, "I must say I am becoming rather worried by all this talk about being self-centered. . . . I'm told that marriage is the only cure for me—and maybe it is! . . . The media will simply not take me seriously until I do get married and apparently become responsible. At the moment I'm convinced that they see me as 'marriage' or 'bird' fodder."

Throughout the seventies, Amanda Knatchbull remained in the picture for Charles. Clearly he admired and respected her, and he recognized that she instinctively understood the demands of the "job." Not long after Mountbatten's rebuke about selfishness, Charles raised the topic of marriage with Amanda, who gently and swiftly turned him down. She grasped all too well the sacrifices that she would have to make as his wife: giving up her independence, losing her identity in the royal family, and exposing herself to relentless scrutiny by the press.

"She was fond of the Prince," noted a man who knew her well, "but she knew the life would be unbearable." Ironically, the very qualities that drove her to rebuff Charles argued for her suitability as his consort: She was secure in her identity, she had no illusions about the monarchy, and she had a realistic view of what she wanted from life. "She is a very attractive and warm woman, very sensible, feet on the ground," her friend continued. "She was much more aware of the duties than Diana was, because the Mountbattens were closer to the throne than the Spencers."

Amanda Knatchbull did not appear to know, however, that Charles had recently renewed his relationship with Camilla Parker Bowles, by then married for six years and the mother of two children, the second of whom was born in 1979. Because of the friendship between the Parker Bowles family and the Queen Mother, Andrew and Camilla had often been invited to the various royal residences, where they spent time with Prince Charles. In many ways, the Parker Bowleses had a typically male-dominated, upper-class marriage. They lived essentially separate lives, he in London with a succession of mistresses, and she in the country, where he would return for hunting and shooting on the weekend. Camilla was no fool; she was aware of her husband's peccadilloes. "It was an open marriage," said a friend of the couple. "He wandered a lot."

By 1979, Charles was having long telephone conversations with Camilla; he had come to regard her as the best friend to whom he could confide his hopes, happiness, anxieties, and secrets. He was drawn, according to Dimbleby, to her "warmth, her lack of ambition or guile, her good humour and her gentleness." They fell in love, and when Andrew left that year for a six-month posting in Zimbabwe (then Rhodesia), Charles and Camilla's relationship again became intimate. Close friends and some family members "began to suppose that they were having a clandestine affair . . . to a point where [Charles] was warned that an illicit liaison would be damaging to his own standing," according to Dimbleby. Yet the Queen, in her customary hands-off fashion, declined to intervene to end the relationship.

Diana Spencer faced another family trauma in September 1978, when her father collapsed at fifty-four from a massive cerebral hemorrhage. He lay in a coma for several months as Raine supervised his care in a London hospital. "The surgeons didn't want to operate because they were sure I was going to die," Johnnie said a decade later. "She told them to 'Bloody well get on with it!' She saved me." When Johnnie contracted pneumonia, Raine used her connections to secure an untested medication from Germany that cured him. "I was the first person after the rats that it was tried on," Johnnie said.

Diana, then seventeen, and her siblings resented Raine's controlling behavior. They felt that Raine kept them from visiting their father in the hospital—with the exception of Sarah, who asserted herself and went anyway. Afterward, Diana believed that her father had become a different person: "estranged but adoring."

The only bright spot evident in that otherwise gloomy autumn was Diana's invitation to attend a dance at Buckingham Palace for Prince Charles's thirtieth birthday on November 14, 1978. Sarah Spencer was naturally invited because of her friendship with Charles, but Diana's inclusion came as a surprise. As she had been when she met Charles a year earlier at Althorp, Diana was intrigued by Sarah's apparent jealousy.

Detecting signals that Diana "hadn't twigged on to," Sarah wondered why her younger sister was included. Diana later said she had not been "intimidated" by Buckingham Palace, although she confessed thinking it was an "amazing place."

As their father left the hospital in January 1979 to begin his long convalescence, Sarah and Diana were invited to Sandringham for a shooting weekend; their sister Jane was part of the house party because of her husband's position as assistant private secretary to the Queen. According to Penny Junor's 1982 biography of Diana, "that weekend was the beginning of Diana's relationship with the Prince of Wales. . . . Diana still nurtured a schoolgirl crush on him, which she had had ever since their meeting in November 1977, which he cannot have failed to notice and be flattered by."

Tabloid reporter James Whitaker had taken up his customary position outside the Sandringham estate that weekend, peering at the royals through binoculars, as was his habit. "They were shooting pheasants," Whitaker recalled, "and [Diana] was a very young girl who stayed very close to the Prince of Wales. Sarah was around, too, but Diana was absolutely at his side, and he was interested. We established that it was Sarah's sister, so we thought she must be there for [his younger brother] Andrew. Still, it was odd that she spent all day close to Charles. She was grabbing Charles's binoculars and pulling him along, pulling at the binoculars and looking through them. It was the kind of thing that would ordinarily annoy him, but clearly it didn't. She was looking at us. She was very relaxed, intimate, not a bit fazed, and Charles was not irritated. There was some chemistry because he didn't object to her pulling his neck off. It was a flirtatious thing."

Penny Junor ventured further in her book, offering two slightly different interpretations of Charles's feelings for Diana. "Charles probably didn't see his relationship with [Diana] as anything other than platonic in those days," she wrote, "but he must have enjoyed her sense of humor and found quite refreshing her ease with him and her lack of sophistication." Further along, Junor turned more categorical, stating, "Charles found himself strangely attracted to her, though not in any consciously physical sense. . . . He found Diana fun to be with. . . . She did liven up the party. She wasn't quite as unpredictable as Sarah but she was irreverently giggly and girlish, yet sensitive. In some ways she was a little girl, in other ways she showed uncanny maturity. It was a curious mixture, which Charles found appealing."

According to Junor's biography, Charles began to see Diana "quite a lot" in 1979—not as a girlfriend, but as part of a group. "He would ring up Cadogan Place out of the blue and ask her out to the ballet or to the opera, often to make up numbers." Diana was considered "good value . . . guaranteed to make everyone enjoy themselves." As a companion, Junor continued, "she was undemanding, she obviously liked to be with him, which was flattering." Yet "no one ever took much notice" of Diana: Those aware of the Prince's activities during that time don't specifically recall her. "She could have been amongst the party and I might not have known it," said Michael Colborne, a close aide at the time. According to Charles's valet Stephen Barry, the Prince was "disorganized about arrangements" and often put together impromptu groups.

Diana turned eighteen in July. After her customary visit to her mother in Scotland, she went to stay with her sister Jane at her cottage at Balmoral, where Charles and his family were spending their holiday. Nothing remarkable occurred during this visit—Charles, at this time, was preoccupied by his growing closeness to Camilla—and Diana returned to London, where she busied herself with her new apartment.

A month later, in August 1979, tragedy hit Charles for the first time. His beloved great-uncle Mountbatten was assassinated by IRA terrorists while fishing off the west coast of Ireland. Mountbatten's fourteen-year-old grandson Nicholas was also killed, along with the Irish boatman, and Doreen, Lady Brabourne, who was the mother of Mountbatten's son-in-law. Mountbatten's daughter Patricia, her husband, John, and Nicholas's twin brother were severely injured. "I have lost someone infinitely special in my life," Charles wrote in his journal that night, "someone who showed enormous affection, who told me unpleasant things I didn't particularly want to hear, who gave praise where it was due as well as criticism; someone to whom I knew I could confide anything and from whom I would receive the wisest of counsel and advice."

Charles had others to console him that fall—Camilla, to be sure, and Amanda Knatchbull, with whom he remained friends. Charles also became infatuated with twenty-five-year-old Anna Wallace, whom he met while hunting in November. The daughter of a millionaire Scottish landowner, she had worked as private secretary to a flamboyant Iranian hostess named Homayoun Mazandi. Known in social circles as the "caviar queen," Mazandi threw lavish parties in her grand six-story house at 46 Chester Square in London. Mazandi's secretary was predictably high-spirited as well, earning the nickname "Whiplash Wallace" from friends impressed by her enthusiasm on the hunting field.

Anna was very pretty, and Charles was smitten—although revelations in Nigel Dempster's gossip column cast doubt on her fitness to be Charles's wife. "There is a risqué picture of Anna in circulation—and I have a copy of it," he wrote on June 10, 1980. "She'll never be Queen of England." The tabloids speculated that Charles asked Wallace to marry him and she said no. Yet a man who knew Charles well said, "I don't think he was interested in marrying her. She wasn't that important." Indeed, Stephen Barry noted that although the Prince was "enormously attracted" to Wallace, "he seemed to be more cautious with her than any of his other girls."

Even as Charles was distracted by his romances, the invitations kept coming to Diana Spencer. In February 1980, she traveled again to Sandringham for a shooting party, this time accompanied by Amanda Knatchbull. One of Sarah Spencer's roommates, Lucinda Craig Harvey, recalled that Diana's excitement was tinged with self-deprecation over the prospect of anything serious developing with the Prince of Wales: "Can you see me swanning around in kid gloves and a ball gown?"

Around the same time, Diana started baby-sitting for Mary Robertson, her American employer, who was struck by her blossoming good looks: "perfect English skin, a slight blush on her cheeks, and clear blue eyes. She simply glowed with youth and good health." Diana's beauty caught the eye of a man who met her for the first time early that year at a twenty-first birthday party for the Duchess of Westminster, the former Natalia Phillips, whom Diana had known since childhood. "I said, 'God, that's a pretty girl,'" he recalled. "Diana was definitely doelike." For all her insecurities, Diana had a disconcertingly bold side as well, and the man at the birthday party was struck that she recognized him as a friend of one of her sisters and introduced herself. "In England, people don't do that," he recalled. "People are so reserved. She seemed to have no 'side' to her: By that I mean she was totally natural."

After a number of "casual encounters" with Diana, Charles "began to think seriously of her as a potential bride," according to Dimbleby, although he had not experienced "any apparent surge in feeling for her" in the more than two years since they crossed paths at Althorp. They next met in July 1980 shortly after Diana's nineteenth birthday, when both were invited to a weekend at the Sussex home of Robert de Pass, whose son Philip ran with the crowd of men she knew in London. "You're a young blood," Philip had said to her. "You might amuse him."

Diana watched Charles play polo during her weekend with the de Pass family, and James Whitaker recalled seeing her at the tournament without linking her with Charles. At the de Pass's barbecue following the polo match, Diana and Charles sat together on a bale of hay, beyond the lenses of the tabloid press. The image of that scene, however, has earned nearly as prominent a place in their saga as the initial meeting in the plowed field.

Diana's description of this encounter was filled with Charles's mixed signals and her own disquieting interpretations: "He was all over me . . . and it was very strange," she recalled. "I thought, 'Well, this isn't very cool.' I thought men were supposed not to be so obvious. I thought this was very odd."

She told him how sad he had looked during Lord Mountbatten's funeral, and that her heart had bled for him. "The next minute," she recalled, "he leapt on me, practically, and I thought this was very strange, and I wasn't quite sure how to cope with all this." Yet after expressing alarm about his being too physical with her, she seemed distressed by Charles's evident restraint when he seemed content only to talk. "Frigid wasn't the word," she said. "Big F when it comes to that."

Charles was touched by Diana's compassion for his grief over Mountbatten, and he recalled "how she had sensed his loneliness and his need for someone to care for him." Several weeks later he spilled out his feelings to a close friend, in all likelihood Lady Susan Hussey, a woman somewhat older than Charles who had been lady-in-waiting to the Queen for two decades. "It was to Lady Susan that he talked about his girlfriends and his problems," explained Stephen Barry. "She was always at the palace." In late July 1980, Charles told his confidante that "he had met the girl he intended to marry," wrote Dimbleby. "He spoke of Diana Spencer's easy and open manner, of her warmth, of her enthusiasm for rural life and of her background, through which she knew a little of his family and certainly enough, he presumed, to have few fears of marrying into it."

By then, Charles had spent more time with Diana in different settings. They had danced together at the Goodwood Ball, and they met again when she traveled to Balmoral shortly after the de Pass weekend to stay with her sister Jane and her new baby. Diana was "as soft, cheerful and bouncy as ever, still dancing attendance, still hanging on his every word, enjoying his company, boosting his ego, and still waiting for some show of affection from him, like a puppy underfoot," Junor wrote in her 1982 biography. Diana seemed completely comfortable with country life, giving "the impression to the Prince's family and friends," according to Dimbleby, "that she was one of nature's 'tomboys.' " During this private interlude at Balmoral, Charles and Diana got to know each other better, which fortified his feeling that she was the one.

"The summer of 1980 was all rosy for Diana," said her cousin Robert Spencer. "She was in great heart, on good terms with her parents. She had a new flat and plenty of money. She may have had the Prince of Wales in her head, but she was not in the position to do anything about it until that summer when the cards were stacking in her favor. When she went to stay with Jane, that was the crucial visit. The romance didn't start, in my opinion, until she went up there. She had visited me earlier in the summer, and she said nothing at all about Prince Charles."

At Charles's invitation, Diana joined his group on the royal yacht *Britannia* during the first week in August for the Cowes yacht races—the capstone of the English summer social season. Diana's recollection was once again faintly uneasy, touched by her mistrust and insecurity: She was disconcerted by his older friends, who were "all over me like a bad rash." Somewhat cryptically she said she sensed that "obviously somebody was talking."

Tabloid reporters would later write about the way Diana showed off while waterskiing, flirtatiously bumping into Charles's windsurf board. But Diana's real impact seemed more subtle. "Lady Diana's presence struck me right away," wrote Stephen Barry, who detected her variable moods. She combined "a natural maturity with a charming artlessness," he observed. "She seemed quite different from any of the other ladies who had ever engaged the Prince's attention." Barry recalled that she was "shy and confident at the same time," "wonderfully good-looking," and instantly popular with the crew, who were taken by her refreshing friendliness. Charles "didn't seem to take too much notice of her at the beginning," noted Barry, "though her eyes followed him everywhere."

Charles persisted in his own way, inviting her to Balmoral during the Braemar Games in early September. Although she had visited her sister Jane there several times previously, Diana recalled, "I was terrified—shitting bricks. I was frightened because I had never stayed at Balmoral, and I wanted to get it right." Perhaps she was indeed fearful, because for the first time she was asked to stay at the castle, although she later said she was "all right once I got in through the front door."

Charles was surrounded by his closest friends that weekend, including Camilla and Andrew Parker Bowles. Another couple, Patty and Charlie Palmer-Tomkinson, were impressed by Diana's vivacity and apparent enjoyment of the sporting life as she slogged through mud during their deer stalking, and learned how to fish on the River Dee. "She was a sort of wonderful English schoolgirl who was game for anything," Patty Palmer-Tomkinson said, "naturally young, but sweet and clearly determined and enthusiastic about him, very much wanted him."

Diana seemed attuned to Charles's needs. She quizzed Stephen Barry about the Prince's likes and dislikes and was "always buying him little presents," according to Barry, including shirts and ties to "spruce up his wardrobe." She had an "instinctive understanding of Prince Charles," Barry observed, and in the early days, she looked to his valet for guidance on whether she was "doing the right thing. . . . She picked up my signals amazingly quickly," he noted. "The only time I perhaps needed to slightly raise an eyebrow was when she wanted to giggle and he wanted to be quiet. The Prince needs periods of silence. Then Diana would quickly pick up a book or the tapestry work she loves to do and sit silent herself."

In September, Charles "confided to one of his friends that though he did not yet love her, she was lovable and warmhearted, and he was sure he could fall in love with her." He also had the somewhat antiquated notion that "as her first love, he would also be her last," and he felt that, at nineteen, she was sufficiently malleable to learn her role as his consort.

In later years, Charles's critics accused him of cynicism in his courtship of Diana, an impression abetted by Diana, who described herself to Morton as "the virgin, the sacrificial lamb"—an intriguing choice of words, since a year before their interviews Morton had written in *The Sunday Times* that Diana had been "the sacrificial virgin bride." Because of his complicated feelings for Camilla Parker Bowles, Charles was certainly conflicted in his approach to Diana. Yet he seemed less cynical than tangled in his theoretical model of marriage and blinded by the peculiarities of his status as Prince of Wales—"not a position but a predicament," wrote Alan Bennett in the play *The Madness of George III*. Clive James, an avid fan of Diana's, considered Charles "a man as good and honest as I have ever met," but James pointed out that Charles was "born to a life in which people magically appeared when needed."

Like many men of his generation and class, Charles had not been raised to nurture a wife—a deficiency compounded by the essential selfishness bred into him as heir to the throne. He could not envision an equal partnership; he expected to be listened to, respected, and even obeyed. He wanted a soulmate, a country girl of intelligence and wit, willing to share his hobbies, embrace his passions, and honor his values; a wife who was loyal, committed to duty, and who, as he said to Alistair Cooke, was willing to mold herself to him and walk two steps behind. That was the royal way, and above all, he needed the support of a woman who would be consistent and dependable.

Charles also believed in the notion that an "arranged" marriage could work, as it had for his grandparents the Queen Mother and George VI, who grew to love each other deeply. "He often used to say that he wanted to have the same kind of long and happy marriage which his grandmother had," said his friend Patty Palmer-Tomkinson. "To a detached or untutored nonestablishment observer, his approach seems bizarre in that he wouldn't think in terms of passion," said a man close to Charles. "This is a romantic age where passion is important. He was aware of the fact that he was inviting someone to do a job, and . . . over and above the normal tests of marriage, he always felt, 'Who would ever want to do this job?' That explains his diffidence."

If Diana had read any of Charles's various statements on marriage, his expectations and attitudes about a helpmeet would have been clear. But she had no interest in doing that sort of homework. Finding a husband was much on her nineteen-year-old mind after her sister Jane had her first child and her sister Sarah had been married the previous May. Diana's rivalry with Sarah remained a backdrop to her interest in Charles. Years later, Diana told her friend Elsa Bowker that Sarah "resented it terribly because I accepted to go out with Prince Charles." At the time, Diana confided to her employer Mary Robertson that she was unnerved by Sarah's constant inquiries about the relationship. "I don't even dare to pick up the telephone at my flat for fear it might be Sarah," said Diana.

Diana seemed to have scant reason for such wariness, but it was ingrained in her temperament. It didn't matter that Sarah was now spoken for, having settled on Neil McCorquodale, a wealthy gentleman farmer and former Coldstream Guards officer, described by a friend as "solid, very steady, private, quiet, with a good sense of humor." He was in many ways the opposite of Sarah, who was ebullient and enterprising, with an unpredictable streak and a fondness for the limelight. Just weeks before her wedding day, in February 1980, Sarah called it off only to reschedule it three months later. "Sarah was smart enough to know she needed a man like Neil," said a friend of the couple. "He was the sort of man Diana should have married, but Diana went for ambition."

Diana idealized marriage as a fantasy that contrasted sharply with Charles's elaborately considered view. "I had so many dreams as a young girl," she recalled. "I wanted, and hoped . . . that my husband would look after me. He would be a father figure, and he'd support me, encourage me, say 'Well done' or say, 'No, it wasn't good enough.' But I didn't get any of that. I couldn't believe it. I got none of that. It was role reversal." Diana also believed that since Charles had to marry "forever," she would be safe from the possibility of divorce, and she saw the royal household as a place where she would be protected. In contemplating marriage to Charles, Diana supposedly told friends that she felt secure for the first time in her life.

While Charles envisioned a loving partnership in which he called the shots, Diana longed for a selfless man to fill her emptiness and offer continuous devotion. Her expectation was particularly unrealistic given Charles's busy public life and time-consuming hobbies, as well as the nature and restraints of the royal family. Women had "never dominated" Charles's life, according to Stephen Barry. "The only thing that dominates Prince Charles is his work, and then his sporting activities. Girls come third."

Diana's detractors have accused her of manipulating Prince Charles during their courtship and fooling him into thinking she was something she was not. Diana proceeded "with great cunning," wrote Penny Junor in her 1998 book about Prince Charles. She "professed great interest in everything he said and did, and manifested great sympathy and understanding for the trials and tribulations of his life. . . . She talked about her love of the country and of shooting and of her interest in taking up horse-riding, and she liked his friends. . . . But it was all a sham. Diana didn't like any of these things. She hated the countryside, had no interest in shooting, or horses, or dogs, and she didn't even really like his friends. She found them old, boring and sycophantic."

Like so much written about Charles and Diana, this judgment seems unduly harsh. Diana's disillusionment with Charles's friends—"oiling up, basically, kissing his feet," she said—was fairly predictable. She often started out enthusiastic, then readily found grounds for criticism and suspicion. Similarly, her embrace of Charles's interests seemed to reflect her intense feelings, rather than calculated maneuvering. "When you fall in love, you often suddenly say you like things when you may not really like them," explained Charles's former aide Michael Colborne.

Diana failed to comprehend—or even give much thought to—the range of duties she would have to take on. As she said years later, on her wedding day "[she] realized [she] had taken on an enormous role but had no idea what [she] was going into—but *no* idea." During the courtship, she seemed enchanted mainly by the idea of becoming a princess. "She had a romantic view of life," said a childhood friend, "but Barbara Cartland books didn't prepare you. They were cloud cuckooland, all very romantic escapism, and she was very impressionable." Even Diana's employer Mary Robertson worried that the infatuation was "based on her romantic image of him, combined with his lofty position." Diana struck one unsettling note early on, during her visit to Balmoral in July 1980. A friend recalled that Diana had been dazzled by the perfection of a royal picnic lunch complete with linen, silver, and a menu card. "Oh! This is the life for me!" she exclaimed. "Where is the footman?" Diana's reaction was endearingly refreshing, yet ominously childish.

For all the talking Charles had done about the nature of marriage, he seemed unable to apply his high-minded principles to Diana with a clear eye. If anything, he wasn't calculating enough in choosing her. If he had been, he would have found that she passed muster in only half of his basic marital requirements: she was indeed "pretty special" in her appealing combination of noble birth, natural dignity, refreshing informality, and a virginal image; her love of children showed she could be a good mother in a "secure family unit"; and she had the sort of affectionate nature he wanted from a nurturing wife.

Yet in other crucial ways she fell short. Charles indulged in wishful thinking when he believed that the proximity of their families had prepared Diana for understanding his world or the role she would play in it. He seemed to have forgotten the concern he had voiced six years earlier about the "risky" consequences if a young woman "didn't have a clue" about the royal role. Nor did he recognize that beyond Diana's apparent enjoyment of rural life, her engaging sense of humor, and appreciation for classical music, they had few interests or ideas in common. He also seemed oblivious to Diana's history of willfulness, which showed she might well be reluctant to live in his shadow. Had Charles given the relationship more time or probed into Diana's past in a meaningful way, he would surely have found evidence of psychological fragility that might well have given him pause.

According to one Palace aide who knew him for a number of years, Charles's emotional reaction clouded his judgment. Diana arrived at the right time, and as an older man, Charles found the adoration of a pretty and superficially eligible young woman irresistible. "He accepted her infatuation and saw it as a charming part of her approach and character," said the aide. "She had a sweet and affectionate and amusing side to her, so he let that carry him along and didn't examine it." In short, although Charles said he wouldn't let his heart rule his head when it came to marriage, he did precisely that.

Chapter 7

H E'S IN LOVE AGAIN! LADY DI IS THE NEW GIRL FOR CHARLES blared *The Sun's* headline on September 8, 1980. The story, by Harry Arnold, described Lady Diana Spencer as "a perfect English rose," and asked "Is it the real thing for Charles at last?" The answer left no doubts, and Arnold offered one surprisingly shrewd hunch: "Some observers believe the Prince will follow a pattern set by several royals of marrying a friend he can learn to love."

Arnold, it turns out, hadn't even been at Balmoral for the all-important sighting. It was Arnold's chief rival, James Whitaker, who spotted her with his binoculars. She was slipping behind a tree while Prince Charles fished in the River Dee, and Whitaker didn't immediately identify Diana, but he could see that she was watching him in the mirror of her compact. " 'What a cunning lady,' I thought," Whitaker later wrote. "This one was clearly going to give us a lot of trouble. . . . You had to be a real professional to think of using a mirror to watch us watching her."

As a courtesy to Arnold, who was 200 miles away, Whitaker picked up the telephone and gave him a briefing once he had discovered Diana's identity. Whitaker's own paper at the time, the *Daily Star,* buried his story inside, but *The Sun* went all out on page one. "They exaggerated it," grumbled Whitaker. " 'He's in love' was based on nothing except there was this woman." Indeed, Stephen Barry, Prince Charles's longtime valet, would later write that "there was certainly no obvious romance" during that Balmoral visit. "The Prince and Diana seemed to like each other, but there were no clues to a budding love affair."

The Sun claimed the scoop the tabloids had been hungering for since 1976. Its bold words typified Fleet Street's increasingly aggressive approach toward the royal family. What had once been a cozy relationship shifted largely because of the influence of Australian media baron Rupert Murdoch, owner of two of the most popular tabloids, *The Sun* and *News of the World*, as well as *The Times* and *The Sunday Times*. The *News of the World*, published on Sundays, was the lowest of the downmarket papers, specializing in tawdry stories of sex and violence. *The Sun*'s trademark was a picture of a bare-breasted woman on page three.

Murdoch was an admitted antimonarchist, and his recipe for tabloid journalism included generous servings of royal gossip. After a decade in English journalism, Murdoch turned his attention in the late seventies to America, where he was buying up newspapers and magazines. "Because we had a foreign proprietor with Murdoch's attitudes, it allowed us freedom," said Andrew Neil, who edited *The Sunday Times* in the eighties and early nineties.

The most important beneficiary of Murdoch's latitude was Kelvin MacKenzie (variously nicknamed MacFrenzy and MacNasty), who moved up to editor of *The Sun* in June 1981. "Kelvin is a natural troublemaker," said Neil. "Under Kelvin, *The Sun* started giving the royal family a degree of scrutiny and irreverence that permeated all newspapers." Roy Greenslade, who worked for MacKenzie at *The Sun* and later competed against him as editor of the *Daily Mirror*, recalled, "Kelvin would adopt at a conference in the morning a mock-and-shock look and say, 'I'm afraid we've upset the Palace. How can we do it today?' "

Terrifying adversaries, the tabloids routinely turned tiny incidents into sensational page-one stories that were picked up around the world. The tabloids happily ignored prevailing standards of accuracy, in large part because the royal family declined to acknowledge—much less comment on—the manner in which they were covered. Most important, in those years the royal family did not sue, although they would later on.

Having watched the press destroy her sister Sarah's chances with Charles, Diana was attracted and repelled by the hacks. The Fleet Street pack pursued Diana relentlessly in the fall of 1980. Although she had little sense of her own worth, she did have the confidence of her upper-class background, combined with the down-to-earth openness she inherited from her father. Unlike the royal family, Diana paid attention to the reporters. When they camped out on the doorstep of her London apartment building, she was invariably polite, addressing her stalkers by name and taking their phone calls in the middle of the night, even when she had nothing to say. "She made a decision that they were going to be around, so she had to tolerate them," said one of her relatives. "She took a pragmatic view." When tabloid photographers embarrassed her by snapping pictures with sunlight silhouetting her legs beneath a sheer skirt, she wept privately but assured them, "I understand all your problems, and there are no hard feelings."

The tabloid men (and they were, with a few exceptions, male) fell in love with Diana. They were smitten by her drop-dead looks, gleaming smile, infectious giggle, and natural manner. To Harry Arnold, Diana "had a way . . . of taking scalps. She used to collect men . . . in the old-fashioned romantic way. She would give you a look with lowered eyes. . . . You knew deep down it was a game she played, and a very clever one in a way, not cynical, but by doing this, she won everybody over." The hacks decided almost immediately, as Whitaker later wrote, that Diana "fitted perfectly . . . She was the most likely candidate to be future queen that I had seen in years."

Like Charles, the hacks were content to skim Diana's lovely surface, judging her by the most obvious selling points: her beauty, her venerable family, and her pristine image. Captivated by the effusive press coverage, the public fell in love with Diana, too. As the courtship developed, Whitaker and other reporters became Diana's fierce advocates, and she began looking to them for approval.

The leaders of the tabloid pack were Whitaker and Arnold. Others included Ross Benson of the *Daily Express* and Andrew Morton, who would take over at the *Daily Star* following Whitaker's move to the *Daily Mirror* in 1982. Also in the mix was the bombastic *Daily Mail* gossip columnist Nigel Dempster.

"James and Harry," said Morton, "were like the Labrador and the Jack Russell." Whitaker was thirty-nine and had been a royal hack for thirteen years when he first spotted Diana. Florid and heavyset, with a nimbus of curly hair, Whitaker was the son of an executive at the Sperry Rand Corporation. "People talk about me as if I'd come from nowhere," he once told a reporter. "But my father owned race horses. We've always had good cars." After graduating from The Elms at Colwall, a boarding school, Whitaker touched down briefly at Cheltenham College and did a stint as an accountant before landing in journalism.

Whitaker's flamboyance was legendary, both in his columns and his frequent television appearances. He spoke loudly and emphatically, but he redeemed his pomposity with a measure of self-deprecation, describing himself as a "master of trivia." He admitted to joining the royal beat after tasting the high life while covering a polo match where champagne and smoked salmon were being served.

Whitaker once followed Diana and Charles to Ascot with his *Daily Star* editor Peter McKay. Both men were in morning dress, but Whitaker had enlivened his formal attire with a shirt that he described as "absolutely scarlet, with a white collar." "His face was beet-red," said McKay, "which went very well with the shirt." The two men sneaked into the tent reserved for White's, the exclusive men's club, where the aristocratic members were *not* wearing red shirts. "We were just about to be chucked out," said McKay, "when Charles and Diana came in, and Diana walked straight up to us, smiling. She called us by our first names, so the people in the tent figured we were okay."

From the beginning, said McKay, "Whitaker both proclaimed himself a royalist and reserved for himself the right to expose everything he could." Whitaker would lie for hours on a rock overlooking Balmoral, a picnic lunch nestled at his side as he trained his binoculars on the royal residence. Whether Diana was at a polo match or the opera, or even just across the room at a reception, Whitaker would invariably peer at her through his high-powered Nikons. "I know binoculars are intrusive," said Whitaker, "but I could see all sorts of things."

To win Diana's confidence, Whitaker wooed her with blandishments, bouquets of roses, and even homeopathic remedies, claiming later that he had "a bond" with Diana resulting from "several intimate chats." She nicknamed him the "Big Red Tomato."

Equally competitive but somewhat less blatant was Harry Arnold, the terrier of the two. He was a year younger than Whitaker, with a "resemblance to a London taxi driver," wrote Douglas Keay in his book, *Royal Pursuit: The Palace, the Press and the People.* Arnold was a natty dresser, with such flashy touches as gold rings and gray-tinted lenses in his glasses. Having reported on murder trials before covering Diana for *The Sun* and then the *Mirror,* Arnold considered himself more of a probing reporter than Whitaker. Although he professed to support the monarchy, he was known to be politically liberal and to take a dim view of the upper class.

Andrew Morton grew up in Yorkshire and earned a degree in history from Sussex University. When the *Daily Star* appointed him royal correspondent at twenty-eight, it was assumed his six-foot-four height clinched the position, since he could see well in crowds. Square-jawed and bespectacled, he was mocked for his resemblance to Clark Kent, which once prompted him to wear a Superman costume on assignment. From the beginning, he was starstruck by Diana: "Her blue eyes gaze straight into yours with a look that is frank, friendly, . . . and sexy," he once reported.

Ross Benson of the *Daily Express* secured his bona fides by attending Gordonstoun, where he was in the same class as Prince Charles. Benson liked "to think they were friends, but I'm not sure they were," said his wife, Ingrid Seward. Handsome and impeccably attired, Benson was the most ardent royalist of the bunch. Seward was the editor of *Majesty,* the premier fantasy magazine about royal life. Observed Benson, "If they do a feature about Prince Charles's cuff links, it will be the most authoritative article that you have ever read about the royal family's cuff links."

Even more riveting than Benson's coverage of the royal family was his long-running feud with *Daily Mail* gossip columnist Nigel Dempster. Not only did they expose errors in each other's columns, they lashed out with personal insults. To Dempster, Benson was "the Pompadoured Poltroon," and to Benson, Dempster was "the Tonsured Traducer." An Australian who immigrated to Britain at age six, Dempster left Sherborne, a boarding school, when he was sixteen. He married a daughter of the 11th Duke of Leeds, which gave Dempster the best aristocratic connections of the tabloid crowd. Yet he made his mark with sharp-edged gossip about the aristocracy—not the "old established" grandees he admired, but those who would "abuse that privilege—the ones who are unkind to waiters."

Although technically Dempster didn't follow the royal beat, his *Daily Mail* column became a magnet for nuggets about the royal family. With his customary immodesty, Dempster condemned the entire tabloid pack. "[They] knew no one," he said. "No one in journalism, apart from my good self in those days, had input from the royal family. [Princess Margaret] had been a very good friend of mine, so I had great input. Prince Charles's office was also in my pocket."

It was Dempster who broke the story in September 1980 that Prince Charles's "new choice of girlfriend" had been approved by "the two happily married women who influence [him] most on personal matters, Lady Tryon and Camilla Parker Bowles." Diana confessed that she had read the column, but she withheld comment. From September onward, the tabloids filled their front pages with descriptions of every glimpse they could get of Charles and Diana: a horse race in Shropshire, a fiftieth birthday party for Princess Margaret ("back in each other's arms," wrote Whitaker, Charles and Diana "danced the night away"), and riding on the Berkshire downs.

They trailed Diana to her job at the kindergarten and even to a Knightsbridge shop owned by a "romantic underwear expert." "If I go to a restaurant or just out shopping in the supermarket, they're trying to take photographs," she complained to Danae Brook, a *Daily Mail* reporter who lived in her apartment building. On the weekend of Charles's November 14 birthday, the pack followed Diana to Sandringham, forcing her to remain indoors the entire time and ultimately to leave early. Stephen Barry said she was "very depressed" as a result.

Diana learned to evade the hacks, and she and Charles managed to slip away for a series of weekend meetings that would be reported by the tabloids only after the fact—thanks to tips from low-level staff. Beginning with his use of Broadlands as a "safe house" in the seventies, it had been Prince Charles's custom to conduct his courtships at the homes of friends. He took Diana several times to Broadlands and to the home of the Parker Bowleses in Wiltshire, and Camilla "encouraged the romance," wrote Stephen Barry. Observed Whitaker in November 1980, "It's almost as if the Parker Bowleses must ensure that the path of true love runs as smoothly as possible."

It is unclear precisely when Charles and Camilla ended their intimacy. Jonathan Dimbleby, the most authoritative source, wrote that "from the moment of [Charles's] engagement in February [1981], he saw Camilla Parker Bowles on only one occasion and that was more than four months later to say farewell. His feelings for [her] had not changed, but they had both accepted that their intimacy could no longer be maintained." Dimbleby was silent on whether the couple had remained intimate once Charles began his romance with Diana in July 1980. In her 1998 book on Charles, however, Penny Junor asserted that the affair had stopped when Charles started seriously courting Diana, although Camilla remained "his best friend."

Charles had essentially made up his mind during the summer of 1980 that he wanted Diana as his wife, and the courtship became an exercise in reassuring himself that he had made the right choice. With the press so avidly embracing Diana's cause, Charles had no room for second thoughts. "The pressures on the prince began to seem like a tidal wave sweeping towards an inevitable destiny," wrote Dimbleby.

Diana came across as mature and levelheaded during this period, and she made no secret of her devotion to him. "She was most certainly in love with her prince," said Stephen Barry. "She was always available when he called, and she always fitted in with his plans." When Charles proudly showed her Highgrove, the country home eleven miles from the Parker Bowleses' that he had purchased the previous June, Barry sensed her disappointment that the house didn't live up to the grandeur she was used to at Althorp, but Diana hid such feelings from Charles. Somewhat primly, she was offended by Charles's request that she help decorate the house although they weren't engaged; she felt that Charles was acting improperly.

After a month or so, the tabloid reporters began to describe Diana's character with growing authority. In one of the more evenhanded early assessments, *Mirror* reporter Paul Callan described her as "quietly captivating . . . modest . . . not a great conversationalist, a trifle nervous, seemingly cool . . . a great laugher . . . she can look intensely serious one moment, then if someone cracks even a mild joke, her face lights up . . . she is quietly spoken, not particularly posh even . . . [with] a pleasant, even classless accent." A more speculative but provocatively intuitive appraisal came from an astrologer's reading in the *Daily Star* around the same time: Diana tended to "rely on instinct . . . to 'feel' what is right," and was naturally inconsistent, wrote astrologer Lena Leon. "Every morning will be different— giddy or giggly, sulky or silky . . . coldness will suddenly be followed by warmth . . . trust is . . . terribly important."

Yet much of the tabloid reporting about Diana consisted of distortions and outright inventions, which set the template for the emerging portrait of Diana that included traits she couldn't recognize and overstated her familiarity with the royal way of life.

James Whitaker, for example, described Diana's "reputation as a demon driver . . . scooting around London at a surprisingly nippy speed," omitting the fact that she was speeding to avoid the pursuit of Whitaker and other hacks. (Whitaker even boasted later about "an 80-mph car caper in which he drove alongside the car she was driving while a photographer snapped her picture.") Within days, other reporters picked up on Diana's "erratic driving record." Harry Arnold contributed to the misimpressions by exaggerating "the friendship which Charles and Diana have shared for years." Arnold likewise incorrectly asserted that Diana "has been groomed from childhood to join the Balmoral set."

The tabloids also distorted the role of the Queen Mother and Diana's grandmother Ruth Fermoy, presenting them as the conspiratorial architects of an arranged marriage. Charles's "choice of bride," wrote Andrew Morton in one representative account, "was engineered by the machinations of the grandmother he reveres and of Diana's grandmother." While both the Queen Mother and Ruth Fermoy strongly endorsed the marriage, the two women chipped in only after the relationship was already on track. Lady Fermoy signaled her approval that autumn when she accompanied Diana and Charles to a performance of Verdi's *Requiem*, with dinner afterward at Buckingham Palace.

The speculation about the cabal of the grandmothers began shortly after Diana's October 1980 visit to Birkhall, the Balmoral residence of the Queen Mother, where Lady Fermoy was in attendance. "Both grandmothers know each other well," wrote Anne DeCourcy several weeks later. "It is tempting to think that there has been a certain amount of 'Wouldn't it be nice, if.' " In the British press, it was but a short leap from "It is tempting" to the unshakable notion that the two elderly women orchestrated the marriage, which became a pillar of the Diana myth.

In fact, Ruth Fermoy had doubts about the match. "She never dared say anything," said a man close to Charles, "but she thought Diana was unsuitable, and that she was an unreliable girl." Shortly before her death in 1993,

Lady Fermoy revealed her unspoken doubts. "If I'd said to [Charles], 'You're making a very great mistake,' " she said, "he probably wouldn't have paid the slightest attention because he was being driven." Even Diana recalled that during the courtship Ruth Fermoy registered some caution by telling her that the royal family's "sense of humor" and "lifestyle" were "different" and might not suit her.

Some of the mistaken assertions by the tabloid reporters deliberately cast Prince Charles in a harsh light to boost Diana. He "never sent flowers," wrote Whitaker indignantly, although the *Daily Mail*'s Danae Brook reported the delivery of two dozen dark-red roses from Charles to Diana's door. "I often felt sorry for her," Whitaker wrote, because Diana "had to . . . drive hundreds of miles . . . to be with him. . . . No normal boyfriend would ever get away [with] treating his girl[friend] in such a cavalier manner." Yet Charles's valet Stephen Barry later described at length the number of times during the courtship that he met Diana at her sister's or grandmother's home in order to avoid the press before driving her to meet Charles in the country, then returning the following morning in a "dawn dash."

Inevitably, a few minor negatives popped into the developing picture of Diana. A butler at Althorp told the *Daily Star* that Diana had been "a bit of a nuisance" as a girl, but predicted that "with some training she could fit into the strict rules and regulations of a royal household." Judy Wade of *The Sun* dredged up a 1976 interview with Raine Spencer in which she said Diana and her sisters had snubbed her. But for the most part, the press beat the drum on Diana's behalf, virtually ordering Charles to propose, as Whitaker recalled, "or the whole country would lynch him." "The time has come when Prince Charles should get married," thundered Whitaker in the *Daily Star* on November 10. "It is his duty."

The months before her engagement were Diana's first major test of character, and she impressed the tabloid hacks with her imperturbability—one account praised her "remarkably cool and mature approach"—during their siege. They were witnessing her self-professed ability to "put on the most amazing show of happiness" however "bloody" she might be feeling. They had no idea that she actually crumbled under the pressure very early. As she said years later, the reporters were "unbearable. . . . I cried like a baby to the four walls. I just couldn't cope with it." Diana revealed her feelings only once at the time, in her interview with neighbor Danae Brook of the *Daily Mail*. "I'm not so much bored as miserable," said Diana. "It's quite tiring and it's been going on for two weeks now, solid."

While Charles limited his newspaper-reading to *The Times*, Diana read "everything she [could] lay her hands on," according to Stephen Barry. After several months of publicity, a *Daily Mirror* reporter observed, "It seems that . . . Lady Diana . . . has come to enjoy recognition." There were moments when Diana seemed to invite attention. In December 1980, Charles's former girlfriend Anna Wallace married Johnny Hesketh at the Guards Chapel in London. To the astonishment of one of her friends, Diana showed up near the chapel pushing a child in a stroller. "I said, 'For God's sake, there are three hundred press crowded round. My God, you'd better get out of here,' " recalled her friend.

In her Morton interviews, Diana bitterly criticized Prince Charles for being unsupportive. She remembered that he seemed only concerned for Camilla Parker Bowles, who had to fend off a handful of reporters at her home—versus thirty-four outside Diana's door. Yet Stephen Barry disclosed that Charles was actually "more concerned" than Diana about the effects of press harassment on her. In earlier years Charles had been quite cordial to the press, but he had turned sharply against reporters when they began stalking his various girlfriends. "He used to say to me, 'I wish the bloody press would leave [Diana] alone,' " according to Barry. At one point in early December, Charles publicly attacked the British media's "sensationalism" and lack of moral values. Encountering the pack at Sandringham, Charles blurted out, "I should like to take this opportunity to wish you all a very happy new year and your editors a particularly nasty one."

Diana claimed that she considered it inappropriate to complain to Charles about the press, so she remained silent. She added that she had asked him and the Buckingham Palace press office for help, but that they had rebuffed her: "They just said, 'You're on your own.' " Yet her employer at the time, Mary Robertson, related a different and more revealing story. In November 1980, Diana told Robertson that her grandmother Lady Fermoy "had suggested . . . that she seek help from Buckingham Palace in dealing with the press." When Diana asked what she should do, Robertson gave her some advice that Diana unfortunately heeded—one of many examples of well-meaning but ill-informed guidance from people who didn't grasp the extent of Diana's problems. "I wouldn't ask for help if I could possibly manage without it," Robertson told her. "If the palace thinks you can't handle the pressure now, they might think you couldn't handle it once you're part of the royal family. If you're serious about this romance, you should try to struggle along on your own."

Much has been made of Diana's anxiety about being photographed. Still, she seemed to know instinctively what to do in front of photographers, perhaps because she was more at ease than she let on. Growing up, she had loved posing for her father's ubiquitous camera. "She would automatically sort of make gestures and strike poses," her brother Charles recalled. "She was a natural performer." Even as a child, he said, she had "star quality, the way she just reacted to the camera."

Felicity Clark, then the beauty editor of *Vogue*, knew both of Diana's older sisters from their jobs at the magazine. When Diana was sixteen, Clark had heard that she was "really pretty" and tried to photograph her as one of the "young new faces" to watch. "Diana had been quite eager," said Clark, but had been forced to cancel when she came down with appendicitis.

When the stories began circulating about Diana and Charles in the fall of 1980, Clark asked again, and Diana agreed to be photographed by Lord Snowdon, the husband of Princess Margaret, for a feature in the February 1981 issue. Using what Clark described as "cloak-and-dagger" methods, *Vogue* arranged for Diana to be transported undetected to Snowdon's studio for the shoot. Clark couldn't help noticing that Diana was "strung up in general . . . terribly nervous because the press were all over her." Despite Diana's inexperience, Clark was also struck that she "wasn't nervous about what she was doing with us." Significantly, it was a controlled environment that soothed Diana's anxieties, and the attention boosted her self-esteem. "She felt comfortable with Snowdon," said Clark. "He knew what he was doing and he made it easy."

The low point in the courtship occurred on November 16 with the *Sunday Mirror*'s publication of a sensational page-one scoop headlined ROYAL LOVE TRAIN. The story claimed that Diana had twice met Prince Charles late at night earlier in the month on the royal train. The two reporters, Wensley Clarkson and Jim Newman, claimed that she had made a "100-mile dash" from London to Wiltshire in a "blue Renault car" and had been ushered through a police barricade. The following night, according to the *Sunday Mirror*, Diana had traveled to the "country home of the Prince's close friend and confidante," Camilla Parker Bowles, before "dashing once again to the same lonely siding." The story was heavy with innuendo, noting that Diana "spent a number of hours in the carriage normally used by the Duke of Edinburgh" and "left in the early hours of the morning."

When the *Sunday Mirror* called Diana the night before publishing the story, she emphatically insisted it was untrue (a denial they did not even print), and in subsequent days she repeated her assertion that she had been at home with her roommates, all of whom backed her up. According to Whitaker, she said that she stayed in because "I was feeling frail and hungover" after the birthday party for Princess Margaret the night before. She told Roger Tavener of the Press Association wire service that she "had some supper and watched TV before going to bed early . . . I never moved out of the flat," although she firmly denied "a newspaper story today that she had

had a hangover from the party . . . 'I never get hangovers.' " After issuing another denial to the *Daily Mail*, Diana seemed defeated: "The trouble is," she said, "people do believe what they read."

Since Diana was not a member of the royal family, or even a fiancée, Buckingham Palace was not officially obliged to protect her. But the Queen and the Prince of Wales were incensed by the report and its implication of a sexual liaison. Instead of ignoring the story, as the tabloids expected her to do—and as she had previously done—the Queen countered with an unequivocal denial from her press secretary Michael Shea: "With the exception of the fact that the Prince of Wales . . . used the royal train on the two nights in question, any other suggestion made by you is a total fabrication . . . The only guests on board the train on either night were the Secretary of the Duchy of Cornwall, his successor and the local Duchy land steward."

The royal train story took a further bogus turn in James Whitaker's 1993 book about the Wales marriage, which accepted that Diana had not been on the train. But even after firsthand denials that *any* woman had been present, Whitaker added his own new sensational twist by insisting that "a blond woman was hurried onto the train. . . . The woman on the train was Camilla Parker Bowles."

Part of Whitaker's evidence was a telephone log from the royal train showing "that a call had been made to . . . the nearby home of the Parker Bowleses." But Camilla's husband, Andrew, told Ross Benson that Prince Charles "rang me from the train. The call was about hunting arrangements for the weekend. Nothing else."

Whitaker's tale has also been contradicted by key people in a position to know the Prince's whereabouts. "There was no foundation to it," said Michael Colborne, then a close aide to the Prince of Wales. Charles's valet Stephen Barry was equally emphatic when he said, "I myself was on the train with him, plus . . . two policemen. . . . There was no lady on his train, not Lady Diana nor anyone else."

Despite overwhelming evidence to the contrary, the royal train story became part of the mythology surrounding Diana, with some believers contending that Diana had been present, while others insisted it was Camilla. Diana later traced her mistrust of Camilla to this period, although she didn't specifically cite the royal train story. Diana recalled feeling "there was somebody else around" when Camilla seemed so well informed about the course of Charles's new romance.

Those close to Diana could see that the media coverage was taking a toll on her. Frances Shand Kydd was sufficiently alarmed to write a letter to *The Times* early that December denouncing the "inexcusable" lies printed about Diana (although she rather strangely sanctioned "fanciful speculation . . . in good taste"). Did the Fleet Street editors, she asked, "consider it necessary or fair to harass [her] daughter daily, from dawn until well after dusk? Is it fair to ask any human being, regardless of circumstances, to be treated in this way?" A month later, Diana's father made his own plea: "Things have been getting very overwrought for her," he told reporters who followed her to his estate. "Let her have some peace and quiet."

On her own, Diana tried to defend herself by selectively enlisting the help of the hacks. In the same month the train story appeared, Roger Tavener of the Press Association caught up with her at the Young England Kindergarten. His subsequent dispatch made headlines when he quoted her as saying, "I'd like to marry soon. . . . I don't think nineteen is too young. It depends on the person." Panicked by her evident indiscretion, Diana angrily disavowed the quote. According to a report in the *Daily Express,* "Lady Diana Spencer last night asked the *Express* to 'help set the record straight. . . . I didn't say any of this. I never said anything about marriage.' . . . Her blue eyes blazed as she read through the agency account. . . . 'We only spoke about two minutes. I hardly said a word.' " After checking Tavener's notes, David Chipp, editor in chief of the Press Association, affirmed the accuracy of the story. But by striking back quickly, Diana had succeeded in blunting the interview's effect.

Diana's family knew that she had "difficulty telling the truth," as her brother once said. Early in their relationship the tabloid reporters began to suspect this tendency as well. Although for public consumption James Whitaker wrote that Diana "never lied to me," he believed otherwise. "The whole thing was enormously complicated," said Whitaker. "She was not straightforward at all. She was very tricky."

Despite the mutual suspicion, Diana and the hacks kept up cordial relations. They could see that Diana was infatuated with the Prince of Wales, so they redoubled their campaign on her behalf. The reporters promoted and protected her, declining to print comments that might damage her cause and even offering advice on what she should and should not say. Said Whitaker, "Diana was very aware that if she was going to progress with Prince Charles she needed the press on her side . . . saying how wonderful she was and what a dope he would be if he wouldn't marry her."

Sometimes their efforts backfired, as when Whitaker quoted her uncle Lord Fermoy as saying, "I can assure you, [Diana] has never had a lover," an intrusion into Diana's privacy that Whitaker afterward admitted "horrified" her. Two weeks later, however, Diana fell into the same undignified trap, telling the *Daily Mail* that she didn't have "a background of leaping in and out of bed with people" that "everybody else seems to have."

By any reasonable standard, Charles and Diana should have spent enough time together to get to know each other in depth and to see each other in a range of circumstances. But the public spotlight made a normal courtship impossible, and as 1980 drew to a close, Diana's anxiety began to show. "I will simply die if this doesn't work out," Diana confided to Mary Robertson. "I won't be able to show my face." The closest Charles came to a proposal was shortly before Christmas during a visit to the Parker Bowleses, when he said, "If I were to ask, what do you think you might answer?" Diana responded with a giggle. The next month, when she stayed at Althorp, Diana's distress over the continuing uncertainty was obvious. "I rang up and spoke to Raine," recalled Elsa Bowker. "I said, 'How is Diana?' Raine said, 'She is very sad. She is in the park and she is walking alone, and she is crying because Charles is not proposing.'"

It was an article of faith in the tabloids that Prince Philip began haranguing Charles to get married well before Diana. "He'd been saying for some time that if Charles didn't hurry up and find a bride there would be no one suitable left," observed Stephen Barry. Now that the royal train story had cast Diana in a bad light by implying that she and Charles had slept together, Philip weighed in more forcefully that Charles should propose or end the relationship. "He counseled his son that he could not delay a decision for much longer; that to do so would cause lasting damage to Diana Spencer's reputation," wrote Dimbleby. "The Prince interpreted his father's attitude as an ultimatum."

Against this backdrop of urgency, two friends—Penny Romsey and Nicholas Soames—approached Charles in January 1981 to voice their reservations about Diana. Penny Romsey, who was married to Mountbatten's grandson Norton Romsey, had "sensed the absence of intensity in [Charles's] feelings for Diana," wrote Dimbleby. Penny pointed out how little the couple had in common, and she worried that Diana seemed to be courting tabloid photographers, posing for them "to her best advantage." Her biggest concern was that Diana had apparently "fallen in love with an idea rather than an individual" and acted as if she were "auditioning for a central role in a costume drama" instead of grasping "the enormity" of her role as consort. Norton Romsey backed up his wife's impressions more forcefully, which only angered the Prince. Still, Penny Romsey's observations were significant, according to a friend of Charles's, because she was "one of the sharpest and most closely observing friends of the Prince. She felt something was wrong. It was an intuitive sense."

Nicholas Soames expressed his annoyance to a Palace official that Philip had imposed "such a terrible mismatch on his son." A former equerry to Charles, Soames so identified with the Prince that his house was "a monument to their relationship, with the Prince of Wales feather motif on everything and Prince of Wales pictures everywhere," said a friend of Soames. To risk Charles's displeasure under those circumstances indicated how strongly Soames felt. Soames was not known for his perceptiveness about women, but he told Charles that he and Diana were "too completely unalike," according to Soames's friend. "Nick thought Diana wasn't up to Charles's weight, to use a riding expression. She was pretty childish and very unformed."

Between the pressures and the misgivings, Charles told another friend that he was in a "confused and anxious state of mind. . . . It is just a matter of taking an unusual plunge into some rather unknown circumstances that inevitably disturbs me, but I expect it will be the right thing in the end." Finally, after a skiing holiday in Switzerland with his friends the Palmer-Tomkinsons, whose "support helped to steel his nerve," he invited Diana to Windsor Castle on the evening of February 6, where he asked her to marry him and she accepted instantly.

Diana's description of the proposal was both tormented and contradictory, offering a revealing snapshot of her quickly shifting feelings. Her words should also be viewed through the prism of her insecurities, along with her later animosity toward Charles. "There was never anything tactile about [Charles]," she complained. "It was extraordinary." When Charles proposed, she recalled laughing and thinking "This is a joke," a fairly inappropriate reaction to a moment she had been openly longing for.

In her interviews with Morton, Diana several times invoked the "voice inside" that seemed to propel her almost against her will, an expression of the unusual detachment she said she had felt since childhood. In this instance, "a voice said to me inside, 'You won't be Queen but you'll have a tough role.'" At another point, she said, "From day one, I always knew I would never be the next Queen." Yet in her 1995 *Panorama* interview, Diana cast doubt on her earlier recollection: "As for becoming Queen," she said, "it was never at the forefront of my mind when I married my husband. It was a long way off, that thought." To add further contradiction, Morton himself wrote in a 1991 article that Diana said to her friends, "After everything I've been through, I'm determined to be the next Queen of England."

By Diana's account, when she told Charles after his proposal that she loved him, he only replied, "whatever love means." She remembered, possibly with sarcasm, "So I thought that was great! I thought he meant that!" Moments later in her recollection, she swung 180 degrees and said, "I thought he was very much in love with me, which he was, but he always had a sort of besotted look about him." Then she turned just as rapidly to add, "It wasn't the genuine sort," hinting at her persistent fears of rejection. Diana's feelings of isolation and confused identity were equally apparent in another puzzling observation: "Who was this girl who was so different? But he couldn't understand it because his immaturity was quite big in that department."

Several days after the evening at Windsor Castle, Diana went to Australia to begin making arrangements for the wedding with her mother. Diana took this separation badly, calling it a "complete disaster." While she missed Charles terribly, she later claimed he never called her on the phone, and when she tried to reach him he wouldn't call her back. But Stephen Barry remembered that Charles and Diana "spoke constantly but guardedly on the telephone. . . . Generally, she called him. His engagements were booked so far in advance she knew where to find him." Charles himself recalled, in a television interview, what happened when he first rang Australia—where Frances Shand Kydd had carefully hidden her daughter from the press—and asked to speak to Diana. "We're not taking any calls," came the reply. It took some rather heated persuasion to convince them that he was in fact the Prince of Wales. Diana's statement that he didn't call, which became significant evidence of callousness in her case against Charles, was a classic illustration of the way she lashed out when she felt abandoned—a pattern that would repeat itself throughout her marriage.

The engagement announcement came on February 24, and the television interview given by Charles and Diana that day became bigger news than the engagement itself. The couple both looked exceedingly nervous as Diana bit her lip and Charles grimaced. "Can you find the words to sum up how you feel today?" asked a questioner. "Difficult to find the right sort of words," Charles said, glancing at Diana as she nodded. "Just delighted and happy. I'm amazed that she's even brave enough" (turning to her and grinning) "to take me on." With that, they both laughed as the interviewer asked, almost offhandedly, "And I suppose in love?" "Of course," said Diana, with a half-grimace, half-smile as she rolled her eyes. "Whatever 'in love' means," said Charles, smiling, as Diana giggled and echoed, "Yes." "Put your own interpretation on it," added Charles. Commented the interviewer, "It means two very happy people." Replied Diana, "As you can see," nodding her head and smiling.

Out of that brief exchange, with all its body language and conspicuous embarrassment, Charles's four words—"Whatever 'in love' means"—have been played back endlessly over the years to portray him as chilly and aloof. Diana told her astrologer Debbie Frank that she had been "shocked" by his answer in the interview—although Diana also claimed that Charles had used similar words the night of his proposal. "She told me it . . . was the first real indication . . . that Charles didn't think or feel like ordinary people," said Frank. Seen in full context, with Diana's mild eye-rolling mockery as she said, "Of course," and her very distinct "yes" following Charles's uncertain words, his response seemed less offensive than many have implied.

Given the number of times Charles publicly discussed the meaning of love and marriage, his reply was consistent with his tendency to intellectualize matters of the heart, especially when they intersected with his sense of duty. "It was an idiotic question," said a man who was a friend of Charles and Diana, "and the answer was typical of [Charles's] self-doubting, probing personality. It was an awkward attempt at introspection." Like any upper-class male, Charles also shrank from the sort of public display of emotion demanded of him. "He was very good at hiding what he was thinking," noted Stephen Barry. "He always had his feelings under control."

Yet the question of whether they were in love remains unanswered to this day—for her as well as for him. According to one theory, propounded by James Whitaker and royal biographer Anthony Holden, Charles's feelings shifted when he traveled to Australia after the engagement. "Wherever he went, he would see her image on the TV," recalled Holden, who was part of the press pack. "James and I think we saw him fall in love with the idea of her at a distance."

Charles was notably restrained in writing to friends that March: "I am very lucky that someone as special as Diana seems to love me so much. I am already discovering how nice it is to have someone round to share things with." Charles didn't appear to be "in love" with Diana at the outset. He was fond of her, and he hoped that his feelings could grow into love through a deepening of shared values and interests.

Diana's view of Charles's feelings fluctuated wildly, and over the years she offered varying versions to friends, depending on her mood at the moment. When she felt she had been a "sacrificial lamb," she dismissed Charles for choosing her only to produce a male heir. During her first meeting with astrologer Penny Thornton in 1986, Diana spoke of her "unrequited love for Charles" and recounted how devastated she was before her wedding by a "categorical denial" from Charles of "any love for her." A year later, according to Thornton, Diana told her "unequivocally that the marriage was arranged . . . by her grandmother . . . and the Queen Mother" and that the romance "was created purely by the media."

At other times, Diana expressed resentment of those who doubted Charles's love. "What really hurt [her] was the claim that Charles never loved her," said astrologer Debbie Frank. Diana insisted to Frank: "He did love me and I loved him. It wasn't all arranged." According to one of her close friends, "Diana said he was in love with her at the beginning, but that his idea of love was a bit different from hers."

Charles could see that Diana was infatuated with him, but even he was unsure how deep her feelings ran, as he indicated when he observed to friends that she "*seems* to love me so much [emphasis added]." Asked if Diana might have been more in love with her fiancé's title than with him as a person, her brother Charles replied "nobody with insincere motives could look that happy." Diana's mother also saw in Diana and Charles "genuine happiness and deep affection for each other." "When she first fell in love," explained one of Diana's close friends, "of course part of it was that he was the Prince of Wales, but he was lovable in many aspects. . . . He really was her first love, the only man who really impressed her."

Yet if Diana's later recollections were an authentic gauge of her mood in 1980 and early 1981, she felt intense resentment, anger, fear, depression, and jealousy behind her expressions of affection. Diana needed to be consoled and cared for, and had she felt secure, her disquieting undercurrents might have subsided. But life with the royal family behind palace walls only offered the illusion of protection. Diana was an emotionally bruised adolescent without a clear identity, and royal life, with its rigid protocol and fishbowl confines, would become a source of anxiety rather than a safe haven.

She had to leave her friends, her work, her comforting routines—an environment in which she did as she pleased and avoided entanglements ("I couldn't handle [them] emotionally. . . . I was very screwed up") that threatened her fragile self-esteem. She had to commit herself to an intimate relationship with a powerful man, to fill a demanding role for which she was unprepared, and to submit to the harsh and unceasing judgment of the intrusive press. Inevitably, she would be overwhelmed by her inadequacy, and she would experience disappointment as well as a sense of betrayal. Her fears of rejection would turn into a pattern of self-destructive behavior and emotional withdrawal that would stun not only the royal family but Diana herself.

Chapter 8

"It's a relief that she is going to have protection from Buck-ingham Palace at last. . . . I'm sure being Princess of Wales won't change Diana in any way. For me she'll always remain my sweet lovable little sister."

—SARAH SPENCER MCCORQUODALE,

in the *Daily Mail*, February 25, 1981

ONCE the engagement had been announced, Diana moved into Clarence House, the home of the Queen Mother. That night Diana dined with Charles and his grandmother—an occasion Diana did not mention when she subsequently complained that "nobody" was "there to welcome me." Three days later, Diana settled into her own apartment in Buckingham Palace, where she was to stay until the royal wedding on July 29.

In theory, the palace was filled with people who could help ease Diana into her role. As her sister hoped, Buck House, as it is often called, did provide a wall behind which Diana could hide from the invasive press, but her sense of security ended there. With its endless rooms and more than 200 employees, Buckingham Palace is a forbidding place, more like a large apartment and office building than an embracing household. Each member of the royal family has a separate apartment, and a sense of isolation is almost inevitable, since the royals spend a great deal of time alone when they are in residence, often dining separately. "At the door you are met by footmen and then you walk down echoing corridors and you don't see anyone except the occasional cleaner," said a man close to Prince Charles.

Diana had a suite consisting of a sitting room, bedroom, bathroom, and small kitchen. She was assigned a maid and footman, and although she had grown up with servants, the footman remarked to Charles's valet, "What shall I do? Lady Diana never seems to ask for anything." By her own later admission, her view of royal life had been astonishingly simplistic: "I had my own money and lived in a big house, so it wasn't as though I was going to anything different."

She occupied her time with wedding preparations such as shopping, making lists, and writing thank-you notes, assisted by her mother or her new private secretary, Oliver Everett. She was so eager for company that she sought out footmen and maids to chat with, showing an informality unheard of in the royal family. (Though in keeping with her need to maintain control, she bristled when any servant took the liberty of addressing her in an overly familiar way.) But much of the time she was by herself, watching soap operas, doing needlework, or tap dancing for hours—to the point, recalled Charles's valet Stephen Barry, that she "quite ruined the music room parquet."

"The Prince of Wales has made everything far easier for me," Diana told reporters a few days before her wedding. Reflecting back on this period in later years, however, Diana spoke in withering terms about the royal family and the courtiers of the royal household—the high-level staff who served the family. She said they treated her coldly, and she complained that no one helped her learn the ropes: "I was just pushed into the fire." She hastened to add that she managed by dint of her upbringing, although her behavior indicated otherwise. In her first official appearance, she said she was confused about such basics as which hand to use for holding an evening bag, and whether to precede Charles when making an entrance. Said her former employer Mary Robertson, "Diana told me . . . she'd received virtually no support or advice from the royal family, ever."

Diana came from a family of courtiers; her own father had been an equerry to King George VI and to the Queen, and her Spencer and Fermoy grandmothers had been ladies-in-waiting to the Queen Mother. The top layer of courtiers have traditionally been upper-class men drawn from the elite public schools and the officer corps of the military. They serve as private secretaries—actually chief advisers to each member of the royal family—press secretaries, equerries who help plan and supervise official trips, and an array of assistants. One level below are officials who work as accountants and office managers; the bottom rung in the household is occupied by footmen, maids, butlers, and other servants who operate "below stairs."

The various ladies-in-waiting to the Queen and other female members of the royal family also come from aristocratic backgrounds, but their positions are not as prestigious as the male courtiers. "The lady-in-waiting is part secretary and part servant," said a woman close to the royal family. "She is responsible for answering correspondence, and when someone like me comes to visit, the lady-in-waiting has to offer me a drink and carry my bags."

Pay for the senior courtiers has historically been low, but the prestige and the perks are considerable. Courtiers often receive free lodging in "grace and favor" apartments attached to the royal residences, travel widely, and carry a sense of importance that comes with proximity to royalty. It is a culture that encourages sycophancy when dealing with members of the royal family. As Stephen Barry noted with understatement, "Few people voice criticism of what the Prince of Wales chooses to do."

The conventional wisdom is that Diana received "less training in her new job than the average supermarket checkout operator." Yet there is ample evidence—including effusive letters of gratitude from Diana—to indicate that she received a great deal of help from the moment she entered Buckingham Palace. Jonathan Dimbleby described the way several advisers tried "to instruct her in the ways of the court and what they saw as her duties. . . . They explained that her future role as consort . . . would be more complicated than she might have realized, and that her husband would not be at her side as often as either of them might have wished. They also told her that . . . she would always be expected to walk somewhat in his shadow."

Diana seemed to take in these instructions while actually feeling overwhelmed and resentful, an attitude that grew out of her insecurity, her determination to stick to her old habits and patterns, and her reflexive mistrust of those around her. The courtiers and members of the royal family were tentative in their dealings with her. "I don't think any of them really helped her," said Michael Colborne, who was an aide to Prince Charles at the time. "They didn't resent her, but they were apprehensive about her. Was she going to be molded?" The courtiers may have thought they were doing the right thing, but they misunderstood the profound challenges posed by a vulnerable young woman.

The courtiers assigned to Diana were of the highest caliber—a signal that the Queen wanted her to be thoroughly tutored. Susan Hussey, who had been close to Charles since his boyhood, was a trusted lady-in-waiting to the Queen. Hussey was intelligent and experienced, with a strong personality and a no-nonsense view of life. Because of her long-standing affection for Charles and the Queen, whom she had served since 1960, Hussey took her assignment seriously. She offered Diana advice on protocol and other aspects of royal life. "I know from talking to her at length that she helped Diana," said a former Palace aide.

At the time, Diana seemed to regard Hussey as an elder sister—or at least, she wrote her letters to that effect—but she later claimed to have felt quite differently. "She thought Susan Hussey was slightly in love with Charles," said one of Diana's close friends. "Diana felt Susan loathed her from the moment she walked in." With the benefit of hindsight, it seems obvious that Susan Hussey's friendship with Charles would create a wedge—as Michael Colborne said, she was "two hundred percent behind the Prince of Wales"—and that her powerful personality would intimidate Diana. "She wasn't sympathetic, and she would not tolerate anything that didn't conform to royal behavior," said a friend of the Queen Mother's.

Another high-ranking courtier tapped to assist Diana was Edward Adeane, a punctilious bachelor nine years older than Prince Charles who had been his private secretary since 1979. Like the Spencers, the Adeane family had served the royal family over the years; Edward's father, Sir Michael, had worked as the Queen's private secretary. Known for his serious intellect and rigid personality, Edward Adeane was an austere figure whose temperament was less than ideal to tutor a skittish nineteen-year-old. Although Diana later said she admired and got along with him, she made it known at the time that she considered him too formal for her taste.

Diana fared somewhat better with Francis Cornish, Adeane's thirty-nine-year-old assistant, and Oliver Everett, another Buckingham Palace veteran summoned by Charles from a diplomatic post in Spain to be Diana's first private secretary. Both men were veterans of the foreign service. They instructed Diana on the public requirements of her role; Everett in particular made himself available to listen to her concerns and brief her about events she would attend and people she would meet. "Before the wedding, Oliver was very supportive to her," said a fellow Palace aide.

Yet Diana felt vaguely uncomfortable with all of them—at times, with good reason, because they couldn't help being patronizing. To Diana, they seemed stuffy and reserved, with the exception of Michael Colborne, Charles's personal secretary who handled his financial accounts and helped organize his private life. After serving with Colborne in the navy, Charles had hired him as an aide in 1975. "I was not the usual type of person to do that job," Colborne said—he was the first to have been to grammar school. "I was known as a rough diamond, and I was."

Twenty-five years her senior, Colborne was a soothing presence for Diana. "I was Uncle Michael to her," he recalled. She shared an office with Colborne, and she spent many hours unburdening her apprehensions to him. "She was very unnerved by it all," Colborne recalled. "At one point she said, 'Do you think I'll change?' I said, 'You will change in five years. You will be a b-i-t-c-h because you won't be able to help it. You will expect people to wait on you.' "

At first, Diana was completely intimidated by the Queen. When Robert Runcie, the Archbishop of Canterbury, sat between Diana and her future mother-in-law at a meeting on the eve of the engagement announcement, he could see that "Diana was terrified of her." In her own fashion, the Queen tried to help Diana relax. "I hope to see her every now and then," the

Queen wrote to a friend, "but I hope she will feel free to come and go as she pleases." Unfortunately, Diana was too intimidated to walk unbidden through the Queen's open door.

Along the way, Diana's new family did give her some tips on royal behavior, such as the "royal wave"—cupping the right hand and swiveling it from side to side, "like screwing a lightbulb, it was all in the wrist," observed Diana's future sister-in-law Sarah Ferguson after her first try—and the art of the curtsy. The Queen Mother offered advice on instructing staff and remembering faces in a crowd. She also showed Diana how she would pause during official visits to ask for the date before signing a visitor's book; as she lifted her head to inquire, she gave photographers a good picture. The Queen and Prince Philip demonstrated, by example, their techniques for interacting with the public. The Queen was diligent about memorizing names and places, and Prince Philip was known for making people feel important by asking them what they did, then repeating back to them what they had just said. ("Ah, you're the baker, are you?")

Their approach was hardly systematic, however. The royals avoided involvement in one another's lives, and they assumed that newcomers would work things out on their own. Since their duties were second-nature, they expected Diana to take the initiative and adapt. "You don't get training to be Princess of Wales," said the Queen's press secretary Michael Shea. "There was never any question of that. It's a matter of making information available if she wants it. Being Princess of Wales is an education in itself."

All the experts and briefing papers and instructions only disoriented Diana: "I was terrified, really. Everything was all over the place," she later said. Diana considered it unfair that she had to conform to strict royal rules. "The royal family are not like us," said a friend of the Queen who knew Diana well. "They cannot be, bless their hearts. It is difficult to find yourself in that world and have your wings clipped." When Diana attended royal receptions and garden parties, she could no longer simply enjoy herself; she had to charm and converse with hundreds of people while enduring the piercing gaze of the tabloid press. "For Diana, royal life was like a movie," said her friend Roberto Devorik. "She thought royalty was one thing when she was growing up. Then she opened the back door of royalty and couldn't cope with it."

Instead of protecting her, the palace walls became a formidable barrier, preventing her from leading her old life and blocking spontaneous visits by her roommates and school friends. "It was as though she had been whisked off to an ivory tower . . . never to be seen again," said her friend Carolyn Bartholomew. It wasn't quite that bad, because Diana did entertain them from time to time at small lunches in her sitting room, usually along with her mother and her sister Jane. But all visitors had to arrive through the front gates and cross the vast expanse of the forecourt, in full view of gawking tourists, to an entrance guarded by a footman. It was an intimidating experience for Diana's young friends, so they didn't come as often as they might have. "I missed my girls so much," Diana said. "I wanted to go back there and sit and giggle like we used to and borrow clothes and chat about silly things." Perhaps most telling of all, she said she yearned to be "in my safe shell again."

Like the rest of his family, Prince Charles saw no particular need to coddle Diana, but he did make a sincere effort to give her pointers. He taught her to conserve energy during a public event by shaking hands with every fifteenth person in a crowd; to bite the inside of her lip to stifle inappropriate laughter; to toss out a general question ("Do you all come from around here?") toward a group as a conversational stimulus; and to use a pleasant smile to extricate herself from a tedious conversation.

In many circumstances, Charles understood how to be thoughtful. According to Dimbleby, he was known for "the care with which he nurtured personal friendships and the compassion he revealed when . . . [his] staff found themselves in personal misfortune." Yet Charles's character had a strain of self-absorption that came with being royal. A natural introvert, he was set in his ways. "It would take a lot to pull him out," said a longtime friend. Charles was obsessive about his work—overseeing his charities, meeting with government officials, making speeches—at least in part because he was constantly trying to prove himself and justify his role. On weekends he buried himself in paperwork when he wasn't off hunting, shooting, fishing, or playing polo. "The Prince of Wales was always working at something," said Charles's aide Michael Colborne. "He was endlessly writing letters or painting."

Charles tended—literally—to run from one place to another, and he grew impatient with those who couldn't keep his pace. "The trouble is," he once told a friend, "I always feel that unless I rush about doing things and trying to help furiously, I will not (and the monarchy will not) be seen to be relevant and I will be considered a mere playboy!" He frequently phoned his staff when they were off-duty, expecting them to produce instant answers. If they failed to please him, he could be short-tempered, and he seldom complimented their successes. "He isn't cynical," said one of his friends, "but, like other royals, he is used to getting what he wants and having his own way."

Preoccupied by his schedule of official duties and customary activities, Charles seemed scarcely aware that Diana was beginning to unravel.

"When you don't read and are not interested in current affairs, you get lonely and upset," said Michael Colborne. "She wasn't educated. She was an empty vessel, a pretty empty vessel, but empty nevertheless." Lacking even hobbies or sporting pursuits to divert her, Diana had to confront the sort of enforced solitude that she had striven since childhood to avoid. She was disoriented by Buckingham Palace, where everyone seemed distant and unwelcoming, and she felt hemmed in. Years later she told her friend Roberto Devorik that during these months she began having a recurring dream about Charles's coronation: His crown fit perfectly on his head, but when a crown was placed on her head it was the wrong size, which she took as a sign that she would never be Queen.

Diana fretted about Charles during his frequent absences, reminiscent of her persistent childhood worry when her father left for long stretches. She sometimes threw temper tantrums, became moody and unpredictable, and suffered bouts of depression. "She went to live at Buckingham Palace and then the tears started," said her former roommate Carolyn Bartholomew. "She wasn't happy. She was suddenly plunged into all this pressure and it was a nightmare for her. She was dizzy with it, bombarded from all sides. It was a whirlwind and she was ashen, she was gray." Although Diana had shown signs of depression in her childhood, she insisted that until her engagement, "I didn't know about jealousy or depressions or anything like that."

Diana had enormous difficulty dealing with Charles's inflexible devotion to duty, even in the face of her obvious anguish. When he had to leave for an engagement, "she didn't like it all," said Colborne. "She couldn't understand why he wouldn't stay with her, why he couldn't do what he wanted." Diana even felt anxious when Colborne left her alone in the office. "Every time I went to lunch, she didn't like it because it was the only time the phone didn't [ring], and she didn't like that," said Colborne. Charles considered her objections unreasonable, and he tried, as his close advisers did, to explain his obligations.

Just one month after the engagement announcement, Charles left for a five-week tour of Australia and New Zealand, followed by quick stops in Venezuela and the United States. It was, he confided to a friend, a "much regretted" trip that he undertook to fulfill long-promised commitments. Diana wept publicly when they parted at the airport, and Charles tried to reassure her by telephoning every day. The trip deepened Diana's fears of abandonment and gave her far too much time alone to worry.

Diana's suspicions of those around her hardened during her fiancé's absence. As she later said, "I was told one thing but actually another thing was going on. The lies and deceit." In her insecurity, she focused on Charles's former girlfriends and took to quizzing Michael Colborne and

Francis Cornish about them. At the time, she seemed unduly worried about Dale "Kanga" Tryon, a vivacious Australian friend of Charles's who had married Anthony Tryon, an English baron close to Charles. Diana actually banned Kanga during the engagement, prompting Kanga to complain to Stephen Barry, "I can't understand why we're never invited." When Kanga turned up at Buckingham Palace for a royal event, Barry told Diana she was there. "Oh, is she?" Diana replied with a blank expression, "How nice." Commented Barry, "[Diana] did not go and see her. She [was] still young enough to be slightly anxious that someone might interest him more than she [did]."

Diana fixated even more fiercely on Camilla Parker Bowles. She told Colborne and Cornish that she had asked Charles if he was still in love with Camilla and that he had given her an ambiguous answer. When she asked the two men how she should react, both declined to offer advice, in part because they couldn't speak for Charles. In Diana's imaginings, these well-meaning evasions became "lies and deceit." She later claimed that Charles had responded to her inquiries by telling her that his former girlfriends were "safe" because they were married.

Her instincts were correct to zero in on Camilla's special relationship with Charles. Her tearful parting from Charles at the airport, she said, had "nothing to do with him going," but was prompted by a call from Camilla the previous evening. The phone rang while Diana and Charles were talking in the library, and while there was nothing surreptitious, the idea of Camilla's call on the eve of a journey undid Diana, who left the room to "be nice" and let them talk, although she later said "it broke my heart."

While Charles was away, Diana and Camilla had lunch at Camilla's suggestion. Their time together was cordial, by Camilla's reckoning, but Diana recalled an encounter filled with portents. Diana later concluded that Camilla—"very tricky indeed"—was fishing for information. The older woman particularly wanted to know if Diana planned to take up hunting. Because she had no plans to do so, Diana came to believe that Camilla had designated the hunting field as her "communication route" to Charles after he married.

In his typically earnest, somewhat naive fashion, Charles came clean with Diana, telling her that Camilla had been "one of his most intimate friends," but he assured her that with his engagement and marriage there would be no other woman in his life. He declined to go into "unnecessary detail," assuming that Diana would take him at his word. This was a perfect moment for a secure and confident woman to thank him for his candor and reassure him that she trusted his love: such sweet forgiveness would doubtless have inspired Charles's respect. But Diana was neither secure nor confident, and Charles lacked the insight to realize that Diana would become even more paranoid about Camilla once she knew the truth of the relationship.

Diana didn't acknowledge Charles's frankness, later saying that she had "worked it all out" about Charles and Camilla on her own, adding vaguely that she "found the proof of the pudding, and people were willing to talk to [her]." Diana went further when she confided to her friend Elsa Bowker in 1994 that "she didn't know about Charles and Camilla until she broke open Charles's desk and found love letters from Camilla." According to Bowker, Diana said she made her discovery about six months after the wedding. When asked about Diana's claim, Michael Colborne said he had not seen any evidence to indicate Diana had done such a thing.

Diana's friends often wondered why she didn't simply seize on her advantages—her beauty, her youth, her natural charm—and concentrate on eradicating Camilla from Charles's thoughts. But that strategy assumed a level of self-assurance absent in Diana. Instead, Diana alienated Charles by urging him to sell his new country home, Highgrove, because it was only eleven miles from Camilla's house. In constant turmoil, Diana became obsessive, perhaps even delusional. She later said that Charles had sent Camilla "flowers when she had meningitis. 'To Gladys from Fred.' " Michael Colborne wasn't aware that Charles sent flowers with such a card, or that "Gladys" and "Fred" were nicknames used by Charles and Camilla. Diana's account, he said, was "a bit muddled."

The severity of Diana's torment and the violence of her emotions shocked Charles—who called them "her other side"—and he visibly worried about her. "Whenever the Prince came back from engagements, his first question was, 'Is Lady Diana all right?' " recalled Stephen Barry. Charles saw that he was trapped in a mismatch, but he couldn't call off the wedding without inflicting great damage on Diana. At that stage, he didn't share his apprehensions with his family, or even with friends; only his aides witnessed Diana's behavior. "I was used to temper with him," said Michael Colborne. "But her mood swings were quite frightening in a nineteen-year-old. [They] came from total despair."

In her own recollection, Diana actually accused Charles of the volatility *she* experienced. "He was obsessed with me," she said. "But it was hot and cold, hot and cold. You never knew what mood it was going to be, up and down, up and down." Projecting one's own unpleasant characteristics onto others is known in psychotherapy as a "primitive defense." Its appearance in Diana showed how disturbed she had become.

When Diana and Charles met with Robert Runcie, the Archbishop of Canterbury, that spring for premarital instruction, they couldn't hide the troubles in their relationship. Runcie recalled that his assistant, Richard Chartres—"a very observant man"—noticed that Charles was "seriously depressed. You [could] tell from his voice." Runcie and Chartres concluded that it was an arranged marriage, but Runcie believed Diana would "grow into it." Runcie was fond of Charles, and considered him "highly sensitive" and "capable of hidden acts of kindness." The Archbishop was touched that Charles "encouraged [Diana] a lot when she looked a little anxious and wan." Runcie noted perceptively that Diana was "very tender, very un-formed," yet "had a sort of shrewdness and was tremendously obser-vant . . . of anything about you." In Charles's presence, Diana seemed awed. "He's very deep, Charles," Diana told Runcie with childlike adora-tion.

No one, not even Charles, knew that Diana suffered from severe bulimia nervosa from practically the moment they were engaged. In her childhood and adolescence, Diana had shown a low tolerance for stress and a need for a safe environment where she would be accepted and encouraged. Given her vulnerabilities, Diana now found herself in the worst possible place—with a fiancé who couldn't completely devote himself to her, a family that couldn't support her, and a press and public that clamored for her atten-tion, expecting her to perform perfectly.

When Diana had faced a previous highly stressful situation—her O-level exams—she had fallen apart and failed. When she felt strain in her personal life, she had turned to food for relief. The pressures of being the prospective bride of the Prince of Wales were too much, and her bulimia relapse seemed almost inevitable. "There are circumstances which bring difficulties to the surface," said a leading British psychologist. "Some have been mild or never very apparent. I could imagine if she had been in a sup-portive situation it might have been different."

Diana later blamed Charles for the onset of her bulimia a mere week after their engagement, telling Andrew Morton, "It was all very strange. I just felt miserable. . . . [Charles] put his hand on my waistline and said, 'Oh, a bit chubby here, aren't we?' and that triggered off something in me—and the Camilla thing. I was desperate, desperate." Charles's unthink-ing mockery may well have pushed a button. According to eating disorder expert Kent Ravenscroft, "comments like that can set teenage girls into a cycle of bingeing and purging."

Yet larger forces were also at work, as even Diana's close friends con-ceded. Said one, "All these terrible memories of her childhood, and all these insecurities, came back and she became very ill." In the view of another friend, "her bulimia was triggered by the responsibilities of being a public figure. She was a perfectionist, and her bulimia was created by lots of different reasons. But to get people on her side, it was better for them to think Charles caused the bulimia than other things like her public responsibilities and expectations."

A crucial catalyst was Diana's preoccupation with her portrayal in the press. On March 9, Diana appeared at her first royal engagement, a benefit for the Royal Opera at historic Goldsmiths' Hall. She wore an extravagant black strapless taffeta dress, with a décolletage displaying her ample bosom. According to former *Vogue* editor Felicity Clark, Diana had put on weight since being photographed by Snowdon for *Vogue* the previous fall. Clark, who later visited Buckingham Palace regularly as part of a *Vogue* team helping with her wardrobe, said that Diana had chosen the dress because there wasn't time to have a ball gown made. The design was too bold for the occasion, and Diana miscalculated by choosing black, which royals traditionally only wore for mourning. "It is what happens when you first wear grown-up clothes," said Clark. "You dream of how you look in something. I am sure she wanted to create a sensation. She wanted to look fantastic. She knew the eyes of the world would be on her."

She made the hoped-for splash, "but then she was rather overwhelmed by the attention," said Clark. Behind the tabloid headlines (DI'S DARING DEBUT in the *Daily Express* and DI TAKES THE PLUNGE in the *Daily Mirror*) reporters applauded the dress, but Jean Rook in the *Daily Express* noted the "ounce or two of puppy fat" under Diana's arms. Diana had already expressed dismay about her image on television, hiding her head in her hands and moaning, "Oh, God, I look awful." Now that her weight had been criticized so directly, Diana was even more agitated.

Diana's descriptions of her bulimia were informed by language honed on the therapist's couch: "my escape mechanism." The first time she was sick after her engagement, she recalled, "[she] was so thrilled because [she] thought this was the release of tension." She likened bulimia to "a secret disease. You inflict it upon yourself because your self-esteem is at a low ebb, and you don't think you're worthy or valuable. You fill your stomach up four or five times a day—some do it more—and it gives you a feeling of comfort. It's like having a pair of arms around you, but it's temporary. Then you're disgusted at the bloatedness of your stomach, and then you bring it all up again, and it's a repetitive pattern which is very destructive to yourself."

She confessed that "when you have bulimia you're very ashamed of yourself and you hate yourself, so—and people think you're wasting food, so you don't discuss it with people." She also claimed that "the thing about bulimia is your weight always stays the same, whereas with anorexia you visibly shrink. So [with bulimia] you can pretend the whole way through. There's no proof." But in Diana's case, there was plenty of proof. From the time her bulimia reemerged in March 1981 until the wedding in July, Diana's weight dropped nearly fourteen pounds—from 140 to 126—and her waistline contracted from twenty-nine inches to twenty-three-and-a-half inches. As she herself said, "I had shrunk to nothing."

Diana vacillated between bulimic bingeing and purging and anorexic self-starvation, much as her sister Sarah had done. Both anorexia and bulimia are linked by a morbid fear of fatness, which Diana and Sarah shared. Yet Sarah was basically an anorexic who periodically controlled her weight by purging, in addition to fasting. Diana was primarily a bulimic who engaged in binge eating and compensated for her gluttony with forced vomiting, fasting, excessive exercise, and later, colonic irrigation. Although the conditions are closely related, psychiatrists believe it is likely that women with bulimia nervosa are "psychologically different" from those with anorexia nervosa, which seems to have been the case with Sarah and Diana.

Diana's abuse of food was not deliberately self-destructive, but a way to quell inner turmoil. In a letter to a relative five months after her marriage, Diana wrote, "I am ashamed to think I ate everything in sight [during a recent lunch], but if it's any consolation, felt so much better with a stomach filled." Vomiting, like vigorous exercise, releases endorphins, the chemicals secreted by the brain that have a tranquilizing effect. "It's a good antidepressant and antianxiety mechanism," said Dr. Kent Ravenscroft. "Some people become addicted in part because of the secondary physiologic[al] effects."

The signs of Diana's obsession with food seem all too clear in retrospect. Even before her engagement, Charles's valet observed that "she loved eating sweets. She always got into the car with her Yorkie bars or bags of toffees." After she moved into Buckingham Palace, her puzzling eating habits became more conspicuous. "Lady Diana never ate properly then," Stephen Barry said. "She picked like a bird at chocolate, yogurts, and cereal. She never dr[a]nk but [ate] lots of fruit, and in those days she was always running down to ask the chefs for an apple or any sweet leftovers made by the pastry cooks. It seemed funny to us. She wasn't adjusting to being royal. The Prince hasn't been to the kitchens for years. They are right at the back of the palace and miles from anywhere. It seemed a long way to go for an apple." Most tellingly, Diana ate copious amounts of ice cream, which bulimics often consume before eating other kinds of food so they can induce vomiting more easily.

Diana's immediate family might have been expected to detect her condition before anyone else. Her mother, Frances, later said that because of her experience with Sarah, she had "recognized all the symptoms very quickly with Diana"—although if she knew during the engagement period, she didn't sound an alarm, nor did she directly intervene in Diana's illness as she had with Sarah. As she rather weakly explained, "There are an enormous number of reasons for anorexia and bulimia taking hold and you have to know those reasons to be able to help." Diana's mother remained in the dark about the reasons, either because Diana refused to tell her or Frances declined to ask. "It's a very difficult area," Frances said, "because you're told you mustn't pander. That can accentuate the problem, but if you don't take enough notice, that can be damaging, too."

During the months before the marriage, Frances spent more time with Diana than she had in many years. By some accounts there was friction between mother and daughter, which wouldn't have been surprising under the circumstances. Frances took Diana shopping several times a week and helped out in the office. Diana's sister Jane also came by regularly to give whatever assistance she could, and Diana periodically stayed at Jane's apartment in Kensington Palace. Diana was then closest to Jane, and relied on Jane's husband Robert Fellowes for guidance.

Diana's father stayed in the distance, but he and Raine made some remarks after the engagement that could only have put more pressure on Diana. Commenting on Diana's fortitude in the face of media scrutiny, Earl Spencer told *The Times,* "She never breaks down because Diana does not break down at all." Raine defensively added that Diana was neither highly strung nor prone to depression.

Diana's parents and siblings had too much of a vested interest in a successful royal marriage to probe her feelings. The excitement was contagious, and it carried them all along. "If she had been in a united family, it would have been all right," said Michael Colborne. "During the engagement her mother came into my office every day. It was helpful, but I don't think Diana had ever experienced that before. They got on, the adrenaline was flowing."

By all appearances, Diana was enjoying herself, especially the most visible aspects of being a princess. She loved inspecting her wedding presents; when she saw the suite of sapphire jewelry—a bracelet, watch, necklace, and earrings—sent by King Faisal of Saudi Arabia, she exclaimed, "Gosh, I'm becoming a very rich lady!" She also immersed herself in building her wardrobe, an activity that Charles encouraged.

Through her sister Jane, Diana met the four editors from *Vogue* magazine who helped her select a wardrobe, gave her tips on makeup, and taught her techniques for walking through crowds and posing for the cameras. "At the beginning the people at *Vogue* would tell her, 'You should wear this for this occasion and these other things for another occasion,' and she was listening and learning a lot," recalled Roberto Devorik, who worked with the *Vogue* editors. "Diana seemed to enjoy the new glamour." *Vogue* editor Felicity Clark remembered that "Charles was very interested in her clothes. He participated occasionally in choosing things. It was lovely and nice."

Diana showed off her newly glamorous image in a series of public appearances—dining with the Saudi king, promenading at Ascot, watching polo at Windsor and tennis at Wimbledon—all of which received blanket coverage in the press. LADY DI-ET! proclaimed *The Sun,* marking its approval of Diana's more svelte figure.

The ever-vigilant hacks detected a few hints of tension. James Whitaker noted that, during Ascot, Diana left Charles to spend time with an old friend named Humphrey Butler, and that Charles had gone home alone. Several weeks later, Whitaker quoted some tart remarks Diana made to tennis star Chris Evert Lloyd about Charles: "He can never sit still," Diana complained. "He is like a great big baby. But one day I hope to calm him down."

Charles was trying to change his habits to accommodate a woman who needed far more attention than he had anticipated, and he showed his apprehension in a joint television interview taped for broadcast several days before the wedding. "I tend to lead a sort of idiotic existence of trying to get involved in too many things and dashing about," he said, "and this is going to be my problem—trying to sort of control myself and work out something so that we have a proper family life. It isn't easy." When interviewer Angela Rippon said, "You'll have a wife by your side. That's obviously going to make an enormous difference to you," Charles replied, "Well, it's marvelous to have a lot of support," prompting Diana to quietly murmur—as if giving herself a grim reminder—"Better like it."

In late June, Charles and Diana attended a twenty-first birthday party for Prince Andrew at Windsor Castle, where Diana was reported to have "requested rock numbers and flung herself about energetically to Shakin' Stevens numbers." "She was in great form that night," recalled a member of Diana's family. "She looked radiant."

Behind the scenes, Diana's anxieties took on a new and unfortunate focus in mid-July. Charles had asked Michael Colborne to help him organize gifts for various friends as tokens of gratitude. "There were more than a dozen [gifts] that [Charles] was giving to Lady Tryon, Camilla, and others," recalled Colborne. At the suggestion of a friend, Charles came up with a special keepsake for Camilla: a gold bracelet with a blue enamel disk stamped GF, which stood for "Girl Friday," Charles's nickname for her.

Colborne ordered the bracelet, which was delivered to his office along with the other gifts. Diana later claimed that Colborne had told her about the bracelet, but he insisted that Diana had found the box on his desk and opened it. As a friend of Charles's explained, "If you make a habit of opening parcels and letters out of curiosity, thunderbolts do strike." Diana was convinced the initials stood for "Gladys" and "Fred," which would have symbolized Camilla and Charles as a couple. "I was devastated," Diana recalled.

According to Diana, Colborne let slip that Charles planned to give Camilla the gift that evening. In a "rage, rage, rage," Diana confronted Charles, who tried to explain the gift, but she was unmoved. They had a bitter fight when Charles told her he was determined to deliver the bracelet to Camilla as a graceful and courteous farewell gesture. Diana accused him of dishonesty and later said, "he cut me absolutely dead."

Charles decided to present the bracelet to Camilla at lunch on Monday, July 27. On Saturday, July 25, during a polo match at Tidworth, Diana's public facade of cheerfulness cracked when she burst into tears and rushed off. Prince Charles caught up with her at Broadlands, where she had gone to rest. "It was easy to see that he was worried," said Stephen Barry. The next day's newspapers were filled with stories of her breakdown, which Charles explained by saying the crowded polo match was "just a bit too much for her." All the hacks showed up on Sunday when Diana was due to watch more polo at Windsor Great Park. Under the headline THAT'S BET-TER!, Whitaker described Diana at her "radiant best," while the *Daily Mail* said she "kept her composure and her smile."

Only John Edwards in the *Daily Mirror* broke from the party line of a quick recovery to describe a darker mood: "The radiance for television at the end of the day couldn't change things," he wrote. "Something had gone wrong for sure. Diana was mostly tired and tense. . . . She hardly smiled." He noted how she had lingered in the Queen's private enclosure, "twisting a white cardigan in her hands, peeping nervously from behind the door at the crowds." Later, he observed that Diana "turned her head uneasily from side to side. . . . She rubbed her forehead with both hands and looked disturbed. She was never relaxed."

Edwards read her body language correctly, because Diana was dreading Charles's meeting with Camilla the next day. That Monday, as he was delivering the bracelet, Diana had lunch with Sarah and Jane, and later recalled telling her sisters that she couldn't go through with the wedding, to which they replied, "Well, bad luck, Duch, your face is on the tea towels, so you're too late to chicken out." Diana incongruously recalled being pleased by this response because her sisters reduced her anguish to a laugh. In such exchanges, Diana showed how she could shift quickly from a mood of serious distress to one of jocularity, causing others to feel puzzled about which signals they should heed.

Later, Diana and Charles went to St. Paul's Cathedral for their final wedding rehearsal, this time under the television lights. Afterward she broke down again. "The tension had suddenly hit me," Diana recalled. "I sobbed my eyes out. Absolutely collapsed, and it was collapsing because of all sorts of things, the Camilla thing rearing its head." Reinhold Bartz, the husband of Diana's first cousin Alexandra Berry, later said that Diana's distress continued during a small reception in the early evening for family and friends. He said her "eyes were swollen as if she'd been crying," leading him to conclude that "she had cracked under the strain." At a grand ball given by the Queen that evening, Diana was all smiles once more as she and Charles greeted well-wishers at the top of a staircase.

That night, "in the hours leading up to his marriage to Lady Diana Spencer, Prince Charles lay in bed at Buckingham Palace with Mrs. Camilla Parker Bowles," James Whitaker announced on the first page of a book he wrote about the Wales marriage in 1993. Calling Charles's actions "the grossest deceit on his future wife," Whitaker asserted that "Diana was simply there to make a marriage of convenience." According to Whitaker, Charles had taken Camilla to his bed on Monday, July 27, while Diana slept at Clarence House following the Queen's ball.

It was one of the most damaging charges made against the Prince of Wales, and, by all reliable accounts, it was wrong. Whitaker cited two sources for his information: an unnamed informer and Stephen Barry, who was dead by the time the book came out. But in his own book, *Royal Service: My Twelve Years as Valet to Prince Charles,* published in 1983, Barry had written, "Buckingham Palace was totally unsuitable for anything secret to take place." Michael Colborne, who was part of the team working night and day at Buckingham Palace to prepare for the wedding, said the assignation "didn't happen, that is for certain. It couldn't have happened without a lot of people knowing. It would have been impossible—and suicidal. It was not in the Prince's character to do something like that."

Camilla was at the ball that Monday night with her husband, Andrew, who later denied to Nigel Dempster that his wife had stayed at Buckingham Palace. What's more, Diana and Charles left the ball together, and she slept in her apartment at the Palace as usual, not Clarence House. The following night, her wedding eve, Diana did move to the Queen Mother's residence, and after the evening's fireworks celebration, Charles stayed up late to talk with Susan Hussey. As he looked out the windows of Buckingham Palace, Charles was "in a contemplative mood," according to Dimbleby. He was "not at all elated, but aware that a momentous day was upon him," and he was "clear about his duty and filled with concern for his bride at the test she was to face." When Charles was back in his room, he watched the people gathered on the steps of the Victoria Memorial, singing "Rule Britannia." "It really was remarkable," he recalled in a 1985 television interview. "I found myself standing in the window with tears pouring down my face."

Like the royal train fabrication, the prewedding assignation story leached into the mythology of the Prince and Princess, and Diana tormented herself by taking it to heart. As early as March 1986, when Diana first consulted astrologer Penny Thornton, she recounted a variation of the story, saying that not only had Charles "spent the night before the wedding with this woman," but that he had told Diana, the same day, "categorically that he did not love her"—an assertion Diana would later disavow.

Diana was distraught the night before her marriage, although she hid her worries from Jane, who stayed with her at Clarence House. She had a severe bulimic attack, eating "everything I could possibly find, which amused my sister." Neither Jane nor anyone else could begin to grasp Diana's problem. "It was very hush-hush," Diana recalled. "I was sick as a parrot that night."

Her wedding day was no less emotional. Diana's later description was typically equivocal, one moment expressing happiness at the adoration of the crowds, the next saying, "I don't think I was happy." She described her "deathly calm" and sense of dread as a "lamb to the slaughter," yet said she was "so in love with my husband that I couldn't take my eyes off him. I just absolutely thought I was the luckiest girl in the world." She remembered that she had concentrated on guiding her father—unsteady from the damage done by his stroke—up the aisle, but she also said she had been searching for Camilla. When Diana finally found her, she saw a "pale gray, veiled pillbox hat, saw it all, her son Tom standing on a chair. To this day . . . vivid memory." It was her only sighting of Camilla that day, because at Diana's request, Camilla and Kanga Tryon had been excluded from the guest list for the wedding breakfast.

Years later, when asked about the worst moment of her life, Diana made a chilling comment about her wedding day: "The day I walked down the aisle at St. Paul's Cathedral, I felt that my personality was taken away from me, and I was taken over by the royal machine." At a time when she might have experienced love, happiness, and exultation at her position in the world, she could only recall feeling utterly defenseless.

To family and friends, as well as to the press and the public, Diana projected an impressive serenity. Charles Spencer remarked that she was "very composed . . . happy and calm." Frances, who told her children after the ceremony, "Now we can go back to normal life," also observed that her daughter seemed "incredibly calm and unfazed by it all. I really don't think she suffered any nerves." But sharper eyes might have spotted a manic edge to her behavior. After the wedding breakfast, the photographs, and the appearance on the Buckingham Palace balcony before thousands of wellwishers, Diana paused on the platform of the Waterloo train station and impulsively kissed Sir "Johnnie" Johnston, comptroller to the Queen, and Lord MacLean, the Lord Chamberlain, the two senior officials who had organized the wedding. It was a distinctly unroyal gesture that, for all its poignant sweetness, summed up in an instant the unpredictability that would increasingly define Diana.

Chapter 9

CHARLES and Diana spent a long stretch of time together at the beginning of their marriage—a two-week Mediterranean cruise on the royal yacht *Britannia*, followed by two-and-a-half months at secluded Balmoral, Charles's favorite retreat. It seemed an ideal plan. Without the interruptions of Charles's duties or the intrusions of the press, they could build their relationship and develop the shared values and interests that sustain a happy marriage over the years.

By all outward appearances, the cruise was a great success. As Diana wrote to her former nanny Mary Clarke, "I adore being married and having someone to devote my time to." When they boarded in Gibraltar, the newlyweds stood on the aft deck and waved to the cheering crowd, Charles holding Diana tightly. Lady Hassan, wife of Gibraltar's chief minister, was touched that Diana was so overcome by emotion "she was almost in tears." The only other public glimpse was in Egypt, where Charles and Diana disembarked, smiling and waving, to dine with Egyptian president Anwar Sadat and his wife—after which Diana unexpectedly kissed each of them good-bye.

Charles's valet Stephen Barry, one of four private staff aboard, gave an eyewitness account of the couple's days together that conjured tranquillity and harmony. They "spent most of their evenings alone on the royal deck," he reported, "and we never knew at what time they went to bed." Charles and Diana often had "intimate" meals together in their sitting room and watched videos after dinner, including tapes of their wedding. Many days they went off to deserted beaches for picnics, swimming, and sunbathing. The crew of more than 200 men, noted Barry, at all times tried "to keep a discreet distance." While Charles rarely left his deck, Diana frequently roamed around, giggling and chatting with the sailors and snapping photographs. She joined in sing-alongs with the crew and once even played "Greensleeves" on the piano for the delighted men.

For reasons no member of *Britannia*'s crew could possibly have fathomed, Diana was actually in a bad way. When she and Charles were alone together, she would suddenly flip into different moods, from extreme anguish to extreme anger. Diana's sporadic depression turned chronic, and, unknown even to Charles, her bulimia became "appalling," as she later described it, "rife, four times a day on the yacht." Ironically, Diana fell apart when she was under minimal external pressure; the hacks couldn't reach the royal couple, and she scarcely had to appear in front of crowds. (Diana later said she hated the strain of having to entertain the ship's officers at dinner.) But the sharp contrast between her public and private selves that had emerged during the engagement now settled into a disturbing pattern.

Charles found it difficult to know what would set Diana off. With almost touching obliviousness, he had brought a stack of books for his enjoyment and Diana's edification during the honeymoon: works by Laurens van der Post, an elderly mystical philosopher who had become a guru to Charles, and by psychoanalyst Carl Jung, another of Charles's favorites. Charles assumed that, as with his sporting pursuits, Diana would enjoy sharing the books that he loved. On the second night, Charles produced his books, to the dismay of Diana, who called it the "worst moment" of the honeymoon. By her account, his Pygmalion-style effort "slashed" her "tremendous hope" (for happiness, presumably) and created a "grim" atmosphere. According to Diana, Charles insisted on discussing his latest reading with her every day at lunch. Later, at Balmoral, Charles would read aloud from van der Post and Jung. But reading aloud from treatises on spiritualism and psychology was far removed from Diana's own marital reverie: "the idealized bride, cooking suppers and darning socks for her husband."

Charles was no intellectual, but he had developed a searching intelligence. He earnestly probed spiritual puzzles, dabbled in psychology, and enjoyed debating theories of environmental and social policy. He was fundamentally serious-minded, while Diana had superficial interests and no inclination to explore weighty topics. She also had an inferiority complex about her intelligence, and was easily cowed by bright people. "When you began on abstract ideas," recalled Archbishop Robert Runcie, "you could see her eyes clouding over, her eyelids become heavy." But Runcie also grasped how to draw Diana out, an insight that eluded Charles and his family: "It was a matter of encouraging her through talk about people, about personalities, and she was very receptive to that."

Still, even the gap in their intellects might have mattered little if Diana or Charles had been able to nourish the other. Both of them wanted the marriage to succeed—Diana to avoid going through a traumatic divorce, and Charles to fulfill his duty. "Marriage is something you ought to work at," Charles had said several years earlier. "I intend to work at it when I get married." Yet neither had the temperament to accommodate the other's needs. "She didn't understand him, and he didn't understand her," said Michael Colborne. What's more, Diana and Charles were far more interested in being understood than trying to understand.

Since his school days, Charles had savored solitude and privacy. He required a measure of tranquillity in his life that Diana couldn't comprehend. Diana had tried joining him in salmon-fishing at Balmoral, but was too impatient to endure standing for hours in a chilly river. Nor did she retain the tolerance she had shown during their courtship for sitting silently during his extended periods of quiet contemplation. On their honeymoon, Charles was perfectly content to stay in his cabin writing long letters or curled up with one of his books, reading. "Diana dashes about chatting up all the sailors and the cooks in the galley, etc., while I remain hermitlike on the verandah deck, sunk with pure joy into one of Laurens van der Post's books," he wrote to one friend, unwittingly emphasizing the gulf between them.

Diana wanted Charles's undivided attention, and misread his preoccupation as rejection. Such fears reflect a common anxiety, but only the most deeply disturbed would act out their worries the way Diana did: "Anything I could find I would gobble up and be sick two minutes later. . . . That slightly got the mood swings going in the sense that one minute one would be happy, the next blubbing one's eyes out. I remember crying my eyes out on our honeymoon." Charles remained mystified by Diana's mercurial moods, but he blamed postwedding nerves and assumed her misery would recede.

More than ever, Camilla was the focal point of Diana's angst. Diana recalled being undone twice by jealousy of her rival during the cruise. The first time, she said, two pictures of Camilla fell out of Charles's calendar; the second time, Diana spotted him wearing cuff links with entwined C's. When Diana asked if Camilla had given him the cuff links, Charles admitted that she had, but only out of friendship. Charles's honesty once again fueled Diana's outrage, provoking another fight.

Diana's emotions intensified when they arrived at Balmoral in late August and she confronted the everyday reality of a married royal. "This was going to be her life," said Colborne, "spending wet days shooting, and she hated it." She had persistent nightmares about Camilla, and found herself "obsessed by Camilla totally. Didn't trust him, thought every five minutes he was ringing her up, asking how to handle his marriage." Charles confided to friends that Diana had a fixation on Camilla that he couldn't dislodge.

Despite Charles's repeated assurances that he had closed the book with Camilla before the wedding, Diana refused to accept his word, telling him, according to Dimbleby, that she was "convinced that [he] was still deceiving her. . . . She more than once exploded into a tirade of anger from which he retreated in bewilderment and despondency." At the same time, Diana felt bereft when Charles went off to fish by himself, or to stalk deer with friends. However much he infuriated her, she couldn't bear to see him leave.

Diana kept her bulimia hidden, but her weight continued to drop. Since February she had lost 28 pounds, and she now weighed slightly less than 8 stone—alarmingly low for her five foot ten frame. "Everybody saw I was getting thinner and thinner, and I was being sicker and sicker," Diana recalled. She slept poorly and wept for hours—sitting in a chair, with her head on her knees. "She would almost cry privately in front of you," said a friend who witnessed her bouts of weeping in later years. "You couldn't help her. She would be wrapped up in herself. Nobody spoke to her or touched her because they knew they could not." At one point in the fall of 1981, Michael Colborne tried for an entire day to console Diana as she alternated between tears and silence, her head buried in her hands.

One problem in offering Diana help was her combination of fragility and defensiveness. She wanted to be soothed, yet invariably rejected efforts to comfort her—especially when they came from Charles. Her silences, which often signaled reproach, were especially difficult to read, as they arose from Diana's inability to articulate what was troubling her.

Largely because Diana's behavior was so unpredictable, Charles's responses were inconsistent, even counterproductive. "He was totally unaware that people suffered as his wife was suffering," said Michael Colborne. "He was totally unable to cope." Charles found it easier to deal with her mute sulks than with her tears. When she wept, he would knead his hands in frustration and say, "What is it now, Diana? What have I said now to make you cry?" Whether she was angry or tearful, he usually temporized—capitulating to her demands, beseeching her to cheer up, staying by her side for long stretches to offer consoling words that she frequently ignored even as she insisted he remain. Other times he withdrew in exasperation, reinforcing her abandonment fears. Diana would then react either by retreating or by lashing out yet again. If Charles seemed unflappable, she would become even angrier.

As Diana challenged Charles's devotion, she tested her own limits as well. Occasionally Charles rebuked her, but neither he nor anyone around him called Diana to account for her behavior. Urging her to pull herself together was as ineffective as efforts to coax her out of her unhappiness.

Charles's fondness for Diana had not evolved into deeper feelings as he had hoped. He was protective of her and genuinely sorry for her, but when he felt suffocated by her possessiveness, he tended to pull away. The more he withdrew, the more she tried to bring him back with her demands and entreaties, which pushed him further away. Charles couldn't tell her what she needed to hear—that he loved her unconditionally—so he compensated by yielding to her wishes. Diana was astute enough to know he was humoring her, so she resorted to even more extreme behavior to get Charles's attention.

When he felt he couldn't manage Diana, Charles sought help from others. He invited Laurens van der Post to Balmoral to offer his counsel, but Diana couldn't connect with the philosopher and felt he misunderstood her. Charles arranged for Diana's old roommates Virginia Pitman and Carolyn Bartholomew to visit, hoping they would distract and entertain Diana. At one point Charles even took Diana to a more remote Balmoral location, a lodge called Craigowan, so they could be alone, and she momentarily brightened. Observed Stephen Barry, "The princess was happier at Craigowan, as she was out of the royal system and could run the house."

The royal family and their employees couldn't avoid witnessing Diana's distress as she grew more vocally defiant. "I heard of Diana's moods early," recalled a relative of the royal family. "She suddenly refused to come to dinner. The Queen asked Charles to persuade her, and he returned red-faced and said he could not. I was fascinated. I could not imagine doing that. It did happen, and everyone was vastly embarrassed." Yet, the relative continued, "[The royals] didn't see her as ill. Mental illness they do not understand."

It is difficult to imagine life inside the royal family. While the rest of England views the world as a social hierarchy, the royals divide the world into "us" and "everyone else," making no essential distinction between the Duke of Devonshire and the local grocer. They also firmly adhere to their own rules. Duty always prevails, everyone defers to the Queen, emotions are kept private, and personal matters are not discussed. The royals have an ingrained sense of entitlement; when offered a concert ticket purchased by a friend, for example, a member of the royal family wouldn't think of paying for it. "The royals are spoiled, but not by the common definition," said Mark Lloyd, a London entrepreneur with friends in the royal family. "They are spoiled by deference. They go through life being 'yessed' to. A royal makes a vague joke, and everyone roars. Then when people disagree with a royal, he finds it intolerable."

In her last interview before she died, Diana said, "From the day I joined that family, nothing could be done naturally." Yet the royal family regards its habits and customs as routine: they know no other way. For much of the year, they follow their own schedules. The Queen and her husband could easily breakfast together, only to discover later on the staircase that they were about to visit the same part of London. But at certain times—August, September, and October at Balmoral, December and January at Sandringham, and June at Windsor, they gather as a clan and share the timeless rituals of sporting pursuits, barbecues, teas, concerts, picnics, cocktail hours, and large formal dinners.

General conversation tends to be quotidian and bland; if anyone brings up a personal dilemma or disagreeable topic at dinner, the response is usually silence. "It's a strange family, the royal family," Robert Runcie told his biographer Humphrey Carpenter, "because conversations aren't followed up. I think it's also that survival is the overarching priority, and you have to prove yourself as a safe person with whom to be a friend, not a man who enjoys boasting about his position with them."

Even in little ways, Diana had trouble relating to the royals. "You cannot judge them by our standards," explained a friend of Diana's whose family served the royal family. "They live on another planet. Things that we get excited about, the royals just wouldn't . . . because they don't even notice. They are oblivious." They are also notoriously tightfisted, while Diana tended to be extravagantly generous. She later told friends about being nonplussed during her first royal Christmas that the family took pride in giving each other inexpensive gifts, making hers seem inappropriately lavish by comparison. Although Ruth Fermoy had warned her granddaughter that the royal family's sense of humor was "different," Diana later said she was nevertheless put off by what she called their "silly" inside jokes. Paradoxically, in a December 1981 letter from Sandringham, Diana praised the family's "generosity" and seemed to enjoy the royal sensibility, noting, "Even though thirty of us were here, it was all laughter."

Diana treated the Queen with respect, but privately betrayed a tinge of animosity. After the engagement, Diana felt the Queen viewed her as a threat, for reasons Diana couldn't quite explain. Diana's hostility could be petty; when the family gathered for drinks, Diana was irked that Charles correctly deferred to his mother and grandmother by serving them first. "Fine, no problem," Diana grumped. "I always thought it was the wife first—stupid thought!" Nor could Diana abide the Queen's adoration of her dogs, a prevailing royal preoccupation. "The Queen is always surrounded by corgis," she once said, "so you get the feeling you are standing on a moving carpet."

Despite her reedy voice and matronly looks, the Queen has a powerful mystique. By a simple turn of her head she can cut off a conversation, and her rigid self-control commands attention. "It is hard to be natural with the Queen, because she is very frightening," said a friend of the Queen Mother. "The truth is, she is frightened of us, too." The Queen's fear—shyness, really—creates an unsettled atmosphere in which people often feel ill at ease. "The Queen is not a demonstrative person," said a former courtier. "She is not 'touchy-feely.' But she is kind and warm. She is very shy by nature and has mastered that." Diana would later resent Sarah Ferguson, the Duchess of York, for her easy rapport with their mutual mother-in-law; Fergie was more of an extrovert than Diana, which appealed to the Queen.

Clever and noncommittal, the Queen gave away very little in dealing with her family. She was fundamentally sympathetic, but she had no tolerance for self-indulgent whining. "The Queen is the opposite of Diana," said a former courtier. "She is the least self-obsessed person you have ever met. She doesn't think it is interesting to talk about herself, and she is not interested in other people's efforts to talk about themselves." She could register disapproval with a stern glance, but otherwise, it was not in her nature to confront problems. "Regardless of how rude Princess Margaret is to [the Queen], she never says anything," said a longtime friend of the royal family. "That is her policy. She never says anything to her children. She is a very decent person, but she won't intervene with anyone."

Diana considered herself the outsider, and made little effort to ingratiate herself with the royal family. She showed her emotions and flouted royal protocol with her informality, causing comment among the courtiers from almost the first day. In a sense, she was laying down her terms and conditions, assuming she would prevail. "Diana was raised without a mother," explained one of her friends, "and I don't think she understood the idea of duty toward a husband's family and toward a husband."

"Her willfulness was a direct result of her insecurity," said aide Michael Colborne. Royal houseparties intimidated her, just as gatherings of people outside her circle had unnerved her, growing up. "Suddenly people were hanging on her every word," recalled her friend Rosa Monckton, to whom Diana confessed, "Only I had none." She couldn't bear that the Balmoral guests just "stared at [her] the whole time, treated [her] like glass." Fearful of being judged inadequate, Diana would sometimes leave meals abruptly, or not appear at all. She later explained her behavior by saying she regarded the regimentation of royal life old-fashioned and boring, claiming it made her feel claustrophobic. She said she loved Scotland but hated the stressful atmosphere at Balmoral because she constantly detected "undercurrents" of "all their moods," and the family depleted her strength.

Diana may have been daunted by the royal family, but in a curious way she also felt superior to them, which stoked her defiance. She had what Paul Johnson called "the toughness of Whig women." Explained historian Andrew Roberts, "Because her family looks down on the royal family, she thought of them wrongly as German parvenus."

When Diana began behaving erratically, members of the royal family chose not to notice in the hope that the problem would disappear. "They are a very matter-of-fact family," said a friend of the Queen. "They would find it difficult to understand a difficult girl who was very young and having a hard time learning to cope. But someone should have done something." As Jonathan Dimbleby explained it, "[The family] had witnessed symptoms of the princess's distress, but not wishing to interfere, they had become accustomed to averting their gaze." The royals even have a name for their ability to ignore the unpleasant: "ostriching." "Maybe I was the first person ever to be in this family who ever had a depression or was ever openly tearful," Diana said. "Obviously this was daunting, because if you've never seen it before, how do you support it?"

But their failure to acknowledge her pain, much less to sympathize with and comfort her, made Diana feel more isolated and wounded than ever. Her reaction summoned up all her memories of rejection: "She told me, 'I am unwanted. I was born and they wanted a boy. I married Charles and I was unwanted, then the royal family didn't want me,' " said her friend Elsa Bowker. Quite understandably, Diana felt the royal family had cast her adrift emotionally, as she had been in childhood by her parents' divorce.

In October 1981, after many days of rain, Diana was "about to cut my wrists," as she put it, when Charles finally persuaded her to go to London for professional help—a significant step, given his family's discomfort with mental illness. But Diana could be neither diagnosed nor treated properly because she refused to admit her bulimia, an essential symptom along with her mood swings and spells of depression. Diana saw "all the analysts and psychiatrists you could ever dream of," but she was a mistrustful patient, unwilling to concede that she was seriously ill.

Instead of prescribing an antidepressant, the doctors gave her the tranquilizer Valium, which she rejected, believing that they only wanted to remove her as a problem by sedating her. In recalling these first encounters with psychiatrists, Diana revealed her rage, resentment, and denial: She spoke in the third person, as if about someone else. "The Diana that was still very much there had decided it was just time, patience, and adapting were all that were needed," she said. She believed she was only given pills so the doctors could rest easily, knowing that "the Princess of Wales wasn't going to stab anyone."

Diana returned to Balmoral no better than before, and even more wary. "She was brought down to London and seen, but she resisted it because she was frightened," said Michael Colborne, who believed she was more gravely afflicted than anyone realized. "You get fed up with people giving you advice, and you do what you want to do and then find you can't. She knew she had problems but she wasn't willing to take help."

Just at that moment, amid all the turmoil, Diana learned that she was one month pregnant, which she considered a "godsend" because it "occupied [her] mind." According to a friend of Charles, the pregnancy relieved him as well, because he thought it would stabilize and focus Diana, and assure her that the marriage had a future. On the other hand, a quick pregnancy robbed the couple of more time to settle down together, and imposed yet another role on an immature woman struggling to come to terms with herself.

At the end of October, Diana and Charles went to Wales for their first official visit, three days in cold, rainy weather—a punishing schedule of seven stops the first day, eight on the second, and eight more on the third. Despite Diana's pregnancy and her delicate mental state, the trip proceeded according to plan. Diana performed superbly, facing overwhelming crowds, shaking hands indefatigably, even delivering brief remarks—three sentences in English and one in Welsh. Neither Charles nor Diana had seen anything like the turnout in Wales, and it unnerved them both. Charles smiled proudly as she went through her paces, but for the first time an unsettling dynamic became clear. "We want Diana," the people chanted whenever the Princess was on the other side of the road. "You will have to make do with me, I'm afraid," Charles said. "Poor Charles," noted Douglas Keay, who covered the royal beat. "Not a single photographer was taking his picture, he who had known all his life what it was like to be the focus of everyone's attention."

Behind the scenes, Diana was a wreck, "sick as a parrot" with bulimia, convinced that she was doing everything wrong. Between engagements she wept in the car, terrified of facing the crowds again. Charles encouraged her to "get out and do it," so she did, drawing on her ability to put on a face despite how awful she felt. Later, she expressed her bitterness that she "never got any praise" from Charles—although Charles commended her publicly at the Lord Mayor's banquet in London: "The response of the people in Wales during our visit there was entirely due to the effect my dear wife has on everybody."

She was also aggrieved that no one in the royal family gave her credit for doing well. If the Queen offered approval at all, it was usually by way of an aside or a chance observation. "Diana couldn't understand why nobody said, 'Well done,'" recalled a former Palace aide. "The reason is that they all do their duty, and they wonder what is so unique. It's a 'been there, done that' attitude. At the time, she said she never got any praise, but it isn't in their nature. This amazed Diana, who needed it more than most."

Diana feared making any public appearances on her own, to the extent that the mere thought gave her tremors. She did one solo engagement—switching on the Christmas lights on Regent Street in London, which required a three-sentence greeting. "I was shit-scared," she said later. Otherwise, she stayed by Charles's side when she ventured out.

Shortly after their return from Wales, they attended the opening of the "Splendours of the Gonzagas" exhibit at the Victoria and Albert Museum. The director of the museum, Roy Strong, was seated next to Diana and had been specifically asked by Edward Adeane to look after her. To Strong, Diana seemed nervous. She was "like a young colt, immensely well-meaning, unformed." Charles seemed, by contrast, "assured and mature . . . with a wonderful sense of humor and great warmth of personality (which she [had], too)." Significantly, Strong observed, "I did not think that he looked after her enough."

Instead of calming her down, Diana's pregnancy made her even more volatile. Her bulimia continued, complicated now by severe morning sickness. In the first two weeks of November, she had to bow out of four official engagements, once because Prince Charles insisted she stay in bed. She lost her appetite and had even greater difficulty sleeping. "People tried to put me on pills to stop me from being sick," she said. "I refused. So sick sick sick sick."

At formal dinners with the royal family she had to excuse herself periodically. "I either fainted or was sick," she recalled, feeling like an outcast for having morning sickness in a family unfamiliar with such an ailment: In fact, the highest value was placed on one's ability to leave a sickbed to attend an official engagement. She believed they saw her only as a "problem" and a "nuisance," yet she recalled resisting any suggestion to retire to her room and lie down when she was ailing. "I felt it was my duty to sit at the table," she said. "Duty was all over the shop." Her dilemma was complicated by what she described as Charles's unwillingness to advise her.

"In some ways she was crying out for someone to say, 'You don't have to do anything,' " said a former Palace aide. "You come up against doctors who leave it to you to do what you feel up to. But in her position she was longing, in hindsight. If someone could have told the doctors to say '[you] mustn't do that,' she could have stopped doing things, with a clear mind. The awful thing was she came from a family where her father raised her not to let people down, and she married into a family where duty was even more important, where you never canceled anything, and they didn't comprehend the idea that people do feel unwell."

The press, meanwhile, was operating on a parallel track, keeping the fairy-tale drama rattling along. The only brief exchange between the royal couple and the tabloid hacks occurred on the fourth day of the honeymoon at Balmoral, when they posed for pictures and took brief questions. The *Daily Express,* in the first of many similar pronouncements over the years, said Diana "showed a confident new face to the world . . . gone were the shy smiles and the lowered head of prewedding days." The couple had their arms around each other and Charles gallantly kissed her hand, but he seemed solemn and fidgety—perhaps because shortly before the arrival of the press Diana had suddenly refused to participate, then just as quickly changed her mind. When asked how she was enjoying married life, Diana smiled and said, "Highly recommend it," but when someone shouted to Charles, "Have you cooked her breakfast yet?" Diana tersely replied, "I don't eat breakfast," while Charles said nothing.

Less than three weeks later, the press picked up the scent of unhappiness, thanks to tipsters inside Balmoral. In the increasingly competitive arena of royal reporting fanned by the Murdoch papers, tabloids had begun paying for information, and disgruntled former and current staff members were willing to tattle for cash payments that could not be traced. Stuart Higgins, formerly editor of *The Sun,* was unapologetic about the policy. "*The Sun* has often paid royal sources for stories," he said. "There were people that were leaving, like butlers, or there were junior staff who knew little things."

James Whitaker initially dismissed the hints of marital trouble, writing in the *Daily Star,* "Diana has been laughing at recent suggestions that she is suffering from the strain of being Charles's wife," but the *News of the World* and *The Sun* persisted. Diana, said the *News of the World,* "goes for lonely walks or a paddle on the River Dee" in an effort to "get away from the stuffed-shirt atmosphere of formal royal functions." *The Sun* went even further, reporting that Diana "has reached a personal crisis in her new lifestyle as a royal. She is known to be deeply unsettled."

The newspaper noticed that she had continued to lose weight, was finding it difficult to adapt to the royal routine, and was feeling the pressure to live up to "all that [was] expected of her." Among the danger signs cited were her unwillingness to attend shooting parties, her premature departure from long evening meals, and Charles's decision to take her off to Craigowan—all accurate indicators of her malaise.

After the triumphant trip to Wales and the announcement of Diana's pregnancy, however, any concerns raised during their stay at Balmoral drifted away—a pattern of press coverage that would persist throughout the marriage. The trip reinforced the image of a happy couple, and as long as Diana was performing well, the tabloids assumed that she was fine. Still, the Queen was evidently more aware of Diana's mental fragility than she let on, because she authorized her press secretary, Michael Shea, to invite twenty-one editors from Fleet Street, along with representatives of radio and television, to a highly unusual meeting in Buckingham Palace that December—the first such gathering in twenty-five years.

Shea spoke candidly about the concern felt by the Queen and the members of the royal family over invasions of Diana's privacy. He said Diana was growing "despondent" that she could no longer go outside her front door without being snapped by the army of photographers staking out her homes. She was young and newly pregnant, and she was entitled to a private life. When Barry Askew, editor of *News of the World*, wondered if he was hinting that Diana was on the verge of a nervous breakdown, Shea said he intended no such suggestion.

The newspapers continued to cover the royal couple nonstop, but the photographers backed off, and a period of relative calm followed. Charles and Diana spent a quiet holiday at Windsor; he gave her a beautiful emerald-and-diamond ring, which she noted in a letter at the time, "I spend most of my time looking at in a stupid gaze." As Charles wrote to a friend, "We've had such a lovely Christmas—the two of us. It has been extraordinarily happy and cosy being able to share it together."

At the same time, the tabloids offered their own rhapsodic speculation about the couple. James Whitaker wrote in the *Daily Star* that while "Diana [had] felt desperate at times, trapped and very unhappy . . . now she is sophisticated and elegant. She has learned to turn herself on for the camera. When it suits her she 'flirts' with photographers," though he unhelpfully observed that "she has learned to use makeup to hide her too-large nose." The royal couple, reported Whitaker, "are very much in love. . . . It is the loving soft side of Diana and the romantic side of Prince Charles that brings the two of them the greatest pleasure. He is a man who goes in for flowers, light music . . . soft lights and extreme tenderness. . . . She gives him shirts and ties . . . He gives her chocolates, bath salts and bottles of scent. . . . I am told the prince regularly gives her flowers and leaves gifts for her under her pillow at nighttime." This depiction of Charles is sharply at odds with Whitaker's later judgment that the Prince had been unfeeling and cynical.

The path of mental illness follows a jagged line, and Diana's melancholy had not in fact lifted, despite the hopeful signs at Christmas. As she went out to events with Charles, she seemed at times to enjoy the enthusiasm that invariably greeted her, yet at other moments she appeared bewildered. Sometimes she would refuse even to appear before reporters and photographers, confounding her staff.

Her celebrity simultaneously bolstered and bothered her, and she felt disconnected from the superstar she saw on television and in the newspapers each day. In her mind, she later said, "I was a fat, chubby, twenty-year-old, twenty-one-year-old, and I couldn't understand the level of interest." She was painfully aware of the difference between her public and private selves. In public, she said, "they wanted a fairy princess to come and touch them," while Diana "was crucifying herself inside, because she didn't think she was good enough."

To Charles and their staff, Diana seemed apathetic, her tearful spells protracted, and she was sometimes paralyzed by despair about the future. According to Dimbleby, "She spent long hours with the Prince's friends and advisers, talking about the plight in which she found herself, the loss of freedom, the absence of a role, the boredom, the emptiness in her life, the heartlessness of her husband. They listened and did their best to offer comfort and reassurance."

Charles had his obligations to attend to, as always, which Diana continued to resent and resist. For a while, though, she had legitimate tasks to divert her, including the redecoration of Highgrove and their Kensington Palace apartment; according to a former courtier, "she was rushing around like a demented flea moving house." But once she was settled, Diana could find little to fill her days other than shopping excursions and luncheons with friends. "She was trying to find a role for herself," said the former courtier. "She was very soon expecting William, so she didn't do a lot of public things. She didn't take on new things, so she didn't have enough to do. She was lonely in little ways that manifested themselves. There were undercurrents of instability all the time."

When gripped by her extreme mood swings, Diana took to impulsive, even dangerous behavior. One night she left home in an agitated state and jumped into her car, heading out alone without telling anyone her destination. This incident was kept quiet, but others like it filtered out into the press. The most famous was the Sandringham staircase scare, early in 1982.

New leaks about discord between Charles and Diana surfaced in early February with an account that they had a "blazing public row" during a pheasant shoot. A week later, *The Sun* and the *Daily Mail* reported that shortly after the new year Diana had fallen down half a flight of stairs at Sandringham, causing a "clearly worried" Prince Charles to summon the local doctor. Charles sat with her until the doctor's arrival, and after an examination turned up no injuries to mother or baby, Diana rested for several hours before Charles took her with him to a royal barbecue.

Nine years later, Diana told Andrew Morton that she and Charles had been fighting that day, and when he wouldn't listen to her, she had thrown herself down the staircase to "get [her] husband's attention." By Diana's account, Charles had told her, "You're crying wolf," before she ran to the staircase. After the fall, which left the Queen "shaking" and "horrified," Diana said that Charles left to go riding and when he returned, his attitude was "just dismissal, total dismissal." She added that she "knew" she wasn't going to lose the baby, although she didn't reveal how she knew.

Diana's account, which Morton reported as an attempted suicide, was at variance with what she told a woman who was close to her at the time. "I talked to her afterwards," said the woman, "and she said she tripped and fell down the stairs and landed at the feet of the Queen. I didn't get the impression it was more than an accident. The way [it] came across to me was she had fallen, a doctor had been called as a precaution, and it was no big deal. Nobody told me anything like, 'You ought to be aware, this was a suicide attempt.' What struck me as so inconsistent in what she told Andrew Morton is that she would not have done anything to harm herself and that baby."

The story Diana related to her friend meshes with the contemporary newspaper reports, so the Morton version seems to have been designed to make a point: that Charles disregarded Diana and treated her callously. To add a further twist, Diana later told her friend Elsa Bowker, it was around this time that she claimed to have broken into Charles's desk drawer and discovered an exchange of letters between Charles and Camilla—a claim that Michael Colborne has disputed. "She said that this is why she threw herself down the stairs at Sandringham," said Elsa Bowker. "She said she didn't think it was worth living or having a baby." As with so much concerning Diana, her state of mind—at the time of the fall as well as during the various retellings—was probably turbulent and quite possibly unreliable.

Soon after the revelation about Diana's fall at Sandringham, she and Charles took a vacation at Windermere Island in the Bahamas. The tabloids lapsed into their customary misbehavior, as James Whitaker and Harry Arnold each supervised a "smudge" (an especially intrusive picture) of Diana by their photographers with long lenses from a nearby beach. The resulting shots of Diana, five months pregnant and wearing a bikini, were accompanied by Whitaker's observation that "her sensational figure has not gone out of shape" and Arnold's comment, "Carefree Di threw royal caution to the wind to wear her revealing outfit."

The Queen denounced the tabloids' "unprecedented . . . breach of privacy," and the newspapers halfheartedly apologized—although Whitaker admitted, "I've never done anything as intrusive in my life, but it was a journalistic high." Whitaker also later disclosed that while watching from his concealed surveillance post, he had been reassured to see Diana and Charles looking "blissfully happy" as they stood in the water "kissing constantly"—an observation he had withheld from his *Daily Star* readers, for whom he only noted that "Charles led Diana into the water for a cooling swim. The Princess laughed with delight as the cold waves splashed against her."

The vacation had, in fact, been good for Diana—at least until the smudge—as she had been able to unwind. Still, it was clear to their hosts, Penny and Norton Romsey, that the relationship between Charles and Diana was shaky. Even in the presence of the Romseys, Diana objected when Charles wanted to read or paint, and she openly expressed her boredom with his conversation.

Diana seldom appeared in public as her pregnancy progressed, and when she did, her demeanor raised questions. At the Cheltenham races in March, the tabloids again caught her in a glum mood. As an edgy Charles "fired a series of questions" at her, "shocked racegoers saw her shake her head to each one, then gloomily turn away." During the race, she "looked aimlessly around at the countryside." Within weeks, the predictable follow-up appeared in *The Sun*: "Why Di Keeps Throwing a Wobbly," an article that listed examples of her "odd behavior" and offered a London cardiologist's theory that "the pressures on the princess are just too great."

On June 21, the longest day of the year, Diana gave birth to William Arthur Philip Louis. Labor was induced, as Diana was beginning to crumble under the strain of constant press speculation about the baby's arrival. With Charles by her side throughout, she had a difficult sixteen-hour labor that nearly ended in a cesarean section. Afterward, Charles described the event to his godmother, Patricia Brabourne, as "an astonishing experience. . . . I really felt as though I'd shared deeply in the process of birth." A decade later, Diana's memory had a sadly sour aftertaste: She sarcastically recalled that the date was chosen so "Charles could get off his polo pony for me to give birth. That was very nice, felt very grateful about that!" But back in June 1982, she was genuinely thrilled, and she and Charles shared in the joy of a healthy son. "It was a great relief because it was all peaceful again," she said years later. "And I was well for a time."

Chapter 10

THE peace after William's birth was short-lived. Diana breast-fed for only three weeks, and opposed Charles's effort to bring in his favorite childhood nanny, Mabel Anderson, to help care for the baby. Instead, Diana chose a nanny herself. By the time William was barely a month old, Diana was hit with depression even worse than what she had experienced during her honeymoon and pregnancy. "You'd wake up in the morning feeling you didn't want to get out of bed," she recalled. "You felt misunderstood and just very, very low in yourself." At the same time, Diana's abandonment fears grew more acute. "Boy, was I troubled," she said. Diana panicked when Charles didn't arrive home on time, which drove her to tears because she thought "something dreadful had happened to him." Yet Charles didn't witness her panic, according to Diana, who concealed it by sitting quietly when he returned.

Diana said that the two years between the births of William, in June 1982, and of their second son Harry, in September 1984, were "totally darkness" to her. She claimed she could remember very little because she had "blotted it out, it was such pain." This was the beginning of what she called her "dark ages," yet she actually recounted vivid memories of this period, many of them bad, but with bright moments, too. She often told friends that the two months before Harry's birth were the happiest of her marriage.

After waving and smiling sweetly on leaving the hospital, Diana went into seclusion for a month, emerging for a service at St. Paul's in late July. The press coverage was enough to drive her back into hiding, as the tabloids insensitively carped at her for looking plump ("Her shape," said the *Mirror*, "was, to put it kindly, generous") and for behaving inappropriately ("Diana fidgeted [and] whispered incessantly to a rather embarrassed-looking Prince Charles," noted the *Daily Express*).

For the rest of the summer and into the autumn, Diana stayed out of the public eye, sinking into a deep malaise. She scarcely marked her twenty-first birthday on July 1, quietly lunching with Sarah Ferguson, whom she had known since their teenage years: their mothers had gone to Downham together. Felicity Clark, *Vogue*'s beauty editor, also saw Diana that summer when she assisted in Lord Snowdon's photo shoot of Diana and William at Kensington Palace. Clark detected no black moods, but she was struck by "a wistfulness about her in general." At William's christening in early August, Diana's anguish was more apparent. She later complained that she hadn't been consulted about the timing of the ceremony and that she had been "excluded totally" by the royal family. "I wasn't very well," she said, "and I just blubbed my eyes out." The only other time she ventured forth was an unexpected trip to Monaco for the funeral of Princess Grace, whom Diana had met once and admired greatly. The tabloids interpreted Diana's public tears—unusual in a member of the royal family—as a sign that she was "endearingly human," with a "big heart."

On August 14, the day Charles, Diana, and William left for the royal family's annual holiday at Balmoral, the tabloids broke a story that added to Diana's misery. For Gordon Honeycombe's new biography of Diana, her mother had made an "exclusive statement" detailing the events surrounding her separation and divorce fifteen years earlier. The tabloids seized on Frances's "rash" choice of words: that Johnnie had "insisted" the children remain with him, and "refused" to allow them to return to London with her—thus placing the blame on Johnnie for being stubborn and cruel, and portraying herself sympathetically. The newspapers also printed Johnnie's condemnation of Frances's statement as "very unkind" and "cheap publicity" that could "only hurt Diana" by reopening old wounds. Diana was indeed "deeply distressed" to revisit her parents' acrimony in such a public fashion.

At Balmoral, Diana was plagued by insomnia—at one point she went for three nights without sleeping—and continued to binge and purge. Once again, her weight dropped alarmingly. She sensed that members of the royal household knew about her bulimia, but she decided that they preferred to ignore the problem and even considered it "quite amusing" that she ate such large quantities without gaining weight. However, Michael Colborne recalled that "she kept the bulimia a secret," and "no one suspected it." Those around Charles and Diana were puzzled by her "disconcerting propensity to consume large quantities of junk food (ice cream, biscuits and popcorn)," yet neither Charles nor anyone else identified her eating disorder.

Nor had Diana's obsession with Camilla abated; Camilla continued to embody Diana's anxiety about being rejected by Charles. Despite Charles's denials, Diana persisted in accusing him of maintaining the affair. Diana's suspicion, Dimbleby noted, "continued to grow to the point where it became a canker between them, destructive of every effort on both their parts to draw closer together." In her interviews with Morton, Diana claimed that her worst fears had been confirmed when she stood outside Charles's door to deliberately eavesdrop, and overheard him on a cordless telephone in his bath, telling Camilla, "Whatever happens, I will always love you." Although Diana didn't attach this conversation to any particular time, Morton wrote that it occurred soon after William's birth, and that she had overheard Charles "accidentally."

This incident occupies a pivotal place in the saga of Diana and Charles, which makes it worth scrutinizing. Jonathan Dimbleby wrote unequivocally that once Charles became engaged, he "had made virtually no contact with Camilla Parker Bowles for over five years," and that Charles had seen Camilla only "fleetingly" at "social gatherings." They had conversed by telephone "a few" times during the engagement and "only once" after his marriage, when he called in the autumn of 1981 to tell Camilla that Diana was pregnant. By Dimbleby's account, Camilla and Charles had not spoken after William's birth—in fact "had not talked to each other at all" until they resumed their relationship in 1986.

Others close to the situation also said that while Charles had indeed ended his relationship with Camilla, it is likely that the former lovers continued communicating in some form, by direct or indirect means. Stuart Higgins, editor of *The Sun* from 1994 to 1998, conducted regular off-the-record conversations with Camilla Parker Bowles from 1982 to 1992, when he was a reporter and junior editor. He had first known her when he was covering weekend sporting events, and when he returned from an assignment in the United States in 1982 he got in touch with her.

"I talked to her once a week for ten years," said Higgins. "I talked to her about Diana and Charles. She guided me on things that were not true, or things that were off the beam. Everything was behind closed doors, and I didn't write about her, although I spoke to her all the time during that period. I didn't sense that she and Charles were out of touch. I felt she was involved, but not necessarily in a romance or affair with Charles. I never sensed that she was out of contact, though I definitely believe there was a cessation in the relationship and that Charles put an effort into the marriage."

Camilla spoke reliably about Charles and Diana, and she became a trusted source for Higgins, who protected her by keeping their relationship confidential. "Our relationship was two ways," said Higgins. "We had some long conversations. She was trying to really gauge whether the press was on to her [and Charles], so it was a question of her keeping in touch, too."

It is conceivable that Diana heard the sort of conversation she described to Andrew Morton. She had a disconcerting tendency to listen at doors, and Charles, for all his public restraint, often spoke and wrote with great affection to his close friends. "He has a habit of saying things like 'Masses of love,' 'I adore you,' and 'Whatever happens I'll look after you' if someone has been going through a hard time," said a friend of Charles. In Diana's turbulent state—and given her predisposition to imagine the worst—she could have jumped to the conclusion that Camilla was the recipient of such endearments when they were completely innocent. Alternatively, the exchange might have been Diana's own invention; the circumstances of the conversation she described could only have occurred some years later, because Charles was reported to have purchased his first cordless phone in August 1986.

Regardless of the truth of the matter, Diana's imaginings had a profound impact on the relationship, and on her own behavior, which took an alarming new turn in Scotland during the autumn of 1982: She began to injure herself with sharp objects. By Diana's later description, she tried to cut her wrists, and she slashed her arms and legs using a lemon knife with a serrated edge as well as fragments of glass from windows she broke. A series of these incidents occurred at Balmoral, the most dramatic of which took place when Diana and Charles were once again on their own at Craigowan. As an indicator of how rapidly her mood could shift, she seemed quite calm when the couple first arrived. In a letter to a relative on September 21, Diana remarked, "We are now installed [in the lodge], which is marvelous and very relaxing."

The provocation for her violent actions, she later said, was her feeling that "no one's listening to you. . . . You have so much pain inside yourself that you try and hurt yourself on the outside because you want help." The intent was not "attention-seeking"; rather, in her confusion, "I was actually crying out because I wanted to get better." It was her "desperate cry for help," she said, because she wanted "people to understand the torment and anguish going on in my head." She also "didn't like" herself and felt shame "because I couldn't cope with the pressures." She didn't characterize her actions as suicide attempts, although they were portrayed as such in the press when Morton's book disclosed them. Diana did later say that she had tried to commit suicide a number of times without naming the specific incidents.

Self-mutilation is one of the most severe symptoms of mental illness, and "cutting" is the most prevalent form, accounting for nearly three-quarters of cases. According to a 1986 survey, ninety-seven percent of self-mutilators are women. Mental health professionals generally agree that such self-destructive behavior is seriously pathological and requires prompt and thorough psychiatric evaluation—and frequently hospitalization.

Self-injury sometimes accompanies bulimia, but more often indicates an even more wide-ranging psychological disorder. It springs from depression and hopelessness, and—as Diana indicated—is a desperate plea for rescue, a way to demonstrate the extent of internal suffering. Even more disturbingly, self-injury can signal someone's wish to experience pain as an alternative to numbness. One 1986 study of self-cutters showed that they knew when to stop because after a certain point they felt soothed. Twenty-three percent of those in the study experienced only moderate pain and sixty-seven percent little or none. When self-injury occurs in front of someone else, there is usually a corollary intention to punish that person.

Diana enacted some of her self-mutilation in Charles's presence, implying that he showed a lack of concern by failing to understand the reasons for her actions. Based on what she later told them, Diana's friends judged Charles even more harshly: Morton quoted one who asserted that Charles's "indifference pushed her to the edge." But Diana's distressing behavior greatly worried Charles, who shared his anxieties with a few of his closest friends and advisers. Fearful of leaks, he was extremely careful about confiding such explosive information. "The trouble is one day I think some steps are being made uphill," he wrote in a letter to one of his confidants on October 10, 1982, "only to find that we've slid back one and a half steps the following day. . . . This afternoon a heavy feeling descended."

After Charles consulted with his confidants and talked with Diana, they agreed that she should undergo psychiatric counseling. (Neither the Queen nor any other member of the royal family was privy to these discussions.) Charles was still unaware of Diana's eating disorders, so the impetus for treatment was her self-mutilation. As a friend of Charles explained, "They were at a loss and knew she needed psychiatric care. They wanted to do something, but bulimia wasn't the buzzword."

On October 17, a week after Charles's letter confessing his despair about Diana's condition, he took her, along with William and the nanny, to London so Diana could begin treatment. She did not return to Balmoral that fall. As Charles had done a year earlier when he urged Diana to find professional help for her depression and mood swings, he showed that he considered her symptoms serious enough for special care.

The day after Charles and Diana left for London, James Whitaker reported in the *Daily Mirror* that Diana had been depressed at Balmoral following two-and-a-half weeks of rain. After "complaining and sulking," Diana had announced that she wanted to go to London to shop and see her friends, provoking a "blazing row" with Charles. Her abrupt return to London "caught many royal aides on the hop." Andrew Morton followed in the

Daily Star along similar lines, describing Diana as "bored to tears" in Balmoral and adding that she was "reported" to be on a "shopping spree" at Harrods.

Over the following months, these small drumbeats became an extraordinary cacophony, beginning on November 13, 1982, when Diana committed an inexplicable faux pas by showing up late at the British Legion Festival of Remembrance at the Royal Albert Hall, presided over by the Queen and other members of the royal family. ("No one, but no one, is EVER late for the Queen," Whitaker thundered.) Prince Charles had already announced that Diana was "unwell" and wouldn't be attending, when Diana unexpectedly turned up looking out of sorts. It was clear to everyone around them that a fight between the royal couple had preceded her arrival. "I will never forget it," said a woman who was sitting in an adjacent box. "Diana and the Prince of Wales had a row right there. I wanted to pinch Charles and caution him that someone might be able to read lips. Prince Philip was looking daggers at Diana. It was agonizing." The following day the tabloids were full of comments on Diana's gaunt appearance and flustered demeanor.

It took the two tabloid rivals, James Whitaker and Harry Arnold, to make a leap that set off a whole new round of speculation. Each of them put several elements together: Diana's "unpredictable" behavior at Balmoral and the Remembrance event, her weight loss, her sister Sarah's battle with eating disorders. The conclusion: Diana was suffering from anorexia nervosa.

IS IT ALL GETTING TOO MUCH FOR DIANA? asked a *Daily Mirror* headline over a November 15 story by Whitaker, who noted that Charles was so concerned, he went "out of his way whenever possible to join Diana for lunch." Whitaker also stumbled on fresh evidence of Diana's compulsive tidiness when he quoted a "family friend" (later revealed by Whitaker to be Diana's press secretary, Vic Chapman) who said, "If . . . her shoes are cleaned, she wants them put back precisely in line in her cupboard. She is obsessed that everything and everybody around her should be perfect."

In his report the same day, Arnold said Prince Charles was "seriously concerned" and had "taken top medical advice." Both Arnold and Whitaker were onto something, although they had offered only a partial picture by highlighting anorexia, and Arnold didn't know what sort of medical help Charles had really sought.

Almost immediately, other newspapers ran stories in which a Buckingham Palace spokesman denied that Diana was suffering from anorexia and said she was "fit and well . . . and in sparkling form." The most emphatic disavowal came from Nigel Dempster, writing several days later in *The Mail on Sunday.* Dempster scolded *The Sun* and the *Mirror* for running speculative stories that exaggerated the "inevitable stresses" of the Waleses' marriage. He went on to undercut his own denunciation by listing various signs that Diana was "cracking," quoting a member of the "inner circle" as saying "quite simply she has freaked out." Dempster continued, "My sources tell me that the Princess has become so disorientated by the type of exposure that she may have to seek psychiatric assistance."

These pronouncements sparked a wave of stories discrediting Dempster. Andrew Morton wrote in the *Daily Star* that Dempster was just a "sniper" and dismissed such "professional knockers" as "wide of the mark." Several days later, the *Daily Express* ran a piece headlined LOOKING GOOD, FEELING GREAT that described Diana's "new lease of enthusiasm and energy" as she undertook thirteen official engagements in three weeks, on her own for the first time. "It was Diana herself who decided that the time was indeed right to make her solo run," the paper reported.

The amazing denouement of this surge of overheated coverage was an appearance by Dempster on ABC's *Good Morning America* in early December 1982. Barely two weeks after his plea to the tabloids to "give her a chance," Dempster launched into a vicious tirade, calling Diana a "fiend" and a "monster." "Diana is very much ruling the roost," he said. "Charles is desperately unhappy . . . because Fleet Street forced him into this marriage." Sixteen years later, Dempster was as confident of his information as ever. "I got it straight from one of Prince Charles's staff," he said.

Predictably, his tabloid competitors furiously denounced him. The *News of the World* called his remarks "the greatest howler of all time for the balding 41-year-old columnist." Yet within weeks, the same tabloid returned to the fray with an account in early 1983 that said Diana was "near to tears much of the time . . . and her quick temper never far from the surface." Her basic problem, according to the tabloid, was that she could not handle being left alone, leading to concern that "she might well be heading for some kind of breakdown."

Andrew Morton countered the bad news once again, this time with six pages in the *Daily Star* dismissing the "nonsense" about Diana "teetering on the brink of a nervous breakdown." Charles has, Morton wrote, "acted as her guide and mentor. [He] is very seldom away from Princess Diana for any length of time." Morton based his account on a "heart-to-heart talk" with a "reliable source close to the Palace" whose pattern of speaking was virtually identical to Michael Shea's, the Queen's press secretary. According to this authoritative source, Charles and Diana had "occasional spats" and "a few fireworks." "It's a rumbustious marriage," said the source, who also emphasized that Charles and Diana were "very fond of each other."

With that final burst of positive spin, the press frenzy subsided. But Diana, who took her coverage all too seriously, had been badly battered.

She was hurt that the press had called her names and admitted that she "did take criticism hard." "One minute I was a nobody," she recalled, "the next minute I was Princess of Wales, mother, media toy, member of the family, and it was just too much for one person at that time."

The Spencer family was noticeably absent during Diana's acute psychological crisis. As Diana said, "None of my family knew about [my bulimia, self-mutilation, suicide attempts] at all. . . . I never leant on anyone"—a sad admission of the distance she felt from her parents and siblings. The public squabble between Frances and Johnnie about their divorce had hurt and embarrassed Diana, who held her mother responsible for generating the bad publicity. Even before then, relations between mother and daughter had cooled. Her mother was busy with her own life, splitting her time between Scotland and her farm in Australia. "I am a firm believer in maternal redundancy," Frances had told the *Daily Mail* in June 1982, shortly after William's birth. "When daughters marry they set up a new home, and they don't want mothers-in-law hanging around. They should be free to make their own decisions and maybe to make their own mistakes."

While Frances's sentiments reflected her own confidence and independent spirit, they revealed how little she seemed to understand her daughter, given the reports of Diana's unstable behavior that began leaking out of the royal household only weeks after the marriage. What Diana needed—as she later told her friends—was unconditional support and reassurance from her mother.

Johnnie Spencer told his cousin Robert that Diana had been "upset" after William's birth by the "constant attention." But Johnnie's view of his daughter's situation was as clouded as Frances's, though in his case by the certitude of being a Spencer. "I know the royals can appear to swallow people up when others marry in," he said in a 1983 interview, "but that could never happen to us. We can cope with the pressures." Little grasping how confused his daughter was most of the time, Johnnie affirmed his belief that Diana would prevail as Princess of Wales because she "knows her own mind."

During the flurry of speculative articles about Diana's health, James Whitaker quoted "a close member of the Princess's family" who revealed, "I am extremely worried about her. . . . I can't say for sure that Diana has anorexia. . . . Somebody at some time has to sit down and talk to her." Some years later, Whitaker dropped his pledge of confidentiality by naming Diana's sister Sarah as his source. "She told me then they were very, very worried," he said. "I couldn't name her at the time." By Diana's account, neither Sarah nor Jane seemed to offer more than perfunctory sympathy. Although Diana considered Jane "wonderfully solid," she said that if she called with a problem Jane would say, " 'Golly, gosh, Duch, how horrible, how sad and how awful.' " Sarah would reply along similar lines: "Poor Duch, such a shitty thing to happen."

Diana's relationship with her family "sort of went in cycles," said one Spencer relative. "That was how she treated her family, but it was not a problem because they were the ones she could let off steam to and not worry about being betrayed. Someone was always in and out of favor. The other thing was, they were the only ones to tell her the truth."

It was for this very reason, in the view of one of Diana's friends, that she couldn't be closer to her immediate family: "She didn't have anyone to turn to. Diana was very up and down with Jane and Sarah. Diana and I discussed it, and she said, 'I envy you so much the relationship you have with your family.' It was love-hate in her family, up and down, never steady or constant. The sisters were of a different emotional kind. Diana wanted to be listened to and loved and told she was doing the right thing. She wanted to be told she was wonderful, and the family brought her down to earth."

The one family member Diana began to strongly mistrust was her grandmother Ruth Fermoy, with whom she had never enjoyed a close relationship. Ruth Fermoy's first loyalty was the royal family, and early in the Wales marriage she began to express her dismay about Diana's treatment of Charles, who she believed needed "a woman to love and be cared for by." During a dinner at Balmoral in March 1982, Ruth Fermoy observed to her dinner partner Roy Strong that Diana "had a lot to learn" about royal life. Lady Fermoy was even more pointed with Robert Runcie, a close friend of hers. "Ruth was very distressed with Diana's behavior," Runcie recalled. "She was totally and wholly a Charles person, because she'd seen him grow up, loved him like all the women of the court do, and regarded Diana as an actress, a schemer."

Chapter 11

O N March 20, 1983, Charles, Diana, William, and their entourage left England for their first major royal tour—forty-five days in Australia and New Zealand. The trip was a defining moment for Diana, although perhaps not for the conventional interpretation, that she developed a "new maturity." In the battle between the strong elements of Diana's character and the fragility of her temperament, her character prevailed under extreme stress. Because of the demands made on both Charles and Diana, and the enormous pressure to perform flawlessly, the trip also proved an important bonding experience for them as a couple. But in other ways, it drove a greater wedge between them. The experience deluded the press and the public into believing that Diana had become the superwoman she still could not be—as long as her fundamental psychological problems were not fully addressed.

The tour took the couple to every state in Australia, from scorching heat one day to chilly rain the next. As a veteran of more than fifty overseas visits by age thirty-four, Charles knew how heavily he had to support his inexperienced and emotionally vulnerable twenty-one-year-old wife; even for someone twice Diana's age with a solid sense of herself, the pressure of being "on" for forty-five straight days would have been daunting. As Charles himself admitted in a letter to a relative, "The great problem is . . . keeping our enthusiasm . . . when everything is so exactly the same each day. After three weeks a strange feeling overcomes you, and when you see another crowd all you want to do is scream and run away as fast as possible!"

On what Charles called their "Antipodean Odyssey," all eyes were on Diana: She had to watch every word, smile incessantly, and show excitement for everyone and everything she encountered. Charles rarely left

Diana on her own, gently steering her from place to place. He was often seen lightly squeezing her hand to bolster her confidence. In her later bitterness, Diana bemoaned that "nobody ever helped me *at all*" during the tour. But in a letter to a friend at the time, she praised Charles for encouraging her when she felt overwhelmed, and she expressed admiration for his ability to inspire others with well-chosen words. What's more, staff members like her press secretary Vic Chapman were soothing and supportive. "He was very good at talking her through things," said a former courtier. "He would brief her about what to expect. He would say, 'You will get out of the car, and there will be four thousand screaming children.' "

The crowds in Australia and New Zealand were staggeringly large; in the city of Brisbane, more than 100,000 people turned out. During that stop, Diana was nearly mobbed as sweat poured down her face in the 86-degree heat. Charles quickly intervened by wrapping his arm around her waist and guiding her into a room where she could rest: It was the closest she came to losing her public composure. She moved informally among the people on "walkabouts," shaking hands (6,000 by one estimate) and offering down-to-earth comments. She complained from time to time about the heat, but if she felt bored, she didn't show it, and her emotional state seemed steady. "She has a wonderful way of dealing with people," Charles wrote to a relative. "Her quick wit stands her in excellent stead." Occasionally, her impish humor got the better of her: When she greeted a man with one arm, she blurted out, "I'll bet you have fun chasing the soap around the bath!" Diana managed to be so endearing that he didn't take offense.

One of the more perceptive assessments of her public persona was from Simon Hoggart of *The Observer:* "The Princess was plainly ill at ease," he wrote. "This I suspect is partly the cause of her astounding international celebrity. Her voice is ordinary and a little flat. . . . Her face, with its self-deprecating little smiles and giggly grimaces, signals that she is really just another nice and nervous girl. She is somehow gawky and graceful at the same time. She is both princess and commoner, the living embodiment of a million fantasies."

The extraordinary adulation for Diana that the royal couple first experienced in Wales turned into a tidal wave Down Under, and once again, Charles took second billing. After applauding his arrival, the crowds erupted into cheers and screams when they caught sight of Diana. Charles took these lopsided greetings in good humor: When Diana's fans begged him to bring her over to his side of the street, and she continued chatting on her side, he cracked, "You can't tell a woman to do anything these days." In his moments of privacy, Charles coped with the strain of these encounters by listening to his favorite classical music and immersing himself in Ivan Turgenev's *First Love* as well as Carl Jung's *Psychological Reflections.*

These activities, he confided to a friend, helped "preserve my sanity and my faith."

Charles took pride in Diana's performance, although he was mildly disturbed by her reaction to the crowds. Sometimes they frightened her, but she also found pleasure in the sense of power they gave her. Charles understood the dangers of giving credence to such idolatry, because he understood the fickle nature of celebrity. "The terrifying part," he wrote to a friend, "is that [the crowds] construct the pedestal, they put you on top of it, they expect you to balance on the beastly thing. . . . [Then] along come the demolition experts amongst them who are of the breed that enjoy breaking things down."

Although he masked it well, Charles also felt resentful, and Diana knew it. "All you could hear was, 'Oh, she's on the other side,' " Diana recalled. "Now, if you're a man, like my husband a proud man, you mind about that if you hear it every day for four weeks." In a letter to a friend written on April 1, Diana described the situation but emphasized that they were supporting each other. In her reminiscences, though, Diana took a harsher view, claiming that not only did Charles fail to share in her success, he was "jealous" and "took it out on [her]"—although there is no evidence that he did so.

By all accounts, Charles publicly showed his delight in her popularity, while he privately agonized about the impact of the disproportionate adoration. "I do feel desperate for Diana," he wrote to a friend on April 4. "There is no twitch she can make without these ghastly and, I'm convinced, mindless people photographing it. . . . Can't they see . . . what it is doing to her? How can anyone, let alone a twenty-one-year-old, be expected to come out of all this obsessed and crazed attention unscathed?"

Diana's toughest moments occurred during the first week of the tour, when she was nearly overcome by the pressure. She was sick with bulimia, she wept to her twenty-nine-year-old lady-in-waiting Anne Beckwith-Smith, and she begged to go home. Gradually, she began to relax and concentrate on her job as a royal representative. In a letter written nearly two weeks into the trip, Diana told a friend that her depression had lifted, and she expressed remorse about her earlier behavior in London and Balmoral, which she characterized as "selfish." Diana was comforted by having William nearby. When she and Charles periodically visited him at the sheep station where he stayed with his nanny, it provided a welcome escape. "We were extremely happy there," Charles wrote to his friends the van Cutsems. "The great joy was that we were totally alone together."

Diana and Charles openly showed affection for each other—as one writer described it, "his hand resting on hers, her glance towards him, those sort of telling things." During a tree-planting in New Zealand, Diana winked at Charles, he tossed away the shovel, heaved her over his shoulder, and carried her into a nearby building as they dissolved in laughter. And when a photographer accidentally encountered the couple in an elevator in Melbourne, Charles pointed to Diana and reportedly said, "Isn't she absolutely beautiful? I'm so proud of her."

At the end of the tour, Diana and Charles escaped for a nine-day rest on Windermere Island, and this time the tabloids left them alone. Once recharged, they were off again on a seventeen-day visit to Canada, but without William. Diana again acquitted herself well under considerable pressure. "Not a moment to breathe," Diana confided in a letter to a relative. "I find the endless receptions quite difficult, as people tend to ask extraordinarily personal questions." She could also spot the absurdity in their situation, as in her description of greeting children chewing bubble gum: "When trying to drag a sentence out, all we actually see is a bright pink thing, turning round and round, like a washing machine inside."

Diana and Charles missed William's first birthday on June twenty-first. Somewhat surprisingly, Diana wrote to her relative, "I haven't missed William as much as I'd thought," and revealed a flash of media savvy on her son's birthday: "I smiled myself stupid all day, as the press were quite determined to see a 'sad mama.' "

Brian Peckford, the premier of Newfoundland, commented that Diana was "very witty" and "asked questions about what we may consider simple things but they are really the ones that count." He also praised her ability to relate to patients during a hospital visit: "She sat down on every single bed to talk to people. She speaks very softly. She does not raise her voice. She makes people come down to her decibel level, and it is lovely."

More significantly, Peckford revealed that Diana had said to him, "I am finding it very difficult to cope with the pressures of being the Princess of Wales. . . . I have learnt a lot in the last few months . . . [and] feel I am doing my job better now than I was before. I have matured a lot recently and got used to coping with things." Only days earlier, Diana had confessed to a Halifax newspaper owner that her royal life was agonizing at times. "When they write something horrible," Diana said, "I get a horrible feeling right here," pointing to her chest.

At the time, nothing "horrible" was being written about Diana. Broadsheets and tabloids alike hailed Diana's mastery of her royal role. "Prince Charles is largely responsible for this newfound confidence," James Whitaker declared, "but it is Diana herself who can take most of the credit." Andrew Morton proclaimed in the *Daily Star* that Diana was "a big girl now . . . a far cry from the nervous young woman who twice burst into [public] tears before her marriage when the pressure got too much. As she celebrates her twenty-second birthday tomorrow, she'll be saying good-bye forever to Shy Di, and hello and welcome to a self-assured and poised princess."

The rosy assessments of Diana's progress were based on little more than the appeal of her charm and looks, and her ability, through practice, endurance, and determination, to learn the royal drill. A relative of the royal family who attended a public event with Diana that year recalled, "She was saying, 'I'll take five deep breaths and plunge in and talk to all those people.' She did it well." Diana had clearly benefited from the boost to her public confidence provided by her reception on the two tours. But her later assertion that she had returned from Australia a "different person" was an illusion. She was fooling herself and the public by learning to function well in her public role. The symptoms of her emotional disturbance—mood swings, bulimia, self-mutilation, depression—could persist privately while she functioned well outwardly.

By the autumn of 1983, Diana had long since given up her psychiatric therapy. She had stuck with treatment for several months, but ended it early in the year, saying she no longer needed it. "The therapy appeared not to be delivering a solution for her," according to a friend of Charles. Because Diana still didn't admit to her bulimia, her diagnosis was incomplete, which limited the effectiveness of her therapy. She had been to at least two therapists: Dr. Allan McGlashan, a Jungian specialist friendly with Laurens van der Post who focused on dream analysis, and David Mitchell, who probed her reactions to daily events and her conversations with Charles. Diana's sessions with Mitchell at Kensington Palace often brought her to tears. She didn't think her therapists genuinely understood her, and without that essential trust, her treatment could not succeed.

In some ways, Diana did seem better that fall, largely because she was performing her royal duties so reliably. But according to Jonathan Dimbleby, "her swings of mood continued, and there were periods of distress that were exhausting to both [Charles and Diana]." She still suffered from attacks of weeping, during which Charles spent "hours comforting and reassuring her."

In February 1984, Diana made her first solo foreign trip—an overnight to Oslo, where she captivated the Norwegians. She became the patron of seven new organizations, in addition to the five she had previously adopted—ranging from ballet and opera companies to schools and groups combating childhood cancer and other ailments. Out of seventy-six public engagements in 1983, forty-five had been without Charles. Years later, Diana complained that because so much attention was directed at her, "my husband decided that we do separate engagements, which was a bit sad for me, because I quite liked the company. But there again, I didn't have the choice." Like other statements Diana made for revenge, this one seems untrue and sadly unfair. When she first went solo at the end of 1982 (before the Australia trip), press reports made clear the initiative was hers.

Much of the perception of Diana was based on her glamorous image. "The combination of style and glamour has always been explosive," observed *Woman's Own* magazine in January 1984, "and Diana's brand is positively atomic." Every account of her public appearances included detailed descriptions of her clothing, usually accompanied by critiques of her latest fashion statement. She made her share of blunders, but she availed herself of the best advisers, and she had great flair. After the first year, Diana stopped relying on the *Vogue* editors and chose her own clothing. "She was terribly keen and interested in fashion," said former *Vogue* editor Felicity Clark. "She knew what she liked and didn't like. At the beginning, she would not wear a short skirt because she didn't like them, and she consciously wore very low heels so she wouldn't tower over her husband. She bought hats because she liked hats. One of our useful functions was editing the collection. She made mistakes when she started going to collections on her own and saw the whole thing. Most designers have a few mistakes, and once or twice she chose them."

It took only a couple of years in the public eye for Diana to begin appreciating the clout of her celebrity, especially her ability to command attention with a dramatic new look. Because she so frequently yielded to this impulse, her image lacked consistency. Sometimes out of insecurity, at other moments simply to capture the limelight, she constantly changed her appearance. Early in the marriage, Diana began her habit of combing through the tabloids to scrutinize her photographs. She could sit for as long as an hour, exclaiming that the tabloids were trying to make her look awful, inviting compliments from staff members on the flattering shots and reassurance about other images that bothered her.

Beyond her place as "queen of fashion," Diana had no specific role. No one had thought out in detail what she would do, and she offered the Buckingham Palace courtiers scant guidance on her interests, which were still quite limited. Her inclination was, as *The Times* described it, toward "visiting the very young, the very old, and the sick, to whom she brought a touching directness." By putting her in familiar, comfortable settings, the royal schedulers could rely on her natural abilities, first developed when she did community service in boarding school.

Diana later said that Charles had not allowed her to have interests: "I think I've always been the eighteen-year-old [*sic*] girl he got engaged to." But Charles, according to one of his friends, "wanted her to find things she enjoyed doing," and he tried to help her develop some skills. In 1982, Charles had brought in his friend Eric Anderson, the headmaster of Eton who had been his drama instructor at Gordonstoun, to assist Diana with her writing skills and spark some intellectual leanings. "It was to educate her," said a former Palace aide. "He would come and talk to her about poetry and Shakespeare." These once-weekly sessions at Kensington Palace lasted less than six months, however. "She was enthusiastic about it," said the courtier, "but only for a short time. I don't know why, but it petered out in a matter of months. This was a pattern."

In those early years, Diana balked at getting too involved in anything. "She worried about being bored by her public duties," said a former Palace official. When aides presented Diana with lists of charities and descriptions of what they might mean to her, she showed no inclination to learn about them in any depth. "She couldn't understand the requirement of duty, that you had to be sitting next to an architect or a don, and that you had to prepare yourself for it," said Michael Colborne. "Diana was intelligent enough," noted another former courtier. "You could give her a brief, and she could read through it. But it was a matter of intellectual discipline and application. She didn't have sustained concentration for anything. She was disciplined in other ways. She wouldn't let people down."

Diana's erratic behavior took a heavy toll on the royal staff. In the first four years of the marriage, some forty officials left the Waleses, among them butlers, valets, private secretaries, bodyguards, and chauffeurs. Stephen Barry, Prince Charles's longtime valet, was one of the first to go, explaining philosophically that it was "understandable [Diana] would not wish to have around herself and her husband those who had known him at earlier times, when there were other girlfriends."

Some staff members retired or left for a better job, but quite a few were pushed out by Diana's displeasure. Sometimes there was poor chemistry, as with several bodyguards who "made her feel nervous." But more often, the dismissal followed a predictable sequence of events. Diana would draw a staff member into her confidence, burdening him with intimate details of her anxieties that caused him discomfort. Misreading her familiarity, he would then overstep an invisible line or say something that struck Diana as inappropriate or disloyal, and she would, without warning, cease speaking to him or even acknowledging his presence.

While Charles was upset over the departure of loyal staff, he was disheartened that Diana compelled him to exile some of his closest friends, a number of whom he had known since his boyhood. As even the Queen's press secretary, Michael Shea, conceded, "Certain friends had to go— because they just didn't fit anymore, and Charles and Diana began to make new friends together as a couple." The Parker Bowleses and the Tryons topped the banned list for obvious reasons, but Diana was equally adamant about the banishment of the Brabournes, the Romseys, the Palmer-

Tomkinsons, and Nicholas Soames, with whom Charles had been accustomed to speaking almost daily on the telephone. The Palmer-Tomkinsons were in the cold for three years, Soames for more than two.

Diana felt these friends were against her from the start, a misguided impression, according to one friend of Charles: "They thought she was a young person who needed help to make her way," said the friend. "There was no animosity toward her, no coven saying, 'She's a new witch and we don't like her.' Early on, they were extraordinarily helpful, but then she quickly turned against them."

Diana had little use for Soames, a Conservative member of Parliament known for his large size and pungent views ("Pass the port, he's not my sort") whom Diana disparaged as "heavy furniture." The others, she was convinced, were colluding with Charles in the relationship she believed he was continuing with Camilla or were simply against her in some way. By one account, she turned on the Romseys after she learned that the couple had counseled him not to marry her. Because of the awkwardness of the situation, Charles shrank from directly telling his friends why he could no longer see them. Instead, he stopped calling and sending them invitations to country weekends and Balmoral holidays.

Those friends who stayed in favor—among them Hugh and Emilie van Cutsem, Charles and Antonia Douro, Rick and Libby Beckett, and Gerald and Tally Westminster—along with newer friends from the polo world, such as Galen and Hilary Weston, and Geoffrey and Jorie Kent—had to deal with Diana's range of disturbing symptoms and the self-pity her moods stirred in Charles. Many of them tried in the beginning to befriend Diana. "In many ways, I fell in love with her the way Charles did, but she was the most difficult woman in the world," said one friend. "To sit next to her at a dinner party was such hard work. She just wouldn't respond. You would ask her questions and she just wouldn't reply. She wasn't interested in reading anything, in learning anything. She didn't make an effort. She would throw food and do childish things. She could be spontaneous and endearing, but in some basic ways she never matured."

Several of the wives became Diana's confidantes—Emilie van Cutsem, in particular. A contemporary of Charles who was born in Holland, Emilie had old-fashioned attitudes, taking the view, for example, that "jeans are workman's clothes." She established herself as a mother figure to Diana, who poured out her troubles and asked for advice. "Emilie was very helpful to Diana early on," said a former Palace aide. Antonia Douro, the wife of the heir to the Duke of Wellington, was a powerful London hostess who also befriended Diana. When Diana was once portrayed in the press as domineering and demanding with Charles, Antonia offered a spirited public defense.

Both Emilie and Antonia were also close friends of Camilla Parker Bowles, and when Charles returned to Camilla in 1986, Emilie and Antonia helped facilitate the affair. Antonia supplied them with a cottage in Scotland, and the van Cutsems invited Charles over from Highgrove. "Diana discovered that when she would leave the van Cutsem house, Camilla would arrive," said one of Diana's friends. "It shattered Diana. She felt they behaved according to a double standard." Diana often discovered evidence of such treachery through subterfuge, because she didn't fundamentally trust anyone. "She steamed open letters and listened in to telephone conversations," said a friend of Charles. "These were just letters from friends. There is a sorting postal system, and she used to on occasion take letters out, and if addressed to him she would steam them open. With the letters, she was caught red-handed quite early."

On Valentine's Day 1984, Charles and Diana announced that she was expecting their second child in September. The pregnancy seemed to progress more smoothly this time, although Diana twice said publicly—in March and June—"I haven't felt well since day one." "It was a good year," said Michael Colborne. "The second child was coming, things were going well, they had done good tours, she wasn't as sick as she had been with William."

William's presence was an important stabilizing factor. Even with a nanny in residence, Diana took an active role in caring for her toddler, allotting three hours in the morning for him before beginning her official schedule. Diana also seemed more focused on maintaining her emotional balance through exercise: two to three times a week, she went to Buckingham Palace, where she would swim laps "very energetically for about half an hour," according to her press secretary Vic Chapman. Also vital to her mental stability was her full schedule of official engagements—primarily visits to hospitals and other medical treatment and research centers. Only once did she falter publicly, when she had to leave midway through a performance of *Aïda* at the Royal Opera House, feeling ill.

In a departure from her customary reticence, the Queen made a point that April of praising Diana publicly with an official statement through a Buckingham Palace spokesman: "The Queen could not be more pleased with her daughter-in-law. She is very proud of the Princess's activities around the world and at home." By then, Diana and her mother-in-law had developed an easier relationship. When Diana came to the palace to swim, she would usually bring along William afterward to play in the garden while she visited the Queen.

Charles had his own busy official schedule, which included three major trips abroad—five days in Brunei in February, a month in Africa in March, and a week in Papua New Guinea in August. Otherwise, the royal couple attended the usual charity concerts and other royal events. But according to Dimbleby, they were living "within the shell of a normal marriage," and "still lacked the intimacy and mutual understanding without which the relationship could not grow. As they shared no common interests there was little to talk about except the mundane arrangements that are necessary when two people share the same roof."

Nearly three years into Charles and Diana's marriage, the full extent of their incompatibility was more obvious than ever. Their differences have usually been cast as matters of taste and preference: she loved the city, and he thrived in the country. She adored Elton John and Abba; he listened endlessly to opera. She enjoyed the company of film stars, and he gravitated to philosophers and academics. She loved everything trendy; he cherished tradition, right down to the clothing he wore for shooting: an unfashionable Norfolk jacket identical to those worn by his father and grandfather.

Even their styles of letter-writing showed their disparities: Charles was known for settling down and composing five- or six-page letters punctuated with passionate outbursts and bold underlinings. His letters were intensely engaged with the recipient's predicament, or his own situation. "His letters were anguished, concerned, and also extremely funny," said one friend. "They showed his character, beliefs, hopes, what disturbed and pleased him, what made him despair, and made him optimistic."

Diana's approach was more brief, chatty, and girlish, redeemed by sly flashes of flippant humor ("a lot of tiara functions, which left the head sore"). She wrote effusively, with simple descriptions of what she was doing and how she was feeling at a given moment, sprinkled with an "occasional spelling or grammatical mistake or a crossing-out," according to her former employer Mary Robertson. "One winced when one got letters sometimes," said a longtime friend. "She wrote 'lots of love,' with little smiles inside the o's for hugs. The little faces were a trademark, and the words were slightly archaic." Nevertheless, her letters could be entertaining, full of charm, and often touching.

If their letters reflected sharply divergent personalities, Charles and Diana provoked even more striking reactions in people who met them. Charles tended to be more rigid and programmed, especially when he was with Diana. He sometimes appeared uncomfortable, while she seemed at ease anywhere. His charm was quiet and contained, while she had the glow, the magic, the magnetism, the energy, and the spontaneity. Charles used to notice that, after he left a party, the noise level immediately rose. "What happened after I went?" he would frequently ask. "The real point of Diana

Diana Spencer in 1968 at age six, several months after her mother left home to marry Peter Shand Kydd. [2]

Diana at age thirteen in western Scotland during a visit to her mother. [1]

Diana with her brother, Charles Spencer, in 1980 when he was a student at Eton. [3]

Diana mugging for photographers in the autumn of 1980, after the press had proclaimed her "the new girl for Charles". [4]

Above: Johnnie Spencer and his second wife, Raine, at Althorp, the family's ancestral home, after their marriage in July 1976. [5]

Left: Diana in the stands at Tidworth Polo Club on Saturday, July 25, 1981, shortly before she burst into tears and rushed off. [6]

Right: Diana and Camilla Parker Bowles, Prince Charles' former lover, at a steeplechase in which he was riding in 1981. [7]

Below: Diana and Charles on the steps of St Paul's Cathedral after their wedding rehearsal on Monday, July 27; moments earlier, she had broken down again. [8]

Above: Diana and Charles in late August, on the fourth day of the continuation of their honeymoon at Balmoral, posing for pictures and taking brief questions from the press. [9]

Left: Diana and Charles leaving the hospital after the birth of William on June 21, 1982. [10]

Above left: The Queen joining Diana and Charles at the Braemar Highland Games near Balmoral in September 1982. [11]

Above right: Diana, six months pregnant with their second son, smiling at Charles during a polo game at Windsor on June 6, 1984. [12]

Below: Diana and Charles with her sisters Jane (right) and Sarah (far right) and her brother, Charles, at his twenty-first birthday party in May 1985. [13]

Left: On their second trip to Australia in November 1985, Diana wearing a £2 million emerald-and-diamond choker across her forehead as an Indian-style headband. [14]

Below: In December 1985 at the Royal Opera House, Diana performing a four-minute routine with dancer Wayne Sleep that she had secretly choreographed as a surprise for Charles. [15]

Top left: Captain James Hewitt, with whom Diana began a five-year love affair in November 1986 when Charles was touring the Middle East. [16]

Top right: Car dealer James Gilbey, Diana's frequent companion beginning in the summer of 1989. [17]

Above: Diana and her sister-in-law Sarah Ferguson (Fergie), to whom she had grown close as they struggled with their marital problems, in 1991. [18]

Charles leaving Cirencester Hospital with Diana on July 1, 1990 – her twenty-ninth birthday – after he had broken his arm in two places during a polo match. [19]

is that when she walked into a room, she lifted the temperature," said one of her longtime friends. "The general rule in England is when a royal arrives at a party it goes stone dead, but she put all the men on their mettle and they began performing."

The basic polarities between Charles and Diana showed a clash of attitudes and values, but in some areas they did find common ground: Diana had grown up with classical music and developed a love of opera, and she came to share Charles's interest in alternative medicine as well. In other ways, the couple had the potential to learn from each other and find compromises. Long after their marriage had broken up, Diana told friends that she and Charles could have made an "amazing team." "They had strengths and weaknesses she was aware of," said film producer David Puttnam. "She felt they could have made a good team because of their complementary abilities." But their different temperaments—Diana's persistent suspicion, insecurity, possessiveness, and unpredictability set against Charles's inability to cope with her problems and his continuing need to be nurtured—proved too great an obstacle.

Throughout 1984, the press promoted the fairy-tale marriage by seeking evidence of harmony, such as the "lingering look and quick kiss" at a polo match on their third wedding anniversary. In an assessment headlined DI OF A THOUSAND DAYS, Judy Wade of *The Sun* declared in April that Diana "leads conversations . . . and if anything, dominates the discussion with Charles." This was patent nonsense, as Andrew Neil, the editor of *The Sunday Times,* discovered when he and the editor of *The Times,* Charles Douglas-Home (a cousin of Diana's), had lunch with the Waleses that month at Kensington Palace. "It was clear the royal couple had very little in common," wrote Neil. "Charles roamed far and wide on the issues of the day. . . . Diana played little part in the conversation. . . . Charles made no attempt to involve her."

Neil tried to draw out Diana by noting that she had attended a Dire Straits concert the previous evening. "Then she got animated," recalled Neil. The only other time she chipped in was when they talked about Ronald and Nancy Reagan's coming visit to London. Diana called Reagan a "Horlicks," a Sloane-Ranger term for a boring old person, and she said Nancy Reagan was only interested in being photographed with the royal family. "That surprised me a bit," said Neil. "She was bitter in her comments."

Diana withdrew from public activities in July, and the royal couple left for their annual Balmoral visit in late August. She was jolted by the suicide of her uncle Edmund Fermoy that month at age forty-five, and she wept openly at his memorial service. Only days later, when Charles drove off into the Highlands for a fishing trip, Diana breezily wrote to a friend, "Can't stand being away from him, in case I lay my egg." Although these were her "dark ages," the summer months before Harry's birth were also the time when Diana later said she and Charles were closer than they had ever been.

Nevertheless, Diana incongruously failed to share one vital fact with her husband. Ever since Diana's ultrasound the previous April, she had known she was carrying a boy, but she kept the sex of their child a secret. (Both Diana and Charles had been quoted in the press that spring as wanting a girl: Diana said she was "hoping" for one, and Charles said it "would be nice" to have a girl.) "Diana said that all the royal family always had a boy and then a girl," said a former courtier. "She had it in her mind he wanted a girl, and she kept it from him that she was having a boy. She was obsessed about it."

Diana was still preoccupied by Camilla as well—a fixation that had become a permanent part of the marital dynamic. Over the years, Diana contradicted herself so frequently regarding her suspicions about her husband that it is nearly impossible to know what she was thinking at any given time. She variously said she believed that Charles never stopped seeing Camilla, that he cynically went back to Camilla after the royal wedding, and that she actually agreed with Charles that the affair with Camilla had resumed in 1986 after the Wales marriage had "irretrievably broken down." In discussing the birth of their second child, Diana told Andrew Morton: "By then I knew he had gone back to his lady, but somehow we'd managed to have Harry."

The conflicting messages sent by Diana to Charles grew even more complicated after the arrival of Henry Charles Albert David on September 15. Diana later said she was shocked by the disappointment she heard in Charles's voice when he said, "Oh God, it's a boy," followed by, "and he's even got red hair." At that moment, said Diana, "something inside me closed off. . . . It just went bang, our marriage, the whole thing went down the drain." Yet a man close to Charles said Diana had gravely misinterpreted the moment: "To have said something like that in disgust or dismay was not in his character. He may have squealed 'Ooooohhh, red hair,' teasingly. But when he was told about this at the time of the Morton book, he was horrified by the interpretation."

Friends of Charles and Diana viewed Diana's "closed off" remark to mean the end of their sexual relationship. "She said [the marriage] all went badly wrong after Harry's birth," said a friend of Diana's. "She always maintained to me she didn't know why." Yet a friend of Charles said that he didn't spurn Diana after Harry's birth. "That simply doesn't square with the available evidence," said the friend. "By this point, there was practically nothing anyone could do to make her feel her needs were being met. With her problems, mere demonstrations of kindness and trying to make it right would not have been enough."

Chapter 12

A LIGHT may have switched off in Diana, but it was by no means clear that the marriage had fallen apart. Rather, the relationship seemed to enter a downward drift, hastened along by hostile press coverage. Charles continued to try to cope with Diana's mystifying volatility. She moved between shadow and light, her despairing mood punctuated by periods of deceptive calm. Her "interludes of happiness" were usually brought on by her two sons, whose antics caused her to shriek with laughter. At other times, Diana disintegrated over imagined slights or critical headlines in the morning tabloids.

As far as the public knew, Diana had adjusted to royal life and settled into her role as wife and mother. As *The Sunday Telegraph* reported, "Professional Diana-watchers will tell you that 1984 was really the year when the princess became her own woman, knowing just who she is and how to cope with the phenomenal pressures upon her." While Diana's carefree public appearances were little more than performances, her fondness for motherhood was genuine. Her hairstylist Kevin Shanley arrived several days after Harry's birth to find her "in such good form . . . overjoyed with Harry." With William she had stopped breast-feeding after only three weeks, but with Harry she continued for nearly three months.

Nor did she suffer a debilitating postnatal depression, partly because she resumed a busy schedule of public engagements in November, visiting centers for the deaf and blind, inspecting a new preschool playground, and christening a cruise liner. She seemed determined to hold herself together. She rose early, took a daily swim, seldom went out in the evenings, and got to bed early.

Yet her insecurity about Charles appeared to intensify. A few of Charles's friends became alarmed by the degree to which she demanded his constant presence, and they worried, as Dimbleby described it, that "she sought to possess him, but only in order to reject him." At Diana's insistence, Charles had already curtailed his hunting and shooting; during the previous year's shooting season, from October through January, he left his guns at home, and he went fox-hunting only occasionally, compared to a twice-weekly routine before his marriage. Contrary to the popular tabloid theory, Diana's objection to these pursuits wasn't a philosophical opposition to blood sports; rather, she found them tiresome to watch, and she resented the amount of time they took Charles away from her.

Diana disliked polo as well. She considered the sport rough and boring—an antipathy that deepened on the day Charles brought her home from the hospital with Harry, then left to play a game at Windsor. Despite Diana's hostility, Charles stubbornly kept up with the game, which he once said was "very important to my physical and mental well-being, and makes me feel incredibly well afterward . . . one of the best ways I know, aside from my painting . . . of forgetting the pressures and complications of life. It's the intense concentration required that is, funnily enough, what makes it so relaxing."

After Harry's birth, Diana asked Charles to cut back his official calendar to be at home more with the boys. Diana even advised the starchy Edward Adeane that he shouldn't expect to meet with Charles in the early mornings—when the private secretary had been accustomed to working undisturbed with Charles—because her husband needed to be in the nursery. Adeane took a dim view of her communiqué but did not protest. Although Charles felt guilty about shirking his public duties, he went along with Diana's wishes.

As a result, Charles drew closer to both of his boys. Diana later said that Charles had enjoyed helping to care for his young sons, feeding them bottles and playing with them, and that he had done these tasks well. Inevitably, the eagle-eyed tabloids began to chart Charles's absences from the public arena. They kept a running tally based on the "Court Circular" page at the back of each day's *Times* and *Telegraph:* listings of the day's appearances by members of the royal family. Periodically, the tabloids published a scorecard to compare the royals' relative devotion to duty. When Charles came up with only fifteen engagements during a three-month period, compared with fifty-six for his indefatigable sister, Anne, the tabloids didn't hesitate to point out his shortcomings. Anne's "peak of royal productivity," noted the *Daily Express,* "has coincided with her brother's sizable withdrawal from the royal round" because of "his desire to spend as much time as possible with his children."

In early January, Edward Adeane abruptly resigned, and the press unfairly tarred Diana as the reason. Adeane's friends, reported the *Daily Ex-*

press, "are in no doubt that it is the Princess of Wales who drove him out of royal service." The razor-tongued Nigel Dempster proclaimed Charles "so wet you could shoot a duck off his back" and said Diana had "every single opportunity of becoming a first-class bitch." Adeane's discomfort with Diana was a contributing factor, but the resignation was actually precipitated by a philosophical difference with Charles. Adeane had been accustomed to obedience when he advised the Prince to avoid controversy in his role, but Charles wanted to voice his unconventional views on important issues such as urban planning, an outspokenness that Adeane couldn't abide.

Two weeks later, Diana stormed off the ski slope in Liechtenstein after she became annoyed with photographers during a prearranged picture session. "I'll get it in the neck for this," Charles mumbled. Andrew Morton stitched together Adeane's firing, Diana's outburst, and Charles's new image as a househusband and produced an article asking if Charles was a "dithering wimp" at the mercy of "his diamond-hard wife"—a "royal mouse" or a "Thoroughly Modern Man." After trotting out the circumstantial evidence, Morton concluded that "while Diana has the upper hand on the home front, Charles is firmly in the driving seat in the official royal world." Contrary to the impression of weakness, Morton said Charles had "iron in his soul" and was in fact "a mouse that roars."

Other tabloids saw the relationship differently, with one calling Diana "the real ruler" and Charles "a thoroughly henpecked husband." *The Sun* said that Diana was a "prima donna," and a "woman of steel" who didn't "seem to give a damn" if she humiliated her husband in public. "No man can have tried harder to please a woman," Harry Arnold and Judy Wade wrote. "She must allow the man who will one day rule the country to rule the roost."

In April 1985, the royal couple spent two weeks in Italy, where the crowds thronged to glimpse Diana, and the Italian press covered her relentlessly. Charles was transported by what he called Italy's "great flights of human spirit," and the *Daily Mail* optimistically predicted that the trip would make Diana "more of a companion to Charles in the intellectual sense." Diana, however, was less than enthralled, though she hid her lack of interest behind her poise and her smiles. Touring a garden in Florence, Charles spotted Diana walking toward an archway and shouted, "Mind your head." "Why?" Diana cracked. "There's nothing in it." Charles found himself resenting Diana's popularity, but he buried his insecurity in the beauty of the art and architecture around him.

Before the Waleses left England, the tabloids had speculated about the small fortune Diana was spending on her wardrobe for the Italian trip. Then, when she wore too many familiar outfits, the press called her "secondhand Rosa." The Italian fashion critics declared her "unsophisticated," especially her collection of what one commentator called "heinous hats." But the public, primarily women, couldn't get enough of Diana's procession of new looks. She was like a paper doll come to life, playing dress-up to feed women's fantasies.

As the press and public came to view her as a fashion avatar, she indulged in ever-more daring surprises—an ankle-length fuchsia, pink, and turquoise silk dress in the style of a dressing gown, a silver lamé dress that upstaged Joan Collins's, a specially altered black dinner jacket from Charles's closet, a backless dress with a string of pearls "the wrong way round," and one of her most dramatic inspirations: a $3 million emerald-and-diamond choker that she wore across her forehead as an Indian-style headband. "She would go out and do things to court press attention," a former Palace adviser said, "whether it was wearing something new and outrageous rather than an old dress, there would be something flashy and different and stylish. She knew how to play it."

These stunts attracted applause, but they also created a perception of frivolity and exhibitionism. "Being a princess, even if you marry into the royal dynasty, means more than creating an image," huffed The Times. Diana grew more insecure and ambivalent about how she was perceived, even complaining to her friend Roberto Devorik when she was complimented for being beautiful or chic. "She said, 'Why don't they say what a beautiful human being I am?' " he recalled.

In all the hullabaloo that winter and spring, the press missed an important development in the life of Diana and Charles: the quiet departure on January 1 of Charles's aide Michael Colborne after ten years of service. Colborne had been a solid support to both Waleses, mainly because he knew how to be responsive without overstepping the invisible royal barrier, especially with Diana. But his position inevitably made him a referee between warring parties, which sapped his enthusiasm for the job. The turning point had actually come during the Canada trip in mid-1983.

One day, when Charles was out on his official rounds, Diana remained behind on Britannia and asked Colborne to meet her. She was lonely and wanted his company—a role he had played many times to keep her calm. After completing some arrangements for Charles, Colborne spent the afternoon with Diana. When Charles returned, he summoned Colborne to his cabin and exploded in anger, accusing his trusted aide of giving short shrift to princely needs. Charles wouldn't be mollified by Colborne's explanation that assisting Diana was in everyone's best interests. When Charles ended his outburst, he opened the door to find a tearful Diana eavesdropping.

Although Charles later apologized, Colborne decided he could not continue. He was pained by Charles's "stress and disruption," while Diana's behavior "seemed something out of a nightmare, beyond all reason and out of control." Colborne resigned in April 1984, but Charles and Diana persuaded him to remain until after the birth of their second child. "To both of them, my resignation was a bit hard," Colborne said. "I didn't realize it was going to upset him so much, and when she saw me going, she had the two children, her engagement calendar was filling up, and she couldn't change him. She could see what was happening. She could see her future."

By mid-1985, the word was spreading in aristocratic circles that the gloomy reports about the Wales marriage were more than just tabloid tittle-tattle. Princess Michael of Kent, a neighbor of the Waleses in Kensington Palace, was known for her indiscretion as well as her powers of observation. She also had an ax to grind, since Diana had supplanted her as the most glamorous royal. During an event at the Victoria and Albert Museum, Princess Michael unloaded some intelligence on museum director Roy Strong that took him aback. She called Diana a "catastrophe" and expressed pity for "poor Prince Charles, who had bought Highgrove to be near his former girlfriends. Nothing was happy. Diana was hard. There was no pulling together, no common objectives, and it was misery for him. . . . And Diana has become a media queen, which only makes it worse." Charles, Princess Michael told Strong, was "increasingly isolated, the Queen is withdrawn." With some prescience, she characterized Diana as a "time bomb."

Fed by leaks from assorted staffers, the tabloids kept dancing around the edges of the unraveling Wales marriage. The first serious doubts about the marriage were raised, ironically enough, by an American publication, *Vanity Fair*. Because the article was written by Tina Brown, then the magazine's British-born editor in chief, it attracted instant attention back home. Essentially, the article pulled together themes that had run through the tabloids earlier in the year, added new information and provocative interpretation, and presented it all in a glossy package. Titled "The Mouse That Roared," the story turned Andrew Morton's earlier portrayal on its head, declaring Diana, not Charles, the "iron mouse," and concluding, "the heir to the throne is, it seems, pussy-whipped from here to eternity." The article noted Diana's "obsession with her image" and cautioned that her "adversary mood toward the press" was "the first stage in the removal from life that fame inflicts. The second stage is 'Graceland,' when the real world melts away altogether. There is a danger that this has started to happen to Diana."

Buckingham Palace dismissed the story as "nonsense," and the tabloids predictably jumped on "snobby *Vanity Fair*" for its "astonishing," "amazing," and "horrid" attack, all the while meticulously detailing the particulars. The *Daily Mirror,* while denouncing the "ratbag of gossip," conceded that "parts of it are very plausible, and it's all too easy to believe." The *News of the World* insisted that Charles was not a "royal wimp," but added its own evidence of further tension in the marriage. In the end, recalled Deidre Fernand, former royal correspondent for *The Times*, " 'The Mouse That Roared' had an impact, but people thought it wasn't true, just bitchy New York gossip."

Charles and Diana were sufficiently stung that they felt compelled to respond in a much-anticipated television program shown in late October. The program had been in the works since the previous summer, when Palace courtiers decided it was time for the couple to give an extensive interview to counteract stories circulating about their marriage; a companion documentary to be broadcast a year later would include footage of the couple at home and at work. The 1985 interview, conducted by Sir Alastair Burnet, touched on topics ranging from their public duties to their press coverage, from Charles's eccentricities to Diana's eating habits and taste in fashion.

Diana was almost phobic about public speaking, so Charles enlisted film director Richard Attenborough to coach her. (Earlier in the year, when asked to introduce a campaign on drug abuse education she got so tangled she could only blurt, "Oh, gosh . . . well . . . er . . . fingers crossed.") Attenborough worked with Diana on how to move while on camera, how to sit attentively while being questioned, and how to speak slowly and clearly. To calm her nerves, Burnet gave Diana a full rehearsal.

Sitting side by side on a silk sofa, Diana and Charles appeared confident and charming before a television audience of 20 million. When asked if she had been hurt by the malicious reports on their private life, Diana looked directly at the camera and spoke revealingly of her anxieties: "Well, obviously. You feel very wounded. You think, 'Oh gosh, I don't want to go out and do my engagement this morning. Nobody wants to see me, help, panic.' But you have got to push yourself out." Regarding the charge that she ruled the roost, Diana pleaded not guilty, admitting only to being a "perfectionist with myself but not necessarily with everyone else." To dispel her image as a trendy airhead, she insisted that "my clothes are not my priority," though she admitted, "sometimes I can be a little outrageous." She also said, "I'm never on what's called a diet. . . . Maybe I'm so scrawny because I take so much exercise." Diana's most important role, she said, was "supporting my husband whenever I can and always being behind him, and also most important, being a mother and a wife."

Charles admitted to "becoming more eccentric as I get older," but said his interest in alternative medicine reflected his desire to be "open-minded." He responded most forcefully to critics of his effort to voice his outspoken views on architecture. The previous year he had given a speech blasting the "monstrous carbuncle" proposed as an addition to the National Gallery—a vivid metaphor that led to a highly praised replacement design. "I just feel sometimes, not too often," he said, "I can throw a rock into a pond and watch the ripples create a certain amount of discussion and hopefully to see whether something better can come out."

Both Prince and Princess showed flashes of self-deprecating humor, Diana when she defended the size of her wardrobe for foreign tours by saying, "I couldn't go round in a leopard skin," and Charles by calling himself an "ancient old thing." When Diana said she was learning sign language to communicate with the deaf, Charles interjected, "I shall look forward to her teaching me. She says I am deaf anyway."

There was only one glimmer of mild irritation, when Burnet asked if they argued. "I suspect that most husbands and wives find they often have arguments," Charles admitted. "But we don't," countered Diana. "Occasionally we do," Charles insisted. "No, we don't," she said. The exchange was described as a "friendly tiff" by the *Daily Mail,* but Diana's insistent denial of such an obvious truth seemed peculiar.

Compared with her awkward, monosyllabic demeanor in the engagement interview, Diana appeared poised and articulate; if anything, she was slightly more voluble than her husband. All the tabloids awarded them high marks and drew extravagant conclusions about the state of the marriage. "What a smashing royal couple they are," James Whitaker wrote in the *Daily Mirror.* "There is no kinder, more considerate person in the world than Prince Charles." *The Sun* declared, as if it were July 1981 all over again: "Di and Charles are so very much in love."

After their television triumph, the couple took another overseas tour, returning to Australia and visiting the United States for the first time. Charles and Diana gazed at each other as they danced to Stevie Wonder's "Isn't She Lovely" in Melbourne. In Washington and Palm Beach, their dance partners stole the show: John Travolta and Clint Eastwood with Diana at the White House and Joan Collins with Charles in Florida ("unbelievable cleavage. . . . Eye wander was a problem!" he wrote to a friend).

One of the more poignant moments in the Wales marriage occurred in late December, during the Christmas benefit for the Friends of Covent Garden at the Royal Opera House. The annual variety show featured Covent Garden performers doing offbeat singing, dancing, and theatrical routines. The previous year, Charles had made an engaging appearance as Romeo in a Shakespeare vignette, and this year, Diana had decided to surprise him by showing her own talent. "She was trying to please him," one of her friends recalled, "to make him proud of her." In October she contacted dancer Wayne Sleep, who at five foot two was eight inches shorter than Diana, and asked him to choreograph a duet with her to the Billy Joel song "Uptown Girl."

Diana secretly rehearsed the routine, and at a designated time on the night of the benefit, she excused herself from the royal box. She changed from her red velvet gown into a clingy, low-cut white satin dress and appeared onstage with her diminutive partner as the audience gasped. Their four-minute number drew applause at every step. Although Diana towered over Sleep, at one point he lifted her above his head and carried her twenty feet across the stage. Covent Garden photographer Reg Wilson called Diana's performance "provocative and sensuous. . . . She kept looking up at Charles. There was an enormous sense of fun between the two of them." Charles was stunned, but he smiled and clapped enthusiastically through the eight curtain calls. Afterward, Charles told Sleep that Diana was a "terrific" dancer, but privately, he had been discomfited by Diana's Salome routine. "He was perhaps a little concerned about the decorum and felt she should have worn something different. The dress was a bit slinky," a friend of the couple said. "She was trying hard to impress him, but possibly it backfired."

In 1985, the Waleses still presented a united public front—even carrying on with playful kisses after polo matches—but they now seldom socialized together. From the earliest days of their marriage, Diana had shown little enthusiasm for entertaining, primarily because she lacked confidence as a hostess. Diana tended to avoid people who seemed too clever. She took to complaining about the "heavies," the Foreign Office and political types who dutifully talked to her about issues when she landed next to them at dinner. Her self-consciousness in unfamiliar settings even extended to children's parties. "She would hardly bother to say hello to the mothers," one of her friends said. "If she was in a good mood she would talk to the nannies and play with the children. If in a bad mood, she would just play with the children."

Diana and Charles began showing the first signs of following different paths in their private lives. Diana appeared at several parties on her own, where she seemed visibly more relaxed than in her husband's company. At one weekend house party with old friends, she danced until four A.M. Afterward, the host, a captain in the Coldstream Guards named Richard Clowes, was reported to say that Diana "was in sparkling form." Charles had also resumed seeing his exiled friends, including Nicholas Soames, the Brabournes, Romseys, Palmer-Tomkinsons, and even Kanga Tryon. The rapprochement with Kanga conspicuously included Diana, who gave her blessing with a visit to the clothing boutique Kanga owned on Beauchamp Place, where she bought several dresses. Before long, the two women were spotted having lunch together. Diana may well have had an ulterior motive, since Kanga was known to be "blue with jealousy for Camilla" in her rivalry for attention from Charles, said London interior designer Nicky Haslam. "Camilla had a fallout with Kanga during the eighties," said *Sun* journalist Stuart Higgins, who spoke to Camilla regularly.

At some point in 1985—it is impossible to know precisely—Diana decided to look beyond Charles for affection and support. In the late spring, a new bodyguard had come aboard, Sergeant Barry Mannakee. He was an unlikely prospect for romance: slightly plump, with thinning brown hair and a working-class background. But he had a jocular personality, and he put Diana instantly at ease. She first drew close to him when he comforted her during bouts of weeping and depression. He described to another staff member how she had collapsed in tears before making a public appearance, insisting she couldn't go through with it. He had no choice, he said, but to embrace and soothe her so she would stop crying and pull herself together.

Diana came to rely on his compassion, and she looked to him for approval when she was feeling uncertain. She often asked him how she looked: whether, for example, her jewelry was becoming or her dress flattering. He poured on the compliments, usually with an amused grin, and in front of the other staff they bantered about "fancying" each other. Diana flirted with him, listened to him attentively, and shared private jokes with him. Eventually they became intimate, and Diana was often alone with him at Kensington Palace, when she would dismiss the rest of the staff.

Diana was so smitten that a decade later she told Anthony Holden, a biographer of her husband, that Mannakee had been "the love of my life," the same words she had used to describe Charles in conversations with a few close friends. As Charles had already learned, involvement with Diana meant submitting to her overpowering possessiveness. In her fear of rejection, she believed that if she didn't have someone's total attention, she couldn't count on him at all. Barry Mannakee was married and had two children, and although he sympathized with her neediness, he couldn't give her the constant support she wanted. "Once it began, [Mannakee] was very distraught about being caught up with her," a friend of Charles's said. "She was so intense, and he found it very difficult to handle."

The relationship between the guard and the guarded is, by definition, unusual, especially for a woman employing a male security officer. "It is intense and strange," a friend of Diana's explained. "The bodyguards knew the most personal things. They went with her to the dentist, and the doctor, and to Marks and Spencer to buy knickers and bras." For that reason, their tenure was usually limited to four or five years, when they were reassigned by Scotland Yard to traditional police duties.

When Barry Mannakee was suddenly transferred to another job in July 1986 after scarcely a year, the staff speculated that he and Diana had become "too close," as one courtier described it. Mannakee had been warned by the senior protection officer, Colin Trimming, that his familiarity with Diana was unseemly, and he should put an end to it. Mannakee couldn't control Diana's behavior, however, and every time she spoke an endearment to him or gave him an affectionate squeeze, Trimming took note. Given the pressure Mannakee was feeling from Diana, his reassignment was for the best, because it defused a hopeless—and potentially explosive—situation. Nevertheless, Diana was disheartened by his transfer.

For all the signs of familiarity witnessed by the staff, Charles knew nothing of Diana's involvement with Mannakee at the time and only learned about it some years later. He was by nature incurious about such matters, in typical royal fashion. "I don't want to spy on [Diana] or interfere in her life in any way," Charles wrote to a friend. Consequently, another friend said, "It is absolutely untrue that there was any cause and effect regarding his going back to Camilla. He went back to her for completely different reasons."

On the question of why Charles resumed his romance with Camilla, Jonathan Dimbleby's biography is considered definitive. According to former courtiers, Charles read the book line by line before its 1994 publication, as did his private secretary Richard Aylard, who checked all the facts. The book is indisputably Charles's perception of events, with some shadings by Dimbleby.

By this account, Charles felt after five years that his marriage was beyond repair. Instead of diminishing, Diana's rages intensified: "There appeared to be a terrible conflict inside her that would suddenly erupt in anger or grief. As her public prestige soared, she grew correspondingly anguished in private." Worn down by Diana's ragged emotions, Charles finally gave up: "There was no specific incident that precipitated the end of the Prince's effort to hold his marriage together; it collapsed gradually. . . . By 1986 their marriage had begun slowly to disintegrate."

The most visible evidence that Charles had, according to Dimbleby, "started to withdraw the support which . . . had drained his reserves of sympathy and compassion" came during their tour of Canada and Japan in May 1986. Diana had virtually no appetite and seemed unusually tense; Charles was more brooding than ever. Picking up signs of their disaffection, the Canadian press had turned hostile, calling Charles "bat ears" and accusing Diana of having a "plastic smile." Diana and Charles were visiting an exhibition in Vancouver when Diana suddenly fainted. As she slid to the floor, she was caught by two men on her staff, who helped her into a nearby room to be revived by a physician and several aides. "I didn't know anything about fainting," Diana said, although by her own admission she had fainted numerous times during pregnancy.

Diana later spoke bitterly of Charles's insensitivity: "My husband told me off," she said, when he rebuked her for not withdrawing to a private room when she began feeling faint. She also said he insisted she go out later in the evening to avoid speculation that she might be seriously ill. While Charles's behavior didn't strike their aides as blatantly cruel, they did detect, in the words of a former Palace official, "for the first time a real lack of sympathy. It was obvious that something had gone from the relationship. He wasn't that caring, and he had been before."

The Waleses' domestic staff also noticed a new chill. "Even together," Dimbleby wrote, "they were apart." Diana and Charles had been sleeping in separate bedrooms for some time, and they kept different hours as well, she retiring early, he staying up late, listening to opera and doing paperwork. Now, when Diana fled to her room from the breakfast table in tears, Charles declined to follow. They arrived at Highgrove in separate cars; Charles would come a day early and depart on Mondays, while Diana would leave with the boys on Sunday afternoons, often weeping so hard she could scarcely say good-bye. After an altercation with Charles, she would retreat into silence for several days, or she might blister members of her staff in frustration. Sometimes Diana slammed the door in Charles's face or called him names. At other times, she would unexpectedly run to embrace him while he was busy in his garden; when he didn't reciprocate immediately, she would retreat in despair. Small wonder that the staff took to shouting "storm stations" or "hard hats" when they sensed trouble coming.

At the nadir of his "desperation," Charles wrote to a friend in 1986, "I feel nowadays that I'm in a kind of cage . . . longing to be free. How awful incompatibility is. . . . This extraordinary drama has all the ingredients of a Greek tragedy." In his paroxysms of introspection, Charles blamed himself for the failure. "I never thought it would end up like this," he wrote to a friend. "How could I have got it all so wrong?"

Charles turned to Camilla at that point because, according to Dimbleby, she offered "the warmth, the understanding and steadiness" that "he had never been able to find with any other person." For her part, Camilla was still coping unhappily with her chronically unfaithful husband, and still in love with Charles. The relationship rekindled with telephone calls, which led to Camilla's visits to Highgrove, typically with her husband or other friends of Charles: "The opportunities to be alone with each other for any length of time were infrequent. That they loved each other was not in any doubt."

Had Camilla simply disappeared from Charles's life, she might have faded from his imagination. But one of the odd consequences of jealousy is its elevation of the object of that jealousy. With her constant complaints and questions, Diana kept Camilla in Charles's thoughts. He was married to a woman beloved by the entire world, yet she was fixated on a rival who was older and less beautiful, as if she saw something in Camilla that Charles had missed.

Charles understood the extent of Diana's obsession; Camilla had become the "canker" in his marriage. Yet Charles took up with Camilla, well aware that the relationship could cripple Diana's tenuous hold on stability once she figured out the situation—as she surely would. Charles knew all too well that Diana had good antennae, and that she eavesdropped and opened mail. Perhaps Charles believed he had no other options, but his decision to resume his intimacy with Camilla took him down a dangerous path.

It wasn't long before Diana confirmed her long-standing suspicions. In her somewhat cryptic answers on *Panorama,* she said that in 1986 she had "knowledge" of Charles and Camilla "from people who minded and cared about our marriage." The household at Highgrove had caught on fairly quickly. Only the security officers knew at the outset, but other staff understood their boss's destination when he went out on Sunday nights for dinner. He dispatched his loyal manservant Paddy Whiteland to deliver notes, flowers, chocolates, and other gifts to Camilla's home, and Camilla's housekeeper kept a tally of Charles's visits, which she passed on to the Highgrove groom.

Diana also said she noticed "the change of behavior pattern in [her] husband, for all sorts of reasons that a woman's instinct produces. . . . It was already difficult, but it became increasingly difficult." Although Diana didn't yet mention Camilla by name, she began voicing her unhappiness. "It was into the mid-eighties before she started talking," one friend recalled. "In 1986, it was mostly the lack of ability to communicate with Charles or get the sympathy and understanding she needed." When Diana first met astrologer Penny Thornton that March, she referred to Charles's affair with "a certain woman." Diana contacted Thornton at a moment, she said later, when she felt "I've got to get out. I can't bear it any longer." Around this time Charles wrote to a friend about Diana's unhappiness: "It's agony to know that someone is hating it all so much. It seems so unfair to her."

Diana told Thornton she wanted to escape "the whole royal 'setup,' " but Thornton dissuaded her from leaving. After reading Diana's chart and talking with her for four hours at Kensington Palace, Thornton advised Diana to stop "berating Charles for seeing another woman" and to "make a friend of her opposition." Her advice was sensible though futile, given Diana's mental state, but she did succeed in defusing the crisis. Later that evening, Thornton heard from Sarah Ferguson, who had introduced her to

Diana, that Prince Charles was grateful for her help. It turned out that Diana had packed her bags that morning before meeting with Thornton.

Diana's certain knowledge of Charles's affair with Camilla was "pretty devastating," she later said. Her bulimia became "rampant," and she was consumed with "a feeling of being no good at anything and being useless and hopeless and failed in every direction." She would later confide to one of her future lovers, James Hewitt, that she had been "terrified" that her bulimia would be discovered when she fainted in Vancouver. On a holiday that summer with King Juan Carlos of Spain and his family, Diana felt exhausted and "spent my whole time with my head down the loo." She recalled feeling resentful of Charles because the king and his wife Sofia "were all so busy thinking Charles was the most wonderful creature . . . and who was this girl coming along?" Showing further evidence of confusion about her identity, she recalled knowing "there was something inside me that wasn't coming out, and I didn't know how to use it, in the sense of letting them see it." At Balmoral afterward, Diana's new sister-in-law Fergie couldn't help noticing Diana's disturbing symptoms: "She was teary and reclusive and out of sorts."

When Diana had her portrait painted that summer, she was vibrating with tension. Sitting periodically for portraits was a ritual for every member of the royal family, and Diana had already been painted seven times in the five years since her marriage. In early 1986, Richard Foster had spent sixteen hours painting her and had found her surprisingly uncertain about the sort of image she should project. Only months later, Diana was posing again, six one-hour sessions with Emily Patrick, who was disconcerted by Diana. "She was tense down to the very nails," Patrick recalled. "She never stopped moving . . . and she always wanted to talk about dieting." To Patrick's trained eye, it was obvious "Diana was uncomfortable with herself and was hiding so much it was difficult to do a good portrait"—a problem encountered by other artists as well.

Perhaps it was Camilla, or the reassignment of Barry Mannakee, but by the summer of 1986, Diana had relapsed into her most acute symptoms. Sometime during that period, by Diana's account, "after five years of being married," she was visited by her sister Jane (a Kensington Palace neighbor) "to check on me." The previous evening, during a fight with Charles, Diana had grabbed a penknife off his dressing table and "scratched myself heavily down my chest and both thighs." Although there was "a lot of blood," Diana claimed Charles "hadn't made any reaction whatsoever." When Jane inquired about the marks on Diana's chest, Diana replied, "Oh, it's nothing," and when Jane pressed, "What is it?" Diana still wouldn't tell her.

Diana was all of twenty-five years old, and had been exhibiting signs of mental illness for more than five years. As in the autumn of 1981 and 1982, this was a moment when it was vital for someone to intervene and find a long-term treatment for Diana, yet there was no evidence of such an effort by Charles or anyone else. According to Diana, after fainting in Canada, she had confided in the doctor about her bulimia. But she recalled that he couldn't help her because he didn't understand the severity of her problems. Instead, she said, "he just gave me a pill and shut me up." A footman at Balmoral reported that a psychiatrist visited Diana a few times that September, after fights between the Waleses had grown particularly fierce. But again, Diana's immediate family and in-laws appeared incapable of dealing with her situation.

Diana suspected Charles's friends of conspiring against her, and she feared being sent away for treatment—a reasonable course of action, given the severity of her symptoms. "Friends on my husband's side were indicating that I was again unstable, sick, and should be put in a home of some sort in order to get better," she recalled. In her view, their intention was only to "dismantle" her personality by isolating it.

Luckily for Charles and Diana, the media spotlight during much of 1986 turned to the July wedding of his younger brother Prince Andrew and Sarah Ferguson, known to all as Fergie. Their romance had begun in June 1985 when the Queen invited Sarah to join her Windsor house party for Ascot. Diana had suggested Fergie to the Queen—Fergie later called her "matchmaker Diana"—and ensured that Sarah was seated next to Andrew at lunch. Fergie was exuberant, even boisterous, which appealed to Andrew, who was noisy but somewhat passive. Their courtship proceeded quietly, abetted by Diana and Charles, who invited Sarah to Highgrove, Kensington Palace, and skiing in Klosters. When Andrew proposed to Sarah in February 1986, Diana was delighted. With her own marriage fraying, Diana was eager for a sympathetic contemporary inside the palace.

After five years of family gatherings at Sandringham, Balmoral, and Windsor, Diana's dealings with the royals ranged from cordial to unsatisfactory. She once said that the royal family sucked her dry, and that her in-laws put her under such stress that her bulimia invariably worsened when she was around them.

Diana had settled into a correct if not overly warm relationship with the Queen, though she felt uncomfortable with Prince Philip, whom she called "The Greek" behind his back. (Diana's irreverence even extended occasionally to the Queen, when she would refer to her as "Brenda," *Private Eye*'s nickname, when joking with friends.) Philip, who had an eye for beautiful women, was enchanted by Diana at first. "I remember a party for Prince Philip when the Waleses came in late," recalled a friend of the royal family. "Diana greeted Philip and they lingered holding hands. I thought,

'How lovely.' It couldn't have been put on." Philip eventually became disenchanted with Diana's behavior and considered her difficult.

From the beginning, Diana was unnerved by the Queen Mother, for several reasons: her closeness to Ruth Fermoy, who Diana said "tried to lacerate me"; the Queen Mother's complete devotion to Prince Charles, which caused tension as the Wales marriage grew more estranged; and her longstanding friendship with the Parker Bowles family. "[Charles's] grandmother is always looking at me with a sort of strange look in her eyes," Diana once said. "It's not hatred. It's a sort of interest and pity mixed in one. . . . She's sort of fascinated by me, but doesn't quite know how to unravel it."

Despite the Queen Mother's image as a plump, smiling matron, she was tough, sharp-tongued, and smart. "The Queen Mother has a big heart," a friend of the royal family said, "but she is very rigid about many things. She believes if you marry into the royal family you have to act a certain way, you have to carry on, you have to be in control all the time, you cannot show your feelings." When Diana failed to measure up in each of these important areas, she lost the Queen Mother's support.

Diana's most sympathetic in-law was the Queen's sister, Princess Margaret, whom Diana called "Margo." To some extent, Diana identified with her aunt by marriage. As a young woman in 1955, Margaret had fallen in love with Group Captain Peter Townsend, who, like Wallis Simpson, was a divorcé. Ultimately, Margaret rejected Townsend as unsuitable, and the tabloids made much of her being forced to submerge her happiness for the sake of duty. When Margaret married photographer Anthony Armstrong-Jones (later Lord Snowdon) several years later, they departed from the royal stereotype by leading a jet-set life with fashionable friends outside the British establishment. After eighteen years of marriage, Margaret and her husband divorced in 1978 on the grounds that their relationship had "irretrievably broken down."

"Diana related to Margaret because she was an unhappy person," one of Diana's friends said. Margaret was often prickly and demanding, but she could be teased into a good mood, and her friends attested to her loyalty. "Diana sometimes said Princess Margaret should have been her mother-in-law," Diana's friend Roberto Devorik said. "She admired the way Margaret had worked within a broken home. Diana knew Margaret was always in the shadow of her sister, but she was always a fighter." Diana was also drawn to Margaret's love of ballet and her waspish wit, and she got on well with Margaret's two children, David Linley and Sarah Armstrong-Jones. Margaret, in turn, found Diana's sense of humor appealing, and she was touched by the spontaneity of Diana's affection.

Among Charles's siblings, Diana was most comfortable with Andrew. Behind his bluff demeanor, Diana said she sensed "something troubling" and felt he got "squashed" by his family. She related to him because his family "dismissed" him as an "idiot," although Diana found him to be quite shrewd. While her assessment was close to the mark, Diana underestimated Andrew's favored position with the Queen, who was enormously proud that he had served in the Falklands war as a naval officer.

Edward, the youngest of the Windsor children, initially got on well with Diana, although they weren't close. He was bright and sensitive, somewhat on the shy side, which Diana found attractive. Over time, however, they grew more distant, as Edward seemed to pull away from her when he felt that she was undermining the royal family.

Diana had the trickiest relationship with Princess Anne, and the tabloids periodically set them up as rivals, even enemies. Anne's failure to appear at Harry's christening sparked great speculation about her reported "pique" at not being asked to be a godmother. Anne and Diana were certainly not close and seldom socialized, although Highgrove was only twenty minutes away from Anne's country house. Diana and Anne had little in common. Anne was plain and unfashionable, a countrywoman who loved to ride. While Diana was secretive, insecure, and unpredictable, Anne was straightforward, confident, and consistent. As a young woman, Anne was considered contentious (her nickname in the press at one point was "Her Royal Rudeness") and more concerned with horses than people, but she turned her image around by zeroing in on one cause, the Save the Children Fund, which became her life's work.

Anne became a professional and efficient princess who even wrote her own speeches. Diana admired Anne's dedication, as well as her lively mind and independent spirit. Still, Diana admitted that she didn't like to "rattle her cage" and tended to "keep out of her way." When Diana's glamour stole the headlines, it was often Anne whose good work was overlooked. For the most part, Anne kept her displeasure to herself, but once, when Anne had been tramping through farms in Ulster, Diana appeared that evening in a low-cut burgundy dress at a Barbican gala in London. The next day, Diana's image was everywhere, and Anne was ignored in all papers except *The Daily Telegraph*, which noted on its fourteenth page: BOVINE SALUTE FOR PRINCESS ANNE IN ULSTER. By one account, Anne was "hopping mad and quite indiscreet in saying so."

Compared with the chill of Diana's sister-in-law Anne, Sarah Ferguson was a warm breeze. Their friendship, however, would turn out to be particularly turbulent, even for Diana: a blur of giddy, girlish pranks, support and affection, deep jealousy, astonishing lapses of judgment, and unhealthy paranoia about Palace conspiracies against them. Fergie introduced Diana to new friends, as well as the world of astrologers, psychics, and alternative therapists. Their exploration of this territory came to define their relationship and delude them both. In the end, their destructive synergy had a profound impact on the Wales marriage. "I wonder what would have happened if Sarah had not been there," a former Palace adviser said, "because the two of them were trying to break the system."

Diana was much more grand than Fergie, who characterized her background as "country gentry, with a bit of old money." Her father, Major Ronald Ferguson, came from "a long line of distinguished gentleman soldiers," but he left the service to play polo, run the Guards Polo Club for Prince Philip, and eventually become Prince Charles's polo manager. Fergie's mother, the former Susan Wright, was from a well-established Irish family that once owned a large estate near Dublin.

Despite the difference in their backgrounds, Fergie and Diana had one important thing in common: besides being schoolmates, their mothers had both left their husbands for other men and had moved to distant locales, Fergie's mother to Argentina with another polo player, Hector Barrantes. Although the marriage of Fergie's parents had been shaky for a while, she "never heard [them] argue," and they didn't separate until Sarah was thirteen. Until then, she had a relatively happy childhood with a mother who involved herself in the lives of her two daughters, teaching them to ride and taking them on skiing holidays.

Sarah adored her father, a feckless sort who didn't fully deserve such admiration. He was often away playing polo, and as Fergie put it, he had been "gone too often and strayed too far." Fergie later grew closer to her mother, despite the geographic distance, and developed strong ties with her stepfather, Hector.

Fergie had her share of emotional problems, including low self-esteem complicated by persistent worries about being overweight. She had an excessive need for approval, and an eagerness to please that played out as infinite adaptability. She sought attention by playing the fool, and often acted impulsively and without regard for consequences. But she was far more outgoing than Diana, and she became a good-time girl, eager to try anything. She worked in a London art gallery and scouted projects for a publisher of art books. She spent six months traveling around South America and the United States, at one point cleaning lavatories to earn money for her bus fare. When Sarah met Andrew, she was dating a widower twenty years her senior.

Fergie remembered becoming friends with Diana a year before the wedding to Charles, keeping Diana company at Buckingham Palace in her loneliness during the engagement, and being invited to the Wales wedding but being hurt by her exclusion from the Queen's luncheon afterward.

Diana's interpretation of the origins of the friendship was somewhat cattier. During the courtship with Charles, Fergie "kept rearing her head for some reason," Diana recalled, "and she seemed to know all about the royal setup. . . . She suddenly appeared, and she sat in the front pew of our wedding."

When the tabloids discovered Sarah Ferguson, they fell in love with her, just as they had Diana. At age twenty-six (two years older than Diana), Fergie won over reporters with her unpretentious manner and ebullient personality. Not only did Diana become jealous of the press coverage, she resented that Sarah was succeeding with the royal family in ways she had not. Sarah was a country girl who adored Balmoral because it "set me free"—away from the strictures of city life. She could march around in what one of Diana's friends called the "pissing rain," stalking and shooting, fishing and hunting. "I was robust and jolly and not too highly strung," Sarah recalled. Soon enough, the hurtful comparisons began.

"Why can't you be more like Fergie?" Charles said to Diana during their first ski holiday in Klosters in February 1986. Fergie could ski the expert slopes, while Diana still wobbled along. "It must have been hell for Diana," Sarah admitted. At Sandringham in the fall of 1986, Diana grew even more envious, particularly when she saw the instant connection Sarah formed with the Queen. "Diana felt the Queen was much warmer to Fergie, gave more chances to Fergie," Roberto Devorik said. As Sarah described their relationship, "our common interests and acquaintances dated back. . . . The Queen and I both doted on horses and dogs, on farming and open air." Fergie rode horses with the Queen, and said she "felt favored and blessed." After listening to the praise for her sister-in-law and reading her favorable press coverage, Diana grew more insecure and decided, "maybe I ought to be like Fergie."

In the tabloids, Fergie was, as she put it, "flavor of the month," while the press was taking a dim view of Diana once again. Aside from the routine reports on her public appearances, the tabloids paid scant attention to Diana's official role. They took a far greater interest in charting Diana's appearance and eating habits, which they began to pursue aggressively again in March 1985 when her weight had once more dropped below 8 stone. Her shoulder blades jutted sharply through her clothing, and her skin seemed translucent. Diana's weight became headline news during the 1986 Canada-Japan tour when her fainting spell prompted speculation about diets and anorexia.

The tabloids had no knowledge of Charles's unsympathetic reaction to Diana's collapse—indeed, James Whitaker called him "a tower of strength to her; no woman could have a more caring and understanding husband"—so they chose instead to blame the victim. The *Daily Express* criticized Diana's "near obsession about how she looks and what people are saying and writing about her. She behaves like a top fashion model." James Whitaker in the *Daily Mirror* rebuked her for "the cold indifference on her face as she defied the photographers" and complained that she "lacked the sparkle we have come to expect."

With the focus continuing only on her possible anorexia, Diana seemed almost to taunt the press when she periodically showed how much she could eat. In Japan she conspicuously downed a ten-course meal, telling Japanese journalists "I don't know why there are all these stories saying I am too thin. I am eating a lot." Back in England touring a health center, she proclaimed, "It doesn't matter what I eat. I never put an ounce on!" as she stared at a black cherry cheesecake and several pizzas and said, "I could eat all that!"

At midyear, two tabloids moved closer to the truth. Judy Wade in *The Sun* wrote that "fasts and feasts" were beginning to worry Diana's staff. Wade described how Diana ate little in public—one member of her household said she would refuse to eat for days after being criticized—but that at home she was known to feast: "At night she cannot resist gorging on her old favorites—ice cream and chocolates." Though there was no mention of vomiting, a staff member observed that "indulging in these sweet treats always seemed to make her feel guilty. Afterwards she would barely eat a thing for days." In the *News of the World*, Fiona MacDonald Hull concentrated more on Diana's "weeping self-doubts, nerves and desperation," but noted that her staff "always believed her emotional nature has stopped her eating, rather than a desire to diet. . . . She finds it difficult to swallow food even when she is relaxed."

Given the usual half-life of ideas launched on tabloid pages, these perceptive observations evaporated without further comment. They were replaced by another burst of schizophrenic coverage of the Wales marriage, this time prompted by the Majorca vacation with King Carlos in August 1986. When Diana wasn't periodically escaping to "put [her] head down the loo," she sunbathed and swam while photographers snapped away. The tabloids did handsprings over their pictures of the happy family: "Nothing like a touch of Spanish sun to put the shine back in a marriage!"; "Having a wonderful time!"; and most absurdly, "Recent worries about starvation dieting can be banished," because Diana "has filled out in just the right places."

When Charles flew off to Balmoral, leaving Diana and the boys to finish out the vacation, the naysayers were ready. ARE CHARLES AND DI MOVING APART? asked *The Sun*, asserting that the couple now had a special agreement to allow Diana more time on her own "for the things she enjoys and Charles doesn't." The gist was that Diana was "growing restless" and had taken to "repeatedly embarrassing Charles with such complaints as 'My husband doesn't approve of the books I read.' "

No one knew about the severity of Diana's emotional problems, or, for that matter, about Camilla. Not even Stuart Higgins of *The Sun*, in his regular conversations with Camilla, understood what was going on. "Whether that was bad journalism or she was very good at hiding things, I don't know," he said. The *News of the World* may have stumbled on a case of mistaken identity when it reported that "Charles spends long hours on the phone to Kanga [Tryon] . . . calling her on his private line from his soundproofed study." With his new cordless phone, he would also go for long walks at Highgrove, "making calls from the middle of a field."

If the details of such reports were often stretched or fanciful, Charles and Diana's tense body language was sufficient evidence of their marital difficulties. Before the Balmoral holiday, two tabloids captured a startling incident after a polo match: Charles lightly cuffed Diana on the back of the head, prompting her to unexpectedly turn and kick him, and Charles to push her against their car. After Diana leaped into the driver's seat, Charles took a final swipe at the back of her neck. It was all supposed to have been playful, but the public display of anger was all too real.

That fall, the companion documentary to the 1985 interview with Alastair Burnet appeared on British television. Unlike the previous effort, this intimate view of the Prince and Princess was unsuccessful. The consensus of critics, according to the *Daily Mail*, was that "Diana seemed to be permanently having fits of the giggles and wasn't overbright, with Prince Charles being humorless and taciturn." Both Charles and Diana made statements that would subject them to endless ridicule, and that neither would live down. In talking to a boy at a children's home, Diana said, "I never got any O levels: brain the size of a pea, I've got." When asked about his garden, Charles said, "I just come and talk to the plants, really. It's very important to talk. They respond, don't they?"

It would be their last joint television program. Though they tried to appear devoted to each other, their unhappiness was obvious. But this was the marriage of the heir to the throne, and Diana and Charles were locked into position. They would both keep pretending, without fully understanding the consequences of their charade.

Chapter 13

IN November 1986, Diana invited a cavalry captain named James Hewitt to dine with her at Kensington Palace. She had met Hewitt in the late summer at a London cocktail party, and over the following four months, he had been giving her riding lessons in Hyde Park. At twenty-eight, Hewitt was three years older than Diana, who had an admitted weakness for men in uniform. Copper-haired and slender, Hewitt was as meticulous about his appearance as Diana was about hers. He redeemed his evident vanity with ornate manners, and he was skillful at attracting a woman with the sort of studied attentiveness that made her feel "as if no other woman matters—which, of course, is not the case," said his embittered former girl-friend Emma Younghusband. In some of his mannerisms—grimacing as he gathered his thoughts, fiddling with his signet ring, shying from showing too much emotion—James Hewitt even bore an eerie resemblance to Prince Charles.

Diana had found Hewitt attractive, charming, and sufficiently sympathetic to tell him about her fear of horses dating from a childhood fall. When she asked if he might help restore her confidence on horseback, he said he could arrange lessons down the road from Kensington Palace at the Knightsbridge Barracks, where he was in charge of the stables for the Household Division of his regiment, the Life Guards. Only days after their meeting, Diana called to accept his offer.

Accompanied by Hazel West, a lady-in-waiting who was an accomplished horsewoman, Diana rode with Hewitt in the early mornings once or twice a week. Hewitt patiently instructed Diana, and afterward they had lengthy talks over coffee in the Officers' Mess. Before long, Diana unburdened herself to Hewitt, telling him that she and Charles had drifted apart and were now living separate lives. As she confessed her marital unhappiness and her childhood insecurities, Hewitt responded with comforting words. When she returned home, she called to thank him for being supportive, and afterward phoned him whenever she needed cheering.

She invited him to dinner following the royal couple's state visit to the Middle East. Diana and Charles had successfully toured Oman, Qatar, Bahrain, and Saudi Arabia, and when Diana left for England, Charles had continued on *Britannia* through the Suez Canal to Cyprus—which is where he was when James Hewitt arrived at Kensington Palace. Having dismissed her staff for the evening, Diana asked Hewitt to open a bottle of champagne, and she served him from a buffet laid out in the dining room. They talked about the Middle Eastern trip, and after coffee in her sitting room, Diana first sat on Hewitt's lap, then led him by the hand to her bedroom, where they became lovers. "It wasn't a typical seduction scene with me as the big white hunter going after a princess," Hewitt later said.

Thus began a five-year affair that remained secret for a surprisingly long time. Diana reached out to Hewitt because she needed attention, but she was also reacting to her husband's behavior. It was the traditional aristocratic solution to a troubled relationship: with three in the marriage already, Diana made it four. Diana showed little sign of guilt, either with Hewitt or her friends who knew of the relationship. "Charles was involved with Camilla, and she felt that what was good for the goose was good for the gander," Hewitt recalled.

From the moment Diana met Hewitt, she controlled the relationship, taking the initiative, making the demands, intensifying or drawing back as her feelings dictated. For all his apparent confidence, Hewitt was in many ways the wrong man for Diana, which fit her pattern of choosing partners who were bound to disappoint her. "I always want the unobtainable in men," she told astrologer Debbie Frank. Hewitt was weak, emotionally immature, and self-pitying, and, like Diana, suffered from a deep sense of inadequacy, for which he compensated by womanizing.

A middle-class man with upper-class pretensions, Hewitt was the son of a Royal Marine officer and a simple countrywoman who taught riding. His father was often away during Hewitt's youth, so he grew up in the company of women: his mother, his twin sister, and a sister eighteen months older. He became an accomplished equestrian, but he performed miserably in school. He was diagnosed with dyslexia, and at age thirteen, when he went to Millfield, the progressive boarding school in Somerset, he said later, "I couldn't read and assumed it was my lot in life to be dumb and stupid. I was always at the bottom of the class." Hewitt was also a late-blooming adolescent: only five feet tall until age seventeen, when he shot up to his adult height of six feet. "I had red hair, was short, slow, very quiet, and had absolutely no confidence," Hewitt recalled. As a consequence, he still felt "very small and inadequate" well into his thirties.

During his school days, Hewitt used sports to make up for his inferiority complex. He competed in fencing, swimming, running, and rowing, and his horsemanship led him to learn polo. Despite his learning disability, Hewitt passed six O levels, but he dropped out of school to become a riding instructor. At nineteen, he joined the 5th Royal Inniskillen Dragoon Guards, an upper-class regiment where Hewitt was known as a "temporary gentleman," an expression dating from World War I that described socially ambitious officers. Hewitt trained at Sandhurst and polished his skills on horseback by riding six hours a day at the École Nationale d'Equitation for a year. While he was abroad, his parents divorced, and although he was twenty-six, he took the news unusually hard. "He lost his trust in people and relationships," according to his biographer, Anna Pasternak, and retreated from emotional intimacy.

Diana's friends believed she was drawn to Hewitt precisely because he was insecure, and he didn't intimidate her with complicated ideas as Charles did. Diana did not know, however, that Hewitt was unfaithful as well; throughout the relationship with Diana, he was involved with Emma Stewardson (later Younghusband)—as a "decoy," Emma later said. Emma knew about Diana and tolerated her rival even when Hewitt "was holding long whispered conversations with the princess while I was in his company."

The torrid ("She let her fingers mingle momentarily with his, and he felt a voluptuous thrill shoot up his arms") version of Diana's relationship with James Hewitt was recounted in Pasternak's *Princess in Love,* published in 1994. Hewitt later said that he had "trusted" the Oxford-educated Pasternak (Russian novelist Boris was her great-uncle) and "cooperated with her, but the book was not the kind I imagined." For her part, Pasternak said that Hewitt, whom she had known "vaguely, socially," had approached her to write his story under two conditions: that the book be published before a follow-up volume by Andrew Morton, with whom Hewitt had declined to cooperate on *Diana: Her True Story,* and that it be a "love story." Pasternak wrote the book in five-and-a-half weeks; when it was published three weeks later, it was widely ridiculed for its overheated prose.

Diana acknowledged the affair in her 1995 *Panorama* interview ("Yes, I adored him. Yes, I was in love with him") and admitted that the Pasternak book contained "factual evidence," although she added that "there was a lot of fantasy." As with the Morton and the Dimbleby books, *Princess in Love* has to be regarded as the perspective of one person, James Hewitt. But aside from the book's audacious mind reading ("She knew that somewhere, lurking frightened and embarrassed, was a hungry capacity for sexuality, a need to feel a fulfilled and potent woman . . .") and self-serving, misguided assertions ("It was with James Hewitt's unswerving devotion and patience that she managed to conquer her bulimia and embark on the long and often arduous journey of self-discovery"), the essential narrative stands as a generally accurate chronicle of events.

Diana's romance with Hewitt intensified in the months after the evening at Kensington Palace, although its components remained essentially the same: long telephone calls, once or twice a day, which Diana filled with quotidian detail that Hewitt listened to without complaint. She solicited his comments on her clothing, and constantly asked for reassurance about her looks. According to Hewitt, Diana told him that she "spent hours lying in bed at night dissecting her body, endlessly enumerating to herself its deficiencies, telling herself that she was not good enough."

The relationship had an unhealthy imbalance, with Diana simultaneously clingy and controlling, as Hewitt willingly assumed subordinate status. "I was with her because she needed me," he recalled. "I was prepared to give up my life for her. . . . I could have been for her what Camilla has become for Charles, I would have accepted that supporting role." This meant riding along with her mood swings to provide a "release from the tension that characterized her daily life."

Diana's "emotional roller coaster" frightened Hewitt. In the beginning she would sit, as she had with Charles during their courtship, and watch Hewitt read—although she herself was disconcertingly unable to read because she was too excited and restless. The more time they spent together, the more mood gyrations Hewitt witnessed. Just when she seemed calm and balanced, she would be overcome by "violent paroxysms of despair." She generally hit bottom at the end of their weekends together, growing agitated at the prospect of his departure, which "struck her as a form of rejection."

Hewitt confided to his father that "he had never seen anyone so distraught, so churned up . . . that he really feared that she might even take her life if he tried to end their relationship." Perhaps most disquieting was the sense of detachment Diana had experienced since childhood: "Often she felt as if she was perching on the doorstep of life peering in, an onlooker while everybody else . . . was a participant." Six months into their affair, in the spring of 1987, she told him about her bulimia. Although Hewitt read about the affliction and tried to understand it, her "lack of control" and "seemingly unmitigated greed" baffled him.

Hewitt responded to Diana differently than Charles, who tried to calm her down through cajolery, followed by irritation when he failed. Hewitt expressed his love and pledged to take care of her. In the short term, Hewitt's approach helped Diana, who couldn't help talking about him to her staff. "She was crazy about him," a former Palace adviser said. "He was a big support for her. He tried to make her feel better, to give her a good time with little things. She was happy with him, and happy is not a word you can use about her often."

Yet over time, Hewitt couldn't be as open with Diana as she wanted. When Diana would beg him to share the anxieties tucked behind his reserve, he couldn't reveal how shocked he was by her volatility, or how burdened he felt by the responsibility of keeping her stable. Diana could detect when Hewitt was withholding his feelings, which left her feeling defeated.

Hewitt was also more obtuse than Charles about Diana's need for expert professional help. "I view depression as a sign of weakness. . . . I believe in the stiff upper lip," Hewitt once said. Psychological counseling was anathema to him. "Some people go to psychiatrists or take drugs," Hewitt said. Diana "needed love and support, she needed to know and be told that it would all be all right."

Diana expressed her affection by showering Hewitt with gifts, including a diamond tie pin and a gold-and-silver alarm clock from Asprey, as well as countless articles of clothing; she would later boast to her friend James Gilbey that she dressed the army officer from "head to foot. Cost me quite a bit." Hewitt read her passages from Tennyson or Wordsworth and took to calling her "Dibbs." Together they would read issues of *Country Life* and pick out dream houses. They periodically met for lunch at Diana's favorite restaurant, San Lorenzo; he introduced her to his father, and Diana traveled to Devon for weekends with Hewitt and his mother. Diana's West Heath friend Carolyn Bartholomew also knew of the romance and spent several weekends with the couple.

In the spring of 1987, Hewitt was promoted to the rank of major and moved to the Combermere Barracks near Windsor Castle. Diana continued to ride with Hewitt there, and brought William and Harry, then aged four and two, for a tour of the barracks. When Charles was away, Diana and Hewitt had assignations at Kensington Palace and Highgrove. These were risky encounters, since William and Harry might easily have come into Diana's room during the night. The household and security staff felt as awkward about the situation as they did about Charles and Camilla. At least one maid worried about what to say if Charles made any inquiries. He did not, a friend explained, because he "had a tremendous gift for not observing what was not desirable to observe."

Hewitt believed that, during the first months of their affair, Diana still had not entirely given up on Charles, and that "she would try anything to win him." During that period, some friends of Diana and Charles made efforts to patch up the marriage. Film producer David Puttnam and his wife, Patsy, were invited to several dinners that were "an attempt by others to help the Prince and Princess by getting them out," recalled Puttnam. "What was noticeable during those dinners was how hard Diana was working at the relationship, to be a good wife. She was affectionate, and she was trying hard to be special."

But faced with what she perceived as continued rebuffs, Diana not only gave up, she began to tell Hewitt she hated Charles. She also started to boycott dinner parties planned by her husband. When their guests arrived, Diana would stay upstairs, leaving him to explain lamely that she was feeling ill and couldn't join them. During a dinner for eighteen to honor patrons of the Royal Academy, Diana was spotted swimming outside while the group was having drinks. Charles didn't display similar hostility toward Diana, only persistent anguish that his marriage had fallen apart so completely. "That is the total agony about the situation," he wrote to a friend in October 1987.

The fights between Charles and Diana grew less frequent as their chill hardened into a cold war, stripped of basic civility except in the presence of their sons. At Highgrove, Diana would take vigorous swims each morning (even Hewitt couldn't help noticing that swimming had become "an obsession for her. Whenever she felt overemotional she would pound up and down the pool") and then retreat to her room to watch movies with the boys or talk on the phone while Charles lost himself in the garden.

If Diana and Charles had been tougher, they might have been able to publicly maintain the illusion of a happy marriage. But both were too sensitive—albeit in different ways—to prevent the stress from showing. As always, the press played a pivotal role. Simon Jenkins, editor of *The Times* from 1990 to 1992, said reporters sensed it was "the biggest story they'd ever got. It was the love story gone wrong, and as we all know, the only thing that's a better story than a love story is a love story gone wrong." At this point, the tabloids assigned Diana her heroine role and began vilifying Charles in earnest. Lacking solid information about what was really going on, the tabloids relied on body language, hunches, and tips to launch a new wave of speculation about the Wales marriage. For five years, beginning in 1987, the press published what Jonathan Dimbleby called "a version of the facts . . . which bore more than a passing resemblance to reality," though many details were inaccurate.

The first significant clue came during an official visit to Portugal in February 1987, when the news leaked that Charles and Diana had taken separate rooms. Diana actually told Andrew Morton that the Portugal trip was "the last time we were close as man and wife," which seemed to contradict her other assertion that the marriage "closed off" and "went down the drain" after the birth of Harry. In the following months, the press tracked the amount of time the couple spent apart, culminating in a thirty-nine-day stretch at the end of the summer.

Charles had resumed shooting and hunting, the pursuits he had previously renounced to please Diana, and he took an increasing number of holidays on his own—several trips to Italy, four days in the Kalahari Desert, a retreat on a Hebridean island to herd sheep, long sojourns at Balmoral. These escapes into solitude for thinking and painting invariably prompted rebukes from Diana for abandoning her, and from the press for being a neglectful husband and father. After Diana and the boys returned to London from Scotland in September 1987, while Charles remained in Balmoral for three weeks on his own, some tabloid reports even hinted unfairly and incorrectly that Charles was having affairs with two of his guests, Kanga Tryon and Sarah Keswick, the wife of Sir Chippendale Keswick, chairman of Hambros Bank, who were friends of both Waleses.

With his fortieth birthday a year off, Charles went into full retreat, according to Dimbleby, "eclipsed by the Princess, resentful of the public adulation of her and wounded by the media's contempt for him." He became more temperamental, introverted, and gloomy—"I can't see a light at the end of a rather appalling tunnel at the moment," he wrote one friend in the fall of 1987—and relied even more on his friends, "unable to turn to his parents to discuss the misery either of his private life or his public persona," wrote Dimbleby. As Charles said, "When marriages break down, awful and miserable as that is . . . it is your friends who are most important and helpful and understanding and encouraging. Otherwise you would go stark, staring mad."

Instead of turning inward, like Charles, Diana began to acquire new friends and new activities. She took up tennis and tried to get Charles to build a court for her at Highgrove. When he refused—partly due to the expense, but also because a court would mar the aesthetic of his carefully planned gardens on the estate—she joined the exclusive Vanderbilt Racquet Club in London. For three years, she played a regular doubles game there with a group that included Antonia Douro, whose alliance with Camilla she had not yet discovered. Diana wasn't good at the sport, and as with so much she took on, she lacked the discipline to practice and improve her skills with lessons; her aim was more to socialize in a place where the photographers couldn't find her.

But Diana's private life revolved primarily around Hewitt, whose presence soothed her, although his usefulness as a safety valve only worked when they were together: "The very fact that she felt he relieved her of responsibility for herself meant that when he was not with her, her panic could grow worse than before," Pasternak wrote. "Sometimes her fear of coping with her own instabilities would grow so great, create such hysteria, that the only answer was to escape from herself. Then, she would frantically dial James's number, eager to hear him, anxious for him to calm her and restore her balance."

Diana's instability was particularly evident in May 1987, when she learned that her former lover Barry Mannakee had been killed in a motorcycle accident, just a year after he had been transferred out of his job with the Waleses. As the royal couple prepared to leave Kensington Palace for an evening at the Cannes Film Festival, Charles and members of the couple's staff learned about Mannakee's death. Charles told her about Mannakee when they were alone in their limousine en route to RAF Northolt, where they boarded their plane in private. On the flight to Cannes, Diana wept inconsolably as Charles and her lady-in-waiting tried to comfort her.

A report by Penny Junor that Diana "slashed herself" during the flight, requiring her dress for Cannes "to be adjusted to hide the damage," was an exaggeration, however. If Diana had mutilated herself, the wounds were not apparent to her staff, and the long gown she brought for the evening's festivities was singularly unadjustable: a pale-blue strapless chiffon that revealed her pristine arms, back, chest, and shoulders. She wore a matching pale-blue chiffon scarf draped softly across the nape of her neck and trailing down her back—not tied securely, as it might have been, to conceal telltale cuts. A small gust of wind or an inadvertent snag could have easily dislodged it.

The most striking aspect of Diana's behavior was her ability to put on a sunny facade as soon as she reached Cannes. In fact, she was ebullient that evening when she met TV personality Clive James, master of ceremonies for the dinner. "She was like the sun coming up," James wrote. "Coming up giggling." She mischievously flirted with James, laughing about the clips from Japanese game shows that he screened on his weekly program. "You are *terrible*," she teased, then rapidly changed the subject as she glimpsed media tycoon Robert Maxwell across the room. "Ooh. There's that odious man Maxwell over there. Don't want to meet *him* again. Yuck."

In the following weeks, Diana showed no evidence of lingering upset over Mannakee's death, nor did the tabloids learn of her distress during the trip to Cannes. But beginning early in 1987, they did get wind of a series of incidents involving Diana that, taken together, indicated a pattern of disconcerting public behavior, some of it involving other men. By her own admission, she was trying on a newly exuberant, Fergie-like identity, but she was displaying her confusion as well. The commotion Diana created proved irresistible to the press.

During a February ski holiday in Klosters, Diana and Fergie drew attention to themselves by jokingly pushing each other around on the ski slopes, causing the *Daily Mail* to pronounce the two women "undignified." In subsequent months, Diana blurted out to a group of reporters that she was thinking of taking a "black lover"; she smirked while reviewing a parade of cadets at Sandhurst; and, during Ascot, she and Fergie poked a rolled umbrella into the backside of Lulu Blacker, a friend of Fergie's.

But it was Diana's public flirtatiousness that drew the most pointed comment—beginning on her Klosters holiday, when "sexy" Diana danced at discos without "grumpy" Charles. Unknown to the press, Diana's bulimia had again become acute, and each evening in Klosters, she was calling James Hewitt to complain about her loneliness and declare how much she missed him.

Two of the men in Diana's company that winter became the subject of endless conjecture in the coming year: Guards Major David Waterhouse and banker Philip Dunne. Both were introduced to Diana by Sarah Ferguson, and they were part of the lively new set that formed around the Princess. Waterhouse and Dunne were solid establishment figures. Dunne's parents, Captain Thomas Dunne, Lord Lieutenant of Hereford and Worcester, and his wife, Henrietta, were great friends of the Queen. Dunne's sister Camilla, who also became friendly with Diana, married Nicholas Soames's brother Rupert. Waterhouse was the son of Hugo Waterhouse, a Life Guards major, and Lady Caroline Spencer-Churchill, the sister of the Duke of Marlborough and a friend of the Queen's as well.

The tabloids went into a frenzy over Diana's behavior with Philip Dunne during the wedding reception for the Marquess of Worcester and actress Tracy Ward in June 1987. Diana spent the evening dancing wildly with an assortment of partners including a "mystery fat man" later identified as David Ker, a happily married London art dealer. Most conspicuously, Diana danced with Dunne. According to the tabloids, she was seen "running her hand through [his] hair and planting a kiss on his cheek." Charles left the party at two A.M. ("stormed off" by one account, "in a huff" by another) after spending his time talking with former girlfriend Anna Wallace. Diana continued dancing until dawn, and for weeks afterward, the press went into overdrive probing the nature of her relationship with Dunne.

There was something almost too showy about subsequent sightings of Diana with Philip Dunne and David Waterhouse—at concerts, films, house party weekends, and fashionable London restaurants. She was deeply entangled with James Hewitt, and titillating press reports about a string of other men served as a convenient diversion. Still, as one of Diana's friends observed, "Diana lit a fire that occasionally burned out of control." The tabloids castigated Diana for being a "tease," a "flirt," and a "pampered princess" who "loves being the center of attention." The hacks also made life miserable for Dunne and Waterhouse, combing through their lives in forensic detail—to the point that Waterhouse declared to *The Sun,* "We are *not* having an affair."

Although the press paid greater attention to Dunne, perhaps because he was better looking, Diana was actually quite close to Waterhouse, who happened to be in James Hewitt's regiment. In his book on Charles, Dimbleby singled out Waterhouse among Diana's friends during this period as a "frequent visitor to Kensington Palace, arriving accompanied by his dog to spend long hours with the Princess." Waterhouse also visited Diana at Highgrove when Charles was away. Hewitt was jealous of Waterhouse, and Diana "repeatedly tried to reassure [Hewitt], telling him over and over that she and David were just friends," according to Pasternak.

The tabloids were so preoccupied by the Wales marriage that they barely acknowledged much of what Charles and Diana did in their official roles, which especially galled Charles, who grew less tolerant of Diana's fixation on her press coverage. His irritation at her distress over negative articles became a major source of friction between them. Charles refused to read what he considered rubbish—although aides gave him abridged briefings on the coverage—and accused Diana of encouraging the tabloids by paying such close attention to them. In a letter to a friend, Charles railed about the "positive hurricane of self-righteous, pontificating censorious claptrap in the newspapers."

By the autumn of 1987, both Diana and Charles were profoundly unhappy. They spent several weekends at Highgrove with Diana's mother, who helped persuade the couple to keep their marriage together and Diana to comport herself more properly in public. A group of advisers to Charles outlined the terms of a proposed truce: that the couple continue with separate but discreet social lives while they worked harder to present a united front through more joint engagements.

Diana later said she had her own epiphany that fall about the need to erase her image as "Disco Di," the femme fatale. After making what she called "so many cock-ups," she told herself, "Diana, it's no good, you've got to change it right round, this publicity. You've got to grow up and be responsible. . . . You must adapt to the position and stop fighting." Diana had decided to "rediscover the real Diana Spencer." She and Charles settled on an arrangement she described to astrologer Penny Thornton as giving each other a "comparatively civilized 'space' ": She would use Kensington Palace as her base, and he would use Highgrove as his.

The Waleses' new resolve was on display the following January during a trip to Australia for the country's two hundedth anniversary. "They were back in sparkling form for the first time in almost a year," the *Sunday Mir-*

ror declared. Diana took the trouble to learn Australia's national anthem, which she sang heartily, as Charles, who did not know the words, "glanced affectionately at his wife as he tapped along to the beat." James Hewitt, watching the royal couple on television as they danced together, felt mystified that Diana could seem so happy with the man he believed "she now hated with a vitriolic intensity."

The trip seemed to benefit Charles and Diana, at least temporarily; on their return to England they appeared to their staff more calm and civil in private than they had been. But for Diana, periods of peace couldn't last long: when she and Charles traveled to Klosters for their third skiing holiday in the Swiss resort, Diana's bulimia was again severe. She was on the phone constantly to Hewitt, who sensed her mood was "worse than her usual melancholy."

On the afternoon of March 10, 1988, Diana and Fergie were together in their chalet, Diana ill with a cold and Fergie, who was four months pregnant, recovering from a spill she had taken earlier in the day. During a run down some little-used slopes, Charles and his friends Hugh Lindsay and Patty Palmer-Tomkinson were caught in an avalanche. Charles escaped without injury, but Lindsay was killed, and Palmer-Tomkinson was gravely injured with multiple fractures.

Charles acted heroically, staying by Palmer-Tomkinson's side, digging her out of the snow with his hands, holding her head and talking nonstop to keep her conscious until the rescue helicopter arrived. But when he returned to the chalet he was shattered. As Diana recounted the day's events to Penny Thornton, she had offered to comfort Charles, but he wanted to grieve alone. Instead of accepting his reaction as the predictable way he would deal with such strong emotions, Diana felt rejected. "He just pushed me aside," Diana told Thornton, who recalled, "She felt that if Charles had fallen into her arms . . . their relationship would have turned round completely."

Diana took pride in the fact that she organized the logistics of their return to England. "I felt terribly in charge of the whole thing," she recalled. She insisted that they take Hugh Lindsay's body home immediately to his widow, overruling Charles's arguments for staying longer. Diana viewed her ability to make decisions and take control as a signal that she could fight Charles's effort to make her feel "so inadequate in every possible way."

The tabloids used the occasion to praise Diana and condemn Charles anew. IN THE MIDST OF GRIEF, OUR FUTURE QUEEN STOOD TALL, read the headline in the *Daily Express*. "We cried for Prince Charles, who wept for himself," the *Express* said. "But nobody patted Diana on the 26-year-old back she held so straight. . . . Unlike her husband, she hadn't been able to join in the struggle to save their friend. . . . Diana has suffered in silence from her apparently now emotionally frozen husband, who has turned less to her than into his own private grief . . . At Klosters she showed . . . inner strength."

The message could not have been lost on Diana, who read every word in the tabloids. In her own mythology, the Klosters tragedy took on outsize importance: "the beginning of a slow process of awakening to the qualities and possibilities which lay within herself," wrote Morton. Diana did deal effectively with people in distress, so her reaction to the accident was quite natural, just as those around her rose to the occasion. But her imagination magnified her actions to symbolize the confident and capable woman she wanted to be. After the weekend in Klosters, she was no more mature than she had been before, and her general behavior didn't perceptibly change, but she did feel she had achieved something, even if it was at Charles's expense.

Back in England with Hewitt, Diana wept and vented, and for the first time turned her anger toward her lover instead of Charles. She and Hewitt were at his mother's home in Devon for the weekend when she felt he was ignoring her during a lunchtime picnic. She lashed out, saying he had tired of her and considered her inadequate. When Hewitt explained that he was only trying to rest, she ran across the fields in a fury, and Hewitt didn't pursue her. She eventually returned in a sullen mood. Only after fulsome reassurance from Hewitt—she was the "most beautiful woman alive" and "of course he found her attractive"—did she settle down.

In recalling this period, Diana maintained that her years of bulimia had not affected her looks. She said that her skin hadn't been damaged, nor her teeth, despite years of acid from her forced vomiting. But by 1988, people had begun to notice that underneath heavy makeup, her complexion appeared rough and unhealthy. Those particular observations didn't make it into the tabloids, but after only glancing references to her figure for more than a year, the press began noting that she was again "painfully thin, almost gaunt."

In the spring of 1988, Diana "suddenly woke up and realized what I was going to lose if I let go." Her friend Carolyn Bartholomew actually jolted her awake by intervening with the sort of decisiveness Diana needed. After Diana finally confided in her old schoolmate about her bulimia, Carolyn warned that her gorging and purging were draining her system of vital minerals. Carolyn gave Diana an ultimatum: If she did not immediately call a doctor, Carolyn would call the press and tell them the entire story.

The threat worked. Diana phoned Dr. Maurice Lipsedge, a psychiatrist based at Guy's Hospital in London who dealt frequently with eating disorders. It had been five years since Diana had abandoned her last round of therapy, but she had a connection to Lipsedge, who had treated her sister Sarah. Diana was reassured by Lipsedge's combination of sympathy and directness; she considered him a "sweetheart, very nice." When he asked her how many times she had tried to commit suicide, she blithely told him "four or five." She agreed to his proposed treatment—an hour of talk therapy once a week, plus books to educate her on eating disorders. Lipsedge's approach seemed effortless to Diana, who recalled that he promised she would be better in six months if she learned to keep her food down.

Diana told Andrew Morton in her 1991 interviews that her therapy with Lipsedge made her feel "born again," and her bulimia had "finished" in 1989. In the next breath, she acknowledged that she still suffered from the symptoms in 1990 when she binged and purged every three weeks instead of four times daily. The sad reality was that Diana gave up on Lipsedge, as she had with her previous therapists, in a matter of months. The eating disorders persisted, along with her other symptoms of psychological problems.

Oddly enough, in the spring of 1988, no one seemed to fully consider the example of Diana's sister Sarah, who only overcame her eating disorder after checking herself into a clinic for a six-week stay. But residential treatment was not an option for Diana, who feared the stigma of being considered mentally ill, and whose high profile guaranteed that word of her condition would be leaked and sensationalized by the tabloids.

Chapter 14

INHERENTLY wary of psychiatry, Diana could not bring herself to make the long-term commitment required for effective therapy. But she knew she needed help dealing with her mood swings, depression, and self-destructive behavior, and after she dropped Maurice Lipsedge, she began shopping for easy salvation in the alternative-therapy bazaar.

"In the late eighties and early nineties she was with every different sort of person," a former Palace official said. "They marched in and out, and I don't know how they got there, but once you get into that scene, it's a cry for help." Diana sent confusing signals to her chosen "therapists," none of whom was trained to grasp the full extent of her problems; as in other areas of her life, she maintained tight control of these relationships. When she called, they jumped. "She'd never ask if she was disturbing me when she rang out of the blue," astrologer Debbie Frank said. Diana "tended to seek out people who would tell her what she wants to hear," astrologer Penny Thornton recalled. "Her instability makes it difficult for her to make rational decisions." Diana also lacked the analytical skills to determine whether her "healers" were doing her any good.

Diana's approach suggested a classic adult response to childhood neglect as described by psychologist Hugh Missildine, author of *Your Inner Child of the Past:* The behavior pattern, according to Missildine, includes moving "from one person to another, hoping that someone will supply whatever is missing," and feeling "restless and anxious" due to an inability to find emotional satisfaction. "Anyone who offers admiration and respect has appeal," Missildine noted, "and because [the] need for affection is so great, [the] ability to discriminate is severely impaired."

Diana had already begun her search in 1986 by consulting Thornton, and three years later, she added Debbie Frank. When Diana first called in

February 1989, Frank was surprised that the Princess "immediately began to pour out her troubles, as if she had known me all her life." This indiscriminate tendency of Diana's seemed inconsistent with her strong streak of mistrust, but in fact it showed how powerfully impulsive she could be. Two years later, Diana brought in still another astrologer named Felix Lyle, who felt that Diana was "easily defeated," "self-destructive," and unpredictable, although he underestimated her willfulness when he concluded that she was readily "dominated by those with a strong character."

Diana's view of astrologers was ambivalent, and she moved from one to another to find the answers she wanted. An overriding theme was whether she could win back Charles to revive her marriage. "What is going to happen to me? Will I ever be happy?" she would ask Frank, who, to her credit, urged Diana to "see a proper therapist." Diana relied on astrologers mostly when she was too uneasy with herself to make a decision on her own. "Diana believed in astrology," one of her friends said. "She opened up to the astrologers in a way she would not open up in a drawing room, where word could get around," another friend said. "Then if the astrologers betrayed her, she could dismiss them by saying they were just trying to make money off of her."

Diana said that she would listen to astrological predictions, but added that she didn't "believe [astrology] totally. It's a direction and a suggestion rather than it's definitely going to happen." But she seemed to have greater faith in astrology than she let on. "She was not ruled by every prophecy," Morton wrote, but "her belief [was] at times all-consuming." Diana invoked her astrologers in conversations, telling her friend James Gilbey (who shared her fascination with reading the stars) that Debbie Frank predicted he would "go through a transformation" and that the message to Diana from another astrologer was "anything you want you can get next year."

Diana was equally credulous with the spiritualists she embraced. Psychic Rita Rogers, who, like Penny Thornton, was referred by Fergie, recognized that Diana was "willful and capable of making up her own mind." Rogers tried to give Diana "inner strength" by connecting her to dead relatives and friends. Through Rogers and other clairvoyants, Diana believed she communicated with her grandmother Spencer—who looked out for her "in the spirit world"—as well as her uncle Edmund Fermoy and former lover Barry Mannakee. Still, Diana was reluctant to talk to friends and family about her spiritual contacts because she feared being branded a "nut."

Betty Palko, who did monthly tarot card readings, said that Diana "had deep emotional problems," but in her attempt to help, Palko reinforced Diana's insecurity. "I think the most important thing I used to say at a reading was to be careful in whom she placed her trust," Palko said. "I could see a lot of deceit around her at that time."

For four years, energy healer Simone Simmons made weekly visits to Diana. During their first session together, Simmons claimed to have extracted "truckloads of negative emotional waste" from Diana when she "analyzed her aura." While Simmons "rarely met anyone so greatly in need of physical and emotional repair," and routinely fielded eight-hour phone calls from the Princess, she felt that Diana "always seemed completely compos mentis to me."

Diana's spiritual advisers abetted her "magical thinking," another kind of primitive psychological defense that produced a false sense of power. Diana claimed to experience déjà vu when she encountered places she thought she had been before or people she had met in an earlier incarnation. "I know this sounds a bit crazy, but I've lived before," she told James Gilbey. By one account, she said that in a former life she had been a nun, and she told Penny Thornton that she had been a martyr in the time of Christ. She spoke of voices that pushed her to take certain actions or think certain thoughts, and she talked of having premonitions such as her "strange feeling" that her father would "drop down" the day before he suffered a stroke.

Diana also experimented with a variety of other nostrums. She used hypnotherapy to "visualize" her anger by "throwing it up an imaginary chimney and burning it"; "anger release" therapy, in which she would scream, shout, and pummel a punching bag; and most controversially, colonic irrigation, to "take all the aggro [aggression] out of me." According to Simone Simmons, Diana and Fergie would schedule their irrigation appointments together "so that they would be in different rooms of the same clinic at the same time and then giggle afterward." In effect, colonic irrigation was another form of purging, "a peculiar mixture of trying to get the bad things out and trying to get rapid transit to lose weight," in the view of eating disorder expert Kent Ravenscroft. Physicians take a dim view of the practice in the absence of medical supervision.

Diana suffered from back pain that may have been stress-related, and for treatment she turned again to alternative practitioners: an osteopath, who used massage, and a chiropractor, who manipulated her spine. For physical and mental solace, she used reflexology, a foot massage designed to reduce pain and tension in various parts of the body; aromatherapy massage, with aromatic oils; tai chi chuan, a slow-moving exercise to increase energy; and acupuncture, the ancient Chinese therapy in which needles are inserted in strategic spots to relieve pressure and pain. Acupuncture "helps me to keep calm and relax," Diana once said. "In my job I cannot afford to panic." Diana was least successful in her efforts to meditate; she was too fidgety to remain still.

Her principal "mind-body" therapist was Stephen Twigg, a onetime tax accountant who specialized in deep massage, diet consultation, and new-age advice based on problems he claimed to detect below the surface of the skin. When Twigg first came to Diana in December 1988, "she had reached a very low point indeed," he recalled. She had "intensely painful emotions and thoughts, muscular tension, digestive problems and other physical problems." He said he taught Diana how to "work her way out of the hole into which she had dug herself" and claimed to have ended her bulimia in 1992—although other therapists encountered the problem in subsequent years. Acupuncturist Lily Hua Yu treated Diana as late as 1996 for depression and "an eating disorder which in Chinese terms is caused by disharmony between the stomach and the spleen."

As Diana zigged and zagged through the world of alternative treatments, there is scant evidence that any of them actually eased her problems, with the possible exception of acupuncture, which research studies have shown to alleviate mild to moderate depression. At best, her range of treatments kept her occupied and distracted, offered any number of sympathetic listeners, and staved off her fear of losing control. Whatever extravagant claims her various healers may have made, Diana's symptoms carried through to the end of her life. Diana was vulnerable and gullible, and she leaned on her therapists as she did her friends and lovers, phoning them, as psychic Rita Rogers recalled, "just to tell me what she had been through that day." Astrologer Debbie Frank found Diana's manner in these frequent calls surprisingly childlike. "Most of all," Frank said, "she needed someone to talk to, to tell her problems to."

From the early eighties, when Diana first began exploring a public role, she had gravitated toward soothing the sick and dying, work that became a source of her own comfort as much as it was others'. When she would "support and love" people, she said, "they weren't aware just how much healing they were giving me, and it carried me through." It was often said that Diana "created a new royal role" by reaching out to victims and using her position to promote important causes, yet both her husband and his sister had long been similarly engaged, Charles with the disadvantaged in the inner cities, Anne with children in the Third World. Diana's impact was more a matter of style: her down-to-earth manner and heartfelt empathy contrasted with stiff royal formality. Diana had no grand plan to immerse herself deeply and build an expertise in one or several causes. Rather, she reacted to events and found views that she embraced passionately for a time before moving on. Though she had genuine feelings for these causes, her unstable temperament prevented her from sustaining her support—which often left those who counted on her disappointed and confused.

Diana's pursuit of a meaningful public role was bound up in her effort to understand who she was. "I want to feel I am needed," she said. "I want to do, not just be." As she strove to redefine herself, she frequently felt indecisive about which direction to take, succumbing to feelings of fraudulence for achieving celebrity when her actual achievements amounted to little. "She was up and down in terms of her morale and her self-worth," a former Palace official said. "She was sometimes confident, but sometimes unsure of her own abilities and her own worth, and had questions about her impact as a human being."

The turning point in Diana's public role occurred in April 1987, when she made an enormously symbolic gesture by shaking the hand of an AIDS patient without wearing a glove. Her work for AIDS awareness was a cornerstone of her official life, and her first step was typically described as an act of singular courage in her quest to help the outcasts of society. According to the prevailing mythology, Diana disregarded the advice of friends and defied Buckingham Palace courtiers by launching a crusade for a marginal disease associated with homosexuals. The *Sunday Express* called it "the toughest battle of her royal life" after "royal advisers . . . warned her it would harm her position as the future Queen."

In fact, her AIDS activities were carefully orchestrated and approved by the Palace, and her initial decision was motivated by personal considerations, rather than by an ambitious urge to take on a societal problem. The emotional tug of AIDS came from Diana's friendship with a London art dealer named Adrian Ward-Jackson, whom she met in London in the mid-eighties during a ballet gala performance at Sadler's Wells. Ward-Jackson was personable and erudite without being threatening. "He had a connoisseur's knowledge of ballet," said a man who was close to Ward-Jackson.

Around the time they became friends, Ward-Jackson learned he was HIV-positive, which he confided to Diana almost immediately, and she became interested in the disease. "He more or less said, 'It would be very nice if you would help me through this,' " a friend of Ward-Jackson said. "She said, 'Of course I will.' Sort of a pact was established before many of Adrian's friends knew he was HIV[-positive]." "Diana was a good friend of Adrian and also his partner Harry Bailey," said William Haseltine, an American research scientist and early advocate of AIDS education. "She was with them a lot before they deteriorated. Harry died first, and she knew very well Adrian had AIDS too."

In January 1987, Diana met Michael Adler, a London doctor working with AIDS patients, who asked if she would help him change the public perception of the disease. "She was very, very nervous," Adler said. "AIDS was still a very controversial disease." That month, Middlesex Hospital announced that Diana would open the first dedicated AIDS ward the following April. In describing Diana's task, Adler requested that she wear no protective clothing, such as a surgical mask or gown, but assured her that she would be in no danger. "We hope if people see the Princess of Wales opening the ward it will help to demystify and destigmatize AIDS," Adler said at the time.

A few weeks later, the *Daily Mirror* ran a story quoting a doctor named Graham Sharp, who said, "Princess Diana should shake hands with an AIDS sufferer" in order to allay public fears about how the disease is transmitted. This was a period of widespread fear about catching the disease by touching, sharing a swimming pool, or sitting across a dinner table; there were even suggestions that those infected with the virus be quarantined. A simple handshake with someone of Diana's stature could indeed have important consequences.

Adler proposed to Buckingham Palace that she not only shake the hand of an AIDS patient, but that her gesture be photographed. "It was highly programmed and rehearsed," Adler said. "We were concerned about patient confidentiality and privacy, so we ran a proposal past the Palace, and we agreed on a photo over the patient's left shoulder, with only one pool photographer [designated to supply pictures to all the newspapers]. So the whole thing was set up, and it was not a relaxed visit, not spontaneous. I don't think Diana knew what she was taking on when it was agreed she would do this. Suddenly she found herself at the center of attention in an area that was controversial, with people who were marginalized." The photograph had a worldwide impact, and profoundly affected Diana: "I found myself being more and more involved with people who were rejected by society . . . and I found an affinity here."

By 1988, after the truce between Charles and Diana took effect, and Diana decided to "grow up and be responsible," the tabloids started to focus on the latest manifestation of a "new Diana." "The caring princess has thrown herself fully into her work," *Today* reported in May 1988. Four months later, Georgina Howell, in *The Sunday Times,* proclaimed "a cooler and more independent Princess of Wales," followed by the *Daily Mail*'s Richard Kay, who announced the "fully fledged emergence of a new princess" eager to express opinions with a "confidence and maturity that have surprised observers."

Diana had still done little public speaking, confining herself to brief remarks that she hurried through in a breathy monotone. When Turning Point, a patronage of Diana's devoted to treating drug and alcohol abuse, asked her to speak at their conference in May 1989, she sought coaching from Richard Attenborough, the film director who had prepared her for the 1985 interview with Alastair Burnet. Attenborough helped Diana cast the speech in her own idiom, and she spent several days rehearsing each phrase, replaying her words on a tape recorder to hone her delivery. Diana spoke for all of six minutes about the damage alcohol and drug addiction can do to families, saying at one point, "the line between recreational use and creeping addiction is perilously thin." In keeping with the tabloids' customarily lavish praise for Diana, Richard Kay of the *Daily Mail* called her talk "remarkable."

Behind the hyperbole, Diana was actually showing signs of progress in her public duties. She was working harder—250 engagements in 1988, compared with 153 for Fergie and 665 for Princess Anne—and she showed a greater willingness to do the necessary preparation. She still couldn't absorb complex documents, but she paid closer attention to the materials prepared by her staff. "Reading briefing papers was not her idea of fun," a former Palace official said, "but she had a natural street wisdom, and a natural intelligence to ask the right questions." She had also learned how to turn to her advantage aspects of her personality that others might have seen as defects. An avid viewer of TV soap operas such as *Coronation Street*, she would talk about the shows during her public engagements: "I say, 'Did you see so and so?' 'Wasn't it funny when this happened or that happened?'" By making such connections, Diana tried to break down the barrier between royalty and ordinary people and move "immediately" to "the same level."

Another courtier who worked with her recalled her visiting an AIDS ward. "She was very good. Most people would think, 'I have an hour, what in the world do I say?' I would say, 'There are five who are nearly dead, and you can't talk to them; six with relatives; eight more who are in pretty good shape,' and so on. She would then calibrate everything and know how much time to spend with each of them so that she would fill the hour."

She also made a greater effort to keep herself informed about her charities. "I would have an ongoing thing of seeing her and telling her what was going on with AIDS," Michael Adler said. "After a conference, I would tell her about it. She didn't ask penetrating questions, but she was strong when she was feeling a person's problems." William Haseltine, who briefed her about AIDS as well, said she "fulfilled her public function perfectly. When she was on, she did what she was supposed to do, was knowledgeable and friendly and chatty and warm but proper."

The key to engaging Diana's attention was ensuring she had an emotional connection to an issue. "I used to write her the most outrageous briefing notes," said Vivienne Parry, the national organizer of Birthright, the research group concerned with preventing premature births. "I knew that if I wrote 'So and so was chairman of the finance committee 1979 to 1983,' those details would mean nothing, so I wrote character sketches of people, which gave me enormous pleasure, as it did her when she was able to come up with some small personal detail when she was talking to somebody, and the person just lit up and glowed with pleasure because here was the Princess of Wales remembering a detail about them."

Diana had strong feelings about other causes that she took on in the late eighties: drug and alcohol abuse, the hospice movement, mentally handicapped children, leprosy, and most intriguingly, marriage counseling. In 1988, Diana began visiting centers operated by Relate, a counseling group for troubled couples. She sat in on sex therapy sessions, played the role of an overwrought mother, and expressed an interest in working with couples facing divorce. "She was totally involved," said Rose Spurr of the Bristol branch of Relate after Diana's role-playing. It was no small irony that she and Charles had not engaged in marital counseling themselves, and Diana gave all the appearance of trying to educate herself through her work with Relate. She even kept a copy of the *Relate Guide to Marital Problems* on her bedside table.

During these years Diana's unusual rapport with strangers, including those with deformities and terminal diseases, became more evident. Through a combination of natural warmth and curiosity about people, the gentle use of touch, and her laserlike intensity, Diana could make instant connections. "Some people find it very difficult to confront people who are seriously disabled," said Roger Singleton of Barnardo's. "It's something she takes on board in a very direct and open way." Father Alexander Sherbrooke, a Catholic priest who was a friend of Diana's, said he had to prepare himself intellectually before he could visit the sick and dying. Diana, by contrast, "was completely intuitive and saw something special in every human being."

Over the years, Diana came to believe she had a special healing power after watching her effect on others. "She did have a powerful persona," Michael Adler said. "You could believe she felt she had a magic touch, and in a sense she did. She had real qualities. She absolutely had a heart." "Her charisma was not normal," one of Diana's close friends said. "Her visits would bring light into sick people's lives, and they felt better." This friend recounted the time Diana visited a man who had been wounded by a land mine: "He changed while she was there. He had been hugely depressed, curled up in bed, but when she left he was so happy. Since then he went up and up. He was happy she had singled him out."

Diana's complicated temperament added a psychological component to her interaction with sufferers. Her uncanny empathy grew out of her tenuous sense of herself. She could shed her own troubles, compensating for her own emptiness, by losing herself in others' traumas—in effect, she could "be" another person, if only momentarily—even as she delivered the sort of compassion she desperately wanted for herself. This was the positive extreme of Diana's sensitive personality; at other times, she couldn't fill her emptiness in a constructive way, and would feel abandoned. Imagining that others were thinking the worst of her, she would react with panic or anger.

Diana could visibly strengthen while comforting those even more fragile than she. "This morning I arrived in a filthy mood," she once told Christopher Spence, president of the London Lighthouse, but after visiting the dying patients, she said, "I'm leaving on top of the world." One of her friends remembered accompanying Diana to a hospital ward when "an Indian gentleman had a major heart attack, and his family were there, not knowing what to do. Diana took control and said 'You sit next door, you go in, do this.' She had a natural sense of authority."

In such situations, Diana displayed a false maturity, because, as her astrologer Debbie Frank pointed out, "She often felt powerless to do anything when it came to her own life." In a hospital, "she knew exactly what to do and say," said her friend Cosima Somerset. "It was all right when she had a role. But in social situations she didn't find it easy." Most of her empathy was directed at those she felt closer to than her social peers: children, the elderly, social outcasts, and the dying, whom she found "more open and more vulnerable and much more real than other people."

Diana had become the "caring princess" whose image plastered the tabloids almost daily. But as press approval of Diana soared, the image of her friend Fergie collapsed. Although Diana and Fergie often showed affection for each other, their relationship was strained by rivalry: Diana dominated the tabloid front pages unless Fergie did something outrageous.

The hacks had pinned the blame on Fergie for Diana's reckless behavior in 1987, and by the end of that year, the Duchess of York, by her own admission, "was declared a loser." As Fergie recalled, Diana's rehabilitation "opened a vacancy on Fleet Street for 'the bad royal.'" Behavior that had previously been lauded as refreshing and exuberant became "appalling . . . crass, rude, raucous and bereft of all dignity," Fergie said. She was mocked mercilessly for being overweight, most memorably in the cruel headline DUCHESS OF PORK! Fergie's troubles were compounded in mid-1988 when her father was caught in a London massage and sex parlor.

Prince Andrew was away much of the time in the navy (by Fergie's tally, he came home only forty-two days a year), and she was stuck living in a gloomy Buckingham Palace apartment "as cozy and personal as a railway hotel." Besides his £35,000 salary from the Royal Navy, the Yorks depended entirely on the largesse of the Queen and Prince Philip. Diana and Charles, on the other hand, lived independently on £1 million in annual disposable income from the Duchy of Cornwall—128,000 acres of land in nine counties that included 1,500 dwellings in London, administered solely for the benefit of the Prince of Wales. Charles also had income from more than £2 million in investments that he had accumulated over the years, using unspent income from the Duchy.

"Sarah should have lived the life of a naval officer's wife in Dorset, made a home there and done a few things, but instead she wanted to emulate Diana," a former Palace official said. "There was a lot of jealousy. Diana was able to live a more exotic life and have what she wanted." Sarah tried to keep up, said the courtier, "by going on one spending spree after another, and [she] resented the powers who were trying to restrain her spending." Fergie was amassing a debt that would eventually run well into six figures, and she was battling Palace aides she called the "gray men" who disapproved of not only her spending habits, but her "hopelessly erratic" behavior. To further complicate matters, her chief adversary became Robert Fellowes, private secretary to the Queen, who was both her father's first cousin and Diana's brother-in-law. "Robert Fellowes would come into Fergie's office and slam down the papers and say, 'We haven't done very well today,' " said a friend of Fellowes.

Diana began to realize that Fergie's jealousy sometimes translated into disloyalty. In a conversation with her friend James Gilbey, Diana called Fergie "the redhead," and noted that she was "actually being quite supportive . . . I don't know why." Recalled another friend of Diana's, "I remember Fergie and Prince Andrew coming to a dinner when there was a lot of talk about the York marriage, and Fergie saying, 'If only they knew what is happening at Kensington Palace.' " By the late 1980s, Diana's suspicions that Fergie took advantage of their friendship prompted her to pull away. Diana knew, according to one of her friends, "the Fergie association brought criticism, and she couldn't take any more criticism."

Chapter 15

AFTER his 1987 truce with Diana, Charles could more freely take separate holidays—Africa for safaris, Italy and Turkey for painting, Switzerland for skiing, along with his usual interludes at various royal residences—and Diana began to do the same, traveling to Italy and the Caribbean. Since they irritated each other if they were together for any extended period, Charles and Diana structured their schedules to minimize the time they would both be at Highgrove or Kensington Palace. They showed scant interest in each other's activities, and their phone conversations focused primarily on William and Harry. Sometimes they would let weeks go by without talking, and when they happened to sit down over a meal, Diana might well leave in tears.

Diana's moods continued to fluctuate. Although she would seem resigned to their arrangement, at times she disintegrated into resentment and anger. She absorbed yet another emotional blow in June 1988, when she learned that her mother and stepfather were divorcing. Peter Shand Kydd left Frances for another woman, which so shattered Frances that it took her four years to recover. "I was very bad about getting my act together, it took a long time," she said later. Frances blamed unrelenting tabloid scrutiny as the principal factor. "The media descended on [Diana] . . . and have never left me since," she said. "I think the pressure of it all was overwhelming and finally impossible for Peter. . . . I became Di's mum and not his wife. You could say the marriage wasn't strong enough in the first place, but that's rather like saying the house wasn't strong enough after a hurricane has gone past."

When Diana and Charles made an official visit to France in November, they put on an adroit performance of public amicability. Diana showed her seriousness about AIDS research by visiting the Pasteur Institute, and her beauty and style enchanted the French. "You have seduced every man in France," said Jacques Chirac, the mayor of Paris. Diana delighted the tabloid hacks by performing an impromptu "sexy dance" for Charles after dinner in a French chateau, when she started "wiggling her hips and shim-mying until both she and her husband dissolved with laughter." Still, for a change, it was Charles's statesmanship that dominated the headlines. "We got the balance right," a staff member said. The tabloids were upbeat about what one paper called a "triumphant tour" that included a "romantic" can-dlelit dinner cruise on the Seine. Three years after the fact, the *Mirror*'s James Whitaker finally reported that the riverboat cruise had actually been a "disaster." There had been a "sourness in the air," he wrote, and Charles and Diana had "never once looked at one another all evening."

In mid-November, 1988, the Waleses were together again for Charles's fortieth birthday ball at Buckingham Palace. Diana managed to include James Hewitt among the three hundred guests, and he spent the evening stewing because he couldn't get near her. He thought she put up a "valiant front," and he felt jealous every time he saw her dancing or laughing with friends. Finally, Hewitt captured her for one dance, which they carried off by feigning indifference.

Clive James met Diana that evening for the second time and noticed a change from their first encounter at Cannes, eighteen months earlier. James was well aware that Charles and Diana "were sticking together for the sake of the monarchy and the children, but were otherwise going their separate ways." Although Diana was cordial enough, James saw that "the lights in her face were dimmed down to about three-quarter strength. . . . She was still there physically, but her soul had gone AWOL, and without that soul, the party had no life."

The following month, masseur Stephen Twigg began trying to help Diana deal with her "painful emotions and thoughts." By then, Diana had redoubled her fixation on Camilla. With no discernible provocation, Diana had become vocal about her rival, speaking openly about her to friends and staff. Diana's initial consultation with astrologer Debbie Frank early in 1989 was primarily to deal with the "presence of Camilla," Frank said. "It became a complete obsession," a former Palace official said. "It was all anger against Camilla. 'How dare she do this?' " If that anger happened to flare up before a public engagement, Diana's aides had to work fast. "She would get into the car all steamed up," a former Palace adviser said. "I would try to calm her down. You just absorbed it. You would listen, sympathize, you would agree, or disagree, and she would eventually calm down."

Diana decided to meet the enemy face-to-face that February when she and Charles were invited to a fortieth birthday party for Camilla's sister Annabel Elliot at the home of billionaire tycoon James Goldsmith and his wife, Annabel. The invitation had been sent with the expectation that only Charles would come, but at the last minute, Diana opted to join him because "a voice inside me said, 'Go for the hell of it.' " Perhaps she was emboldened by the trip she had recently made to New York, her first official solo visit overseas. Before her arrival, the *New York Post* had called her "the most famous welfare mother in the world," and *Women's Wear Daily* had pronounced the visit "out." Three days later, Diana overcame the skepticism by balancing a charity gala with tours of a Bowery homeless shelter and Harlem Hospital, where she hugged a toddler dying of AIDS. At the end, the New York tabloids were calling her DI-VINE.

Before making her final decision about the Goldsmith party, Diana consulted James Hewitt, who urged her to go, on the grounds that she should "hold her head high." Diana later said she concluded that she would "come away having done her bit." In the car, en route to the party, Diana recalled, Charles "needled me the whole way . . . needle needle needle." The Goldsmiths' house on Ham Common in Richmond was filled with friends of Charles and Camilla, and Diana felt instantly out of place. Still, Diana "looked ravishing, and charmed everyone. She was full of energy," one guest said. After dinner, Diana noticed that Charles and Camilla had disappeared. She sat for a while with two of Charles's friends, Christopher Balfour, chairman of Christie's Europe, and Rick Beckett, whose wife was the sister of David Waterhouse. After more than an hour, Diana decided to go to the downstairs dining room to locate Charles.

When she spotted Charles, Camilla, and another friend, Diana joined the conversation "as if we were all best friends." Diana recalled asking the two men if she could speak privately to Camilla. Charles and his friend headed upstairs, where Annabel Goldsmith intercepted Charles and took him on a tour of paintings by her daughter Jane Birley. Charles politely followed, but it was clear that he was edgy and eager to return downstairs.

By Diana's account, she told Camilla that she "wasn't born yesterday" and was well aware of the affair. Diana said she realized she was "in the way," but she resented that Charles and Camilla treated her like an unknowing "idiot." Her approach to Camilla that evening wasn't aggressive, Diana recalled, but "calm, deathly calm." Shortly afterward, Charles and several others returned to find Diana and Camilla sitting at the table together. "There was not a ripple," one guest said. Diana and Charles left shortly afterward, and according to Diana, Charles reprimanded her in the car.

"It was . . . seven years' pent-up anger," she recalled. "I cried and cried and cried." After a sleepless night, Diana still felt anger and jealousy, but not as intensely as the previous evening. Several days later, Diana told Charles that, in the conversation with Camilla, "I just said I loved you."

When one of Diana's friends asked her about the encounter soon after the party, she related a less dramatic but more poignant version. "Diana said that not much happened," her friend said. "She said she more or less said humbly to Camilla, 'What am I doing wrong? What is wrong with me? What makes him want to be with you and not me?' " Said Diana's friend, "She was desperate to get him back, and she didn't know how to do it."

It didn't seem to occur to Diana that her anger at Camilla might be inconsistent with her own romance with James Hewitt, to whom she gave a detailed account of the Goldsmith party the following day. After more than two years, Diana's affair with Hewitt had settled into its own rhythm that depended entirely on Diana's emotional state: "For a few weeks she would feel better, exhilarated, with newfound health," wrote Pasternak, "and then it was as if she had pushed herself too far too soon, and suddenly her reserves were depleted," and "she would sink back into what seemed a deeper trough than before."

The principal difference between Charles's romance with Camilla and Diana's with Hewitt was that Diana kept Hewitt tightly under wraps. Diana could preserve secrecy because he was not from her world, while Camilla was part of Charles's social set. Still, it was remarkable that Hewitt repeatedly visited Kensington Palace and Highgrove, and dined with Diana at the San Lorenzo restaurant, without being detected. Diana did flirt with danger, however, when she invited Hewitt to Raine Spencer's sixtieth birthday party at Althorp in May 1989.

With five hundred guests, the dance was large enough for Hewitt to get lost, and Prince Charles didn't come. But Diana was considerably more reckless than she had been at Charles's fortieth. She took Hewitt for a guided tour of Althorp, and then danced, talked, and drank champagne with him. At the end of the evening, she led him out to the pool house, where they made love. Once again, nothing appeared in the press, and their romance remained sub-rosa.

Toward the end of 1989, Hewitt was posted to Germany for a two-year hitch. When he broke the news to Diana, she was upset, and begged him not to leave. He explained that he had to follow his career, but Diana viewed it as abandonment. She stopped returning his phone calls, although after he went to Germany, she resumed calling him.

Historian Paul Johnson, a friend and fan of Diana's, once compared her to a seventeenth-century beauty named Madame de Chevreuse, paraphrasing a description in the *Memoirs of Cardinal de Retz*: "She loved with an everlasting love but was always changing its object." With James Hewitt off in

Germany, Diana was ready to change objects when she was reunited with a car dealer from the Gilbey gin family, whom she had originally known when she first came to London. At age thirty, James Gilbey was slender and handsome, his dark brown hair starting to recede from his forehead.

In the summer of 1989, Diana and Gilbey were guests at a thirtieth-birthday party in Berkshire for their mutual friend Julia Samuel. According to one of her friends, Diana was disconcertingly out of sorts that night. "She was miserable," her friend said. "Gilbey was just coming on the scene, and Diana was very edgy. You'd have thought she'd be dancing. All her friends were there, and Charles was not. But she sat at a table with her sister Jane." According to Andrew Morton, who enlisted Gilbey's cooperation for his book with Diana's permission, Diana and Gilbey eventually got together during the Samuel party and talked about "their respective love lives . . . he about a failed romance, she about her fading marriage."

Diana and Gilbey started to see each other over the following months. They often met at San Lorenzo as Diana had with Hewitt, assisted by the restaurant's owner Mara Berni. In late October, the *Sunday People* blew Diana's cover by reporting that she had been seen on a "secret late date," ducking into Gilbey's apartment building in London's chic Lennox Gardens. A flustered Gilbey acknowledged that Diana had visited him but insisted that she was part of a bridge group. "It's very hard for the Princess to keep up any of her old friendships," he said. "It's given me a lot of grief." After besieging him for several days, the hacks backed off, and the relationship went underground.

In December 1989, under circumstances that remain unclear, telephone conversations between Diana and Gilbey, as well as Charles and Camilla, were tape-recorded and later passed along to several London newspapers. Both conversations are filled with embarrassing sexual innuendo, and both offer snapshots of the state of the Wales marriage. Gilbey was speaking on a mobile phone to Diana on New Year's Eve at Sandringham, where she was spending yet another unhappy holiday with the royal family. They gossiped about mutual friends, compared horoscope readings, and spoke irreverently of the royal family. Most strikingly, they conversed with easy intimacy as he repeatedly called her "darling," "honey," and "Squidgy." They blew kisses into the phone, said they missed each other, and at one point lapsed into phone sex when they each referred to "playing with yourself."

Gilbey took the lead in making suggestive remarks, and Diana concurred ("I love it" to Gilbey's "This sort of feeling. Don't you like it?") or briefly commented. "I had the most amazing dream about us last night. Not physical, nothing to do with that," said Gilbey. Cracked Diana, "That makes a change." When Gilbey said, "I'm wrapping you up, protecting you," Diana responded "Yes, please." As they discussed meeting two days later, both said they wanted to "fast-forward" to the moment when he would be "just holding you so close to me." Diana, who by all accounts no longer had a physical relationship with Charles, also told Gilbey, "I don't want to get pregnant," and mentioned an episode of the soap opera *East-enders* in which one of the main characters "had a baby. They thought it was by her husband. It was by another man."

The tone of their banter was affectionate (she told him he was "the nicest person in the whole wide world") and flippant (he called her "old Bossy Boots" and complimented her on the "shit-hot" pink top she wore in a tabloid picture) more than seriously passionate. Even Diana's "all the love in the world" before hanging up had the lighthearted note of the "lots of love" sign-off commonly used among friends. Not surprisingly, Diana maintained control as Gilbey reflexively reassured and complimented her: "You don't need to encourage me to think about you. I have done nothing else for the last three months. . . . That smile comes on and the charm comes out. . . . Underneath there is such a beautiful person in you. . . . *You* make people happy. It's what you give them."

The conversation opened a few small windows into Diana's character. She showed her skill at deception, concocting various cover stories: To explain her phone calls, she told Gilbey, "Say one of your relations is not very well, and your mother is just ringing in to give you progress." To justify her trip to London to see Gilbey, she said, "I shall tell people I'm going for acupuncture and my back being done." She just as casually dissembled to Gilbey when he asked, "You don't mind it, darling, when I want to talk to you so much?" and she replied, "No, I *love* it. Never had it before." She also revealed her preoccupation with her newspaper image after Gilbey pointed out the day's tabloid photos and she replied, "I'm always smiling, aren't I? I thought that today."

She was especially revealing when she displayed the extent of her bitterness toward the royal family. Christmas at Sandringham that year had been typically fractious. Diana told Gilbey that she had nearly broken down at lunch when feelings of sadness overtook her: "I thought, 'Bloody hell, after all I've done for this fucking family.' " She spoke of wanting to do "something dramatic because I can't stand the confines of this marriage," and she recounted a drive in the car with Charles in which they barely spoke to each other. "It's just so difficult," she said, "so complicated. He makes my life real torture, I've decided."

Clearly Diana and Gilbey were on intimate terms, although two people who were close to her said that it wasn't a full-blown love affair. One called it a "flirtatious relationship," and the other said, "I know it sounded bad on the tape, but they were very good friends." Diana confirmed the authenticity of the conversation in her *Panorama* interview, but she denied an "adulterous relationship" with Gilbey, while admitting her affair with Hewitt. "Of course they had a romance," another close friend of Diana's said. "Gilbey was attractive to her. Why she admitted [her relationship with] Hewitt was bizarre. He was the most sacrificial one, from outside the circle. Also, he had already spilled in his own book."

Charles's tape-recorded phone conversation with Camilla, which had taken place several weeks earlier on December 18, 1989, was only a third as long as what became known as the "Squidgy" tape. It had none of Diana's rancor, some of Gilbey's goofy sexual playfulness, and considerably more sexual passion. Aside from Charles's infamous musings about living in Camilla's trousers or spending his life as a tampon, he and Camilla spoke in more explicitly sexual terms: of filling her up, and of pressing her "tit." "God, I wish I was," Charles said, "harder and harder."

Their expressions of longing were anguished, and they frequently voiced their abiding love for each other. Camilla took care to prop up Charles's ego ("Those sort of people do feel very strongly about you") and Charles to express gratitude for Camilla's love and loyalty ("You suffer all these indignities and tortures and calumnies"). Like Diana and Gilbey, Charles and Camilla spoke almost clinically about ways to organize their subterfuges: which homes of friends they should use for rendezvous, how long they needed to travel, whom they could and could not trust.

Around the time of these conversations, the tabloids elevated the Princess of Wales to "Saint Diana." She and Charles had recently been to Indonesia, where Diana had visited her first leprosy mission. "Faced with the horror of leprosy," wrote the *Sunday Mirror*, Diana "shook a little girl's hand" and showed "no hesitation as she grasped the gnarled, bent fingers of the patients," "touched the bloody bandages of an old man," and "stroked a woman's arm."

In one respect, the following year was "fulfilling" for Diana, as she told Gilbey her astrologer had predicted. The tabloids continued to gush about her at Charles's expense. Diana, noted the *Daily Express* in July 1990, "turns a blind eye to . . . how incredibly selfish Prince Charles is." They wrote extravagantly of her "star quality" and good deeds. The few criticisms of Diana tended to be trivial: a flurry of comment over her new short "heatwave hairstyle" (though only the *Daily Star* called it a "disaster"), and Andrew Morton's report that she spent £100,000 a year on clothing, which she dismissed as "ill-informed." Otherwise, Diana had little to complain about.

The Buckingham Palace staff had even begun to relax somewhat about the Wales marriage. As one said, "We all felt things were not well, but that it would either get better, or they would develop a modus vivendi, make compromises." But in June 1990, circumstances changed for the worse after Charles suffered a serious accident playing polo. He fractured his right arm in two places, which left him in such agony that he required a second operation in September to pin the bones and prevent crippling.

During his four-month convalescence at Highgrove and Balmoral, Charles was frustrated by his inactivity and worn down by his pain. Diana sat by his bedside during his hospital stays, but she spent little time with him at Highgrove and none in Scotland. According to Penny Thornton, Diana felt that Charles had "brushed aside" her efforts to offer him affection and care, and she knew Camilla was filling that role. Camilla was a frequent visitor to Highgrove, as were his other close friends, including Nicholas Soames, the Palmer-Tomkinsons, van Cutsems, and Romseys, who spent hours cheering up Charles.

For the most part, Camilla was mentioned as just one of many friends who rallied around to help Charles "snap out of the gloom." A long excerpt in *The Sunday Times* that September from a new Andrew Morton book called *Diana's Diary* even put a positive gloss on the Wales marriage. According to Morton, Diana had found "an affectionate accommodation within her marriage. . . . Divorce is not an option. . . . The royal couple have reached a friendly alliance. . . . Understanding companionship has supplanted mutual indifference. . . . Their marriage is based on trust."

Yet newspaper editors were aware of Charles's affair with Camilla. Early in 1990, the *News of the World* had received "blackmail-style notes" containing details of alleged meetings between Prince Charles and Camilla. The notes, always hand-delivered, were either stenciled or made with letters and words cut out of newspapers. Partly for legal reasons, partly out of restraint, the tabloid declined to pursue these mysterious leads, as did the mainstream *Telegraph* when it was given information about the affair in a more straightforward fashion.

"I knew about Charles and Camilla," said Max Hastings, then editor of *The Daily Telegraph,* despite "a concerted effort by the Prince of Wales's people to deny it. At one point, a friend of the Prince's said to me, 'You have to get your mind around the fact that there is only one woman in the Prince's life, and that is Camilla.' This was in 1990, when everyone knew there was trouble, but there was still no idea of a divorce."

In November 1990, the Waleses traveled to Japan for what a former Palace official termed a "brilliant visit. Diana was back on top, and she was radiant." But her private torment continued. Over the Christmas holidays she wept frequently and screamed at Charles, to the point that their staff worried she might be suicidal.

As it turned out, Diana had a lot on her mind. One immediate worry re-sulted from some alarming news she had recently heard about her New Year's Eve chat with Gilbey. Earlier in 1990, *The Sun* had been handed a tape-recording of the conversation. Stuart Higgins, then an editor at the paper, oversaw the verification of the tape. "We went through the various people mentioned," Higgins said, "and at some point we confronted Gilbey. We were never one hundred percent confirmed, but the circum-stantial evidence made it inconceivable that it was not Diana and Gilbey." Fearful of the damage that disclosure of the conversation could do, Rupert Murdoch and his lieutenants decided to keep the tape in a safe. "I was con-vinced it was authentic," Higgins said. "Other powers were at work to en-sure we kept it under wraps"—which is where it would remain for more than two-and-a-half years.

Murdoch's top executive, Andrew Knight, chairman of News Interna-tional, was primarily responsible for keeping the lid on the Gilbey tape and other stories about the Wales marriage that had come over the transom. Besides the Camilla blackmail notes, *News of the World* had a story about Diana's affair with James Hewitt based on revelations by Lance Corporal Malcolm Leete, Hewitt's disaffected valet. "Patsy Chapman, the editor, wanted to publish the Hewitt story on at least a half-dozen occasions," Knight recalled. "I said absolutely not. I didn't believe it. Patsy told me she had the story that Hewitt had been Diana's lover, and she could stand it up. I said, 'I don't like the sound of it, and we are not publishing it.' As time went by, it became harder to resist, and on the last occasion we didn't pub-lish, I had to get Rupert Murdoch's help in stopping the story."

There is no indication that Diana caught wind of the Leete tale, but she did hear of the Gilbey tape. "Diana certainly knew the contents and had seen a transcription, but I cannot say how," Stuart Higgins said. "It was probably sometime in late 1990 or early 1991 that she learned about it, as we were corroborating the authenticity." By then, another copy of the tape had made its way to Richard Kay of the *Daily Mail.* Kay had contacted "someone very close" to Diana, who authenticated her voice. Kay then con-sulted his editors, who agreed they shouldn't disclose it. Kay "put it away, thinking it would never appear in a British paper." Still, Diana knew that the Gilbey tape couldn't stay hidden forever, and she wanted the story of Charles and Camilla to come out first, but she couldn't quite figure out how to accomplish her goal.

James Gilbey was still in the picture for Diana, but James Hewitt was very much in her thoughts. Since Iraq's invasion of Kuwait the previous

August, she had become overwrought about the situation in the Persian Gulf, mostly for fear that Hewitt might be sent into battle. By January 1991, as the United States, Britain, and other allies prepared for war with Iraq, Diana was tuning in to news bulletins on radio and television whenever she had a chance. Throughout the autumn, she had been calling Hewitt in Germany, and when he returned to England briefly before Christmas, they resumed their intimacy during a reunion at Highgrove, when he gave her a pair of emerald-and-diamond earrings.

After Hewitt flew to the Gulf, Diana began writing letters to him, addressed to "Dearest James," "Darling James," or "My darling James," and signed "Diana," "D," "Julia," or "Susie." Diana wrote once or twice a day, sometimes four times: "long, flowing letters over endless sheets of paper," according to Pasternak, who saw them. "Every thought that flooded into her mind poured onto the pages. She held nothing back." It was the same kind of unbridled outpouring with which she had responded to stress in childhood and adolescence.

During the bombing of Iraq and the subsequent ground war, Diana was glued to the television coverage, staying up all night to catch news about Hewitt's unit. She read about military strategy, spent many evenings by herself at Kensington Palace, prayed in church, and even visited Hewitt's mother in Devon. In her letters to Hewitt, Diana described the despair brought on by her solitude, but assured him that she was "finally trying to understand herself." Somewhat more ominously, she said she felt frantic that "the truth about Charles and Camilla . . . had not become public knowledge." If it did, she said, she believed people might understand her better. Diana constantly vacillated in her thinking about her marriage, from saying she hated Charles and could not bear being in the same room with him to wanting him to beg her forgiveness and start over.

Diana no longer seemed willing to acquiesce to the truce she had struck with Charles three years earlier. She told Hewitt that she could not stand the deception and that she had given Charles an ultimatum: "Something had to be done about their marriage." Indeed, according to Fergie, to whom Diana had again grown close as they both struggled with marital problems in 1991, "we first put the words to the unspeakable idea . . . that one or both of us might leave the royal family. We burned the phone wires into the night trading secrets . . . that no one else would understand."

Diana's affair with James Hewitt was seriously compromised that February when Nigel Dempster disclosed that she had "cause for concern" because her "good friend" James Hewitt was stationed in the Gulf—the first public mention of Hewitt. Dempster revealed that Hewitt had not only taught Diana how to ride, he had joined her "on picnics or for tea while at Windsor Castle when the Prince of Wales was away." The scent for Hewitt had been laid down, and when he reached Diana by telephone, he was nervous, even after Diana reassured him that the tabloids had lost interest.

It took only a month for Hewitt to be exposed when his estranged girlfriend Emma Stewardson sold her story to the *News of the World*, revealing that Diana had been sending letters and gifts to Hewitt in the Gulf and that Hewitt was so besotted with Diana he had once broken a lunch date with Emma so he could spend the day at Highgrove—though Emma stopped short of saying that Hewitt and Diana were lovers. The *Daily Mirror* blamed Hewitt for these unflattering disclosures, saying "Diana cannot afford to be the subject of any rumors, however false."

When Hewitt returned to England several months later, following the liberation of Kuwait, Diana invited him to Highgrove. Hewitt was now a target of press surveillance, so he had to hide in the boot of a car driven by one of the Highgrove staff. With his exposure in the press, Diana had effectively lost control of their relationship. After a tearful reunion, she grew cool toward him, and finally ended the relationship, leaving Hewitt feeling "rejected" and "used." "She simply stopped ringing and taking my calls," Hewitt said years later. "There was no cutoff. I never had a chance to say good-bye."

Publicly, Diana kept playing the royal game. On a tour of Brazil that spring, the Waleses offered what the *Sunday Express* called a "glimpse of the old magic" and the *Sunday Mirror* described as "a united front to the world. . . . Their closeness sent a shiver of excitement around the massed ranks of media men and women." This impression came as no surprise to a veteran Palace adviser. "Sometimes the Prince and Princess were relaxed with each other even when things were not going well," the aide said. "It was by no means the case when they were together that they were always tense. They were often relaxed."

Both Charles and Diana were pleased and engaged by the agenda for the Brazilian trip. Charles had worked hard to convene a group of important environmentalists, including Environmental Protection Administration chief William Reilly and Senator Al Gore, for an international seminar to prepare for the Rio Environmental Summit the following year. The seminar was a big success, as were Diana's visits with AIDS babies and orphaned children.

On the flight back to England, Reilly was struck by Diana's ebullience and the rapport she seemed to have with Charles. "I walked in, and Diana and Prince Charles were laughing together," Reilly said. "I had never seen him laugh like that. Diana was describing various things she had done that day, and he seemed genuinely amused. Maybe they were putting on a show, but they seemed to enjoy each other's company." Yet Lucia Flecha de Lima, wife of the Brazilian ambassador to Britain, came away with a different view after her first encounter with Diana. Lucia, who subsequently became one of Diana's closest friends, said that Diana had been "very tense. The marriage was difficult, and there were other problems. She was not well and did not give the impression of being very well."

Such contradictory views were nothing new, but they showed how much one's impression turned on Diana's mood of the moment. "Not all public events would lead to [tears]," a former Palace official said. "It was a time in her life when all sorts of things would trigger her unhappiness, and our role was to help. She was a real professional, and she had a lot of fun doing a big visit like Brazil. But after prolonged public exposure and even a period of a good time, often a downer would follow. It was not automatic, but after the strain of keeping up—not a false appearance but of being expected to be in public and apparently happy—even if she was having a good time, she would need to unwind. That was a sad unwinding for her most of the time."

Behind Diana's public compliance, she increasingly competed with Charles, in almost passive-aggressive fashion, by trying to outdo him in their everyday official roles. "In 1991, she suddenly increased her patronage," a former Palace official recalled. "She had sixty [charities] and suddenly it zoomed to over one hundred. To her it was a competition, the more charities the better, because she wanted attention. And so she planned more engagements, figuring, 'I'll come out topping the league and maybe someone might thank me.' " As a result, Diana's effectiveness decreased. "We wanted her to stay with some things," the Palace aide said. "We were concerned that she was not getting in-depth experience. But Diana didn't want that. We tried to impose that, but she needed a flash of publicity that she could give and then move on."

Diana frequently employed that publicity to upstage Charles. "If Charles was off to see an African leader, she would be at a big ball and wipe him off the headlines," said Andrew Neil, then editor of *The Sunday Times*. More troubling was the way Diana manipulated publicity to create the impression that she was an affectionate, devoted mother and he a cold, distant father. Charles played into her hands with his obliviousness to appearances and dogged devotion to duty.

In April, for instance, Diana took her sons on an outing to Thorpe Park. CHARLES THE ABSENT ROYAL FATHER: WHY THE PRINCE SHOULD SPEND MORE TIME WITH HIS SONS, said the *Daily Mail* the next day, pointing out that Diana "often has to act as surrogate father. . . . Why do we not see from him the demonstrations of warmth, affection or closeness Diana so freely displays toward her sons in public?"

James Whitaker, in the *Daily Mirror*, was equally pointed several weeks later when he reported on Diana's ski trip with her sons to Lech, Austria, in a story headlined WISH YOU WERE HERE PAPA. "Charles insists that his royal duties come before everything else—even his young sons," Whitaker wrote. "Sadly, his absences from the family scene have become a habit."

After such pounding coverage, it is difficult to fathom why the Prince's aides weren't more alert to the implications of a decision he made two months later. On June 3, 1991, Diana was interrupted at lunch in London, and Charles was alerted at Highgrove, that William had been struck in the head with a golf club at Ludgrove, his boarding school. Both parents were terribly worried when they arrived at Royal Berkshire Hospital in Reading, but they were relieved to see William sitting up and alert. The doctors found a "depressed fracture" in his forehead where the golf club left an indentation, so they decided to send William to Great Ormond Street Hospital for Sick Children in London for surgery to "pull those depressed bones out and smooth them off."

Diana and Charles accompanied William to London, where the surgeons reassured them that the operation carried little risk. At that point, Charles decided to proceed with his scheduled commitment for the evening, a performance of *Tosca* at Covent Garden, where he had longstanding plans to entertain a group of European and British officials. Afterward, he traveled overnight to Yorkshire for a morning engagement before returning to London to visit William following the successful surgery.

The damage to Charles's reputation was clear in that day's tabloids. The *Daily Mirror* contrasted Diana's "bedside vigil" with Charles's "astonishing departure." In subsequent days, the tabloids piled on: WHAT KIND OF DAD ARE YOU? asked *The Sun;* noting that "a fractured skull is not a trivial matter"; the *Daily Express* branded Charles a PHANTOM FATHER; and *Today* described THE EXHAUSTED FACE OF A LOVING MOTHER. Diana later told Morton that Charles blamed her for exaggerating the severity of William's injury and contributing to the negative coverage.

The morning after the surgery, a friend called Diana, and she actually "made light of it," the friend recalled. "It is a very English reaction. You wouldn't make a big thing of it." But Diana worked up some outrage of her own to match the tabloids'. She complained about Charles to James Gilbey, who later said that Diana's response to the accident was "horror and disbelief . . . [it was] a narrow escape. She can't understand her husband's behavior, so as a result, she just blocks it out." Diana told her friend Adrian Ward-Jackson, "I can't be with someone who behaves like that."

In the months leading up to Charles and Diana's tenth wedding anniversary on July 29, the tabloids put the royal marriage under their murky microscope, shifting back and forth between indignant defenses and sensational exposés. By May, Andrew Morton had sharpened the focus in *The Sun,* under the provocative headline CHARLES MAKES IT SO OBVIOUS HE PREFERS TO BE WITH CAMILLA. Morton wrote: "Since the Prince broke his right arm . . . last summer, he has turned to his own circle of friends. . . . Prominent among them is Camilla Parker Bowles, the woman he once loved and lost. During Diana's frequent absences Camilla . . . acted as hostess at Highgrove dinner parties . . . and often made daytime visits to comfort the invalid Charles . . . even sunbathing in her bikini in the Highgrove gardens. . . . Friends say [Diana] feels humiliated that her husband prefers to spend so much time with Camilla rather than her." Most telling of all, "What irks [Diana] even more is that while little is said about Prince Charles's relationship with Camilla, every time [Diana] speaks to an unattached male, it causes headlines."

Morton had aired Diana's deepest grievance, but it still wasn't enough. "Diana was bitter, vengeful, at a low ebb," said a former Palace official who worked with her at that time. Her experience after William's head injury left her feeling utterly estranged from Charles. "He ignores me everywhere," she said later that year. "Ignored everywhere and have been for a long time. . . . He just dismisses me."

In late June, Diana made her first overt effort at news management by leaking a story to the *Daily Mail* about plans for her thirtieth birthday on July 1. At that stage, Diana had engaged in few direct dealings with the press, but she knew where her allies were: One of the many oddities of the coverage of Diana and Charles was the complete absence of objectivity. "It was an open secret that the press was divided into Diana and Charles camps, with the Princess enjoying by far the most support," wrote tabloid columnist Peter McKay. The large pro-Diana contingent included James Whitaker, Harry Arnold, Anthony Holden, Richard Kay, and Andrew Morton. On Charles's side were Ross Benson and Nigel Dempster.

Diana understood the importance of the *Daily Mail,* her favorite newspaper. Of all the tabloids, the *Mail* had been the most consistently in her corner—with the exception of Dempster, whose gossip column was often critical. Under the editorship of David English, the *Mail* succeeded in winning over the middle class, particularly women, by emphasizing human-interest features; it also had a substantial following among the aristocracy. "All Diana's friends read it," a man close to Diana said. "It was the privileged woman's tabloid, and it was important for her friends to read the right things about her."

Unlike the other top editors, David English had managed to develop a relationship with Diana. After having lunch with her in 1990, English "came back very excited about a story," said Sue Douglas, then a deputy to

English. "Diana had talked about her problems, and he was sure she was telling him things were going wrong." The paper couldn't come up with confirmation, so nothing was published, but Diana knew that English and his paper were sympathetic to her cause, so when she wanted the word out about her birthday, the *Mail* was the obvious conduit.

Headlined HAPPY BIRTHDAY DARLING, I CAN'T COME TO THE PARTY, the article on June 28, 1991, by Emma Wilkins, recounted that "Princess Diana is to spend her 30th birthday apart from her husband. She will be in London on Monday, lunching at the Savoy and hosting a party for close friends. Charles plans to stay at Highgrove." "That was straight PR from Diana," Nigel Dempster said, "and we all swallowed it."

Two days later, Dempster received a late afternoon call from a friend of Prince Charles's. "It was a well-bred lady's voice," Dempster recalled, "and she said, 'It is quite the opposite. Prince Charles has offered her anything for her birthday—lunch, dinner, a ball—whatever she wanted, but she has refused, because she wants to be a martyr.'" Dempster came out in another two days with a front-page story in the *Daily Mail*—CHARLES AND DIANA: CAUSE FOR CONCERN—describing how Diana had thwarted Charles's plans and noting the "growing coolness" in the marriage.

Andrew Morton volleyed back the next day in *The Sun:* "The sad truth about the royal birthday party that never was . . . [is that] Princess Diana preferred to spend her 30th birthday alone rather than attend a High Society ball in her honor planned by her husband." Based on a conversation with "one of her closest confidantes," Morton wrote that Charles's "guest list comprised all his stuffy old friends rather than her younger pals, and she simply couldn't face it."

After the birthday brouhaha had subsided, the principals and the press tried again to conjure an illusion of harmony. The *Evening Standard* declared that Diana's "friendship with Hewitt has been innocuous," and the *Daily Mail* concluded that Charles "finds Mrs. Parker Bowles a mature, pleasant, understanding companion, but no threat [to Charles] intellectually or emotionally. She has hosted dinner parties for the Prince at Highgrove. The Princess has often found these occasions tedious and a shade too earnest."

The end of July brought reports of the Wales's anniversary "supper for two" and hopeful mutterings about their future together. The retreat was best summed up by TRUCE, the headline in *The Sunday Times* on a Morton article that proclaimed, "Charles and Diana's summer of discontent erupted into a storm . . . but now the air has cleared."

Eighteen months after the furor, Lord McGregor of Durris, the chairman of the Press Complaints Commission, unequivocally blamed Diana for manipulating the press reports. "I was told that both the Prince and

Princess had been involved in making statements about their marriage," he said. "I did not at any time, nor have I subsequently received any evidence for any involvement by the Prince in leaking to the press anything of that nature. I made inquiries to the editors of newspapers and was satisfied the intrusions were contrived by the Princess herself."

Bitterly displeased that the media had accepted what she viewed as a false rapprochement, Diana decided in the summer of 1991 to cooperate with Andrew Morton. According to several of Diana's friends, she was equally disappointed that the press had been unwilling to identify Camilla as Charles's lover. As one of her close friends said, "She was absolutely desperate that people should know what Camilla had done."

Chapter 16

WHEN Diana and Charles shared a "cozy supper" at Highgrove to mark their tenth anniversary on July 29, 1991, Diana had already embarked on an enterprise that would have profound consequences for her and her marriage. Two weeks earlier she had begun a series of tape-recorded interviews for Andrew Morton's book. "She thought she was a wise soul," her friend David Puttnam said, "and she thought she was a clever game player . . . I don't think she was. . . . I think it was just pure instinct. . . . Once or twice she got it horribly, horribly wrong."

Besides her fixation on exposing Camilla Parker Bowles, Diana was still apprehensive about the Squidgy tape. She had also been hearing reports that some of Charles's friends were calling her the "mad cow" (after BSE, or "mad cow disease") at fashionable dinner parties, and she sensed what her friend Vivienne Parry called "a huge amount of hostility . . . from those within the Palace . . . not just the royal family but those in the establishment at the Palace." Parry said Diana believed there was a "whispering campaign: This woman is a cracked vessel. This woman is potty. This woman is a danger to the royal family." Diana later told her friend Roberto Devorik that she had even approached the Queen and Prince Philip for help during this time, only to be told that "everything was in her imagination and she should consult a psychiatrist and maybe go to a psychiatric cure."

Diana told friends that she believed the Queen should have intervened to end Charles's affair with Camilla and to help Charles and Diana stay together. Diana's frustrations were understandable, but her expectations were unrealistic given the nature of the royal family. "I don't think Camilla was regarded as a big threat in the royal family," a source close to the family said. "It is easy with hindsight to say, 'Why not send them away [by arranging to transfer the couple to a foreign military post]?' Really, the royal family saw an impossible marriage and figured it was better for Charles to have a shoulder to cry on. But no one thought it would break up the marriage. They thought that for centuries the royal family and the aristocracy had had mistresses, and people went on with their marriages and their duties."

In the summer of 1991, Diana felt that "the lid was being put down on her," Morton said. "She was terrified she would be publicly labeled an impossible lunatic," one of her friends recalled, "and if so, she could lose a fight over custody. She was terrified of character assassination and angry that some of her own hanky-panky would be released without the extent of Charles's infidelity revealed." Still suffering from bulimia and depression, Diana was "at the end of my tether," as she said on *Panorama*.

By unhappy coincidence, Diana sat for another portrait—her tenth—during this period, and the artist, Douglas Anderson, could not avoid capturing what he called her "horrible sadness" on canvas. It was "the very worst time," he recalled of her five sittings over several weeks. "She was on the verge of a nervous breakdown. I painted what I saw. She was on the edge, and it was draining. She was very preoccupied and constantly on the verge of crying. I had the feeling that if she left the room she might be in floods of tears."

Feeling under siege, Diana decided to launch a preemptive strike against Charles. "She was a woman scorned," said Andrew Roberts. "She couldn't or wouldn't stop herself. She thought, 'Oh, God, I'm the story, not the Crown.' To a great extent she brought everyone down." She needed to justify herself to the public, which "she regarded . . . as an extension of her family," one of Diana's friends said. "She had to explain her suffering. Deep down, she needed to be understood, and she craved approval. I remember telling her to be like Jackie O., that if she did, people could interpret but there would be no certainty. She agreed with me, but that was before the book."

Diana shared her grievances with a group of trusted friends, who encouraged her to tell her side of the story. "Most people who knew her for years figured it couldn't get any worse for her," Morton explained. "She was living a lie, and they thought she might as well lance the boil." Among those she consulted were James Gilbey and Adrian Ward-Jackson, who proved a crucial catalyst.

Ward-Jackson became bedridden with AIDS in April 1991. To honor their pact that she would care for him through his illness, Diana made frequent unpublicized visits to his home to keep him company. "Around the sickbed, a lot happened," a friend of Ward-Jackson's said. "Adrian was deeply intrigued by the state of the marriage. She confided in him. What she projected was confusion, hurt, resentment, and anger. He was sympathetic, and she sought advice. She would talk about these things to pass the time. It was very useful for him. Instead of thinking of himself, he would listen to her problems."

Through Ward-Jackson, Diana grew close to his friend Angela Serota, a former ballet dancer who was supervising his care. Serota was separating from her husband at the time, and she and Diana formed a close bond. When Diana poured out her anguish about her marriage, Serota listened. As Diana debated whether to go public, "Angela was very important," Morton said. "She could see the pain Diana was in."

Diana had been confiding as well in Dr. James Colthurst, a radiologist who had been her friend since they met in 1979 on a ski trip. Back in 1986, he had invited her to visit his London hospital, St. Thomas's. During that visit Colthurst had met Morton, who was there with the royal press pack. The two men struck up a friendship that included a regular squash game. According to a man close to Diana, it was Colthurst who suggested that she entrust Morton with her story.

Still, it is difficult to know precisely why Diana settled on the veteran tabloid man as her "conduit," as Morton described himself. It was not in Diana's nature to conduct a rigorous analysis of Morton's abilities and his body of work. But she knew that Morton was, as he said, "nibbling around" the idea of writing a biography about her. He had been on Diana's radar even after he left the *Daily Mail* in 1988 to write freelance articles and books (*Diana's Diary: An Intimate Portrait of the Princess of Wales* and *Inside Kensington Palace*).

In fact, Morton was perfect for Diana's purpose. He had been captivated by her from the moment he joined the royal beat in 1982 and attacked Nigel Dempster as a "royal sniper." Although he had shifted back and forth between apologist and alarmist in his coverage, he never wavered in his adoration of Diana. Even when dealing with potentially negative material, he turned it to her advantage, as in a 1986 story on reports that Diana had been insulting Charles: "It is just another indication of how a strong-willed princess is steadily winning her battle to bring the royal family to heel."

Most recently, Morton had been Diana's champion in her undeclared war on Charles, venturing further than any reporter toward unmasking Camilla. He had a slick, commercial writing style and chameleon-like qualities, moving easily from tabloid to broadsheet: His articles on the Wales marriage in *The Sunday Times* had given him a patina of respectability.

Andrew Morton's biggest advantage was his outsider status. He could disappear from sight, as he did in July 1991, without explaining himself or attracting attention. As a freelancer lacking a formal newspaper affiliation, he could be trusted to keep Diana's role a secret, and he would be eternally grateful for her gift of a sensational story. In other words, he could be controlled.

Diana dispatched her friend James Colthurst to sketch out her story for Morton. Over bacon and eggs in a North London cafe, Colthurst told the writer about the unraveling royal marriage, including Diana's bouts of bulimia and attempts at suicide—all of which, Diana contended, resulted from her problems with Charles and his infidelity with Camilla Parker Bowles. Morton was staggered by the sensational revelations. "I didn't know about the bulimia, the suicides," he recalled. "Who did? It shows how many secrets can be held." Morton later freely admitted that Diana was in charge. "People make out that I am a tabloid hack who conned her, that she didn't know what she was getting into, that I teased information out of her, the poor girl who would have lived happily ever after," Morton said. "That is from the Goebbels book of best-selling stories. The fact is, she sought me out."

Around this time, Colthurst introduced Diana to a new astrologer, Felix Lyle, who was also a friend of Morton's. By one account, Diana only proceeded with the project after Lyle gave her the green light. But as was so often the case with Diana's advisers, Lyle simply reinforced what Diana was already determined to do. "She didn't see him until late summer, after the project was under way," Morton said. "She didn't have second thoughts, and as the project progressed, she became more enthusiastic."

Morton and Colthurst devised a scheme to give Diana "deniability" about her part in the book; if asked, she could say she and Morton had not even met. Morton submitted lists of questions to her for a series of interviews, which Colthurst tape-recorded. "James was always with her during the interviews," Morton said. "She would answer the questions as best as she could. Sometimes she ignored them. It was a ramshackle way to do a book."

The first interview was a "confusion," Morton said. "Everything just tumbled out." Recognizing the delicacy of broaching such intimate topics as bulimia and suicide, Morton "would send James off with two sets of questions, one if she started being one way, otherwise, go for [the other] line [of inquiry]." Morton later admitted that Diana misled him about James Hewitt, and although Morton interviewed James Gilbey, the still-secret Squidgy tapes never came up.

By definition, the arrangement precluded follow-up questions and the freedom to challenge Diana's version of events. "The classic was the suicides," Morton said. "You are dealing with a very delicate area. I asked questions about when, where, what. Afterwards she said, 'He's pretty well written my obit.' "

Morton described how her moods slipped between the energy and "breathless haste" she often showed in the mornings and the deflation at other times. The "hit and miss" aspect was aggravated by Diana's tendency to schedule interviews on short notice, when Morton would hurriedly assemble his queries and "hope for the best." Despite her obvious fragility, and the history of mental illness she described, Morton "had doubts about her veracity but not about her stability." He said he tried to cross-check whenever possible by talking to her friends. A conspicuous flaw in this method, later pointed out by friends of Charles, was that Morton had to rely on people who had heard only Diana's side of the story.

One of the trickiest areas for Morton was Charles's relationship with Camilla, which for legal reasons he ended up calling a "secret friendship" rather than adultery, "much to Diana's annoyance and in spite of overwhelming evidence." To help establish that proof, Diana unearthed revealing letters in August 1991. Morton said, "She procured them because I wanted them. She didn't know about letters when we started to talk. They were not on the kitchen notice board. She got them because I was hesitant about the Camilla business, and they underpinned what she told me and made me feel happier about using it. The letters I saw were notes from Camilla to Charles, written at that time in 1991. It upset Diana to see them."

In the early autumn, Diana approached a group of friends to ask them to cooperate with Morton. The first was Angela Serota, who consulted another friend who would become vital to Diana's project: Andrew Knight, Rupert Murdoch's chief executive, a close friend of both Serota and Ward-Jackson. Like Diana, Knight had been a frequent visitor to Ward-Jackson's bedside during the summer of 1991, although Knight said he and Diana never met there. Diana heard about him from Ward-Jackson and Serota. According to a man close to her, Diana came to regard Knight as "on her side."

"Angela rang me and said Diana was asking her and others to cooperate with Andrew Morton on a book," Knight recalled. "Diana wants to end the fairy tale," Serota told him. "There are dramatic things that we know," although Serota declined to say what they were. "Angela is a very private person," Morton said. "She wasn't interested in speaking to me. All these people needed convincing. They didn't even know how closely Diana was involved in the project, that she was giving interviews." When Serota asked Andrew Knight if she should help, he said, "Yes, if [Diana] says so, you should do it."

Serota also confided to Knight that Diana was "worried" that the book would be serialized in the *Daily Mail*. "She wants it in *The Sunday Times*," Serota said. Despite her affinity for the *Mail*, Diana was sufficiently media-savvy to understand that a *Sunday Times* excerpt would give the book the credibility and authority that even a midmarket tabloid could not. Knight told Serota he would "lobby Andrew Neil about this book and say *The Sunday Times* should take it seriously."

Diana controlled Morton's access to her friends, who would not sit for interviews without her permission. She included just one member of her family, her brother Charles, whose innate wariness she could count on. In fact, Charles agreed to be questioned only about her life until the age of eighteen. As the project advanced, Diana brought in her father to give Morton his choice of photographs from the family albums Johnnie had compiled over the years, but she excluded the women in her family. Her sister Jane was off-bounds for the obvious reason that her marriage to the Queen's private secretary required her to be kept in the dark. Both Sarah and Frances Shand Kydd had a history of making unhelpful comments to the press.

These arrangements yet again pointed up the absence of a solid family foundation that might have prevented Diana from risking the Morton book. Her father lacked the subtlety to fathom the extent of her problems and could do little more than say, "Just remember we always love you"—an important and heartfelt reassurance, but insufficient when she needed crucial guidance. In his public comments, Johnnie perpetuated the myth of a happy royal marriage, calling stories of marital discord "trivial, like mosquitoes." At one point, Johnnie expressed his concern that Diana was working too hard, but he couldn't help admiring her celebrity. "Someone said to me recently that the two most famous people in the world are the Pope and my daughter," Johnnie said in 1989. "I am so proud."

In September 1991, Diana and her father had one of their few public spats when she and her siblings objected to the way Raine Spencer was orchestrating the sale of art and heirlooms to finance their lifestyle at Althorp. Asked for comment, Johnnie angrily denounced his children for "ingratitude," saying pointedly, "Diana doesn't understand about money. She has no experience of money. She's too young."

Such disagreements were more common in Diana's uneven relationship with her mother. Though Frances was not the recluse that the tabloid press often described, she relished her independent existence far from sophisticated society, befriending nuns, fishermen, and plainspoken Scots who respected her privacy. "I love people for what they are," she once said. "You won't find me at the smart dinner parties. . . . I have nothing to do with London society. . . . I don't mix."

At times, Frances and Diana giggled together like sisters, but they might not communicate for extended periods. "It was not an easy relationship," tabloid reporter Richard Kay said. Frances had managed to help

Diana and Charles in the fall of 1987, but from 1988 through 1992—the years when Diana's marriage was fracturing—Frances was despondent about the breakup of her own marriage, so neither woman could offer much support to the other. One friend of Diana's remembered when Frances "would call three times a day, and Diana would talk a lot to her. Diana tried on the phone to be caring, but then she would blow up. She thought her mother would only call with her own problems." The nub of Diana's predicament, according to this friend, was that "with her own mother, Diana was afraid to give her love and be rejected. That is why it was such a difficult relationship."

Diana also feared her mother's volatility. "Diana's mother would get too emotionally involved," one of Diana's friends said. "Frances is not a woman who worries about speaking her mind." That impetuous streak was evident when Frances periodically popped up to make disconcerting, sometimes incoherent statements to the press that embarrassed Diana. "I don't understand why I have to be attacked all the time," Frances said in an outburst to the *Sunday Express*. "They say I turned my son Charles and Diana against their stepmother. That is very damning stuff. . . . I am well versed in being crucified. Why can I just not be me? I am well aware that if I was caught speeding, Myra Hindley would look like a Girl Guide."

Part of Morton's bargain with Diana was her right to read and comment on his manuscript. To disguise her role, he altered some quotes to the third person, attributing them to "a close friend," or he used her direct quotes that "she told friends." "There were 4,000 of her words in the book," Morton said. "She approved it, including her first-person speech." According to Morton, she also "made a number of alterations of fact and emphasis." One odd request changed a significant fact in the staircase incident at Sandringham in January 1982: it was the Queen who found Diana at the foot of the stairs, but Diana asked Morton to substitute the Queen Mother's name, "presumably out of deference" to her mother-in-law. Otherwise, Diana's marginal comments were minor, and sometimes touching. When Morton referred to Charles as "the man she longed to marry," Diana wrote "was in love with." The book was "to all intents and purposes her autobiography," Morton said.

For the first two months of the Morton project, Diana was in a state of considerable agitation over the condition of Adrian Ward-Jackson, who was declining fast. Angela Serota tightly coordinated his visiting schedule, and Diana came three or four times a week. Diana was attentive and compassionate, but also excited by the scene in the Mount Street apartment. "It was a frenzied atmosphere," another visitor said. "Once Diana was visiting, everyone more assiduously visited as well. It became an event." A friend of Ward-Jackson's recalled that Diana "kept saying in a girlish way that it was the first time she monitored someone dying. There was a kind of morbid interest for everyone. She saw it as a part of growing up, and an interesting experience."

By August, it became too difficult to administer a morphine drip at home, so Ward-Jackson was moved to St. Mary's Hospital. At that point, Diana's visits became public knowledge. Ward-Jackson had secured her promise to be at his deathbed, but he hadn't counted on the media circus that surrounded her visits. His brother arranged a private route into the hospital for Diana, but she declined to take it. "She said, 'I am not going to be intimidated,' " a friend said, "Then she would change her outfit every day and enjoy it. She was like a young girl who wanted to avoid the paparazzi but flirt[ed] with them."

When Angela Serota called Balmoral to say Ward-Jackson was dying, Diana rushed to London, arriving at four A.M. Over the next four days, Diana spent hours at his bedside, but she was en route to the hospital when he died. The tabloids splashed the deathwatch story on page one, calling her compassion "extraordinary" and marveling that she spent six and a half hours "consoling his grieving family." (Actually, she didn't meet his parents until the funeral, several days later.) The funeral turned into a media spectacle when Diana arrived in defiance of protocol, which held that senior members of the royal family didn't attend funerals of commoners. "Diana's tears flowed during the service," wrote *The Sun,* as they did two months later at Ward-Jackson's memorial service.

Diana's overwrought behavior hampered her work for AIDS when she drew fire from reactionary columnists such as John Junor (the father of Penny), who wrote in *The Mail on Sunday,* "What do you suppose can explain her preoccupation with the disease? Could she really want to go down in history as the patron saint of sodomy?" She also alienated members of the establishment, including some of her friends discomfited by what they viewed as her theatrics. "The whole episode was very bizarre," a longtime friend said. "She adopted Adrian like a sick dog. It did her great damage in the establishment. She went sort of mad, and she lost some allies because she was too over the top."

Afterward, Diana wrote to Angela Serota that caring for Ward-Jackson gave her a "more positive and balanced" view of life, although her subsequent actions didn't indicate a new level of maturity. She had come to similarly optimistic conclusions before, but lost sight of them during periods of personal adversity. "Afterward she didn't rather mention Adrian," said a woman who knew her well. "For her, that was not odd. It was intense and current, and then when it was over, that was it: out of sight, out of mind." "She was extraordinarily affected at the time," one of Ward-Jackson's friends said. "But she absorbed pretty superficially. I don't think she learned long-term lessons."

Diana carried on with her duties, living with the subterfuge of the Morton book. By then, deception had become second nature. In August, she joined Charles and the boys for a Mediterranean cruise on a yacht owned by John Latsis, a wealthy Greek friend. The tabloids were appropriately moonstruck, pronouncing it a "second honeymoon," and the Waleses "two lovebirds" who were "happier and closer than for ages . . . scotching rumors of a big freeze." Charles and Diana were also reasonably successful maintaining appearances on an official visit to Canada with William and Harry in October, immortalized by one of Diana's favorite photographs of herself: smiling with arms outstretched as she ran up the gangplank of *Britannia* to greet her two sons.

Meanwhile, the Waleses were navigating their daily life through their private secretaries. As James Gilbey summed up their existence at the time, "Their lives are spent in total isolation." Diana had a successful four-day solo tour of Pakistan that fall, giving the tabloids another opportunity to draw pointed contrasts. "While the caring princess meets crippled Afghan child refugees," Ashley Walton wrote in the *Daily Express*, "Charles will be fishing and stalking deer with friends."

A month later, Penny Junor, who earlier in the year had authored a book saying the Wales marriage was "actually very healthy," wrote a magazine article on Diana pronouncing 1991 "the greatest year of her life," when she became "the new Diana, the complete woman." Charles and Diana, Junor wrote, "are together far more than you would believe from reading the reports in the tabloid press."

Diana was eager to send the opposite message the following February during the couple's tour of India. A memorable image of Diana sitting alone in front of the Taj Mahal, the tomb built by a Mogul emperor for his wife, was the most vivid example up to then of her use of photographs to make a point. On a visit many years earlier, Charles had vowed to bring his future wife to the romantic monument. Palace officials planning the schedule for the Indian trip had no knowledge of the Prince's pledge and didn't give a second thought to Diana's solo visit. It was only the day before, when they saw the tabloid pack's excitement, that they realized the photographers wanted a picture to fit the story they planned. Diana understood, too, and obligingly posed in "wistful solitude" (*Daily Mail*) as a "poignant reminder of the royal wish that did not come true" (*Daily Mirror*). Her message, Dimbleby wrote: "The marriage was indeed on the rocks."

As it turned out, the photograph was the first in a run of potent images crafted by Diana that spring. The next day in India, when Charles tried to kiss her after a polo match, she turned her head so the cameras would catch him awkwardly pecking her neck. Diana was well aware the tabloids were hoping for a proper smooch; she and her aides even discussed the photo opportunity beforehand, and the *Evening Standard* set the stage by saying "all eyes will be on them." OH COME ON YOU CAN DO BETTER THAN THAT CHARLES! blared the *Daily Mirror*'s front-page headline, placing the blame for the botched kiss on the hapless Prince. But the *Mirror*'s man James Whitaker later admitted, "It was she who seemed to make sure it didn't work. She knew that there would be a lot of judgment on it." On a solo visit to Egypt several months later, Diana echoed her Taj Mahal shot by posing in solitude in front of the Pyramids. "Here she was again, the innocent victim," *The Sunday Times* noted. "And once again, the image was carefully created."

In March 1992, Johnnie Spencer died unexpectedly of a heart attack at age sixty-eight while the Waleses were skiing in Lech, Austria. Even in her grief, Diana wished to cut a lone figure, agreeing to travel home with Charles only after their staff argued at length that if they went separately they would suffer a "tabloid mauling." For her father's funeral, however, they arrived and departed on their own, at Diana's request. The press showed some restraint in its interpretation this time. Charles had a meeting in London afterward, "leaving Diana to attend her father's cremation without him," noted the *Daily Mail*.

As Diana put distance between herself and Charles, she was already worrying about the consequences of the Morton book, which was due to be published on June 16. Some Palace officials were aware of the project, but not the extent of Diana's involvement. The previous November, Diana's friend Roberto Devorik had met with Patrick Jephson, Diana's recently appointed private secretary, over lunch at Mark's Club in London. Devorik had heard Diana was cooperating with a book and that she had sanctioned a previously unpublished photograph by French photographer Patrick Demarchelier for the cover. Devorik recalled, "I asked, 'Are you aware of this book?' Patrick [Jephson] said, 'This is my nightmare.'" By January, Robert Fellowes and other top Palace aides were poking around to figure out what line they should take. They got nothing from Diana because she could truthfully say she had no contact with Andrew Morton, but she was unnerved by the inquiry.

Diana gave a speech on AIDS that March at a monthly dinner gathering of high-powered media executives called the Thirty Club. About 150 members showed up at Claridges, and although Michael Adler, chairman of the National AIDS Trust, was by Diana's side, she was extremely nervous—so much so that she was visibly shaking. But she rose and talked about the incidence of AIDS among women, and afterward fielded questions from the likes of *Telegraph* owner Conrad Black and *Mail* owner Lord Rothermere. "It was a hard-boiled crowd," Andrew Knight said. "She spoke well, but it was awfully stilted, and she didn't say much. During the question period, she would say something sweet, and Michael Adler would add chapter and verse. But overall, she did awfully well."

The most revealing part of the evening occurred before her speech. At dinner, she was seated next to film producer David Puttnam, who was a friend, though not part of her intimate circle. Perhaps as a result of her nervousness, "suddenly she started confiding in me how unhappy things were in her marriage," Puttnam recalled. "She said, 'Neither of us has been perfect, but I've done a really stupid thing. I have allowed a book to be written. I felt it was a good idea, a way of clearing the air, but now I think it was a very stupid thing that will cause all kinds of terrible trouble.' She said, 'I would like to reel the movie back. It is the daftest thing I have ever done.' "

In May, the rumors began to surface as *The Sunday Times* announced it would serialize the book starting on June 7. When Morton's publisher, Michael O'Mara, had first taken the book to Andrew Neil in March 1992, the *Sunday Times* editor had replied, "I think it would be better off in a tabloid." Neil was intrigued by O'Mara's description of the book's disclosures, along with his assurance that it had been "effectively" authorized by Diana, yet Neil at first "did not believe it," he later said. "It seemed too fantastical."

Morton then came to see Neil to persuade him otherwise. "He started going through and naming sources, even those not named in the book," Neil recalled, "and he said, 'I have a lot more backup.' I was impressed." Neil dispatched his deputy Sue Douglas to read the manuscript. Although she was put off by the "gushing prose," she was jolted by the revelations, but even more by O'Mara's tip that the photos had come from Diana's father and that some of her best friends had spoken to the author. Douglas spoke to Andrew Knight, who revealed Angela Serota's role and vouched for her as a "person of integrity." "We have something serious on our hands," Douglas told Neil, who agreed to consider publishing excerpts if Douglas and a task force could independently verify the allegations.

Based on his knowledge of Serota's involvement—and recalling Diana's request—Knight lobbied for publication. "I was able to say to Andrew Neil, 'I think you are right to get more interested in this book, because I have been following it through one person, and she is completely trustworthy, and she and Diana are close.' I knew it was a huge story which was sure to break in one paper or another, and *The Sunday Times*'s function over the years was to break that kind of story without favor." Douglas's task force corroborated the book to their satisfaction. A number of the major sources had signed statements certifying their quotes, and the photos from the Spencer family confirmed Diana's authorization. "I never had any doubt that this was a reasonably accurate version of what she believed to be the truth," Neil said. When Neil went to Rupert Murdoch to say *The Sunday Times* was prepared to publish, "Rupert said, 'I'll back you on whatever you do, but remember, if you do this they will try to destroy you.'"

The *Daily Mail* had also read the manuscript and made a bid, but *The Sunday Times* upped the ante to £250,000 and secured the rights. By then, Neil, Douglas, and others believed Diana had read the manuscript. Douglas knew "there were large chunks of tape-recordings. Andrew Morton let me believe these were friends being briefed by Diana and taped by him." Morton had also told Stuart Higgins of *The Sun,* "Treat that book as though the Princess had signed every page."

Given the number of journalists aware of Diana's fingerprints, it was probably inevitable that an article of unsettling accuracy about the Morton book would appear only weeks before publication. "It is believed," said the *Daily Express* in early May, that "the author has had close cooperation with the Princess and her family to produce startling revelations about her marriage . . . The Princess is already reported to have read the proofs and has the power to make amendments. . . . Officials are also concerned that pictures in the book have come from the Princess's family and will be seen as more evidence of her tacit approval."

A few days later at a dinner at the British ambassador's residence in Cairo, Diana startled her fellow guests by announcing, "I still see myself as Lady Diana Spencer." When someone asked what would happen when Charles became king, she replied, "I think I will still be Lady Di." It was an uncomfortable moment that turned reckless a few moments later when an Egyptian said, "Here we can change our royal family every few years." Catching his words, Diana shouted across the room, "In our country, we are stuck with ours."

The misgivings she had expressed to David Puttnam seemed to have vanished, and Diana was again emboldened. Weeks away from her thirty-first birthday, she was on the verge of seeing her "true" story in print, buttressed by the respectable imprimatur of *The Sunday Times.* It is impossible to know what she expected: certainly sympathy for how she had been treated and understanding of her problems, as well as the ruination of Camilla Parker Bowles. She also seemed to think that the press would accept her story and move on, that she could preserve her marriage, and that she could maintain her innocence. "The Princess hoped by putting her side across with the Morton book that the press would do her a favor," said Robert Hardman of *The Daily Telegraph.* "She was very wrong."

Chapter 17

THE uproar that followed the serialization and publication of Andrew Morton's book in June 1992 shocked everyone, including Diana. By exposing her emotional torment and mental illness, the book created enormous sympathy for her, but nearly destroyed Charles by blaming him for her problems and portraying him as a callous and unfaithful husband, as well as an insensitive parent. Perhaps the most wounding quote of all came from Diana's close friend James Gilbey, who said, "She thinks he is a bad father, a selfish father; the children have to tie in with whatever he's doing."

Diana may have explained herself to the public, but she had alienated her husband, his family and their retainers, members of her own family, and the establishment, whose support she needed. She had exposed a group of her friends to press harassment. Most of all, in creating new story lines for the inquisitive press, she had invaded "her own privacy," as Lord McGregor, Chairman of the Press Complaints Commission, put it. "There was no commercial advantage to holding back once we got an inkling of how bad things were," said Max Hastings, then editor of *The Daily Telegraph*.

In the weeks before the book's publication, senior advisers in the Palace had believed it increasingly likely that Diana had colluded in some way with Morton, but she had deflected their efforts to pin her down. Three days before the first excerpt appeared in *The Sunday Times, The Sun* ran an article saying that Diana was "coming under strong pressure . . . to publicly disassociate herself" from the book, even as Morton and Buckingham Palace "strenuously denied" that she had cooperated. Nevertheless, the tabloid pointed out that "other royals" had begun to question Diana's role after learning about the inclusion of pictures from Spencer family albums and her approval of the cover photograph. Morton later characterized the atmosphere as "a war situation. I felt very much on her side."

Diana's brother-in-law Robert Fellowes asked her directly, not once but several times, if she had cooperated with the book. Each time she assured him that she had not, and he believed her.

Fellowes had served the Queen for fifteen years, and since 1990 had been her private secretary, the highest position in the courtier ranks. A former Guards officer educated at Eton, Fellowes was regarded as intelligent, steady, and deliberate in his work. Fealty to his sovereign was paramount: He devoted himself to protecting the Queen's interests and took the heat on her behalf whenever necessary. Since their marriage in 1978, Robert and Jane Fellowes had been an exemplary couple, living modestly and avoiding the limelight. "Robert is absolutely incorruptible," one of his friends said. "He's the sort who bicycles to work with his father's old battered leather briefcase. He isn't interested in money or power. He is not fashionable today because he is so straight."

Behind his Bertie Wooster manner, however, Fellowes could be astute and worldly, and in his own quiet way he was trying to modernize the monarchy—helping to ease the Queen into paying income tax, for example. But he had a blind spot when it came to Diana and, recognizing that Diana was troubled, he tried to give her the benefit of the doubt. "Perhaps if Robert had been more Machiavellian, it might have served him better," said another of his friends. He might have profited from more imagination as well. When Diana denied cooperation with Morton, Fellowes took her at face value, assuming she had responded straightforwardly (as he would have), and disregarding evidence that indicated otherwise.

The first *Sunday Times* excerpt on June 7 highlighted Diana's bulimia, suicide attempts, and Charles and Camilla's secret relationship. Although clearly one-sided, the article was persuasive in its details and its naming of Diana's friends as sources. After reading it, one of Diana's close friends called her immediately. "She pretended to me it had nothing to do with her," said her friend. "But my heart sank, reading it, because I could see she had. One thing gave it away, that quote, 'He was all over me like a bad rash.' But I never brought it up again." Dining with another friend a few days later, Diana said, "I couldn't stop my friends talking." As the friend recalled, "It was fantastically disingenuous. If you are a friend of the royal family, you don't talk unless they tell you to."

"I HAVE NOT COOPERATED WITH THIS BOOK IN ANY WAY," announced the *Daily Mirror*'s page-one headline on June 8, quoting Diana. That day, Lord McGregor of the Press Complaints Commission contacted Robert Fellowes, who assured him, as did the Queen's press secretary Charles Anson, that Diana had no involvement in the Morton book. McGregor then drafted a statement condemning press coverage of the Wales marriage as an "odious exhibition of journalists dabbling their fingers in the stuff of other people's souls." Before releasing the statement, McGregor checked once more with Fellowes about persistent rumors that Diana had leaked information on the Wales marriage. Fellowes said the rumors were baseless.

Prince Charles first read the excerpt over breakfast at Highgrove on Sunday, but when he tried to talk to Diana about it, she fled to London in tears. Charles and Diana met at Kensington Palace the next day to discuss what to do next. Diana recounted her version of that meeting to Morton's middleman James Colthurst, who recorded her description in a diary: "Diana and Charles agreed that they were incompatible, and decided on a parting of the ways. . . . He was being reasonable, grown-up and himself. No tears. First time Diana slept through night without sleeping pills."

On Tuesday, News International's Andrew Knight wrote what he later described as a "pompous" letter to McGregor, insisting that *The Sunday Times* had serialized the book only after establishing its authenticity. According to Colthurst's diary, Robert Fellowes called Diana that day to probe her further about the book, saying "she was making his life unbearable." Diana also told Colthurst she had talked to friends about finding a lawyer and had drawn up "a shortlist of five."

Lord McGregor phoned Knight on Wednesday the tenth. "Are you really telling me the Princess knew?" McGregor asked. "She did know," replied Knight. "She authorized it." Only moments earlier, Knight had heard from Kelvin MacKenzie, editor of *The Sun,* who said, "You'll never guess what today's story is. We've been phoned and told there is a photo op with Diana at the home of one of her friends."

At Diana's direction, the tabloids had been alerted that in the evening she would be visiting her friend Carolyn Bartholomew, one of the named sources in the book. "This was Diana's elaborate way of authenticating the source," Knight said. Knight relayed this information to McGregor: "What would you say if in tomorrow's newspapers there are photos of the Princess of Wales visiting Carolyn Bartholomew in an orchestrated way?" McGregor "was absolutely amazed," Knight recalled.

While trying to protect herself with repeated denials, Diana had exposed everyone else who helped Morton. "She was under huge pressure from her friends, including Carolyn Bartholomew, to show a public display of support," *Sunday Times* editor Andrew Neil said. "Gilbey and Carolyn in particular were getting a terrible pounding from their other friends, who said, 'How could you do that to Diana?' They were becoming social outcasts. They said, 'You have to help us,' and that is why she went to Carolyn Bartholomew's house."

Thursday's tabloids splashed the photographs of Diana greeting Carolyn at her doorstep. McGregor reached Fellowes in Paris, where the Queen was on a state visit, to blister him for misleading the Press Complaints

Commission. Fellowes knew at once how profoundly Diana had deceived him, and not only apologized to McGregor, but offered his resignation to the Queen as well. McGregor understood that Fellowes had behaved honorably, and the Queen refused to let him resign. But Diana had mortified her brother-in-law and, as McGregor wrote later in a letter, "embarrassed the commission and undermined the purpose" of its statement to the press. Although Diana and her brother-in-law remained on speaking terms, their relationship was irreparably damaged, and Diana and Jane grew more distant.

Until then, according to Jonathan Dimbleby's biography, Charles had believed the marriage could survive. Like Fellowes, Charles had continued to cling to "the thought that the Princess might be innocent of involvement in such malice." He changed his mind after Diana refused to sign a statement prepared by Richard Aylard, his private secretary, that condemned the book for its inaccuracies and distortions. When Charles learned of Fellowes's apology to Lord McGregor, he understood that Diana was deeply implicated in the book.

After the Carolyn Bartholomew pictures appeared, Diana received a stern message from Prime Minister John Major saying he couldn't help her "if she tried to manipulate the press." That afternoon, Diana burst into tears while visiting a hospice; her tangled cover story was coming apart, and she was beginning to crack. After tacitly approving her friends' cooperation and refusing to sign the Aylard statement, she kept just a small fig leaf of personal deniability; her direct role would be revealed by Morton only after her death.

While the Queen was in Paris, she discussed the Morton book with her top advisers. Although the material was devastating, the Queen could also see that Diana was desperately troubled. The Queen's first impulse, backed by Prince Philip, was to focus on salvaging the marriage—for the sake of William and Harry, but also because it was a royal union with constitutional and succession questions at stake. According to Dimbleby, Charles and his parents had not discussed his marriage until the Morton book, and only then after the Romseys, van Cutsems, and several other friends had revealed to the Queen and Prince Philip, presumably in a way Charles himself could not, the details of his marital ordeal. At that point, Charles's parents abandoned their neutrality and "rallied to the Prince."

As Diana later admitted, the royal family was "shocked and horrified and very disappointed." Among those most dismayed was Diana's staunchest royal friend, Princess Margaret. "Until the Morton book, she liked Diana," one of her friends said. "But [with] any attack on the Queen . . . Princess Margaret reacts violently. She has not said enough bad things since then about Diana." The rest of the royal family quickly shifted from shock to outrage. "The Morton book was something everyone thought was a despicable way of airing dirty linen in public," a relative of the royal family said. "After that, the wheels began to turn. The book was the most public thing that had happened in the royal family since the abdication, and the fact that it was in print for anybody to read made it even worse."

As the second Morton excerpt rolled out on June 14, the Queen and her family were at Windsor for the races at Ascot. Two days earlier, Charles had first discussed with his mother the pros and cons of seeking a separation. At a meeting in Windsor Castle on the fifteenth, the Queen and Prince Philip talked to Charles and Diana. The idea of divorce came up but was rejected, and the Queen "was led to believe that the Princess would stand by the Prince and suggested a six-month 'cooling-off period.' "

Diana gave an emotional account of this meeting to Colthurst, who wrote in his diary: "Left her shaken rigid. They accused her of having done the book." Diana said they asked if she had helped, and again she lied, with "a lot of tears." Philip, she said, was "angry, raging, and unpleasant," and Charles wouldn't raise his earlier conversation with Diana about a "parting of the ways," even when she urged him to: "He stood there absolutely *stumm*. . . . He couldn't speak for himself when his parents were present. His physical proximity leaves her cold." Diana also told friends that Philip said if she divorced Charles she would lose her title. Recalled her friend Elsa Bowker, "Diana said, 'When I came here, I had my title. I don't need your title.' The meaning was, though she didn't say this, 'I am from a better family than you are.' "

Prince Philip took his own "tough love" approach by writing Diana a series of four letters that were part reprimand, part entreaty. Without knowing the truth about Diana's role in the Morton book, he rebuked her for cooperating with the author and permitting her friends to talk, but he also admitted his disappointment in his son's behavior, and he made an appeal to her sense of duty.

"He tried to bring the sides together in his own way," said a close friend of Diana's who discussed the letters at length with her. "He wrote about duty to the family, how he felt when George VI died and [Philip] had a career he loved that he had to give up for duty. Diana had her ups and downs with Prince Philip, but she recognized his role in the family. Some of the letters were hurtful about the Morton book, and at first I thought he was outrageous to blame her, but then I realized she was behind the book much more than I thought, and I realized he was correct. The trouble was, he never touched Diana's heart. He couldn't, because he argued in terms of duty and not love."

Diana reacted defensively to her father-in-law's letters, hiring a lawyer to help her draft replies explaining her mistreatment by the royal family.

Her interpretation of Prince Philip's letters—"stinging," "wounding," "irate"—along with details of the contents, surfaced in an updated paperback of Morton's book that was published later in the year. It seemed unlikely that the leak had come from Prince Philip.

Charles had given his friends strict instructions not to return Diana's fire. Some couldn't help themselves. David Frost, who had been friendly with both Charles and Diana, defended Charles on his morning television program, *Frost on Sunday,* as "caring and compassionate" and denounced the Morton book as "one-sided and infuriating. . . . The real picture of the Prince has been lacking."

After the considerable heat *The Sunday Times* had taken for publishing such a tendentious version of the Wales marriage, editor Andrew Neil assigned several reporters to present Charles's side. They made little progress because of Charles's injunction against speaking out—until Andrew Knight happened to meet Charles's close friend and cousin Norton Romsey at a cricket match. Romsey "was very upset and outraged," Knight recalled, but said he was powerless to say anything publicly. Knight called King Constantine of Greece, a longtime friend also close to Charles, who seconded Romsey's views ("You should have seen them when they were together; she would talk to him like a fishwife") but said he had pledged silence as well. Nevertheless, Knight alerted Sue Douglas, the editor in charge of the article, who called both Romsey and Constantine. Although their views informed the article and they were listed as sources "spoken to" by the newspaper, they weren't quoted directly.

THE CASE FOR CHARLES appeared in *The Sunday Times* on June 28 and offered little to redress the imbalance. It mostly recounted how unfairly Charles's friends felt he had been depicted, noting that he had requested a "dignified silence . . . because he fears that to deepen the crisis would hurt his children." *The Sunday Times* offered a few illustrations of Diana's difficult behavior, including her efforts to organize William's first trip to Wales without her husband's knowledge, and her unwillingness to stay with Charles while he recuperated from his broken arm in 1990. The most revealing insight, however, was a quote from a "close friend of the Prince" that showed a possible way out for Diana: "He is annoyed that the Princess is half-denying she cooperated with the book. He wants her to admit her involvement, and admit it was a mistake."

Instead, Diana viewed the *Sunday Times* article as evidence of a larger conspiracy, a "campaign of derision and disdain" by Charles's friends and aides. Her paranoia only increased at the end of August when transcripts of the Squidgy tapes were finally published—first in the American supermarket tabloid the *National Enquirer,* then in the *Sunday Express,* and finally in *The Sun* on Monday, August 24, under the headline MY LIFE IS TORTURE.

Diana, who was at Balmoral when the Squidgy story broke, later said the publication "was done to harm me in a serious manner . . . to make the public change their attitude towards me."

Barely a week later, Diana's conspiratorial suspicions surfaced again when *The Sun* ran an article alleging that Diana and James Hewitt "had enjoyed a 'physical relationship.' " Photographs of them together were analyzed for intimacy in their body language. Hewitt immediately sued the paper for libel, and while he never took the case to court, his indignant denials took some of the sting out of *The Sun*'s allegations. Still, now that Hewitt had been named along with Gilbey, the possibility of adultery by Diana was harder to dismiss, and friends reported she felt "destroyed" by the coverage.

The one potential benefit of the Morton book was that it publicized Diana's severe symptoms of psychological distress. Unfortunately, the book said that Diana had come through the "dark ages" to vanquish her problems; as a result, Diana didn't seek help, and no one offered her any. By Morton's account, she had achieved the "flowering of [her] true nature" through her display of "courage and determination," and she was steadied by her "growing sense of self-belief." In fact, Diana was in despair, on an "emotional roller coaster," as Morton well knew—and her behavior in public became ever more erratic.

Initially, Diana had regarded the book as a public relations coup, but by the autumn she came to see it as "the beginning of the end," said one of her close friends. She told friends of her regrets and constructed a new version of the book's origin. "She said to me that things went out of her control," one close friend recalled, "that Andrew Morton talked to people she didn't want him to talk to, and that they told him things she didn't want to get out. She had a little control in the beginning, and then she lost it."

This disavowal extended to the friends she had recruited to help with the book. According to journalist Richard Kay, who became Diana's confidant some months after the Morton book, "She dropped most of the people who cooperated with Andrew Morton. She went into denial and had to distance herself from everyone involved. Gilbey was cast to the outer darkness, and Angela Serota, too. Carolyn Bartholomew endured, but they weren't terribly close." At the time, Kay reported in the *Daily Mail* that Diana had dropped these friends because she was "incensed . . . at what she perceived as a massive show of disloyalty" by cooperating with Morton's "inflammatory book."

Yet Diana made one fascinating exception in James Colthurst, who remained her "unpaid adviser," according to Morton's publisher, Michael O'Mara, until 1994. Through Colthurst, Diana kept secretly feeding information to Morton. "James Colthurst was still my intermediary," Morton admitted, citing a long article about Diana he wrote late in 1993 for *The Sunday Times:* "She called James Colthurst, and I did that piece based on her spin."

Palace officials couldn't begin to grasp the labyrinthine way Diana operated, though they now knew she was capable of treachery when she felt cornered. They were constantly wary, because they recognized she was at once highly visible and utterly unpredictable. One moment she would be contrite, the next she would be furious. Because she didn't operate logically, she remained beyond their control. Much of the time, they couldn't fathom whether she wanted in or out of the Wales marriage, and they feared the consequences of crossing her.

Three years later, Diana spoke of this period in a curiously passive fashion—as if someone else had been responsible for the Morton book and its aftermath. "What had been hidden, or rather, what we thought had been hidden, then became out in the open and was spoken about on a daily basis," she said. "The pressure was for us to sort ourselves out in some way. Were we going to stay together or were we going to separate? And the word[s] 'separation' and 'divorce' kept coming up in the media on a daily basis. We struggled along. We did our engagements together. And in our private life it was obviously turbulent. My husband and I, we discussed it very calmly. We could see what the public were requiring. They wanted clarity of a situation that was obviously becoming intolerable."

By the autumn of 1992, Charles and Diana were each consulting lawyers; according to several accounts, their face-to-face discussions often ended in tears and anger. Dimbleby recounted that after Diana began "openly talking about a separation," Charles contacted Arnold Goodman, longtime legal adviser to prominent members of the British establishment. Yet Charles was unwilling to initiate formal proceedings. "He was struggling on, but in despair. I don't think either wanted a separation," said a relative who talked with him that fall.

Diana had also been conferring with her lawyer, Paul Butner, but in her usual cloak-and-dagger fashion. She used a code name—"Mrs. Walsh"—and met him secretly at friends' apartments and obscure restaurants before inviting him to Kensington Palace. Her principal concern, as it had been for a while, was losing custody of her sons and being "exiled" by the royal family.

While Diana vacillated and Charles hesitated, events forced decisive action. For some months, Diana and Charles had been committed to an official visit to Korea in November, but during the Balmoral holiday in August, Diana had suddenly withdrawn from the trip. Only after the Queen intervened did Diana agree to travel with Charles. Before they departed in early November, Charles's private secretary Richard Aylard tried to set a positive tone by telling the editor of the *Express* that the trip showed a new harmony between the Waleses. The newspaper obediently ran an article headlined WHY CHARLES AND DIANA ARE BACK TOGETHER.

But as soon as the Waleses arrived in Seoul, Diana made it clear she was there under duress. Her expressions ranged from indifferent to miserable, and according to Dimbleby, she was "often distraught . . . in a state of desperation, overcome by nausea and tears." According to one of her former aides, "Diana felt she no longer needed to disguise what she felt." Charles did his best to deflect attention from her obvious anguish, but he was at times visibly uncomfortable. The tabloids nicknamed them "The Glums." As Charles wrote to a friend at the end of the trip, "The strain is immense. . . . I feel so unsuited to the ghastly business of human intrigue and general nastiness. . . . I don't know what will happen from *now* on but I *dread* it."

While they were away, the tabloids had published stories about Morton's updated book, including his revelations about Prince Philip's "stinging" letters. Diana had been on the phone with friends about the reports, and on her return to London, she felt compelled to distance herself from Morton's account with a brief statement denouncing the "recent wave of misleading reports about the royal family. . . . The suggestion that the Queen and the Duke of Edinburgh have been anything other than sympathetic and supportive is untrue and particularly hurtful."

Within days, the tabloids were filled with still another tape scandal when the *Daily Mirror,* quickly followed by *The Sun,* published abbreviated extracts of the intimate telephone conversation in December 1989 between Camilla and Charles that became known as "Camillagate." (Unlike the Squidgy tape, which had been in tabloid hands for nearly three years before publication, the tape of this conversation had only landed at the *Mirror* a few weeks earlier.) The Palace remained silent, as it had after the Squidgy tape came to light, but the snippets ("I'll just live inside your trousers") left no doubt about Charles and Camilla's intimacy, and prompted questions about Charles's fitness to be king.

Prince Charles finally "snapped" that week when Diana tried once again to stymie plans he had made for William and Harry. The family had been slated to gather on November 19 at Sandringham for Charles's annual three-day shooting party when Diana abruptly told him that she would be taking the boys to Windsor or Highgrove that weekend. Her decision evidently was not sudden; she had told her butler Paul Burrell weeks earlier that she couldn't face a weekend with her husband. Charles felt her actions, only days before the weekend, underlined the impracticability of their situation. "Unable to see any future in a relationship conducted on these terms," biographer Jonathan Dimbleby wrote, "[Charles] decided he had no choice but to ask his wife for a legal separation."

Once Charles had made up his mind, events moved swiftly. On November 25, less than a week later, Charles sat down with Diana at Kensington Palace to tell her of his decision. Despite all her provocations, Diana later said it was "not at all" her idea to separate because, as she said, "I come from a divorced background, and I didn't want to get into that one again." But Diana readily agreed, their lawyers exchanged documents, and Diana went to Ludgrove, the boarding school that William and Harry attended, to tell them the news. On December 9, Prime Minister John Major announced the separation to the House of Commons. Diana, who was out on a round of official duties, "heard it on the radio, and it was just very very sad." In public, Diana looked "carefree, glossy and utterly content," wrote Lynda Lee-Potter in the *Daily Mail*. She spent the evening at the home of some close friends, where she was sad and subdued. She expressed no relief, but said she hoped that somehow her life could change for the better. When James Hewitt phoned to bolster her, he said later, "Diana sounded flat and low. . . . She did not think that it would ever be possible for her to have what she really wanted."

The newspapers—broadsheets as well as tabloids—devoted pages to analyzing the causes and implications of the separation. Not surprisingly, they absolved themselves of responsibility. Forgetting the obsessive and often reckless coverage of Diana over the years, the *Daily Mail* observed, "The media did not mismatch the royal pair nor split them asunder. This marriage has died from within as marriages do." The *Evening Standard* explained that the media were only trying to "report the truth about the royal marriage" when "every difficulty was put in their way. . . . The newspapers were right to say that Prince Charles and Princess Diana were an unhappy couple. . . . This turn of events is a vindication of the press."

In assigning blame, the tabloids pointed to Charles. Paul Johnson, writing in the *Daily Mail*, best reflected the prevailing sentiment: Diana, he wrote, had the "royal magic" and "could have proved to be the biggest asset." For Charles to "throw away this treasure . . . reflects very badly on his judgment."

Chapter 18

As Diana considered what to do after the separation, she turned to her diverse collection of friends for solace and advice. Her friends later talked about how Diana kept her friendships exclusive. She would rarely see two or three friends together, and then only if they already knew one another. This practice was unusual in the British upper class, in which social life typically revolved around group activities such as house parties. Indeed, Prince Charles socialized with a tightly knit clique widely known as the "Highgrove Set."

Some of Diana's relationships were well known, but when Diana died, many of her friends were stunned to discover who else she had been close to. "She lived her life in so many tight compartments," her friend Rosa Monckton said. "She didn't introduce her friends very often. You know she was just so scared of losing people or of people rejecting her."

Diana's attitude toward friends reflected her complicated temperament—her mistrust, insecurity, and penchant for secrecy, as well as her warmth, humor, and impetuous generosity. By keeping her friends apart, she always maintained the upper hand. Fashion entrepreneur Roberto Devorik once suggested that she gather a half-dozen friends for a weekly lunch "to discuss the things you're not sure about and directions you might take." Diana would have none of it, because "by dividing you rule," said Devorik. She said different things to different friends—yet another reason she preferred that they not compare notes. "Everyone knew a piece of her," a close friend said. "But no one knew the whole. I think it started because she couldn't afford to trust one person completely, and then it became a way to be."

Diana had an aversion to pushy people. "She liked to be the one who offered rather than hav[ing] people offer to her," said Marguerite Littman, an American expatriate living in London who knew Diana well in the nineties. "I watched her watch people stand back, and she would go to them. She didn't like it when people came to her." Although Diana was susceptible to flattery, she often befriended people facing tough times; after they had recovered she sometimes drifted away, although one friend recalled that Diana stopped speaking to her "when I was at my lowest and could not have been more vulnerable. She may not have known it."

Diana idealized each new friend as someone who could do no wrong. She gave large bouquets of roses, scented candles, Herend animal figurines, and enamel boxes as tokens of her affection. (One box in the shape of a shopping bag said "Shop 'Til You Drop.") When the boyfriend of one of Diana's friends had to leave England for several months, Diana sent flowers to her friend, with a note that read, "Hang in there." "She needed to be liked and she wanted to please, to get feedback," said businessman Mark Lloyd, a friend during her last few years.

People were attracted to Diana initially by her beauty, charm, and celebrity, and they remained attached because of her vulnerability, spontaneous affection, and ebullient sense of humor. "The mistake people made," said one friend who lasted over the years, "was to get deeply involved. They got obsessed by her and she did by them, and then when it went wrong, it did [so] big-time. She had a paranoid side."

Diana expected her friends to be instantly available, and to listen to her long, emotional phone calls. "She couldn't relax," one of her friends said. "If something was bothering her, she would talk about it over and over and over with her friends. She really valued relationships, but her intensity would cause problems that disrupted the relationships: her torment, her interpreting and reinterpreting another's act. She lived her life trying to be one step ahead, always on her guard."

Some friends resisted the temptation to "get inside her net," as one man put it, and give her total devotion. In doing so, these friends endured far longer. With selected friends she gossiped, with others she didn't even whisper another friend's name. "It was totally one-to-one," said Cosima Somerset, who had an intense friendship with Diana a year before she died. "We didn't talk about other people, only what was going on in her life and my life."

Diana was easily wounded and quick to feel patronized. "If something happened and it was her fault, she would not accept blame," a friend said. "And if you said something critical, she would think you disapproved of her." The unpredictability of her reactions made her friends fearful of saying anything that might offend, although this injunction didn't extend to witty irreverence, which she enjoyed, mostly from men. She had one male friend who teased her continually, making her laugh by calling her other friends impudent nicknames (Lucia Flecha de Lima was "Pressa de Fle-sha,") and mocking her choice of lovers (red-haired Hewitt was "Ginger").

As swiftly as Diana took up with people, she would drop them, usually without explanation or even obvious provocation. "She would be disap-pointed, not over big things, but little things," one of her friends said. She retreated if she sensed a friend was trying to take control, or if she felt too dependent and feared someone might reject her. Diana also was especially quick to see—or imagine—disloyalty. Although Diana occasionally got into heated arguments with friends, the end was usually marked by si-lence—unreturned and uninitiated phone calls, averted eyes at social gath-erings. "She had difficulty solving her own problems," one of her friends explained. "She wanted to please, but for her it was easier to cut off a prob-lem than to solve it."

Most of the time, people withdrew if Diana dropped them. "Because of who she was, people were reluctant to get in touch," a friend explained. In some cases, as if on a whim, Diana would call an exiled friend after a period of months and resume as if nothing had happened. However, when friends made her face the consequences of her actions, she would lower her de-fenses and relent. After Diana's *Panorama* interview, David Puttnam wrote a letter advising her how to pick up the pieces. His criticism was gentle, and his advice sound, but she didn't reply and cut him from her Christmas card list. A year later, they met at a luncheon. Puttnam bluntly told her how her rudeness had hurt him, and when she "made up a story" as an excuse, he wouldn't accept it. He told her that if she had any questions about his loyalty, she should simply call him: "I said, 'When you do things like that, you are not like other people. I couldn't call you. You have a peculiar ability to call me.' " Like a father with a remorseful daughter, he then made her repeat several times, "David, I am very sorry. If ever I have a worry in the future I will pick up the phone." Recalled Puttnam, "She charmed me. Having absorbed being told off, she behaved like a child."

Interior designer Nicky Haslam took a more direct approach. After five years of friendship, Diana had dropped him after he displayed her light-hearted thank-you note for a pair of Turkish slippers ("They are the perfect size for my giant clodhopping feet") in the window of his shop. When he saw her at a cocktail party and she ignored him, he spent the rest of the evening glaring at her. Finally, she sent a mutual friend over to ask, "Why are you sending daggers at Diana?" "The bitch is cutting me," Haslam replied. The friend scurried away to confer with Diana, and soon after-ward, the Princess "flew across the room and said, 'I wasn't cutting you. I was just saving you till last.' "

The nature of female friendship—offering emotional support, sharing experiences of children and husbands—was particularly important to

Diana. More than most women, Diana fit her friends—male and female—into specific categories. "She was very clever to give roles to us," Roberto Devorik said. There were holiday friends, companions to share giggles over lunch, friends who broadened her horizons, mothers with children the ages of her sons, soul mate friends, avuncular friends, fraternal friends, maternal figures, and friends outside her upper-class milieu. "I was not on the same social circuit as other friends," said Diana's energy healer Simone Simmons. "There was no danger of me blurting out things to people to whom she might have been sending out different messages from her complicated private agenda. . . . She carved out a very precise box for me in her life."

Diana's maternal figures, who filled the gap created by her inconsistent relationship with her own mother, formed an especially influential group. Having an array of maternal figures was an arrangement that reflected Diana's neediness as much as her power to command such a lineup. If one woman wasn't available, Diana could always turn to another, or if one wasn't listening carefully, Diana could find an alternative. "She was better behaved with the older women, probably because they were more patient with her," a friend said. "It was more difficult with her contemporaries because they couldn't give her that kind of attention."

Diana's collection of surrogate mothers emerged in the late eighties and early nineties, and included Annabel Goldsmith, Lucia Flecha de Lima, Hayat Palumbo, and Elsa Bowker—formidable women in their own right, but all living outside the conventional world in which Diana had been raised. They eclipsed Diana's original maternal friend, Mara Berni, owner of the San Lorenzo restaurant. During the eighties, Mara had functioned as a spiritual counselor, giving Diana "prophecies," advice on her love life, and guidance about astrology and clairvoyance. Diana's mother figures were anywhere from twenty to fifty years her senior; even within the maternal category, they occupied different niches.

Lucia Flecha de Lima was foremost among these maternal figures. The two women met during the Waleses' tour of Brazil in April 1991, when Lucia was forty-nine and Diana twenty-nine. Afterward, Diana became a regular visitor at the Brazilian ambassador's residence on Mount Street in London. One of nine children, Lucia was the beautiful, privileged daughter of an heiress and a doctor who specialized in tropical disease research. Diana once described Lucia as "the mother I would have liked to have had."

A mother of five and grandmother, Lucia pulled Diana into her lively family life; on a number of occasions, Diana joined them for Easter, Christmas, and Boxing Day when her sons were with Charles. One of Lucia's daughters, Beatrice, became a close friend as well. "Diana loved going to their house and feeling the warmth of a close-knit family," one of Diana's friends said. Lucia was down-to-earth and nurturing, always a willing listener. Since her own children were grown, she had the time to dedicate to Diana. "It required her to be there when Diana called, and to go to lunch when Diana called," a friend said. The two women spoke at least once a day, even after the Flecha de Limas moved to the United States in November 1993.

As a Latin American, Lucia had a different sensibility from the British upper class that Diana found refreshing; for example, she was less judgmental about openly expressed emotion. Diana appreciated that Lucia was an outsider with no strong feelings for or against the royal family, but because Lucia didn't completely understand the British mentality, her advice was sometimes limited. What Lucia gave Diana above all was unconditional love: Lucia voiced her opinions but didn't press them; the two women argued from time to time, but Diana didn't drop Lucia as she dropped so many others.

Annabel Goldsmith had solid credentials in the British establishment. The daughter of the Marquess of Londonderry, she had known both Frances and Johnnie in her youth. (In the hereditary peerage, a marquess ranks just below a duke, and one rung above Diana's father, Earl Spencer.) Annabel's friendship with Diana began the night of her party in 1989, when Diana confronted Camilla. Initially, Diana tried to pump Annabel about Camilla, but when Annabel offered scant information, Diana gave up. Although their relationship had a mother-daughter quality, it was more lighthearted than Diana's friendship with Lucia. Annabel and Diana often met over lunch, and laughter was "the essential ingredient in our relationship," Annabel wrote in the *Daily Mail* after Diana's death.

Once or twice a month, Diana went to the Goldsmith home on the outskirts of London for Sunday lunch. She would call on Saturday and inquire, "Is the madhouse on?" Like the Flecha de Limas, the Goldsmiths offered Diana a family atmosphere. Diana frequently brought her sons, who enjoyed the Goldsmith children.

Although Annabel came from Diana's aristocratic milieu, she was not establishment in her outlook, and her husband, Jimmy, the iconoclastic billionaire businessman, was profoundly antiestablishment. The family was also decidedly unconventional: Jimmy and Annabel shared a life in England, and he openly lived with a mistress (by whom he had two children) in France. On the other side of Goldsmith's Parisian house lived his first wife. This combination of familiar and daring enabled Diana to unwind at the Goldsmiths' more completely than anywhere else.

"At lunch at Annabel's, Diana was at her most relaxed and giggly," said Cosima Somerset. The Princess would tell stories, joke with the staff, swim in the pool, and help wash the dishes. In quieter moments, Annabel listened to Diana's laments, yet Diana was reluctant to admit her deepest insecurities to Annabel. "She minded what Annabel thought of her," a friend said. "She was like a child who wanted to be seen at her best, without a flaw."

Elsa Bowker was the oldest of Diana's surrogate mothers—into her eighties when they met in 1993. Her cosmopolitan background appealed to Diana much as Lucia's did. Elsa was born in Egypt to a French mother and Lebanese father. After World War II, she married Christopher Bowker, a British diplomat, and they lived in Burma, France, Germany, and Spain before returning to Britain. "She liked my way of living, my experience, and she could tell me everything," Elsa said. "She became more and more affectionate. She treated me as a mother that she did not have. She told me she didn't understand her mother." A friend of Elsa's called her a "wise old bird," and added, "She gave Diana a lot of advice, although I'm not sure she took any of it."

Elsa did her best to reassure Diana, but felt powerless when Diana was distraught. "To be her friend was difficult," Elsa recalled. "In my case, when she wanted to see me eagerly, I had to abandon everything. Once I put my foot down, and she came three hours later." While Elsa felt great affection for Diana, she considered her "unbalanced" after witnessing her extremes of mood, and she was uncertain what to believe. "Sometimes I would see her face when she was telling me this or that, and I would say, 'Is that the truth?' It wasn't always. She was frightened of what one would do to her if she told the truth. You could tell when she wasn't [telling the truth] by the way she looked and the way she remained silent."

Diana came to know Hayat Palumbo through her husband, Peter, the multimillionaire chairman of the Arts Council. Like Elsa, Hayat was from the Middle East, a Lebanese whose father was a Shiite Moslem and owned a newspaper in Beirut. When Hayat was sixteen, her father was assassinated by terrorists. Before meeting the widowed Palumbo in the 1980s, Hayat had been unhappily married to a wealthy Lebanese businessman. Although Hayat was only a decade older than Diana, she assumed a maternal role, and her husband took a paternal interest. "Hayat is very clever, full of experience, very artistic," a friend said of her. "She is strong, but her life has made her harder."

The Palumbos shared the trappings of their wealth with Diana, flying her in their private jet, entertaining her on their yacht *Drumbeat,* and at their homes in England and France. Peter Palumbo put Diana in contact with the prestigious lawyer Lord Mishcon, whose firm took over her divorce negotiations, as well as Gordon Reece, a public relations adviser who tried to help Diana. Not incidentally, Palumbo was an erstwhile friend of Prince Charles, who had sabotaged one of Palumbo's ambitious development projects with his savage architectural criticism, calling it a "glass stump." "Peter took the approach, 'My enemy's enemy is my friend,' and went straight to Diana," said gossip columnist Nigel Dempster.

It was Lucia Flecha de Lima who introduced Diana to Rosa Monckton, the managing director of Tiffany's in London. Lucia's daughter Beatrice worked for Tiffany's, and the Flecha de Limas shared with Rosa a devout Catholicism. This religious connection was enough to set off a wave of press speculation (PALACE DENIES SPIRITUAL CRISIS) in 1993 that Diana might convert to the Catholic faith. Close friends said that Diana didn't consider conversion, but she was attracted to the good works of Catholic humanitarians such as Mother Teresa and Cardinal Basil Hume, both of whom she met with on a number of occasions.

The daughter of Viscount Monckton of Brenchley, Rosa had a unique perspective on royal crises. Her grandfather, Walter Monckton, had been a close friend and legal adviser to King Edward VIII. When the King abdicated in 1936 to marry divorcée Wallis Simpson, Monckton helped write the King's famous speech renouncing the throne for "the woman I love." Rosa was also married to Dominic Lawson, editor of *The Spectator* and later *The Sunday Telegraph*, a relationship that sometimes circumscribed Diana's conversations with Rosa, but that proved an advantage at other times. Strong and articulate, Rosa served as a sounding board for Diana, who occasionally took offense at Rosa's advice. After the disastrous Korea trip in November 1992, Rosa rebuked Diana for "her sulky public behavior," and Diana didn't call her for four months. Like other friends, Rosa was someone Diana could call and "simply cry [until she was] totally drained and completely exhausted." As a friend of Prince Charles said, "Rosa was tough-minded and analytical about Diana, but entirely devoted to her nevertheless."

Diana and Rosa were closest when Rosa miscarried, then subsequently gave birth to a daughter named Domenica who had Down's syndrome. Rosa recalled that Diana was "compassionate and practical" in the extensive help she gave her and her daughter. "Diana was there for her," a friend of Rosa said. "Diana got some kind of strength from that." Diana offered to be Domenica's godmother, which led to another brief falling-out when Rosa invited photographers from *Hello!* magazine to the christening. Whenever anyone seemed to be exploiting a friendship with her, Diana took it as betrayal. "Diana was very angry about that; I don't know how Rosa could have made that mistake," another friend said. The two women repaired the relationship, but the episode left Diana uneasy.

Another friend sometimes identified as a maternal presence was Marguerite Littman, probably because she was of the same generation as Diana's own mother. The Louisiana-born wife of an English barrister,

Marguerite founded the AIDS Crisis Trust and met Diana through Adrian Ward-Jackson, vice chairman of the trust. "I would have loved to have been a mother figure," Marguerite said. "But we were much more like play-mates." Known for her droll humor and numerous connections in Holly-wood (where she lived in the fifties while coaching actors in Southern dialect), New York, and London, Marguerite often had lunch with Diana at Harry's Bar, Kensington Palace, or Marguerite's home in fashionable Chester Square.

"I deliberately didn't get into situations where she would ask me for advice," Littman said. "She would confide in me about little things, but she had enough people to confide in. You end up resenting people you confide in, because it gives them power. She told me her opinions of people, which was much more dangerous. That kind of thing she trusted me with. When I was with her, I liked everything to be as light as I could make it. If I had anything to tell about myself, it would have weighed on her. We were hav-ing a good time, talking about serious things but keeping it light."

These new friends of Diana's overshadowed the "girlfriends" she had met in the mid-eighties—Kate Menzies, Catherine Soames, and Julia Samuel. After the separation was announced, it was Catherine and her son Harry who joined Diana and her two boys on the Caribbean island of Nevis. Catherine, an heiress whose family controlled the Hong Kong–based Jardine Matheson Holdings, a multinational conglomerate, was the former wife of Nicholas Soames, Charles's friend whom Diana disliked. Diana skied each spring in Lech, Austria, with Catherine and Kate, and vaca-tioned at the home of Kate's parents in exclusive Lyford Cay in the Ba-hamas. Kate was also from a wealthy family whose fortune was built on the John Menzies newsagency chain.

"Diana was terribly giggly with Catherine and Kate," a friend said. "They talked in little innuendos and private jokes and shorthand." They even gave Diana a new nickname: "Princhey." "Originally everyone called her Duch, so Princhey was an upgrade," a friend explained. Since both Kate and Catherine were independently wealthy, they were less deferential than they might otherwise have been. "They didn't want to be ladies-in-waiting to Diana," another friend said. Although Julia Samuel was known for her lively parties, her relationship with Diana had a more serious cast, since she had trained as a therapist. "Julia was a helping sort, a great listener, who[m] Diana gravitated to," a friend of Diana's said.

Diana also had a group of male friends who played specific parts. One avuncular friend described himself from Diana's viewpoint as "an old fart who was open-minded." They teased each other, and he felt a duty to "cheer her up." In later years, he gave her advice, which she declined to take, and he noticed a pattern to their friendship: "You could tell when she was up to something. You wouldn't hear from her. I would hear from her in between, when she was under pressure."

Wealthy Argentine Roberto Devorik, who first met Diana when he supplied clothes from his fashion business for her wedding trousseau, considered himself "like a brother to her. She was very British, and proud to be British, but she was fed up with the coolness and hypocrisy of the English upper class. I come from a middle/upper-class background, and I am Latin." Devorik organized dinner parties and lunches for Diana with a glittering social set drawn from the worlds of film, theater, and fashion. He also organized several of her trips to the Caribbean. "My aim was to make her laugh in life," Devorik said.

Diana's up-and-down friendship with Fergie was unique in their shared antipathy for the royal family. Fergie's path in 1992 had been nearly as bumpy as Diana's, and by the year's end, she was outside the fold as well. Fergie's marriage to Andrew had begun to fray even before the birth of their second daughter in 1990. "By 1989, [Andrew and I] were sharing less and less," Fergie recalled. "I should have asked Andrew to leave the navy." Fergie clashed repeatedly with the Palace hierarchy over her spending habits, and her husband was absent too often to give her much help.

Although Andrew and Fergie remained fond of each other, Fergie ran into trouble when she turned to other men. The first was Steve Wyatt, a wealthy Texan she had started seeing in 1990; in January 1992, the *Daily Mail* reported that a maid had found a packet of compromising photographs in Wyatt's London apartment showing Fergie with Wyatt on a Moroccan holiday. A week later, Fergie suggested to Andrew that they part company, and in mid-March, Buckingham Palace announced their formal separation.

By then, Fergie was already involved with another American, John Bryan, formally known as her "financial adviser." In August 1992, Fergie and her two young daughters went on vacation with Bryan at a secluded villa in Saint-Tropez. It was this holiday that prompted one of Diana's friends to remark that Fergie had a "judgment bypass." While hiding in some nearby foliage, Italian paparazzo Daniel Angeli snapped nearly 200 pictures of a topless Fergie nuzzling and kissing Bryan. *The Mirror* bought more than fifty of the photos and published them in late August (just three days before the Squidgy story broke) when Fergie was with the royal family at Balmoral. In one shot, Bryan was shown kissing the top of Fergie's foot, an image that transmuted into royal lore as the infamous "toe-sucking picture." Fergie's position in the royal family had become untenable and divorce inevitable.

Diana and Fergie had formed what Fergie called a "potent confederacy" in the year before they left the royal family, prodding each other in various acts of defiance. "If it hadn't been for Fergie's example and her encouragement to separate, Diana might have acted differently," one of Diana's close friends said. Even so, Diana had few illusions about her sister-in-law; her jaundiced view of Fergie had been evident in the spiky comments she made to Andrew Morton in the summer and fall of 1991 for his book. But by 1993, the two women were reunited in their outsider status, fueling each other's worst conspiratorial view that, as Fergie put it, the royal "firm" was doing "its level best to isolate us." Neither woman had the capacity to see beyond her own perspective, and any action seemed a plot against them.

Diana's sister Sarah moved closer to her after the divorce as well, as Jane receded following the Morton debacle. Diana made Sarah a lady-in-waiting, and took her along on two foreign trips in the months following the split from Charles. "She's the only person I know I can trust," Diana said at the time. Sarah's brisk wit struck a note of levity when Diana began to descend into self-pity; Diana also drew on her sister's strength, practicality, and efficiency. But the role of lady-in-waiting proved difficult; Sarah chafed at having to stand aside holding Diana's purse during official engagements instead of mingling with the guests. "Sarah loves the limelight," one of Diana's friends said. "It was a mistake to make her lady-in-waiting. Sarah doesn't have the personality to play second fiddle."

At the same time, Diana had a major falling-out with her brother Charles. With the loss of Highgrove for weekends, Diana faced the practical problem of finding a country retreat where she could take her two sons. Charles, by then the 9th Earl Spencer, offered her a home at Althorp, where he was living with his wife and children. She immediately chose Garden House, a "Palladian jewel" inside the walls of the estate, where Jane and Robert Fellowes had lived for a decade before moving to a house in Norfolk. Charles initially agreed, but after the royal security service recommended an elaborate alarm system and thrice-daily sweeps of the property by dog patrols, Charles became concerned about the privacy of his family.

Charles offered Diana a choice of 120 other homes in the Spencer holdings in lieu of Garden House. He recommended Wormleighton Manor, the Spencer family's original fifteenth-century manor house, which offered complete privacy: It was surrounded by a wall, with a gatehouse for bodyguards. But Diana had set her heart on Garden House, and she was furious that her brother denied her wishes. She told her friends how much he had hurt her, the press was soon decrying her brother's unfeeling behavior, and she refused to speak to him—what he later characterized as a "brief but bitter silence."

It may have been no coincidence that Diana abruptly chose that moment to reconcile with Raine Spencer, her sworn enemy. Only four years earlier, Diana had confronted Raine at Charles Spencer's wedding and sputtered, "I hate you so much. If only you knew how much we all hated you for what you've done."

Diana and Raine had met by chance in May 1993 at Claridge's, where Diana was attending a charity luncheon. Afterward, Diana invited Raine to Kensington Palace, and the two women began to meet periodically for lunch. As word of their friendship spread, it caused endless comment, and at least one angry exchange between Diana and her mother.

When Diana encountered Raine, "she felt remorse," recalled Elsa Bowker. "Diana's sisters and brother were very cross with her [for reconciling]. Diana had been the one who hated her the most, but she decided to be nice. Diana did a great imitation of Raine. 'Let me take you to a private lunch in a quiet place,' Raine said to her. Diana said, 'Look where she took me, to Claridge's, and all she did was wave to people when they went by.' " But Diana had come to recognize that Raine had been good to her father, and she was amused by Raine's flamboyant presence, fascinated by her cleverness, and titillated by her gossip. "Diana felt Raine was fun and amazing," a friend of Diana's said. "She took Raine as she was, and didn't judge her."

Chapter 19

DIANA's effort to define herself took on greater urgency after her official separation from Charles in December 1992. Her life as a mother had changed several months earlier when eight-year-old Harry went off to boarding school at Ludgrove, leaving her to cope with an empty nest and the loss of day-to-day family responsibilities. She was no longer a wife, except on royal occasions when her presence with Charles was required. She was left with the overwhelming portfolio of public responsibilities she had built up helter-skelter in her competition with Charles over the previous two years. By 1993, she was the patron of 118 charities that had come to depend on her to attract attention and money.

The mythology was that Diana drew "new strength" from the failure of her marriage, and that her official separation was "the trigger for her to complete her metamorphosis from despairing princess to confident new woman," as reporter Richard Kay described it in the *Daily Mail*. As had so often proved the case, the "new strength" was a tabloid fantasy; even Richard Kay admitted years later, "I never found her strong."

Diana was a creature of impulses—both good and bad—who was as surprised as anyone by the consequences of her actions. She had no specific plan other than to use her position to comfort the afflicted—a genuine desire that gave her a sense of purpose. Unfortunately, her ability to articulate her mission was hampered by persistent suspicion of her estranged husband and his allies. Rather than thoughtfully crafting a positive role, she worried about imagined intrigues against her. "I was a problem," she said. "I was a liability. . . . My husband's side [was] very busy stopping me."

One way Diana tried to combat her "husband's side" was in making speeches. She hadn't conquered her terror of public speaking, but she had learned how to use highly visible forums to send coded messages directly to her "public." She may no longer have been an official representative of the royal family, but she had become a singular phenomenon: a celebrity princess who understood her power to command attention and even sway popular opinion.

Diana had made her first speech with clearly personal overtones in the fall of 1991. Addressing a convention of child and adolescent psychiatrists, Diana spoke of the legacy of an unstable childhood created by parental neglect: "Parents sometimes desert families, leaving their children bewildered and bereft with no explanation. . . . Many children even travel through life feeling responsible in some ways for their parents' separation. . . . To travel through life with unbalanced emotions can feel like carrying a heavy rucksack of rubbish." Diana emphasized the need for parents to "hug" and "cuddle" their children to protect them from psychological distress, and to allow children to express their emotions openly. As expected, the press saw Diana's words as a veiled reference to her own unhappy childhood.

A year later, in November 1992, only weeks before her formal separation, Diana made her allusions even more pointed, and the media read her cues as an attack on Prince Charles (THE REAL PAIN OF A BROKEN MARRIAGE in *Today;* DIANA: THE PAIN OF BEING UNLOVED in the *Daily Mail*). In a speech to launch European Drug Prevention Week, she elaborated on her previous year's theme to say that the best prevention against drug abuse was parental affection. Lines such as "children are not chores" but "souls to love and cherish," and "there are potential huggers in every household," seemed like a "lecture on good parenting"—delivered directly to Charles.

Once again, the tabloids went to the thesaurus of superlatives, calling Diana's remarks "astonishing" and "extraordinary." Actually, the speech was a collection of sweet-sounding bromides, delivered somewhat haltingly. Diana's hand was evident in the scrambled syntax and unpolished, even childlike language. But what mattered in Diana's case was the transmission of feelings, something she instinctively knew how to do. The tabloids also missed the underlying shrewdness in Diana's oblique delivery. Had she forthrightly spoken about herself, she might not have received such a positive response. By approaching her subject sideways, she could get her message across without being branded as self-pitying.

Early in 1993, Diana began working closely with her new public speaking coach, Peter Settelin, a former soap opera actor. She had sixty sessions with Settelin, who tried to teach her how to relax and speak more conversationally. Diana asked for his guidance on a speech she had agreed to give at Britain's first conference on eating disorders at the end of April. Settelin helped her write something "that didn't actually say she suffered from [bulimia]," he recalled, "but made the connection in a way that people knew she knew what she was talking about."

In her eight-minute address, Diana spoke with evident passion: "I have it on very good authority that the quest for perfection in society can leave the individual gasping for breath at every turn." As Richard Kay wrote in the *Daily Mail,* "the 'authority' was herself," pointing to some key phrases that "were all Diana's": calling bulimia a "shameful friend," and describing childhood feelings of "guilt, self-revulsion and low personal esteem creating . . . a compulsion to dissolve like a Disprin and disappear."

It was another "astonishing" effort by Diana, leading the tabloids to conclude that her words "showed she had beaten the disease." She had not, and when Susie Orbach, a well-known psychotherapist, described her feminist approach to eating disorders in the keynote address, Diana was listening carefully. Orbach, the author of several best-selling books on eating disorders, had become a therapist after ten years of what she once characterized as "dieting, bingeing, and self-hatred."

Orbach's remarks that day were thick with psychological jargon ("the body as the personification of culture"), but she struck some themes that would appeal to Diana: the need for therapists to see the world through the eyes of their "food-refusing, mouth-stuffing, vomiting, laxative-using" patients; the unhelpful impulse to dismiss victims of eating disorders as "willful, manipulative and resistant"; the need to recognize that an eating disorder victim wants a therapist "who will understand her, who will respect her. . . . She is scared of being patronized, of having control wrested away from her."

In one of the tabloid reports on the conference, Orbach remarked that Diana was "someone who had learned and thought a lot about the problem." But all that Diana may have learned, all of her friends' ministrations, and all the distractions of her healers and spiritualists were insufficient to dispel her symptoms of depression, bulimia, and self-injury. After hearing Orbach's words, Diana decided to undergo therapy once again. The most important factor in Diana's decision was Orbach's own struggle with eating disorders, which would allow her to connect with Diana's emotional turbulence.

Diana contacted Orbach soon after the conference, and began to see her twice a week. Orbach had a narrow agenda: Compulsive eating was "*not* about lack of self-control or lack of willpower," but "a response to the inequality of the sexes." Yet she also used Diana's bulimia to examine other problems, including the warping effects of her celebrity. "I think Susie Orbach helped Diana try to sort herself out," one of Diana's friends said.

Diana made one more major speech that spring—perhaps her most controversial—to a conference run by Turning Point, a charity devoted to treatment of drug and alcohol abuse. In some ways her remarks were more revealing than her bulimia speech, because they reflected her fears about the treatment of mental illness with prescription medication. Diana had rejected tranquilizers prescribed early in her marriage by psychiatrists, but in subsequent years she had agreed to try several medications to soothe her insomnia and depression.

By 1993, she had been taking prescription sleeping pills nightly for several years, a dependence that made her uneasy. She had also tried Prozac, the "miracle" antidepressant available since 1988, but she had quickly abandoned the medication. A close friend recalled, "She said she was afraid to keep taking it because she saw herself as an addictive person. So she was afraid, and she quit. I don't know whether it helped her or not."

That ambivalence was the subtext of Diana's speech in June 1993 on the perils of drugs prescribed to treat women for depression. In strongly feminist language, she described the "haze of loneliness and desperation" that turned too many women into "anxious zombies" hooked on "tranquilizers, sleeping pills and antidepressants," the "mother's little helpers" that "doomed" women to a "life of dependence." Yet Diana declined to reveal her own dependence on prescription sleeping medications. "Perhaps we need to look more closely at the cause of the illness, rather than an attempt to suppress it," she said—an admirable impulse, but a serious disservice to patients who depended on psychopharmacology, especially during periods of crisis.

❧

Despite this rather glaring defect, Diana's speech, like all her public pronouncements, received extensive and mostly positive coverage in the press. In the year following her separation, Diana continued to be portrayed heroically while Charles was either vilified or mocked. When the full text of the Camillagate tape was finally published in January 1993, a poll in *Today* showed that sixty-eight percent of those surveyed thought Charles's reputation would be badly damaged, and forty-two percent thought William, not his father, should be the next king.

Unlike Fergie, whose separation cut her off from official engagements, Diana was free to continue with her royal calendar. (Fergie regarded the move as arbitrary, based only on the courtiers' view of her as the "Bad Witch" and Diana the "Good Witch," although the difference probably had more to do with Diana's special status as mother of the heir to the throne.) Diana was precluded only from representing the Queen on official visits overseas, a logical restriction given Diana's estrangement from Charles. Foreign Secretary Douglas Hurd encouraged Diana's role as unofficial ambassador, and the Foreign Office helped with logistics.

Diana kept a frenetic schedule. Week after week, she stole headlines from Charles and other royals more than ever, with her well-timed speeches and visits with victims. Diana made successful trips to Nepal and Zimbabwe as a representative of several charities. The press corps trailing her around Nepal included a team from *Vogue,* along with the usual contingent of hacks. Diana's celebrity even eclipsed the speeches and meetings of Lynda Chalker, the Overseas Development Minister who accompanied her to Nepal. While Chalker's mission to oversee the spending of $17 million in foreign aid was ignored, the trip became THE TRIUMPH OF DIANA, as the *Express* proclaimed. Skiing in Klosters, Switzerland, that week, Charles spotted only one reporter and asked where everyone had gone. "Nepal," he was told.

Diana received occasional barbs in the press. Woodrow Wyatt, the colorful *News of the World* columnist, said Diana was "addicted to the limelight . . . it's like a drug"; *Daily Mail* columnist Lynda Lee-Potter wondered if Diana's "relentless" work with victims had become her escape from dealing with the crucial issues of her life; a *Mirror* poll showed that eighty-one percent of its readers felt Diana was a "hypocrite" for taking luxurious vacations after doling out gruel to poor people in Africa; and *Tatler*, which Diana read avidly, ran a cover story titled DIANA: MONSTER OR MARTYR, with a poll saying forty-four percent thought "monster" and thirty-eight percent "martyr."

Those articles were the exceptions in a year of glowing coverage. Even so, Diana insisted that she was the victim of "dirty tricks" by the Palace to "downgrade" her role and "marginalize" her. Palace officials denied operating against her. Even Richard Kay, who promoted Diana's Palace conspiracy theories on a number of occasions, had to admit by July 1993, "Palace plots against her have been forecast and rumored . . . yet never materialize."

The tabloids kept up the conspiracy line anyway; the continuing marital rift made more compelling reading than an amicable relationship between the Waleses. Thanks to the Morton book, the media also had a limitless license to report on Diana's private life. Diana still had Palace officials to front for her in dealing with these intrusions, but since she was convinced the "gray men" were operating against her, she sought more direct contact with the press on her own. She was the first member of the royal family to deal with the media without regard for protocol.

Through James Colthurst she continued her secret connection to Morton, who was writing a sequel scheduled for publication in the fall of 1994. "I acknowledge that she had to keep her distance from me," Morton said. "But it is a willful misunderstanding to say she didn't want a second book." Diana also wanted a hand in day-to-day coverage, a far trickier business. British press critic Stephen Glover once compared the tabloid press to a "many-headed hydra, not a monster with a single will. It is mercurial and fiercely competitive." Diana "may have thought she could control the beast," Glover wrote in *The Daily Telegraph*.

To exert that control, Diana turned to Richard Kay, the lead royal reporter on her favorite newspaper, the *Daily Mail*. Like Morton, Kay had clearly staked out his position on Diana's side against Charles. Kay was thirty-six, only four years older than Diana, which made him more accessible than grizzled reporters like James Whitaker and Harry Arnold. Kay appealed to her personally as well as professionally. Tall and lanky, he had the tousled good looks of the well-born men she had known since childhood. Raised in Kent, he had opted out of college. At eighteen, he began working in newspapers and joined the *Daily Mail* in 1980 at age twenty-three. He had worked the royal beat since 1986, and Diana's siblings had gotten to know him five years later when he did a series of articles about their disagreements with Raine Spencer.

Diana made her move on the return flight from Nepal in March 1993 when she invited Kay to join her for what he later described as "our first serious and lengthy conversation." Afterward, Kay recalled, "I realized how inadequately I had served my readers in purporting to be an expert on her and on the royal family. We knew bugger-all." It was the beginning of a relationship that lasted until Diana's death. "I saw her at her happiest and in her darkest moments," Kay said. "There were moments of confusion and despair when I believed Diana was being driven . . . almost to the point of destruction."

From the beginning, Diana set the terms of their relationship. "I wanted information," Kay explained, "but she was not someone I could phone up and say, 'Give me a story.' The contacts came from her side." They spoke frequently on the phone and occasionally saw each other. "When I was at the *Mail*, Richard Kay and I would have lunch at a restaurant where Diana was," recalled Richard Addis, who later edited the *Express*. "She would sit at a different table, and I realized the reason was that she wanted to talk to Richard Kay. If she got the chance, she would go to Richard's table for a cup of coffee." The tabloid press mocked Kay for his role as what Andrew Morton called Diana's "unofficial press officer."

Decoding Kay became a new, British form of Kremlinology. One former Palace official called Kay's *Daily Mail* reports "Diana's own dead-letter drop." "I couldn't disclose that the information had come from her," explained Kay. "Her position would have been untenable in the Palace. In the British press we have conveniently used this device over the years: 'A friend' said this. If the information was accurate, it would work for you, and people would know you were talking to someone. I had no problem saying 'a friend' when it was Diana."

The degree to which Diana had become tethered to her press coverage was evident when she went on vacation with Lucia and Beatrice Flecha de Lima and Rosa Monckton in August 1993. "I want to get away from it all," Diana told entrepreneur Mark Lloyd, asking his help in finding a haven where she could escape into anonymity. Lloyd had a business partner with a string of hotels in Indonesia, and he made elaborate arrangements for them at Amanwana, a new hotel of "twenty luxury tents" on the remote island of Moyo near Bali. Since the resort hadn't yet opened, Diana and her friends would have it to themselves. To avoid a commercial flight, Lloyd arranged for a private jet belonging to Saudi Prince Khalid to transport them.

"It was totally secure," recalled Lloyd, who gave Diana's bodyguard a satellite phone as their sole link to the outside world; "it was the first time Diana ever completely disappeared." But after only a few hours on the island, Diana wanted to move to Bali because she said she was "bored, and hated the isolation." Whenever Diana was away from England and felt out of touch, she became anxious. "She thought people might do something against her [when] she was not there to protect herself," one friend explained.

"Once Diana made up her mind, she was very difficult to change," Lloyd said. He arranged for the women to go to a villa on Bali and then, as he recalled, "the scales fell from my eyes. This was the first time I realized Diana was in touch with Richard Kay. He called my office and asked if we could have a picture of Amanwana. I said, 'How in God's name did you know that?' The only people Diana called were Fergie and Richard Kay." The four women went to Bali, where they walked down a public beach, and Diana was immediately recognized and written about. Recalled Lloyd, "When Diana came back she said to me, 'Wonderful time, Mark. . . . Such a pity it was in the papers.' "

The tabloids began remarking during the summer of 1993 that Diana's frantic pace seemed to be wearing her down, reporting that she was "suffering from stress and exhaustion." When she blew up at an intrusive photographer in early August, shouting, "You make my life hell!," the tabloids concluded that she was about to crack. Two months later, she showed up at the theater "looking angry and strained," and the tabloids ran photos of her with droopy eyes headlined PAIN OF A PRINCESS: IS THE STRAIN GETTING TO DI? and DI'S AT BREAKING POINT AS CHARLES WINS THE PR WAR. "This is the face of a woman under extreme pressure," James Whitaker wrote in the *Daily Mir-*

ror, and Stuart Higgins noted in *The Sun* that an "increasingly emotional and unhappy" Diana had been worn down by the "campaign against her by pro-Charles courtiers."

A meeting on October 20 at Kensington Palace between Diana and John Major to discuss her role, along with an official visit by Diana to Brussels, seemed to belie any concerted campaign to derail her. But Charles was clearly irked by her chronic ability to grab the headlines. Diana later told *Sunday Times* editor Andrew Neil that when she and the Prime Minister talked, he had approved of her proposal to become a humanitarian ambassador for Britain along the lines of actress Audrey Hepburn's longtime work for UNICEF. "Diana told me that Prince Charles had gone mad about that, and had gone to the *Financial Times* and said *he* wanted to be the ambassador," Neil recalled. "She said the Prime Minister had contacted her and said, 'This is getting too messy.'"

Charles did give the *Financial Times* an interview, but not until late November, five weeks after Diana's meeting with Major, and Diana's interpretation was a willful misreading of his words. Citing his recent visit to the Middle East as an example, Charles spoke of his efforts to promote British trade and business overseas—a far different role from what Diana envisioned for herself. Charles also said his work on behalf of British commerce reflected his long-standing interests: "The idea I am searching to redefine my job is rot. It is just that, since the day I got married, people have chosen to ignore the things I continue to do, day in and day out."

Diana was easily thrown off-balance, and the month of November brought a series of provocations that nearly undid her. As the month began, the Flecha de Limas left for the Brazilian Embassy in Washington; on the same day, Diana's chauffeur, Simon Solari, told Diana he was moving to Charles's staff. That evening Diana arrived at a charity performance red-eyed and distraught, and an hour later she left in tears.

The next day, Diana's favorite bodyguard, Ken Wharfe, was moved by Scotland Yard to another position. "Diana leaned on Ken a lot for advice, and he lightened things up," said one of her friends. "But she would draw her staff in too close and then put them in their place. She did that with Ken." According to another friend, Diana mistreated Wharfe when she suspected him of briefing the press. Nevertheless, Diana was extremely distressed when he left, prompting Barbara Cartland to announce on television that her stepgranddaughter had gone on a "prolonged eating binge." This moved Diana to show a "rare public display of her frustration" by telling a luncheon for WellBeing, the charity concerned with the health of mothers and infants, "I was supposed to have my head down the loo for most of the day. . . . I thought I might postpone my nervous breakdown for a more appropriate moment."

Energy healer Simone Simmons began working with Diana during this period and found that, behind her friendly manner, the Princess was a "pathetically damaged creature. . . . She felt abandoned, rejected, and broken." Simmons was "shocked" to see "traces of the scratches and scabs of recent self-mutilation." In Simmons's view, some of Diana's alternative therapies—the osteopathy, reflexology, acupuncture, shiatsu, colonic irrigation, and aromatherapy that she continued even as she was seeing Susie Orbach—"were counteracting each other, possibly harmfully . . . She was misreading . . . confused and conflicting advice she was offered from every quarter. . . . Diana's bright but rather manic conversational manner was an expression of tension and panic."

In that unhappy state, Diana decided to announce at a charity luncheon on December 3 that she was withdrawing from public life. Although she had hinted to Palace officials for several weeks that she might pull back some of her activities, Dimbleby recounted that they found "it proved impossible to discover exactly why or how the Princess intended to do this." Once Diana arrived at her decision, "in a gust of emotion," as a friend of Charles's described it, she was determined to make a dramatic announcement. The Queen and Prince Philip, after asking her to reconsider, urged her to pull back quietly and gradually instead, which would give her maneuvering room. Charles advocated the same course, to no effect; neither could he determine Diana's "real purpose." "It was an emotional decision," said an official who worked with her. "That was a low time for her. She was very estranged from Charles."

Diana offered a few clues several years later. "The pressure was intolerable," she said. "I was constantly tired, exhausted." But she referred again to the "campaign" against her that "was being successful." Her decision to withdraw "did surprise the people who were causing the grief—it did surprise them when I took myself out of the game. They hadn't expected that. And I'm a great believer that you should always confuse the enemy . . . the enemy was my husband's department because I always got more publicity." Diana felt she needed to declare her intentions rather than quietly withdraw, she said, "because I owed it to the public."

Diana's remarks at the luncheon to benefit the Headway National Head Injuries Association took less than five minutes. The first half sounded like a valedictory, reviewing the benefits of her public service for the previous twelve years. She did not close the door, as she had originally intended, leaving a "little light," as several friends and advisers suggested. "I will be reducing the extent of the public life I have led so far," she said. "I intend to focus on a smaller range of areas in the future. Over the next few months I will be seeking a more suitable way of combining a meaningful public role with, hopefully, a more private life." Her "first priority" would be William and Harry, "who deserve as much love, care and attention as I am able to give"—although her intentions didn't entirely make sense, since the boys were at boarding school and Diana's vacation time with them had been mapped out months earlier.

The reason for her departure, she said unequivocally, was the "overwhelming" media attention, especially to her personal life, which was "hard to bear." In that spirit, she asked to be given the "time and space that has been lacking in recent years." She emphasized that her decision had the backing of the Queen and Prince Philip, "who have always shown me kindness and support," but she conspicuously omitted reference to Prince Charles.

Diana's manner magnified the melodrama of the moment. After finishing her remarks, she sat down, and "the tears started to flow. The Princess sat with her head down, biting her lip and blinking furiously," according to the *Evening Standard*. Even if her words indicated she would return to the public stage sooner rather than later, she acted as if she was in fact leaving—and with enormous sadness. The pages of tabloid coverage contained all the shock and sorrow appropriate to a final farewell.

The tabloids again made Prince Charles the scapegoat, using Diana's failure to mention him as proof he was at fault. CHARLES FORCED DIANA TO GO: SAD PRINCESS QUITS PUBLIC LIFE, announced *The Sun,* capturing the coverage's general drift: that the "campaign to downgrade" Diana by Charles and his "sophisticated propaganda machine" had "driven her out and left her no choice but to step into the shadows."

But the decision had been Diana's, and it had as much to do with her backbreaking schedule as with pressure from the media and her desire to "confuse" her enemies in the Palace. In one sense, she was trying to assume some control over her life by removing herself from the royal regimen. But losing the structure of royal routine also removed the discipline and constant distractions of a busy life. For Diana, "time and space" brought the dread and anxieties that overtook her when she was alone.

Diana was fed up as well with being the fund-raising magnet at endless charity engagements. Although she would have better served the charities by admitting she had assumed too much responsibility and was now scaling back her obligations to a realistic number, she left her 118 charities hanging by writing to each with an offer to resign or continue in a nominal way. Hoping to be among those she would pick up again, charity officials declined her resignation and jockeyed to stay in her good graces. Indeed, Mike Whitlam, the Director-General of the British Red Cross, had met with her the day before she made the announcement. Only weeks earlier, Diana had become a vice president of the British Red Cross, and Whitlam, like other charity officials, was determined to maintain a working relationship with her.

Some commentators accused Diana of hypocrisy in blaming the media. "Carping newspaper columnists and even intrusive newspaper editors have proved . . . to be Diana's closest allies," wrote Anne Robinson in *Today;* when Diana wanted to expose the rift in her marriage, "it was a journalist she turned to." Other critics expressed skepticism about Diana's ability to lead a genuinely private life, even for a few months. Ninety-two-year-old Barbara Cartland predicted that Diana would be "bored stiff" outside the public eye. "The only books she ever read were mine," Cartland said, "and they weren't awfully good for her." As *The Times* pointed out, Diana "does not know what her role should be, and no one seems able to tell her. . . . Watching her . . . one had the overwhelming impression that she was making this announcement to her only real friends . . . the ordinary and extraordinary people she has met on her walkabouts and in her charity work. . . . What this is all about is a love affair with the public."

Diana was ready for the critics within two days. "We can reveal today that one proposal of pivotal significance has quietly emerged about her future," wrote Richard Kay in the *Daily Mail.* Because of Kay's special relationship, his report carried Diana's imprimatur. The plan called for the establishment of a Princess's Trust that would fund programs and research around the world to help the disadvantaged. According to Kay, Diana would *not* want a "film-star photo opportunity role" similar to Audrey Hepburn's—of the sort she had described to John Major—instead, she wanted to be a "chief executive, chairing policy and planning meetings, making decisions and guiding philosophy."

Aside from the unsuitability of such a role for someone like Diana, who thrived on contact with ordinary people and hated the dreariness of boardrooms, the proposal was an exercise in wishful thinking that had come up before and would emerge again. Earlier in the year, David Puttnam had organized a lunch for Diana at Claridge's with "the great and good of TV and movies" to discuss setting up a Princess of Wales Trust. "She loved the idea," Puttnam recalled, as she did each time it was presented to her over the years. Nothing ever came of it because it didn't fit Diana's style of operating: find a cause, bring it to light, and let someone else carry it forward.

Diana was thirty-two at the end of her first year of separation from Charles. As unsure of her purpose as she had been at the outset, she clearly hadn't thought through the implications of her "retirement." "I don't think she knew her own mind about it," said Michael Adler, Chairman of the National AIDS Trust, one of Diana's patronages. "When she retired, she didn't know whether or why she needed to do it, and the moment she did it, she regretted it and missed the limelight."

Chapter 20

EVEN when Diana's stated reason for doing something was perfectly valid, any number of hidden factors were often involved. In the case of her retirement from public life, the unacknowledged factor was her entanglement with a married man. Some tabloids had caught the scent. "There is one man at the moment who has been seeing Diana for some time," reported the *Daily Mirror* only days after the announcement—although the tabloid did not name him.

The man was Oliver Hoare, a wealthy dealer in Islamic art who had met the Waleses in the mid-eighties during a house party at Windsor. Hoare was distantly related to the prosperous Hoare banking family but had come from modest circumstances. His mother, Irina, had emigrated from Czechoslovakia, and his father, Reginald, had been a career British civil servant who left only $2,000 when he died in 1964. Irina and Reginald scraped enough money together to send their son to Eton, where he was captain of the boxing team, and then to the Sorbonne.

After college, Hoare met an Iranian princess named Hamoush Azodi-Bowler, who took him on as her "protégé," inviting him to live in her home in Tehran so he could "study and excavate and read Arabic and Persian script." In Tehran, Hoare mingled with a cosmopolitan crowd that included David Sulzberger, from the American publishing family, who would later become Hoare's business partner. Sulzberger introduced him to a number of figures in the world of ballet, including Rudolf Nureyev. In Iran, Hoare began collecting Middle Eastern art and antiquities, and he embraced Sufism, the mystical branch of Islam that emphasizes the quest for divine love and knowledge through ecstatic dancing and other meditative rituals. On returning to London, he joined Christie's auction house, where he headed the Islamic art department.

Hoare was known as a ladies' man. He was handsome—with eyes of "deep velvet-brown . . . fixed on the spellbound object of his conversation"—and his manner combined what *Sunday Times* columnist Taki Theodoracopulos called "an old-fashioned politesse" with a hint of the bohemian. As a struggling college student, Hoare had grown his hair long and played guitar in Parisian cafés. As a figure in the London art world, he was known for wearing mismatched colored socks and discussing the spirituality of Iranian mosques. As a sideline, Hoare advised wealthy clients on their collections.

In 1974, he met Diane de Waldner, a beautiful and elegant heiress to a vast French oil fortune. Diane's mother, Louise de Waldner, counted the Queen Mother among her friends, and she owned an estate in southern France where Prince Charles came to paint. Diane and Oliver were married in 1976, the same year he left Christie's to open his own London gallery dealing in Islamic art. In the art trade, many thought him overly awed by money and glamour. "Oliver is half child and half old man," his mentor Hamoush once said. "Like a child, he is very impressed by unimpressive things."

From 1985 to 1989, Oliver had an affair with Ayesha Nadir, a wealthy Turkish beauty with a house in London and a villa near Istanbul. The romance ended when Hoare refused to leave his wife and family, and Ayesha moved to Turkey. The Hoare marriage stabilized, thanks largely to Diane's patience and discretion.

It was Diane's family connection to the Queen Mother that brought the couple to Windsor Castle during Ascot week in 1984, where Charles and Oliver, who was three years older than the Prince, struck up a friendship based on their love of art and fascination with mystical Eastern religions. Hoare was also close to Camilla Parker Bowles, and he and his wife entertained Charles and Camilla in their home. Hoare and the Princess of Wales had a kinship as well, sharing an interest in ballet and a number of mutual friends, among them Adrian Ward-Jackson.

When the Wales marriage began to rupture in 1991, Hoare offered his services as an intermediary. "Oliver tried to help Diana to understand Prince Charles—his passion for architecture, his sense of history, and that he was a hardworking man," said a friend who knew Diana and Hoare well. "He wanted to keep her with Prince Charles." But in 1992, as the rift between the Waleses proved irreparable, Hoare abandoned his efforts. "He is not a man to insist," their mutual friend said. "He is a bit of a sybarite, not in the bad sense, but he likes to live well and not make a huge effort."

It had also become obvious that Diana, then thirty-one, was infatuated with the forty-seven-year-old Hoare, who was in turn fascinated by Diana. "He was flattered that Diana had a crush on him, and he encouraged her without knowing it," said the mutual friend. "To some extent, she misread his signals, but he genuinely liked her. The motivation for Diana was partly that he was Prince Charles's friend, and she was intrigued. She wanted to have something that belonged to Prince Charles. There were mixed motivations and mixed signals." Another friend took a less benign view: "Oliver was naughty. He led her on. She was besotted with him because he is very attractive."

Diana and Hoare spent increasing amounts of time together at Kensington Palace and the homes of friends. Diana began visiting Hoare's mother as well, much as she had befriended James Hewitt's mother. She spoke to friends of the new interest in Islamic philosophy that she had picked up from Hoare. As she did with others close to her, Diana frequently called Hoare on the telephone. "Sometimes she could phone more than twenty times a day when we were in the car driving around London," said Hoare's former chauffeur Barry Hodge. "If she only called five or six times, we thought of it as a quiet day. The sheer number of calls she made used to get Mr. Hoare down. Whenever his wife was in the car, he'd carefully pull the plug out just a fraction to break the connection."

Diana first met Elsa Bowker, a friend of Hoare's through Middle Eastern connections, one evening in 1993 when Hoare brought her to dinner at Elsa's Belgravia apartment. The next morning, a royal courier delivered a thank-you note filled with affection; as Elsa recalled, "She wrote the letter at midnight, saying, 'I can't go to sleep. I want to tell you that you had such an impact on me, you are someone who understands me. I want you to be my friend.' "

In Elsa's view, "there was great love on both sides" between Diana and Hoare. Diana told Elsa she wanted to marry Hoare, and to buy a house with him in Italy. "She was willing to leave England with him," Elsa recalled. Hoare told Elsa he thought Diana was "radiant inside, and he loved that. . . . He did a lot for her. He helped to give her confidence, but it was never enough. Diana had wonderful qualities of heart, but she was terribly possessive. If she loved someone, he had to leave everything, including children. Her possessiveness frightened men. Everything became drama."

The Hoare marriage had already become strained due to anonymous telephone calls to their home. The calls began in September 1992 and numbered as many as twenty a week, some as late as midnight. Each time, the caller remained silent, lingering until Oliver Hoare asked, "Who's there? Who's there?" and hung up. "Whoever it is just wants to hear the sound of my voice," Hoare said later. Finally, in October 1993, Diane Hoare demanded that her husband ask the police to trace the calls. He did, and the police equipped their phone with a computerized code that could activate tracers.

The relationship between Diana and Hoare eventually precipitated a crisis in his marriage. "It was like a war zone," chauffeur Barry Hodge recalled. "Diane Hoare is no fool, and she can smell another woman a mile off." Toward the end of 1993—when Diana was on the verge of making her "time and space" speech—Hoare moved into a friend's apartment in Pimlico to "cool off."

After Hoare had made the move, he confronted the magnitude of Diana's insecurities one evening when his wife was out of town. For Hoare, it was an alarming moment consistent with the experiences of Prince Charles and James Hewitt. "Oliver told Diana he had to see his daughter, who had a fever," Elsa Bowker recalled. "She suspected he was really going to see his wife, and nothing he said could convince her otherwise. She was very suspicious and mistrustful. They were in the car, and he was taking her home. At one point she was so upset that she opened the door as if to jump out. He pulled her back, and a little while later they were in a traffic jam in Sloane Square. Suddenly Diana did jump out, leaving behind her bag and her money and everything. Oliver was so distraught he never saw his daughter. He drove all over London for three hours and finally found Diana weeping in the park next to Kensington Palace."

Diana was repeating other destructive patterns from her relationship with Charles. In late 1993, energy healer Simone Simmons concluded that the marks of self-injury she had seen on Diana "had been made essentially to call Hoare's attention to her . . . need for him." Later, Simmons warned Diana that she was "asking for trouble" by continuing with Hoare, and that she couldn't expect him to leave his family for her. Diana took exception to what Simmons described as her "sharp words of warning," and stopped calling her for a time.

The anonymous phone calls ceased during Hoare's two-month absence from home, but they resumed on January 13, 1994, after he returned to his wife. Over the next six days, the police tracked a dozen silent calls ranging from before 8:00 A.M. to nearly midnight. To the astonishment of the police and the Hoares, all the calls originated from four lines, three in Kensington Palace (as the police report described them, "rented by the Office of HRH Prince of Wales") along with Diana's mobile telephone. "Mr. Hoare believes that the calls are being made by Princess Diana," noted the police report. When Hoare told police he wanted to call Diana, they advised instead that he wait for the next silent call and then "ask her by calling her first name." According to a later account of the episode, Hoare took the advice, and when Diana heard her name, she began crying and said, "Yes, I'm so sorry, so sorry. I don't know what came over me."

The phone calls stopped for several days but then started up again. This time they were traced to phone booths in Kensington and Notting

Hill, both neighborhoods in the vicinity of Kensington Palace, as well as Sarah McCorquodale's home. Scotland Yard alerted the head of the Royalty Protection Squad, who called a top official in the government. He in turn spoke to a senior official at the Palace who transmitted a message to Diana's office: The phone calls had to stop because the police were involved, and prosecution under nuisance call laws was being considered. At that point, the calls ended.

Hoare's relationship with Diana weathered the incident, and they became even more visible around London. In December 1993, a reporter for *Today* had already seen them sitting together in her car for nearly an hour, "her head rested trustingly on Mr. Hoare's shoulder." They were also spotted having breakfast together at 7:00 A.M. at the Chelsea Harbour Club where Diana worked out each day—"enough to start speculation about their relationship," noted the *Telegraph Magazine*. When photographers finally caught them in March 1994 driving into Kensington Palace, reports appeared in the next day's tabloids about their evening out with Beatrice Flecha de Lima at a Chinese restaurant. "The Princess has been a regular visitor" to Hoare's art gallery, reported *Today*, adding, "she has tearfully poured out her heart to her loyal friend."

Five months later, on Sunday, August 21, 1994, speculation about the nature of their relationship splashed across the tabloids with the *News of the World*'s "world exclusive" headlined DI'S CRANKY PHONE CALLS TO MARRIED TYCOON. Over five pages, the tabloid recounted in detail, with times and dates, the results of the police investigation into Hoare's silent calls the previous January. The story implicitly questioned Diana's stability and suggested that she and Hoare were having an affair.

Both Hoare and Diana had learned of the impending story on Saturday. They conferred by telephone, and Diana asked Richard Kay for help. Kay spoke to Clive Goodman, the royal reporter for the *News of the World*, telling him that the phone calls had probably been made by "some very loyal, and perhaps misguided people working for her, [who] took the matter into their own hands." Diana's employees were concerned, according to Kay, because Diana had so often been tearful after Hoare's efforts to broker a reconciliation in her marriage. "Anger can make people do strange things," Kay told Goodman. In his *News of the World* story, Goodman attributed Kay's statements to "a close friend and adviser to Princess Diana," and in a fascinating effort to shield Kay's identity, used the pronoun "she" instead of "he."

On Saturday afternoon, Diana arranged a clandestine meeting with Kay in Talbot Square. After Diana hopped into Kay's car, he drove her around for several hours as she "poured out her anger and unhappiness" over the accusations the Sunday tabloid was about to publish. Her intention was to have Kay attribute her comments, as usual, to a "friend" of the Princess of Wales. But when they returned to Talbot Square, two photographers lay in the square's garden, cameras poised. They had been tipped off by someone who had identified Diana's parked car, and when they saw her with Kay, they clicked off a series of pictures. An elderly man spotted the photographers, shouting to Diana and Kay, "Do you know you're being photographed?"

Recognizing that he couldn't use his conventional disguise, Kay told Diana he would have to quote her directly. That Monday's *Daily Mail* billed its "unprecedented interview" with the page-one headline WHAT HAVE I DONE TO DESERVE THIS? Diana did herself damage by overreacting—"They are trying to make out I was having an affair with this man or had some sort of fatal attraction. It is simply untrue and so unfair"—and telling one transparent lie. When asked whether she had called Hoare from telephone booths in her neighborhood she said, "You can't be serious. I don't even know how to use a parking meter, let alone a phone box."

The Observer pointed out the "neurotic nonsense" of such claims, and *The Times* observed that this "thoroughly modern princess" had known how to use the "last-number redial button" on her husband's phone to track his phone calls to Camilla. The *Telegraph Magazine* recalled a photo taken earlier in the year showing her "hunting for change for a parking meter in Knightsbridge," and *The Sun* printed a diagram instructing her how to use a public phone by inserting a shiny coin "with a picture of your mother-in-law on it."

Diana fell back on her customary defense, suggesting to Kay that Palace enemies were behind the tabloid leak. "I feel I am being destroyed," she said. "Someone is going to make out that I am mad, that I am guilty by association, that the mud will stick . . . I know there are those whose wish is apparently to grind my face in it." At the same time, she abandoned her earlier effort to blame her own employees for the dozen calls that clearly came from her telephone. Instead, she denied making six calls by producing alibis ranging from a dinner with "an elderly titled lady in Eaton Square" and lunch at a Mayfair restaurant to massages and hairdressing appointments. These claims later proved to be shaky: the Mayfair restaurant was closed on the day in question, and no witnesses came forward to publicly back Diana's assertions.

Kay covered himself by acknowledging that Diana had been "in the habit of ringing Mr. Hoare around the time the tapping was being carried out. It is possible that she would have replaced the receiver if his wife answered." *The Sunday Times* called this admission "bizarre." Such a confession of furtive behavior seemed to suggest an illicit relationship between Hoare and Diana instead of putting the idea to rest. *The Sunday Times* pointed out previous examples of Diana's silent phone calls, including James Hewitt's admission that he had received ten silent calls over three weeks the previous summer. "I reckon she has phoned other people the same way," Hewitt said. "I feel very sorry for her."

By early September, the tabloids began misstating the nature of the allegations as "300 silent nuisance calls," although the original report had not estimated the number of calls made in the sixteen months before the tracing began. In October, Richard Kay also weighed in with THE TRUTH ABOUT THE CRANK CALLS. According to Kay, the calls traced to telephone booths had probably been made by a teenage boy who knew one of Hoare's sons. Kay reiterated Diana's belief in the "whiff of conspiracy" against her and further muddied the evidence of the traced calls by dismissing them as "a mere 12 calls over a three-month period"—although, in fact, they had been made over six days.

Diana pulled together these threads of doubt in her *Panorama* interview a year later to issue a denial that further misstated the facts to deflect attention from her own behavior. "I was reputed to have made three hundred telephone calls in a very short space of time," she said, "which, bearing [in mind] my lifestyle at that time, made me a very busy lady. No I didn't, I didn't. But that again was a huge move to discredit me, and very nearly did me in." She added that she had done her "own homework on that subject and consequently found out that a young boy had done most of them. But I read that I'd done them all." She also said that she had phoned Oliver Hoare "over a period of six to nine months, a few times, but certainly not in an obsessive manner."

The press jumped on Diana's accusation and tracked down the "young boy" fingered as "the source of up to 300 nuisance calls." According to their reports, he was a sixteen-year-old student at Stowe, the boarding school attended by Hoare's sons. As Kay had reported a year earlier, these accounts asserted that the boy had "made a lot of calls from phone boxes . . . the ones some people suspected Diana was using . . . the calls were . . . a form of harassment." It took the boy's mother, contacted by the *Daily Express,* to expose the essential flaw in the charge. During late January 1994, when police traced the calls, her son had been away at boarding school.

By that time, logical explanations were beside the point. What mattered was Diana's sorrowful denial on television, which turned sympathy toward her and attention away from the facts. She had undeniably made silent phone calls to the Hoare household, behavior that carried serious psychological implications. Diana privately had admitted to Elsa Bowker that "she rang him seventy times." Elsa believed Diana called Hoare because "she was so highly excited. She couldn't control herself." It is impossible to know whether Diana needed to stay connected with Hoare by hearing his voice or whether she succumbed to an urge to invade and disrupt his marriage—perhaps both.

Immediately after the "phone pest" scandal broke in August 1994, Diana had asked Hoare to make a public statement, but he had opted to say nothing. Diana felt betrayed by Hoare's failure to back her publicly, even if it would have meant misstating the facts. "She said he was a weak man," Elsa Bowker recalled. Yet Diana kept up their relationship. According to Simone Simmons, "as late as 1995," Diana had a habit "of parking her car near his home and waiting for a glimpse of him." In February, Hoare's former chauffeur Barry Hodge went to the *News of the World* with details of the affair, and again Hoare made no public comment. At that point, Diana decided to drop him. The rejection came via some harsh words in a Richard Kay article. "The truth is, she views Hoare as a pretty spineless creature," Kay wrote in the *Daily Mail*, citing the ubiquitous "close friend." "Ever since his failure to help her over the nuisance calls business, the friendship has been a one-way street. He is very much more besotted with her than she is with him." Kay misleadingly wrote that allegations that "[Diana] had plagued Hoare with silent phone calls . . . proved groundless," pointedly noting, "but Mr. Hoare remained silent."

Hoare reacted in gentlemanly fashion. He wrote Diana a letter and enclosed a gift she had given him: a pair of her father's cuff links. "He put them in a brown envelope and on the front of the envelope he drew a crown with a big 'D' in it," recalled Elsa Bowker, to whom he delivered the envelope with instructions that she pass it along to Diana. When Elsa called, Diana said, "I will send Paul [Burrell, her butler] to take the cuff links, but destroy the letter." After Burrell had retrieved the cuff links, Diana called back and said, "Have you torn up the letter?" Elsa said, "No, I am going to open it and read it."

The one-page letter "thanked Diana for all the happiness she gave him," Elsa recalled. A friend of Elsa's who also read it described Hoare's words as "poetry, so beautifully written. He thanked Diana for giving him the cuff links, but they were such treasures he couldn't possibly keep them."

While Diana was juggling her still-private romance with Oliver Hoare in early 1994, Jonathan Dimbleby, a prominent television interviewer, was working on a documentary about Charles, along with a companion biography. As these projects progressed, Diana was growing increasingly anxious that both would cast her in a bad light. Charles's chief aides had initiated the film and book at the end of 1992 to mark the twenty-fifth anniversary of his 1969 investiture as Prince of Wales. The primary focus was on Charles's good works, although the larger purpose, particularly after the Morton book, was to display the complexities of his character so the viewer and reader could judge him fairly. Dimbleby's crew sat through meetings, trailed Charles on official engagements, and captured him with his sons on the slopes at Klosters and the highlands of Balmoral. The capstone of the film was Dimbleby's interview with Charles at Highgrove in April 1994.

Before Dimbleby conducted the interview, he arranged a luncheon meeting with Diana in March at the home of a mutual friend. He tried to ease her worries by assuring her she would be treated respectfully in the film, but Diana remained suspicious. When he asked her what sort of role she planned following her "retirement" speech, she said only, "The important thing is to keep them guessing."

Dimbleby's filmed conversation with Charles touched on the Prince's views of public service, child-rearing, the monarchy, the Church of England, architecture, the armed services, politics, and the press. Charles was especially caustic on the press, which he said had manufactured much that had been attributed to him. "It's clearly much easier to invent all this and say it all comes from some close friend or a member of the staff or some person, and it's all rubbish," he said. "I've learned over the years . . . you just don't read it. Otherwise you go bananas." But it was Charles's response to Dimbleby's question about marital fidelity—all of several seconds in a two-and-a-half-hour documentary—that would be the most memorable moment.

When Dimbleby asked about the "damaging charge" that Charles had been "persistently unfaithful" to Diana "from the beginning" of the marriage, Charles replied, "There is no truth in so much of this speculation." He said Camilla Parker Bowles was "a great friend . . . she has been a friend for a very long time . . . and will be a friend for a very long time." Dimbleby probed further: "Did you try to be faithful and honorable to your wife when you took on the vow of marriage?" "Yes," Charles replied. "And you were?" pressed Dimbleby. "Yes," Charles said, "until it became irretrievably broken down, us both having tried."

Moments later, Charles added, "It's the last possible thing that I ever wanted to happen. . . . It's not as if I went into marriage with the intention of this happening or in any way in a cynical frame of mind. I mean, I'm on the whole not a cynical person. Sorry to sound self-righteous, but I have on the whole tried to get it right . . . and tried to do the right thing by everybody." He said the breakdown of his marriage was "deeply regrettable" and "a dreadful thing" that had caused "a certain amount of damage." Although Charles didn't specify with whom he was unfaithful, Dimblebly later told reporters, "the clear context was that we were talking about Camilla Parker Bowles," and the date of the marital breakdown was 1986.

The documentary was scheduled for broadcast on June 29, 1994, and two days earlier, an evening newscast disclosed that Charles would admit his adultery. By then, Charles had briefed Diana as well as the other members of the royal family on the points that the program would cover. Buckingham Palace officials had advised Charles to duck the matter of adultery by simply saying that his marriage was a private matter. Charles had opted instead for the "let-it-all-hang-out" approach advocated by his private secretary, Richard Aylard. Dimbleby later said he would have been dishonest to omit the question after the Morton book had exposed the affair and the Camillagate tapes had revealed embarrassing intimacies. By answering the question, Charles hoped "to kill off the speculation that he had been unfaithful to the Princess from the moment of their marriage and also scotch the myth that he had never intended to make his marriage work."

The night the documentary was broadcast—to an audience of 13.4 million, 63 percent of those watching British television that night—Diana showed up at a fund-raising dinner for 300 at the Serpentine Gallery in a stunning black dress: off-the-shoulder, showing significant cleavage, skirt well above the knees, a dramatic pearl choker around her neck. It was an outfit calculated to steal the next morning's front pages. "She bounded out of the car in that wonderfully athletic way she had . . . in the 'I'll-show-you' dress, and she was radiant," recalled Peter Palumbo, chairman of the gallery of which Diana had just become patron.

Inside the Serpentine, Diana was seated between Lord Gowrie, chairman of the Arts Council after Peter Palumbo, and Graydon Carter, editor of *Vanity Fair,* sponsor of the evening. Neither Charles nor the documentary came up in Diana's conversation with Carter. "I didn't exactly feel like saying to her, 'Why aren't you home watching television?' " Carter recalled. Diana did have a particular preoccupation she wished to discuss. The most recent issue of *Vanity Fair* had run a cover story on Jacqueline Kennedy Onassis, who had died earlier in the year. "Diana had read it and she wanted to know more about how badly the Kennedy family had treated Jackie after Jack died," Carter said. "She said to me, 'I know all about being treated like that.' "

As the evening went on, Lord Gowrie evidently had greater difficulty than Carter conversing with Diana, because his wife approached Christopher Hitchens, the magazine's British-born columnist, to say, "You have to help us out. She's not even engaging in small talk. See if you can get her talking." Hitchens walked up to Diana and said in a deep voice, "Ma'am, we're all republicans here," eliciting a burst of appreciative laughter from the Princess.

The tabloids decorated their coverage of the Dimbleby documentary with archly captioned photographs of Diana. THE THRILLA HE LEFT TO WOO

CAMILLA ran in *The Sun* alongside a less flattering shot of Camilla in a similar dress and necklace. Commenting on Diana's sunny demeanor as she arrived at the Serpentine, the *Daily Mail* noted, "Here was a woman at ease with herself, confident in her own attractiveness, and who didn't really care about her estranged husband's public soul-searching." Only *The Daily Telegraph* injected a note of skepticism about Diana's behavior: "She could have watched a video . . . and curled up in bed, but we wouldn't have known, would we? . . . She fled her self-imposed purdah . . . to bury the hatchet—in the back of her estranged husband."

While Charles spoke earnestly on camera about his projects and duties, he seemed surprisingly ill at ease. He grimaced, squirmed, and wrung his hands, clearly uncomfortable with intimate topics. His tortured delivery contrasted with the popular portrayal of Charles as a cavalier and indifferent character. Within days it became apparent that the public had sympathized with Charles. One poll showed that eighty percent of respondents supported him, and another conducted by *The Sun* tracked a rise in popularity from fifty-four percent to sixty-three percent. CHARLES RULES OK, said a subsequent headline in *The Sun*.

The commentators overlooked the program's most striking feature. Even after the ferocity of the accusations leveled by the Morton book, Charles only referred to Diana obliquely. He indicated that he and Diana talked about their two sons without rancor, and he declined to discuss the possibility of divorce, saying, "It is something that I think is very personal and private between my wife and myself." He even expressed sympathy for the incessant scrutiny Diana had endured in her marriage: "I do think those people who marry into my family find it increasingly difficult . . . The strains and stress . . . become in some cases intolerable. . . . Just look at the level of intrusion, persistent endless carping, pontificating, criticizing, examining, inventing, the soap opera constantly trying to turn everybody into celebrities. If you're not a celebrity, well, what's the point?"

Camilla maintained a discreet silence, although her father told one tabloid that Charles came across as "very fair-minded and sincere" and showed "honesty and courage" in commenting on his marriage. Rosalind Shand said her daughter had done "remarkably well, considering some of the terrible things written about her."

Diana was reportedly "crowing" over Charles's admission, sure that he had badly damaged his image. "I haven't seen the program, and I never will," the *Daily Express* said she told friends. Yet for all her bravado, Diana later said she had been "pretty devastated . . . but then I admired the honesty, because it takes a lot . . . to be honest about a relationship with someone else, in his position. That's quite something." Charles's confession actually had the practical effect of removing his relationship with Camilla from the realm of innuendo. "The public was sympathetic, and for the media, it stopped the story," said a friend of Charles's. Barely a week after the documentary aired, it had dropped off the media's radar. From Diana's standpoint, the story was far from over, although the Dimbleby documentary had done her little damage compared with what she had already inflicted on herself.

Less than two months later, the tabloids were running with the Hoare phone story, and by now the troubles in the royal marriage were so well known that the broadsheets joined in as well. Only a month into their coverage, they got wind of even bigger revelations coming in *Princess in Love*, by Anna Pasternak, James Hewitt's amanuensis. Diana had known about the book since mid-August, when the news ruined her Martha's Vineyard vacation with the Flecha de Limas, prompting her return to London three days later. By then, Diana was estranged from Hewitt and was powerless to derail the book. When she called him, he told her, "I don't regard myself as a friend anymore."

Hewitt felt bitter about Diana on two counts: She had "dumped him," and she had double-crossed him. After leaving the army the previous March, he had sold the *Express* a sanitized version of his relationship with Diana for more than £100,000. He claimed that Diana had backed this untruthful effort to portray their affair as an innocent friendship. "It was a preemptive strike," Hewitt said, but "the rumors grew stronger than they were before." Despite the account's sugar coating, Hewitt was widely criticized for cashing in on his connection to Diana. "Diana was happy for it to go out," Hewitt said, "but once it backfired, the support I got from her was nonexistent. . . . Diana told me she was sorry that it turned out that way, but when it got too hot . . . she decided to drop it."

Anna Pasternak had written the "anodyne" *Express* account, but she knew from numerous conversations that the story of Hewitt and Diana was far more explosive. She later said that Charles's televised adultery confession had left her so indignant she was determined to tell what she characterized as a love story "too beautiful . . . to remain a secret." By late July, Pasternak had signed a deal with Bloomsbury Publishing, the highbrow London house, to be Hewitt's ghostwriter. She resigned from the *Express* and disappeared to the country to turn out 80,000 words by early September so Hewitt could beat Andrew Morton's sequel to the bookstores. While Hewitt insisted that he had not profited financially from the book, *The Mirror* later published bank statements showing he had received £130,000. At the time of publication, Hewitt was suddenly able to pay £245,000 for a Georgian mansion in Dartmoor.

Pasternak found Hewitt's story thoroughly convincing. The "proof" that he and Diana slept together was in Diana's letters, which Hewitt shared with her. Hewitt also gave the publisher a sworn affidavit "affirming the truth" of the events described by Pasternak. The writer's intent was to "set the record straight" in a "thoughtful, dignified," and "sophisticated" fashion—three adjectives that failed to emerge in any of the reviews of *Princess in Love* when it was published on October 3. The book was roundly ridiculed, with perhaps the most pungent comment coming from Lord St. John of Fawsley, Master of Emmanuel College, Cambridge, and a longtime friend of Johnnie Spencer's. He called the writing "clogging, nauseating and overblown . . . It makes Barbara Cartland sound like George Eliot. Once you put it down, you cannot pick it up again."

The tabloids condemned Hewitt with every imaginable pejorative they could stuff into two-inch-high headlines: TRAITOR (the *Daily Express*), LOVE RAT and CAD (*The Sun*), BRITAIN'S BIGGEST BOUNDER (the *Daily Mail*). "He is a revolting creep," the *Mirror* editorialized. "Horse-whipping would be too good for him." Yet the tabloids slavered over Pasternak's prose, reprinting extensive excerpts. The *Daily Mirror* ran five pages, and *The Sun* seventeen, including an "Eight-Page Special on the Book That Betrayed Diana," with such stories as "They Did It at Althorp"; "They Did It in the Bathroom"; "She Begged to Do It on Dartmoor"; and "Page-by-Page Guide to the Juiciest Bits." With no evident irony, *The Sun* explained its coverage with, "Our distaste at Hewitt's hustling is tempered by concern for Diana's well-being. That is why we print his story at length. The truth may be painful and unpleasant, but closing our eyes to it helps no one." For good measure, *The Sun* went on to indict the royal family for failing to provide Diana with a "shoulder of theirs to cry on."

Princess in Love profoundly embarrassed Diana, Charles, and the entire royal family. Buckingham Palace dismissed it as "grubby and worthless," and Diana's lawyer Lord Mishcon called it "wretched," but the Palace refrained from challenging the book's claims. Significantly, Diana did not step forward with a public denial. Instead, she resorted to her habit of letting "friends" speak for her. Richard Kay dutifully reported that she was "bitterly hurt" by Hewitt's "invasion of her private life," and "despite the flowery descriptive passages . . . Diana firmly maintains that she and Hewitt were never lovers." In the *Daily Express,* a "friend" described the book as the product of Hewitt's "fevered imagination."

Barely a year later, Diana contradicted these disavowals by admitting on *Panorama* that her relationship with Hewitt had indeed been adulterous. She also said Hewitt had assured her ten days before publication that "there was nothing to worry about," and that when the book arrived, "the first thing I did was rush down to talk to my children, and William produced a box of chocolates and said, 'Mummy, I think you've been hurt. These are to make you smile again.' "

Diana had still more explaining to do when excerpts from Jonathan Dimbleby's biography of Charles appeared in *The Sunday Times* on October 16, 1994. Charles had told Diana what to expect in the book, which on the whole was restrained and sober. Dimbleby described Diana's bulimia and mercurial behavior by way of explaining the marriage's breakdown, but Charles offered no negative judgments of his wife, directly or indirectly. One rigid ground rule for the project had been Dimbleby's pledge to exclude anything critical of Diana.

It was the *News of the World*'s headline, CHARLES: I'VE NEVER LOVED DIANA, that wounded Diana. Charles had said no such thing to Dimbleby, who wrote guardedly about the Prince's feelings for Diana: He found her "lovable" and "warmhearted" and "was sure he could fall in love with her." Dimbleby also acknowledged that Charles had proposed under pressure from the media and his father and had approached his marriage feeling uneasy about Diana's shifting moods. Dimbleby emphasized that even as the marriage was collapsing, Charles tried to make the relationship work, and when Diana remained inconsolable, he would "insist he was to blame, that if it were not for him she would not be in such a state of misery. . . . It was too much to expect anyone to be the wife of the heir to the throne."

The day after the *Sunday Times* excerpt, Diana went to see William at Ludgrove. When William asked why the marriage had broken up, she recalled telling him, "Well, there were three of us in the marriage, and the pressure of the media was another factor, so the two together were very difficult. But although I still loved Papa, I couldn't live under the same roof as him, and likewise with him." By blaming Charles, Diana seemed unlikely to reassure her twelve-year-old son, but she insisted that she had "put it in gently, without resentment or any anger."

Diana was indeed angry about what she saw as a "picture portrayed in the book . . . of a wife who was both unreasonable and unstable." Perhaps more than the television interview, Diana viewed the book as a "revenge attack." Of course, Diana herself had graphically described her eating disorders, depressions, and self-injury to Morton, but she was upset by Dimbleby's portrait of her volatile behavior. "She feels the furor over the biography has wrecked her chances of building a new private life," reported *The Sun*.

Andrew Morton's sequel, which appeared on the heels of Dimbleby's book, seemed almost anticlimactic. As early as August, Diana had distanced herself from the project, saying that she "had not had any contact with Morton for more than three years." Left unmentioned was her friend James Colthurst's continuing role as a middleman for Morton. When the book came out in November, she dismissed it as a "mishmash of tedious secondhand gossip assembled by Morton for his own benefit." No wonder, since *The Times* characterized the sequel's portrait of Diana as "bitter, jealous, and lonely . . . obsessed with . . . alternative therapies . . . and increasingly isolated."

The sequel sparked a run of tabloid stories on Morton's most sensational assertions: another self-mutilation—a gruesome account of Diana slashing her arms while traveling on the Queen's airplane and smearing her blood on the seats and walls—and her use of Prozac, which he said had controlled her bulimia. In fact, Diana's experiment with Prozac had been short-lived, and the bulimia symptoms persisted. After publication, James Colthurst's status as an "unpaid adviser" to Diana came to an end.

Nearly a year after Diana's "retirement," some of the British press were taking a more jaundiced view of her than they had before. Even die-hard supporters such as *The Sun* had begun to carp, with headlines like TWO FACES OF TORMENTED DI, over a story about her "Jekyll and Hyde" personality. In its April 1994 issue, *Tatler* magazine had pronounced her wardrobe "dead common," and other publications had begun to mock her, even when she showed signs of emotional fragility. "She has been given of late to frequent bouts of weeping: the Princess of Wails," wrote *The Observer*.

Until she became tangled in her own evasions and deceptions with the Hoare and Hewitt stories, Diana's principal sin had been snubbing and sometimes snarling at photographers, who had grown more aggressive after she dropped her security detail early in 1994 along with her schedule of royal obligations. Once she was on her own, she became unpredictable with the royal hacks as well. "She was schizophrenic, which caused problems," said Robert Hardman of *The Daily Telegraph*. "People didn't know where the goalposts were. One minute she was jokey, then she made anguished pleas for privacy. You didn't know if she did, if she didn't, if she was pretending or what."

When Diana's coverage started turning sour, she began a methodical campaign to get the press back on her side, working from the top down. She dined regularly with newspaper proprietors such as Lord Rothermere of the *Mail* and his top lieutenant David English, *Telegraph* owner Conrad Black, and News International's Rupert Murdoch. Most of the time, Diana didn't tell Buckingham Palace officials about these get-togethers with owners and editors until the last minute, or after the fact.

She continued to feed information to Richard Kay, but she began establishing contacts with other reporters and editors who might be useful to her. One was Anthony Holden, Kay's colleague at the *Daily Mail*, who intrigued Diana because he was a critical biographer of Charles as well as an outspoken republican. Since the Morton book, Holden had written especially supportive articles about Diana for the *Daily Mail* and other publications. "I got a call from a mutual friend, a male, saying 'come to San Lorenzo at twelve-forty,' " Holden recalled. "The table next to mine was the only one with flowers, and pretty soon in came Diana with the boys and their nanny." As she did with Kay, Diana suggested that Holden join her. "This was the first in a series of lunches in public places," Holden said. "There was always subterfuge, and always, 'Oh, I'm so glad to see you.' " Her off-the-record remarks "informed the stuff I wrote," Holden said.

At her friend Peter Palumbo's suggestion, Diana also consulted with Andrew Neil, whose *Sunday Times* had published the original Morton excerpts in 1992. They met in February 1994 during a luncheon at Palumbo's country house. Palumbo had asked Neil to help give Diana some direction. "She wanted me to touch base," Neil recalled, "and Peter was worried about her, almost to the extent he was afraid he would wake up and find she had killed herself. He never quite voiced that, but I would say it, and he would nod grimly and never dissent. Peter said to me, 'How can we help this woman get a more normal life and not spend all her time working out,' which was an indication of a bulimic personality."

Neil found Diana changed from their meeting a decade earlier when Charles had dominated the conversation. "She was talking about the royal family with a bitter sense of humor," Neil said. "What surprised me was that despite her limited brainpower and lack of education, she had developed street smarts. She was talking about the future of the royal family, and she was making sense." Neil tried to impress on her that she should find a full-time job. "You need to get up and get out and do something and then come home," Neil said, but he suspected she wasn't interested.

Diana felt she should reach writers she considered unfriendly as well. "She wanted to win them over," Richard Kay said. "Her line was, 'These people write about me but they don't know me. Maybe if they knew me they wouldn't write those things.' I thought it was a dangerous strategy."

Still, she made some impressive conversions, especially among men of a certain age. She won over the crotchety Auberon Waugh during a lunch at Kensington Palace. "I've been walking on air ever since," he declared. She further endeared herself to Waugh when she read a self-deprecating limerick at his annual *Literary Review* lunch, after apologizing for being a "notorious illiterate" who "made time between therapy sessions and secret trysts" to compose her verse. Waugh henceforth "took Diana's side unreservedly because he fancied her," said Richard Ingrams, former editor of *Private Eye*. "That is the crude explanation. But he was touched."

Max Hastings, editor of *The Daily Telegraph* until 1995, when he moved to the *Evening Standard,* offered an especially daunting challenge to Diana. The *Telegraph* had taken a pro-Charles line, and Hastings himself had a number of friends in the Prince's sporting set. Physically imposing at six foot five, Hastings had become a Fleet Street legend for his derring-do in covering eleven wars, including India-Pakistan, Vietnam, and the Falklands. Diana decided in 1995 to approach Hastings through a good friend who was his neighbor. "Come to dinner Friday night in the country," the friend said to Hastings. "Diana wants to see you." While his host and hostess sat in the corner, "Diana talked her game," Hastings recalled. Like Andrew Neil, Hastings saw "a bitter woman speaking, but she was witty, and it was skillfully done. She had my undivided attention."

Diana appealed to journalists in part because she dealt with them on a human level. She was scrupulous about thanking them for favors, and made thoughtful gestures—such as the letter she wrote to Richard Kay's mother after his father died, followed by tickets to the ballet. Prince Charles, on the other hand, could sail through a long meeting with a journalist without inquiring about his children or even his sporting interests. "The Prince felt too ill at ease with anyone in the media to play the game as she did," Hastings said. "She asked the right questions, took an interest in your affairs. I would lap up Diana, who knew how to make people feel good."

"She was the kind of person you could feel on intimate terms with quickly," said Paul Johnson, another prickly character who came to lunch at Kensington Palace and was enchanted by Diana. Johnson hadn't been one of her consistent fans, but he took an even more jaundiced view of Charles, which interested Diana. Johnson produced several memos advising her about the press. "Don't think you can manipulate them, because they will manipulate you," he told her. "Don't tell them a confidence because down the line they will break it." Conceded Johnson, "She didn't listen to me."

Diana's ability to ingratiate involved what Clive James described as a "tacit bargain": "You tell me what you don't tell anyone else, and I'll tell you what I can't tell anyone else, and then neither of us can tell anyone else what we said. . . . I suppose it was a mind game. There must have been dozens of people that she played it with. . . . She would make each of her platonic cavaliers believe, or at any rate want to believe, that he was the only one."

Diana began to take pride in her techniques of influencing coverage. During a luncheon at the Goldsmiths', she described one ploy to journalist and historian Andrew Roberts. Although he was a Diana skeptic, he couldn't help admiring her "native cunning about the press." He recalled,

"She said one good way of scotching a rumor about to come out is to tell a slightly different version of the same story to the opposition. So if the *Express* was coming out with something, she would call Richard Kay and give him a version with the facts altered, not necessarily honestly, so neither newspaper would know what the truth was. The real story would slip through the cracks. That was very clever, and she did it repeatedly."

Sometimes Diana went too far and her efforts backfired. In May 1994, representatives of a displeased Prince of Wales told the press (including Kay at the *Daily Mail*) about Diana's extravagant annual expenditure of £160,000 for "grooming," which included some £91,330 for clothing, £9,350 for hairdressing, and £7,306 for alternative therapies. That day, Diana had a previously scheduled lunch with Peter Stothard, editor of *The Times,* as part of her outreach campaign. The moment they sat down, Diana began venting about the coverage. "My husband said it at a dinner party last week, where it got to Ross Benson and to Nigel Dempster, and now there's all this stuff," she told Stothard, who later wrote, "To my horror, she began to set out a complicated story about how she had helped a tramp who had fallen into Regent's Park Canal."

Puzzled by her account, Stothard failed to take the bait. Later that afternoon, Diana's chauffeur called Richard Kay with the story of the rescue. The next day's *Daily Mail* ran Kay's page-one feature under the headline DIANA RESCUES DROWNING MAN, which goaded other papers to knock down its inflated claims of Diana's heroism. Kay later insisted that he trusted Diana's chauffeur and that Diana "played a role and got her feet wet," although he acknowledged that the headline was a stretch.

Richard Kay's role as Diana's Boswell became public knowledge in early May. Diana had just returned from a weekend holiday in Spain with her friends Kate Menzies and Catherine Soames. They had been besieged by paparazzi, one of whom took five pictures of Diana sunbathing topless and put them on sale for £1 million. Back in London, Diana contacted Kay, who interviewed her in her car behind Harrods.

The next day, quoting a "friend," Kay reported in the *Daily Mail* that Diana considered the paparazzi invasion of her privacy "like a rape." Unknown to either Kay or Diana, a photographer had snapped them conferring in her Audi and sold the picture to *The Sun,* which ran its second headline about the "two faces" of Diana. *The Sun* blasted Diana for her "hypocrisy and double standards . . . supposedly speaking through a 'friend,'" and for sunbathing topless, adding, "You can't marry a prince and then expect to live like a typist."

Diana's favoritism with Kay often worked against her in unexpected ways. "She didn't understand what happens when you give an exclusive story," explained Kay's *Daily Mail* colleague Peter McKay. "This causes the others to rip the exclusive story apart. This is partly rage that someone has been given something exclusive, and also you have to take a different view. Diana never understood that she caused envy and hatred at the other papers if she was cooperating with one."

According to Richard Kay, Diana "hated" being described as "manipulative," as she often was in later years. In her view, manipulation was management by another name, and she had a right to do whatever it took to shape her coverage. "It was manipulation," said Clive James, "but what else does a marionette dream of except pulling the strings?"

Chapter 21

No matter how much the tabloids criticized Diana's private life, they kept pressing her to take on a larger public role. "It was always push push push," said Jane Atkinson, an adviser on press relations toward the end of Diana's life. "The media always wanted to know, 'What did she mean by wanting to be an ambassador?' I said, 'Can't you see she doesn't know?'"

In her "retirement" speech, Diana had promised that after several months she would articulate "a more suitable way of combining a meaningful public role with, hopefully, a more private life." In 1994, she sharply reduced her official duties, turning up at only ten royal events compared with 198 the year before. But in 1995, she was back on the royal calendar, appearing at 127 official engagements, ensuring that she would be on display for photographers and reporters roughly two times a week.

Whatever her official schedule, Diana had achieved a level of celebrity that kept her constantly in the public eye. The quotidian events of her life—going to her health club, meeting friends for lunch, taking a vacation—would turn up in one newspaper or another, often on page one. While she professed dismay at the press coverage, Diana was also drawn to it. In the space of eighteen months, she appeared on the cover of both British *Vogue* and *Harper's Bazaar,* and cooperated with two television documentaries. In the first of these programs, in March 1994, about a shelter for battered women, Diana participated in a group therapy session and made a tantalizing reference to her inability to come up with "something positive" she had done the previous week: "If you'd asked . . . what the negative aspects of the week had been, you would have been flooded." Throughout the two years after announcing her "retirement," Diana also took frequent trips, often on the spur of the moment. Her most common destination was the United States, which she visited more than a half-dozen times, mostly to see her friend Lucia Flecha de Lima.

Diana later characterized her activities during this time as "a lot of work . . . underground, without any media attention," but in fact Diana courted publicity. When she made a "hush-hush" visit to Ulster in April 1994, the tabloids contained photographs and accounts of her meeting with British troops. As Richard Addis, editor in chief of the *Express* newspapers, recalled, "There were phone calls to our picture editors when someone would say, 'If you want a picture, go to this address at such and such a time, and you will find Diana coming out.' She would always be there."

Richard Kay and other followers reminded their readers at regular intervals of Diana's "secret" charity activities. That April, for example, Kay wrote that although Diana had made only one official appearance to date, "she has been attending many other events in a private capacity." In a later report on the "hidden life" of Diana, he recounted the specifics of "dozens of visits" to the ill and dying. Charles Rae reported in *Today* that Diana carried out this work "without the trumpet blowing." Even in the din of the tabloid brass band, Diana could be heard tooting her own horn, the most dramatic example being her attempt to publicize her role in the "drowning tramp" rescue, which left her open to mockery as "Super Di."

Diana's mixed signals only encouraged the paparazzi. Most of the time, the photographers would wait outside the gates of Kensington Palace to follow her to her destination, where they would capture the day's quota of pictures. "A normal day [I] would be followed by four cars, a normal day [I] would come back to my car and find six freelance photographers jumping around me," she said. Yet Diana wanted their attention when she wished to make a point, as she did the night of the Dimbleby documentary in her knockout dress.

Diana dispensed with her security guards at the beginning of 1994: she found the guards' constant presence oppressive, and longed to lead a "normal" life. Instead, she got constant surveillance from the paparazzi, who considered stalking Diana an exciting game. Two of the most aggressive "snappers," Glenn Harvey and Mark Saunders, published a book called *Dicing with Di* in which they gleefully boasted of reducing her to tearful "wobblies" and mocked her as "The Loon" when she lashed out at their intrusiveness. "Sometimes a Loon attack would entail Diana sprinting towards a photographer, forcing him to leap out of her way," Harvey wrote. "At other times she would run at full pelt away from snappers. . . . But a worse kind of Loon attack was when Diana just stood dead still, eyes welling with tears, head down, giving the silent treatment. Invariably, these happened after she had visited one of her many therapists."

In September 1994, Diana announced a "relaunch" of her public life—

primarily to counter her bad publicity—with a series of high-profile events, including the opening of a new clinic affiliated with the National AIDS Trust, one of her charities. When trust chairman Michael Adler first asked her to participate, he was surprised by her response: "I said, 'I know you retired, but as a personal favor would you open our new outpatient department? I guarantee there will be no press. It will be a private visit.' She said, 'I'd like the media, the more the better.' "

A TV documentary several weeks later about her "new role as a behind-the-scenes charity worker" included "affectionate scenes with her sons" and chats with the homeless in what the tabloids described as a "secret solo visit." Her last—and splashiest—appearance of the year came at Versailles, where she "dressed to thrill" in a low-cut, figure-hugging, sequined gown with a skirt split up to her thigh. The dinner was a fundraiser for a Parisian children's charity, which, with Diana as the main attraction, pulled in some £500,000. Commentators couldn't help comparing her dazzling step-out with her "tearful retreat" only a year earlier.

Diana's accelerated 1995 schedule included three official trips abroad (Japan, Russia, and Argentina) as well as fund-raisers in Hong Kong, Venice, Paris, and New York. Yet she remained ambivalent about her role. In May 1994—five months after the "retirement" speech—Diana had announced she would join the policy and planning committee of the International Red Cross, a "real working appointment," that required her to read reports, develop strategy, and attend meetings—none of which was her strong suit.

The Red Cross was the ultimate establishment charity, and for that reason, Diana was initially reluctant to get involved. But Mike Whitlam, the antiestablishment Director-General of the British Red Cross, convinced her that the organization could fulfill her desire to play a substantive role in public life. "She is more interested in the mechanics of the operation, less in being the fund-raising figurehead," he said late in 1994.

As it turned out, Diana attended only three meetings of her International Red Cross committee. "She got bored, and who wouldn't," said one of her former aides. "We have to do boring things in life, and she had no tolerance for that. Her strength was people. It was a waste for her to sit in a darkened room somewhere."

Diana had also promised to be a Red Cross ambassador overseas, a commitment she fulfilled only once, making a stop at the Red Cross offices in Tokyo at the end of her visit to Japan in February 1995. Diana's Japanese visit was a success, but measured only by her popularity, which, the *Evening Standard* noted, had "rocketed overnight. . . . Her four-day tour shows every sign of turning into a major step on the road to rehabilitation for the Princess's public image."

Subsequent overseas trips did not include Red Cross activities. In fact, her choice of places to visit had more to do with her friendships than anything else. In April 1995, for example, she was unexpectedly back in the Far East on a three-day "fact-finding mission" organized by Hong Kong entrepreneur David Tang, to whom Diana had been introduced by Sarah Ferguson. Known to his friends as "Tango," the Chinese millionaire had attended boarding school in Britain and studied philosophy at London University before making his mark as the owner of a fashionable Chinese club and a department store.

In Hong Kong, Diana visited a cancer treatment ward, a shelter for homeless youths, and a drug rehabilitation center; she also appeared as guest of honor at dinners to raise money for leprosy and cancer treatment. Although she was accompanied by Governor Chris Patten, the trip was David Tang's show. He hosted the dinner for the Hong Kong Cancer Fund at his China Club, where he introduced her by saying, "Your presence here today is like winning a lottery." To secure Diana's help as a fund-raiser, Tang underwrote most of the costs of her trip, which included a suite at a luxury hotel. Scarcely six weeks later, Tang was at Diana's side again, this time in Venice, similarly orchestrating her appearance as a fund-raiser for the Serpentine Gallery. By then, Diana's association with the International Red Cross was "in abeyance."

Because she was so involved with the drama of her own life, Diana had been spending less time focusing on Camilla. But when Camilla and Andrew Parker Bowles announced in January 1995 that they would divorce, Diana once again attacked her rival. Richard Kay reported Diana was "uneasy" that her sons might spend time with Camilla, whom she blamed for "destroying" the Waleses' marriage. Diana also offered a new version of her own marital breakdown. Contrary to what she had told Andrew Morton, that "something inside me closed off" and "our marriage . . . went down the drain" after the birth of Harry in 1984, Diana now maintained that in 1986, when Charles said the marriage had "irretrievably broken down," she had been "hoping for a third child." As Diana told Kay, "Getting baby number three on board" could have revived their marriage, which was "in trouble but . . . far from over," had it not been for Camilla.

By early 1995, Diana had been in therapy with Susie Orbach for nearly two years, and she was talking a brave game to tabloid reporters, telling them she felt "stronger than ever." In fact, her temperament had shifted into one of its more volatile cycles. Energy healer Simone Simmons recalled Diana's "grim mood swings and tantrums. . . . Her despondency might last for days." One measure of Diana's insecurity was her habit of carrying as many as four mobile phones in her pocketbook and according to Simmons, "spending nearly every free minute of the day on the telephone."

Diana's ongoing struggle with bulimia prompted her to contact Peggy Claude-Pierre, a Canadian whose intensive treatments for eating disorders Diana had seen on television. At Diana's invitation, Claude-Pierre met with her for four hours in Kensington Palace. "She was hurting because she couldn't express who she was," Claude-Pierre recalled. Diana confided her feelings of inadequacy and loneliness, and said she needed human contact to feel stronger. Diana asked countless questions, "imploring as a child does. . . . She said, 'I know that the more I know, the more I can deal with myself.' "

During this period, Diana broke off her friendships with Catherine Soames and Kate Menzies: On their annual ski trip to Lech, Austria, in March, Diana decided that the two women were disloyal. Neither Catherine nor Kate fully understood what happened, but one reason for the rupture may have been their criticism of Diana's behavior. In the aftermath of the Hoare and Hewitt scandals, Diana had struck up a friendship with Will Carling, captain of the English rugby team, whom she had met during workouts at the Harbour Club and had started seeing for coffee afterward. At first, he just gave her pointers on her training routine, but soon they began to confide in each other. Diana found Carling easy to talk to, and she enjoyed his company; he was married, however, and when he began calling Diana's suite at Lech, Kate and Catherine took exception.

"Diana was doing things the average person wouldn't approve of," recalled another friend who was in Lech at the time. "If you were her friend, it was natural to say 'Be careful.' But Diana didn't like being told what to do. There was a falling-out. Diana started eating in her room. She didn't come out." Barely a month later, one of the tabloids took note of Diana's failure to attend Kate Menzies's thirty-fifth-birthday party, and the following February, when Kate married restaurateur Simon Slater, Diana was overseas. Since Diana didn't tell either Kate or Catherine directly what had bothered her, they could only guess, and like others dropped by Diana, they were reluctant to confront her. When another friend asked Diana for an explanation, "She said she had reached a different point in her life, a different era, a different phase."

Just as Diana had decided to cooperate with Andrew Morton when she was especially mixed-up in 1991, four years later she began to seriously think about doing her own television interview in response to Charles's documentary with Dimbleby. Emboldened by her skill at dealing with journalists one-on-one, Diana had come to consider herself more clever than she was. "She thought she had a fine analytical mind, but she misled herself," said her friend David Puttnam. "She mistook her very good intuition for strategic shrewdness. Listening to her chatter at lunch, [it would seem] she had worked out a chess game, but she hadn't really. She'd had a notion only fifteen minutes before, although she was telling you she had worked this out six months earlier."

Diana's confusion was captured eerily by Henry Mee, who painted her final portrait in the summer of 1995. Mee's image was a shocking contrast to her previous portrait, painted only a year earlier by American artist Nelson Shanks. Her sittings with Shanks had taken place during the Dimbleby and Hoare publicity, and Shanks recalled that "there was no day when her mood didn't change. She would be laughing one moment and the next minute in tears." Shanks's aim had been "to acknowledge that she was injured," but "to paint her beauty and soul." He dressed her in a romantic ruffled blouse, and conveyed a mood of dewy wistfulness. The Shanks portrait, with its suggestion of martyrdom, had become Diana's favorite.

The same could not be said for Mee's interpretation, which one columnist compared to Myra Hindley, the most infamous inmate at Broadmoor, the maximum-security psychiatric hospital Diana had taken to visiting as part of her private charity work. It is a spooky image, larger-than-life, with gray hair and brown streaks shadowing the left side of Diana's face, the eyes hinting despair: a fragmented personality on the verge of disintegration. "Diana was raw," Mee recalled. "On several occasions her eyes were red, and she had clearly been up all night crying. She was having trouble holding it all together." Diana told Mee that "all her portraits had been condemned as an extension of herself, and she was sure that this one would be, too."

That summer, Diana selectively canvassed media-savvy friends about taking her troubles to the airwaves. The wiser among them tried to impress on her the power of silence. "She was slightly juvenile," David Puttnam said. "She would say, 'I always have surprise on my side because the Palace acts in such predictable ways.' She said, 'I have offers to do a long interview on television.' I said, 'Don't even think about it. It will look like tit for tat, which is not attractive. And your only power is your ability to do it. The moment you have done it, you have lost your option. Not only is it a bad idea, it is bad tactics.'"

Clive James counseled her against an interview as well. "I said if that happened, the two-camps thing would go nuclear, and continue until there was nothing left," he later wrote in *The New Yorker*. "She would be on the run forever. . . . She seemed convinced, but of course she was pretending. She had already decided."

At that stage, Diana had been approached by Barbara Walters, whom

she had met during her visits to the United States. Walters had also cultivated Patrick Jephson, Diana's private secretary. "He would ask me about
various charitable events she was going to attend," Walters recalled. "When
we first met, he was extremely uptight and protective and very fond of her.
Over time, he loosened up."

Jephson had worked for Diana since 1987, first as her equerry, and
since 1991 as her private secretary. A graduate of Cambridge and a former
lieutenant commander in the navy, Jephson was five years older than
Diana. He tended to be enigmatic—"Patrick's pulling the shutters down
again," friends would say—but he was quick, witty, and efficient. "He knew
how to deal with Diana," said one of Diana's friends. "He never trespassed,
and he was never patronizing. To be patronizing to her was a disaster."

Jephson was the custodian of Diana's image. "He tried to filter out
nonsense and get her into a serious position," said Michael Adler of the National AIDS Trust. "He protected Diana from the outside world and from
herself. He could see the elephant traps a long way away."

Perhaps for that very reason, Diana decided to exclude both Jephson
and her press secretary Geoffrey Crawford from her interview plans, taking
her advice from those who reinforced her impulses. Chief among them was
Sarah Ferguson. Throughout the spring and summer of 1995, Diana and
Fergie met for many Sunday afternoon lunches at Fergie's rented home in
Surrey. Fergie told Diana how much she had benefited from a candid television interview she had given in March 1993. "She encouraged Diana to
go ahead," said reporter Richard Kay.

As she had done with Morton, Diana settled on an interlocutor introduced to her by someone she trusted. At the end of August, her brother
Charles had a meeting at Althorp with thirty-two-year-old Martin Bashir,
a producer for *Panorama,* the BBC's preeminent current affairs program.
Bashir was a little-known sportswriter and television reporter who had
worked on the program for a few years. He contacted Charles Spencer as
part of an investigation into suspicions that some of Earl Spencer's former
employees had been paid by newspapers for leaks about Diana and her
family. In their meeting, Bashir told Spencer that the British intelligence
service M.I.5 was carrying out "dirty tricks" on Diana.

Spencer met with Bashir several more times, and in one of those meetings Bashir allegedly produced a bank statement—later discovered to be
fraudulent—that showed a payment from News International (Rupert
Murdoch's media conglomerate) to Allen Waller, Spencer's former head of
security at Althorp. While Bashir later said he didn't use the false bank
statement to land an interview with Diana, Charles Spencer found the producer's evidence persuasive at the time—especially since he had heard similar charges from one of his friends.

In late September, Spencer asked Diana to get together with Bashir at a friend's apartment in London. During that meeting, Bashir laid out his findings and made the absurd allegation to Spencer and Diana that he had statements for a "front company" controlled by employees of both Prince Charles and Diana, showing them to be paid informers, but he didn't name the source of the funds. Quite apart from those charges, Bashir also told Diana that she shouldn't trust Catherine Soames, Kate Menzies, and Julia Samuel. He probably figured that all three women were independent-minded as well as discreet, and would have cautioned Diana against cooperating with him. Although Diana hadn't repaired relations with Kate and Catherine, she was still on speaking terms with their mutual friend Julia. "But that was the death knell," said another friend of Diana's.

Spencer did not see Bashir again; he became suspicious when he compared the notes he had taken at the earlier meetings with what Bashir said in Diana's presence and found discrepancies in the details. But Bashir had struck a nerve with Diana, who had long suspected she was being spied on by the royal family. Over the next month, she and Bashir discussed the terms of a wide-ranging interview. "She was off on her own bat, having had her various insecurities fed by Bashir very cleverly," said a man who knew her well; among other things, he said, Bashir convinced Diana that her apartment was bugged.

Bashir also benefited from the consequences of a *News of the World* report in early August that Diana was having "secret trysts" with England rugby captain Will Carling at Kensington Palace. The source of this information was Carling's former personal assistant Hilary Ryan, who had no evidence of any intimacy between Diana and Carling, but said, "he's been running around after her like a puppy."

The implication was that Diana had another affair with a married man. "I have done nothing wrong," Diana said. "We were never alone together." But comments by Carling and his wife, Julia, to several tabloids undercut her denial. Julia said that her marriage was strong, "however much someone is trying to destroy what you have." She added: "This has happened to [Diana] before, and you hope she won't do these things again, but she obviously does." Will Carling publicly pledged not to see Diana again and said, "It was flattering that the Princess of Wales was interested in me—and that is probably where I made my mistake." Admitting he had hurt Julia, he said, "That is unforgivable."

On September 24, the *News of the World* asserted that Diana and Carling were still seeing each other. The evidence was trumped-up—a visit Carling made to Kensington Palace to deliver rugby shirts for William and Harry when Diana wasn't even at home, and a chance encounter in a London health club. But less than a week later, the Carlings announced their separation, and once again, Julia pointed the finger at Diana, saying, "Recent pressure and tensions have produced this situation. . . . It hurts me very much to face losing my husband in a manner which has become outside my control."

The press lambasted Diana. *Today* asked, "Is Will Carling merely another trophy for a bored, manipulative and selfish princess?" *The Sun* called her a "homewrecker," and the *Daily Express* wondered, "Is no marriage and no man safe from the wife of the heir to the throne?"

Several years after the fact, Carling said in his memoir, *My Autobiography,* that Diana had started their friendship by inviting him for coffee at the Harbour Club, then regaling him with gossip about famous people: "She said she found President Bill Clinton impressive in private, but she considered Hillary, his wife, to be overambitious." "Out of the blue" in mid-1995, Carling said, "she asked me about my marriage to Julia," and he confessed he was unhappy. "Her remark broke the ice. . . . That was her gift: Inoffensively and humorously, she had shown her concern." While Carling admitted he had been "very attracted to [Diana]," he said, "I never made a pass at her," which left open the possibility that Diana had taken the initiative as she had with Hewitt. Carling deepened the ambiguity by adding, "If I had a sexual relationship with her, I wouldn't say I had."

Diana insisted to close friends that she did not have a physical relationship with Carling. "She always denied an affair," said one friend. "I believed her because she admitted to others." Clearly Diana didn't have the same strong attachment for Carling she had felt for Hewitt and Hoare. "She made a lot of jokes about Carling," recalled a friend who spoke to Diana frequently at the time. "She would answer the phone, 'Mrs. Carling.' But then she realized it was getting out of control." Within weeks of the first tabloid disclosure, Diana had dropped Carling "like a hot brick," in the words of *Today*. Afterward, Diana gave no sign of missing him.

The Carling scandal reinforced Diana's desire to show herself in a good light on television. Toward the end of October, Diana and Martin Bashir had agreed on an interview plan—ironically enough, only days after public relations adviser Gordon Reece gave a dinner party to introduce her to Lord Wakeham, the new chairman of the Press Complaints Commission. Diana told Wakeham that she favored a privacy law to protect people from media intrusions, even as she was secretly plotting her own invasion of the royal family's privacy.

Diana and Bashir agreed to tape on November 5, Guy Fawkes Day, when her staff would be away from Kensington Palace. The program was scheduled to air November 20—the forty-eighth wedding anniversary of the Queen and Prince Philip. For Diana's purpose—to demonstrate her strength and her independence—the timing seemed perfect. She even had an idealized new image to show the world, her first *Harper's Bazaar* cover. The magazine's editor, Liz Tilberis, said she had originally been unaware that Diana had arranged the cover to coincide with *Panorama,* but then realized that Diana "knew exactly what she was doing." Indeed, the shoot with Diana's favorite photographer, Patrick Demarchelier, was on October 13, far along in Diana's scheme with Bashir. Diana had planned another symbolic event two days after the transmission date: her arrival in Argentina for a four-day "working visit."

Diana told neither her close aides nor her close friends about the interview; no one in her family knew, either, not even Charles Spencer. She did consult her psychic Rita Rogers, however. "I supported her choice," Rogers later said. On November 5, Diana opened the door at Kensington Palace herself, further proof of the project's secrecy. The four-man crew took two hours to set up and spent three hours filming the interview, which was edited down to fifty-five minutes.

"Diana was a very unusual interviewee," one of the BBC filmmakers told the *Sunday Express.* "She was behaving like she was an extra producer." Diana insisted to one close friend that she had not rehearsed, although she said she had known all the questions in advance. But according to Barbara Walters, who discussed the interview with Diana after ABC paid $642,000 for the U.S. broadcast rights, "*Panorama* was very well planned. All the questions were submitted in advance, and she rehearsed. I thought it was a superb performance."

Signs of her preparation were evident in contrived lines such as "three of us in the marriage" and her unattributed quotation of a passage from *An Evil Cradling,* the book by former hostage Brian Keenan: "There's no better way to dismantle a personality than to isolate it."

At one point during the interview, a member of the BBC crew joked, "It's a different kind of birthday present for Charles," to which Diana replied, "That is exactly when I want you to announce it in public." On the morning of November 14, Charles's forty-seventh birthday, just after she opened a new patient center at Broadmoor, Diana called a senior Buckingham Palace official to inform him of the interview.

The royal family was stunned that Diana would conduct a television interview behind the back of the Queen and her top advisers. Since they still didn't know the full extent of her cooperation with Andrew Morton, this was her first overt breach of trust, and the royal family viewed her actions as unforgivable.

In the days before the November 20 broadcast, Diana tried to reassure various friends, telling them over and over, "You will be proud of me," and "There is nothing controversial." Palace officials noted Diana's apparent sincerity. As Richard Kay explained to his *Mail* readers, Diana believed the film would "counter hostile media portrayals of her by showing a patient, rational woman." She defended her secrecy by telling Kay, "If the Queen knew, then the Palace would know and . . . the program's very idea would have been crushed."

The interview was more devastating than anyone imagined. Before an audience of 15 million in Britain and many millions more around the world, Diana discussed the misery of her marriage, excruciating details of her bulimia, Charles's infidelity with Camilla, her doubts about his fitness to be king, and her adultery with James Hewitt. She confirmed the legitimacy of the Squidgy tape, although she went out of her way to deny adultery with James Gilbey. While she admitted she had allowed her friends to talk to Andrew Morton, she denied giving him any "personal help," saying "I never met him." She specified that she did not want a divorce, and she emphasized her wish to be "a queen of people's hearts" and an ambassador for Britain who would "give affection" and "help other people in distress." She used the word "strong" to characterize herself four times, and she defiantly proclaimed, "She won't go quietly, that's the problem. I'll fight to the end." When Bashir asked if Diana would rather see William succeed the Queen than Charles, she said simply, "My wish is that my husband finds peace of mind, and from that follows other things."

Diana spoke calmly, but she looked haunted, her eyes rimmed with dark makeup. People who knew her were thunderstruck. One friend was mystified by Diana's "psychobabble." "When I heard her talking, it wasn't Diana talking," he said. He also considered it "her suicide note: brilliant and terrifying." Rosa Monckton, one of Diana's closest friends, later wrote in *The Sunday Telegraph* that *Panorama* "was born of some basic desire to hurt those whom she felt had betrayed her. . . . It was Diana at her worst."

Most of her friends interpreted her comments about Hewitt as pure revenge against Charles. "I said, 'You said you adored Hewitt. How could you say that so openly?' " recalled Diana's friend Elsa Bowker. "She said, 'I have to vindicate myself.' " According to another friend of Diana's, "She said she loved Hewitt because she thought love would make things seem better." Yet another friend said that Diana made the comment about Hewitt "only to annoy Oliver Hoare."

The only member of Charles's set to speak out was Nicholas Soames, who said on television after the broadcast that Diana showed "the advanced stages of paranoia." He also characterized parts of the interview as "toe-curlingly dreadful." Since Soames was Defence Minister in the Conservative government, Downing Street hastily pointed out that he was speaking "in a personal capacity"; Soames then retreated from his harshness, saying he was "not questioning the Princess of Wales's state of mind."

Press reaction was nearly as forceful. Even Richard Kay was moved to write, "Everywhere was the stench of revenge. She laid waste her husband and her love rival with the skill of a woman betrayed." Andrew Neil said in the *Daily Mail* that Diana "must now expect the wrath of the Establishment to come down on her head." Paul Johnson sprang to her defense in the same newspaper, declaring that "manipulative she may be, but she is in no way nuts." But *The Daily Telegraph*'s venerable columnist William Deedes wrote that "some part of her performance appeared to confirm . . . her reputation for being unstable. . . . Virtually the entire programme was devoted to her analysis of a broken marriage. It was not so much an interview as an inquest." Pondering her statement that she would "not go quietly," Deedes wondered, "How in the world could she believe that expressing herself in that way would enhance her stature?"

The public reacted quite differently. Three-quarters of the respondents in a Gallup survey said she was right to appear on television, and forty-six percent had a better opinion of Diana than before. Eighty-five percent believed she should be given an ambassadorial role for Britain. Only fourteen percent saw revenge as her motive, while seventy-seven percent thought she just wanted to present her side of the story. Eighty-four percent regarded her as truthful, seventy-four percent found her strong, nearly a third found her manipulative, and a quarter thought she was unstable. Diana's comments about Charles did him significant damage. In the summer of 1993, only thirty-three percent of Gallup respondents considered him unfit to be king, but after *Panorama,* that number had risen to forty-six percent.

Diana was jubilant over her popular support. Richard Kay reported that she had "no regrets" over "any element" of the interview, and that she believed she had "finally won the independence she has craved." As the interview was broadcast, Diana appeared at a glamorous fund-raising gala for cancer research looking "radiant and unfazed," in the words of one guest. Yet all was not right with Diana. The next morning, she went to her colonic irrigation clinic, where she spent two hours having her bowels purged.

When Martin Bashir asked Diana why she decided to speak out on television, she gave her most revealing—and disturbing—answer. She said she was concerned that the public perception of her had become "very confusing" and "turbulent," and she feared that "many people doubt me. . . . I want to reassure all those people who have loved me and supported me throughout the last fifteen years that I've never let them down. . . . The man on the street, yup, because that's what matters to me more than anything else." This connection strengthened when Diana received 6,000 letters from "desperately unhappy" women in the first week after the TV broadcast. "I'm overwhelmed by their response," Diana said. "I'm trying to respond to or meet as many as I can."

She had crossed a line. Diana Spencer was long gone, and so was the traditional royal princess. Diana had been carried away by her celebrity. She couldn't sustain relationships with friends or lovers, and her sons were pushing toward adolescence and its accompanying separation. Like an aging, isolated Hollywood star, she sought the love of an amorphous "public," and no one around her seemed capable of restraining her growing need for popular adulation. Not only did Diana believe in her celebrity, she had grown accustomed to using it, as both a weapon and a palliative.

By describing herself in *Panorama* as the "queen of people's hearts," Diana didn't know quite what she meant beyond providing love to people in need: the ultimate global nurturer. In a sense, she was assuming her traditional childhood role—first comforting her father and brother, then other children. She had intended to take care of Prince Charles as well, but her instability had prevented her from carrying that out. She had immediately been thrown into motherhood, which brought her great satisfaction, but it wasn't enough. So she had taken to ministering to the sick and needy, first in Britain, then throughout the world.

Diana's preoccupation with celebrity meant she would not have a moment's peace. Had she decided to spend every day toiling in a shelter or hospice in East London—much as the disgraced politician John Profumo had done for decades—the photographers and reporters would have quickly disappeared. But Diana needed to alight, spread her magic, and move on. The magic might have withered if she had shed her glamorous mystique to pursue a life of quiet dedication. She also would have lost the ability to see her reflection each day in the press. The camera was kinder than the mirror.

Chapter 22

DIANA swept into Argentina in an ebullient mood. "If she had regretted *Panorama* she never would show it in front of her friends," said Roberto Devorik, her Argentine friend who accompanied her on the trip. "She was quite confident in what she had done at that stage. She called London several times, so she was aware of the uproar."

The decision to visit Argentina had its origins in her friendship with Devorik. The idea had emerged the previous May during a luncheon at Devorik's London home with Rogelio Pfirter, the Argentine ambassador. "She wanted to meet my family and friends, and she was interested in seeing the country," Devorik said. "Her goal was to be an ambassador for the world, so she decided to see the state of charities in Argentina."

Pfirter relayed Diana's words to Argentine president Carlos Menem. Relations between Britain and Argentina had ruptured thirteen years earlier when they went to war over the Falkland Islands. Argentina's resounding defeat led to the end of military rule and restoration of democracy in 1983, and since then, Argentina had worked to rebuild its relations with Britain. The prospect of a high-profile royal visitor gave Carlos Menem a chance to smooth out the Anglo-Argentine relationship before he made an official visit to Britain. The Argentine government found a suitable charity, the Association for the Prevention of Infantile Paralysis, to issue an invitation to Diana and give her visit a plausible pretext.

Although Diana's schedule focused on hospital and clinic visits, the British Foreign Office worried that Menem would exploit her presence or that she would misspeak and spark a diplomatic incident. No crisis materialized, primarily because Diana kept quiet. But the *Panorama* interview overshadowed her efforts to be taken seriously as an ambassador when she was greeted with Argentine tabloid headlines such as THE ADULTERESS DI AR-

RIVES ON A MISSION OF CHARITY and LADIES LOOK AFTER YOUR HUSBANDS: THE SEDUCER LADY DI ARRIVES TODAY. Diana seemed unconcerned about her notoriety as she made her way around Buenos Aires, and in the end, Menem was able to score political points when he entertained Diana at lunch and said, "Argentina has gradually regained a position in the world it had lost."

Back home, the Queen initially responded to *Panorama* by sending conciliatory signals when Diana returned from Argentina. Buckingham Palace advisers met with Diana to discuss her future role and asked for a written description of her ambitions that they could submit to the Queen. But diplomats and politicians remained skeptical that Diana could handle tricky questions of protocol, much less articulate complicated government policies. While Prime Minister John Major said that as mother of the heir to the throne Diana should have a "dignified" and "worthwhile" public position, Foreign Secretary Malcolm Rifkind specifically ruled out a formal ambassadorial role.

Diana soon reinforced these misgivings. Ten days after her television appearance, a photographer from the *News of the World* caught her outside Royal Brompton Hospital after midnight. Instead of fleeing, she posed for pictures and then impulsively gave a twenty-minute interview to Clive Goodman, the newspaper's royal reporter, on the photographer's mobile phone. She explained to Goodman that she was a regular midnight visitor to the hospital, spending sometimes four hours a night comforting terminally ill patients, often three times a week. "I try to be there for them," Diana said. "I seem to draw strength from them. They all need someone. I hold their hands, talk to them, whatever helps."

Making the midnight interview all the stranger was the fact that only hours earlier she had met with the Queen's private secretary, Sir Robert Fellowes, and the Queen's press secretary, Charles Anson, to discuss her press relations. "She again demonstrated her willingness to abandon protocol and infuriate Buckingham Palace," the *Evening Standard* declared. The interview "has led to fears that the Princess could not be relied on to exercise wise judgment in a politically sensitive situation and should remain on a tighter rein." Her actions, the newspaper added, smacked of a "personal publicity campaign."

On December 7, four days after her *News of the World* interview, Diana gave an emotional speech—her first public remarks in two years—at a luncheon hosted by Centrepoint, a charity for the homeless that she supported. She spoke about the plight of "young people who have suffered abuse and have run away from home; young people whose families neither know nor care where they are; young people who have taken far too much upon their shoulders, far too young; young people forced to leave home because of family poverty and overcrowding."

In its tone, language, and simplicity, Diana's speech-making hadn't advanced much in the two years since her retirement announcement. She still couldn't manage a speech longer than about ten minutes, and despite extensive coaching, her delivery remained stubbornly awkward. Perhaps because of nerves, Diana took in air when she should have been breathing out, and paused at odd moments. "Her timing was wrong, she sounded false, and it got worse," said Jane Atkinson, who advised Diana on media relations in 1996. Diana continued to draft most of her own remarks, but the tabloid cadences were no accident. Not only was Richard Kay her principal advocate in the press, he had also started helping her with speeches. As energy healer Simone Simmons explained, "He knew her so well and understood her natural vocabulary and speaking rhythms so acutely that he was able, with her cooperation, to prepare many a public statement."

The Centrepoint luncheon caused a furor, but not because of Diana's remarks or delivery. On the platform with her was the Labour party's Jack Straw, the Shadow Home Secretary, who blistered the Tory government for its homeless policies. Not only was Diana's presence a tacit endorsement of his position, she conspicuously applauded his remarks. Her actions underscored her political naïveté and embarrassed John Major. "It is almost unprecedented for a senior royal to be linked so closely to such an attack," noted the *Evening Standard*.

By that time, the Queen had already talked to Major and her top advisers about the futility of the Wales marriage in light of Diana's televised attack on Charles and the royal family. If the Morton book had been the beginning of the end, *Panorama* was the end: Diana may have won the hearts and minds of the public, but she had irretrievably lost the support of her in-laws. That much was evident when Diana received a stern letter from Princess Margaret criticizing her behavior. According to Simone Simmons, the letter hit Diana hard.

Neither Charles nor Diana wanted to make the first move and file for divorce, so the Queen took matters into her own hands. On December 12—three years and three days after John Major had announced Charles and Diana's formal separation—the Queen told her prime minister that she would write to her son and daughter-in-law to request that they agree to an "early divorce . . . in the best interests of the country." With Diana's agreement, Charles could file for an uncontested divorce after a two-year separation. If she refused to go along, they could still be divorced after five years. As one possible inducement to Diana's agreement, Charles took Major's suggestion and publicly announced that he would not remarry.

Diana, meanwhile, had just returned from a triumphant trip to New York, where former Secretary of State Henry Kissinger had given her the "Humanitarian of the Year Award" at a dinner for 1,000 to benefit the

United Cerebral Palsy Foundation. Kissinger had praised her "luminous personality" and called her a "princess in her own right [who] aligned herself with the ill, the suffering and the downtrodden." In her brief remarks, Diana said being humane required a "sharpness of mind," "kindness of heart," and "loving our neighbors as ourselves"; she quoted a two-line verse that concluded, "Just being kind is all the sad world needs."

The high-powered Manhattan audience, which included Colin Powell and Rupert Murdoch, gave her a standing ovation "in adoration of its new saint," wrote Richard Kay in the *Daily Mail*. It didn't hurt that the saint looked like a star. Since the night of the Dimbleby documentary, Diana had taken to wearing ever more revealing dresses to major events. So it was on this evening, when dinner guests stared slack-jawed at the plunging neckline on Diana's clinging black velvet gown. The next day, Rupert Murdoch's *Sun* ran a page-one photo aimed down her cleavage, under the headline PRINCESS AND HER BIG PAIR WOW 'EM IN BIG APPLE.

For all Diana's public radiance, she was showing signs of unraveling in private. One telling outburst took place at the annual Christmas party that Charles and Diana put on for their staff. Diana approached Alexandra "Tiggy" Legge-Bourke, a thirty-year-old member of Charles's staff who helped care for William and Harry, and said, "So sorry to hear about your baby," implying that the unmarried woman had undergone an abortion. The malicious taunt was entirely without foundation, but Legge-Bourke was so shocked she had to be helped to another room, where she broke down and wept.

For two years, Diana had been nursing a grudge against Legge-Bourke, the daughter of a merchant banker and a Welsh aristocrat who grew up on a 6,000-acre estate in Wales. The Legge-Bourkes had been friendly with the royal family for years; Tiggy's mother was a lady-in-waiting to Princess Anne. Charles had known Tiggy since she was six, and he appreciated her enthusiasm for shooting and fishing, which made her an enjoyable companion for the two young princes. She had also briefly run her own nursery school. "She is the closest thing to a lady-in-waiting [Charles] has," said his private secretary Richard Aylard. Diana only grew resentful whenever she saw photographs in the tabloids of Legge-Bourke with William and Harry.

The tabloids made mischief with Diana's jealousy. During 1995, they ran exaggerated stories about a few affectionate pecks Charles gave Legge-Bourke on the cheek, as well as her sudden weight loss and attractive new figure. "The word is that Tiggy is slimming to please Prince Charles," wrote Richard Kay in July 1995. In fact, Tiggy was suffering from celiac disease, a gluten intolerance that causes severe abdominal pain as well as rapid weight loss. Diana somehow became persuaded that Charles and Legge-Bourke were having an affair, and that she had aborted his baby—none of which was true, but which prompted the Christmas party calumny. Legge-Bourke was so upset by Diana's remark that she instructed her lawyer to request an apology from the Princess and a withdrawal of her "false allegations."

Legge-Bourke's attorney delivered his letter to Kensington Palace on December 18, the same day Diana received the Queen's handwritten request for a divorce. While Diana expected Legge-Bourke to seek redress, she was stunned by the Queen's letter. Diana's reply to both her mother-in-law and Charles was noncommittal: She would now "consider her options," she said. On Christmas Eve, Diana had an appointment with her therapist, Susie Orbach, then spent Christmas day alone in Kensington Palace, and visited Orbach again on the twenty-sixth. When Diana retreated the following day to the exclusive K Club on Barbuda in the Caribbean, her companion was neither friend nor relative but her twenty-six-year-old personal assistant Victoria Mendham—another measure of her growing isolation.

Diana should have foreseen that divorce would be the ultimate consequence of her *Panorama* interview, but instead she believed the interview would earn her respect and "independence" on her terms while she remained married to Charles. Diana had even consulted with psychics, who assured her that she and Charles would be reunited. "When she had to face the bitter truth from the Queen, Diana fell apart," energy healer Simone Simmons said. "She couldn't sleep at night and started taking very strong sleeping pills. She was constantly in tears."

As 1996 began, Diana turned her attention to achieving the best possible divorce settlement. She was tense and suspicious, "aggressive and defensive all at once," said Simone Simmons. Leaving a session with Susie Orbach in early January, Diana collapsed in sobs against her car for a full minute as photographers surrounded her to take pictures. "Is she indeed perilously close to a complete breakdown?" asked John Junor, one of her sharpest critics, in *The Mail on Sunday*. Two weeks later, she offered her answer at a luncheon in her honor given by the Association of American Correspondents, telling them she was "very stable." The following month, Diana sought out Dr. Lily Hua Yu for acupuncture to treat her bulimia and depression. "Diana's life was in turmoil," Dr. Hua Yu recalled.

After the initial exhilaration over *Panorama*, Diana realized she had lost more than she had gained. As she had done after the Morton book, she began to tell certain friends that she regretted much of what she had said. "She felt it hurt the boys, very much so," said one of Diana's close friends.

"The *Panorama* interview left her deeply depressed," said *Daily Telegraph* columnist William Deedes, who came to know her in the following year.

From a practical standpoint, *Panorama* exposed Diana to even greater press intrusion. "All bets were off, because she had bared her innermost thoughts in the most amazing way," said Piers Morgan, editor of the *Mirror*. "She had no right to claim privacy after what she had said. You can't dance with the devil and not expect to be pricked by the horns." She also opened herself up to satire, especially with her "queen of people's hearts" comment. Rory Bremner did a wicked imitation of her, and when she later appeared on television wearing a surgical mask to watch an open-heart operation, she drew not only harsh criticism from the medical establishment, but derisive laughter from columnists for the image's ghoulishness.

As a result of *Panorama,* Diana lost the support of two loyal, knowledgeable professionals: first her press secretary Geoffrey Crawford, who had been so mortified he had resigned immediately after the interview aired, and then her private secretary Patrick Jephson—nicknamed "my rock" by Diana—who left in January 1996 after eight years of service. His departure coincided with the public disclosure of Diana's slur against Tiggy Legge-Bourke, which was widely misinterpreted as the precipitating factor; in fact, it was *Panorama.* Jephson had stayed on after the broadcast because he felt Diana needed him, although he was upset and "diminished" because she had kept him in the dark.

In January, Jephson told Diana he wanted out. "She was shocked," said one of Diana's friends. "She never expected him to leave. They had a big argument and said hurtful things to each other. She trusted Patrick, and he was devoted to her. After Patrick left, she was alone." One indicator of Diana's faith in Jephson had been her appointment of him as an executor three years earlier when she made out her will; after his resignation, she replaced him with her sister Sarah.

Two days after Jephson departed, Diana appointed her new media adviser, Jane Atkinson, who came aboard as a consultant rather than a Palace employee. At forty-eight, Atkinson was a seasoned public relations professional who had worked for clients that included Gillette and Duracell. Atkinson had been "bemused" by Diana in their interview, and considered her a challenge. "She was almost the same as she had been on *Panorama*," Atkinson recalled. "She sat with her head cocked, and she was very fey and breathless. She was mostly interested in talking about herself. She told me how she was canny with the media, and she had a strong sense of self-preservation, a sixth sense of what was right for her."

Although Atkinson saw room for improvement in Diana's public speaking, she was impressed by her other skills on the public stage. "If she could have held on to her professionalism in her work, she would have been incredible," Atkinson said. "She could work a room or a lunch or an audience." Diana's unwillingness to study diligently for her appearances remained a problem, however. "Unless you gave her what she wanted, she would not pay attention," said Atkinson. "She worked to her own agenda whether it was right or wrong. Maybe she couldn't deal with abstractions or new ideas. Someone as lovely as that, and with a powerful image, you wanted to have the intelligence to go with it. Was she dim and didn't get things, or was she dealing with so much in her private life that she couldn't pay attention? I didn't know. I was dealing with her at a difficult time of her life. In my dismissive moments I would say she was dim, and in my generous moments I would say she was depressed."

Atkinson prudently avoided being drawn in too deeply by Diana, speaking to the Princess about professional matters and confining herself to what she needed to know to deal with the press. Atkinson would call Diana each morning to discuss what was in the papers; they generally spoke four or five times more in a day. "I said to her the best thing is not to read the papers," Atkinson recalled. "I will be your outside ears and decide what to respond to." Atkinson soon realized that Diana read everything anyway.

Diana turned out to be a more unusual client than Atkinson could have predicted. "She was quite secretive," Atkinson said. "She would get advice from someone, but she wouldn't say from where. She wouldn't say what a normal person would, which is, 'I spoke to Alan and his view was this.' Rather, she would talk to Alan and present what he said as her idea. In my view, this was an insecurity. She felt she couldn't trust anyone, and she needed to have control."

Atkinson viewed her role as guarding Diana's image during the difficult divorce negotiations for a fair settlement. To that end, Atkinson set up a series of luncheon meetings with newspaper editors, but with Jephson gone and Diana keeping her cards close to the chest, Atkinson was operating in a vacuum. "I thought this was the first time she met a lot of these people," Atkinson recalled.

From her original involvement with Morton back in 1991, Diana had been dealing directly with journalists for some five years. She benefited from a lack of distinction between downmarket tabloid reporters and the more prestigious broadsheet journalists, as her impromptu interview with *News of the World*'s Clive Goodman had shown. Beyond her early appreciation of the *Daily Mail*'s ability to reach "Middle England" as well as her aristocratic friends, Diana now grasped the importance of the red top tabloids for getting the word out to her "public." "She was keen to keep the *Sun* and *Mirror* at bay," recalled *Mirror* editor Piers Morgan. "She knew

...ana in front of the Taj Mahal on February 11, 1992. [20]

...e following day, Diana deliberately turning her head as Charles tried to kiss her after a polo
...atch in Jaipur. [21]

Top: Diana and Charles in November 1992 during a visit to South Korea, when the tabloids nick-named them "The Glums". [22]

Diana and her mother, Frances Shand Kydd, at Wimbledon in July 1993 during a tranquil period in their up-and-down relationship. [23]

Above: Diana and her sons, William (left) and Harry (right), with her friends Catherine Soames (left rear) and Kate Menzies (right rear), riding in a sleigh while on a ski vacation in Lech, Austria, in March 1994. [24]

Right: Accompanied by her friend Peter Palumbo (centre), Diana greeting Graydon Carter, editor of *Vanity Fair*, at a fund-raising dinner at the Serpentine Gallery on June 29, 1994, the night Jonathan Dimbleby's documentary about Prince Charles was shown on television. [25]

Diana leaving the home of her psychotherapist, Susie Orbach, in May 1995. [26]

Diana in front of her last formal portrait, painted in the summer of 1995 by Henry Mee. [27]

Above: Diana as she appeared during her Panorama interview with Martin Bashir on November 20, 1995. [28]

Right: Hasnat Khan, the Pakistani surgeon with whom Diana had a romance during the last two years of her life. [29]

Below: Diana on television in April 1996 as she watched open-heart surgery, one of a number of operations she witnessed as a result of her romance with Hasnat Khan. [30]

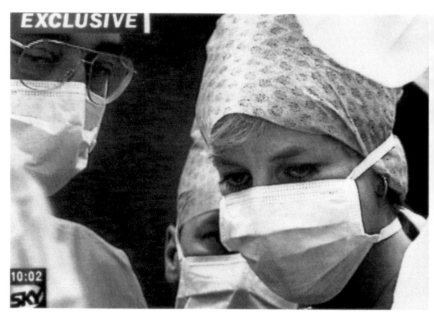

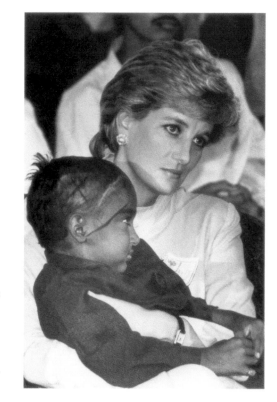

Diana conducting an impromptu press conference with surprised tabloid reporters on July 14, 1997, the third day of her holiday with the Fayeds in the south of France. [33]

Diana and Dodi in the back seat of their Mercedes limousine in Paris shortly after midnight on August 31, 1997, only minutes before the car slammed into the wall of a tunnel, killing them both. [34]

twenty million people read those two papers every day. If she wanted to appeal to the masses she needed a level of tolerance from the red tops."

The Sun and the *Mirror* covered Diana in sensational fashion. Originally, both papers had been on her side, but *The Sun* had become critical, so Diana arranged a lunch with its editor Stuart Higgins. Diana let Higgins know that "she considered the *Sun* readers her friends that she could reach out to." At the same time, Diana gave Higgins personal background information. "It was understood that things you had been told would come back in some way," said Higgins, "but not as harmfully as if they were in the newspaper the next day."

Aside from the *Daily Mail,* the *Mirror* had been the most consistently sympathetic to Diana, so she was eager to solidify a relationship with editor Piers Morgan, who at age thirty was four years younger than she. When Morgan arrived at Kensington Palace in early 1996, he found Prince William at the table with Diana and Atkinson. Diana "was keen to know what I thought of [her son]," Morgan said. "She was thinking that I was a young editor and might well be covering William when he was beginning to get the sharp end of press attention." Morgan could see that Diana's relationship with William "was extremely close, not unnaturally, but he knew everything about her life, which was surprising." Morgan got along with Diana, he later said, because he "treated her less than reverentially, and she liked it."

Diana was less successful with the editors of the midmarket *Daily Express* and *Sunday Express.* Richard Addis of the *Daily Express* was the sort of man who might have intimidated her—a Cambridge graduate with supreme confidence. Addis felt that she "manipulated through her looks and the way she talked." Still, he confessed to admiring how she "talked directly and bravely to me. She had the courage of a cornered rabbit." He was perplexed when Diana invited him several more times to Kensington Palace for coffee. Each time, she reeled off a list of statements about her in his newspaper that she claimed were untrue. "Her manner would be on the verge of bursting into tears and getting nasty at the same time," Addis recalled. Once, when Diana's assistant Victoria Mendham phoned to complain, Addis replied that Diana was just a "whinger"—a chronic complainer. "I am not a whinger," said Diana, who had been silently listening on another extension.

Sue Douglas, the former *Sunday Times* deputy who had become editor of the *Sunday Express,* was the only woman among the editors invited to Kensington Palace. "For me it was a difficult conversation," Douglas said. "If you were male, she would be flirty and interested, but being female made it difficult. It was hard work." In the end, Douglas was unmoved by

Diana's lament: "She talked a lot of crap about being the princess in the gilded cage, how she couldn't go out because the Charles camp made it so difficult for her. But then she would contradict herself and talk about having been to the theater or having taken a walk around Kensington. She had a clear notion of being a tragic heroine, but she was inconsistent."

Diana was so determined to shape her coverage that she even agreed to meet journalists in groups—the sort of encounters with clever people that so often filled her with terror. During a luncheon at the *Evening Standard,* the novelist and columnist A. N. Wilson told Diana about a picture he had seen of a royal from an earlier century wearing only his underwear. As the rest of the group wondered if Wilson had offended her, she smiled and said, "Did it turn you on, Mr. Wilson?," prompting what columnist Peter McKay described as a "great roar of laughter."

Diana worked on the press in an ad hoc way as well. Taki Theodoracopulos, the "High Life" columnist for *The Spectator,* had written harshly about Diana before they met at a party given by Jimmy and Annabel Goldsmith in 1995. " 'Do you think I'm mad?' " Diana asked. "I was drunk and said, 'All I know is I'm mad about you,' " Taki recalled. "She turned me like that." Taki wrote glowingly about her, and beginning in 1996, invited her to dinner parties with other journalists.

One guest at those dinners was Charles Moore, editor of *The Daily Telegraph,* whose cerebral manner and sympathy for Charles unnerved Diana. In the aftermath of *Panorama,* Moore tried to impress on Diana that the *Telegraph* couldn't look favorably on her unless she affirmed Charles's fitness to be king. Instead, Diana insisted that Charles didn't want to rule, saying, "He wants to live in Italy and look at beautiful things"—a refrain she repeated to a number of journalists. "She was careful not to say, 'I don't want him to be king,' " Moore said, "but it was difficult to see what else it could be other than revenge, and it was linked to her promotion of Prince William to be king."

Diana achieved mixed results in her continuing campaign to win over the press. "She gave us more information, and we understood her thoughts, but our coverage didn't change in the sense that she offered a revelation that made us see her differently," Moore said. For her part, Diana persisted in complaining about her coverage. "She couldn't understand when we ran stories that were not on her side, so she would go out of her way to deny them," said Stuart Higgins of *The Sun.* She had more success with Piers Morgan of the *Mirror,* who used his Kensington Palace luncheon to establish an amicable relationship that benefited both of them.

"I would deal every day with her office, and she would usually be in the background," Morgan said. "It was an ongoing working relationship, and for that, we gave her a more sympathetic hearing. I would speak to her in the early morning, and she would be well informed about what everyone had done. We had pretty good relations, although you would write a headline she didn't like and you would be frozen out. Then you would do something nice, and there would be a thaw. As long as you were broadly sympathetic, you had a good relationship."

In one respect, "Diana held all the cards because she knew what was coming up," said *Daily Mail* columnist Peter McKay. But Diana's ability to shape her coverage was limited by competition, commerce, and the kinds of stories she generated. "If a story concerned what she was doing and thinking, and it was in her control, she could be effective," Stuart Higgins said. "But when other factors were at work, with loose cannons like James Hewitt or the Oliver Hoare matter ending up with the police, it was beyond her control." Max Hastings, editor of the *Evening Standard,* admitted to being a "sucker" for Diana's "Bambi eyes," but only up to a point. "We sympathized with her as a woman," Hastings said, "but she still did silly things, and we reported that."

Chapter 23

O N February 18, 1996, word leaked in the tabloids that Diana was planning a "secret trip" to Pakistan the following week to visit a cancer hospital run by Imran Khan, the forty-three-year-old former Pakistani cricket star married to Jimmy and Annabel Goldsmith's twenty-two-year-old daughter, Jemima. Through Annabel, Diana had become friendly with Jemima, who had shocked English society the previous year by converting to Islam and moving to Lahore.

Diana wanted to see the hospital and its patients, but another important reason underlay her interest. Since the previous September, Diana had been in love with a Pakistani heart surgeon named Hasnat Khan—"Natty" to his friends, no relation to Imran—who worked at the Royal Brompton Hospital where Diana had been paying mystifying midnight mercy visits to patients. Khan was five years older than Diana and several inches taller; he was described in the press as "Doctor Dishy," "a dark-skinned Tom Selleck look-alike," and the "dashing medic whose looks echo movie heart-throb Omar Sharif." Diana herself said he was "drop-dead gorgeous."

In truth, Khan didn't quite measure up to the superlatives. Although he was mustachioed and dark-eyed, he had a visible paunch and "enjoyed many of the 'wrong' foods," in the words of energy healer Simone Simmons. Diana and Khan had met at the Brompton when Diana was visiting her friend Joseph Toffolo, whose triple bypass operation Khan had assisted. Khan was so absorbed in his patient that he didn't even recognize Diana, who was instantly smitten. Turning to Joseph's wife Oonagh, her acupuncturist at the time, Diana said, "His name is Hasnat Khan. It's written on his shoes." Commented Oonagh, "Those eyes of hers had not missed a thing."

For the next eighteen days, Diana sat at Joseph Toffolo's bedside and got to know Khan. She asked the surgeon to introduce her to other patients needing comfort, and in the following months, he accompanied her on her visits throughout the hospital late at night when he was on duty. "She was very well known there," said press relations adviser Jane Atkinson. Diana sometimes stayed long into the night to shadow Khan at work, and she watched him perform open-heart surgery at least a half-dozen times.

To Diana, Hasnat Khan represented the idealized nurturing man of her dreams. She was captivated by "his wit, his intelligence, and his dedication to work which she knew to be truly important," said Simone Simmons. "He was a male version of what she wanted to do—save lives and give to people," said one of her close friends. Diana also "relished the . . . sense of 'forbiddenness' that surrounded their affair," said Simmons. Diana's fascination with Eastern cultures had begun with Oliver Hoare, and after a string of bad experiences with Englishmen, she was open to a more exotic friendship with a man she felt she could trust.

Mostly, Diana was drawn to Khan's kind, down-to-earth manner. The surgeon was "the first man who was completely unimpressed by her glamour," said her friend Cosima Somerset. "He liked her for herself." With her customary intensity, Diana threw herself into the relationship. She took to studying *Gray's Anatomy* and reading surgical reports as well as books on the Muslim faith. She bought a custom-made wardrobe of brightly colored silk shalwar kameez, the tunic and trouser ensembles worn by Pakistani women, and she burned scented joss sticks at Kensington Palace. All the while, Diana's friendship with Jemima Khan intensified as Diana focused on finding out everything she could about marriage to a Pakistani man.

The tabloids had caught up to Hasnat Khan in mid-December 1995 when the *News of the World* identified him as the "inspiration" for Diana's nighttime hospital visits. But the tabloid discounted any notion of romance, emphasizing that Diana's relationship was purely professional and that she even called him "Mr. Khan." One reason for the unusual reticence might have been their preoccupation with speculating about Diana's "new hunk," real estate developer Christopher Whalley, who was actually a casual friend from the Harbour Club.

When the Whalley relationship proved too insubstantial to pursue, the tabloids began tracking Khan. By the end of January 1996, they had confirmed Diana's dinner dates with the surgeon in Stratford-upon-Avon— where the couple visited Khan's uncle Omar and Omar's British wife, Jane—as well as a lunch at Kensington Palace. The further disclosure of Diana's planned trip to Pakistan—DIANA'S LOVE TRIP SECRET—reported that Hasnat Khan would be joining her, which proved untrue. Diana declined to give Jane Atkinson any details about her connection to Hasnat, but she didn't ask her media adviser to categorically deny the relationship, either.

Diana's plans upset the Foreign Office, but not because of Hasnat Khan. Rather, they were disturbed by the link to Imran Khan, who was laying plans to form a new political party that would run against Prime Minister Benazir Bhutto on an anticorruption platform. Diana informed Buckingham Palace and government officials only a few days before her departure, and she asked for no formal assistance, since she was flying on Jimmy Goldsmith's plane and would be staying at the Lahore home of a friend of Jemima and Imran's. Palace courtiers were so fearful of being portrayed as conspiring against Diana that they lodged no objections, but diplomats were concerned that the visit could harm Anglo-Pakistani relations. That concern deepened when Diana rebuffed an invitation from Bhutto to stay in her guest house, and it turned out that the Prime Minister would be excluded from Imran Khan's fund-raising dinner.

The trip was noteworthy for its photographs of Diana in striking native garb, embracing cancer-stricken children. "Her mission to reach out to the poor and suffering achieved almost Biblical proportions," wrote James Whitaker in the *Daily Mirror*. "Never once did she falter as wave after wave of children came up to her for comfort."

On February 15, several days before her departure for Pakistan, Diana had met with the Queen at Buckingham Palace to discuss progress toward divorce. The Queen's deputy private secretary, Robin Janvrin, had attended the meeting as well, and had taken notes. In the two months since receiving the Queen's letter, Diana had kept silent, until tabloid reports surfaced in early February about various "demands" Diana would make. The most important concerned her desire to retain "Her Royal Highness" in her title as a condition of divorce. The "HRH" designation, as well as the question of custody of William and Harry and Diana's residence in Kensington Palace, were ultimately the purview of the Queen.

Diana did not say explicitly what had passed between her and the Queen, but she indicated to Jane Atkinson that her mother-in-law had been noncommittal about "HRH" and had urged her to sort out that matter and others in a meeting with Prince Charles. "The Princess never expressed to me that she didn't want to keep the title," Atkinson recalled. Yet in conversations with friends, Diana said that in the Buckingham Palace meeting she had offered to give up "HRH" because she assumed the Queen would wish her to.

At Charles's request, Diana agreed to meet in St. James's Palace late in the afternoon on February 28—just the two of them, with no one taking notes. As she entered the meeting, "she wanted to have things sorted, that was her mood," Atkinson said. "She wanted to resolve things so they would move forward." The estranged couple talked for forty-five minutes. "It was as difficult a meeting about divorce as one can be," Atkinson recalled. "There were a lot of things to resolve."

Diana received Charles's assurance that their discussion would be private, and they agreed on a few points. Diana then went to her office where Jane Atkinson and Diana's lead lawyer, Anthony Julius, awaited her. Diana said she wanted to make an announcement immediately because she was convinced that Charles's side would leak. Atkinson agreed that "if [Diana] wanted to write the agenda, she should issue the information on her own terms rather than having to respond." Diana's statement indicated that she had consented to Charles's request for a divorce, and they had agreed that she would continue to be involved with all decisions regarding the children, that she would live at Kensington Palace and keep her offices at St. James's Palace, but that she would give up "Her Royal Highness" and be known as Diana, Princess of Wales.

Just as Atkinson was releasing the statement to the press, Diana was calling the Queen to agree to a divorce. When the Queen, Prince Charles, and Buckingham Palace officials learned of Diana's unilateral announcement, they were incensed by her breach of confidentiality. The Palace swiftly issued its own statement, insisting that what Diana had characterized as "decisions" were merely "requests," and details about the divorce "remain to be discussed and settled." Diana instantly shot back on the grounds that her release of the information "cultivate[d] the image of a strong woman and wanting to be in control of the message." The language was entirely Diana's; Atkinson considered the term "strong woman" to be "protesting too much."

As with *Panorama,* Diana initially felt elated that she had the upper hand. But again she went too far, using Richard Kay to transmit her accusation that the Queen and Prince Charles had pressured her to drop "HRH"—a direct contradiction of what she had told Jane Atkinson earlier. Diana also leaked to the *Daily Mail* that in their discussion she had told Charles, "I loved you and I will always love you because you are the father of my children."

The Palace strenuously denied Diana's account, even allowing the Queen's press secretary, Charles Anson, to be quoted by name rather than as a "royal spokesman." "The decision to drop the title is the Princess's and the Princess's alone," Anson said. "It is wrong that the Queen or the Prince asked her. I am saying categorically that is not true. The Palace does not say something specific on a point like this unless we are absolutely sure of the facts." *The Times* noted pointedly that the Queen was irritated that the "Princess's camp" had been providing "carefully selected insights" about the meeting with Charles.

As the public disagreements escalated, Diana dropped out as the guest of honor at the final gala for the 125th birthday of the British Red Cross. The lavish event on February 29 had been billed as Diana's "first step in building herself a new role as an ambassador for humanitarian causes," but Diana was too emotionally fragile to play her assigned role. "She felt she would meet people who would express sympathy, and she said to me, 'I'll just cry,' " said Jane Atkinson. "She could see what would happen, and what pictures would be in the papers. She needed space to function in public again."

In an atmosphere of ill will, negotiations between Charles's and Diana's lawyers proceeded slowly. There was general agreement about joint custody of William and Harry, as well as Diana's continued residence at Kensington Palace. The sticking points involved money (Diana initially asked for a lump sum of $70 million), the location of her office, her future role, and her title, which Diana had seemed ready to give up, but belatedly recognized its vital role in her identity and special status. Without it, she would be required, among other things, to curtsy to such "minor" royals as Princess Michael of Kent.

The question of her role as goodwill ambassador confounded everyone, including Diana. At times, she wasn't even certain she wanted to travel the globe on behalf of good causes. She told some of her friends that she would be happy working with Hasnat Khan in some capacity. She had an equally impassioned conversation with Paul Johnson about wanting to be a therapist.

The roving ambassador notion "was put into her head," Johnson said. "She had no idea what an ambassador did, and it wouldn't have suited her. She said to me, 'I would like to be a therapist, a psychological counselor.' I said, 'It is very hard work. You have to knuckle down. You wouldn't be able to go off on trips.' She said, 'Oh, I wouldn't mind.' But she never got down to it. The spirit was willing but the flesh was weak. She would have been very very good, but she was never brought up to discipline herself."

After her February trip to Pakistan, Diana made few public appearances until June, when she took a three-day trip to Chicago to raise money for cancer charities. After Lucia Flecha de Lima's move to Washington at the end of 1993, Diana's regular visits to the United States had offered a refuge. While Diana had a growing number of detractors in Britain, her popularity was undimmed in the United States, and she often spoke of her fondness for American informality—as Richard Kay put it in the *Daily Mail*, "that engagingly enthusiastic way Americans have."

Diana even talked about moving to the United States, but had developed several misconceived notions of what life would be like for her in America. She believed that she would have a "chance to prove herself," to be judged as a person rather than by her position, and she figured that there were so many celebrities she would be able to "disappear." She didn't fully appreciate that, in America, she would be lionized as a celebrity even more than in Britain.

Everywhere she went in Chicago, Diana attracted large, enthusiastic crowds that recalled the earliest days of "Di-Mania." She spoke briefly at Northwestern University about cancer, "the dreaded C-word" that "seems to strike out of nowhere, destroying lives at will, leaving devastation in its wake." She toured hospitals, attended a symposium on breast cancer, and was the guest of honor at fund-raising lunches and dinners.

Seated between *Today* show cohost Katie Couric and novelist Anna Quindlen at the luncheon for 500 women, Diana seemed out of her element. "I have never seen this many women in one room in my life," Diana said. "She was disconcerted by it," said Quindlen, who was surprised that Diana appeared "incredibly young. I could see a bell-jar effect. It seemed as if she had stopped growing once she married the Prince of Wales." When Quindlen thanked Diana for helping the cancer charities and observed that "probably no one else could have raised the money you have raised in two days," Diana "ducked her head and shrugged and made a face," Quindlen recalled. "It was the way a thirteen-year-old would respond to a compliment. By age thirty-five, you assume someone would say something like, 'Thank you very much. I was glad to be able to do it.' "

Chicago's embrace boosted Diana, but she couldn't shake her gloomy moods. On the evening of her arrival, Diana and her entourage were tackling the mountain of presents that had been delivered to the hotel. "It was a very funny twenty minutes," Jane Atkinson said. "Lighthearted and girlie and laughing about the notes and trying on hats. Suddenly she switched off and left for her room. It was the only time I saw anything that abrupt. She was outgoing, and then she completely shut down."

Upon Diana's return to London, the press declared her trip a major success, and the *Daily Express* singled out Atkinson for her organizational skills. Knowing that Diana disliked sharing the spotlight, Atkinson asked the *Express* reporter not to write the article, and finally cooperated only to verify facts and give one statement emphasizing the trip's "team effort."

Diana called Atkinson the next morning to express her displeasure. Later that day, *Daily Express* editor Richard Addis came for a previously scheduled lunch with Diana. He reassured Diana that Atkinson had nothing to do with the article. But Diana had made up her mind that Atkinson had betrayed her, and even told friends that Atkinson had been leaking negative stories about her to *The Sun*, which was untrue. From that point on, Diana stopped consulting Atkinson, and used her only as a mouthpiece.

At the end of June 1996, Diana made a final bid to preserve "HRH" by leaking to Richard Kay that Buckingham Palace now insisted she keep the title. Kay characterized the turnabout as an "odd twist" predicated on the Queen's belief that as the mother of the future king, Diana "must have appropriate status." The leak was simply Diana's wishful thinking. The Queen had already decided that Diana was unworthy of the title because of the Morton book, the *Panorama* interview, and her dalliances with the tabloid press.

On July 4, three days after Diana's thirty-fifth birthday, Prince Charles presented her with his settlement offer. Diana would receive a lump sum of £15 million—much of which would be underwritten by the Queen, since the Prince was forbidden by Parliament to sell any of his nearly £100 million in Duchy of Cornwall assets—plus more than £400,000 a year to underwrite Diana's office. Charles would partly finance that expenditure with a loan, and his £1.5 million annual income after taxes and staff expenses would pay for the rest. Diana's title would be "Diana, Princess of Wales," and a statement issued by the Palace emphasized that she would be "regarded as a member of the royal family."

As a semi-royal, Diana would be invited to state and national occasions, and in those circumstances would be treated as if she still had the "HRH." She would live in Kensington Palace, where her office would also be located. Her public role would be "for her to decide," although any working trips overseas—representing charities, for example—would require consultation with the Foreign Office and the Queen's permission, which was standard practice for members of the royal family. (For private holidays, no permission was necessary.) Diana would keep several important perks—access to royal aircraft and the state apartments at St. James's Palace for entertaining—and she would have the use of all her royal jewelry, eventually to be passed on to the wives of her sons. As part of the settlement, both Diana and Charles would sign a confidentiality agreement precluding them from discussing divorce terms or any details of their life together.

The terms were generous, and Diana formally agreed to them just four days later. Besides her lawyers, Anthony Julius and Maggie Rea, Diana had received behind-the-scenes help from her friend Jimmy Goldsmith. "He told her to hang tough, don't settle" until she got the money she wanted, according to John Tigrett, Goldsmith's business partner for more than three decades. The evening she received the settlement terms, Diana joined the Goldsmith family at the Dorchester Hotel for a gala to raise money for Imran Khan's hospital. "We made the deal today," Goldsmith told Tigrett.

The last stumbling block was losing "HRH," which Diana had resisted until the end. She may have been justified in doing so, because the solution imposed by the divorce was complicated and ambiguous. Diana was in a unique position as mother of the heir to the throne, and for that reason alone was probably entitled to full royal status. She finally decided to give up the "HRH" after she asked Prince William whether he would mind if she no longer had it. When he said it made no difference, she told her lawyers to agree to the terms.

Coverage of the final agreement on July 12 was mixed. The *Daily Mail* called it HER ROYAL HUMILIATION, and the *Daily Mirror* termed it THE FINAL BETRAYAL, accompanied by a photograph of Diana looking haggard. "It is the face of a woman utterly destroyed," said the tabloid. Other papers were less judgmental, with *The Daily Telegraph* announcing PRINCESS TO GIVE UP HRH STYLE and *The Times* declaring GO-AHEAD FOR 15 M POUND SETTLEMENT. Diana spent much of the day with Lucia Flecha de Lima, who had flown from Washington to console her.

On July 15, Charles and Diana filed their "decree nisi," the document declaring that the marriage would be officially dissolved in six weeks on August 28. For all her transgressions, Diana still held the public's sympathy. The sentiments expressed in the *Mirror* caught the popular mood: Diana may have been well compensated, but she had been mistreated—and ultimately humiliated and punished—by the icy royal family.

Scarcely twenty-four hours later, Diana managed to squander some of that goodwill when she unexpectedly announced that she had given up nearly one hundred of her charities and would keep formal affiliations with only six: the homeless charity Centrepoint; the Leprosy Mission; the National AIDS Trust; the English National Ballet; Great Ormond Street Hospital for Sick Children; and the Royal Marsden Hospital. The announcement created a furor because her actions seemed precipitous and unfeeling. Some charities even had to read about her decision in the press.

Diana's decision had not actually been sudden. She had made up her mind in mid-June to maintain ties with charities that reflected her own emotional needs. Atkinson had urged her to keep the English National Ballet to "give her something lighthearted to do," which Diana readily agreed to because of her lifelong love of ballet. The National AIDS Trust had special significance because AIDS had given Diana her first meaningful public role. When a friend questioned her choice of the Leprosy Mission, Diana joked, "It's the travel, stupid." The rejoinder was typical of Diana, and her interest in the disfiguring disease did take her to exotic locales. But according to Atkinson, Diana felt the leprosy charity needed her prominence to remain in the public eye. Both the Great Ormond Street and Royal Marsden hospitals kept her in touch with the sick and dying, and Centrepoint gave her a link to the dispossessed.

The most glaring omission from the list was the Red Cross. That relationship had gone through its ups and downs, and in the end, Diana decided that the charity had a high enough profile without her. As newspaper articles tallied the financial toll on the charities she had "ditched," Diana told Atkinson to issue a clarifying statement that was illogical as well as false: "The move is entirely because of her loss of royal status. . . . The loss in her standing will not be beneficial to those charities, and her pulling power must be diminished. She can no longer give them the strong position they are entitled to." Atkinson told Diana the statement made no sense because it implied that the remaining six charities would be similarly harmed by her reduced status, but Diana insisted she release it anyway.

The announcement did not get the kind of press coverage that Diana expected. "It was all bad, and she accused me of saying the wrong things," Atkinson recalled. Within a few days, it became clear that the relationship between Diana and Atkinson had broken down, and a week later, Atkinson resigned.

Diana nearly cut loose Richard Kay around the same time. The divorce negotiations had made Diana more sensitive than ever to her image. Energy healer Simone Simmons, who had become friendly with Kay through Diana, said that Diana "decided that Richard's draft speeches were too long and complicated." Diana decided to use Martin Bashir, the *Panorama* interviewer, who had offered his services. Diana had stayed in touch with Bashir much as she had maintained a link to Andrew Morton following his 1992 book. "Martin Bashir is a humble man, and he would turn on quite a bit of charm," explained Diana's butler Paul Burrell. "He is a flattering person." Richard Kay was "dreadfully upset" to be displaced by Bashir, according to Simmons, but he swallowed his pride and didn't protest, which ensured the continuation of his friendship with Diana, and his role as her conduit to the *Daily Mail*.

The press speculated that Diana would emerge in the autumn with an ambitious plan for her six charities. According to one account, she would fulfill three charity engagements a week compared with her once-monthly commitment during the previous year. As before, these expectations proved mistaken. In the final year of her life, Diana was associated primarily with causes outside her chosen half dozen. Her promotion of a ban on antipersonnel land mines was the most publicized, but her affiliations also included an Australian research center associated with Hasnat Khan, and American charities supported by two relatively new friends, Katharine Graham, the influential head of *The Washington Post*, and *Harper's Bazaar* editor Liz Tilberis.

Whenever Diana shifted her attention, she left those behind feeling puzzled and wounded. "In [her] last two years, she was totally unpredictable in terms of her professional relationship with the organizations of which she was patron," said Michael Adler, chairman of the National AIDS

Trust. "When she reduced from one hundred to six organizations, on the whole she didn't do much even for the six. She did less and less for us. We couldn't get her to do something. We would write to her, try to talk with her. But she was interested in other things, which is fair enough. That is life. But if you are a patron, you have responsibilities that go with patronage that you must fulfill. Diana had very special qualities, but she was totally reactive."

Chapter 24

D URING the last year of her life, Diana presented herself in public as a
strong single woman advancing worthy causes. In private, it was a different story. Caught in her desperate love affair with Hasnat Khan, she behaved erratically, even to the point of wearing disguises. Her final
downward trajectory began two months before her death, when she accepted the hospitality of Egyptian businessman Mohamed Fayed and his
family.

In the late summer of 1996, just after her divorce became official,
Diana decided to make a dramatic public gesture to break with her past.
She called her American friend Marguerite Littman, head of the AIDS Crisis Trust, and said, "I have decided to give you my clothes." "I didn't think I
dressed that badly," cracked Marguerite. Diana explained that she and
Prince William had been talking about what she might do with her life, and
he had suggested she auction the clothes she no longer wanted and donate
the proceeds to charity. "Don't you think this would be a good idea for your
charity?" asked Diana. "Come to lunch if you want them, tomorrow or the
next day."

Diana's choice of beneficiary was significant: Marguerite Littman's
AIDS Crisis Trust, with which Diana had no affiliation, instead of the National AIDS Trust, which, only weeks earlier, Diana had endorsed as one of
her six remaining patronages. The rationale for her decision remained
mysterious. She had made a publicized visit to a National AIDS Trust clinic
the previous June, and Michael Adler had praised Diana for her dedication
to the AIDS cause. The visit had attracted some negative publicity because
Diana was accompanied by AIDS victim Aileen Getty, an American cru-
sader for the dangers of the disease to heterosexuals. "We'd love Di more if
she didn't let herself be used," *The Sun* complained. Diana had been

knocked more harshly many times, so media criticism seemed an unlikely cause for her defection. Still, Diana's June visit turned out to be her last contact with the National AIDS Trust.

The most likely explanation was Diana's affection for Marguerite Littman, along with her organization's more glamorous profile. AIDS Crisis Trust raised funds primarily through film premieres, and its patrons were more social than Adler's group. The social aspect interested Diana, who suggested to Marguerite that they take the dresses to Los Angeles and New York for a "road show, something fun that would make money." "Diana had a childlike love of celebrities," said one of her friends, noting how much the Princess enjoyed meeting film stars like Tom Hanks. Diana and Marguerite selected Christie's auction house because its chairman, Christopher Balfour, was a mutual friend, and they chose June 1997 for the sale in New York City.

Michael Adler did not learn about the auction of seventy-nine evening dresses until it was announced in the press six months later. By then, he had even greater reason for dismay over Diana's rebuff: "The National AIDS Trust was nearly bankrupt," Adler said. "Not only was she sending the wrong sort of message to our community, that she was giving her dresses to an organization that had film premieres, but the organization of which she was a patron was about to go into liquidation."

As Diana planned her gala charity auction, she made another important decision about her public role in the first months after her divorce: joining the movement to ban antipersonnel land mines. She later told reporters that she had been alerted to the problem when "a lot of information started arriving on my desk about land mines, and the pictures were so horrific that I felt it would help if I could be part of the team raising the profile around the world." Left unsaid was the role another friend played in alerting Diana to the issue: her energy healer Simone Simmons had visited a Red Cross worker in Bosnia during the summer of 1996. When Simmons returned from her ten days in Tuzla, she brought back photographs of mine victims to show Diana. "Do you think I could make a difference?" Diana asked.

Having dropped the Red Cross so dramatically in mid-July, Diana reversed course and returned to the organization because it was conducting a worldwide campaign to eradicate land mines. When Diana asked if the Red Cross would sponsor her on an overseas trip to raise awareness of land mine victims, director-general of the British Red Cross Mike Whitlam offered to be her official escort. At the same time, filmmaker Richard Attenborough, who had known Diana off and on for more than a decade, invited her to be the guest of honor at the premiere of his new film, *In Love and War,* to raise money for the British Red Cross Land Mines Appeal.

With Attenborough's encouragement, Diana decided to make her own documentary on the subject, and he helped her negotiate a deal with the BBC that would enable camera crews to film her overseas trip. The Red Cross first suggested that Diana go to Cambodia, but the Foreign Office said her presence could interfere with delicate negotiations over a British hostage there. The British government vetoed Afghanistan as too dangerous, so Diana settled on war-ravaged Angola, where the grim statistics included one land mine for each of its 12 million inhabitants. The Foreign Office approved Diana's trip in January 1997. "In a sense, the land mine issue was a dead lucky pick," said the *Daily Telegraph* columnist William Deedes, an eighty-three-year-old anti–land mine campaigner with whom Diana consulted. "She hit the subject, and the fact that all the victims die or are crippled singly meant there was never any public indignation."

As indicated by Diana's reliance on Prince William's idea for the dress sale, along with his role in breaking the "HRH" logjam, she had come to lean on her sons more than ever—both as confidants and as supports when she was lonely and perplexed. By the fall of 1996, William and Harry were fourteen and twelve; William had been away at boarding school for six years, and Harry for four. William was intelligent and self-possessed, and like his mother, sensitive and instinctive. Diana considered him a "deep thinker." He had begun showing signs of adolescent moodiness as well, and was clearly mature beyond his years. "He had the weight of the world on his shoulders," said one friend of Diana's. Harry, by contrast, was more high-spirited and mischievous. Both boys had learned to be "respectful but not ridiculous," and had "natural manners," in the view of one Palace official.

Diana had been living in an empty nest since the autumn of 1992, when Harry left to join William at Ludgrove, but Diana's sons were often in her thoughts and conversation. When Nelson Shanks painted her portrait in 1994, he recalled that she talked of her sons "incessantly," an observation shared by many of her friends. "Her world was illuminated by the boys, and her life revolved around them," her friend Peter Palumbo said. Even at the peak of her royal duties, Diana made certain to carve out private time with her sons, and she frequently arranged her schedule to accommodate their activities. "She was always dashing down to Ludgrove to see if the boys were all right, to watch them perform in a drama," recalled one of her friends.

Diana was probably no more devoted to her boys than any good mother, but she had a special gift for connecting with them. "She was attuned to what William and Harry felt, and she kept in close touch with them," said her friend Cosima Somerset. "She really listened to her children and would value their opinions." In the view of her friend Carolyn Bartholomew, Diana was "very responsible and responsive to their individual natures, and aware of their character differences."

Above all, Diana wanted her sons to feel loved. "I hug my children to death," she told Andrew Morton. "I always feed them love and affection." Some critics accused Diana of smothering, but her friends felt her demonstrative ways were laudable given her background. "No one was the parent to her that she was trying to be to the boys," said David Puttnam. Indeed, having her sons reciprocate her affection was vital to Diana. "The constant bear hugs and showerings of kisses were mutually beneficial," in James Hewitt's view. "She needed pure unconditional love as much as they did. . . . [It] reassured her that no matter what, she was fulfilling her role as a mother to the very best of her abilities."

At times, Diana could be quite childlike, reveling in thrill rides at amusement parks in a way Prince Charles could not have managed. "She loved being with children," said one of her friends. "In a way, she was very simple." Once, on a visit with William at Ludgrove, she was so excited she jumped from one bed to another in his dormitory. After the mortification of the Gilbey tapes, her sons took to calling her Squidgy, "and she roared with laughter," recalled a friend. Sometimes her enthusiasm exceeded good judgment, most notably when she exhorted William and Harry to race go-carts around Highgrove during a downpour.

Most of the time, Diana handled her boys in a responsible way. When Puttnam invited her to bring them to Pinewood Studios, he noticed how "attentive and smart" she was. "She wanted them to be like well-behaved, normal kids, to line up in a queue for lunch, not to be served." Another time, when she took Harry to the movies, he ordered a glass of mineral water at the concession stand. When the saleswoman handed him sparkling water, he asked for still water instead. Afterward, Diana rebuked him, telling him "he should simply have thanked her for what he had been given," because she didn't want him to engage in behavior "that gave the royal family a bad name for being difficult."

Diana was determined that her sons grow up in a more "normal" fashion than was customary for members of the royal family. She took them to McDonald's and local cinemas, and she introduced them to people from all walks of life. "I want them to have an understanding of people's emotions, people's insecurities, people's distress, and people's hopes and dreams," she said in her *Panorama* interview. To that end, she took the boys to homeless shelters, and to see dying AIDS patients. Although William was developing a full-blown antipathy toward the press, Diana recognized that he needed to understand the tabloid mentality, so she introduced him to Piers Morgan of the *Mirror*. "She was trying so hard to teach her sons how to cope with media attention, how to accept that it was something they were going to have to live with," said Liz Tilberis of *Harper's Bazaar*. "William understood her fury with them, and he also understood that she courted them from time to time."

Yet Diana's powerful emotions had a profound impact on her sons, who in their formative years overheard numerous fights between their parents and grew accustomed to the sight of their mother weeping. One of the indelible images of William's childhood was his reaction when Diana cried after a bitter disagreement with Charles early in 1992. Nine-year-old William followed his tearful mother upstairs, where she locked herself in the bathroom. Pushing tissues under the door, he said, "I hate to see you sad." Beyond what they witnessed, William and Harry also had to cope with the searing Morton and *Panorama* revelations about their mother's disturbing behavior.

Diana's insecurities got the better of her when she dealt with various nannies. She grew resentful of Barbara Barnes, who joined them after William's birth, because she felt the nanny was trying to usurp her maternal authority. Barbara Barnes's successors, Ruth Wallace and Jessie Webb, also left after running afoul of Diana's shifting moods. From the outset Diana mistrusted Tiggy Legge-Bourke, who came aboard after the separation, because Diana imagined that the young woman was trying to supplant her in her sons' affections. According to Richard Kay, "[Diana] raged that Tiggy always seemed to be having fun with the boys."

Diana's rivalrous behavior with Charles caused the most serious problems for the two boys. Starting in the mid-eighties, Diana had tried to portray Charles in a poor light as a father—a campaign that culminated in her hurtful comments in the Morton book. She competed with Charles directly for the boys' affection as well. When she and Charles were going through one of their bad periods, she would take the boys to her room for dinner, leaving Charles to eat alone in the dining room. As she told Andrew Morton, "I get into bed with them at night, hug them and say, 'Who loves them most in the whole world?' and they always say, 'Mummy.'" This rivalry played out increasingly in various excuses and pretexts that prevented Charles from seeing his sons. Indeed, it was Diana's refusal to allow William and Harry to join their father at Sandringham that triggered Charles's decision to seek a separation.

After the separation, Diana became more dependent on her eldest son as a confidant. "Diana had a mother-and-son relationship and a mother-and-husband relationship with Prince William," said her friend Roberto Devorik. "She told me she had with her son William very private and very profound conversations, and he was an extraordinary moral support." Beyond William's solace, Diana sought his guidance. "Diana used to ask William for advice all the time, about what she should do with her life," said her friend Elsa Bowker. Diana felt compelled to unburden herself, according to her friend Rosa Monckton, because she "wanted William to hear the truth from her about her life, and the people she was seeing, and what they meant to her, rather than read a distorted, exaggerated, and frequently untrue version in the tabloid press." But by confiding in William as much as she did, Diana was placing a significant emotional burden on an adolescent boy.

Diana was aware that her status was directly tied to William's position as heir to the throne, and she didn't disguise her desire to see Charles bypassed as king in favor of William. She told Andrew Morton as early as 1991, "William is going to be in his position much earlier than people think now." Diana added that she hoped Charles would "go away with his lady" and leave her with the two boys "to carry the Wales name through to the time William ascends the throne."

Between his duties and his urge to escape an unhappy marriage, Charles had probably spent too much time away from his sons from the mid-eighties until the separation in 1992. But in his own way, Charles had been a good father. When they were younger, the boys had loved playing "Big Bad Wolf" with him, and during Highgrove weekends, he spent hours with them outdoors. They followed him around in the gardens, and he talked to them about plants and animals. Diana often rebelled at such moments, retreating to her room to listen to music, read magazines, and talk on the phone.

Charles approached children on a more adult level than Diana did, explaining, querying, and drawing out their ideas. As they grew older, he took the boys to Shakespeare productions at Stratford-upon-Avon. He also showed sensitivity to their moods; once, when William was apprehensive about returning to Ludgrove after Christmas vacation, Charles spent considerable time boosting his son's confidence.

As teenagers, both boys clearly preferred their father's country pursuits—hunting, shooting, and fishing—to Diana's urban life of movies, shopping, and dining out. "Diana said to me, 'All William wants to do is have a gun in his hand,'" one of her close friends recalled. "She could see that. But I don't think she would have made them go to an AIDS hospice rather than go shoot with their father. She wouldn't punish them in that way."

In her *Panorama* interview, Diana defined the boundaries of her life with "I've got my boys, I've got my work." According to Richard Kay, Diana regarded her sons as "the only men in her life who had never let her down and never wanted from her anything except for being herself." That kind of standard was difficult to sustain, and as William and Harry became more independent, friction seemed inevitable. In the meantime, Diana tried to keep them close, calling them nearly every day at boarding school and taking them on vacations whenever she could.

Besides her sons, Diana looked to a dwindling number of friends she felt she could count on. Most of the castoffs didn't know why she let them go, but the trigger was some kind of slight or betrayal, usually illusory. Those who remained trod carefully and yielded to Diana's impulses for fear of disrupting the friendship.

She still depended on Annabel Goldsmith, Elsa Bowker, and Lucia Flecha de Lima as maternal figures, but had fallen out with Hayat Palumbo. While Lucia may have lived an ocean away, she continued to make time for Diana on the phone, adjusting her habits to accommodate their different time zones. Lucia would frequently stay up past midnight, reading and waiting for Diana to call when she awakened early.

Rosa Monckton and Marguerite Littman made themselves available as well, although Diana occasionally got perturbed when she sensed that Rosa "had other priorities." Diana picked up a new friend in Cosima Somerset, a niece of Annabel Goldsmith's, and for nearly a year they were extremely close, until Diana inexplicably dropped her. Since Diana's 1993 reconciliation with her stepmother, Raine Spencer had occupied a unique niche, keeping company with Diana at lunches in Mayfair restaurants, providing entertainment and advice.

Several alternative therapists—energy healer Simone Simmons, psychic Rita Rogers, astrologer Debbie Frank, and two acupuncturists, Oonagh Toffolo and Dr. Lily Hua Yu—remained important to Diana, but she told friends that she had stopped seeing psychotherapist Susie Orbach in the spring of 1996. According to reporter Richard Kay, Diana said she ended the therapy "because she found herself analyzing the therapist's problems rather than her own." Media adviser Jane Atkinson recalled that Diana "talked about wanting to leave Susie Orbach, but she was terrified to reach her because Susie Orbach would have said, 'Come and see me,' and Diana didn't want to. Then [Diana] did go to see her and was proud of the fact that she had finished. Whether she had finished, I don't know, but she wanted everyone to think she had finished." In fact, Diana did continue seeing Orbach at irregular intervals.

The autumn of 1996 also brought Diana's final rupture with Sarah Ferguson. Diana and Sarah had formed a tight bond in the years leading up to their divorces, and Diana had become a regular Sunday visitor at Sarah's home. "Sarah Ferguson was a very, very useful friend to the Princess during the months before the divorce," said Jane Atkinson. "The Princess was very fond of her. If she hadn't had her house to go to, she would have gone mad.

'Sarah makes me laugh,' she said." Diana and Fergie had been together the day before the *Panorama* interview, and they had vacationed in France following the July announcement of Diana's divorce.

But Sarah overstepped the bounds of friendship when she published her autobiography in November, and Diana cut her off without a word. The book's references to Diana were mostly positive, although one passage patronizingly pointed out Diana's "teary and reclusive" manner around the royal family at a time when Fergie was in their good graces. Fergie also tastelessly revealed that she had contracted warts from wearing Diana's shoes, a story Diana considered "unkind." During her book tour in the United States, Fergie answered personal questions about Diana—after Diana had specifically asked her not to. Not only did Diana stop speaking to Fergie, she wouldn't permit Fergie's name to be mentioned in her presence, and she refused to answer Fergie's letters or take her phone calls. Nine months after the start of what their mutual friend David Tang called the "arctic freeze," he tried to get them together at a dinner in Diana's honor. "The Duchess of York is the one person who would not be welcome," Diana replied.

Diana saw little of her immediate Spencer family after her separation. "She wasn't as close," said Richard Kay. "She was moving away from her own family, and from the royal family. She was looking for something else. She was very restless, even until the end." Diana's brother, Charles, had relocated to South Africa; her mother seldom ventured from her remote redoubt in Scotland; and the estrangement from her sister Jane persisted. When Diana told one of her friends that she wasn't speaking to Jane, he said, "This is an absurd situation," and quoted the biblical admonition: "You mustn't let the sun go down upon your wrath." Diana replied, "I know. I know," but her friend didn't feel she had taken in his advice. Sarah remained the closest of the siblings, still joining Diana on occasional trips as a lady-in-waiting. But Sarah had her life in the country, although she tried to maintain contact with Diana by phone most days.

Professionally, Diana suffered from the lack of an adviser experienced in politics and public relations. After Jane Atkinson's departure, Diana hired Michael Gibbins, a fifty-three-year-old former accountant, as her private secretary. While Gibbins had the financial expertise Diana needed to manage her divorce settlement, he was less experienced in negotiating with government bureaucrats and Palace courtiers, nor did he have the public relations savvy to deal with the tabloids.

For help in fielding press inquiries, Diana turned to her junior assistant Victoria Mendham, and Paul Burrell, her butler. As Diana's staff diminished, Burrell had become a jack-of-all-trades, and Diana took to calling him "my rock," as she had with her former private secretary Patrick

Jephson. Burrell had been fiercely loyal since siding with Diana in the breakup of her marriage. He was skilled at assessing her moods, and he continued to call her "Your Royal Highness." In the year after the divorce, he found himself conveying messages to certain members of the press when Diana couldn't do it herself. "I was a go-between," said Burrell. "I dealt with Clive Goodman [of the *News of the World*], and in general with people whenever she needed me."

Outwardly, Diana's single status did not affect her relationship with Hasnat Khan. Because of his aversion to publicity, they remained underground. It was during her romance with Khan that Diana took to wearing disguises, including an array of custom-made wigs and glasses with nonoptical lenses. They went undetected to jazz clubs and restaurants in Soho or Camden Town, but they spent most of their time together at Kensington Palace. Since Diana's Pakistan trip in February, the tabloids had left Khan alone—with the exception of one sighting by the *News of the World* in August, when a photographer caught Diana and Khan in a "furtive roadside rendezvous" near the Royal Brompton Hospital, which Khan had left several months earlier to work at Harefield Hospital thirteen miles outside London.

The relationship between Diana and Khan deepened after her divorce, and she considered him a vital anchor in her life. "She was emotionally more stable when she was with him," said a friend of Diana's. "He taught her that she could be loved." Diana told friends she was especially pleased that Khan admired her empathy with the sick. As Diana confessed to Elsa Bowker, "I found my peace. He has given me all the things I need."

But as was so often the case with Diana, love was accompanied by possessiveness. This time, she tried to advance Khan's career and, in the process, the prospects for their life together. When Diana went to Rimini, Italy, in October 1996 to accept a humanitarian award, she befriended South African heart surgeon Dr. Christiaan Barnard, another award recipient. Diana told Barnard about Khan and asked if the surgeon could help find him a position in South Africa. Diana revealed to Barnard that she wanted to marry Khan and "have a pair of girls. There was no doubt in my mind that she was very much in love with Khan and would've wed him if he'd agreed," Barnard recalled. "She said she wanted to move away from London with him. South Africa was her first choice because her brother was here."

On Diana's return to London, she telephoned, faxed, and wrote to Barnard about job possibilities for Khan. Barnard came to Kensington

Palace twice to talk further with Diana, and he met Khan at London's Grosvenor House hotel. "In the meeting I had with him I could not work out whether he loved her in the same way, but he clearly knew she loved him very much," Barnard recalled. "He just told me he couldn't handle the publicity."

As with Charles and other lovers, Diana tried to control Khan, fearing he would reject her. Energy healer Simone Simmons remembered when Diana "was so impatient to have Hasnat's undivided attention that if he used the Kensington Palace telephones to speak to his family or friends in Pakistan for more than ten minutes, Diana would turn her music up or dance before him to distract his attention." Diana also frequently phoned Khan at the hospital and "was often upset if he was in the operating theater and couldn't talk to her," Simmons said.

Diana even traveled halfway around the world to demonstrate her dedication to his work. She announced her planned trip to Australia the day after her divorce became final. She was to be the guest of honor at a dinner to raise money for the Victor Chang Cardiac Research Institute in Sydney on October 31, 1996. The charity was hardly a household name in Britain, and Diana's choice prompted some head-scratching. She didn't mention that Chang, a cardiac specialist, had been Hasnat Khan's mentor during his early surgical training in Australia. In a bungled kidnapping attempt, Chang had been murdered, a traumatic experience for Khan.

Buckingham Palace officials raised no objections to Diana's trip, although privately they were displeased that it would coincide with the Queen's state visit to Thailand that had been scheduled for more than a year. Diana acquitted herself well on her four-day trip, with the usual round of hospital visits and charity engagements—"from triumph to triumph . . . she was magnificent," said James Whitaker in the *Daily Mirror*. But the trip was poorly organized, and Diana was perturbed that some sponsors of fund-raising events had sought to financially exploit her name through commercial endorsements. Even worse, the *Sunday Mirror* burst into print with a "world exclusive" that Diana was in love with "shy caring heart surgeon" Hasnat Khan and wanted to "have his babies." The tabloid revealed that Diana had even entertained Khan's grandmother at Kensington Palace.

Knowing how much Khan hated publicity, Diana vehemently denied the report, but in an unintentionally cruel manner. Not only did she tell Richard Kay that she and Khan were "friends . . . in an entirely professional way," but she characterized the notion of being in love with Khan as "bullshit" and said she and her aides were "laughing ourselves silly" over the idea. That comment injured Khan, and afterward, Simone Simmons asked of Diana, "Why didn't she just tell Richard the truth? . . . Her reply was sad. . . . How, she asked, could she start telling the truth *now*, when to do so would expose all the lies of the past?" The tabloids backed off, and the romance survived, propelled by Diana's fantasy about making a new life with a simple middle-class Pakistani who only wanted to get on with his work.

During the remainder of 1996, Diana popped up unpredictably in various places around the world. One day she was darting off to Greece on a Learjet to attend the funeral of a twenty-seven-year-old man who had died of cystic fibrosis; she had often visited him at the Royal Brompton Hospital, and she described him as a "dear friend." Another day she was in Italy receiving her humanitarian award with Dr. Christiaan Barnard and making a short speech on the need to appreciate the elderly for their "wisdom and experience" and to reject the definition of old age "as a disease."

She visited the United States twice, first to raise money at a Washington gala for the Nina Hyde Center for Breast Cancer Research, a charity named for *The Washington Post*'s late fashion editor and backed by Diana's new friend Katharine Graham. Before a sellout crowd of 800 luminaries from society and fashion, Diana read a favorite verse, as she had the previous December in New York: "Life is mostly froth and bubble, two things stand in stone: kindness in another's trouble, courage in your own." Graham also honored Diana at a luncheon, and Hillary Clinton did the same at a White House breakfast for 110, where Diana received a standing ovation.

Three months later, Diana was back in the United States as the guest of honor at a benefit for the Costume Institute at the Metropolitan Museum of Art, a tribute to designer Christian Dior chaired by editor Liz Tilberis of *Harper's Bazaar*. Tilberis had first met Diana ten years earlier when she became editor of British *Vogue* and subsequently supervised several photo shoots of the Princess for the magazine. The two women became friends at the end of 1993, when Tilberis was diagnosed with ovarian cancer, and Diana provided moral support with frequent phone calls. As a favor to Tilberis, Diana had traveled to New York in early 1995 to give the editor an award at the Council of Fashion Designers of America dinner. When Tilberis requested her presence again at the Costume Institute, several friends advised Diana to decline because another such event might make her seem frivolous when Diana was trying to appear more serious.

Diana made no remarks at the museum gala, but she created a stir with a $15,000 Dior gown of midnight-blue satin trimmed with lace that resembled a close-fitting nightgown. Diana later told an acquaintance that the John Galliano–designed dress had initially been too tight, but that she had easily lost three pounds in three days so it would "fit like a glove." She didn't mention how she shed the weight, but such a sudden loss was commonplace for victims of eating disorders. Diana sat through the dinner for

900 (ticket price: $1,000) and then slipped out a side door at 11:00 P.M., disappointing an additional 2,000 guests who had paid $150 each to see her at the after-dinner dance. I'M OUT THE DIOR, said the headline in the next morning's *Daily Star*.

By year's end, Diana had appeared at just three events in five months for her chosen charities: a conference for Centrepoint, where she talked about homeless runaways; the annual meeting of the International Federation of Anti-Leprosy Associations, where she cautioned against complacency about the disease; and a benefit dinner and performance by the English National Ballet at St. James's Palace, the first time she used the state apartments for a charity function.

The ballet fund-raiser was especially significant, but not for Diana's commitment to her charity. During the dinner, she announced that the company's new production of *The Nutcracker* would be sponsored by Harrods. Mohamed Fayed, owner of the famous department store, beamed with pleasure. He had underwritten other causes that were important to her—the Royal Brompton Hospital and the Great Ormond Street Hospital for Sick Children, for example. The previous March, Diana had attended a fund-raising dinner at Harrods that Fayed gave to support the work of Hasnat Khan's supervisor, the heart surgeon Sir Magdi Yacoub. But this was the first time Fayed had played such a public role as her benefactor. Two weeks later, at Fayed's invitation, Diana hosted her annual staff Christmas party in the Georgian Restaurant at Harrods.

By 1996, Mohamed Fayed was one of the more notorious figures on the British scene. He had a famously foul mouth, and he was known to make outrageously insulting statements. ("They're all fuggers, these politicians," he once exclaimed.) The Egyptian-born son of an Alexandria schoolteacher, Fayed started his career at a furniture-importing company owned by Adnan Khashoggi, his Saudi Arabian brother-in-law who would later become a multimillionaire arms dealer. After falling out with Khashoggi, Fayed built an international business by investing in ships, hotels, and real estate, and he made his fortune by constructing a commercial port in Dubai to handle the country's burgeoning oil business.

In 1979, he bought the Ritz Hotel in Paris, and in 1985, took over Harrods after a bruising fight with rival tycoon R. W. "Tiny" Rowland. At Rowland's urging, the Department of Trade and Industry investigated the circumstances of Fayed's purchase. In 1988, the DTI issued a devastating 752-page report concluding that Fayed had significantly misrepresented his background and business practices. Among the findings was Fayed's false claim to have been born into an old Egyptian family enriched by shipping, land, and industry, and his phony aristocratic affectation, calling himself "Mohamed al Fayed."

Fayed was subsequently denied his application for British citizenship, and he sought revenge on the Tory government by revealing that he had paid prominent Conservative members of Parliament to raise questions in the House of Commons relating to his business interests. This "cash for questions" scandal sullied Fayed as much as it did Prime Minister John Major's government. A subsequent *Vanity Fair* profile of Fayed published in 1995, over which he sued for libel, described his racism, sexual harassment of women, telephone bugging, and mistreatment of staff.

Yet Fayed's unsavory reputation didn't seem to faze Diana, who had been acquainted with him for some years. He had cultivated her father and Raine from the time he bought the Ritz. The couple stayed at the hotel frequently, and Fayed always made certain they received red-carpet treatment. Harrods also happened to be Johnnie's favorite store, where he was a cosseted customer. The Spencers entertained the Harrods board for lunch at Althorp, and in 1991, when Fayed produced a book about the history of the store, Johnnie made the introductory speech at the publishing party. According to Tom Bower's book *Fayed: The Unauthorized Biography,* Fayed "showered gifts" on Johnnie and Raine, who was especially enamored of Fayed's generosity and hospitality. In 1996, Raine became a paid director of Harrods International, which supervises the store's duty-free shops as well as outlets in Japan.

Diana had not known Fayed directly through her father and Raine; she had actually met the Egyptian businessman during the eighties at polo matches sponsored by Harrods. But Fayed often said that before Johnnie Spencer died in 1992, he had asked Fayed to "keep an eye" on Diana and her siblings. Fayed frequently took liberties with the truth, and there was no way to verify what he said. Still, around the time of the Wales separation, Diana became friendly enough with Fayed to visit him from time to time when she shopped at Harrods. Through their conversations, Fayed claimed to have engineered Raine's rapprochement with Diana in 1993. "He helped bring them together," said former *Sunday Times* editor Andrew Neil, who worked as a consultant for Fayed. "He wanted to build a new environment for Diana, and he helped facilitate the reconciliation."

"Diana liked Mohamed's outrageousness," said Mark Hollingsworth, who collaborated with Fayed on a proposed memoir in 1998. "I don't think he cleaned up his language at all for her. She would go and pour out her heart to him." Andrew Neil believed that Fayed "made friends with Diana by cultivating the idea that both were outsiders and had the same enemies." Fayed further ingratiated himself with Diana by supporting her causes, and after her divorce, he began regularly inviting her to tea on the Harrods terrace to "talk about their common interest in various charities."

Fayed misstepped once that September when he asked Diana to join the Harrods board. She politely turned him down, explaining that she couldn't be involved in any commercial enterprise. At that point, Fayed tapped Raine instead. Fayed also frequently proffered invitations to Diana to take vacations at his homes in Gstaad, Scotland, and the south of France, all of which she declined. Yet when she was later asked about their relationship, she defiantly proclaimed Mohamed Fayed a "close friend."

Chapter 25

As 1997 began, Diana seemed no closer to finding herself or her place in British life. Yet again, the tabloid press spun stories of her apparent new confidence, independence, and maturity. She was still a royal of sorts, an international celebrity, and a magnetic fund-raiser. But she didn't quite resemble an aspiring ambassador, and her self-described role as "queen of people's hearts" required little more than shows of empathy. After her string of overseas appearances to raise money for cancer and heart research, *The Daily Telegraph* had even tried out an ungainly new label: "roving health educationalist."

Then Diana announced in early January her plan to visit Angola to publicize the campaign against antipersonnel land mines—under the aegis of the Red Cross, no less. Although Diana had planned her campaign months earlier, her sudden announcement took the public by surprise. "Her dramatic return to the world charity stage left officials in Prince Charles's office astonished," noted the *News of the World*. In the months to come, land mines would provide the most sustained focus for Diana's public life since she left the royal family.

The land mine crusade gave a big lift to her image, which *The Times* had declared "tarnished" only months earlier. It also gave her a sense of mission, at least for the moment; she had not been able to engage exclusively with one cause for long, and there was no reason to believe that land mines would be different. (Indeed, in her conversation with Richard Kay only hours before her death, Diana would once again announce her intention to retire from public life.) As William Deedes, an admirer and fellow activist in the land mines cause, had to admit, "We are trying to give serious purpose to someone who was erratic."

In the meantime, Deedes and others who cared about the issue were quick to capitalize on Diana's ability to generate publicity. Deedes accompanied her on the four-day mission to Angola, where, according to Richard Kay, she wanted "to get her hands dirty" and "find a new level of seriousness for herself." Before leaving, Diana had been briefed by the Foreign Office on the basics of government policy: participation in a worldwide effort to clear mines, to which Britain already had contributed £21 million ($35 million); and a commitment to an eventual global ban, while in the short term retaining the right, in exceptional circumstances, to use new high-tech "smart mines" that would self-destruct after a period of time.

The minute Diana touched down on African soil, she ignited a controversy with a brief statement that she was pleased "to assist the Red Cross in its campaign to ban, once and for all, antipersonnel land mines." This amounted to a call for an immediate worldwide ban, which ran counter to government policy and riled Tory leaders in London. One junior defense minister, the 7th Earl Howe, called Diana a "loose cannon."

Howe's comments threatened to derail Diana's trip and nearly reduced her to tears, but she effectively countered them by going into a minefield wearing a flak jacket and face visor. "I am only trying to help," she told reporters. "This is a distraction that we don't need." She was backed by John Major—in no mood to pick a fight with the popular Princess only months before a national election—who indicated that her comments lined up with the government's ultimate objective. When, on the morning of her second day in Angola, she first heard Howe's accusation, Diana muttered, "idiot minister," but William Deedes, the only journalist within earshot, kept her comments to himself to protect her.

During her tour, Diana wore a microphone and choreographed a series of memorable appearances: walking through minefields in her antimine gear, cheering soldiers engaged in dangerous mine-clearing, comforting dismembered victims of mine detonations. The BBC documentary about the trip caught her struggling to control her emotions after visiting victims, especially a young girl named Helena who had been virtually disemboweled by an explosion. Diana's description to reporters of her encounter with Helena offered an insight into her ability to empathize: "I remember looking at her and thinking that what was going on inside her head and her heart was very disturbing."

In a briefing for the press, Diana announced that she would make further Red Cross visits to Afghanistan, Bosnia, and Cambodia, calling her work on land mines a "long-term commitment." "The fact is, I am a humanitarian figure—always have been and always will be," she said. The *Daily Express* exuberantly proclaimed her "an international angel of mercy."

Writing in the *Daily Telegraph* afterward, Deedes called the Angola trip a "watershed" for Diana; privately, he counseled her to shift her emphasis away from an immediate ban, which neither Britain nor the United States was prepared to advocate. U.S. policy was especially complicated by its position in Korea, where land mines serve a strategic purpose in protecting the border between north and south.

Diana had been asked to give a speech to the Royal Geographical Society in June, and Deedes urged her to focus on the need to remove mines from the earth and care for victims, which would "take her out of controversy." He wrote a speech, and she agreed to deliver it because "she understood she needed to be on neutral ground." In a first step toward this more modulated approach, she appeared at a luncheon in March, where she gave an award to a former army captain named Chris Moon who had lost a leg while clearing mines in Mozambique.

Overall, Diana's new issue played well in the press, as did the announcement in late January of her June dress sale. The auction came off as an ingenious way to make money, as well as a powerful statement that Diana was putting her royal life behind her. In addition to the AIDS Crisis Trust, Diana announced that the Cancer Research Fund for the Royal Marsden Hospital, one of her six charities, would share in the proceeds. The one sour note was struck by the *Sunday Express*, which published an erroneous story that Diana would make a personal profit of more than £1 million from the dress sales. Infuriated by the report, Diana took unusually aggressive action by suing the newspaper and its editor in chief Richard Addis.

It turned out that the newspaper had been hoaxed, and Diana won £75,000 in damages and a front-page apology. Addis offered to donate the settlement directly to charity, but Diana's lawyer Anthony Julius told him, "She wants it for herself." Recalled Addis, "She did that to punish us, because if we had said we were giving it to charity it would have looked better for the *Express*." Diana subsequently announced she would personally donate the funds to charity, although she did not name the recipients.

In a further effort to craft a fresh public profile, Diana considered authorizing a book about her charity work. The idea came from Martin Bashir, who continued to moonlight as a paid speechwriter for Diana. She seemed curiously ambivalent about the project. "She was an anxiety-ridden young woman," said Vivienne Schuster, Bashir's agent. "She felt everything she said and did was subject to misinterpretation by those who watched her."

Schuster found an eager publisher, Random House UK, whose chairman and CEO, Gail Rebuck, met with Diana. They made a preliminary seven-figure deal and came up with a title, *In Faith and Hope*. But Diana soon cooled on the idea, deciding "it was too complicated to deal with," according to Rebuck. The unstated reason was that Diana had broken with Bashir, as she had with so many others, in part because she had been feeling pressure from Bashir to sign the book deal, which would have required permission from the Queen. However, the relationship's end came that spring when Diana's butler Paul Burrell, who mistrusted the *Panorama* man, asked Diana to listen to Burrell's conversation with Bashir on the speakerphone, and Diana felt insulted and betrayed by some of Bashir's comments.

Bashir was the second aide to leave Diana early in 1997. Her personal assistant for the previous seven years, twenty-seven-year-old Victoria Mendham, left abruptly at the end of January over a money dispute. On Christmas Eve, Diana had again taken Mendham to Barbuda, as she had the previous year. The Christmas trip was the fourth vacation on which Mendham had accompanied Diana. For the first two trips, Diana had paid all the costs. After the Barbuda trip at Easter the previous year, however, Diana had asked that Mendham, who earned £25,000 a year, split the bill. Instead, Mendham's half had been paid by royal household accounts—a customary practice for employees, although Diana was furious that she had not been informed. When Diana asked Mendham for her share of the most recent bill, totaling nearly £9,000, the assistant said she couldn't afford it but would pay her airfare. Richard Kay called the resulting altercation over the current and previous bills "the final straw in a deteriorating relationship between the two."

Mendham's departure left Diana with Michael Gibbins, her private secretary; Paul Burrell, her butler; and Caroline MacMillan, another personal assistant who assumed Mendham's duties, to manage her personal and professional affairs. With grim predictability, small aspects of Diana's everyday life kept blowing up in tabloid headlines. In early February, she unexpectedly withdrew a foreword she had written the previous July for a book of photographs, *Rock and Royalty,* which was assembled by fashion designer Gianni Versace to raise money for Elton John's AIDS Foundation. Diana had written the fulsome tribute ("From the optimism that shines from the pages of this book, one can tell that [Versace] loves mankind") without seeing the book, and when she received a copy, she was distressed to see photographs of the royal family juxtaposed with suggestive pictures of naked men. Diana said she was "extremely concerned" that the pictures would offend the Queen, and pulled out of a gala book launch as well. Versace was so mortified he canceled the party, and Elton John was reported to be "devastated." As a result of the incident, Diana cut contact with the singer and the designer.

One rare bright spot that spring was William's confirmation at Windsor. It was the second public reunion for Charles and Diana since the divorce; the first had been in December 1996, for the Christmas carol service at Eton, where William had been enrolled since 1995. Tension between Charles and Diana had diminished noticeably in the months following their divorce. Charles had taken to dropping in from time to time at Kensington Palace, arriving by helicopter. On his first visit, Diana called energy healer Simone Simmons to exclaim, "You'll never guess who just came to see me: my ex!" The Waleses now cooperated well on issues regarding their sons, and she occasionally called to solicit his advice. "Things were better on a basic level," said one of Diana's friends. "The hurt was deep on both sides, but they did a better job at public events together."

Unfortunately, arrangements for the confirmation ceremony dredged up some old acrimony when Diana learned that Tiggy Legge-Bourke, who helped with the logistics, would be among the guests. Diana had not invited members of her own immediate family because she assumed the ceremony would be "brief and straightforward." Still, when she saw the proposed list, she was miffed, and at her insistence, Legge-Bourke stayed away.

Diana's mother seemed rankled by her exclusion as well. When queried about her absence, Frances said she was "not the person to ask. . . . You should ask the offices of William's parents." She pointedly placed a notice in the newsletter of Oban Cathedral, where she had recently converted to Catholicism: "For my grandson William on his confirmation day, love from Granny Frances."

The ceremony came off without incident. Charles and Diana even arrived and left together with their sons, instead of taking separate cars, which had been their habit during the long estrangement. Posing for the official photograph, Diana and Charles did not converse, although they laughed and appeared relaxed. William, however, "showed few signs of mirth," according to one observer.

※

With the departures of so many key aides, Diana now handled most press inquiries herself, or directed them from the background, so her views often appeared in papers such as the *Mirror* in addition to the dependable *Daily Mail*. Some editors found her mercurial ways exasperating. "The confusion was there all the time," said Sue Douglas, editor of the *Sunday Express*. "She was going out with the boys wearing her shorts and a baseball cap, but it would be designer stuff and she would be immaculately made up because she never thought there would not be a photographer waiting."

Nor could Diana restrain herself from reading everything written about her. Said a man who knew her from childhood: "She *had* to read it. There was always an element of insecurity for Diana. She wanted to know that what she was doing was being approved of, and I think she found it mesmerizing." Having witnessed her sensitivity for too many years, her butler Paul Burrell finally began hiding the most unpleasant articles. "I took a strong line when something was personal and upsetting, and thought it best for her not to see it," he said. "I always got a strange look when certain papers weren't there. She would ask for them, but I wouldn't let her see them."

Diana and those close to her believed she had to wage a constant battle for survival with the press, to avoid being swallowed by her own celebrity. At the same time, Diana enjoyed playing games with the press and public. One of her more peculiar practices was what Diana's energy healer Simone Simmons described as " 'hiding' in plain sight"—a surreal exercise for a woman whose identity was already confused. As Simmons explained, "I coached Diana in the art of pretending to be someone who bore a strong passing resemblance to the Princess." The trick was to engage in such mundane activities—hailing a cab, taking money from a cash machine—that observers couldn't believe she was the real Diana. "So confident had Diana become as an impersonator of herself," said Simmons, "that if someone . . . gave her a wide-eyed and puzzled stare, she would smile and wave at them, as if daring them to challenge her."

Diana was now "telling pointless lies more and more frequently," Simmons recalled. "She retained a crazy conviction that since she'd compartmentalized her life and had scattered about different versions of the same story, she would be safe and somehow protected." Diana's deceptions defined her relationships with editors and reporters in her last year.

Not all her lies were pointless, however, as could be seen in May 1997 after a visit she made to Roehampton Priory, a private psychiatric clinic specializing in eating disorders. Diana had been secretly visiting Roehampton and other psychiatric treatment centers since 1994 as a sort of Trojan patient, which allowed her to talk to the residents and get information from professionals without discussing her own problems. This time, however, she spoke frankly about the roots of her eating disorders, and someone tipped the *Mirror*.

When editor Piers Morgan called Diana's office to alert her to the story, Diana immediately got on the line. "I persuaded her that, in order to get it right, she should tell me," Morgan recalled. Diana gave him a detailed forty-minute briefing with "the understanding that I would not quote her directly but do it as reported speech." After publication of the *Mirror*'s five-page report disclosing that she had suffered from bulimia as a teenager, Diana issued a statement to the other newspapers saying she was "deeply disappointed" that a patient had leaked her comments. "The benefits to patients depend enormously on privacy being respected," she said.

Diana's manipulation of the truth had several purposes. By not deny-ing her own twenty-year struggle with bulimia, Diana played for public sympathy without ever asking for it. At the same time, she stressed her con-cern for patients and struck a blow for privacy rights. "I rang her and con-gratulated her on a rather slick operation that distanced her from collusion with the dreaded tabloids and made her look rather good," Morgan said.

For nearly eighteen months, Diana had persistently misled the press about Hasnat Khan. Since her vehement disavowal of a romance during her Australian trip the previous fall, the tabloids had written some reason-ably accurate stories about the relationship based on comments by some of Khan's relatives. The most revealing account, in the *Sunday Express* in Feb-ruary, quoted his father and mother. According to Hasnat's father, Rashid Khan, an economist, Diana "had made all the moves" in the relationship, but Hasnat had said "marriage was not possible." Hasnat's mother, Naheed said her son had been "terrorized" by the media spotlight, which was "ru-ining his life."

Diana, however, was determined to make their relationship work. "She would have converted to Islam, she would have done anything," said Elsa Bowker. Diana miscalculated when she made another spur-of-the-moment visit to Pakistan in May, again billed as a fund-raiser for Imran Khan's hos-pital, where Diana attended a lunch with sixty Pakistani VIPs who paid more than £600 apiece for the privilege.

But Diana's covert purpose for the trip was to meet Hasnat Khan's family and "convince them that she was a nice girl," said Elsa Bowker. Wearing a shalwar kameez of pale blue—pastel colors signal respect in Pakistan—she spent ninety minutes with a dozen of Hasnat's relatives, in-cluding his parents and the grandmother she had entertained at Kensing-ton Palace. "She was obsessional about families and longed to be embraced by them," Simone Simmons explained.

When Diana returned to London several days later, she told friends she had made a good impression, and that marriage was now possible. Inex-plicably, she had not informed Khan beforehand of her visit with his rela-tives. He was dismayed that she had gone so far, and rebuked her for disclosing details to the press. The following week, *Hello!* magazine quoted Hasnat's father expressing doubts that Hasnat and Diana would marry: "There are so many people who meet each other, who respect each other, who love each other, who do not get married."

One evening after Diana and Khan quarreled, she summoned Simone Simmons to Kensington Palace and greeted her friend with "swollen panda eyes and mascara-streaked cheeks. . . . [Diana] was both mortified and panic-stricken because she felt that Hasnat was withdrawing from her." During this period, Diana also went to see Elsa Bowker, who discovered her "weeping in the stairway. She had on no makeup, her hair was not done, she was wearing a baggy sweater and pants. She came into my house and said, 'I am destroyed inside. They have destroyed me.' She never said who 'they' were, but she wept and wept and went through four boxes of Kleenex. I really thought she might commit suicide." The next morning, however, a friend called Elsa to say he had seen Diana "smiling and radiant at Turnbull and Asser buying shirts."

Diana and Khan continued to see each other, though still in secrecy. "Diana was getting frustrated and angry with Hasnat," said one of her close friends. "He wouldn't go out in public with her. Even if he did love her, he couldn't marry her with the press baying at the doorway every time he had to do a heart operation."

For the first time, Diana began appearing conspicuously in public with single men. She had lunch several times with Christopher Whalley, her friend from the Chelsea Harbour Club, and by one account made "no attempt to dodge the paparazzi." One evening she appeared at Mayfair's chic Harry's Bar with an Indian businessman, Gulu Lalvani, a multimillionaire electronics tycoon who was twice divorced. Lalvani, who was fifty-eight at the time, later explained that they were friends through several of her charities, to which he had donated generously. After dinner, Diana danced with Lalvani into the night at Annabel's. Lalvani remarked later on her "air of defiance" that evening: "She pulled me onto the dance floor whenever a song appealed to her." Her night on the town was duly reported in the press. As Elsa Bowker explained, "She knew everyone would see her, and the poor doctor [Khan] was shocked."

Diana's misguided visit to Pakistan seemed to be a turning point. She became more jittery and unpredictable with her staff, friends, and family. She broke off with her longtime acupuncturist Oonagh Toffolo after Toffolo made comments about the Princess in the press, and she came close to ending her relationship with Richard Kay over an article she told Simone Simmons she considered "traitorous." Only when Simmons read the offending article aloud to Diana on the telephone, assuring her that it was fair, did Diana relent and call Kay several days later "as if nothing had happened." Not long afterward, Diana turned around and dropped Simmons, whom Richard Kay regarded as one of Diana's key close friends since the separation. Diana "wasn't willing to let me help her deal with . . . a little of her old damage," Simmons said later.

Diana's private secretary Michael Gibbins also felt Diana's lash, though he remained in place. Toward the end of May, when Diana and Charles were prevented by their schedules from attending a picnic at Eton with William, Tiggy Legge-Bourke had joined the boy instead. Legge-Bourke was photographed pouring champagne, which made Diana "hit the roof," recalled *Mirror* editor Piers Morgan. "She arranged briefings from her office." Diana instructed Gibbins to convey her withering criticism through the press, saying Legge-Bourke had "harmed" fourteen-year-old William, had been "thoughtless" and "foolish," and "made an idiot of herself." "I could hear Diana dictating in the background," Morgan said.

After the comments appeared in several tabloids, Diana reversed course and "put out a statement saying it was untrue, that she admired Tiggy," Morgan recalled. "She named *The Sun* in particular, because they had gone the furthest [in criticizing Legge-Bourke]." According to Richard Kay, Diana's denial had been based on her fear that "her son might believe the attack on Tiggy originated with her." *The Sun* fought back, saying "they would publish the name of who had told them," Morgan recalled. Doubtless with the memory of Diana's earlier slur on Legge-Bourke in mind, "Diana's lawyers and *The Sun* issued a joint statement saying that she had formally reprimanded a senior member of her staff for making unauthorized remarks," Morgan said.

The senior staff member was Gibbins, and the public scolding included her edict, reported by the tabloids, that he "never again . . . speak to the media on her behalf." Diana had humiliated Gibbins, but Kay reflected her spin in a *Daily Mail* report that the loyal aide had been "naive" and had "genuinely had her best interests at heart." According to Kay, Diana had actually been "more than pleased" that Tiggy had attended the picnic in her stead.

Diana's most heartbreaking dispute during her last months was with her mother. On the eve of Diana's trip to Pakistan in May, *Hello!* magazine published the first of a two-part interview with Frances Shand Kydd. Frances spoke at length about her own life, but also offered comments on Diana's childhood, her eating disorders, and her marriage. Much of what Frances said was harmless, and some of her views were sensible, although her comments betrayed how little she understood the deep emotional crosscurrents that prevented Diana from acting reasonably when she was emotionally overwrought.

Frances thought the *Panorama* and Dimbleby interviews were both a mistake. "I felt strongly [Diana and Charles] were going to have to live with those interviews and knew somehow that they were only going to hurt even more," she said. "I think one's dignity is lost if you ever give out blame which becomes gossip. Gossip becomes distorted. If a marriage fails, you should never fall into the temptation of explaining why. Silence is the only course."

Frances also considered it "absolutely wonderful" that Diana had lost her title "HRH" because "at last she was able to be herself, use her own name, and find her own identity." Frances disclosed as well that she remained happily in touch with Prince Charles: "He was my son-in-law for fourteen years, and he will always be the father of two of my grandchildren."

At the time of the *Hello!* interviews, Diana's relationship with her mother was already more precarious than usual, as Frances's exclusion from William's confirmation had indicated. "Diana said her mother was impossible," recalled one of Diana's close friends. "She felt her mother was not able to sort herself out." The previous November Frances had been arrested on a drunk-driving charge and lost her driving license. According to James Whitaker, writing in *The Mirror,* Diana was aware that her mother was "prone to giving colorful and unguarded interviews and comments after a good lunch."

The *Hello!* interviews came as a "complete shock" to Diana. She briefly considered legal action, and she punished the magazine by canceling some "exclusive arrangements" at two of her charity events. She was "appalled and bewildered" by her mother's remarks, and "bitterly disappointed and let down" that the magazine would publish them. When it emerged that *Hello!* had paid Frances £30,000, Diana was even more upset, though Frances earmarked all the money for a Catholic charity. Diana stopped speaking to her mother altogether.

After Diana's death, Frances would not acknowledge the rift, insisting, quite oddly, that she and her daughter could only be close in secrecy. Frances told the *Daily Express* that her "special relationship" with Diana "was built on nobody knowing when we spoke and saw each other, but we did and often." She disclosed to the *Daily Mail* that she and Diana "shared such a sense of joy that we often met in many different places without anyone ever knowing," without saying why secrecy was necessary.

In her comments at Roehampton Priory in May 1997, Diana gave some indication of her recent struggle to maintain equilibrium. Using language similar to that she had used with Andrew Morton six years earlier, Diana insisted she had finally "beaten" her bulimia after "[she] suddenly woke up one day and thought, 'I've had enough of everyone treating me like absolute rubbish; I must stick up for myself.'" Diana claimed she hadn't binged for three years—although her effort to find a new treatment for her bulimia in 1995 had indicated otherwise—and emphasized her use of strenuous exercise as a substitute for bingeing. "My workouts are definitely a great benefit in controlling my anger and emotions," she said. "You just get rid of all the stress and rages building up inside you. It's like a huge release."

Although speaking at an institution where psychiatric therapy was widely used, she took the occasion to denounce psychiatry. "I found in the end that therapy was pointless for me," she said, "because the people trying to help me hadn't been through what I had been through"—ignoring the fact that Susie Orbach had suffered from eating disorders for a decade. "In some cases, I ended up thinking it was they who needed help, not me," Diana continued. "Everyone knows how to treat you when you are vulnerable. But if you show any sign of strength, then it is they who end up feeling intimidated. And they try to squash you back to where you were." Yet Diana did confess that she remained haunted by the possibility of a relapse, which she said would "always be in the back of my head."

On June 3, only days after cutting off relations with her mother and publicly rebuking her chief aide, Diana went to a benefit performance of *Swan Lake* by the English National Ballet at the Royal Albert Hall. Since Harrods had sponsored the company's production of *The Nutcracker*, Mohamed Fayed joined Diana in the royal box and sat next to her at the postperformance dinner at the Churchill Inter-Continental Hotel.

During dinner, Diana bemoaned that she had nowhere to take her sons for a summer holiday; wherever she went, photographers pursued her. Fayed, whose hospitality Diana had turned down many times before, saw an opening. His "instant solution" was a vacation at his home in Saint-Tropez, and he promised it could be "as private as they wished." Diana thanked Fayed and said she would get back to him. She queried several friends, among them Rosa Monckton, who "strongly advised" her not to accept Fayed's hospitality because it might "arouse concern." Diana then turned to Raine Spencer, hardly a disinterested party, given her position on Fayed's board. Raine urged her to accept the invitation, which Diana did on June 11.

June was Diana's busiest month since her divorce. She attended preview parties for her dress sale in London and New York, where she was mobbed by a crowd of Manhattan socialites. The tabloids carried photographs of Christie's UK chairman Charles Hindlip guiding her through the crowd with his hand on her bottom, prompting the *Daily Express* to wonder if he had become "rather unnecessarily tactile." Diana later told a friend that the event made her rue the loss of her title "HRH." Recalled the friend, "She was telling me, 'People were saying, "Di, Di, sign this." It was awful, so familiar.' "

After years of pointedly asking people to "call me Diana," she didn't show her pique in public. "She knocked herself out, talked to everyone, gave so much of herself," said her friend Marguerite Littman, who helped her navigate the Christie's throng. Noted Jane Warren in the *Daily Express*, "Surrounded by drooling middle-aged Manhattan men, Diana pouted, fluttered and peered wide-eyed." Her enchanting performance got results: The auction pulled in $3.26 million, exceeding expectations.

As part of her publicity campaign for the auction, she appeared on the cover of *Vanity Fair,* with eight pages of pictures alongside a two-and-a-half-page article titled "Diana Reborn." Once again, she offered a new look, her hair tousled, her expression come-hither, her partly revealed bosom "apparently unsupported," as *The Daily Telegraph* delicately observed. "Whatever Diana's inward state," noted *Vanity Fair,* "outwardly, she appears to be approaching contentment." Richard Kay couldn't resist asking in the *Daily Mail,* "Is this at last the *real* Diana, the woman she always wanted to be?" He seemed to think so, based on "her cool self-assurance . . . displayed in those cleavage-baring dresses" she had been wearing to the ballet and other events, as well as her insistence that she was "free from stress, her life [was] going well, her children [were] happy, and she [was] getting fulfillment from her work."

Diana was also busy with the land mine crusade, which represented an earnest commitment as well as a diversion from her personal problems. In mid-June, she made speeches days apart in London and Washington, advocating efforts to "quicken the de-miners' work" and help injured victims rebuild their lives. After her Washington speech on behalf of Red Cross assistance to land mine survivors, she flew by private jet to New York to see an ailing Mother Teresa, who left her wheelchair to stroll hand in hand with Diana in the Bronx—"her most amazing walkabout ever." At the end of the month, Diana announced that she would go to Bosnia in August with the Red Cross to visit the "killing fields."

Diana's land mine work was warmly endorsed by Prime Minister Tony Blair, who had been swept into office by the landslide Labour victory in the May 1 general election. After the Labour party took over, Diana met with the new Foreign Secretary, Robin Cook, who announced only three weeks after taking his post that Britain would destroy its stock of land mines by 2005 and redouble its efforts for a worldwide ban. Diana was among the "anti-mines campaigners" credited with shaping Labour's move—a "significant shift from that of the former Conservative government which never made any undertaking to destroy all stocks by a fixed date."

Around the same time, Tony Blair invited Diana and Prince William to lunch at Chequers, the prime minister's official country residence. She and Blair discussed ideas for her role as a goodwill ambassador, much as she had done any number of times with John Major and his Foreign Secretary Douglas Hurd, both of whom had encouraged her. This time, Diana was dealing with a man she found "very charismatic." "At last," she said afterward, "I will have someone who will know how to *use* me."

In the following weeks, Diana shared her perceptions of a possible role. According to her friend Gulu Lalvani, she said she saw herself as a "peacemaker. . . . She seriously felt she could have helped with the Northern Ireland situation." In a luncheon conversation with Tina Brown, then editor of *The New Yorker,* Diana said she was thinking about traveling to China because Blair "wants me to go on some missions. . . . I'm very good at sorting people's heads out." Brown noted in *The New Yorker* that Diana's manner was "devoid of irony."

Such talk showed that Diana was having difficulty seeing herself in a realistic way; she almost seemed to view her purpose as a global therapist. Lacking any reliable advisers, Diana was trying to get by on intuition alone, and her naïveté was breathtaking. The idea that she could "sort out" the likes of Chinese president Jiang Zemin would have been comic were it not so sad.

Chapter 26

DIANA received ninety floral bouquets for her thirty-sixth birthday on July 1, including several dozen lilies from fashion designer Giorgio Armani, but no amount of flowers could dislodge the depression she always felt on her yearly milestone. She was cheered only by a call from Harry, who gathered a group of his classmates to sing a rousing "Happy Birthday" over the phone. After spending the day writing thank-you notes, she was the guest of honor at a fund-raising dinner for 500 at the Tate Gallery. Before leaving for the dinner, she told her hairstylist Natalie Symons, "It's my birthday and I'm going to spend the evening with people I don't know and don't particularly like. The only exception is my brother." Charles Spencer said afterward she "sparkled" at the dinner.

Two days later, she was in good spirits when a visiting friend remarked on the extravagant floral display. "She said, 'I really wish they wouldn't. I wish it would go to charity,' " her friend recalled. "And then she giggled." She told her friend she was going away for a vacation, but refused to say where. "She seemed relaxed, and happier than I had seen her," her friend said. "I don't say happy, but happier."

Diana's mood sank that evening when she saw a TV documentary on Camilla Parker Bowles, who was turning fifty that month. Diana had previously made light of the party Charles was hosting at Highgrove on July 18 in Camilla's honor. "Wouldn't it be funny if I popped out of the birthday cake?" Diana said to Elsa Bowker. The TV program, which focused on Charles's romance with Camilla, removed any trace of levity. "All the grief from my past is resurfacing," Diana told her astrologer Debbie Frank in an anguished phone call. "I feel terrible." "She sounded so tense again," Frank recalled. "So frightened and needy. She sounded breathy, childlike again." Diana's tensions triggered a fierce argument with another employee,

Louise Reid-Carr, hired only months earlier as a personal assistant. After the dispute, Reid-Carr left her position saying, "I have quit, and I am happy now."

A week later, Hasnat Khan broke off his relationship with Diana. The proximate cause was a *Sunday Mirror* article disclosing that Diana and Khan had become "unofficially engaged" after what the tabloid characterized as the "amazing 'summit meeting' with his family" in Pakistan the previous May. "He accused Diana of leaking the story, although she tearfully denied it," said Natalie Symons, who witnessed the drama. "Diana was very, very sore and hurting," recalled one friend she called for consolation. "It was the day before the trip [to Saint-Tropez] with Mohamed, and Diana told me it was over with Hasnat. She said it was no good, hopeless. They couldn't go on. He couldn't live with the pressure of the press, so he decided that was that."

The next morning, Friday, July 11, as Diana packed for her vacation in the south of France, she "was sobbing her heart out," Symons said. "I could tell she was totally distraught because she didn't have any mascara on, and she always puts her mascara on before she does anything else." At noon, a green Harrods helicopter picked up Diana, William, Harry, and one of the detectives assigned to the princes, and by early evening, Fayed's Gulfstream IV had transported them to his ten-acre estate above the sea at Saint-Tropez. Moored nearby were Fayed's three yachts, the *Cujo,* a converted U.S. Coast Guard cutter; the two-masted schooner *Sakara;* and the motor-powered 140-foot *Jonikal,* which had just been purchased. Fayed installed Diana and the boys in the guest house adjacent to the main villa, where they had their own cook, maids, and swimming pool.

It took only a day for the tabloids to surround Fayed's compound with boats filled with hacks and paparazzi. Photographs of Diana and Fayed splashed the front pages of the Sunday tabloids. DI'S FREEBIE, announced the *Sunday Mirror,* noting that Diana had "sparked a political and royal row" by accepting a holiday from the Fayeds. "Good God," said author and politician Jeffrey Archer, a fan of Diana's. "It's Jackie Kennedy and Aristotle Onassis all over again," Archer told the *Mirror.* "Money has to be the main attraction." The *News of the World* quoted an unnamed Buckingham Palace aide who said the royal family considered Fayed "a little unsafe in their terms."

Although initial reports indicated Diana's destination was kept secret from the royal family, it turned out that because she was accompanied by the princes, she had sought and received permission. Given Diana's willfulness, the Palace probably had little choice. After all, Fayed had elaborate security, including bodyguards recruited from the Royal Marines, and William and Harry were shadowed by two Scotland Yard detectives. Diana was scorched in the press, however, for imprudently aligning herself with such a controversial figure—and in so public a setting. "If Diana wanted privacy she could not have chosen a busier time to 'hide away' on the French Riviera," said the *Evening Standard*, "timing her trip to coincide with the biggest national bank holiday weekend and . . . Bastille Day celebrations."

Only ten days earlier, the government had released Sir Gordon Downey's official report on the "cash for questions" scandal. Downey "noted that Fayed was so dishonest that he could not accept his uncorroborated word on anything," wrote *Daily Mail* columnist Simon Heffer. "What Fayed did is shortly to be made a criminal offense. . . . However, he has yet to be punished . . . for attempting to subvert [Parliament's] workings through a systematic campaign of bribery." If Diana had read the Downey report, or even "seen the comments made on those to whom [Fayed] had been hospitable and who had then not secured favors for him in return," said Heffer, "even she might have thought twice."

To counteract the criticism, Diana called the *Mail*'s Nigel Dempster, who, unlike Richard Kay, had previously dealt with Fayed. "Mohamed was having a bad time," recalled Dempster. "So Diana came on the phone and said, 'Nigel, I was offered a holiday. My boys couldn't spend the summer in Kensington Palace, and I wanted to get away. I am enjoying myself. It is an ideal holiday.' Obviously Mohamed had said, 'Ring Nigel Dempster.' " The next day, July 14, Dempster printed Diana's defense, described as comments to "fellow guests," including her assertion of a close friendship with Fayed "for the last five years."

As proof of her loyalty to Fayed, she posed for photographs with her hand on his shoulder and his arm wrapped around her waist—described by *The Sun* as DI'S AMAZING CUDDLE. Richard Kay, in a piece accompanying Dempster's front-page exclusive, expressed his bewilderment: "It is her mood almost of defiance that is puzzling some friends. . . . She has been, as one says, 'quite aggressive about justifying herself and fed up with being criticized all the time for getting things wrong.' . . . Most people think she's got it wrong again."

Diana seemed unconcerned about the photographers tracking her leaps into the Mediterranean and cruises on the *Sakara* and the *Cujo*. "She was happy to be seen," recalled the *Mirror*'s Piers Morgan. "I offered to pull out of Saint-Tropez after two days, and her office said, 'That won't be necessary.' After that, she did daily photo calls."

On Bastille Day, July 14, when the *Mail* ran Diana's endorsement of Fayed, her behavior turned bizarre. After a morning of "relaxed and happy" Jet Skiing with her sons, Diana hopped into a launch with a bodyguard and headed for the *Fancy*, a fifty-three-foot motorboat carrying reporters from the *The Mirror*, *The Sun*, and the *Daily Mail*. Wearing a leopard-print bathing suit, Diana spent ten minutes with the reporters, talking "candidly about the dark side of her life as the ex-wife of Prince Charles," James Whitaker recounted in *The Mirror*.

She revealed that William was "distressed" and "really freaked out" by the press attention. "You are going to get a big surprise with the next thing I do," she said. "My boys are urging me continually to leave the country. They say it is the only way . . . They want me to live abroad. I sit in London all the time, and I am abused and followed wherever I go." Diana further complained that her land mine work had been unfairly denounced. "I cannot win," she said. She reiterated her fondness for her hosts, adding that Fayed "was my father's best friend," and "anyway, to be strictly correct, I am here with his wife."

Diana's floating press conference seemed to flummox the hacks, who prided themselves on being ready for anything Diana threw their way. Writing in *The Mirror*, Whitaker claimed an exclusive interview—despite photographs showing Diana talking to the group—in which she "appeared upset" yet "joked and giggled." Nick Craven of the *Daily Mail* found her "relaxed" and "comfortable." Yet another version, the *Evening Standard*'s, had her "getting increasingly distraught and working herself up."

The next day, Diana's actions were even more confounding. She issued a statement insisting she had no intention of making a "surprise" announcement about her life; she even denied giving interviews to reporters. At one moment, she was crawling along a balcony on Fayed's villa, hiding behind a towel to avoid being seen. Shortly afterward, she was posing at the end of a jetty before skipping up some steps, clapping her hands and singing. Writing in *The Sun*, photographer Arthur Edwards said that in the seventeen years he had been snapping Diana, "[he had] never seen her act more bizarrely. . . . You cannot get much stranger than hiding from the camera one minute and walking around like a supermodel the next."

It is impossible to know what prompted Diana's visit to the tabloid motorboat, but the combination of giddiness and furtiveness she displayed the following morning—the fourth day of her holiday—could probably be explained by the previous night's arrival, just in time for the Bastille Day fireworks display, of Fayed's forty-two-year-old son, Dodi. After a summons from his father, Dodi had bolted from Paris, leaving his fiancée, fashion model Kelly Fisher, with the vague excuse that he had business in London. As Fayed biographer Tom Bower explained it, Mohamed had "glimpsed Diana's current unhappiness and profound loneliness. . . . He perceived the vacancy which he could fill" with "companionship, love and a man. To pamper the princess, he could provide the ideal candidate: his son."

In fact, Dodi Fayed was a poor match for Diana by nearly every measure. "Dodi was many things to many people," said Tina Sinatra, a longtime friend with whom he had a brief romance in the 1980s. "His relationships were very varied and quite inconsistent." A man-child with an estimated monthly allowance of £60,000, he led an aimless life without significant responsibilities. Lacking any real professional distinction, he defined himself by women—the more famous and beautiful, the better—although he had been unable to sustain a meaningful relationship. He had been seriously addicted to cocaine, and he told elaborate lies. He was insecure, unreliable, and impulsive, with a reputation for reneging on commitments to creditors. Intellectually dim and not very articulate, he had little curiosity about the world. At forty-two, he was thoroughly dominated by his father. Most who knew Dodi Fayed called him a "boy" and a "kid."

Dodi's charm rested on a kind of juvenile sweetness, along with his lavish generosity. He was known for sending gifts of caviar, cashmere, and smoked salmon to his friends, and his manner was like a friendly puppy's, always eager to please. "What endeared him was that he was without guile, although not without bullshit," said Peter Riva, who knew Dodi for several decades. Women found Dodi appealing: he stood about five foot ten, had a soft voice with a slight Middle Eastern accent, curly black hair, and expressive light-brown eyes. "I didn't think he was good-looking," said Nona Summers, a friend from London. "But he was nicely dressed, wore lovely cashmere, nice shoes, very soigné. And he smelt nice. He loved to laugh."

Born in Alexandria, Egypt, Dodi's given name was Emad, which in Arabic means "someone you can depend on." Although his father was from a modest Egyptian background, his mother Samira was from the Khashoggi family in Saudi Arabia, where her father had been private physician to the Saudi king. In 1959, when Dodi was four, Mohamed and Samira underwent an acrimonious divorce, and Mohamed received custody of his son, according to Muslim custom. Dodi grew up in Alexandria under the care of relatives and servants, seldom seeing either his father or mother. Mohamed traveled the world building his business and later married a Finnish model, Heini Wathen, and had four more children. Dodi's mother married her cousin and lived in Cairo, Paris, and Madrid.

Shuttling between Egypt and the Côte d'Azur with Mohamed's younger brother Salah—Dodi's principal custodian—the young boy was showered with toys and treated to luxurious holidays, but was essentially lonely and withdrawn, a poor student who finished thirtieth in his class of thirty-eight at the College St. Marc primary school in Alexandria. Most accounts said that Dodi was raised a Muslim, though, oddly enough, he told Suzanne Gregard—his wife for eight months during the 1980s—that he considered himself a Catholic, perhaps the religion of some of the servants who raised him.

In 1968, Mohamed sent thirteen-year-old Dodi to Le Rosey, a small Swiss boarding school famous for its unique three-month skiing term in Gstaad. Dodi left after one year, and even members of his family cannot account for the next five years of his life, when he lived in an apartment at 60 Park Lane in London, a building owned by his father, and received no further formal education.

When Dodi reached nineteen, his father sent him to the Royal Military Academy at Sandhurst for the six-month course from January through June 1974. Dodi disliked the rigors of Sandhurst, although he did enjoy learning how to play polo, a sport that promised social cachet. As a player, however, "he was mediocre," said a woman who knew him well in the late 1980s. "He didn't stick with it. He didn't stick with much of anything, or anyone."

On receiving his Sandhurst commission—the equivalent of a second lieutenant—he served briefly as an attaché at the United Arab Emirates Embassy in London before becoming a full-time playboy. A frequent patron of Tramp, a members-only nightclub, Dodi fell in with a jet set crowd and embarked on a series of romances with actresses including Valerie Perrine, Brooke Shields, Mimi Rogers, and Tanya Roberts; models Marie Helvin, Koo Stark, Traci Lind, and Julia Tholstrup; and celebrities Tina Sinatra (a daughter of Frank Sinatra's) and Charlotte Hambro (a granddaughter of Sir Winston Churchill). He pursued them with unabashed romanticism, idealized them, and sometimes spurned them. "He had the attitude that the woman he was with reflected on him," said his longtime friend Michael White. "He had no discernible ego," recalled Jack Martin, a Hollywood columnist who met Dodi in 1975. "He was painfully quiet and shy."

Dodi had been starstruck since the early seventies, when he befriended Barbara Broccoli, the daughter of Albert R. "Cubby" Broccoli, producer of the James Bond movies. The Broccolis, who lived around the corner from Dodi's apartment, virtually adopted the rootless teenager. Dodi often spent entire weekends watching adventure films, and he loved to visit the James Bond sets at Pinewood Studios with Barbara.

Seeking to capitalize on Dodi's only evident interest, Mohamed worked with Broccoli to set up a film business for Dodi in 1979 called Allied Stars Ltd. Fayed made the financial decisions, while the producers and directors made the artistic choices. "Dodi's role was not very involved," said Clive Parsons, a British producer of Allied's first film, *Breaking Glass*. Mohamed similarly called the shots on the second project, *Chariots of Fire*, which producer David Puttnam had brought to Mohamed. Dodi's role consisted of a few visits to the set and the postproduction facility.

At twenty-five, Dodi was feckless and undisciplined. He began taking cocaine, stayed out late at clubs most nights, and slept until the early afternoon. He ran afoul of the producers of both Allied films when he brought cocaine to the set. Puttnam actually ejected Dodi, telling him, "Don't ever come back again."

Chariots of Fire was a hit on its release in 1981 and won the Academy Award for best picture. With his prominent listing as executive producer, Dodi was poised to be a major player in Hollywood, but instead he did nothing for three years, leading a decadent life in London, Paris, and the south of France. "He was into cocaine," said his friend Nona Summers, whose problems with the drug sent her into a rehab program. "He didn't tell the truth about many things, but he told me he had done it, that he got himself in trouble and stopped." Among his mishaps was a fall down a cliff from a restaurant in Sardinia at 2:00 A.M. that resulted in several broken ribs.

During this period, Dodi spent more time with his Khashoggi relatives, and he tried to get to know the mother he had seen so rarely. He called her frequently and visited her in Cairo, but they didn't become especially close. "When he was around his mother, he was serious, reverential, more quiet than usual," said his friend Jack Martin. "She was a combination of doting and demanding." Samira was "warm but very strong," recalled interior designer Corinna Gordon, a friend for many years. "I think Dodi was a little intimidated." In the mid-1980s, Samira became ill with cancer. When she died in the autumn of 1986, Dodi brooded for a long while. One former girlfriend said he went into an "emotional free fall."

Dodi was back in the film business by then, this time in Hollywood. In 1983, Mohamed had set him up with Jack Weiner, a former Columbia Pictures executive turned producer. Mohamed agreed to provide funding to Weiner and Dodi for options and scripts, while Weiner would guide Dodi through the basics of film production. Their seven-year partnership produced two successes, *F/X* and a sequel, both thrillers about a special-effects man, but only Weiner actually worked on the films. Dodi lacked the discipline to see a film through the difficult stages of budgeting and production, sometimes showing up on the sets at lunchtime and attending the odd meeting. "He had a passion to make movies, but he didn't see his role as being there every day," said Weiner. Scriptwriters and others who encountered Dodi in meetings realized he was simply playacting, "keeping up a particular image," in the words of one producer.

By now in his early thirties, Dodi was more dependent than ever on his strong-willed father, a predicament he found emotionally and professionally crippling. To prove himself to such a formidable father, he would need to work doubly hard, but Dodi never did. Mohamed, in recognizing his son's limitations and trying to protect him, put Dodi in an impossible trap. "It's like when you are training a dog and you use a choke chain," said a producer who worked with Dodi. "You give a little freedom, then you need to give a pull."

Winging his way on private jets and cruising on 200-foot yachts, Dodi had no "real life." His father owned the apartments on Park Lane in London and just off the Champs-Élysées in Paris where Dodi often stayed. Dodi moved from one rented house to the next in Los Angeles, and used his family's vacation homes in Saint-Tropez, Gstaad, and Scotland. "I have no idea where Dodi thought was home," his friend Michael White said. "Around the office we used to always say, 'Dodi is a character in a movie,' " recalled Weiner. A sense of unreality touched everything Dodi did; in many ways, he was the victim of his own misguided, romantic dreams.

Despite his extravagant allowance, Dodi wildly overspent, leasing homes in Beverly Hills and Malibu for $25,000 a month, riding in chauffeur-driven cars and hiring costly security guards—all to impress his friends. A spending binge by Dodi was usually followed by Mohamed's declining to pick up certain bills. "Dodi would commit himself and then the funds were not there, and he would try to talk his way out of it," said a producer in Hollywood. When confronted, Dodi would apologetically promise payment, but frequently, the check would bounce. A number of Dodi's creditors sued him. American Express filed a lawsuit against Dodi for failing to pay a $116,890 debt. Other creditors walked away bitterly, including one prominent Hollywood actress who had to reupholster every piece of furniture in her Malibu beach house because of the damage done by Dodi's dogs.

Even with all his financial travails, Dodi's impulsive generosity became one of his hallmarks. "He was after acceptance, people enjoying his company, or prestige," said his friend Peter Riva. Dodi also indulged himself, collecting expensive cars, including five Ferraris, largely for show. Many of his preoccupations were childish. His Park Lane apartment featured a collection of baseball caps, and he was obsessed with military memorabilia. When he visited Los Angeles, he drove a $90,000 Hummer.

Dodi was fanatically concerned with personal security. Wherever he went, he insisted on having one or more bodyguards and a backup security car in tow. He was also hypochondriacal; like his father, Dodi carried scented disposable hand wipes for fear of germs.

One of Dodi's most perplexing traits was his tendency to exaggerate the extent of his wealth and privilege. When he rented a house, he would say he owned it. "I don't think a word of truth came out when he talked about possessions," said Nona Summers. "He was gentle and kind but a complete liar. He wanted to impress people."

His friends learned to live on "Dodi Time," knowing that he would either fail to appear as promised or arrive hopelessly late. "He didn't have the ability to say, 'No, I can't do that' or 'I don't have that,' " said Michael White. "His way of getting out of things was not to be around or not to answer the phone." His friends' tolerance reinforced Dodi's belief that he could talk his way out of anything.

With the exception of some jilted lovers, the women in Dodi Fayed's life took the most forgiving view of his fantasies and fibs. "He had an innocence that was very appealing, attractive, and gentle," said model Marie Helvin, who was impressed that Dodi—unlike his father—did not use profanities and disliked dirty jokes. Dodi poured out his troubles to Helvin and other women who served as sister/mother figures. But for all the jewelry, furs, and flowers he gave women, he didn't know how to make emotional commitments. "He sabotaged his relationships because he was always looking for a bigger and better deal," said a close female friend.

In the mid-1980s, Dodi met Suzanne Gregard, a twenty-six-year-old model, and he courted her avidly, flying her by Concorde to London for weekends, even buying the adjacent seat so she could have privacy. Dodi worshipped Gregard, who told her brother, "You know, he gets down on the ground and kisses my feet." Shortly before the end of 1986, Dodi proposed, and they were married on New Year's Eve in Vail, Colorado. After a Malibu honeymoon, they settled in a rented Manhattan town house. Gregard tried to make a home for them, but she managed to decorate only the living room, bedroom, guest room, and office, leaving the rest of the house empty.

Although Gregard earned a good living as a model, Dodi insisted on putting her on an allowance, refusing to discuss money with her. She continued her career, and he traveled on his own. After eight months, they decided to divorce. One reason, Gregard later admitted, was the intrusiveness of Dodi's heavy security. "We were never alone," she said.

Following the divorce, Dodi resumed his rootless life in London and Hollywood. In 1989, Mohamed tried to involve Dodi in business at Harrods, but he lasted all of three weeks in the training program in retailing and accounting. Dodi also tried to jump-start his film career after Jack Weiner left Allied Stars in 1990. Although he logged production credits on two movies, *Hook,* in 1991, and *The Scarlet Letter,* in 1995, Dodi had virtually no role in either film beyond writing checks with his father's funds. Dodi's finances had become impossibly tangled during these years. By 1997, the dockets of Los Angeles Superior and Municipal Courts were filled with cases in which Dodi was named as defendant—including suits over back taxes as well as damages to various properties he had rented.

By the spring of 1997, Dodi was still fantasizing about new film projects and earnestly talking about settling down. He had been dating Kelly

Fisher since the previous summer, and by her account, had proposed no fewer than four times. On June 20, Dodi bought Julie Andrews's five-acre compound in Malibu for $7.3 million. (The owner of record was Highcrest Investments Ltd.) According to Fisher, the couple planned to live there as husband and wife.

Three weeks later, Dodi was introduced to Diana in Saint-Tropez by his father. The two had met once briefly, during a polo match in 1987 in which Dodi was playing for the Harrods team, but Diana's knowledge of Dodi was based on his father's glowing reports. "Diana saw Dodi through Mohamed Fayed's words," said one of her close friends. "She never cared to find out anything more." There was little opportunity for Diana to learn much. In July 1997, Dodi was scarcely known outside Hollywood and jet-set circles. His name had sporadically surfaced in gossip columns, and then only in connection with film premieres or liaisons with assorted models or starlets.

Although Diana and Dodi were hardly on their own, they spent some time together in quiet conversation. "Dodi couldn't bear to leave her alone," said Debbie Gribble, chief stewardess on the *Jonikal*. As Dodi listened intently, Diana described her travels to Pakistan and Africa and her work on the land mine campaign. Mohamed's wife, Heini, later said that Diana and Dodi also talked eagerly about movies. On two evenings, Dodi made the oddly flamboyant gesture of renting a disco for William and Harry to enjoy privately. By day, as the group swam, Jet Skied, and relaxed on the *Jonikal*, the paparazzi took numerous photographs, but no one noticed Dodi. "We thought he was a sailor," said Jean-Louis Macault, one of the freelance paparazzi.

On July 16, Dodi greeted his fiancée, Kelly Fisher, in the port of Saint-Tropez. For the next two days, he moved back and forth between the Fayed villa and the yachts *Cujo* and *Sakara*, where he and Fisher alternately spent their first two nights together. Explaining his frequent daytime absences, Dodi told Fisher his father insisted on his presence to keep Diana amused. "I knew his father was important to him, and he had to do what he said," Fisher said. "But I was livid. . . . They basically kept me hidden." Fisher took the *Cujo* to Nice on the eighteenth for a previously scheduled modeling assignment that kept her occupied for three days and freed Dodi to be with Diana.

The paparazzi and hacks were primarily interested in how Diana would behave in the days leading up to July 18, the date of Camilla's fiftieth-birthday party. "We ran postcards to Camilla from Diana, which Diana had faxed [from her London office] and roared with laughter," said Piers Morgan of the *Mirror*. "She found it amusing, and she knew the power of what she was doing." On the morning of the eighteenth, the tabloids were filled with photographs of Diana at play, "stealing the spotlight with a . . . 30-minute nonstop performance" of diving, swimming, and riding behind Harry on his Jet Ski. She "leaned forward, revealing a breathtaking cleavage," wrote James Whitaker in *The Mirror*, "and preened herself on Mohamed's beach."

Mohamed Fayed gave an interview to *The Mail on Sunday* that appeared on July 20. Speaking to Brian Vine, Fayed said, "Diana's attitude to all the criticism is that those people can go to hell if they don't like it. Like me, she can see through all the hypocrisy of some of the critics." He claimed that Diana "felt at home" in the Fayed "family atmosphere," and said, "Diana's sons are having a great time, and any critics can just go and suck lemons." But Fayed went too far when he added, "As for Camilla, Diana doesn't think or care about her. . . . Camilla's like something from a *Dracula* film compared with the vividly beautiful Diana, who is so full of life."

Diana and the boys left at sunset that day. The next morning, Dodi filled her Kensington Palace apartment with pink roses and sent the first of numerous extravagant gifts: a £7,000 gold Cartier Panther watch. Harrods delivered a large box of exotic fruit from Mohamed as well. But Diana said little to her friends about Dodi. "The first I heard of her going off with Dodi was when I read it in the newspapers," said one of her close friends. "She didn't tell me." Diana did tell astrologer Debbie Frank that she had "the best holiday [she'd] ever had," and "I've met someone."

Unknown to Diana, Dodi was still sailing in the Mediterranean with his fiancée. The couple flew to Paris on July 23, and the next day, Fisher traveled, as planned, to Los Angeles, while Dodi returned to London. Diana, meanwhile, flew to Milan on the twenty-second to attend a memorial service for fashion designer Gianni Versace, who had been murdered a week earlier in Miami Beach by serial killer Andrew Cunanan. Diana was seated in the front row next to Elton John. Although she had fallen out with both the singer and his close friend Versace six months earlier, she took the opportunity to repair relations with John. As he sobbed quietly, she comforted him with her hand on his arm.

Three days later, Diana was off with Dodi on a Harrods helicopter to Paris for the weekend. Their visit to Fayed's Ritz Hotel was held in strict secrecy. Dodi gave Diana the £6,000-a-night Imperial Suite and treated her to dinner at the three-star Lucas Carton restaurant. On Saturday, they toured the villa where the Duke and Duchess of Windsor had lived in exile. Eleven years earlier, Fayed had leased the villa, which he had since restored. Dodi and Diana also stopped by Fayed's apartment off the Champs-Élysées and took a midnight stroll along the Seine. On Sunday, July 27, they returned to London undetected.

For the next month, Diana was almost continually on the move. With William and Harry at Balmoral for August, she was free to come and go, which she did more impulsively than usual. She made her first move on Thursday, July 31, stealing away with Dodi for a six-day cruise off Sardinia and Corsica on the *Jonikal,* where their love affair began. Drawing on his penchant for the romantic, Dodi pampered Diana with her preferred diet, which included carrot juice in the morning, fruit at lunch, and fish in the evening, as well as plenty of champagne, caviar, and pâté de foie gras. For background music, he provided two of her favorites, the sound track from the film *The English Patient* and George Michael's album *Older,* plus some Frank Sinatra. The couple talked and whispered nonstop, prompting Dodi's valet Rene Delorm to wonder, "How can people have so much to say to each other?" After several days, Dodi gave Diana a diamond bracelet, and when they went ashore in Monaco, they spent the day shopping for more jewelry. "It was as close to paradise as you can get," said *Jonikal* stewardess Debbie Gribble. But according to Antonia Grant, one of Dodi's chefs, "There was always [Mohamed] Fayed in the background. It was obvious that strings were being pulled."

On August 4, Italian paparazzo Mario Brenna located the couple on the *Jonikal* after receiving a tip-off, probably from someone close to Diana or Dodi. He clicked off a series of shots showing them sunbathing, swimming, and embracing, some taken from a small yacht positioned a mere ten yards away, others with a long lens. After a spirited auction, Brenna and his partner Jason Fraser pocketed more than £1.25 million from the London red tops.

The tabloids broke the story of the romance on Thursday, August 7, the day after Diana and Dodi returned to London. DI'S SECRET HOL WITH HARRODS HUNK DODI, headlined *The Sun.* Dodi was quoted in *The Mirror* as saying with a smile, "We relaxed. We had a great time. . . . We are very good friends." An evidently proud Mohamed Fayed told the *Evening Standard,* "I give them my blessing. They are both adults."

The tipoff came, as usual, from Richard Kay, who wrote in the *Daily Mail* that Dodi was "the first man who can openly be described as a boyfriend. . . . The Princess herself was yesterday astonishingly relaxed over the revelation of their closeness and the prospect of intimate photographs . . . being published." Kay recounted that Diana had said during "despairing moments" in recent months, "I so understand why Jackie married Onassis. She felt alone and in need of protection—I often feel like that." Quoting the ubiquitous "close friend," Kay wrote, "She wants to get a life—a *real* life. She is single and so is he. She's sick of all the cloak-and-dagger stuff. Why shouldn't she have a man in her life, and for people to know about it?"

It was a message meant for one reader, Hasnat Khan, according to Diana's friends. After some eighteen months in hiding with Khan, Diana intended to be as flagrantly public with Dodi as she could—at least in part to provoke Khan. "She was on the rebound from Hasnat Khan," said Elsa Bowker. "She started with Dodi to make Hasnat jealous." Added another close friend, "Dodi was a bolt out of the blue."

Many believed Diana was motivated by a more general urge for revenge as well. What better way to annoy the British establishment than by taking up with a man whose father's garish wealth and business manner made him an outsider among the upper classes? Her choice of the son of an Egyptian father and Saudi mother may have shocked the establishment, but to those who knew the history of Diana's recent attachments, Dodi was consistent with her taste for Eastern friends—from her *Panorama* interviewer Martin Bashir to Hasnat Khan and Gulu Lalvani, as well as women friends Elsa Bowker and Hayat Palumbo. Diana seemed to find an element of comfort and trust in non-Westerners.

Diana was infatuated with Dodi, initially described in the tabloids as "Mr. Perfect . . . caring, rich and irresistible to women." Kay, in the *Mail*, went out of his way to draw distinctions between Fayed and his son. Quoting "a friend," Kay wrote, "Dodi is not his father. He is very different, a gentle and sensitive man and that is part of his attraction for Diana." Dodi, according to his friends, was predictably intoxicated by Diana. For a man whose identity and purpose were shaped by his women, she represented his lifetime achievement. Winning her affection would finally prove Dodi's worth to his demanding father.

Given his preoccupation with security, Dodi may have seemed the sort who could give Diana the "protection" she said she wanted. Yet such a wish seemed strange after the years Diana had chafed under her royal protectors; nor was Dodi intrinsically strong. Rather, it was his vulnerability that appealed to Diana, who readily identified with his feelings. As Dodi said to his friend Barbara Broccoli, "It's so extraordinary that [Diana and I] don't have to *explain* anything to each other."

Although they were from different worlds, Diana and Dodi were damaged in similar ways. They were separated from their mothers at an early age and suffered deep insecurities as a result. Diana had taken refuge in bingeing and purging, and Dodi in cocaine addiction. They were prone to romantic fantasies, using gifts as endearments. Fearing rejection, they had difficulty committing themselves and fled relationships without explanation. They were emotionally immature and intellectually superficial. They hated being alone and compensated by constantly talking on the telephone. Both Dodi and Diana tended to repeat rather than learn from their mistakes, and they took refuge in dishonesty when they were feeling threatened or insecure. It is easy to imagine their compulsive confessions to each other of childhood loneliness and of being misunderstood and abused by the arrogant establishment.

"They were each in love with the fantasy about [the] other," said Dodi's friend Nona Summers. "Both were sweet, but they didn't know what each other was. She made an adorable first impression, but she had intense addictive relationships. Dodi saw himself as the knight on the steed, ready to defend his princess against the paparazzi, Charles, and Camilla. They were in many ways ill-fated and the perfect awful couple."

From Diana's standpoint, the very emptiness of Dodi's life worked to her advantage. Because he had no daily responsibility, he had all the time in the world to devote to Diana. "This was something she had never had in her life," said Lucia Flecha de Lima. He offered her distraction and entertainment: His immaturity came across as playful enthusiasm. He amused her with endless tales of Hollywood stars. They giggled together, and he made no intellectual demands. She told Rosa Monckton she was enchanted by "his wonderful voice," and she said to her hairstylist Tess Rock, "I love his exotic accent, the way he says, 'Di-yana, you're so naughty.' "

Diana's head was also turned by the way the Fayeds spent their money. She had found the stinginess of the royal family irksome, and no man had ever treated her as lavishly as Dodi. Although Diana's generous divorce settlement brought a hefty income, access to royal aircraft, and royal palaces, she was nevertheless impressed by those who seemed even wealthier. (Charles had shown the same weakness, accepting the beneficence of business tycoons Armand Hammer and John Latsis, whose yacht the Prince regularly used for holidays.) Diana wouldn't hesitate to borrow a private plane from her friends the Palumbos or billionaires, such as Teddy Forstmann, who enjoyed doing her a favor. Now the Fayeds were offering her unlimited use of their homes in Scotland, France, England, and the United States, plus yachts, planes, and helicopters.

Diana's pattern with her lovers had been to meld as quickly as she could with their families. She became close to James Hewitt's mother and sisters, and spent time with Oliver Hoare's mother. She visited Hasnat Khan's extended family in Pakistan and regularly saw his relatives in England. Mohamed Fayed made a point of emphasizing togetherness during Diana's stay in Saint-Tropez. "[Mohamed's wife] Heini is an elegant lady," explained Andrew Neil. "There were other kids around, including Fayed's deaf son, who Diana could look after. It was the warm embrace of the extended Arab family."

What Diana failed to appreciate was the subservience required of women in Fayed's world, as well as the oppressiveness of the tightly monitored and security-conscious Fayed lifestyle that Dodi's former wife found difficult to take. It was an atmosphere that would have made the British royal family seem positively easygoing.

The spoiled and thoughtless aspects of Dodi would have doubtless grated on Diana eventually: a stickler for punctuality, she would have found "Dodi Time" intolerable. Nor could she have endured his inability to make decisions on his own, or the learned helplessness that forced his father's aides to clean up Dodi's messes. Dodi's evasions would have stirred her mistrust, and when he tried to control her—as he invariably did with women—she would have withdrawn. In turn, Dodi would have tired of Diana's volatility and her constant need for reassurance; Dodi also wanted to be nurtured, which Diana wasn't equipped to do. But in Diana's case, Dodi was willing to make a greater effort than he previously had with women. This time he could be certain that if he succeeded, his father's money supply would never again be cut off.

Chapter 27

THE evening after her romance hit the tabloids, Diana went to Dodi's Park Lane apartment for dinner. When she emerged before midnight, she faced fifty photographers. The next day, Friday, August 8, she left for Bosnia with columnist William Deedes and her butler Paul Burrell on a jet loaned to her by billionaire George Soros.

The land mine trip had been difficult to put together. At the end of July, Diana had to scrap her original plans after the embarrassing disclosure that the president of the local Red Cross in Bosnia was the wife of war criminal Radovan Karadzic. But Diana was determined to go, so with William Deedes's help, she once again dropped the Red Cross and found new sponsors in the Land Mine Survivors Network and Norwegian People's Aid, organizations devoted to assisting victims of land mines.

After the Foreign Office determined that she could travel safely, the trip was announced on August 5, the day before her return to London with Dodi. Foreign Secretary Robin Cook, reaching out to his Labour constituency by writing "exclusively" in *The Mirror,* said Diana's crusade "has captured public attention over a weapon that strikes hardest at civilians. . . . I publicly support her trip to Bosnia."

But from the moment Diana arrived in Sarajevo, her efforts to call attention to the land mine problem were thwarted by the press's overwhelming interest in her new boyfriend. In Bosnia, she repeated much of what she had done to make her Angola trip such a success: an arduous three days of consoling victims, along with visits to the ruins of homes and the massive cemeteries for the war dead. She created vivid images of land mine destruction, and she provided comfort to people who were suffering, including a mother weeping at the grave of her son. "She was impressive in Bosnia," said William Deedes. "She left thirty minutes for every interview [with victims] and we did eight to twelve of them. She decided on that. She understood they would have a lot to say, and she never cut it short. They poured out everything and she remained amazingly silent. Every now and then, she would put out her hand and touch a face or shoulder. It was brilliant."

Diana's life had long been characterized by disconcerting juxtapositions of glamour and pathos. Four days after Robin Cook's encomium to Diana's good works appeared in the *The Mirror,* the same newspaper's Sunday edition exploded on August 10 with ten pages of photographer Mario Brenna's handiwork: "the most sensational pictures ever," starting with THE KISS on page one, a grainy shot of Diana and Dodi embracing on the luxurious Fayed yacht: LOCKED IN HER LOVER'S ARMS, THE PRINCESS FINDS HAPPINESS AT LAST.

Given the headlines in London, land mines couldn't hold the attention of some one hundred reporters trailing Diana around Sarejevo and its environs. *The Observer* described the "air of farce" that resulted when she tried to deliver a pair of prosthetic feet to an injured man as a *News of the World* reporter shouted, "Isn't it wonderful news about Dodi? What is it like to be in love again?" Noted *The Observer,* "The land mines issue had slipped down the agenda. The Princess in love had triumphed over the mission. . . . The real purpose was forgotten as Diana's love life was laid bare." Among the strangest efforts to bridge this gap was the *Sunday Mirror*'s fanciful report that "film producer Dodi has even decided to make a movie with Diana as coproducer—about an elephant crippled by a land mine."

Although Deedes felt that, professionally, Diana was "finding herself again, talking sense, meaning business, happy in herself," he could also see that she was distracted as she had not been on the earlier trip. "She was on the phone all the time to Dodi," Deedes recalled. Although he could "not be positive about anything about Diana," he couldn't believe the romance was serious. "I think she was figure skating with Dodi," he said.

On Monday, August 11, Diana flew back to London. En route, she and her butler Paul Burrell studied her press coverage from the previous days, including the KISS spread. "She was not at all resentful of the pictures that had been taken of her," Deedes recalled. "She talked about the headlines. She went through the newspapers with Paul Burrell, with me as a witness, and she was not horrified."

By then, the tabloids had begun to sour on Dodi. Detailed reports had already cropped up about his trail of unpaid bills and the myriad legal actions against him in the Los Angeles courts. The same day as THE KISS, *The Mail on Sunday* revealed Dodi's extravagance, as described in the American Express lawsuit, as well as one case that offered a "unique glimpse" into

Dodi's "impetuous nature"—a complicated wrangle over a $500,000 penthouse with a former girlfriend named Amy Diane Brown, who commented, "I would tell Diana to keep hold of the crown jewels and not let them out of her sight or he will sell them. . . . Even after all this time, it is still so terribly painful. I feel he ripped me off."

Days later, the coverage shifted to Dodi's sex life, and the tone turned ugly. *The Mirror* disclosed that he dumped girlfriends by what his friends called "Air Dodi"—a one-way business-class airplane ticket home. A former girlfriend named Denice Lewis dissected his sexual inadequacies in the *News of the World* and concluded: "I would lie there in the dark thinking, 'Is this it?' " But the explosion came on August 14 when a sobbing Kelly Fisher, with her mother and attorney Gloria Allred in tow, announced a lawsuit against Dodi after he jilted her to take up with Diana.

Not only had Fisher suffered the humiliation of a broken engagement (her proof: a sapphire-and-diamond ring that she flashed for the cameras), she also accused Dodi of failing to pay her $440,000 in "premarital support" that, she claimed, he had pledged in return for her giving up modeling. (Exhibit A: a check for $200,000 that Dodi had written on a closed account.) Fisher subsequently sold her story for some £200,000 to £250,000 to the *News of the World* and *The Sun*. Among her claims: that while Diana was at Fayed's home in Saint-Tropez, Fisher and Dodi were on one of the Fayed family yachts, making love. She said that Dodi kept an "astonishing array of weapons," and that he was "flabby and out of shape" and so germ-obsessed that he traveled with oxygen tanks. (After Dodi's death, Fisher would drop the lawsuit.)

Suddenly Dodi was no longer a "gentle soul" (the *Daily Mail*, August 8), an "ideal husband" (*The Sun*, August 8), or a "generous caring spirit" (the *Sunday Mirror*, August 10), but a "Dodi Rotten Cheat" (*The Mirror*, August 15), "Oily Bedhopper" (*The Sun*, August 16), and "Dodgy Dodi" (*The Mirror*, August 18), with "enough skeletons in his cupboard to stock a large graveyard . . . Dodi . . . is simply not good enough for [Diana]. . . . Dodgy [Dodi] is so cynical, shallow and spoilt you feel nostalgic for James Hewitt."

Diana was admittedly in an impossible situation. Any man in her life would be scrutinized, perhaps destroyed by the tabloids. But had she chosen someone more stable than Dodi Fayed, without his decadent past, her romance would not have kicked off such an orgy of salacious coverage.

In their prurient frenzy, the tabloids exceeded anything ever written about Diana—even the earliest days of Di-Mania, the endless speculation about the royal marriage, the exposés of Camillagate, the Squidgy tapes, the phone pest scandal, and the "love rat" James Hewitt. No detail of Dodi's debauchery or financial irresponsibility was too sordid to trot out, and

Diana was torn down in the process. Throughout the three weeks in August after the relationship went public, the tabloids ran photos of Dodi and Diana in bathing suits as they embraced and lounged on the *Jonikal,* cruising the Mediterranean. Leering and snide captions left nothing to the imagination. The most egregious, in *The Sun,* featured dialogue—DODI: "How about a quick dip?" DIANA: "Not here, darling. The staff can see us. Let's go for a swim instead." Everything else about Diana fell away as she became a sexual object—stripped of all respect, discretion, mystery, and taste.

At the same time, the tabloids cheerfully focused on the likelihood of marriage between Dodi and Diana. As early as August 10, the *Sunday Mirror* indicated an engagement was imminent—after Diana and Dodi had spent a mere seventeen days together, ten of them alone. Nigel Dempster and Richard Kay tried to apply the brakes in mid-month by recounting in the *Daily Mail* a conversation Diana had with Taki Theodoracopulos of *The Spectator,* in which she indicated marriage was not on her mind. "It took her a long time to get out of a loveless marriage, and she's not about to get into another," wrote Taki. The speculation persisted anyway.

With the tabloids at a boil, Diana and Dodi retreated for some private moments—a day at Fayed's estate in Surrey, two evenings in London. But the hacks pursued them when they took a Harrods helicopter to visit Diana's psychic Rita Rogers. Shortly after Rogers began consulting with Diana, she had told her client that she would "meet a man with whom she would fall in love, and that they would be together on a boat." When Diana and Dodi were on the *Jonikal* together, Diana had called Rogers to say, "I'm in the Mediterranean, with a man on a boat! Rita, you forecast this. You said this would happen!" Rogers later claimed that in her August 12 consultation she warned Dodi of a black car and a tunnel, which she said he "seemed to be taking in," although Diana "was getting fidgety."

On August 15, the day Kelly Fisher's allegations filled the tabloids, Diana and her friend Rosa Monckton flew off in one of Fayed's jets—at Dodi's insistence—for a five-day vacation in Greece. Two days later, Dodi went to California to consult with his lawyers about Fisher's lawsuit. He stayed in his new Malibu home, kept a low profile, and visited a sick friend at Cedars Sinai Hospital. After thirty-six hours, he left, having accomplished little. Flying back to New York on a private plane, Dodi spoke guardedly about Diana to his friend Mark Canton. "He was happy the romance was blossoming," said Canton. "He seemed superstitious, though. He didn't want to go where it might lead."

Although Diana avidly read the tabloids, she dismissed the negative reports about Dodi. "By the time the stories came out, she was besotted by him and tried not to believe what she was hearing," said one of her close friends. She sought reassurance not only from her psychic but from her astrologer Debbie Frank, who did Dodi's chart. "I am so happy we are compatible," Diana told Frank. "I have never before felt truly happy for more than just one day."

But on her holiday with Rosa Monckton, Diana was beginning to express reservations. "Look at this, Rosa, isn't it awful?" Diana said, pointing to what Rosa described as tacky "plush pink seats" and "green pile carpet covered in pharaohs' heads" in the Fayed jet. Diana said she understood that Dodi's world was "far removed from reality" and she spoke of becoming "truly angry" when Dodi "would ring and recite a list of presents he had purchased for her." As Diana told Rosa, "That's not what I want . . . It makes me uneasy. I don't want to be bought. . . . I just want someone to be there for me, to make me feel safe and secure."

Diana was back in London for scarcely a day before she and Dodi headed out again on August 21 for another cruise on the *Jonikal,* covering the same haunts from Nice to Sardinia. Dodi again treated Diana extravagantly. After spending a morning in Porto Cervo on Sardinia, they carried back a heap of cashmere sweaters—he had bought her one in every color—as well as several pairs of J. P. Tod's shoes. "She only had to look at a thing, and he'd get it," said *Jonikal* stewardess Debbie Gribble.

Dodi also gave Diana a small silver plaque commissioned "from a distinguished silversmith" and inscribed with a poem that he had written. According to Tina Sinatra, Dodi had borrowed such a plaque from her when they were dating in the eighties and never returned it, despite her repeated requests. Sinatra said she would "always wonder" whether it was the same plaque.

As the *Jonikal* zigged and zagged around the Mediterranean for nine days, the paparazzi followed every movement, sending back numerous pictures showing the couple lounging on deck. In most of the shots, Diana was reclining, while Dodi nuzzled her or draped his arm across her. At least two of Diana's friends were struck by the lack of demonstrativeness on her part. "The body language on the boat was wrong," Cosima Somerset said.

On August 26, *Le Monde,* the left-leaning French newspaper, published an interview conducted with Diana the previous June, in which she bitterly attacked the British press for criticizing her humanitarian efforts. Overseas, on the other hand, she said, "I'm welcomed with kindness. I'm taken for what I am . . . without looking for blunders." She spoke of her "destiny" to help "vulnerable people" and said her use of touch "comes naturally . . . from the heart. It isn't premeditated." Once again, her views on land mines created controversy: "The Labour government's position has always been clear," she said. "It's going to do terrific work. Its predecessor was absolutely hopeless."

Tory politicians reacted indignantly to her characterization, prompting Diana to spend several days of her holiday trying to contain the damage. The *Daily Express* called the situation "her most ferocious political row" as "senior Tories warned her to stay out of politics." Diana shot back with a strong statement, insisting Annick Cojean, the French journalist, had misquoted her: "The Princess has made no such criticism." The interview had been conducted partly in person and partly through written questions, and Diana's office produced a copy of the article *Le Monde* had submitted for her approval, which did not contain the offending "hopeless" phrase. The French journalist and her editor countered that Diana had made the comment during the face-to-face interview, and that the phrase had been added after Kensington Palace had seen the draft. "I wrote exactly what she said and what I heard," insisted Cojean.

Diana felt "bitterly let down" and "stitched up". As Rosa Monckton later explained, "The . . . reaction in the British press was disproportionate and fiercely critical of Diana. Her response was cold fury. She postponed her return to England." Instead of flying directly home on Saturday, August 30, Diana agreed to instead spend that night with Dodi in Paris. Monckton last spoke to the Princess on August 28, and as she recounted later, Diana's recurring theme was "betrayal, and being misunderstood."

Diana and Dodi left for Paris at midday on August 30, a change in plans that was approved by Fayed himself. Their jittery comings and goings the rest of that day and evening were relayed to Fayed in England by his Ritz managers as well. Diana and Dodi moved around Paris in rapid bursts, followed always by a large pack of paparazzi. From the airport they went to the Villa Windsor, where they stayed less than a half hour. A Fayed employee took their luggage to Dodi's apartment, where they planned to spend the night, while the couple headed for the Ritz to rest in the Imperial Suite.

That day, according to Fayed spokesman Michael Cole, Diana gave Dodi a gold cigar clipper, inscribed "From Diana with love," and her father's gold cuff links—the same pair she had earlier given to Oliver Hoare. "They were her most precious possession," said Elsa Bowker. "I couldn't believe she gave them to Dodi so quickly." Dodi intended to give Diana a garish diamond-encrusted ring that he purchased for £125,000 from the Repossi Jewelers on the Place Vendôme late in the afternoon. Alberto Repossi said Diana helped choose the ring when they twice visited the jeweler's Monaco store during their *Jonikal* cruises, although her friends protested that it wasn't her taste. Richard Kay called it "vulgar."

In the early evening, Dodi and Diana left via the Ritz's rear door to drive to his apartment. As usual, they rode in a Mercedes limousine driven by Dodi's personal chauffeur Philippe Dourneau, followed by Dodi's Range Rover bearing two security guards, Trevor Rees-Jones and Kes Wingfield. When they arrived at the apartment building, Dodi and Diana had to struggle through a paparazzi mob to reach the front door. Two hours later, the couple left the apartment, intending to have dinner at the fashionable Chez Benoit restaurant. En route, Dodi was so exasperated by the crush of photographers shadowing the car that he abruptly changed plans. Instead of Chez Benoit, they would dine at the Ritz. On their arrival at the hotel, they were again thronged by the paparazzi, some pressing within inches of Diana's face—an indignity she had suffered many times, although such pressure was new to Dodi, who was visibly rattled.

They started out in the main dining room at the Ritz, but when Dodi became agitated by the unabashed stares of other diners, they left after placing their order and ate in their suite upstairs instead. Dodi couldn't face the photographers again, so he devised a subterfuge to avoid them. His Mercedes and Range Rover would act as decoys, revving up at the front door as if readying for Dodi and Diana's departure, while the couple would escape by the back door into another car. Shortly before midnight, Dodi called his father, who approved the plan. Hotel officials alerted the paparazzi at the front to expect Dodi and Diana shortly, as the couple waited inside the rear exit for a rented Mercedes to pull up. A small group of paparazzi lingered in the street behind the Ritz as well. Before Dodi and Diana hopped into the backseat, Henri Paul, their new driver, shouted to the paparazzi, "Don't bother following—you won't catch us." The car sped off at 12:20 A.M. as photographers gave chase on motorbikes and in cars. Five minutes later, the Mercedes slammed into the wall of the Alma Tunnel, killing Dodi, Diana, and Henri Paul, and severely injuring security man Trevor Rees-Jones, who was riding shotgun.

Subsequent investigations showed that Paul, the acting security chief at the Ritz—who was not a licensed chauffeur—had been drinking heavily: an autopsy revealed a blood-alcohol level three times the legal driving limit in France, plus the presence of the antidepressant Prozac and the tranquilizer tiapride. The two drugs were prescribed to treat Paul's alcoholism; taken in combination with alcohol, they could severely impair judgment and reflexes. When Paul zoomed into the Alma Tunnel at high speed, he was incapable of controlling a car. Dodi had insisted on Paul as his driver because he was a security specialist, who could best protect them against the swarm of photographers.

Why hadn't Diana and Dodi simply spent the night in the safety of the Ritz? Dodi had been determined to return to the apartment, he reportedly told his father, because their belongings were there. According to Dodi's valet Rene Delorm, Dodi had said earlier he wanted iced champagne ready for their return because he planned to propose to Diana. These reasons overlook the sensible solution of sending someone to retrieve their luggage and bring it to the Ritz, where iced champagne could have been produced within minutes.

Diana's contribution to Dodi's misguided decisions is unknown, although in the Ritz security video of the couple waiting in the hotel's rear corridor, she appears quiet and withdrawn as Dodi encircles her with one arm. Dodi's habit when faced with a perceived threat was to overcompensate, partly to impress and partly to feel secure. According to Thomas Sancton and Scott MacLeod, *Time* magazine correspondents who wrote a book with the cooperation of Mohamed Fayed about the investigation into the deaths of Dodi and Diana, Dodi "seemed to get more and more excited about his plan" as he and Diana prepared for their supposedly secret exit. "When you were with him, you felt protected," said Dodi's friend Nona Summers. "Ironically, it was overprotective zealousness that was the paradox that led to the disaster. He was trying to protect her from the press. But the reaction was over-the-top. If he hadn't been so overprotective, they would just have been photographed, and nothing would have happened."

Indeed, Diana probably felt she was safe. Since she had taken up with Dodi six weeks earlier, she had lived inside the private world of the Fayeds, with its own security details, stores, restaurants, hotels, homes, yachts, planes, and helicopters—an even more elaborate setup than that of the royal family Diana had so recently shed. But had Diana been traveling with a Scotland Yard bodyguard—the royal privilege she had dropped three years earlier—it seems probable he would have applied some common sense to the events of August 30.

In the months after the tragedy, Mohamed Fayed insisted that Dodi and Diana planned to marry, and that the ring from Repossi was meant to seal their engagement. As further proof, Fayed claimed that on the Saturday afternoon before they died, Dodi and Diana had spent two hours at the Villa Windsor "examining every part" of the house that would be their future home. However, photographs published in *The Sun* from a security camera at the villa proved that Dodi and Diana's visit had lasted less than twenty-eight minutes. What's more, Diana disliked the Windsor house, saying "it has a history and ghosts all of its own, and I have no wish to follow that."

Diana's friends heatedly disputed the notion that Diana would have married Dodi. The day after Diana died, Richard Kay initially wrote in the *Daily Mail* that he had felt marriage was "likely." He had been the last friend to talk to her when she called him from the Ritz six hours before she died. It was during this conversation that Diana declared her decision to retire from public life, telling Kay that Mohamed Fayed had offered to finance a charity for land mine victims, and that she and Dodi had discussed a plan to open hospices around the world—arrangements that would have brought Diana more deeply within the control of Mohamed Fayed. When Diana spoke of feeling a new strength, Kay found her neither strong nor certain, although he sensed that Dodi and Diana were "in love" and that she was "as happy as I have ever known her."

In the following days, Kay "rapidly changed" his view, he later said. After talking with a number of Diana's friends, he concluded that he had been wrong to think Diana would marry Dodi. According to Kay, Diana had not discussed marriage plans with anyone close to her—including her butler Paul Burrell, her immediate family, her sons, or confidantes such as Lucia Flecha de Lima and Rosa Monckton. Even factoring in Diana's fondness for secrecy, she most likely would have confided in at least one person—and certainly would have talked with her sons. As Elsa Bowker observed, "She called William about everything."

Friends who watched the videos taken by Ritz security cameras on Diana's last day were bothered by her demeanor. "I don't like what I saw," said one close friend who had encountered paparazzi with Diana on a number of occasions. "I saw a lot of tension. Why did they go in and out of the Ritz so many times? When Diana was unhappy, she was restless, and she seemed restless. If you are in love and staying at a safe place, why leave it? In the tape, her expression didn't seem right. By her body language, her comings and goings, it didn't make sense."

Diana's friend Annabel Goldsmith also had serious doubts about Diana's commitment to Dodi. Both she and her daughter Jemima had spoken to Diana on the twenty-ninth, the last day of the *Jonikal* cruise. In both conversations, Diana said she was having fun, that she had never been treated so well by a man, and was enjoying it. When Annabel said, "You're not doing anything silly, like getting married?" Diana replied, "Don't worry. I need another marriage like a bad rash on my face"—an expression she also used in her conversation with Jemima.

In *Death of a Princess,* their book published in February 1998, Sancton and MacLeod raised the possibility that Diana was pregnant when she died. The theory caused Rosa Monckton and Richard Kay to write blistering replies in *The Sunday Telegraph* and the *Daily Mail.* Rosa's evidence was the most persuasive: Pregnancy, she said, was "biologically impossible" because Diana was menstruating when she and Rosa were in Greece "ten days before her fatal accident." Kay discounted the possibility because Diana "was obsessive about not having a child out of wedlock" and "could not run any risk of embarrassing or hurting her sons William and Harry."

Diana and Dodi had known each other for only six weeks. They were together on thirty-two of those days, and the days they spent alone were a mere twenty-five. They floated along in an existence that was intense and unreal, detached from the world of everyday decisions as well as their respective friends. The only person from Diana's life who met Dodi was her psychic Rita Rogers. Yet they acted out their romance in view of the cameras, and died trying to escape the men who had tormented and celebrated them. "Diana's life should not be frozen into those last six weeks," Rosa Monckton later said. "It is simply neither fair nor accurate. Diana's legacy is so much greater."

But Diana's final summer was highly revealing. As she gave off numerous conflicting signals, she was publicly playing out her shifting moods, doubts, and insecurities in exaggerated form, for all to see. Diana's willingness to entangle herself with the Fayeds showed how alone she was. Her romance with Dodi was perhaps the clearest evidence that she had made little progress in dealing with her demons. "Diana was a fifteen-year-old, emotionally, where men were concerned," said one of her close friends. In all likelihood, even as a teenager Diana would not have given a second look to a man whose reputation and character were as tarnished as Dodi's. In her neediness, Diana had regressed. "No one can tell me what to do," Diana told Le Monde three months before she died. "I work by instinct. It's my best adviser." Given the number of times Diana's instinct failed her, it was a stark admission that she remained sadly out of touch with herself to the very end.

Chapter 28

DURING Diana's lifetime, few were willing to confront directly the extent of her emotional problems. "She clearly should have had a lot more professional help," said Dr. Michael Adler, chairman of the National AIDS Trust. "I think she needed rather intense professional counseling and psychological support, and I was never certain that she ever had that in a manner that I would have thought was totally helpful."

For the first half of her life, when she was usually in a protected environment, Diana managed to keep her problems in check, except for occasional flare-ups when she was in stressful situations. But after the age of nineteen, Diana was often out of control, her fragile psyche cracking under the strain of public life.

Prince Charles, who witnessed her extreme behavior longer than anyone, lacked the knowledge and temperament to help her deal with her torment. He probably deserves more credit than he has received for trying to get Diana into therapy on several occasions. But his standard responses to her—pleading, giving in, retreating in anger—only seemed to feed her volatility. Diana needed constant expressions of love and reassurance combined with firm reminders that she was expected to behave in a responsible way and that her actions had consequences. Perhaps Charles gave up on Diana too quickly, but he did so out of frustration and ignorance, not for lack of concern.

Her friends and family tended to minimize her problems or focus on Diana at her best—her wit, warmth, spontaneity, and generosity—while recognizing, as her friend Rosa Monckton wrote, that she had "an enormous capacity for unhappiness." Even her persistent depression was dismissed by many as postpartum "baby blues" when it actually had plagued her through her adult life. By denying the extent of her difficulties, everyone around Diana "enabled" her to stay on a self-destructive path.

The press played an especially damaging role by building her up one minute and knocking her down the next. Reporters on the royal beat saw Diana's crack-up at close range but chose to perpetuate her fairy-tale myth; for once, the charge seems valid that the press ignored the truth in order to sell newspapers. The relentless coverage gave Diana two selves to deal with: the one in the newspapers and the one she struggled with every day.

Diana presented two versions of herself to friends as well, shifting between Her Royal Highness and old pal Diana. Friends shied away from offering help for fear of seeming presumptuous or patronizing. "What was most difficult about Diana was her dropping friends," said one. "It was hard to understand how lonely she was and how much help she needed." As Cosima Somerset said: "She could open up at the drop of a hat, almost to her detriment. Then on the other side was a wall. She was completely defended. It wasn't very balanced. She would meet someone for the first time and be very open. But basically she was very secretive. There were lots of things she didn't talk about that were quite important."

Diana's genius at playing princess made it hard for people to appreciate the severity of her problems. Yet the telltales were there for all to see. From the days before her wedding to the end of her life, she wept in public to an unusual degree. Sometimes, as when she was assaulted by the paparazzi, her tears were understandable, but more often than not her obvious sadness was unprovoked. Her habit of crying before and after official events showed how hard she had to work to hold herself together. Her media adviser, Jane Atkinson, believed that the "real" Diana was "withdrawn and detached." "The effort she made to come out of that state of mind was considerable," Atkinson said. "The real Diana was a more brooding person." When Diana dazzled in public, she was also "real," in Atkinson's view, "but she couldn't maintain it."

It didn't help that most Britons, especially those in the upper class, have little sympathy for emotional distress. The much-caricatured stiff upper lip remains an esteemed trait. Therapy, by contrast, is often regarded as self-indulgent whining. "In this culture we haven't used psychology," said a man close to Prince Charles. "Until recently it was inconceivable for most people. Today there is more acceptance, and Diana ironically played a part in legitimizing it."

Whenever the subject of Diana's emotional disturbances came up in the British press, she was invariably derided as "loony," "potty," a "basket case," or "barking mad." Time and again, journalists and their sources implied Diana was to blame for her behavior, refusing to accept that mental illness is neither a moral failing nor a character defect. "Diana should not get help," wrote Lesley White of *The Sunday Times* in November 1995. "She should simply get over it."

The harshness of these characterizations prompted allies of Diana to issue misguided denials that she needed *any* professional help. Stephen Twigg, the massage therapist whom Diana relied on for several years in the early 1990s, told the *Sunday Express* in 1992 that Diana's suicide attempts "could happen to anyone . . . the idea that she is ill, unstable in some way, emotionally unbalanced, is nonsense." Such statements reinforced Diana's aversion to being labeled and must have pushed her further from seeking proper care.

Diana herself had an ambivalent attitude toward psychiatry. She turned to alternative therapists largely because she could control them. She initially resisted psychotherapy and was deeply mistrustful of antidepressants and tranquilizers—although she depended on prescription sleeping pills for many years. Even after discussing her self-mutilation and bulimic bingeing on television, she derided the royal family and Charles's friends for stigmatizing her as mentally ill. Diana also claimed at various times to be "finished" with her bulimia. But the underlying causes persisted, as evidenced by her reliance on colonic irrigation and obsessive exercise.

Even when her symptoms were acute—and dangerous—her position as Princess of Wales precluded her checking into a clinic, as her sister Sarah and her brother's wife Victoria had done to treat their eating disorders. "In a sense, she was finished on the day of the royal wedding," said Michael Colborne, former aide to Prince Charles. "Nobody saw the basics with her, that she had to be looked after." As a result, Diana's psychological problems festered and grew.

Diana underwent psychotherapy on several occasions and mastered psychological jargon along the way. But Diana's treatments were short-lived until she enlisted the help of Susie Orbach, a fellow sufferer as well as a therapist who kept Diana engaged for several years. The treatment did not seem to have lasting effects. As her friend Richard Kay wrote, Diana "was as unsure of herself at her death as when I first talked with her [in the spring of 1993]." Her behavior grew more chaotic, not less, and she repeated her mistakes rather than learning from them. She ultimately denigrated Orbach in particular and psychotherapy in general, telling the patients at Roehampton Priory they were unlikely to find much help from "some psychotherapist or someone just reading from a book." The press, which Diana looked to for approval, applauded these remarks. Writing in the *Evening Standard,* Melanie McDonagh saw a hopeful "backlash against therapy . . . this very modern infantilism."

Given the range and severity of Diana's symptoms, it's not surprising that outpatient psychotherapy failed her. A number of psychiatrists and psychologists have debated Diana's condition in the British press, offering diagnoses ranging from addiction to obsessive-compulsive disorder to narcissism. But none adequately explains Diana's disordered thinking, behavior, and relationships. Nor does pinning everything on her bulimia, which was commonly done by both her friends and journalists. In fact, her eating disorder was a manifestation of her illness, not the illness itself. "Don't make a mistake by focusing on bulimia," said a psychologist familiar with Diana's case. "Bulimia is a window."

To a striking degree, Diana's disturbances conformed to the borderline personality disorder. Neurotics may experience anxiety but still have a clear sense of themselves, while narcissists tend to be self-important and disdainful. Borderline personalities feel inferior and dependent and are typically confused about their identity. They are self-destructive, easily depressed, panicky, and volatile. But on the surface they are apt to be charming, insightful, witty, and lively. As in Diana's case, they tend to be perceptive about other people, and many work as counselors, doctors, and nurses, providing the kind of care they would like to receive. One hallmark of the borderline personality is the ability to appear "superficially intact" while experiencing "dramatic internal chaos." Among other notable figures who exhibited borderline behavior was Marilyn Monroe, who, like Diana, was obsessed with finding her identity, harbored a terror of solitude, and suffered from crushing despair.

The term "borderline" has been around since the late 1930s as a catchall category for people who are more severely ill than neurotics but lack the distortions of reality that incapacitate psychotics. The condition exists on the "border" of long-recognized mental illnesses such as manic depression, anxiety disorders, and schizophrenia. Two leading American psychiatrists, Dr. Otto Kernberg of Cornell and Dr. John Gunderson of Harvard, came up with a definition that was officially recognized by the American Psychiatric Association in 1980 and subsequently by the World Health Organization.

The possibility that Diana suffered from borderline personality disorder was discussed by a few people close to Prince Charles. One of them consulted a psychologist and a psychiatrist, each of whom told him that Diana's behavior "fit the description of the borderline personality in quite extraordinary detail." The suggestion was made publicly as well, most notably in a 1995 column by Nigel Dempster, who reported in the *Daily Mail* a "growing feeling" Diana's symptoms pointed toward a borderline disorder. Yet Dempster undercut the potential helpfulness of his suggestion by using it as evidence of Diana's "predatory," "manipulative," and "egocentric" approach to men. "It can only be hoped that she is not allowed to sink further into the indulgence of the victim or the aggressive manipulation of the predator," he wrote.

While one cannot say with certainty that Diana had a borderline personality disorder, the evidence is compelling. The most important factor setting the borderline personality apart from those with other disorders is early parental loss—in Diana's case the departure of her mother and the emotional withdrawal of her father for several years following the Spencer divorce. Even the timing of the usual appearance of borderline symptoms in late adolescence fit Diana's profile, as did the trigger of intense pressure, which in Diana's case was brought on by her royal marriage and the lofty expectations of the public and the press. Borderlines can frequently maintain a facade of normality "until their defense structure crumbles, usually around a stressful situation," according to psychiatrist Richard J. Corelli of Stanford University.

The borderline personality is also more prevalent than one would expect. According to the *Harvard Mental Health Letter,* an "estimated 2.5 per cent of the American population suffers from borderline personality disorder—six million persons, or three times the number with schizophrenia." From fifteen to twenty-five percent of all patients seeking psychiatric care are borderlines. It is by any measure a major mental health problem, although it remains little known and largely misunderstood.

Many people have the traits of the borderline to one degree or another, but someone with the disorder experiences them severely and chronically, as Diana did. The traits are "intricately connected, interacting with each other so that one symptom sparks the rise of another like the pistons of a combustion engine," wrote Dr. Jerold Kreisman, a leading expert in the study of borderline personalities.

At the core of a borderline's psychology is an uncertain self-image. In his eulogy, Diana's brother Charles referred to her "deep feelings of unworthiness." Diana spoke of her self-hatred to Andrew Morton, James Hewitt, and any number of friends. She constantly sought ratification from friends, the press, and crowds of strangers. Her preferred source of approval was the public, but even after mingling with adoring fans, she felt inadequate. As she once explained to *Evening Standard* editor Max Hastings, she cried after public events "because of the strain of feeling that so much is expected of me."

Diana couldn't accept that her attributes were a fixed part of her personality—a typical borderline reaction. Instead, she relied on the most recent judgment she had heard, whether from her husband, her friends, the press, even people she met in hospital wards. This tendency largely explains

why Diana felt she was
weeks earlier, it didn't m
ment to avoid plunging
James Hewitt felt worn dov
"to the point where he had
words had lost their meaning.

Lacking any firm identity,
bored—another marker of the b
ships to fill the vacuum. Since she
derlines do, this urge to find relief in
But for Diana, the possibility of a dis
able to solitude.

The comfort Diana sought from bu   .ging was
also an example of the impulsive behavior   a borderline. A
number of studies have shown that as man\   ..d of bulimics suffer
from the borderline personality disorder.   Diana's well-documented
episodes of self-mutilation, as well as her suicidal gestures and threats,
were related forms of impulsiveness consistent with the disorder. As Kreisman observed, "self-mutilation . . . is the hallmark of borderline personality disorder . . . more closely connected . . . than any other psychiatric
malady."

The most poignant aspect of the borderline personality is the inability
to sustain close, mutually gratifying relationships. Diana brought a ferocious intensity to her relationships, pleading for attention and time, and
demanding complete loyalty. She showered people with affection and gifts,
then cut them off with little or no explanation. "If you have been rejected
by your mother and then rejected by your husband," Rosa Monckton explained, "you feel that as soon as people get to know you they will reject
you." Diana "was so incredibly insecure, and whenever people got close she
got frightened." Diana actually alternated between fears about intimacy
and anxiety over separation. If people came too close, she felt suffocated; if
they kept a slight distance, she felt abandoned. These problems were invisible to the public. Only intimates saw her worries and erratic behavior.

In her closest relationships, Diana showed the borderline's frantic effort
to avoid abandonment. Jonathan Dimbleby described numerous examples
of this behavior, beginning early in her marriage when Diana repeatedly insisted on Charles's presence "to the exclusion of all else in his life." When
Charles went off to work, Diana interpreted his departure as a lack of love.
James Hewitt, Oliver Hoare, and Hasnat Khan all were the objects of the
same pattern of urgent dependency. To the end, when Diana talked about
her ideal man, she envisioned someone "who would be there for her twenty-
four hours a day," according to energy healer Simone Simmons.

trapped and isolated. After a close
nce, she reacted in a childlike fashion, as if
wouldn't return. She also experienced what psy-
ng effect of time": When she was cut off from some-
was intensely attached, her favorable memory of that
be quickly eroded by feelings of doubt. It may have been to
these misgivings and fears that Diana would call people repeatedly
spend hours with them on the phone. "She had no governor that operated," said her friend David Puttnam. "If you said, 'This is the sixth time
you've called,' she would say, 'No, I've only called once,' "—a form of denial
also typical of the borderline's occasional disconnection from reality.

Always distrustful, Diana listened in on phone conversations, opened
mail, and lingered in hallways to catch comments that proved her worst
suspicions. In some cases, Diana had reason to be wary; plenty of people
took advantage of her. But most of the time she overreacted, mainly because she tended to see people in black or white, a defense mechanism
known as "splitting." It is a classically juvenile response frequently seen in
borderlines who "cannot tolerate human inconsistencies and ambiguities"
or "reconcile another's good and bad qualities into a constant coherent understanding of that person. . . . At any particular moment, one is either
'good' or 'evil' . . . idolized one day, totally devalued and dismissed the
next," a behavior pattern often exhibited by Diana.

At the outset of close relationships, Diana usually screened out negative characteristics in the other person. But, inevitably, the object of her affection would let her down, perhaps by failing to praise her enough. Then
she would see only the worst in that person. Virtually everyone was destined to fail her, because Diana couldn't accept the fact that every relationship has its ups and downs.

Diana's sudden mood shifts typified the borderline personality's "emotional hemophilia," an absence of "the clotting mechanism needed to moderate spurts of feeling." As her friend Clive James wrote, "Clearly on a hair
trigger, she was unstable at best, and when the squeeze was on, she was a
fruitcake on the rampage." Even her sunny side had a slightly manic edge.
"I never thought she was unstable when I first met her," said one of her
friends. "But I noticed as I got to know her better the inconsistencies in her
behavior. She was a tremendous giggler, but her laughter had a touch of
madness, almost uncontrollable. Her giggles were always faintly hysteri-
cal—like a combination of tears and laughter."

By her own description, Diana had felt a sense of detachment ("in the
wrong shell") since childhood, another trait of the borderline, especially in
times of severe stress. "Diana seemed to look at the world through a glass,
and was unable to form relationships while seeing others form relation-

ships, and she was tormented that she couldn't do it too," said a man close to Prince Charles. As is often seen in "high functioning" borderline personalities, tied into Diana's sense of being an outsider were instances of "magical thinking": her belief in premonitions of events in her life such as her father's stroke, her reports of hearing voices that instructed her, and her conviction that she possessed healing powers.

Borderline personalities are notoriously difficult to treat. They are frequently misdiagnosed, and they tend to move from one therapist to the next, as was the case with Diana. Antidepressants such as Prozac can ease some symptoms, but borderlines usually don't take medications as prescribed, at least in part because they view pharmacotherapy—as Diana did—as a form of "mind control." For therapists, treating a borderline can be arduous. The mistrust and inconstancy of the disorder can erode the therapist's professional confidence, not to mention his patience. As a result, the borderline is considered by many in the mental health professions to represent "a kind of 'Third World' of mental illness . . . indistinct, massive, vaguely threatening."

On one level, Diana grasped how close to the edge she lived. *Washington Post* publisher Katharine Graham wrote that Diana had once been asked if she gambled. "Not with cards," Diana replied, "but with life." Such moments of clarity were rare. Most of the time, Diana was too troubled to find appropriate care on her own. Nor was anyone around her able to take charge. Given the complexity of her problems, it would have taken someone of keen understanding, great patience, and unwavering love to keep her on a helpful therapeutic course. The royal family were incapable of dealing with Diana, and her own relatives weren't up to the task. "Her mother wasn't there, and for her father everything Diana did was perfect and wonderful. He wouldn't say boo to a goose," said a relative of the royal family. In the view of Charles's former aide Michael Colborne, "Most people look at it as if it was her fault, but it wasn't. Everyone contributed to her downfall."

Under the right circumstances, Diana could have been helped. She needed to be in a structured and predictable environment, out of the limelight, away from the media's deifying praise and flashes of criticism. She probably could have benefited from practical therapy that avoided delving too deeply into analyzing the past and instead concentrated on managing her symptoms. Borderlines require years of therapy, but they can learn new emotional reflexes in order to deal with stress and relate better to others.

From the time she entered public life, Diana conveyed her vulnerability with her eyes, her gestures, her speech, and her touch. Alongside her beauty, this evident fragility made her a star. Once the breadth and depth of her emotional struggle became known, she struck an even deeper chord: She became the fairy-princess version of the troubled everywoman.

Diana had a certain kind of strength as well. Even under the most extreme pressure, she did not seek a hermit's retreat. Her hunger for the love of her public may have accounted for at least some of that determination to keep going. But she also had a willfulness that prompted her to buck royal proprieties, whether it meant roller-skating through the halls of Buckingham Palace or publicly hugging and kissing the sick and dying. Her defiance won her an even larger place in the public's heart.

Diana talked about a sense of destiny, her need to achieve good by fulfilling a role she had trouble defining. Although her identity was fractured, she kept to her quest and seized opportunities, sometimes willy-nilly, to do her bit for society. But Diana couldn't sustain her good works for the simple reason that her own problems consumed so much of her time and energy. As one of her former aides said, "Her life was her drama, and I am not really sure she could move beyond that." Yet, given the extent to which Diana was ruled by her inconstant emotions, the wonder is that she accomplished as much as she did.

A Note on Sources

THIS book was based on interviews with 148 people as well as numerous books and articles in newspapers and magazines. Sixty-eight of the individuals I interviewed asked to remain anonymous, and though these sources contributed significantly to the book, they do not appear in the chapter notes. All quotations excluded from the chapter notes are from these confidential interviews. In citing periodicals, I have listed only publication names and dates. Page numbers in books cited refer to the U.S. edition.

ABBREVIATIONS

Publications

DEx	*Daily Express*	PE	*Private Eye*
SuEx	*Sunday Express*	ES	*Evening Standard*
Gua	*The Guardian*	DS	*Daily Star*
DM	*Daily Mail*	Sun	*The Sun*
MOS	*The Mail on Sunday*	DT	*The Daily Telegraph*
Mi	*Daily Mirror*	SuTel	*The Sunday Telegraph*
	(*The Mirror* as of 1997)	Ti	*The Times*
SuMi	*Sunday Mirror*	ST	*The Sunday Times*
NOTW	*News of the World*	To	*Today*
TNY	*The New Yorker*	VF	*Vanity Fair*
NYT	*The New York Times*	WP	*The Washington Post*
SuPe	*Sunday People*	WO	*Woman's Own*

Books

Works cited more than several times will be abbreviated as follows:

B-SB   *Royal Service: My Twelve Years as Valet to Prince Charles* (1983), by Stephen P. Barry

B-WB   *The Housekeeper's Diary: Charles and Diana Before the Breakup* (1995), by Wendy Berry

B-TB   *Fayed: The Unauthorized Biography* (1998), by Tom Bower

B-JD   *The Prince of Wales: A Biography* (1994), by Jonathan Dimbleby

B-SF   *My Story* (paperback edition, 1997), by Sarah Ferguson, the Duchess of York

B-PJ1   *Diana Princess of Wales: A Biography* (1982), by Penny Junor

B-PJ2   *Charles: Victim or Villain* (1998), by Penny Junor

B-RK   Although not actually a book, *Diana: The Untold Story,* by Richard Kay and Geoffrey Levy, ran as a twelve-part series in the *Daily Mail* in 1998 and will be regarded as a book to distinguish it from Richard Kay's daily writing.

B-DK   *Royal Pursuit: The Palace, the Press and the People* (1983), by Douglas Keay

B-JK   *I Hate You—Don't Leave Me: Understanding the Borderline Personality* (1991), by Jerold J. Kreisman, M.D., and Hal Straus

B-AM1   *Diana: Her True Story—In Her Own Words* (1997), by Andrew Morton

B-AM2   *Diana: Her New Life* (paperback edition, 1995), by Andrew Morton

B-AP   *Princess in Love* (paperback edition, 1995), by Anna Pasternak

B-MR   *The Diana I Knew* (1998), by Mary Robertson

B-TS   *Death of a Princess: An Investigation* (1998), by Thomas Sancton and Scott MacLeod

B-SS   *Diana: The Secret Years* (1998), by Simone Simmons

B-PT   *With Love from Diana* (paperback edition, 1995), by Penny Thornton

B-JW   *Charles vs. Diana: Royal Blood Feud* (paperback edition, 1993), by James Whitaker

Television Programs

Pano   *Panorama,* Martin Bashir interview with Diana, Princess of Wales, BBC, 20/11/95 (citations from BBC transcript)

JD-Doc   *Prince Charles: The Private Man, the Public Role,* written and presented by Jonathan Dimbleby, ITV, 29/6/94

ITV-Doc   *Diana: Her Life,* ITV, 28/12/97

R&R-Doc   *Royals and Reptiles,* Channel 4 (19/10/97, 26/10/97, 2/11/97)

Miscellaneous

I-FSK   *Hello!* magazine two-part interview with Frances Shand Kydd, 24/5/97 and 31/5/97

I-CS   *Hello!* magazine interview with Charles Spencer, 10/10/92

INTRODUCTION

3   *The Sun* created a sensation: Sun, 21/5/91

3   "misread her friendliness": DM, 18/3/91

3   "Set on separate": ST, 12/5/91

6   "She would tailor": B-SS, p. 107

7   after her death, friends: MOS, 20/9/98; Interview with Anthony Holden

7   "Sometimes she appeared to": Interview with Robert Spencer

7   "she had decided to radically": DM, 1/9/97

7   "My feeling was at that time": Interview with Richard Kay

CHAPTER 1

8   Diana was driving: *McCall's,* 10/84

8   "bizarre": Tribute by Earl Spencer, 4/9/97, Westminster Abbey

9   "She needed to be royal": NYT, 3/9/97

9   "They look so wondering": ST, 30/12/84

9   "She has a sympathetic": WO, 9/4/88

9   "People adore her": SuTel, 30/12/84

9   "I am much closer to": *Le Monde,* quoted in DT, 27/8/97

9   "I don't go by": Pano, p. 34

9   "thick as a plank": Ibid., p. 12

9   "brain the size of a pea": DM, 24/9/86

9   "She was an entirely": Interview with Paul Johnson

10   "she could appear to be talking": Interview with Nicky Haslam

10   "My friend Paolo": Ibid.

10   "The time spent alone reviewing": Ibid.

10   "If you have a mind that doesn't": Interview with David Puttnam

10   "I always used to think": MOS, 1/6/86

10   "If she would say we will": Interview with Roberto Devorik

10   "levelheadedness and strength": Tribute by Earl Spencer

11   "honesty": Ibid.

11   "She had real difficulty": B-AM1, p. 82

11   "At least once . . . she lied": TNY, 15/9/97

11   "I would ask her whether": ITV-Doc

11   "The nice side of her": Interview with Nicky Haslam

11   "Her dark side was that": SuTel, 7/9/97

12   a color tabloid modeled: Andrew Neil, *Full Disclosure* (1996), pp. 96–98

12   "Slowly she is adjusting": DM, 7/11/83

12   new "maturity": A sampling of articles includes DM, 18/4/83; DS, 30/6/83; DM, 7/11/83; DS, 1/7/85; DS, 24/2/87; Sun, 23/6/87; DM, 10/6/89

13   "We would speak for": B-SS, p. 34

13   "ghosthopped": B-SS, p. 23

13   "You could see how she": Interview with Dr. Michael Adler

13   "There was a tremendous fight": Interview with Elsa Bowker

13   "If you look through the record": Interview with Richard Ingrams

13   "We felt we had a responsibility": Interview with Max Hastings
14   "It is an undisputed fact": DM, 28/12/97
15   "the paradigm unhappy woman": WP, 5/9/97
15   "publicly and bloodily fought out": ES, 19/12/92
15   "watched her parents publicly": DM, 18/11/92
15   "a fierce custody battle": MTV: *Biorhythms,* 31/8/98
15   only attracted discreet notices: DT, 16/4/69; ES, 15/4/69. A survey of
       newspaper archives for the periods from 13/12/68, when divorce pro-
       ceedings were initiated, to 15/4/69, when divorce was granted, turned
       up no other coverage. There was a similar silence during the compara-
       ble period in the divorce of Peter and Janet Shand Kydd, and in July
       1971, when Diana's mother reopened custody proceedings.
15   "It was clear to me he did not": B-JW, p. 178
15   "Prince Charles has finally fallen": DS, 27/1/82
15   "three of us in this marriage": Pano, pp. 14–15
16   "From the beginning, Diana": Christopher Anderson, *The Day Diana Died* (1998), p. 41
16   "She lived in an extreme": Interview with Cosima Somerset
16   "wolf pack": B-DK, p. 243; Ti, 28/12/83
16   "I didn't like": Ti, 6/9/97
16   "She remained intact": Tribute by Earl Spencer
17   "Whenever things got too": SuTel, 7/9/97
17   "I think essentially that she": Interview with Dr. Michael Adler
17   "As she expressed it to friends": B-JD, p. 478
17   "She scoured the newspapers": Ibid., pp. 477–78
17   "Her whole life": ITV-Doc
17   "The haircut was a way": Interview with Roberto Devorik
18   "From now on, I am going": B-AM2, p. 155
18   "Whatever I do": DM, 1/9/97

CHAPTER 2

19   "when Mummy decided to leg it": B-AM1, p. 23
19   "sat quietly at the bottom": Ibid., p. 70
19   "I will always remember [my mother]": Sun, 12/1/98
19   "cowering behind a curtain": SuEx, 7/9/97
19   "I remember her telling me": Interview with Cosima Somerset
19   "Her mother left at the moment": Interview with Elsa Bowker
20   The Spencers were one: The history of the Spencer family was drawn
       from various sources, including Ti, 30/3/92; DT, 1/9/97; DM, 3/4/92;
       SuTel, 5/9/93
20   "most serious, exclusive and illustrious": David Cannadine, *The Decline and Fall of the British Aristocracy* (1992), p. 503
20   "Diana was brought up to believe": Interview with Paul Johnson
20   "tended to be populist": Ibid.
20   "Despite their calm": Cannadine, p. 504

21	"It was instinctive": Interview with Paul Johnson
21	"curator earl": Charles Spencer, *Althorp: The Story of an English House* (1998), p. 3; DT, 30/3/92
21	"intolerant of differences": Interview with Fiona Fraser
21	"Jolly Jack": Spencer, p. 109
21	"Grandfather found it hard": Ibid., pp. 6–7
21	a formidable memory: DM, 27/12/97
21	surprising shrewdness: I-CS
21	"I found him to be adorable": Interview with Fiona Fraser
21	Perhaps his most memorable: DEx, 28/4/81
21	"He was in many ways": Ti, 2/4/92
22	"Frances was dominant": Interview with Robert Spencer
22	"rather fast romantic": I-FSK
22	"sweet, amusing": DM, 15/6/93: Angela Levin, excerpt from *Raine and Johnny* (1993)
22	proposed marriage to Frances during: I-FSK
22	"It was a real love match": Interview with Robert Spencer
22	"for four generations": I-FSK
22	"mongrel": Frances Shand Kydd interview with Cathy Macdonald, *V.I.P.* (Scottish) ITV, 20/10/95
22	"It really upsets me when": DM, 20/5/97
22	The Fermoys came from: Various sources on Roche family, including I-FSK; Fiona Fraser; and B-PJ1, pp. 28–29
23	"the most compassionate, sensitive": DM 20/5/97
23	"I don't think I've ever": I-FSK
23	A streak of instability: *Royalty Monthly,* 8/88; NOTW, 19/6/88; DEx, 6/12/97
24	In 1984, at age forty-five: DM, 21/8/84
24	"She has a very quick": Interview with Fiona Fraser
24	"good with people": Ibid.
24	"Frances has an inner strength": Ibid.
24	her mother took Johnnie's: Ibid.
24	"mirages of happiness": I-FSK
24	"immensely happy for a long time": Ibid.
24	"honeymoon baby": Ibid.
24	"enormous sadness": Ibid.
24	"She was very attractive": Interview with Fiona Fraser
25	Frances's substantial inheritance: B-PJ1, p. 36
25	"I was blissfully happy": I-FSK
25	"I never saw him, never held him": MOS 9/3/97
25	"Thwarted in his wish": DM, 15/6/93
25	"for intimate tests": B-AM1, p. 71
25	"It was a dreadful time": Ibid.
25	"instinctive understanding": DM, 15/6/93
25	"One had to keep a stiff": MOS, 9/3/97

25   "The death of John was a deep": Interview with Fiona Fraser
26   "She had been married six years": Interview with Robert Spencer
26   "a perfect physical specimen": B-PJ, p. 37
26   "the girl who was supposed": B-RK, p. 42
26   "nuisance to have around . . . try again": B-AM1, p. 24
26   "Diana was a different soul": DM, 9/3/97
26   "I don't know what to say": Interview with Robert Spencer
26   "was feeling pressure": Ibid.
26   "violent and unhappy": B-PJ2, p. 59
27   "motherless years": B-JW, p. 241
27   "violent scenes which went": Ibid.
27   "a wife beater": Ibid., p. 240
27   "believed to have extended": DM, 27/11/97
27   "Over the last three": I-FSK
27   "We hadn't fallen apart": DEx, 30/11/81
27   "It was never discussed": Interview with Fiona Fraser
27   "showed no evidence": Interview with Robert Spencer
27   "She was a wonderful mother": Interview with Fiona Fraser
27   she would find that Frances: B-JW, p. 137
27   "He was a reasonably intelligent": DM, 15/6/93
28   "There is a thing called": I-CS
28   "I don't touch [Raine]": DEx, 30/11/81
29   "It wasn't love at first": I-FSK
29   Shand Kydd's family: B-PJ1, pp. 44, 48
29   "bohemian": B-PJ, p. 44
29   "bon viveur": B-AM1, p. 77
29   "That's when we realized": I-FSK
29   "Peter wasn't responsible": Ibid.
29   "She fell in love with Peter": Interview with Robert Spencer
29   "It was a terrible shock": DEx, 30/11/81
29   The day after her departure: DEx, 14/8/82
30   "trial separation": I-FSK
30   "It was something I put a lot": Ibid.
30   "playing quietly on the floor": B-AM1, p. 78
30   "Of course there were tears": I-FSK
30   "He refused to let": MOS, 9/3/97
30   "I was devastated": I-FSK
30   "always felt especially bleak": B-SS, p. 52
30   "only through lawyers": I-FSK
30   just two newspapers: Ti, 11/4/68; DT, 11/4/68
30   "adultery by Mr. Peter Shand Kydd": DT, 11/4/68
30   The following June: DEx, 14/8/82
30   That December, Frances filed: Ti, 13/12/68
31   "fearful the details": B-JW, pp. 240–41

31   "In those days, [an accusation of] mental cruelty": Interview with Fiona
      Fraser

31   He summoned a string: DM, 15/6/93; B-PJ1, p. 46

31   It was not until 1982: DM, 16/8/82

31   "Only now is the full story": Ibid.

32   "My grandmother tried to lacerate": B-AM2, p. 65

32   According to the *Evening Standard:* ES, 15/4/69

32   "Adultery was alleged": Ibid.

32   "was granted custody": DT, 16/4/69

32   "The fact that the father was": DEx, 14/8/82

32   Two years later, in July 1971: *Majesty,* 4/95

32   which "unbalanced" Frances: Interview with Robert Spencer

32   "He was really miserable": B-AM1, p. 81

33   "body language was appalling": DM, 15/6/93

33   Diana recalled that not only: B-AM1, p. 24

33   "asking where [my mother] was": I-CS

CHAPTER 3

34   "The emotional drama": Luise Eichenbaum and Susie Orbach, *What Do
      Women Want?* (1984), p. 38

34   "It is hard to imagine": DS, 1/7/81

35   "never been able to become": *The Borderline Child: Approaches to Etiol-
      ogy, Diagnosis, and Treatment* (1983), edited by Kenneth S. Robson,
      M.D., p. 5

35   According to psychiatrist E. James Anthony: Ibid.

35   "I always felt": B-AM1, p. 24

35   "I always had this thing": Ibid., p. 25

35   "I felt I was in the wrong shell": Ibid., p. 68

35   "Between their divorce": I-CS

35   "It was a very unhappy": B-AM1, p. 24

36   Diana recalled that she: Ibid., p. 23

36   "Diana and I had a nanny": I-CS

36   "like a little bee": *Fox Files,* Catherine Crier interview with Charles
      Spencer, 16/7/98

36   "I've got what my mother's got": B-AM1, p. 61

36   "Diana could not be called": B-JW, p. 137

36   "She was very modest": Interview with Fiona Fraser

36   "on the go all day long": B-PJ1, p. 50

37   "long list of questions": Ibid., p. 7

37   "became introverted": DM, 30/9/93

37   "In school I was taught to": DM, 20/5/97

37   "ever so talkative": MOS, 25/5/86: Mary Clarke, excerpt from *Little Girl
      Lost: The Troubled Childhood of Princess Diana by the Woman Who
      Raised Her* (1986)

37   "whether a psychologist would say": B-AM1, p. 82

37   She was so afraid of the dark: B-AM1, p. 24

37   "wasn't particularly happy": I-CS

38   "her early life had indeed been": B-PT, p. 23

38   "trailing after her father": *Birmingham Evening News,* 1/9/97

38   She kept twenty stuffed animals: B-AM1, p. 24

38   a "green hippo": Ibid., p. 25

38   "lay in a line": B-AP, p. 93

38   "a self-contained unit": I-CS

38   an affinity for nicknames: B-AM1, p. 83; Sun, 1/7/98: "Duch" stood for Duchess, which, according to Charles Spencer, came from the Walt Disney film *The Aristocats;* "The Admiral" referred to the admiral's hat Charles wore as a child; and "Ginge" was for Sarah's red hair.

38   "an introspective and shy": Ti, 20/6/98

38   While Diana claimed not to be jealous: B-AM1, p. 30

39   Diana's relationship with her sisters: Ibid., pp. 23, 30

39   "Like me, he will always": Ibid., p. 30

39   Many of their friends thought: I-FSK

39   "I didn't like being a girl with": DM, 18/2/78

39   Diana prided herself on: B-AM1, p. 23

39   "Jane and Diana had this thing": Interview with Felicity Clark

39   "confident about her gracefulness": *Fox Files* interview with Charles Spencer, 16/7/98

39   "She loved to show off": ITV-Doc

39   it has often been said: B-PJ1, p. 104; B-AM1, p. 79

40   "Cheer up and grin and bear": *Birmingham Evening News,* 1/9/97

40   "was a wonderful father": ITV-Doc

40   go into a "panic": B-AM1, p. 26

40   "every step she took": DEx, 28/4/81

40   "My father always said": B-AM1, p. 25

40   "one of [Johnnie's] greatest achievements": I-CS

40   "He was of a generation": ITV-Doc

40   a "very kind, understanding man": MOS, 25/5/86

41   "There were long periods": B-PJ1, p. 60

41   "She did fret about Johnnie": Ibid., p. 56

41   "particularly fond of her father": Interview with Robert Spencer

41   "to be left in the custody": B-JW, p. 241

41   "distant and remote": B-PT, p. 23

41   "Poor Daddy, I feel so sad": MOS, 1/6/86

41   "there were no tears": B-PJ1, p. 56

42   "I can remember Mummy" . . . "devastating": B-AM1, p. 25

42   "make unfavorable remarks": MOS, 1/6/86

42   "After he made them welcome": SuEx, 10/11/96

42   "It was agonizing": Interview with Fiona Fraser

42   "Peter and I had no wish": I-FSK

42   "She never felt good enough": Sun, 12/1/98
42   "Diana said her mother": Interview with Roberto Devorik
42   "totally traumatized": B-AM1, p. 25
43   her "father's favorite": Ibid., p. 30
43   "The problem was": Interview with Robert Spencer

CHAPTER 4

44   "beginning to gain confidence": DT, 29/8/98
44   "bright and chatty": B-PJ1, p. 58
44   "quiet and shy": B-AM1, p. 81
45   "horribly different": Ibid., p. 25
45   The school staff waited: B-PJ1, p. 54
45   "a stable family atmosphere": Ibid., p. 60
45   "I used to make threats": B-AM1, p. 26
45   "those downcast eyes": MOS, 25/5/86
45   "adored": B-AM1, p. 26
45   "She was overtaken by the busyness": B-PJ1, p. 68
45   "a teacher's dream": Ibid., p. 64
45   "I was very naughty": B-AM1, p. 26
46   "Diana has been outstandingly": DM, 2/7/98
46   "I wasn't university material": WO, 8/4/78
47   "wary of adults, often prickly": Ruth Rudge, West Heath Magazine, no.
        85, p. 26
47   "She was wary of people": Interview with Ruth Rudge
47   "ghastly . . . calm and sorted out": B-AM1, p. 27
47   "she must try to be less emotional": DT, 29/8/98
47   "She was a very strong character": Interview with Ruth Rudge
47   "I didn't think you had it": B-AM1, p. 27
47   "I would have been involved": Interview with Ruth Rudge
47   "buoyant and noisy": B-AM1, p. 87
47   "I was always looking for": Ibid., p. 28
48   "The compassion and caring": Ruth Rudge, West Heath Magazine, p. 26
48   "for anyone who has done things": Interview with Ruth Rudge
48   "She had a very caring heart": Interview with Violet Allen
48   "Mostly it was a traumatic time": Ibid.
48   "Most of the girls from": Ibid.
48   "was always very controlled": B-PJ1, p. 65
49   "A terrible terrible wrench": B-AM1, p. 28
49   "a difficult phase": Ti, 17/10/98
49   "a chilling time warp": Spencer, p. 2
49   "never grew to be fond": B-PJ1, p. 82
49   a controversial image: Ibid.
49   one of her cousins: SuMi, 18/5/80
49   "When I met Johnnie": DEx, 30/11/81
49   By the time Johnnie brought Raine: B-AM1, pp. 91–92; B-PJ1, p. 82

49   "In the beginning I was very": Interview with Robert Spencer

50   "used to . . . pour us": B-AM1, p. 28

50   Diana enlisted a friend: B-AM1, p. 92

50   Diana's mistrust of Raine hardened: ST, 17/10/98

50   "resented": DEx, 30/11/81

50   "intense love affair": WO, 8/4/78; B-AM1, pp. 90, 96

50   "domestic upheavals concerning my family. . . . bring it up again": WO, 8/4/78

51   "I sought a lot of medical help": I-FSK

51   "like something out of. . . . I wouldn't admit it": WO, 8/4/78

51   Sarah later acknowledged: Ibid.

51   "Bulimia" comes from the Greek: *Handbook of Treatment for Eating Disorders,* second edition (1997), edited by David M. Garner, Ph.D., and Paul E. Garfinkel, M.D., p. 13

51   Although bulimia nervosa was not: Ibid., p. 11

51   "inappropriate compensatory behaviors": Ibid., p. 25

52   "It started because Sarah": Mi, 8/5/97

52   "I don't think I have": I-FSK

52   "She was often seen lurking": Ruth Rudge, *West Heath Magazine,* p. 26

52   "midnight feasts": ITV-Doc

52   "loved food": B-PJ1, p. 72

52   "I ate and ate": B-AM1, p. 27

52   She recalled sneaking: Ibid., p. 27

53   As the movers were packing up: B-PJ1, p. 81

53   From a very early age: Ibid., p. 50

53   "was always washing or tidying": Interview with Robert Spencer

53   "I would go in sometimes": Interview with Violet Allen

53   "Diana had strong": Interview with Kent Ravenscroft

53   "just came out of the pen": B-AM1, p. 88

53   "always released tremendous": Ibid., p. 28

53   "I didn't allow best friends": Interview with Ruth Rudge

54   On one hand, she recalled liking: B-AM1, p. 28

54   but she was easily distracted: Ibid., p. 26

54   wrote a lot: Interview with Ruth Rudge

54   "Any child from a broken home": Ibid.

54   "At the age of fourteen": B-AM1, p. 24

54   she "froze": Ibid., p. 88

54   "exams made her panic": B-PJ1, p. 71

54   "I never remember walking": Interview with Ruth Rudge

55   "something special": B-PT, p. 31

55   "winding road": B-AM1, p. 68

55   "going somewhere different": Ibid., p. 24

55   to marry a prominent man: Ibid.

55   "it was well known": B-RK, p. 44

55   "according to Diana": B-PT, p. 32

55	"never had her marked down": WO, 9/4/88
56	"something like one hundred twenty letters": B-AM1, p. 30
56	Violet Allen couldn't help: Interview with Violet Allen
56	"If Diana was in a safe and secure environment": Interview with Ruth Rudge

CHAPTER 5

57	couldn't wait to go to London: B-AM1, p. 30
57	"By the late seventies": Interview with Robert Spencer
58	But Diana felt overwhelmed: B-PJ1, p. 99
58	"all the tendons": B-AM1, p. 102
58	injuring her leg "slightly": B-PJ1, p. 100
58	"She did not hang about": Interview with Robert Spencer
58	"velvet hairbands": B-AM1, p. 31
58	"When it came to children, [Diana] had": ITV-Doc
59	"Diana was pure state-of-the-art": Newsweek, 26/10/85
59	"the new school of born-again": VF, 10/85
59	"loner by inclination and habit": B-AM1, p. 99
59	"I kept myself to myself": Ibid., p. 31
59	"You always felt that": Ibid., p. 105
59	"Diana didn't enjoy parties": B-PJ1, p. 106
60	"sexually attractive": B-AM1, p. 105
60	"Lady Diana's life in London": DT, 1/9/97; interviews with William Deedes, George Plumptre
60	Diana explained that she: B-AM1, p. 28
60	"I had never had a boyfriend": Ibid., pp. 33–34
60	"tuck into a good-sized": B-PJ1, p. 99
60	"got terribly fat": B-AM1, p. 31
60	Her friend Rory Scott vividly remembered: Ibid., p. 127
61	"Do you have anorexia? . . . just common sense": WO, 8/4/78
61	"Bulimia ranges from fad": Interview with Kent Ravenscroft
61	"touching side to this friendship": DEx, 18/7/77
61	"He makes me laugh": Sun, 8/11/77
62	"I never thought there was": B-SB, p. 182
62	"His closest friends began to": B-JD, p. 315
62	"When she was twelve": Time, 8/9/97
62	"After the investiture": Interview with Ruth Rudge
62	"His first impression": B-JD, p. 337
63	"The first impact was 'God, what a sad man.' . . . He was charm itself ": B-AM1, p. 31
63	"were seen walking around the corridors": DEx, 17/1/78
63	several weekends later: DM, 2/2/78
63	"show [her] grandchildren one day": Interview with James Whitaker
63	"a romantic who falls in love": Sun, 18/2/78
63	"I'm not in love with Prince Charles": DM, 18/2/78

64	"This is the first time": DM, 18/2/78
64	"What a girl!": NOTW, 19/2/78
64	one of his six pseudonyms: B-DK, p. 88
64	"panicky perspiring figure": DEx, ("William Hickey" column, written by Peter McKay), 5/4/78
64	"thousands of boyfriends": WO, 8/4/78
64	"You've just done something": Interview with James Whitaker
64	"by foul means": DM, 4/4/78
64	"My sister Sarah spoke to the press": B-MR, p. 40
64	"I know who you are": Interview with James Whitaker

CHAPTER 6

65	"He was a complete bachelor": Interview with Michael Colborne
65	"I've fallen in love with": B-DK, p. 213
65	By pushing himself to the limit: B-JD, p. 184
65	As a young boy: Biographical material on Prince Charles was drawn primarily from *The Prince of Wales,* the authorized biography by Jonathan Dimbleby, which is the most reliable source.
66	"deep if inarticulate love": B-JD, p. 59
66	"she was not indifferent": Ibid.
66	"the most intimate of the Prince's": Ibid., p. 19
67	"I simply dread going to bed": Ibid., p. 76 (PC letter 9/2/63 to unnamed recipient)
67	"I'm not a gregarious person": Ibid., p. 44
67	"sensitive musician": Ibid., p. 88
67	"surrogate elder brother": Ibid., p. 102
67	"to find himself": Ibid., p. 107
68	"sow his wild oats": Ibid., p. 220
68	"just the girl": Ibid.
68	"with a searching look": PE, "Grovel" column, 3/7/81
68	"dashed [emphatically] accurate": Interview with Nigel Dempster
69	"With all the intensity of first love": B-JD, p. 221
69	"live inside [her] trousers": SuMi, 17/1/93
69	Parker Bowles was a ladies' man: B-PJ2, pp. 47–49
69	By mid-1972 Charles and Camilla had struck: B-JD, p. 232 (PC letter 27/4/73 to unnamed recipient)
69	In Camilla's company, Charles became: Ibid., p. 222
69	"the last time I shall see her": Ibid. (PC letter 12/72 to Mountbatten)
69	"such a blissful, peaceful": Ibid., p. 232 (PC letter 27/4/73 to unnamed recipient)
70	"I must say, Amanda really": Ibid., p. 230 (PC letter 25/4/73 to Mountbatten)
70	"Perhaps being away": Ibid., pp. 248–49 (PC letter 3/74 to Mountbatten)
70	"Our editor said . . . 'We want": R&R-Doc, Part I, p. 21

70	"You've got to remember": BBC/ITV interview with Brian Connell, 26/6/69
70–71	"His bride needed to have": *Harper's & Queen*, 4/90
71	"choose a suitable": B-JD, p. 248 (Mountbatten letter 2/74 to PC)
71	"A woman not only marries a man": *The Observer*, 9/6/74
71	"My marriage has to be forever": ES, 7/1/75
71	"a secure family unit": WO, 2/75
71	"You must get married at once": Colin Clark, *Younger Brother, Younger Son: A Memoir* (1997), p. 154
71	"beginning on the downward slope": B-JD, p. 316 (Mountbatten letter undated, 1978, to PC)
71	"I must say I am becoming": Ibid., pp. 317–18 (PC letter 15/4/79 to un-named recipient)
72	Clearly he admired and respected her: Ibid., p. 249
72	She grasped all too well: Ibid., p. 322
72	Charles had recently renewed: B-JD, p. 335; B-RK, p. 91; B-PJ2, pp. 48–49
72	"warmth, her lack of ambition": B-JD, p. 335
72	when Andrew left that year: DM, 14/1/93; PE, 4/1/80
72	"began to suppose that they": B-JD, p. 335
73	Yet the Queen, in her customary: DT, 20/10/98
73	"The surgeons didn't want to operate": WO, 9/4/88
73	"I was the first person": Ibid.
73	They felt that Raine kept them: B-AM1, p. 29
73	Detecting signals that Diana hadn't "twigged . . . amazing place": Ibid., p. 32
73	"that weekend was the beginning": B-PJ1, p. 97
73	"They were shooting pheasants": Interview with James Whitaker
74	"Charles probably didn't see": B-PJ1, p. 97
74	"Charles found himself strangely": Ibid., pp. 113–14
74	"quite a lot": Ibid.
74	"He would ring up Cadogan": Ibid., p. 97
74	"no one ever took much notice": Ibid., p. 103
74	"She could have been amongst": Interview with Michael Colborne
74	"disorganized about arrangements": B-SB, p. 111
74	After her customary visit: B-PJ1, pp. 101, 116
75	"I have lost someone infinitely special": B-JD, p. 324
75	The daughter of a millionaire: B-PJ1, p. 117
75	"caviar queen": *Sunday Times Magazine*, 22/12/85
75	"Whiplash Wallace": Mi, 22/8/80
75	"There is a risqué picture": DM, 10/6/80
75	"enormously attracted": B-SB, p. 171
75	In February 1980, she traveled: B-PJ1, p. 117
75	"Can you see me swanning": B-AM1, p. 105
75	"perfect English skin": B-MR, p. 15

76   "casual encounters": B-JD, p. 337

76   "began to think seriously": Ibid., p. 338

76   "You're a young blood": B-AM1, p. 32

76   tabloid veteran James Whitaker: Interview with James Whitaker

76   "He was all over me": B-AM1, p. 32

76   "how she had sensed his loneliness": B-JD, p. 337

76   "It was to Lady Susan": B-SB, p. 184

76–77   "he had met the girl he intended to marry": B-JD, p. 337

77   "as soft, cheerful and bouncy": B-PJ1, p. 119

77   "the impression to the Prince's family": B-JD, p. 338

77   "The summer of 1980 was all": Interview with Robert Spencer

77   She was disconcerted by his older friends: B-AM1, p. 32

77   "Lady Diana's presence struck me": B-SB, pp. 189–90

78   "I was terrified—shitting bricks": B-AM1, p. 32

78   "all right once I got in": Ibid., p. 33

78   "She was a sort of wonderful": B-JD, p. 339

78   "always buying him little presents": B-SB, p. 194

78   "instinctive understanding": Ibid., p. 232

78   "confided to one of his friends": B-JD, p. 339

78   "the virgin, the sacrificial": B-AM1, p. 38

78   "the sacrificial virgin bride": ST, 23/9/90

78   "not a position": *The Madness of George III*, Alan Bennett (1991)

78   "a man as good and honest": TNY, 15/9/97

79   "He often used to say": DM, 20/10/98

79   "resented it terribly": Interview with Elsa Bowker

79   "I don't even dare": B-MR, p. 40

79   Just weeks before: DEx, 7/2/80; DM, 2/4/80

80   "I had so many dreams": B-AM2, p. 155

80   she felt secure for the first time: B-PJ1, p. 134

80   "never dominated": B-SB, p. 177

80   "with great cunning": B-PJ2, p. 58

80   "oiling up, basically": B-AM1, p. 40

80   "When you fall in love": Interview with Michael Colborne

81   "[she] realized [she] had taken on": B-AM1, p. 42

81   "based on her romantic image": B-MR, p. 42

81   "Oh! This is the life": B-JD, p. 338

CHAPTER 7

83   "a perfect English rose": Sun, 8/9/80

83   " 'What a cunning lady' ": DS, 29/6/81

83   "They exaggerated it": Interview with James Whitaker

83   "there was certainly no obvious": B-SB, p. 191

84   "Because we had a foreign": Interview with Andrew Neil

84   The most important beneficiary: S. J. Taylor, *Shock! Horror! The Tabloids in Action* (1992), pp. 217, 343

84   "Kelvin is a natural": Interview with Andrew Neil
84   "Kelvin would adopt at a": R&R-Doc, Part II, p. 7
85   "I understand all your problems": SuMi, 21/9/80
85   "had a way . . . of taking scalps": Taylor, p. 152
85   "fitted perfectly": B-JW, p. 150
85   "James and Harry . . . were like": Interview with Andrew Morton
85   "People talk about me as if": *You,* 22/8/93
85   After graduating: Ibid.; Interview with James Whitaker
85   "master of trivia": B-DK, p. 88
86   "absolutely scarlet": Interview with James Whitaker
86   "His face was beet-red": Interview with Peter McKay
86   "Whitaker both proclaimed": Ibid.
86   "I know binoculars are": Interview with James Whitaker
86   "several intimate chats": B-JW, pp. 155, 160
86   "resemblance to a London": B-DK, p. 61
86   Andrew Morton grew up: Interview with Andrew Morton
86   "Her blue eyes gaze straight": DS, 30/6/83
86   "to think they were friends": ES, 9/10/93
87   "If they do a feature": *Independent on Sunday,* 17/9/95
87   "the Pompadoured Poltroon. . . . The Tonsured Traducer": ES, 3/12/91
87   "old established": *The Independent,* 2/3/96
87   "[They] knew no one": Interview with Nigel Dempster
87   "new choice of girlfriend": DM, 18/9/80
87   "back in each other's": DS, 5/11/80
87   "romantic underwear expert": Mi, 19/1/81
87   "If I go to a restaurant": DM, 24/11/80
87   "very depressed": B-SB, p. 197
88   "safe house": Ibid., p. 178
88   "encouraged the romance": Ibid., p. 185
88   "It's almost as if the Parker Bowleses": DS, 12/11/80
88   "from the moment of [Charles's] engagement": B-JD, pp. 346–47
88   had stopped when Charles started: B-PJ2, p. 71
88   "The pressures on the prince": B-JD, p. 339
88   "She was most certainly in love": B-SB, p. 197
88   Barry sensed her disappointment: Ibid., p. 192
88   Somewhat primly, she was: B-AM1, p. 39
88   "quietly captivating": Mi, 19/11/80
89   "rely on instinct": DS, 13/11/80
89   "reputation as a demon driver": DS, 11/11/80
89   "an 80-mph car caper": *Time,* 28/2/83
89   "erratic driving record": DS, 13/11/80
89   "the friendship which Charles and Diana": Sun, 10/11/80
89   "has been groomed": Ibid.
89   "choice of bride": ST, 23/9/90
89   the two women chipped: B-JD, p. 340

89   "Both grandmothers know": ES, 13/11/80

90   "If I'd said to [Charles]": B-JD, p. 340

90   "sense of humor" and "lifestyle" were "different": B-AM1, p. 36

90   "never sent flowers": B-JW, p. 153

90   the delivery of two dozen: DM, 24/11/80

90   "I often felt sorry for her": DS, 30/6/81

90   Yet Charles's valet: B-SB, p. 192

90   "dawn dash": Ibid., p. 199

90   "a bit of a nuisance": DS, 12/11/80

90   Judy Wade of *The Sun:* Sun, 5/1/81

90   "or the whole country would": Interview with James Whitaker

90   "The time has come when Prince Charles": DS, 10/10/80

90   "remarkably cool and mature": Mi, 19/11/80

90   "put on the most": B-AM1, p. 61

90   "unbearable . . . I cried like a baby": B-AM1, p. 35

90   "I'm not so much bored": DM, 24/11/80

90   "everything she [could] lay her hands": B-SB, p. 110

90–91   "It seems that . . . Lady Diana": Mi, 19/1/81

91   In December 1980: DM, 3/12/80

91   She remembered that he seemed only: B-AM1, p. 35

91   "more concerned": B-SB, p. 191

91   "sensationalism": B-DK, p. 50

91   "I should like to take this": B-PJ1, p. 131

91   Diana claimed that she considered: B-AM1, p. 35

91   "had suggested . . . that she seek": B-MR, pp. 40–41

91   "She would automatically sort of": *Fox Files* interview with Charles Spencer, 16/7/98

92   "really pretty": Interview with Felicity Clark

92   "strung up in general": Ibid.

92   "100-mile dash": SuMi, 16/11/80

92   she emphatically insisted: B-PJ1, p. 126

92   "I was feeling frail and hungover": B-JW, p. 28

92   "had some supper": ES, 28/11/80

93   "The trouble is, people do believe": DM, 24/11/80

93   "With the exception of the": SuMi, 23/11/80

93   "a blond woman was hurried": B-JW, p. 32

93   "that a call had been made": Ibid.

93   "rang me from the train": DEx, 26/7/91

93   "There was no foundation": Interview with Michael Colborne

93   "I myself was on the train": B-SB, p. 194

93   "there was somebody else around": B-AM1, p. 33

93   "inexcusable" lies: B-PJ1, p. 130

94   "Things have been getting very": DS, 12/1/81

94   "I'd like to marry soon": ES, 28/11/80

94   "Lady Diana Spencer last night asked": DEx, 29/11/80

94 After checking Tavener's: B-DK, p. 83

94 "never lied to me": B-JW, p. 158

94 "The whole thing was": Interview with James Whitaker

94 even offering advice: *Time,* 28/2/83

94 "Diana was very aware that": Interview with James Whitaker

94 "I can assure you": DS, 10/11/80

94 "horrified": B-JW, p. 154

94 "a background of leaping in": DM, 24/11/80

95 "I will simply die": B-MR, p. 47

95 "If I were to ask": B-PJ1, p. 133

95 "I rang up and spoke": Interview with Elsa Bowker

95 "He'd been saying for some time": B-SB, p. 197

95 "He counseled his son": B-JD, p. 341

95 "sensed the absence of intensity": Ibid.

95 "such a terrible mismatch": B-JD, p. 342

96 "confused and anxious state": Ibid. (PC letter 28/1/81 to unnamed recipient)

96 "support helped to steel": Ibid.

96 "There was never anything tactile": B-AM1, pp. 33–34

96 "a voice said to me inside": Ibid., p. 34

96 "From day one, I always knew": Ibid., p. 62

96 "As for becoming Queen": Pano, p. 2

96 "After everything I've been through": Sun, 21/5/91

96 "whatever love means": B-AM1, p. 34

97 "complete disaster": Ibid.

97 "spoke constantly but guardedly": B-SB, p. 199

97 "We're not taking any": B-PJ1, p. 136

97 "Can you find the": ITV-Doc

97 "shocked. . . . She told me it": Sun, 11/1/98

98 "He was very good at hiding": B-SB, p. 174

98 "Wherever he went": Interview with Anthony Holden

98 "I am very lucky that someone": B-JD, p. 343 (PC letter 5/3/81 to unnamed recipient)

98 "unrequited love": B-PT, pp. 54–55

98 "What really hurt": Sun, 12/1/98

99 "nobody with insincere motives": B-AM1, p. 117

99 "I couldn't handle [them]": B-AM1, p. 34

CHAPTER 8

100 "It's a relief": DM, 25/2/81

100 That night Diana dined: B-PJ2, p. 67

100 "nobody . . . there to welcome": B-AM1, p. 35

100 Diana had a suite: B-SB, p. 205

100 "What shall I do? Lady Diana never": Ibid., p. 206

101 she bristled when: B-DK, p. 225

101   "quite ruined the music room": B-SB, p. 206

101   "The Prince of Wales has made": DEx, 27/7/81

101   She said they treated her coldly, and she complained: B-AM1, p. 37

101   In her first official appearance: Ibid.

101   "Diana told me . . . she'd received": B-MR, p. 141

102   "Few people voice criticism": B-SB, p. 116

102   "less training in her new job": B-AM1, p. 120

102   "to instruct her in the ways": B-JD, p. 357

102   "I don't think any of them": Interview with Michael Colborne

103   "two hundred percent behind": Ibid.

103   Although Diana later said she admired: B-AM1, p. 47

103   They instructed Diana on: Interview with Michael Colborne

103   "I was not the usual type": Ibid.

103   "I was Uncle Michael": Ibid.

103   "Diana was terrified": Humphrey Carpenter, *Robert Runcie: The Reluctant Archbishop* (1996), p. 225

103   "I hope to see her every": Mi, 20/1/99 (letter from the Queen 5/3/81 to unnamed recipient)

104   "like screwing a lightbulb": B-SF, p. 83

104   The Queen Mother offered: DS, 27/1/82; Mi, 22/7/84; B-DK, p. 226

104   The Queen and Prince: B-DK, p. 181; *Harper's & Queen*, 4/90

104   "You don't get training": *McCall's*, 10/84

104   "I was terrified, really": B-AM1, p. 37

104   "For Diana, royal life": Interview with Roberto Devorik

104   "It was as though": SuPe, 30/6/91

105   "I missed my girls": B-AM1, p. 37

105   He taught her to: DS, 27/1/82; B-DK, p. 227

105   "the care with which he nurtured": B-JD, p. 493

105   "The Prince of Wales was": Interview with Michael Colborne

105   he grew impatient with those: B-SB, p. 105

105   "I always feel that unless": B-JD, p. 492 (PC letter 31/3/87 to unnamed recipient)

105   he could be short-tempered: Ibid., p. 493

106   "When you don't read": Interview with Michael Colborne

106   Years later she told: Interview with Roberto Devorik

106   She sometimes threw temper: B-JD, pp. 343, 345

106   "She went to live at Buckingham": B-AM1, p. 119

106   "I didn't know about jealousy": Ibid., p. 38

106   When he had to leave: Interview with Michael Colborne

106   "much regretted": B-JD, p. 343 (PC letter 29/3/81 to unnamed recipient)

106   Charles tried to reassure: B-PJ1, p. 149

106   "I was told one thing": B-AM1, p. 37

107   "I can't understand why": B-SB, p. 184

107   She told Colborne and Cornish: B-JD, p. 346

107   She later claimed: B-AM1, p. 116

107   "nothing to do with him going": Ibid., p. 39

107   Their time together was cordial: B-PJ2, p. 78

107   "very tricky indeed": B-AM1, p. 38

107   "one of his most intimate": B-JD, p. 346

108   "worked it all out": B-AM1, p. 33

108   "she didn't know about Charles": Interview with Elsa Bowker

108   When asked about Diana's: Interview with Michael Colborne

108   Instead, Diana alienated: DT, 20/10/98

108   "flowers when she had meningitis": B-AM1, p. 37

108   "a bit muddled": Interview with Michael Colborne

108   "her other side": B-JD, p. 345

108   "Whenever the Prince came": B-SB, p. 208

108   Charles saw that he was trapped: DT, 20/10/98; B-JD, p. 343

108   "I was used to temper": Interview with Michael Colborne

108   "He was obsessed": B-AM1, p. 38

108   "a very observant man": Carpenter, p. 223

109   "He's very deep, Charles": Ibid., p. 225

109   No one, not even Charles: B-JD, p. 345

109   "It was all very strange": B-AM1, p. 56

109   "comments like that can set": Interview with Kent Ravenscroft

110   According to former *Vogue* editor Felicity: Interview with Felicity Clark

110   "It is what happens": Ibid.

110   "but then she was rather overwhelmed": Ibid.

110   DI'S DARING DEBUT: DEx, 10/3/81

110   DI TAKES THE PLUNGE: Mi, 10/3/81

110   "ounce or two of puppy fat": DEx, 10/3/81

110   "Oh, God, I look awful": B-PJ1, p. 141

110   "my escape mechanism": Pano, p. 10

110   "[she] was so thrilled because": B-AM1, p. 56

110   "a secret disease": Pano, p. 9

110   "when you have bulimia": Pano, p. 10

111   Diana's weight dropped: Interview with Felicity Clark; NOTW, 23/1/83

111   "I had shrunk to nothing": B-AM1, p. 56

111   Both anorexia and bulimia: *Handbook of Treatment for Eating Disorders*, pp. 9–11, 14, 19

111   "psychologically different": Ibid., p. 23

111   "I am ashamed": Mi, 18/1/99 (Diana letter 12/81 to unnamed recipient)

111   "It's a good antidepressant": Interview with Kent Ravenscroft

111   "she loved eating sweets": B-SB, p. 195

111   "Lady Diana never ate properly": Ibid., p. 207

111   Most tellingly, Diana ate copious: B-AM1, p. 127; *Handbook of Treatment for Eating Disorders*, p. 28; B-JD, p. 398

111   "recognized all the symptoms": I-FSK

112   By some accounts there was: Ti, 4/9/97; *Majesty*, 4/95

112   "She never breaks down": Ti, 25/2/81

112   "If she had been in a united": Interview with Michael Colborne
112   "Gosh, I'm becoming a very rich lady": B-SB, p. 211
112   "At the beginning": Interview with Roberto Devorik
112   "Diana seemed to enjoy": Interview with Felicity Clark
113   LADY DI-ET!: Sun, 13/6/81
113   James Whitaker noted: DS, 20/6/81
113   "He can never sit still": DS, 4/7/81
113   "I tend to lead a sort of": Harper's & Queen, 4/90
113   "requested rock numbers": Mi, 22/6/81
113   Charles had asked Michael: Interview with Michael Colborne
113   he insisted that Diana had found: Ibid.
114   "I was devastated": B-AM1, p. 38
114   "rage, rage, rage": Ibid.
114   Diana confronted Charles: B-JD, p. 347
114   "he cut me absolutely dead": B-AM1, p. 38
114   "It was easy to see": B-SB, p. 212
114   "just a bit too much": Observer, 26/7/81
114   "radiant best": DS, 27/7/81
114   "kept her composure": DM, 27/7/81
114   "The radiance for television": Mi, 27/7/81
114   and later recalled telling her sisters: B-AM1, p. 39
114   "The tension had suddenly hit": Ibid., pp. 40–41
115   "eyes were swollen": NOTW, 19/6/88
115   At a grand ball: Interview with Felicity Clark
115   "in the hours leading up to": B-JW, pp. 19–21
115   "Buckingham Palace was totally": B-SB, p. 169
115   "didn't happen, that is for": Interview with Michael Colborne
115   who later denied to Nigel: Interview with Nigel Dempster
115   What's more, Diana and Charles: B-PJ2, p. 84
115   The following night: B-SB, p. 213; B-AM1, p. 125
115   Charles stayed up late: B-PJ2, p. 85
115   "in a contemplative mood": B-JD, p. 348
115   "It really was remarkable": Alastair Burnet, In Person: The Prince and Princess of Wales (1985), p. 26
116   "spent the night before": B-PT, p. 25
116   She had a severe bulimic attack, eating "everything": B-AM1, p. 41
116   "I don't think I was. . . . girl in the world": Ibid., pp. 40–41
116   "pale gray, veiled": Ibid., p. 42
116   "The day I walked": B-AM2, p. 83
116   "very composed": B-AM1, p. 125
116   "incredibly calm and unfazed": I-FSK
116   Diana paused on the platform: B-PJ1, pp. 177, 181

CHAPTER 9

117   "I adore being married": B-RK, p. 4

117   "she was almost in tears": Mi, 3/8/81

117   "spent most of their evenings": B-SB, pp. 217–21

118   When she and Charles were alone together: B-JD, p. 355

118   "appalling . . . rife": B-AM1, p. 42

118   he had brought a stack: Ibid.

118   as with his sporting pursuits: B-JD, pp. 354–55

118   "worst moment" . . . every day at lunch: B-AM1, p. 42

118   he would read aloud from Laurens: Ibid., p. 43

118   "the idealized bride": B-JD, p. 478

118   "When you began on abstract": Carpenter, p. 222

119   "She didn't understand him": Interview with Michael Colborne

119   Diana had tried joining: B-PJ1, p. 186

119   "Diana dashes about": B-JD, p. 354 (PC letter 3/8/81 to unnamed recipient)

119   "Anything I could find": B-AM1, p. 43

119   When Diana asked if Camilla: Ibid., p. 39

119   "This was going to be": Interview with Michael Colborne

119   "obsessed by Camilla totally": B-AM1, p. 43

120   "convinced that [he] was still": B-JD, p. 356

120   Since February she had lost: NOTW, 23/1/83

120   "Everybody saw I was getting": B-AM1, p. 43

120   She slept poorly and wept: B-JD, p. 360

120   At one point in the fall: Interview with Michael Colborne

120   they arose from Diana's: ITV-Doc

120   "He was totally unaware": Interview with Michael Colborne

120   When she wept, he would knead: B-WB, p. 53

120   capitulating to her demands: B-JD, p. 361

120   Occasionally Charles rebuked: Ibid., p. 399

120   Charles's fondness for Diana: Ibid., p. 400

121   He invited Laurens: B-AM1, p. 43

121   Charles arranged for Diana's: B-PJ1, p. 186

121   "The princess was happier": B-SB, p. 225

121   "The royals are spoiled": Interview with Mark Lloyd

121   "From the day I joined": DT, 27/8/97

122   "It's a strange family": Carpenter, p. 225

122   She later told friends: Sun, 12/1/98

122   "silly" inside jokes: B-AM1, p. 51

122   "generosity. . . . it was all laughter": Mi, 18/1/99 (Diana letter 27/12/81 to unnamed recipient)

122   Diana felt the Queen viewed her: B-AM1, p. 52

122   "Fine, no problem": Ibid., p. 43

122   Nor could Diana abide: B-PJ1, p. 186

122   "The Queen is always surrounded": NOTW, 4/5/86

123   "Her willfulness was a direct": Interview with Michael Colborne

123   "Suddenly people were hanging": SuTel, 7/9/97

123   "stared at [her] the whole time": B-AM1, p. 43

123   She later explained: ST, 23/9/90

123   "undercurrents": B-AM1, p. 64

123   "the toughness of Whig": Interview with Paul Johnson

123   "Because her family looks": Interview with Andrew Roberts

124   "[The family] had witnessed symptoms": B-JD, p. 588

124   "ostriching": DM, 21/10/98

124   "Maybe I was the first": Pano, p. 7

124   "She told me, 'I am unwanted' ": Interview with Elsa Bowker

124   "about to cut my wrists": B-AM1, p. 44

124   "all the analysts and psychiatrists": Ibid.

124   "The Diana that was still": Ibid.

124   "She was brought down": Interview with Michael Colborne

124   "godsend": B-AM1, p. 43

125   because he thought it would: DT, 21/10/98

125   "We want Diana": DT, 31/10/81

125   "Poor Charles": WO, 12/11/81

125   "sick as a parrot": B-AM1, p. 44

125   Between engagements she wept: B-JD, p. 356

125   "never got any praise": B-AM1, p. 44

125   "The response of the people": DEx, 6/11/81

125   the mere thought gave her tremors: B-AM1, p. 47

125   "I was shit-scared": Ibid., p. 48

126   "like a young colt": Roy Strong, The Roy Strong Diaries: 1967–1987 (1997), pp. 291–92

126   In the first two weeks: DS, 16/11/81

126   "People tried to put me. . . . all over the shop": B-AM1, pp. 44–45

127   "showed a confident new face": DEx, 20/8/81

127   Diana had suddenly: SuEx, 7/9/97

127   "Highly recommend it": ITV-Doc

127   "The Sun has often paid": R&R-Doc, Part II, p. 22

127   "Diana has been laughing": DS, 10/9/81

127   "goes for lonely walks": NOTW, 13/9/81

127   "has reached a personal crisis": Sun, 18/9/81

127   "all that [was] expected": Ibid.

127   Still, the Queen was evidently: B-DK, p. 55; Harold Evans, Good Times, Bad Times (1983), pp. 314–15

128   "I spend most of my time": Mi, 18/1/91 (Diana letter 27/12/81 to unnamed recipient)

128   "We've had such a lovely": B-JD, p. 360 (PC letter 26/12/81 to unnamed recipient)

128   "Diana felt desperate": DS, 27/1/82

128   yet at other moments she appeared: B-JD, p. 358

128   "I·was a fat, chubby": Pano, p. 3

128   "they wanted a fairy princess": B-AM1, p. 57

129   "She spent long hours": B-JD, p. 357
129   But once she was settled: Ibid., p. 358
129   One night she left home: Ibid., p. 365
129   "blazing public row": Sun, 2/2/82
129   "clearly worried": Sun, DM, 8/2/82
129   "get [her] husband's attention": B-AM1, p. 56
129   "just dismissal, total dismissal": Ibid., p. 45
130   Diana's account, which Morton reported: Ibid., p. 132
130   "She said that this is why": Interview with Elsa Bowker
130   a "smudge": Time, 28/2/83
130   "her sensational figure": DS, 18/2/82
130   "Carefree Di threw royal": Sun, 18/2/82
130   "unprecedented . . . breach of privacy": Gua, 4/3/82
130   "I've never done anything": Time, 28/2/83
130   "blissfully happy": B-JW, p. 173
130   "Charles led Diana": DS, 18/2/82
131   Even in the presence of the Romseys: B-JD, p. 366
131   "fired a series of questions": Sun, 19/3/82
131   "Why Di Keeps Throwing": Sun, 2/4/82
131   Labor was induced: B-AM1, p. 45
131   "an astonishing experience": B-JD, p. 368 (PC letter 2/7/82 to Patricia
       Brabourne)
131   "Charles could get off": B-AM1, p. 46
131   "It was a great relief": Pano, p. 6

CHAPTER 10

132   Diana breast-fed for only: B-AM1, pp. 53, 138
132   "You'd wake up in the morning": Pano, p. 6
132   "Boy, was I troubled": B-AM1, p. 46
132   "something dreadful had happened": Ibid.
132   "totally darkness": Ibid., p. 51
132   "dark ages": Ibid., p. 61
132   "Her shape . . . was, to put": Mi, 27/7/82
132   "Diana fidgeted [and] whispered": DEx, 27/7/82
133   "a wistfulness about her": Interview with Felicity Clark
133   "excluded totally": B-AM1, p. 46
133   "endearingly human": Mi, 20/9/82
133   "exclusive statement": SuEx, 14/8/82
133   "rash" choice of words . . . "refused": Sun, 16/8/82
133   "very unkind": NOTW, 15/8/82
133   "cheap publicity": DM, 16/8/82
133   "deeply distressed": Sun, 16/8/82
133   at one point she went for three: B-AM1, p. 56
133   "quite amusing": Ibid., p. 57
133   "she kept the bulimia": Interview with Michael Colborne

133	"disconcerting propensity": B-JD, p. 398
134	"continued to grow to the point": Ibid., p. 399
134	"Whatever happens, I will always": B-AM1, p. 37
134	Morton wrote that: Ibid., p. 139
134	"had made virtually no contact": B-JD, p. 480
134	"I talked to her once a week": Interview with Stuart Higgins
135	Charles was reported to have: NOTW, 3/8/86
135	By Diana's later description: B-AM1, pp. 55–56, 133; Pano, pp. 7–8
135	"We are now installed": Mi, 18/1/99 (Diana letter 21/9/82 to unnamed recipient)
135	"no one's listening. . . . wanted to get better": Pano, pp. 7–8
135	"desperate cry for help . . . in my head": B-AM1, p. 55
135	"didn't like . . . with the pressures": Pano, p. 8
135	Diana did later say that she had tried: B-AM1, p. 61
135	According to a 1986 survey: A.R. Faazza and K. Conterio, "The Plight of Chronic Self-Mutilators," *Community Mental Health Journal* (1988), 24, pp. 22–30
136	more often indicates: B-JK, p. 33
136	One 1986 study of self-cutters: Op. Cit., Faazza and Conterio
136	When self-injury occurs: B-JK, pp. 32, 34
136	Diana enacted some of her: Pano, pp. 7–8
136	"indifference pushed her": B-AM1, p. 133
136	"The trouble is one day": B-JD, p. 401 (PC letter 10/10/82 to unnamed recipient)
136	After Charles consulted: Ibid.
136	On October 17, a week after: Ibid., p. 400
136	"complaining and sulking . . . on the hop": Mi, 18/10/82
137	"bored to tears": DS, 19/10/82
137	"No one, but no one": Mi, 15/11/82
137	"out of his way whenever": Ibid.
137	later revealed by Whitaker: B-JW, p. 176
137	"If . . . her shoes are cleaned": Mi, 15/11/82
137	"seriously concerned": Sun, 15/11/82
137	"fit and well": Ti, DT, 16/11/82
138	"inevitable stresses": MOS, 21/11/82
138	"sniper . . . wide": DS, 1/12/82
138	"new lease of enthusiasm": DEx, 9/12/82
138	"fiend. . . . forced him into this marriage": DS, Sun, 11/12/82
138	"I got it straight": Interview with Nigel Dempster
138	"the greatest howler": NOTW, 12/12/82
138	"near to tears much of the time": NOTW, 23/1/83
138	"nonsense": DS, 3/2/83
138	whose pattern of speaking: B-DK, p. 232
139	She was hurt that the press: Interview with Michael Colborne
139	"did take criticism hard": B-AM1, p. 56

139   "None of my family knew about": Ibid., p. 54

139   The public squabble between: Sun, 16/8/82

139   "I am a firm believer in maternal": DM, 24/6/82

139   Johnnie Spencer told: Interview with Robert Spencer

139   "I know the royals can appear": Ti, 14/6/83

139   "a close member of the Princess's": Mi, 16/11/82

139   "She told me then": Interview with James Whitaker

139   "wonderfully solid": B-AM1, p. 64

140   "a woman to love and be cared for": Carpenter, p. 223

140   "had a lot to learn": Strong, p. 317

140   "Ruth was very distressed": Carpenter, p. 223

CHAPTER 11

141   "The great problem is": Mi, 18/1/99 (PC letter 13/4/83 to unnamed recipient)

141   Charles rarely left: DT, 2/4/83; B-JD, p. 401

142   "nobody ever helped": B-AM1, p. 49

142   But in a letter to a friend: B-JD, pp. 402–3 (Diana letter 1/4/83 to unnamed recipient)

142   Charles quickly intervened: Ti, 12/4/83

142   She moved informally: B-DK, p. 233

142   "She has a wonderful way": Mi, 18/1/99 (PC letter 13/4/83 to unnamed recipient)

142   "I'll bet you have fun": SuEx, 14/8/83

142   "The Princess was plainly": The Observer, 17/4/83

142   After applauding his: DT, 2/4/83

142   "You can't tell a woman": SuPe, 27/3/83

143   "preserve my sanity": B-JD, p. 402 (PC letter 4/4/83 to unnamed recipient)

143   Sometimes they frightened: Ibid.

143   "The terrifying part": Ibid.

143   "All you could hear was": Pano, pp. 3–4

143   In a letter to a friend: B-JD, p. 403 (Diana letter 1/4/83 to unnamed recipient)

143   "jealous": Pano, p. 4

143   "took it out on [her]": B-AM1, p. 49

143   "I do feel desperate": B-JD, p. 402 (PC letter 4/4/83 to unnamed recipient)

143   Diana's toughest moments: B-AM1, pp. 29, 143

143   In a letter written: B-JD, p. 403 (Diana letter 1/4/83 to unnamed recipient)

143   "We were extremely happy there": Ibid., p. 401 (PC letter 26/4/83 to the van Cutsems)

143   "his hand resting on hers": B-DK, p. 241

143   During a tree-planting: DS, 30/6/83

144   "Isn't she absolutely beautiful?": DEx, 14/8/83

144   At the end of the tour: B-DK, p. 241

144   "Not a moment to breathe": Mi, 18/1/99 (Diana letter 6/83 to unnamed recipient)

144   "When trying to drag": Ibid.

144   "I haven't missed William as much": Ibid.

144   "very witty": Ti, 27/6/83

144   "When they write something horrible": DEx, 16/6/83

144   "Prince Charles is largely": Mi, 18/4/83

144   "a big girl now": DS, 30/6/83

145   "different person": Pano, p. 3

145   She had been to at least: B-AM1, pp. 140–41

145   She didn't think her therapists: B-AM1, p. 55

145   "her swings of mood continued": B-JD, p. 406

145   "hours comforting and reassuring": NOTW, 23/10/83

145   Diana made her first solo foreign: DEx, 2/2/84; NOTW, 12/2/84

145   She became the patron: Ti, 28/12/83

145   "my husband decided": Pano, p. 12

146   press reports made clear: DEx, 9/12/82; Mi, 7/11/83

146   "The combination of style": WO, 7/1/84

146   "She was terribly keen": Interview with Felicity Clark

146   Early in the marriage: B-JD, pp. 359, 477

146   She could sit for as long: B-WB, p. 24

146   "queen of fashion": SuPe, 4/3/84

146   "visiting the very young": Ti, 28/12/83

146   "I think I've always been": Pano, p. 13

147   lasted less than six: DT, 20/10/98

147   "She couldn't understand": Interview with Michael Colborne

147   "understandable [Diana] would not": B-SB, p. 235

147   quite a few were pushed: B-JW, p. 193; DM, 27/5/83

147   "made her feel nervous": Sun, 29/3/82

147   Diana would draw a staff: B-JD, p. 360

147   he was disheartened: Ibid., p. 406

147   "Certain friends had to go": *McCall's*, 10/84

147   but Diana was equally adamant: B-JD, p. 406; DT, 20/10/98

148   "Pass the port": VF, 10/85

148   or were simply against: B-JD, p. 399

148   By one account, she turned: B-PJ2, p. 102

148   Because of the awkwardness: B-JD, p. 406

148   When Diana was once portrayed: DM, DS, 28/9/85

149   "I haven't felt well": DEx, 24/3/84; SuTel, 30/12/84

149   "It was a good year": Interview with Michael Colborne

149   Even with a nanny: *McCall's,* 10/84

149   "very energetically for about": Ibid.

149   "The Queen could not be": Sun, 12/4/84

150   Charles had his own busy: B-JD, pp. 407–13
150   "within the shell of a normal": Ibid., pp. 405–6
150   Charles was known for: DT, 6/11/98
150   "a lot of tiara functions": Mi, 18/1/99 (Diana letter 6/83 to unnamed recipient)
150   "occasional spelling": B-MR, p. 89
150   "What happened after": B-SB, p. 146
151   "amazing team": interview with David Puttnam
151   "They had strengths": Ibid.
151   "lingering look and quick kiss": DEx, 30/7/84
151   "leads conversations": Sun, 12/4/84
151   "It was clear the royal couple": Andrew Neil, *Full Disclosure* (1997), p. 256
151   "Then she got animated": Interview with Andrew Neil
151   She was jolted: DM, 21/8/84; DEx, 23/8/84
151   "Can't stand being away": Mi, 18/1/99 (Diana letter 24/8/84 to unnamed recipient)
152   Diana later said she and Charles: B-AM1, p. 51
152   but she kept the sex of their child: Ibid.
152   "hoping" for one: DEx, 24/3/84
152   "would be nice": Ti, 28/3/84
152   never stopped seeing: B-JD, p. 399
152   she actually agreed: Pano, p. 14
152   "By then I knew he had gone": B-AM1, p. 51
152   "Oh God, it's a boy": Ibid.

CHAPTER 12

153   "interludes of happiness": B-JD, p. 406
153   "Professional Diana-watchers": SuTel, 30/12/84
153   "in such good form": SuMi, 3/2/85
153   with Harry she continued: B-AM1, p. 53
153   She rose early, took a daily swim: Ibid., p. 57
154   "she sought to possess him": B-JD, p. 367
154   during the previous year's: DS, 21/3/84
154   rough and boring: Sun, 13/8/86
154   antipathy that deepened: Sun, 17/7/84
154   "very important to my physical": *Polo* magazine, Jan/Feb 1998, p. 52
154   After Harry's birth, Diana asked: B-JD, pp. 434, 477
154   Diana later said that Charles: B-AM1, p. 53
154   When Charles came up: B-PJ2, p. 119
154   "peak of royal productivity": DEx, 23/1/85
155   "are in no doubt that it is": DEx, 10/1/85
155   "so wet you could shoot": DS, 10/1/85
155   the resignation was: NYT *Magazine,* 21/2/88; B-JD, p. 434
155   "I'll get it in the neck": DS, 25/1/85

155   "dithering wimp": DS, 24/2/85

155   "the real ruler": NOTW, 3/2/85

155   "a thoroughly henpecked": Sun, 4/2/85

155   "prima donna": Ibid.

155   "great flights of human spirit": DM, 27/4/85

155   "more of a companion": Ibid.

155   Diana, however, was less than enthralled: B-JD, p. 431

155   "Mind your head": DM, 27/4/85

155   he buried his insecurity: B-JD, p. 431

155   "secondhand Rosa": Jayne Fincher, *Diana: Portrait of a Princess* (1998), p. 84

155   "unsophisticated": DS, 23/4/85

156   "heinous hats": VF, 10/85

156   indulged in ever-more daring: DS, 21/3/85; Sun, 27/3/85

156   "the wrong way round": Sun, 4/12/85

156   "Being a princess, even if": Ti, 23/4/85

156   "She said, 'Why don't'": Interview with Roberto Devorik

156   Colborne had been a solid support: B-JD, pp. 296, 435

156   One day, when Charles: Interview with Michael Colborne

156   "stress and disruption": B-JD, pp. 434–35

157   "To both of them, my": Interview with Michael Colborne

157   "catastrophe": Strong, pp. 361–62

157   "iron mouse": VF, 10/85

157   "nonsense": Sun, 28/9/85

157   "snobby *Vanity Fair*": DS, 28/9/95

157   "astonishing": DM, 27/9/85

157   "amazing": Sun, 28/9/85

157   "horrid": DM, 28/9/85

157   "ratbag of gossip": Mi, 2/10/85

158   "royal wimp": NOTW, 29/9/85

158   " 'The Mouse That Roared' had": Interview with Deidre Fernand

158   "Oh, gosh . . . well . . . er": *Newsweek,* 26/10/85

158   Attenborough worked with: Mi, 17/10/85; DM, 24/4/89

158–59   "Well, obviously. You feel . . . No, we don't": DM, 21/10/85; Mi, 21/10/85

159   "friendly tiff": DM, 21/10/85

159   "What a smashing": Mi, 21/10/85

159   "Di and Charles are so": Sun, 21/10/85

159   "unbelievable cleavage": B-JD, p. 471 (PC letter 13/11/85 to unnamed recipient)

160   Their four-minute number: Mi, 23/12/85; DS, 24/12/85

160   "provocative and sensuous": *People,* "The Diana Years" (1997), p. 115

160   "terrific" dancer: *Hello!,* 29/11/97

160   "was in sparkling form": Sun, 4/6/85

160   Charles had also resumed: B-JD, p. 480

160   The rapprochement with Kanga: DM, 24/10/85; SuPe, 2/6/86

161 "blue with jealousy": Interview with Nicky Haslam

161 "Camilla had a fallout": Interview with Stuart Higgins

161 He was an unlikely prospect: B-WB, p. 25

161 "the love of my life": Anthony Holden, *Charles: A Biography* (1998), p. 204

162 Mannakee had been warned: B-WB, p. 25

162 Nevertheless, Diana was disheartened: Holden, pp. 198–99

162 "I don't want to spy": B-JD, p. 482 (PC letter 11/2/87 to unnamed recipient)

162 "There appeared . . . to disintegrate": B-JD, pp. 477–79

162 "started to withdraw": Ibid., p. 479

162 "bat ears": Sun, 7/5/86

162 "plastic smile": Mi, 8/5/86

162–63 "I didn't know anything": B-AM1, p. 45

163 "My husband told me off": Ibid., pp. 55–56

163 "Even together . . . they were apart": B-JD, p. 480

163 they kept different: Descriptions of Charles and Diana's domestic discord are based on confidential interviews, as well as: Sun, 13/8/86; B-WB, pp. 5, 12, 28, 35, 43, 45, 53

163 "desperation": B-JD, p. 480 (PC letter 18/11/86 to unnamed recipient)

163 "I never thought it would": Ibid., p. 481 (PC letter 11/2/87 to unnamed recipient)

163 "the warmth, the understanding": Ibid.

164 "knowledge . . . cared about our marriage": Pano, p. 14

164 other staff understood: B-WB, pp. 12, 57; B-PJ2, p. 103

164 "the change of behavior pattern": Pano, p. 15

164 "a certain woman": B-PT, p. 25

164 "It's agony to know": B-JD, p. 479 (PC letter 11/3/86 to unnamed recipient)

164 "the whole royal 'setup,' ": B-PT, p. 28

164 "berating Charles for seeing": Ibid., pp. 29, 33

165 "pretty devastating": Pano, p. 14

165 "terrified": B-AP, p. 121

165 "spent my whole time . . . letting them see it": B-AM1, pp. 50–51

165 "She was teary and . . . out of sorts": B-SF, p. 98

165 Richard Foster had spent: Hello!, 22/11/97

165 "She was tense down to": ST, 1/11/98

165 "after five years of being . . .tell her": B-AM1, pp. 54–55

166 But she recalled . . . "he just gave me": Ibid., p. 56

166 A footman at Balmoral: B-WB, p. 49

166 "Friends on my husband's side": Pano, p. 15

166 "matchmaker Diana": B-SF, p. 69

166 abetted by Diana and Charles: Mi, 24/12/85; B-WB, p. 38

166 She once said that the royal family: B-AM1, pp. 61, 64

167 "tried to lacerate me": B-AM2, p. 65

167   "[Charles's] grandmother is always": Sun, 24/8/92

167   "Diana sometimes said": Interview with Roberto Devorik

168   "something troubling": B-AM1, p. 53

168   initially got on well: B-WB, pp. 33, 109

168   "pique": DM, 23/1/85; DEx, 22/12/84

168   "Her Royal Rudeness": *Time*, 28/2/83

168   "rattle her cage": B-AM1, p. 54

168   "hopping mad and quite": Mi, 24/3/82

169   "country gentry": Biographical material on Sarah Ferguson is drawn
       primarily from her memoir, *My Story*.

170   "kept rearing her head": B-AM1, p. 58

170   "set me free": B-SF, p. 3

170   "I was robust and jolly": Ibid., pp. 97–98

170   "Why can't you be more": Ibid.

170   "It must have been hell": Ibid., p. 75

170   "Diana felt the Queen": Interview with Roberto Devorik

170   "our common interests": B-SF, p. 97

170   After listening . . . "maybe I ought": B-AM1, p. 58

170   "flavor of the month": B-SF, p. 119

170   "a tower of strength": Mi, 15/5/86

171   "near obsession about how": DEx, 8/5/86

171   "the cold indifference": Mi, 15/5/86

171   "I don't know why there": Sun 10/5/86

171   "It doesn't matter what": DS, 3/7/86

171   "fasts and feasts": Sun, 12/5/86

171   "weeping self-doubts": NOTW, 11/5/86

171   "Nothing like a touch of": NOTW, 10/8/86

171   "Having a wonderful time": SuPe, 10/8/86

171   "Recent worries about": To, 11/8/86

171   "for the things she enjoys": Sun, 13/8/86

172   "Whether that was bad": Interview with Stuart Higgins

172   "Charles spends long hours": NOTW, 3/8/86

172   Charles lightly cuffed: NOTW, 3/8/86; Sun, 13/8/86

172   "Diana seemed to be permanently": DM, 24/9/86

172   "I never got any O levels": Ibid.

172   "I just come and talk": NYT *Magazine*, 21/2/88

CHAPTER 13

173   In November 1986: Descriptions of Diana's affair with James Hewitt are
       drawn primarily from his "as told to" memoir, *Princess in Love*, by Anna
       Pasternak.

173   "as if no other woman": DT, 7/4/98

174   Diana and Charles had successfully toured: DM, 22/11/86

174   "It wasn't a typical seduction": DEx, 3/9/98

174   "Charles was involved with Camilla": DM, 28/11/98

174   "I always want the unobtainable": Sun, 12/1/98

174   for which he compensated: DM, 28/11/98

174   "I couldn't read and assumed": Ibid.

174   "I had red hair, was short": Ibid.

175   During his school days, Hewitt used: Ibid.

175   "He lost his trust in people": B-AP, p. 55

175   as a "decoy," Emma later said: DT, 7/4/98

175   "was holding long whispered": Ibid.

175   "She let her fingers mingle": B-AP, p. 86

175   he had "trusted" the Oxford-educated: DEx, 3/9/98

175   "vaguely, socially": You magazine, 20/9/98

175   it was widely ridiculed: DEx, 3/9/98

175   "Yes, I adored him": Pano, p. 27

175   "factual evidence": Ibid., p. 26

175   "there was a lot of fantasy": Ibid., p. 27

175   "She knew that somewhere": B-AP, p. 75

176   "It was with James Hewitt's unswerving": Ibid., p. xiii

176   "spent hours lying in bed": Ibid., pp. 87–88

176   "I was with her because": DM, 28/11/98

176   "release from the tension": B-AP, p. 34

176   "emotional roller coaster": Ibid., p. 171

176   In the beginning she would sit: Ibid., p. 156

176   "violent paroxysms of despair": Ibid., p. 171

176   "struck her as a form": Ibid., p. 170

176   "he had never seen anyone so distraught": Ibid., p. 138

176   "Often she felt as if she was perching": Ibid., p. 142

176   "lack of control . . . unmitigated greed": Ibid., p. 117

177   he couldn't reveal: Ibid., pp. 124–25

177   "I view depression as a sign": DM, 28/11/98

177   "Some people go to psychiatrists": DEx, 3/9/98

177   Diana expressed her affection: DM, 18/7/91; ES, 13/9/92

177   "head to foot": Sun, 24/8/92

177   At least one maid worried: B-WB, p. 87

177   "she would try anything to win": B-AP, p. 126

178   "an attempt by others": Interview with David Puttnam

178   she began to tell Hewitt she hated: B-AP, p. 127

178   When their guests arrived: B-WB, p. 66

178   "That is the total agony": B-JD, p. 477 (PC letter 24/10/87 to unnamed recipient)

178   stripped of the basic civility: NOTW, 20/9/87

178   "an obsession for her": B-AP, p. 160

178   then retreat to her room: B-WB, p. 69

178   "the biggest story they'd ever": R&R-Doc, Part II, p. 24

178   "a version of the facts": B-JD, p. 574

178   The first significant clue: DEx, DS, DM, 12/2/87

178   "the last time we were close": B-AM1, p. 50
179   Charles had resumed: NOTW, 28/12/86; DT, 28/8/86
179   invariably prompted rebukes: B-JD, p. 483
179   hinted unfairly and incorrectly: Ibid., p. 482; DM, 19/10/87
179   "eclipsed by the Princess, resentful": B-JD, p. 476
179   "I can't see a light": Ibid., p. 483 (PC letter 24/10/87 to unnamed recipient)
179   "unable to turn to his parents": Ibid., p. 476
179   "When marriages break down": Ibid., p. 480
179   tried to get Charles to build: B-WB, pp. 46–47
179   "The very fact that she felt": B-AP, p. 142
180   "slashed . . . adjusted to hide the damage": B-PJ2, p. 137
180   "She was like the sun coming up": TNY, 15/9/97
181   "undignified": DM, 18/2/87
181   "black lover": ST, 23/9/90
181   she smirked while reviewing: B-PT, p. 44; B-SF, p. 124
181   "sexy" Diana . . . "grumpy" Charles: DS, 23/2/87
181   Diana's bulimia had again: B-AP, pp. 144–45
181   Waterhouse and Dunne: SuPe, 28/6/87; DM, 2/11/88; MOS, 17/2/91
181   "mystery fat man": NOTW, 28/6/87
181   "stormed off": Ibid., 21/6/87
181   "in a huff": DM, 21/6/87
181   The tabloids castigated: Sun, 23/6/87
182   "We are *not* having": Ibid.
182   "frequent visitor to Kensington": B-JD, p. 481
182   Waterhouse also visited: B-WB, p. 82
182   "repeatedly tried to reassure": B-AP, p. 260
182   which especially galled: B-JD, pp. 476, 482
182   accused Diana: B-WB, p. 60
182   "positive hurricane": B-JD, p. 483 (PC letter 24/10/87 to unnamed recipient)
182   They spent several weekends: B-WB, pp. 78, 80; SuMi, 14/2/88
182   A group of advisers: NYT *Magazine,* 21/2/88
182   "Disco Di," the femme fatale: DM, 25/9/87
182   "so many cock-ups . . . stop fighting": B-AM1, p. 64
182   "rediscover the real": Ibid., p. 157
182   "comparatively civilized 'space' ": B-PT, p. 52
182   "They were back in sparkling": SuMi, 14/2/88
183   "glanced affectionately at his wife": DM, 27/1/88
183   "she now hated with a vitriolic": B-AP, p. 166
183   they appeared to their staff more calm: B-WB, p. 84
183   "worse than her usual melancholy": B-AP, p. 185
183   Charles acted heroically: Ti, 12/3/88
183   "He just pushed me aside": B-PT, p. 61
183   She insisted that they take: B-AM1, p. 60

183   "so inadequate in every": Ibid.

183   "We cried for Prince Charles": DEx, 15/3/88

184   "the beginning of a slow process": B-AM1, p. 161

184   Back in England with Hewitt: B-AP, p. 186

184   She lashed out: Ibid., p. 191

184   "most beautiful woman . . . found her attractive": Ibid., p. 193

184   She said that her skin: B-AM1, p. 61

184   But by 1988, people had begun: Interview with William Haseltine

184   "painfully thin, almost gaunt": To, 25/3/88

184   "suddenly woke up": B-AM1, p. 61

185   "sweetheart . . . four or five": Ibid.

185   "born again": Ibid.

185   "finished": Ibid., p. 60

185   suffered from the symptoms in 1990: Ibid., p. 61

185   who only overcame: WO, 8/4/78

CHAPTER 14

186   "She'd never ask if she": Sun, 15/1/98

186   "tended to seek out people": B-PT, p. 207

186   "from one person to another": B-JK, p. 78

187   "immediately began to pour": Sun, 15/1/98

187   "easily defeated . . . strong character": B-AM1, p. 208

187   "What is going to happen": Sun, 15/1/98

187   "believe [astrology] totally": B-AM1, p. 66

187   "She was not ruled": Ibid., p. 200

187   "her belief [was] at times": Ibid., p. 237

187   "go through a transformation": Sun, 24/8/92

187   "willful and capable of . . . inner strength": Rita Rogers, *From One World to Another* (1998), p. 246

187   Diana believed she communicated . . . "nut": B-AM1, pp. 65–66

187   "deep emotional problems": B-RK, p. 148

187   "I think the most important thing": ITV-Doc

188   For four years, energy healer: B-RK, p. 148

188   "truckloads of negative": B-SS, p. 19

188   "rarely met anyone": Ibid., p. 18

188   routinely fielded eight-hour phone calls: Ibid., p. 34

188   "always seemed completely compos": Ibid., p. 19

188   Diana claimed to experience: B-AM1, p. 66

188   "I know this sounds a bit": Sun, 24/8/92

188   she had been a nun: B-AM1, p. 243

188   she told Penny Thornton: B-PT, p. 79

188   She spoke of voices: B-AM1, pp. 34, 62

188   "strange feeling . . . drop down": Ibid., p. 29

188   "visualize . . . burning it": B-AM2, p. 14

188   "take all the aggro": Ibid.

188 "so that they would be in different": B-SS, p. 132

188 "a peculiar mixture": Interview with Kent Ravenscroft

188 "helps me to keep calm": B-RK, p. 148

189 "she had reached a very low point": SuEx, 5/7/92

189 "an eating disorder which in Chinese": DM, 24/2/98

189 research studies have shown: WP, 13/10/98

189 "just to tell me what she had": Rogers, p. 241

189 "Most of all . . . she needed": Sun, 15/1/98

189 "support and love": Pano, p. 8

189 "they weren't aware": Ibid.

189 "created a new royal role": DEx, 14/11/89

190 "I want to feel I am needed": SuTel, 7/9/97

190 "the toughest battle of": SuEx, 25/8/91

190 "Diana was a good friend": Interview with William Haseltine

190 "She was very, very nervous": Interview with Michael Adler

191 "We hope if people see": DEx, 10/1/87

191 "Princess Diana should shake": Mi, 29/1/87

191 "It was highly programmed": Interview with Michael Adler

191 "I found myself being more": Pano, p. 4

191 "The caring princess has thrown": To, 24/5/88

191 "a cooler and more independent": ST, 25/9/88

191 "fully fledged emergence": DM, 25/1/89

192 "the line between recreational": DM, 19/5/89

192 250 engagements: DM, 10/6/89; Sun, 9/6/89

192 "I say, 'Did you see' ": B-AM1, p. 66

192 "I would have an ongoing": Interview with Michael Adler

192 "fulfilled her public": Interview with William Haseltine

192 "I used to write her the most": ITV-Doc

193 In 1988, Diana began visiting: To, 30/11/88; DEx, 15/12/88; DM, 21/4/89

193 "She was totally involved": To, 24/5/89

193 She even kept a copy: Sun, 16/4/91

193 "Some people find it very": DT, 17/6/89

193 "was completely intuitive": SuTel, 7/9/97

193 "She did have a powerful": Interview with Michael Adler

194 "This morning I arrived": *Requiem: Diana, Princess of Wales, 1961–1997: Memories and Tributes* (1997), edited by Brian MacArthur, p. 107

194 "She often felt powerless": Sun, 15/1/98

194 "she knew exactly what": Interview with Cosima Somerset

194 "more open and more vulnerable": Pano, p. 4

194 "was declared a loser": B-SF, p. 138

194 "opened a vacancy": Ibid., p. 137

194 "appalling . . . crass, rude": Ibid., p. 138

194 DUCHESS OF PORK!: Ibid., p. 143

194 when her father was caught: To, 23/5/88

194 "as cozy and personal": B-SF, p. 110

194   Besides his £35,000 salary: B-SF, pp. 158–59

194   Diana and Charles, on the: B-JD, pp. 614–15

195   Fergie was amassing: B-SF, p. 159

195   "gray men": Ibid., p. 149

195   "hopelessly erratic": Ibid., p. 154

195   In a conversation with her friend: Sun, 24/8/92

CHAPTER 15

196   Since they irritated: B-WB, pp. 86, 92–94, 107–9, 120

196   "I was very bad about": I-FSK

196   "The media descended": MOS, 9/3/97

197   "You have seduced": Sun, 9/11/88

197   "sexy dance": DM, 11/11/88

197   "We got the balance": TV Times, 11/11/89

197   "triumphant tour": SuPe, 13/11/88

197   "disaster . . . all evening": SuPe, 17/3/91 (The article's byline was
        "Frances Cornwell," one of James Whitaker's pseudonyms.)

197   "valiant front": B-AP, p. 195

197   "were sticking together": TNY, 15/9/97

197   "painful emotions and thoughts": SuEx, 5/7/92

197   "presence of Camilla": Sun, 12/1/98

198   "a voice inside me said": B-AM1, p. 62

198   "the most famous welfare": Ti, 3/2/89

198   DI-VINE: Gua, 13/2/89

198   "hold her head high . . . having done her bit": B-AP, p. 206

198   "needled me the whole": B-AM1, p. 62

198   "as if we were all best": Ibid., p. 63

198   Diana said she realized she was "in the way": Ibid.

198   "It was . . . seven years' pent-up . . . "I just said": Ibid.

199   "For a few weeks she would": B-AP, p. 144

199   She took Hewitt: Ibid., pp. 197–203

199   Diana viewed it as abandonment: Ibid., p. 220

199   "She loved with an everlasting": Interview with Paul Johnson; Memoirs
        of Cardinal de Retz, Vol. 1, pp. 150–51

200   "their respective love lives": B-AM1, p. 188

200   "secret late date": SuPe, 29/10/89

200   "It's very hard": To, 31/10/89

200   "darling": Descriptions of the Gilbey conversation are drawn from the
        transcript published on 24/8/92 in The Sun. The reference to "playing
        with yourself" was not included in the Sun transcription but appeared
        in B-JW, p. 89.

202   "adulterous relationship": Pano, p. 22

202   It had none of Diana's: Descriptions of the Camilla conversation are
        drawn from the transcript published on 17/1/93 in the Sunday Mirror.

202   "Saint Diana": DEx, 14/11/89

202 "Faced with the horror": SuMi, 5/11/89

202 "turns a blind eye to": DEx, 11/7/90

202 "heat-wave hairstyle": DS, 25/7/90

202 Andrew Morton's report: ST, 17/6/90

202 "ill-informed": ES, 26/6/90

203 Diana sat by his bedside: DM, 30/6/90, 5/9/90

203 "brushed aside": B-PT, p. 76

203 Camilla was a frequent: B-WB, pp. 125–26

203 "snap out of the gloom": To, 22/10/90

203 "an affectionate accommodation": ST, 23/9/90

203 "blackmail-style notes": NOTW, 30/8/92

203 "I knew about Charles": Interview with Max Hastings

203 Over the Christmas holidays: B-WB, pp. 134–35

204 "We went through the various": Interview with Stuart Higgins

204 "Patsy Chapman, the editor": Interview with Andrew Knight

204 "Diana certainly knew": Interview with Stuart Higgins

204 "someone very close": Interview with Richard Kay

204 Since Iraq's invasion: B-WB, pp. 130, 136

205 Throughout the autumn: B-AP, pp. 224, 253

205 Diana began writing: Ibid., p. 235; DM, 2/4/98

205 "long, flowing letters": B-AP, pp. 235–36

205 "finally trying to understand": Ibid., p. 239

205 "the truth about Charles and Camilla": Ibid., p. 251

205 Diana constantly vacillated: Ibid., p. 263

205 "Something had to be done": Ibid., p. 252

205 "we first put the words": B-SF, p. 187

205 "cause for concern": DM, 17/2/91, 25/2/91

206 when he reached Diana: B-AP, p. 262

206 his estranged girlfriend: SuMi, 17/3/91; ES, 2/7/91

206 "Diana cannot afford": Mi, 18/3/91

206 When Hewitt returned: B-AP, pp. 270–71

206 "rejected . . . used": Ibid., p. 274

206 "She simply stopped": DEx, 3/9/98

206 "glimpse of the old magic": SuEx, 14/7/91

206 "a united front": SuMi, 28/4/91

206 "I walked in": Interview with William Reilly

207 "very tense. The marriage was": DM, 15/1/98

207 "If Charles was off to see": Interview with Andrew Neil

207 "often has to act as": DM, 4/4/91

208 "Charles insists that his": Mi, 13/4/91

208 "depressed fracture": Mi, 4/6/91

208 At that point, Charles decided: B-JD, p. 576

208 "bedside vigil": Mi, 4/6/91

208 "a fractured skull is not": Sun, 5/6/91

208 PHANTOM FATHER: DEx, 5/6/91

208   THE EXHAUSTED FACE OF A LOVING MOTHER: To, 5/6/91
208   Diana later told Morton: B-AM1, p. 179
208   "horror and disbelief": Ibid., p. 176
209   shifting back and forth: These reports included DEx, 8/2/91, 9/2/91;
      DM, 12/3/91; Sun, 16/4/91; DM 17/4/91; Mi, 6/5/91
209   "Since the Prince broke": Sun, 20/5/91
209   "He ignores me everywhere": B-AM1, p. 57
209   "It was an open secret": Interview with Peter McKay
209   "came back very excited": Interview with Sue Douglas
210   "Princess Diana is to spend": DM, 28/6/91
210   "That was straight PR": Interview with Nigel Dempster
210   "It was a well-bred lady's": Ibid.
210   "growing coolness": DM, 2/7/91
210   "The sad truth": Sun, 3/7/91
210   "friendship with Hewitt": ES, 2/7/91
210   "finds Mrs. Parker Bowles": DM, 18/7/91
210   "supper for two": Sun, 9/7/91
210   "Charles and Diana's summer": ST, 7/7/91
210   "I was told that both": DT, 13/1/93

CHAPTER 16

212   "cozy supper": DEx, 25/7/91
212   "She thought she was a wise soul": ITV-Doc
212   "a huge amount of hostility": ITV-Doc
212   "everything was in her": Interview with Roberto Devorik
212   Diana told friends that she believed: DM, 15/1/98
213   "the lid was being": Interview with Andrew Morton
213   "at the end of my tether": Pano, p. 17
213   "horrible sadness . . . the very worst time": Hello!, 22/11/97
213   "She was on the verge": ST, 1/11/98
213   "She was a woman scorned": Interview with Andrew Roberts
213   "Most people who knew her": Interview with Andrew Morton
214   she and Diana formed: Interview with Andrew Knight
214   "Angela was very important": Interview with Andrew Morton
214   "conduit": B-AM1, p. 14
214   "nibbling around": Interview with Andrew Morton
214   "royal sniper": DS, 1/12/82
214   "It is just another indication": NOTW, 4/5/86
215   "I didn't know about the bulimia": Interview with Andrew Morton
215   who was also a friend of Morton's: B-PT, pp. 120–21
215   By one account, Diana: B-RK, p. 146
215   "She didn't see him until late": Interview with Andrew Morton
215   "James was always with her": Ibid.
215   "confusion . . . that line": Ibid.
215   "The classic was the suicides": Ibid.

216   "breathless haste": B-AM1, p. 17

216   "hope for the best": Ibid., p. 16

216   "had doubts about her veracity": Interview with Andrew Morton

216   "secret friendship": Ibid.

216   "much to Diana's annoyance": Ibid.

216   "She procured them because": Ibid.

216   Like Diana, Knight had been: Interview with Andrew Knight

216   "Angela rang me": Ibid.

216   "Angela is a very private": Interview with Andrew Morton

216   "Yes, if [Diana] says": Interview with Andrew Knight

216   "She wants it in *The Sunday Times*": Ibid.

217   As the project advanced: Interview with Andrew Morton

217   "Just remember we always": B-AM1, p. 64

217   "trivial, like mosquitoes": WO, 9/4/88

217   "Someone said to me recently": Sun, 9/6/89

217   "ingratitude": Sun, 10/9/91

217   "Diana doesn't understand": To, 30/3/92; Sun, 10/9/91

217   "I love people for": DM, 20/5/97

217   they might not communicate: DEx, 6/6/88

217   "It was not an easy": Interview with Richard Kay

218   "I don't understand why I have": SuEx, 11/10/92

218   "a close friend . . . she told friends": B-AM1, p. 136

218   "There were 4,000 of her words": Interview with Andrew Morton

218   "made a number of alterations": B-AM1, p. 19

218   "presumably out of deference": Ibid.

218   "the man she longed to marry": Ibid., p. 11

219   When Angela Serota called: Ibid., p. 174

219   "extraordinary . . . grieving family": DM, 24/8/91

219   "Diana's tears flowed": Sun, 30/8/91

219   "What do you suppose": *Independent,* 30/11/91

219   "more positive and balanced": B-AM1, p. 176

220   "second honeymoon . . . lovebirds": DS, 13/8/91

220   "happier and closer": Sun, 13/8/91

220   Meanwhile, the Waleses: B-JD, p. 579

220   "Their lives are spent": B-AM1, p. 182

220   "While the caring princess": DEx, 23/9/91

220   "actually very healthy": B-JD, p. 585

220   "the greatest year of her life": *Good Housekeeping* (British edition), 10/91

220   "wistful solitude": DM, 12/2/92

220   "poignant reminder of the royal wish": Mi, 12/2/92

220   "The marriage was indeed": B-JD, p. 592

221   Diana was well aware: Ibid., p. 591

221   "all eyes will be on them": ES, 12/2/92

221   placing the blame for: Mi, 14/2/92

221   "It was she who seemed": ST, 16/2/92

221   "Here she was again": ST, 17/5/92

221   "tabloid mauling": B-JD, pp. 579–80

221   they arrived and departed: B-AM1, pp. 180–81

221   "leaving Diana to attend": DM, 2/4/92

221   "I asked, 'Are you aware' ": Interview with Roberto Devorik

222   she was visibly shaking: Interview with David Puttnam

222   "It was a hard-boiled crowd": Interview with Andrew Knight

222   "suddenly she started": Interview with David Puttnam

222   "I think it would be better off": Neil, p. 262

222   "effectively . . . too fantastical": Ibid., p. 261

222   "He started going through": Interview with Andrew Neil

222   "gushing prose": Interview with Sue Douglas

222   "We have something serious": Ibid.

222   "I was able to say": Interview with Andrew Knight

223   "I never had any doubt": Interview with Andrew Neil

223   *The Sunday Times* upped: Neil, p. 263

223   "there were large chunks": Interview with Sue Douglas

223   "Treat that book": Interview with Stuart Higgins

223   "It is believed": DEx, 9/5/92

223   "I still see myself": ST, 17/5/92

223   "The Princess hoped by putting": Interview with Robert Hardman

CHAPTER 17

224   "She thinks he is a bad": B-AM1, p. 184

224   "her own privacy": DT, 13/1/93

224   "There was no commercial": Interview with Max Hastings

224   "coming under strong pressure": Sun, 4/6/92

225   Fealty to his sovereign: *The Spectator,* 23/1/99

225   The first *Sunday Times* excerpt: ST, 7/6/92

225   "I HAVE NOT COOPERATED": Mi, 8/6/92

225   "odious exhibition": B-JD, p. 583

226   McGregor checked once more: Gua, 12/1/93 (Lord McGregor letter 11/12/92 to Sir David Calcutt)

226   Prince Charles first read: B-WB, p. 165

226   "Diana and Charles agreed": B-AM2, p. 29

226   "pompous": Interview with Andrew Knight

226   "she was making his life unbearable": B-AM2, p. 30

226   "Are you really telling me": Interview with Andrew Knight

226   "This was Diana's elaborate way": Ibid.

226   "She was under huge pressure": Interview with Andrew Neil

227   Fellowes knew at once: B-JD, p. 584

227   "embarrassed the commission": McGregor letter, 11/12/92

227   "the thought that the Princess": B-JD, p. 587

227   He changed his mind: Ibid., p. 586

227   When Charles learned: Ibid., p. 588
227   "if she tried to manipulate": B-AM2, p. 31
227   That afternoon, Diana burst: Sun, 12/6/92
227   "rallied to the Prince": B-JD, p. 588
227   "shocked and horrified": Pano, p. 18
228   Two days earlier: B-JD, p. 588; ST, 28/6/92
228   "was led to believe": ST, 28/6/92
228   "Left her shaken rigid": B-AM2, p. 34
228   "Diana said, 'When I came' ": Interview with Elsa Bowker
228   by writing Diana a series: ST, 13/12/92
228   Diana reacted defensively: B-AM2, p. 35
229   "stinging . . . irate": B-AM1, p. 217
229   "caring and compassionate": Sun, 8/6/92
229   "was very upset": Interview with Andrew Knight
229   Although their views informed: Interviews with Sue Douglas, Andrew Neil
229   "dignified silence": ST, 28/6/92
229   "campaign of derision": B-AM2, p. 40
229   when transcripts of the Squidgy: MOS, 18/1/93
230   "was done to harm me": Pano, p. 22
230   "had enjoyed a 'physical' ": Sun, 1/9/92
230   while he never took: ES, 3/9/92, 3/12/93
230   "destroyed": B-AM1, p. 221
230   "flowering of [her] true": Ibid., p. 21
230   "growing sense of self-belief": Ibid., p. 27
230   "emotional roller coaster": Ibid.
230   "She dropped most": Interview with Richard Kay
230   "incensed . . . at what she perceived": DM, 6/5/93
230   "unpaid adviser": DT, 7/10/97
230   "James Colthurst was still my": Interview with Andrew Morton
231   "What had been hidden": Pano, p. 18
231   each consulting lawyers: B-AM2, p. 48; B-WB, p. 166
231   "openly talking about": B-JD, p. 589
231   "Mrs. Walsh": DM, 10/12/92
231   being "exiled": B-AM1, p. 222
231   during the Balmoral holiday: B-JD, p. 592
232   WHY CHARLES AND DIANA ARE BACK TOGETHER: B-JW, p. 129
232   "often distraught": B-JD, p. 593
232   "The Glums": B-JW, p. 130
232   "The strain is immense": Ibid., pp. 593–94 (PC letter 8/11/92 to un-named recipient)
232   Diana had been on the phone: Ibid., p. 593
232   "recent wave of misleading": Ibid., pp. 139–40
232   Within days, the tabloids: Mi, 17/1/93; Sun, 17/1/93
232   the tape of this conversation: DS, 14/11/92; MOS, 17/1/93

232	"I'll just live inside": Mi, 17/1/93
232	prompted questions: DM, 14/11/92
232	"snapped": B-JD, p. 595; B-WB, pp. 169–70
232	"Unable to see any future": B-JD, p. 595
233	"not at all": Pano, p. 19
233	to tell them the news: Ibid., p. 20
233	"heard it on the radio": Ibid., p. 19
233	"carefree, glossy": DM, 11/12/92
233	"Diana sounded flat": B-AP, p. 297
233	"The media did not mismatch": DM, 10/12/92
233	"report the truth": ES, 10/12/92
233	"royal magic . . . on his judgment": DM, 10/12/92

CHAPTER 18

234	"She lived her life in so many": VF, 10/97
234	"to discuss the things": Interview with Roberto Devorick
234	"She liked to be the one": Interview with Marguerite Littman
235	"She needed to be liked": Interview with Mark Lloyd
235	"It was totally one-to-one": Interview with Cosima Somerset
236	She retreated: B-RK, p. 108
236	"I said, 'When you do' ": Interview with David Puttnam
236	"They are perfect": Interview with Nicky Haslam
236	"Why are you sending": Ibid.
237	"She was very clever to give": Ibid.
237	"I was not on the same social": B-SS, p. 18
237	giving Diana "prophecies": B-AM1, pp. 130, 163
237	"the mother I would have liked": DM, 14/1/98
238	"the essential ingredient of our relationship": DM, 4/9/97
238	The family was also decidedly: VF, 5/97
238	"At lunch at Annabel's": Interview with Cosima Somerset
239	"She liked my way of living": Interview with Elsa Bowker
239	"To be her friend was difficult": Ibid.
239	Like Elsa, Hayat was: ES, 2/6/95; DM, 9/5/98
239–40	"glass stump": B-JD, p. 546
240	"Peter took the approach": Interview with Nigel Dempster
240	PALACE DENIES SPIRITUAL CRISIS: Ti, 28/4/93
240	"her sulky public behavior": SuTel, 7/9/97
240	"simply cry [until she was] totally drained": Ibid.
240	"compassionate and practical": Ibid.
240	The Louisiana-born: NYT, 4/4/99
241	"I would have loved to": Interview with Marguerite Littman
241	"I deliberately didn't get": Ibid.
241	since she had trained as: DM, 6/5/93
242	"like a brother to her": Interview with Roberto Devorik
242	"By 1989, [Andrew and I] were sharing": B-SF, p. 163

242   The first was Steve Wyatt: Ibid., pp. 191–92, 198–200

242   "financial adviser": *Esquire,* 6/95

242   While hiding in some nearby: Ibid.; B-SF, pp. 6–10; B-JW, pp. 112–13

242–43 "potent confederacy": B-SF, p. 187

243   "its level best to isolate": Ibid., p. 224

243   "She's the only person I know": B-RK, p. 157

243   "Palladian jewel": Spencer, p. 55

243   after the royal security: DEx, 18/5/93

243   "brief but bitter silence": Spencer, p. 55

244   "I hate you so much": B-AM1, p. 29

244   Diana and Raine had met: DM, 12/5/93

244   As word of their friendship: Mi, 13/7/98

244   "she felt remorse": Interview with Elsa Bowker

CHAPTER 19

245   "I never found her strong": DM, 1/9/97

245   "I was a problem. . . . busy stopping me": Pano, pp. 20–21

246   "Parents sometimes desert": Ti, 12/9/91

246   As expected, the press saw: DT, 4/12/93

246   THE REAL PAIN OF A BROKEN MARRIAGE: To, 18/11/92

246   DIANA: THE PAIN OF BEING UNLOVED: DM, 18/11/92

246   "children are not . . . every household": Ibid.

246   "lecture on good parenting": Ibid.

246   "astonishing": To, 18/11/92

246   "extraordinary": DM, 18/11/92

246   She had sixty sessions: DM, 26/5/93

246   "that didn't actually say": ITV-Doc

247   "I have it on very good": DM, 28/4/93

247   "the 'authority' was herself": Ibid.

247   "astonishing": DM, 26/5/93

247   "showed she had beaten": To, 28/4/93

247   "dieting, bingeing, and self-hatred": Susie Orbach, *Fat Is a Feminist Issue* (1988), p. 13

247   "the body as the personification. . . . wrested away from her": Susie Orbach speech "Protest and Defiance: Surrender and Complicity: Eating Problems in the 90's" (1993)

247   "someone who had learned": DEx, 28/4/93

247   "*not* about lack of self-control": Orbach, *Fat Is a Feminist Issue,* p. 28

248   By 1993, she had been taking: B-SS, p. 93; DM, 24/2/98; B-AM2, p. 108

248   "haze of loneliness": DM, 2/6/93

248   a poll in *Today:* Gua, 23/12/93

248   "Bad Witch . . . Good Witch": B-SF, pp. 187, 196

248   Foreign Secretary Douglas Hurd: B-JD, p. 653

249   Diana's celebrity even eclipsed: Ti, 5/12/96

249   THE TRIUMPH OF DIANA: Ibid.
249   "Nepal," he was told: DT, 23/3/93
249   "addicted to the limelight": B-AM2, p. 80
249   "relentless": DM, 13/7/93
249   a *Mirror* poll: Gua, 23/12/93
249   and *Tatler* magazine: *Tatler,* 11/93
249   "dirty tricks": DM, 3/3/93
249   "downgrade . . . marginalize": DM, 8/4/93
249   "Palace plots against": DM, 30/7/93
249   "I acknowledge that she had to": Interview with Andrew Morton
249   "many-headed hydra": DT, 1/9/97
250   Kay was thirty-six: Interview with Richard Kay
250   "our first serious and lengthy": DM, 1/9/97
250   "I realized how inadequately": Interview with Richard Kay
250   "I saw her at her happiest": DM, 1/9/97
250   "I wanted information": Interview with Richard Kay
250   "When I was at the *Mail*": Interview with Richard Addis
250   "unofficial press officer": B-AM2, p. 137
250   "I couldn't disclose": Interview with Richard Kay
251   "I want to get away from it all": Interview with Mark Lloyd
251   "It was totally secure": Ibid.
251   "Once Diana made up": Ibid.
251   "suffering from stress and exhaustion": SuPe, 25/7/93
251   "You make my life hell!": Sun, 3/8/93; DEx, 3/8/93
251   "looking angry and strained": Mi, 11/10/93
251   PAIN OF A PRINCESS: IS THE STRAIN GETTING TO DI?: Ibid.
251   DI'S AT BREAKING POINT AS CHARLES WINS THE PR WAR: Sun, 12/10/93
251   "This is the face of a woman": Mi, 11/10/93
252   "increasingly emotional": Sun, 12/10/93
252   A meeting on: Ti, 31/10/93; DM, 26/10/93
252   "Diana told me that Prince Charles": Interview with Andrew Neil
252   "The idea I am searching": *Financial Times,* 22/11/93
252   "prolonged eating binge": Sun, 4/11/93
252   "rare public display": ES, 4/11/93
253   "pathetically damaged . . . broken": B-SS, p. 27
253   "shocked . . . self-mutilation": Ibid., p. 19
253   "were counteracting . . . tension and panic": Ibid., pp. 27–28
253   "it proved impossible": B-JD, p. 653
253   "real purpose": Ibid., p. 654
253   "The pressure was . . . owed it to the public": Pano, p. 24
253   "little light": Interview with David Puttnam
253–54 "I will be reducing. . . . kindness and support": To, 4/12/93
254   "the tears started": ES, 3/12/93
254   "campaign to downgrade": Sun, 4/12/93

254   she left her 118 charities: ES, 3/12/93
254   Indeed, Mike Whitlam: To, 4/12/93
255   "Carping newspaper columnists": Ibid.
255   "bored stiff": Sun, 4/12/93
255   "does not know what": Ti, 4/12/93
255   "We can reveal today": DM, 6/12/93
255   "the great and good": Interview with David Puttnam
255   "I don't think she knew her own": Interview with Michael Adler

CHAPTER 20

256   "There is one man": Mi, 5/12/93
256   Hoare was distantly: ST, 18/12/94
256   her "protégé . . . study and excavate": DM, 8/9/94
256   he embraced Sufism: NOTW, 26/2/95
257   eyes of "deep velvet": DM, 22/8/94
257   "old-fashioned politesse": ST, 28/8/94
257   As a figure in the London: DM, 8/9/94; ST, 18/12/94
257   "Oliver is half child": DM, 8/9/94
257   From 1985 to 1989: NOTW, 28/8/94; ST, 18/12/94
257   Hoare was also close to: ST, 28/8/94
257   sharing an interest: DM, 22/8/94
258   Diana began visiting: To, 21/3/94; 24/9/94
258   "Sometimes she could phone": NOTW, 19/2/95
258   "She wrote the letter": Interview with Elsa Bowker
258   "there was great love": Ibid.
258   The calls began in September: NOTW, 21/8/94
258   "Whoever it is just wants": Ibid.
259   "It was like a war zone": NOTW, 19/2/95
259   "Oliver told Diana he had": Interview with Elsa Bowker
259   "had been made essentially": B-SS, p. 98
259   "asking for trouble": Ibid., p. 100
259   The anonymous phone calls ceased: NOTW, 19/2/95
259   Over the next six days: NOTW, 21/8/94
259   "rented by the Office . . . calling her first name": Mi, 30/4/98
259   "Yes, I'm so sorry": NOTW, 21/8/94
260   This time they were traced: Ibid.
260   "her head rested trustingly": To, 24/9/94
260   "enough to start speculation: Telegraph magazine, 29/10/94
260   "The Princess has been a regular": To, 21/3/94
260   Five months later: NOTW, 21/8/94
260   Both Hoare and Diana had learned: DM, 22/8/94; 23/8/94
260   Kay spoke to Clive Goodman: Interview with Richard Kay
260   "some very loyal, and perhaps misguided": NOTW, 21/8/94
260   On Saturday afternoon: Interview with Richard Kay

260   "poured out her anger": DM, 22/8/94

261   "Do you know you're being": Mark Saunders and Glenn Harvey, *Dicing
       with Di: The Amazing Adventures of Britain's Royal Chasers* (1996),
       pp. 114–15

261   "unprecedented interview": DM, 22/8/94

261   "neurotic nonsense": *The Observer*, 28/8/94

261   "thoroughly modern princess": Ti, 23/8/94

261   "hunting for change": *Telegraph* magazine, 29/10/94

261   "with a picture of your mother-in-law": *The Observer*, 28/8/94

261   "I feel I am being destroyed": DM, 22/8/94

261   These claims later proved: DM, 23/8/94; B-PT, p. 204

261   "in the habit of ringing": DM, 22/8/94

261   "bizarre": ST, 28/8/94

262   "I reckon she has": Ibid.

262   "300 silent nuisance calls": Sun, 8/9/94

262   "whiff of conspiracy": DM, 24/10/94

262   "I was reputed to have made": Pano, pp. 22–23

262   the "young boy": *Sunday Independent*, 26/11/95

262   "made a lot of calls": DEx, 27/11/95

262   During late January: Ibid.

262   "she rang him seventy times": Interview with Elsa Bowker

263   "She said he was a weak": Ibid.

263   "as late as 1995": B-SS, p. 91

263   In February: NOTW, 19/2/95

263   "The truth is, she views": DM, 20/2/95

263   "He put them in a brown": Interview with Elsa Bowker

263   Diana was growing increasingly: B-RK, p. 134

264   The primary focus: DT, 6/11/98

264   The capstone of the film: ST, 3/7/94

264   Dimbleby's filmed conversation: JD-Doc

264   "the clear context was": Sun, 2/7/94; SuTel, 3/7/94

265   two days earlier: DM, 28/6/94

265   By then, Charles had briefed: DT, 15/11/95

265   "to kill off the speculation": SuTel, 3/7/94

265   audience of 13.4 million: Gua, 21/11/95

265   "She bounded out": ITV-Doc

265   "I didn't exactly feel like": Interview with Graydon Carter

265   "You have to help us out": Interview with Christopher Hitchens

265–66 THE THRILLA HE LEFT TO WOO CAMILLA: Sun, 30/6/94

266   "Here was a woman at ease": DM, 30/6/94

266   "She could have watched": DT, 30/6/94

266   One poll showed: ST, 3/7/94

266   CHARLES RULES OK: Ibid.

266   "It is something that I think": JD-Doc

266   "very fair-minded": Sun, 1/7/94

266   "crowing": MOS, 3/7/94

266   "I haven't seen the program": DEx, 4/7/94

266   "pretty devastated": Pano, p. 25

267   "I don't regard myself": NOTW, 2/10/94

267   "dumped him": Ibid.

267   "It was a preemptive strike": MOS, 2/10/94

267   "Diana was happy for it": NOTW, 2/10/94

267   "anodyne": DM, 3/10/94

267   "too beautiful": ES, 3/10/94; *Independent*, 4/10/94

267   By late July: ST, 9/10/94; Mi, 3/10/94

267   *The Mirror* later published: SuTel, 25/4/99

267   At the time of publication: Gua, 5/10/94

267   "proof": ES, 3/10/94

268   "affirming the truth": Gua, 6/10/94

268   "set the record straight": *Independent*, 4/10/94

268   "clogging, nauseating": Ibid.

268   TRAITOR: DEx, 4/10/94

268   LOVE RAT and CAD: Sun, 4/10/94

268   BRITAIN'S BIGGEST BOUNDER: DM, 2/10/94

268   "He is a revolting": Mi, 3/10/94

268   "Eight-Page Special": Sun, 4/10/94

268   "grubby and worthless": Gua, 6/10/94

268   "wretched": DEx, 4/10/94

268   "bitterly hurt": DM, 24/10/94

268   "fevered imagination": DEx, 4/10/94

268   "there was nothing": Pano, p. 27

269   CHARLES: I'VE NEVER LOVED DIANA: ST, 13/11/94

269   "lovable . . . in love with her": B-JD, p. 339

269   Dimbleby also acknowledged: Ibid., pp. 341–42, 345

269   "insist he was to blame": Ibid., p. 367

269   Diana went to see William: ST, 13/11/94

269   "Well, there were three": Pano, p. 26

269   "picture portrayed . . . revenge attack": B-RK, p. 134

269   "She feels the furor": Sun, 18/10/94

269   "had not had any contact": DEx, 20/8/94

269   "mishmash of tedious": *The Observer*, 5/10/97

270   "bitter, jealous, and lonely": Ti, 7/11/94

270   another self-mutilation . . . her use of Prozac: MOS, 6/11/94

270   "Jekyll and Hyde": Sun, 4/3/94

270   "dead common": *Tatler*, 4/94

270   "She has been given": *The Observer*, 28/8/94

270   "She was schizophrenic": Interview with Robert Hardman

271   "I got a call from": Interview with Anthony Holden

271   "She wanted me to touch base": Interview with Andrew Neil
271   "She wanted to win them": Interview with Richard Kay
271   "I've been walking on air": ES, 13/4/95
271   "notorious illiterate": DM, 28/9/95
271   "took Diana's side": Interview with Richard Ingrams
272   "Come to dinner Friday night": Interview with Max Hastings
272   the letter she wrote to Richard Kay's mother: DM, 1/9/97
272   "The Prince felt too": Interview with Max Hastings
272   "She was the kind of person": Interview with Paul Johnson
272   "tacit bargain": TNY, 15/9/97
272   "native cunning": Interview with Andrew Roberts
273   In May 1994: DM, 18/5/94
273   "My husband said it": *Requiem,* p. 115
273   "To my horror": Ibid., p. 117
273   Later that afternoon: Interview with Richard Kay
273   The next day's *Daily Mail:* DM, 19/5/94
273   "played a role": Interview with Richard Kay
273   "like a rape": DM, 4/5/91
273   "two faces . . . live like a typist": Sun, 5/5/94
273   "She didn't understand": Interview with Peter McKay
274   Diana "hated" being described: DM, 1/9/97
274   "It was manipulation": TNY, 15/9/97

CHAPTER 21

275   "It was always push": Interview with Jane Atkinson
275   turning up at only ten royal: To, 3/12/94
275   But in 1995, she appeared: DT, 17/7/96
275   "something positive": SuPe, 20/3/94
276   "a lot of work . . . underground": Pano, p. 24
276   a "hush-hush" visit: MOS, 24/4/94
276   "There were phone calls": Interview with Richard Addis
276   "she has been attending": DM, 15/4/94
276   "hidden life": DM, 24/10/94
276   "without the trumpet blowing": To, 20/8/94
276   "Super Di": To, 20/5/94
276   "A normal day": Pano, p. 28
276   "wobblies": Harvey and Saunders, p. 11
276   "Sometimes a Loon attack": Ibid., p. 6
276   a "relaunch": Mi, 23/9/94
277   "I said, 'I know you'": Interview with Michael Adler
277   "new role as a behind . . . solo visit": Mi, 2/11/94
277   "dressed to thrill": DM, 29/11/94
277   "tearful retreat": To, 3/12/94
277   a "real working appointment": DM, 5/5/94

277   "She is more interested": *Telegraph* magazine, 29/10/94

277   "rocketed overnight": ES, 7/2/95

278   Known to his friends: *Money,* 10/97

278   "Your presence here today": *South China Morning Post,* 23/4/95

278   Scarcely six weeks: SuTel, 11/6/95

278   "in abeyance": DT, 21/12/95

278   "uneasy . . . destroying": DM, 11/1/95

278   "hoping for a third": Ibid.

278   "stronger than ever": ST, 23/11/94

278   "grim mood swings": B-SS, p. 141

279   "spending nearly every free": Ibid., p. 34

279   "She was hurting because": *20/20* interview with Peggy Claude-Pierre, ABC-TV, 18/9/97

279   Diana found Carling easy: B-SS, p. 102

279   when he began calling: Sun, 7/8/95

279   one of the tabloids: NOTW, 16/4/95

280   "She thought she had a fine": Interview with David Puttnam

280   "there was no day when": ST, 1/11/98

280   "to acknowledge that she was": Interview with Nelson Shanks

280   which one columnist compared: DT, 2/10/95

280   "Diana was raw": ST, 1/11/98

280   "all her portraits": *Hello!,* 22/11/97

280   "She was slightly juvenile": Interview with David Puttnam

280   "I said if that happened": TNY, 15/9/97

281   "He would ask me about": Interview with Barbara Walters

281   Jephson had worked: DT, 23/1/96

281   "He tried to filter out": Interview with Michael Adler

281   "She encouraged Diana": DM, 16/11/95

281   Bashir was a little-known: DM, 7/4/96

281   an investigation into suspicions: DM, 7/5/97

281   in one of those meetings: DM, 7/4/96; 7/5/97

282   But Bashir had struck: DEx, 16/11/95; ST, 19/11/95

282   "secret trysts": NOTW, 6/8/95

282   "I have done nothing": Sun, 14/8/95

282   "however much someone is trying": Ibid.

282   "It was flattering": NOTW, 24/9/95

282   On September 24: Ibid.

283   "Recent pressure and tensions": Sun, 30/9/95

283   "Is Will Carling merely": To, 7/8/95

283   "homewrecker": Sun, 30/9/95

283   "Is no marriage and no man": DEx, 30/9/95

283   "She said she found President": MOS, 27/9/98

283   "like a hot brick": To, 30/9/95

283   ironically enough, only days: ST, 19/11/95

284   "knew exactly what she was": *Harper's Bazaar,* 11/97

284   Indeed, the shoot was: Memo from Wendell Maruyama, studio manager for Demarchelier, 15/3/99

284   "I supported her choice": DM, 2/4/98

284   Diana opened the door: DM, 16/11/95

284   "Diana was a very unusual": SuEx, 19/11/95

284   "*Panorama* was very well": Interview with Barbara Walters

284   "There's no better way": DT, 22/11/95

284   "It's a different kind": SuEx, 19/11/95

285   "counter hostile media": DM, 16/11/95

285   audience of 15 million: Gua, 21/11/95

285   "personal help": Pano, p. 17

285   "a queen of people's hearts": Ibid., p. 33

285   "give affection . . . distress": Ibid., p. 30

285   "She won't go quietly": Ibid., p. 23

285   "My wish is that my husband": Ibid.

285   "was born of some basic": SuTel, 7/9/97

285   "I said, 'You said you adored' ": Interview with Elsa Bowker

285   "the advanced stages of paranoia": Gua, 21/11/95

285   "in a personal capacity": DM, 22/11/95

286   "Everywhere was the stench": DM, 21/11/95

286   "must now expect the wrath": Ibid.

286   "manipulative she may be": Ibid.

286   "some part of her performance": DT, 21/11/95

286   The public reacted quite: DT, 27/11/95

286   "no regrets": DM, 22/11/95

286   The next morning, she went: Ibid.

286   "very confusing": Pano, p. 36

286   "desperately unhappy": NOTW, 3/12/95

CHAPTER 22

288   "If she had regretted": Interview with Roberto Devorik

288   "She wanted to meet": Ibid.

288–89   THE ADULTERESS DI ARRIVES ON A MISSION OF CHARITY: Gua, 24/11/94

289   LADIES LOOK AFTER YOUR HUSBANDS: SuTel, 26/11/95

289   "Argentina has gradually": DEx, 25/11/95

289   Buckingham Palace advisers met: DM, 22/11/95

289   "dignified": SuTel, 31/12/95

289   Malcolm Rifkind specifically ruled out: Ti, 6/12/95

289   "I try to be there": NOTW, 3/12/95

289   "She again demonstrated": ES, 4/12/95

289   "young people who have suffered": ES, 7/12/95

290   "Her timing was wrong": Interview with Jane Atkinson

290   "He knew her so well": B-SS, p. 58

290   "It is almost unprecedented": ES, 7/12/95

290   By that time, the Queen had already: DT, 22/12/95

290   According to Simone: B-SS, p. 65

290   "early divorce . . . in the best": DT, 21/12/95

290   Charles took Major's suggestion: DT, 22/12/95

291   "luminous personality": Ti, 13/12/95

291   "sharpness of mind": Sun, 13/12/95

291   "in adoration of its new": DM, 13/12/95

291   PRINCESS AND HER BIG PAIR WOW 'EM IN BIG APPLE: Sun, 13/12/95

291   "So sorry to hear": DM, 24/1/96

291   the daughter of a merchant banker: DM, 20/7/95, 30/8/95

291   "She is the closest thing": Mi, 5/1/95

291   "The word is that Tiggy": DM, 20/7/95

291   In fact, Tiggy was suffering: Hello!, 30/9/95

292   "false allegations": DM, 22/1/96

292   "consider her options": DT, 22/12/95

292   instead she believed: DM, 22/11/95

292   "She couldn't sleep": B-SS, p. 136

292   "aggressive and defensive all at once": Ibid., p. 85

292   "Is she indeed perilously": MOS, 14/1/96

292   "very stable": DM, 30/1/96

292   "Diana's life was in turmoil": DM, 24/2/98

293   "The Panorama interview left": Interview with William Deedes

293   "All bets were off": Interview with Piers Morgan

293   when she later appeared: B-RK, p. 164; DT, 24/4/96

293   "my rock": DM, 23/1/96

293   His departure coincided: DT, 25/1/96

293–94 "She was almost the same . . . a lot of these people": Interview with Jane Atkinson

294   "She was keen to keep": Interview with Piers Morgan

295   "she considered the Sun": Interview with Stuart Higgins

295   "was keen to know what I thought": Interview with Piers Morgan

295   "manipulated through her looks . . . not a whinger": Interview with Richard Addis

295–96 "For me it was a difficult . . . she was inconsistent": Interview with Sue Douglas

296   "Did it turn you on, Mr. Wilson?": DM, 1/9/97

296   " 'Do you think I'm mad?' ": Interview with Taki Theodoracopulos

296   "He wants to live in Italy": Interview with Charles Moore

296   a refrain she repeated: TNY, 15/9/97

296   "She was careful": Interview with Charles Moore

296   "She gave us more information": Ibid.

296   "She couldn't understand when": Interview with Stuart Higgins

296   "I would deal every day": Interview with Piers Morgan

297   "Diana held all the cards": Interview with Peter McKay

297   "If a story concerned what": Interview with Stuart Higgins

297   "sucker" for Diana's "Bambi eyes": Interview with Max Hastings

CHAPTER 23

298   "secret trip": SuEx, 18/2/96

298   "Doctor Dishy": Mi, 22/4/97

298   "a dark-skinned Tom Selleck": DS, 24/5/97

298   "dashing medic": NOTW, 7/12/95

298   "drop-dead gorgeous": SuMi, 30/8/98

298   "enjoyed many of the 'wrong' ": B-SS, p. 111

298   "His name is Hasnat Khan": SuMi, 30/8/98

299   She asked the surgeon: NOTW, 22/11/98

299   "She was very well known": Interview with Jane Atkinson

299   Diana sometimes stayed: DT, 23/4/96

299   "his wit, his intelligence": B-SS, p. 112

299   "relished the . . . sense": Ibid.

299   "the first man who was": Interview with Cosima Somerset

299   She took to studying: B-SS, p. 33; SuMi, 9/11/97

299   She bought a custom-made: Sun, 22/2/96

299   she burned scented joss sticks: SuMi, 9/11/97

299   the "inspiration": NOTW, 17/12/95

299   "new hunk": Sun, 15/12/97

299   By the end of January: DM, 30/1/96

299–300 Diana declined to give: Interview with Jane Atkinson

300   they were disturbed by: DT, 19/2/96

300   That concern deepened: Gua, 20/2/96; Ti, 23/2/96

300   "Her mission to reach": Mi, 23/2/96

300   On February 15, several: SuTel, 7/7/96

300   "The Princess never expressed": Interview with Jane Atkinson

300   Yet in conversations with friends: SuTel, 7/7/96

300   "she wanted to have things": Interview with Jane Atkinson

301   "if [Diana] wanted to write": Ibid.

301   The Palace swiftly issued: DT, 29/2/96

301   "it cultivate[d]": Ibid.

301   "protesting too much": Interview with Jane Atkinson

301   her accusation that the Queen: DM, 29/2/96

301   "The decision to drop the title": DM, 1/3/96

301   "carefully selected insights": Ti, 1/3/96

302   "first step in building": DM, 29/2/96

302   "She felt she would meet people": Interview with Jane Atkinson

302   There was general agreement: Ti, 13/7/96

302   "was put into her head": Interview with Paul Johnson

302   "that engagingly enthusiastic": DM, 30/1/95

302   a "chance to prove herself": DM, 30/1/95

303   "the dreaded C-word": DEx, 6/6/96

303   "I have never seen this many": Interview with Anna Quindlen

303   "It was a very funny": Interview with Jane Atkinson

303   the *Daily Express* singled out: DEx, 8/6/96

303   emphasizing the trip's "team effort": Interview with Jane Atkinson

303   He reassured Diana that Atkinson: Interview with Richard Addis

303   even told friends that Atkinson had: Interview with Jane Atkinson

304   "odd twist": DM, 29/6/96

304   The Queen had already decided: SuTel, 7/7/96

304   Diana would receive a lump sum: Ti, 13/7/96; DT, 5/7/96

304   "regarded as a member": "Status and Role of the Princess of Wales," statement from Buckingham Palace, 12/7/96

304   she would have the use of all her: Gua, 13/7/96

304   "He told her to hang tough": Interview with John Tigrett

305   When he said it made no difference: DM, 13/7/96

305   HER ROYAL HUMILIATION: Ibid.

305   "It is the face of a woman": Mi, 13/7/96

305   PRINCESS TO GIVE UP HRH STYLE: DT, 13/7/96

305   GO-AHEAD FOR 15 M POUND SETTLEMENT: Ti, 13/7/96

305   "give her something lighthearted": Interview with Jane Atkinson

305   Diana felt the leprosy charity: Ibid.

306   charities she had "ditched": DM, 17/7/96

306   "The move is entirely because": Ibid.

306   Atkinson told Diana: Interview with Jane Atkinson

306   "It was all bad": Ibid.

306   "decided that Richard's draft": B-SS, p. 58

306   "Martin Bashir is a humble": Interview with Paul Burrell

306   "dreadfully upset": B-SS, p. 58

306   she would fulfill three charity: *Hello!*, 27/7/96

306   "In [her] last two years": Interview with Michael Adler

CHAPTER 24

308   "I have decided to give": Interview with Marguerite Littman

308   "We'd love Di more if she": Sun, 28/6/96

309   "road show, something fun": Interview with Marguerite Littman

309   "The National AIDS Trust was": Interview with Michael Adler

309   "a lot of information started": DEx, 17/1/97

309   "Do you think I could": B-SS, pp. 158–59

309   offered to be her official: DM, 14/1/97

309   filmmaker Richard Attenborough: ST, 19/1/97

310   "In a sense, the land mine": Interview with William Deedes

310   "deep thinker": Pano, p. 26

310   "incessantly": ST, 1/11/98

310   "Her world was illuminated": ITV-Doc

310   "She was attuned to what": Interview with Cosima Somerset

311   "very responsible and responsive": Mi, 19/2/89

311   "I hug my children": B-AM1, pp. 67–68

311   "No one was the parent": Interview with David Puttnam

311   "The constant bear hugs": B-AP, p. 110

311   Once, on a visit with: B-RK, p. 76

311   most notably when she exhorted: B-WB, p. 170

311   "attentive and smart": Interview with David Puttnam

311   "he should simply have thanked": SuTel, 7/9/97

311   "I want them to have an understanding": Pano, p. 32

311   Although William was developing: TNY, 15/9/97

312   "She was trying so hard": Harper's Bazaar, 11/97

312   overheard numerous fights: B-WB, pp. 43, 60, 84, 147

312   "I hate to see you sad": B-AM1, pp. 182–83

312   she felt the nanny was: B-WB, pp. 58, 117, 129, 157

312   "[Diana] raged that Tiggy": B-RK, p. 76

312   When she and Charles were going: B-WB, pp. 153, 155

312   "I get into bed with them": B-AM1, p. 68

312   "Diana had a mother-and-son": Interview with Roberto Devorik

313   "Diana used to ask William": Interview with Elsa Bowker

313   "wanted William to hear the truth": SuTel, 7/9/97

313   "William is going to be in his position": B-AM1, p. 68

313   When they were younger: B-WB, p. 20; B-JW, p. 191

313   Diana often rebelled: B-WB, pp. 20–21, 102

313   As they grew older: B-RK, p. 78

313   once, when William was apprehensive: B-WB, p. 152

313   "I've got my boys": Pano, p. 28

313   "the only men in her life": DM, 1/9/97

314   calling them nearly every: B-SS, p. 145

314   "had other priorities": Ibid., p. 76

314   "because she found herself analyzing": B-RK, p. 149

314   "talked about wanting to leave": Interview with Jane Atkinson

314   "Sarah Ferguson was a very": Ibid.

315   Diana and Fergie had been together: DM, 20/11/95

315   Diana cut her off without a word: B-SS, p. 74

315   Fergie also tastelessly: B-SF, p. 72

315   Diana considered "unkind": SuMi, 2/11/97

315   after Diana had specifically: B-SS, p. 80

315   she refused to answer: Ibid., p. 74

315   "The Duchess of York is the one person": B-RK, p. 111

315   "She wasn't as close": Interview with Richard Kay

315   she tried to maintain contact: B-SS, p. 53

315   Diana hired Michael Gibbins: DT, 28/8/96

316   "I was a go-between": Interview with Paul Burrell

316   Diana took to wearing: B-SS, pp. 123–24

316   but they spent most: Ibid., pp. 112–13

316   "furtive roadside rendezvous": NOTW, 11/8/96

316   "I found my peace": Interview with Elsa Bowker

316   "have a pair of girls": NOTW, 22/11/98

317   "In the meeting I had": DM, 23/11/98

317   "was so impatient to have": B-SS, p. 114

317   She was to be the guest: DT, 30/8/96

317   In a bungled kidnapping: SuMi, 3/11/96

317   privately they were displeased: DT, 30/8/96

317   "from triumph to triumph": Mi, 2/11/96

317   Diana was perturbed: DT, 4/11/96

317   "shy caring heart surgeon": SuMi, 3/11/96

317   "friends . . . in an entirely": DM, 4/11/96

317   "Why didn't she just tell": B-SS, p. 118

318   "dear friend": DT, 19/9/96

318   "wisdom and experience": DT, 14/10/96

318   "Life is mostly froth": DT, 26/9/96

318   Tilberis had first met: Harper's Bazaar, 11/97

318   she created a stir: DM, 11/11/96

318   "fit like a glove": Interview with Vivienne Schuster

319   I'M OUT THE DIOR: DS, 11/12/96

319   Mohamed Fayed, owner of: Hello!, 4/1/97

319   Two weeks later, at Fayed's: Ibid.

319   "They're all fuggers": B-TB, p. 233

319   The Egyptian-born son: VF, 12/97

319   Fayed built an international: B-TS, pp. 80–82; B-TB, p. 16

319   In 1988, the DTI: B-TS, p. 80

320   Fayed was subsequently denied: Ibid., p. 88

320   A subsequent Vanity Fair profile: B-TB, pp. 379, 392: Fayed sued Vanity Fair for libel but withdrew his case two years later when confronted by the magazine's overwhelming evidence for its charges (B-TB, pp. 446–47). On May 6, 1999, the Home Office turned down Fayed's application for citizenship a second time.

320   He had cultivated: B-TS, p. 90

320   "showered gifts": B-TB, p. 274

320   who was especially enamored: Ibid., p. 252

320   In 1996, Raine became: B-RK, p. 170; DM, 20/6/97; B-TS, p. 90

320   "keep an eye": B-TS, p. 91

320   visit him from time to time: Ibid.; Interview with Mark Hollingsworth

320   "He helped bring them": Interview with Andrew Neil

320   "Diana liked Mohamed's": Interview with Mark Hollingsworth

320   "made friends with Diana": Interview with Andrew Neil

320   "talk about their common interest": SuMi, 13/7/97

321   when he asked Diana: Ibid.; B-RK, p. 170

321   Fayed also frequently proffered: B-TB, pp. 274, 411
321   "close friend": DM, 14/7/97

CHAPTER 25

322   "roving health educationalist": DT, 14/10/96
322   "Her dramatic return": NOTW, 12/1/97
322   "tarnished": Ti, 24/9/96
322   "We are trying to give": Interview with William Deedes
323   "to get her hands dirty": DM, 14/1/97
323   "to assist the Red Cross": Ibid.
323   "loose cannon": Ti, 16/1/97
323   "I am only trying to help": Mi, 16/1/97
323   "idiot minister": Interview with William Deedes
323   The BBC documentary about the trip: Sun, 11/2/97
323   "I remember looking": Sun, 17/1/97
323   "long-term commitment": DEx, 17/1/97
323   "an international angel": Ibid.
324   "watershed": DT, 17/1/97
324   "take her out of controversy": Interview with William Deedes
324   In a first step: DEx, 20/3/97
324   an erroneous story that Diana: DT, 25/2/97
324   "She wants it for herself": Interview with Richard Addis
324   "She did that to punish": Ibid.
324   Diana subsequently announced: DT, 3/3/97
324   "She was an anxiety-ridden": Interview with Vivienne Schuster
325   "it was too complicated": Interview with Gail Rebuck
325   "the final straw in a deteriorating": DM, 24/1/97
325   "From the optimism that shines": Mi, 8/2/97
325   "extremely concerned": DM, 8/2/97
325   "devastated": Mi, 8/2/97
326   "You'll never guess who just": B-RK, p. 139
326   "brief and straightforward": DM, 8/3/97
326   "not the person to ask": DT, 10/3/97
326   "For my grandson William": DM, 8/9/97
326   "showed few signs of mirth": DT, 10/3/97
326   "The confusion was there": Interview with Sue Douglas
327   "I took a strong line": Interview with Paul Burrell
327   "'hiding' in plain sight": B-SS, p. 127
327   "So confident had Diana become": Ibid., p. 129
327   "telling pointless lies": Ibid., p. 197
327   Diana had been secretly: DM, 24/10/94
327   "I persuaded her that": Interview with Piers Morgan
327   "deeply disappointed": Gua, 9/5/97
328   "I rang her and congratulated": Interview with Piers Morgan

328   the tabloids had written: Mi, 5/1/97; DM, 10/1/97
328   "had made all the moves": SuEx, 9/2/97
328   "She would have converted": Interview with Elsa Bowker
328   "convince them that she was a nice": Ibid.
328   she spent ninety minutes: Hello!, 31/5/97
328   "She was obsessional about families": B-SS, p. 116
328   she told friends: SuMi, 9/11/97
328   she had not informed: B-SS, p. 116; Mi, 7/8/97
328   "There are so many people": Hello!, 31/5/97
328   "swollen panda eyes": B-SS, p. 117
329   "weeping in the stairway": Interview with Elsa Bowker
329   "no attempt to dodge": Hello!, 7/6/97
329   One evening she appeared: Mi, 7/8/97
329   "air of defiance": B-RK, pp. 107–8
329   "She knew everyone": Interview with Elsa Bowker
329   She broke off with her longtime: DT, 14/6/97
329   she considered "traitorous": B-SS, p. 72
329   whom Richard Kay regarded as: B-RK, p. 99
329   "wasn't willing to let me": B-SS, p. 79
329   Legge-Bourke was photographed pouring: Interview with Piers
       Morgan
330   "harmed . . . of herself": DM, 31/5/97
330   "I could hear Diana dictating": Interview with Piers Morgan
330   "put out a statement": Ibid.
330   "her son might believe": DM, 31/5/97
330   loyal aide had been "naive": Ibid.
330   "I felt strongly [Diana and Charles]": I-FSK
331   "prone to giving colorful": Mi, 28/5/97
331   "complete shock": DM, 28/5/7
331   "appalled and bewildered": Ibid.
331   When it emerged: Mi, 28/5/97
331   "special relationship": DEx, 15/9/97
331   "shared such a sense": DM, 29/9/97
331   "[she] suddenly woke up": Mi, 8/5/97
332   Since Harrods had sponsored: B-TS, p. 94; DM, 14/7/97
332   "instant solution": DM, 14/7/97
332   "strongly advised": SuTel, 7/9/97
332   "arouse concern": DM, 14/7/97
332   which Diana did on June 11: B-TS, p. 96
332   "rather unnecessarily tactile": DEx, 25/6/97
332   "She knocked herself": Interview with Marguerite Littman
332   "Surrounded by drooling": DEx, 26/6/97
333   "Diana Reborn": VF, 7/97
333   "apparently unsupported": DT, 10/6/97

333   "Whatever Diana's inward state": VF, 7/97

333   "Is this at last the *real* Diana": DM, 10/6/97

333   "quicken the de-miners'": Gua, 13/6/97

333   "her most amazing walkabout": DEx, 19/6/97

333   "killing fields": DM, 29/6/97

333   "anti-mines campaigners": DT, 22/5/97

333   Tony Blair invited: VF, 10/97

333   "very charismatic": TNY, 15/9/97

333   "At last . . . I will have": Ibid.

333   "peacemaker. . . . She seriously felt": *Hello!*, 27/9/97

334   "wants me to go on some missions": TNY, 15/9/97

CHAPTER 26

335   Diana received ninety: Mi, 16/11/97

335   "It's my birthday": Ibid.

335   "Wouldn't it be funny": Interview with Elsa Bowker

335   "All the grief from my past": Sun, 12/1/98

336   "I have quit": Mi, 13/7/97

336   "unofficially engaged": SuMi, 29/6/97

336   "He accused Diana": Mi, 9/11/97

336   "sobbing her heart out": Mi, 16/11/97

336   by early evening: B-TS, pp. 97–98

336   Fayed installed: MOS, 20/7/97

336   "sparked a political": SuMi, 13/7/97

336   "Good God": Ibid.

336   "a little unsafe": NOTW, 13/7/97

336   she had sought and received: Gua, 15/7/97

336   bodyguards recruited from: B-TS, pp. 97–98

337   "If Diana wanted privacy": ES, 14/7/97

337   "noted that Fayed was so dishonest": DM, 14/7/97

337   "Mohamed was having a bad": Interview with Nigel Dempster

337   "fellow guests": DM, 14/7/97

337   DI'S AMAZING CUDDLE: Sun, 14/7/97

337   "It is her mood almost of defiance": DM, 14/7/97

337   "She was happy to be": Interview with Piers Morgan

337   "relaxed and happy": Mi, 15/7/97

337–38 motorboat carrying reporters: DM, 16/7/97

338   "candidly about the dark side": Mi, 15/7/97

338   "distressed . . . freaked out": Ibid.

338   claimed an exclusive interview: Ibid.

338   "appeared upset . . . joked and giggled": Ibid.

338   "relaxed . . . comfortable": DM, 16/7/97

338   "getting increasingly distraught": ES, 15/7/97

338   making a "surprise": Ibid.

338   At one moment, she was crawling: DM; Sun, 16/7/97
338   "[he had] never seen her act": Sun, 16/7/97
338   previous night's arrival: B-TS, p. 105
338   Dodi had bolted: Ibid.
338   "glimpsed Diana's current": B-TB, p. 413
339   "Dodi was many things": Interview with Tina Sinatra
339   called him a "boy" and a "kid": Interviews with Jack Weiner, David Putt-
       nam, Michael White
339   "What endeared him": Interview with Peter Riva
339   "I didn't think he was good-looking": Interview with Nona Summers
339   "someone you can depend on": SuMi, 31/8/97
339   acrimonious divorce: B-TB, pp. 14–15
339   Dodi grew up in Alexandria: Ibid., pp. 17–18
339   Shuttling between Egypt and: Interviews with Jack Martin, Jack Weiner;
       Ti, 14/9/97
339   finished thirtieth: B-TS, p. 55
339–40 he considered himself a Catholic: Interview with Suzanne Gregard
340   Dodi left after one year: Interview with Philippe Gudin (Directeur
       Général of Le Rosey)
340   even members of his family: Interview with Michael Cole; B-TB, p. 39;
       B-TS, p. 55
340   Sandhurst for the six-month: Interview with Major Tim Coles
340   he did enjoy learning: B-TB, p. 42
340   he served briefly as an attaché: New York Daily News, 1/9/97
340   A frequent patron of Tramp: Interview with Johnny Gold
340   "He had the attitude that": Interview with Michael White
340   "He had no discernible": Interview with Jack Martin
340   The Broccolis, who lived: B-TS, pp. 57–58
340   Seeking to capitalize: Ibid., pp. 58–59
340   "Dodi's role was not": Interview with Clive Parsons
340   Mohamed similarly called: Interview with David Puttnam
341   He began taking cocaine: B-TB, p. 65
341   "Don't ever come back": Ibid., p. 69
341   "He was into cocaine": Interview with Nona Summers
341   Among his mishaps: B-TB, p. 136
341   Dodi spent more time: Ibid., pp. 136–37; B-TS, pp. 52–53
341   "When he was around his mother": Interview with Jack Martin
341   "warm but very strong": Interview with Corinna Gordon
341   In 1983, Mohamed had set him: Interview with Jack Weiner
341   "He had a passion": Ibid.
342   "I have no idea where Dodi": Interview with Michael White
342   "Around the office we used to": Interview with Jack Weiner
342   A number of Dodi's creditors: Mi, Sun, DEx, 9/8/97
342   "He was after acceptance": Interview with Peter Riva
342   like his father, Dodi carried: B-TB, p. 199; B-TS, p. 73

342   "I don't think a word of truth": Interview with Nona Summers

343   "Dodi Time": Interview with Jack Martin

343   "He didn't have the ability": Interview with Michael White

343   "He had an innocence that was": Interview with Marie Helvin

343   he courted her avidly: Interview with Suzanne Gregard

343   "You know he gets down on the ground": Mi, 12/8/97

343   Gregard tried to make: Interview with Suzanne Gregard

343   Dodi insisted on putting: Ibid.

343   "We were never alone": Ibid.

343   In 1989, Mohamed had tried: B-TB, p. 254

343   Although he logged: Interviews with Jack Weiner, Jerry Weintraub, Jim Hart

343–44   He had been dating Kelly Fisher: B-TS, p. 66

344   On June 20: Interview with Bruce Nelson

344   "Dodi couldn't bear to leave": NOTW, 7/12/97

344   Mohamed's wife Heini: B-TS, p. 107

344   "We thought he was a sailor": Ibid., p. 106

344   "I knew his father was": Ibid.

344   Fisher took the *Cujo:* Ibid.

344   "We ran postcards": Interview with Piers Morgan

345   "stealing the spotlight": Mi, 18/7/97

345   "Diana's attitude to all": MOS, 20/7/97

345   Diana and the boys left: B-TS, p. 107

345   numerous extravagant: SuMi, 2/11/97, 16/11/97; Mi, 21/7/97

345   "the best holiday [she'd] ever": Sun, 12/1/98

345   Dodi was still sailing: B-TS, p. 106

345   As he sobbed quietly, she comforted: DM, Mi, 23/7/97

345   Three days later, Diana was: B-TS, p. 108; B-TB, pp. 418–19

346   stealing away with Dodi: B-TB, p. 419

346   For background music: NOTW, 7/12/97

346   "How can two people": B-TB, p. 419

346   "It was as close to paradise": NOTW, 7/12/97

346   "There was always [Mohamed] Fayed": Interview with Antonia Grant

346   after receiving a tip: B-TB, p. 420; B-TS, pp. 109–10

346   DI'S SECRET HOL WITH HARRODS HUNK DODI: Sun, 7/8/97

346   "We relaxed. We had a great time": Mi, 7/8/97

346   "I give them my blessing": ES, 8/8/97

346   "the first man who can openly be": DM, 8/8/97

347   "She was on the rebound": Interview with Elsa Bowker

347   "Mr. Perfect . . . caring, rich": Mi, 7/8/97

347   "Dodi is not his father": DM, 8/8/97

347   "It's so extraordinary that [Diana and I] don't": B-TS, p. 67

348   "They were each in love": Interview with Nona Summers

348   "This was something she had never": DM, 14/6/98

348   "his wonderful voice": SuTel, 7/9/97

348   "I love his exotic accent": SuMi, 2/11/97
348   "[Mohamed's wife] Heini is an elegant lady": Interview with Andrew Neil

CHAPTER 27

350   At the end of July, Diana had to scrap: DEx, 5/8/97
350   with William Deedes's help: Interview with William Deedes
350   "has captured public attention": Mi, 6/8/97
350   She created vivid images: DT, 10/8/97, 11/8/97
350   "She was impressive": Interview with William Deedes
351   "the most sensational pictures": SuMi, 10/8/97
351   "air of farce": *The Observer,* 10/8/97
351   "film producer Dodi has even": SuMi, 10/8/97
351   "finding herself again": Interview with William Deedes
351   Detailed reports had already: Mi, Sun, DM, 9/8/97
351   "unique glimpse": MOS, 10/8/97
352   "Air Dodi": Mi, 14/8/97
352   "I would lie there in the dark": NOTW, 10/8/97
352   Not only had Fisher: DM, Mi, Sun, 15/8/97
352   "astonishing array": NOTW, 17/8/97
352   "gentle soul": DM, 8/8/97
352   "ideal husband": Sun, 8/8/97
352   "generous caring spirit": SuMi, 10/8/97
352   "Dodi Rotten Cheat": Mi, 15/8/97
352   "Oily Bedhopper": Sun, 16/8/97
352   "Dodgy Dodi": Mi, 18/8/97
353   "How about a quick dip?": Sun, 12/8/97
353   engagement was imminent: SuMi, 10/8/97
353   "It took her a long time": DM, 14/8/97
353   some private moments: B-TS, p. 114
353   would "meet a man": Rogers, p. 249
353   "I'm in the Mediterranean": Ibid.
353   "seemed to be taking in": Ibid., pp. 251, 253
353   Two days later, Dodi went: B-TS, pp. 117–18
353   visited a sick friend: Interview with Nicky Blair
353   "He was happy the romance": Interview with Mark Canton
354   "I am so happy we are compatible": Sun, 12/1/98
354   "Look at this, Rosa": SuTel, 7/9/97
354   they carried back a heap: NOTW, 7/12/97
354   "from a distinguished": Interview with Michael Cole
354   "always wonder": Interview with Tina Sinatra
354   the paparazzi followed: B-TB, p. 422; B-TS, p. 122
354   "The body language on the boat": Interview with Cosima Somerset
354   "I'm welcomed with kindness": DT, 27/8/97
355   "her most ferocious political row": DEx, 28/8/97
355   "the Princess has made no": Ibid.

355   Diana's office produced: DM, 28/8/97
355   "I wrote exactly what she said": Ibid.
355   "bitterly let down": Ibid.
355   "The . . . reaction in the British": SuTel, 15/2/98
355   "betrayal, and being misunderstood": Ibid.
355   relayed to Fayed: B-TB, pp. 242, 246
355   stayed less than a half hour: Sun, 17/3/99
355   A Fayed employee took: B-TS, p. 130; B-TB, p. 425
355   "From Diana with love": Interview with Michael Cole; B-TS, p. 121
355   "They were her most precious": Interview with Elsa Bowker
355   Alberto Repossi said: DT, 17/4/98; B-TS, p. 121
355   "vulgar": Interview with Richard Kay
355   As usual, they rode: B-TS, pp. 128, 132, 134
356   they were again thronged: Ibid., p. 134
356   Dodi became agitated: Ibid.; B-TB, p. 426
356   Shortly before midnight: B-TB, p. 138
356   "Don't bother following": B-TS, pp. 5–7
356   the Mercedes slammed: Ibid., pp. 8–9
356   the acting security chief: Ibid., pp. 6, 128
356   an autopsy revealed: Ibid., pp. 8, 136–38; B-TB, pp. 427–28
356   Dodi had insisted on Paul; B-TB, pp. 427–28; B-TS, p. 8
356   because their belongings were there: B-TS, pp. 126, 133
357   "seemed to get more and more": Ibid., p. 138
357   "When you were with him, you felt": Interview with Nona Summers
357   Mohamed Fayed insisted: B-TS, pp. 122–23
357   photographs published in *The Sun:* Sun, 17/3/99
357   "it has a history": DM, 11/2/98
357   "likely": DM, 1/9/97
358   "rapidly changed": Interview with Richard Kay
358   "She called William about": Interview with Elsa Bowker
358   "Don't worry. I need another": SuTel, 15/2/98
358   "biologically impossible": Ibid.
358   "was obsessive about not": DM, 11/2/98
359   "Diana's life should not be": SuTel, 15/2/98
359   "No one can tell me": DT, 27/8/97

CHAPTER 28

360   "She clearly should have": Interview with Michael Adler
360   "an enormous capacity for": SuTel, 7/9/97
361   "She could open up at": Interview with Cosima Somerset
361   "real" Diana . . . "withdrawn": Interview with Jane Atkinson
361   "loony . . . basket case": DM 22/11/95
361   "barking mad": ITV-Doc
362   "Diana should not get help": ST, 19/11/95
362   "could happen to anyone": SuExp, 5/7/92

362   "In a sense, she was finished": Interview with Michael Colborne

362   "was as unsure of herself": DM, 1/9/97

362   "some psychotherapist or someone": Mi, 8/5/97

362   "backlash against therapy": ES, 8/5/97

363   neurotics may experience: B-JK, p. 9

363   narcissists tend to be: Ibid., p. 24

363   Borderline personalities feel inferior: Ibid.

363   many work as counselors: Ibid., p. 12

363   "superficially intact": *Handbook of Treatment for Eating Disorders*, p. 438

363   Among other notable figures: B-JK, pp. 36, 38, 40

363   the "border" of long-recognized: Ibid., p. 5

363   Two leading American: Ibid., p. 27

363   "growing feeling": DM, 20/8/95

364   Even the timing: DSM-IV Criteria for Borderline Personality Disorder;
       ICD-10 Classification of Mental and Behavioral Disorders, WHO,
       Geneva, 1992: F60.3 Emotionally Unstable (Borderline) Personality Dis-
       order; B-JK, p. 63

364   "until their defense structure": Web site for Richard J. Corelli, M.D.,
       Stanford University

364   "estimated 2.5 per cent": *Harvard Mental Health Letter*, 3/92

364   From fifteen to twenty-five percent: B-JK, p. 4

364   "intricately connected": Ibid., p. 7

364   "deep feelings of unworthiness": Tribute by Earl Spencer

364   "because of the strain": ES, 6/9/97

365   "to the point where": B-AP, pp. 101–2

365   A number of studies: *Handbook of Treatment for Eating Disorders*, p. 438

365   "self-mutilation . . . is the hallmark": B-JK, p. 33

365   "If you have been rejected": VF, 10/97

365   "to the exclusion of all else": B-JD, p. 361

365   "who would be there for her": B-SS, p. 37

366   "paling effect of time": Interview with Kent Ravenscroft

366   "She had no governor": Interview with David Puttnam

366   "cannot tolerate human inconsistencies": B-JK, p. 10

366   "emotional hemophilia . . . clotting mechanism": Ibid., p. 8

366   "Clearly on a hair trigger": TNY, 15/9/97

367   "magical thinking": *Handbook of Treatment for Eating Disorders*, p. 439

367   Antidepressants such as Prozac: Ibid., pp. 441–42

367   "a kind of 'Third World' ": B-JK, p. 5

367   "Not with cards": WP, 7/9/97

367   "Most people look at it": Interview with Michael Colborne

Bibliography

Andersen, Christopher. *The Day Diana Died.* New York: William Morrow and Company, Inc., 1998; London: Blake, 1999.

Barry, Stephen. *Royal Service: My Twelve Years as Valet to Prince Charles.* London: Macmillan, 1983.

Berry, Wendy. *The Housekeeper's Diary: Charles and Diana Before the Breakup.* New York: Barricade Books, Inc., 1995.

Blos, Peter. *On Adolescence: A Psychoanalytic Interpretation.* New York: The Free Press, 1962.

Bower, Tom. *Fayed: The Unauthorized Biography.* London: Macmillan, 1998.

Burnet, Alastair. *In Person: The Prince and Princess of Wales.* Independent Television News Limited and Michael O'Mara Books Ltd., 1985.

Campbell, Lady Colin. *Diana In Private: The Princess Nobody Knew.* New York: St. Martin's Paperbacks, 1992.

Cannadine, David. *The Decline and Fall of the British Aristocracy.* New York: Anchor Books, Doubleday, 1992; London: Papermac, 1996.

Carpenter, Humphrey. *Robert Runcie: The Reluctant Archbishop.* London: Sceptre, 1997.

Clark, Alan. *Diaries.* London: Phoenix, 1994.

Clark, Colin. *Younger Brother, Younger Son: A Memoir.* London: HarperCollins, 1997.

Claude-Pierre, Peggy. *The Secret Language of Eating Disorders.* New York: Times Books, 1997; London: Doubleday, 1998.

Davies, Nicholas. *Diana: The People's Princess.* Secaucus, N.J.: Carol Publishing, 1997.

Deutsch, Helen. *Neuroses and Character Types: Clinical Psychoanalytic Studies.* New York: International Universities Press, 1965.

Dimbleby, Jonathan. *The Prince of Wales: A Biography.* London: Warner Books, 1995.

Eichenbaum, Luise, and Susie Orbach. *What Do Women Want: Exploding the Myth of Dependency.* New York: Berkley, 1984; London: Harper Collins, 1994.

Evans, Harold. *Good Times, Bad Times.* New York: Atheneum, 1984; London: Phoenix, 1994.

Fincher, Jayne. *Diana: Portrait of a Princess.* New York: Simon & Schuster/Callaway Editions, 1998.

Garner, David M., Ph.D., and Paul E. Garfinkel, M.D. *Handbook of Treatment for Eating Disorders: Second Edition.* New York: The Guilford Press, 1997.

Goleman, Daniel. *Emotional Intelligence.* New York: Bantam Books, 1997; London: Bloomsbury Publishing, 1996.

Holden, Anthony. *Charles: A Biography.* London: Fontana/Collins, 1989.

———. *Charles: A Biography.* London: Bantam Press, 1998.

———. *Diana: Her Life & Her Legacy.* New York: Random House, 1997; London: Ebury Press, 1997.

Junor, Penny. *Diana Princess of Wales: A Biography.* London: Sidgwick & Jackson, Ltd., 1982.

———. *Charles: Victim or Villain?* London: HarperCollins, 1998.

Keay, Douglas. *Royal Pursuit: The Palace, the Press and the People.* London: Severn House, 1983.

Kreisman, Jerold J., M.D., and Hal Straus. *I Hate You—Don't Leave Me: Understanding the Borderline Personality.* New York: Avon Books, 1991.

MacArthur, Brian, ed. *Requiem: Diana, Princess of Wales 1961–1997: Memories and Tributes.* London: Pavilion Books Ltd., 1997.

Morrow, Ann. *Princess.* London: Chapmans Publishers, 1991.

Morton, Andrew. *Diana: Her True Story—In Her Own Words.* New York: Simon & Schuster, 1997; London: Michael O'Mara, 1997.

———. *Diana: Her New Life.* London: Michael O'Mara, 1995.

Neil, Andrew. *Full Disclosure.* London: Pan Books, 1997.

Orbach, Susie. *Fat Is a Feminist Issue: The Self-Help Guide for Compulsive Eaters.* London: Arrow, 1986.

———. *Hunger Strike.* London: Penguin Books, 1993.

Paglia, Camille. *Vamps & Tramps.* New York: Vintage Books, 1994; Harmondsworth: Penguin, 1995.

Pasternak, Anna. *Princess in Love.* London: Signet, 1995.

Rhys, Ernest, ed. *Memoirs of Jean Francois Paul de Gondi, Cardinal de Retz, Vol. One.* London: J. M. Dent & Sons, Ltd., 1943.

Robertson, Mary, *The Diana I Knew: The Story of My Son's Nanny Who Became the Princess of Wales.* London: Judy Piatkus (Publishers) Ltd., 1998.

Robson, Kenneth, M.D., ed. *The Borderline Child: Approaches to Etiology, Diagnosis, and Treatment.* New York: McGraw-Hill Book Company, 1983; UK: Jason Aronson, 1997.

Rogers, Rita, with Natasha Garnett. *From One World to Another.* London: Pan Books, 1998.

Rose, Kenneth. *King George V.* New York: Alfred A. Knopf, 1984.

Sancton, Thomas, and Scott MacLeod. *Death of a Princess: An Investigation.* London: Weidenfeld & Nicolson, 1998.

Saunders, Mark, and Glenn Harvey. *Dicing with Di: The Amazing Adventures of Britain's Royal Chasers.* London: Blake, 1996.

Simmons, Simone, with Susan Hill. *Diana: The Secret Years.* London: Michael O'Mara Books Ltd., 1998.

Spencer, Charles. *Althorp: The Story of an English House.* London: Viking, 1998.

Spoto, Donald. *The Decline and Fall of the House of Windsor.* New York: Pocket Books, 1996.

Strong, Roy. *The Roy Strong Diaries: 1967–1987.* London: Weidenfeld & Nicolson, 1997.

Taylor, S. J. *Shock! Horror! The Tabloids in Action.* London: Black Swan Books, 1992.

Thornton, Penny. *With Love from Diana.* New York: Pocket Books, 1995.

Viorst, Judith. *Necessary Losses: The Loves, Illusions, Dependencies, and Impossible Expectations That All of Us Have to Give Up in Order to Grow.* New York: Fawcett Columbine, 1996; UK: Fireside Books, 1998.

Whitaker, James. *Diana vs. Charles: Royal Blood Feud.* London: Signet, 1993.

Wyatt, Woodrow. *The Journals of Woodrow Wyatt.* London: Macmillan, 1998.

York, Duchess of, Sarah, with Jeff Coplon. *My Story.* London: Pocket Books, 1997.

Index

Photo Credits